The Gospel *and the* Gospels

THE GOSPEL *and the* GOSPELS

Christian Proclamation and Early Jesus Books

Simon Gathercole

WILLIAM B. EERDMANS PUBLISHING COMPANY
GRAND RAPIDS, MICHIGAN

Wm. B. Eerdmans Publishing Co.
4035 Park East Court SE, Grand Rapids, Michigan 49546
www.eerdmans.com

28 27 26 25 24 23 22   1 2 3 4 5 6 7

ISBN 978-0-8028-7759-8

Library of Congress Cataloging-in-Publication Data

A catalog record for this book is available from the Library of Congress.

Contents

PREFACE

This book has had a long gestation period, during which many friends and colleagues have provided extremely helpful input. The first impulse for it was a conversation with my former colleague Eamon Duffy in 2010, and his encouragement was invaluable. Francesca Murphy's invitation to contribute a chapter to the *Oxford Handbook of Christology* provided the opportunity for a first stab at the subject of this book, which was then refined into a position paper presented as a plenary lecture at the British New Testament Conference in Manchester in 2014. This lecture then expanded into various series: the New College Lectures at the University of New South Wales in 2016, and in 2017 the Sizemore Lectures at Midwestern Seminary, Kansas City, and the Annual Biblical Studies Lectures at Westminster Seminary, California. Individual parts of the argument were presented as a keynote lecture in a Nag Hammadi conference at the Humboldt University, Berlin, as the 2018 Lagrange Lecture at the École biblique in Jerusalem, and in the Connecting Gospels conference in Durham and a seminar in Oxford. I am particularly grateful for responses and questions to some of these presentations from John Barclay, Markus Bockmuehl, Anthony Giambrone, Matthew Novenson, Dieter Roth, Jens Schröter, and Francis Watson, as well as from numerous anonymous interlocutors. I also benefited hugely from the anonymous readers, commissioned by Eerdmans, who provided feedback: thanks *unbekannterweise* to you all. I am grateful to the *Dupond et Dupont* of Eerdmans past and present, Michael Thomson and Trevor Thompson: to Michael, for encouraging me to publish this book, and to Trevor for his organization of the readers of various chapters and for his patience in seeing it through to the end. I am grateful to my Cambridge colleagues: Judith Lieu provided valuable input on my chapter on Marcion, and James Carleton Paget and Jonathan Linebaugh read far more of this manuscript than anyone deserves to have inflicted upon them. Morna Hooker both offered encouragement and suggested a key point of clarification that has been taken on board here. My former student Bobby Jamieson also provided valuable research assistance and very illuminating discussions, not least on Hebrews. I must also thank Monique Cuany for casting her expert eye on the material on Acts. Dale Allison's feedback on the Matthew chapter was extremely helpful. Matthew Novenson read some of the Mark chapter, and Mark Strauss kindly read some of the material on Luke. Ben Reynolds's comments on my early drafts on John combined the acuity of Rupert Baxter with the affability of Galahad Threepwood. ὁ ἀναγινώσκων νοείτω. Martha Gathercole has been an excellent, if increasingly expensive, proofreader, and Freddie Gathercole's ingenious method of checking the bibliography was extremely useful.

As ever, my greatest human debt is to my wife, Rosie. Having now put up with me for over twenty years, she has been a constant source of joy, a brilliant example and a wonderful fellow worker. Thank you for being an absolute marvel.

Abbreviations

1 Apol.	Justin, *First Apology*
1 Clem.	1 Clement
1 En.	1 Enoch
1Q28b	Rule of the Blessings
1QM	Milḥamah
1QS	Rule of the Community
1QSa	*Rule of the Congregation*
2 Bar.	2 Baruch
4Q161	4QpIsaª
4Q174	Florilegium
4Q246	Apocryphon of Daniel
4Q252	Commentary on Genesis A
4Q266	*Damascus Document*ª
4Q285	Sefer ha-Milḥamah (*olim* Serekh ha-Milḥamah)
4Q375	apocrMosesª (*olim* apocrMoses B)
4Q376	apocrMosesᵇ (*olim* 3 Tongues of Fire)
4Q381	Noncanonical Psalms B
4Q471b	Self-Glorification Hymn
4Q504	DibHamª
4Q521	*Messianic Apocalypse*
4QCatenaª	Catenaª
4QIsaª	Isaiahª
4QIsaᵇ	Isaiahᵇ
11Q5	Psalms Scrollª
11Q13	Melchizedek
ʿAbod. Zar.	ʿAbodah Zarah
Acts John	*Acts of John*
Adam. dial.	*Adamantius Dialogue*
Ag. Ap.	Josephus, *Against Apion*
Alex.	Plutarch, *Alexander*
An.	Tertullian, *De anima*

Ann.	Tacitus, *Annales*
Ant.	Josephus, *Jewish Antiquities*
Ant. rom.	Dionysius of Halicarnassus, *Antiquitates romanae*
Ap. John	*Apocryphon of John*
Apoc. Ab.	*Apocalypse of Abraham*
Apoc. Adam	*Apocalypse of Adam*
Apoc. Pet.	*Revelation of Peter*
Apol.	Melito of Sardis, *Apology*
Aristocr.	Demosthenes, *In Aristocratem*
As. Mos.	*Assumption of Moses*
Aug	*Augustinianum*
Aug.	Suetonius, *Divus Augustus*
Autol.	Theophilus, *Ad Autolycum*
b.	Babylonian Talmud
Barn.	*Epistle of Barnabas*
BBR	*Bulletin for Biblical Research*
BDAG	Danker, Frederick W., Walter Bauer, William F. Arndt, and F. Wilbur Gingrich. *Greek-English Lexicon of the New Testament and Other Early Christian Literature.* 3rd ed. Chicago: University of Chicago Press, 2000
Ben.	Seneca, *De beneficiis*
Ber.	Berakot
BG	Berlin Gnostic Codex
Bib	*Biblica*
BibInt	*Biblical Interpretation*
BJRL	*Bulletin of the John Rylands University Library of Manchester*
CAL	Comprehensive Aramaic Lexicon Project
Can. pasch.	Pseudo-Hippolytus, *Canon paschalis*
CBQ	*Catholic Biblical Quarterly*
CD	Cairo Genizah copy of the *Damascus Document*
CD-B	*Damascus Document*[b]
Cels.	Origen, *Contra Celsum*
Clem.	Seneca, *De clementia*
CMRDM	*Corpus Monumentorum Religionis Dei Menis*
Com. Apoc.	Victorinus, *Commentary on the Apocalypse*
Comm. Diat.	Ephrem, *Commentary on Tatian's Diatessaron*
Comm. Isa.	Jerome, *Commentariorum in Isaiam*
Cor.	Plutarch, *Marcius Coriolanus*
Cyr.	Xenophon, *Cyropaedia*
Dem.	Irenaeus, *Demonstration of the Apostolic Preaching*
Dial.	Justin, *Dialogue with Trypho*
Diatr.	Epictetus, *Diatribai*
Did.	*Didache*
DSD	*Dead Sea Discoveries*
EC	*Early Christianity*
El.	Euripides, *Electra*
Enn.	Plotinus, *Enneades*

Ep. Apos.	*Epistle to the Apostles*
'Erub.	'Erubin
Esth. Rab.	Esther Rabbah
Exc.	Clement of Alexandria, *Excerpts from Theodotus*
ExpTim	*Expository Times*
Gen. Rab.	Genesis Rabbah
Gos. Eg.	*Gospel of the Egyptians*
Gos. Jud.	*Gospel of Judas*
Gos. Marcion	Marcion's Gospel
Gos. Pet.	*Gospel of Peter*
Gos. Thom.	*Gospel of Thomas*
Gos. Truth	*Gospel of Truth*
Haer.	Hippolytus, *Refutatio omnium haeresium*; Irenaeus, *Adversus haereses*
Herm. Sim.	Shepherd of Hermas, Similitude(s)
Hipp.	Euripides, *Hippolytus*
Hist. eccl.	Eusebius, *Historia ecclesiastica*
Hom.	Pseudo-Clementines, *Homilies*
HR	*History of Religions*
HTR	*Harvard Theological Review*
HUCA	*Hebrew Union College Annual*
ICC	International Critical Commentary
Ign. *Magn.*	Ignatius, *To the Magnesians*
Ign. *Phld.*	Ignatius, *To the Philadelphians*
Ign. *Smyrn.*	Ignatius, *To the Smyrnaeans*
IGT	*Infancy Gospel of Thomas*
Int	*Interpretation*
J. W.	Josephus, *Jewish War*
JA	*Journal Asiatique*
JAAR	*Journal of the American Academy of Religion*
Jastrow	Jastrow, Morris, *A Dictionary of the Targumim, the Talmud Babli and Yerushalmi, and the Midrashic Literature with an Index of Scriptural Quotations.* London: Luzac, 1903
JBL	*Journal of Biblical Literature*
JR	*Journal of Religion*
JSJ	*Journal for the Study of Judaism in the Persian, Hellenistic, and Roman Periods*
JSNT	*Journal for the Study of the New Testament*
JTI	*Journal of Theological Interpretation*
JTS	*Journal of Theological Studies*
Jul.	Suetonius, *Divus Julius*
Lam. Rab.	Lamentations Rabbah
Leg.	Augustine, *Contra adversarium legis et prophetarum*; Philo, *Legum allegoriae*
Lives	Diogenes Laertius, *Lives of Eminent Philosophers*
LSJ	Liddell, Henry George, Robert Scott, and Henry Stuart Jones. *A Greek-English Lexicon.* 9th ed. with revised supplement. Oxford: Clarendon, 1996

m.	Mishnah
Marc.	Tertullian, *Against Marcion*
Mart. Ascen. Isa.	*Martyrdom and Ascension of Isaiah*
Mart. Pol.	*Martyrdom of Polycarp*
Meg.	Megillah
Metam.	Ovid, *Metamorphoses*
Midr.	Midrash
Midr. Ps.	Midrash Psalms
Midr. Tanḥ.	Midrash Tanḥuma
Mos.	Philo, *De vita Mosis*
MTSR	*Method and Theory in the Study of Religion*
Nat.	Pliny the Elder, *Natural History*
Nat. Rulers	*Nature of the Rulers*
Neot	*Neotestamentica*
NHC	Nag Hammadi Codices
NovT	*Novum Testamentum*
NRSV	New Revised Standard Version
NTS	*New Testament Studies*
Num. Rab.	Numbers Rabbah
Numen	*Numen: International Review for the History of Religions*
OED	*Oxford English Dictionary*
OLD	Glare, P. G. W., ed. *Oxford Latin Dictionary*. Oxford: Clarendon, 1982
Oth.	Plutarch, *Otho*
OTP	*Old Testament Pseudepigrapha*. Edited by James H. Charlesworth. 2 vols. New York: Doubleday, 1983, 1985
P. Oxy.	Oxyrhynchus papyri
Pan.	Epiphanius, *Panarion*
Pasch.	Melito of Sardis, *Peri pascha*
Pesaḥ.	Pesaḥim
Pesiq. Rab.	Pesiqta Rabbati
Pesiq. Rab Kah.	Pesiqta de Rab Kahana
PG	Patrologia Graeca [= Patrologiae Cursus Completus: Series Graeca]. Edited by Jacques-Paul Migne. 162 vols. Paris, 1857–1886
PGL	Lampe, Geoffrey W. H., ed. *Patristic Greek Lexicon*. Oxford: Clarendon, 1961
Pirqe R. El.	Pirqe Rabbi Eliezer
PL	Patrologia Latina [= Patrologiae Cursus Completus: Series Latina]. Edited by Jacques-Paul Migne. 217 vols. Paris, 1844–1864
Praescr.	Tertullian, *De praescriptione haereticorum*
Prom.	Aeschylus, *Prometheus vinctus*
Prot. Jas.	*Protevangelium of James*
Ps.-Clem.	Pseudo-Clementines
Pss. Sol.	Psalms of Solomon
QE	Philo, *Questions and Answers on Exodus*
Quest. Barth.	*Questions of Bartholomew*

RAC	*Reallexikon für Antike und Christentum*. Edited by Theodor Klauser et al. Stuttgart: Hiersemann, 1950–
RB	*Revue biblique*
Recogn.	Pseudo-Clementines, *Recognitions*
ResQ	*Restoration Quarterly*
Rom.	Plutarch, *Romulus*
Sanh.	Sanhedrin
SecCent	*Second Century*
Šabb.	Šabbat
Sib. Or.	Sibylline Oracles
SJT	*Scottish Journal of Theology*
Somn.	Philo, *De somniis*
Song Rab.	Song of Songs Rabbah
Soṭah	Soṭah
Spec. Laws	Philo, *On the Special Laws*
StPatr	Studia Patristica
STRev	*Sewanee Theological Review*
Strom.	Clement of Alexandria, *Stromateis*
T. Ab.	*Testament of Abraham*
T. Dan	*Testament of Dan*
T. Levi	*Testament of Levi*
Ta'an.	Ta'anit
Tanḥ.	Tanḥuma
Testim. Truth	*Testimony of Truth*
Tg. 1 Chr.	Targum 1 Chronicles
Tg. 2 Sam.	Targum 2 Samuel
Tg. Hab.	Targum Habakkuk
Tg. Isa.	Targum Isaiah
Tg. Mic.	Targum Micah
Tg. Neof.	Targum Neofiti
Tg. Neof. Gen.	Targum Neofiti Genesis
Tg. Ps.	Targum Psalms
Tg. Ps.-J.	Targum Pseudo-Jonathan
Tg. Song	Targum Song of Songs
Tg. Yer.	Targum Yerušalmi
Tg. Zech.	Targum Zechariah
Theog.	Hesiod, *Theogony*
TLG	Thesaurus Linguae Graecae
Tract. Ps.	Jerome, *Tractatus in Psalmos*
Treat. Res.	*Treatise on the Resurrection*
Tri. Trac.	*Tripartite Tractate*
TS	*Theological Studies*
TynBul	*Tyndale Bulletin*
VC	*Vigiliae Christianae*
Vir. Ill.	Jerome, *De viris illustribus*

Vit. Plot.	Porphyry, *Vita Plotini*
y.	Jerusalem Talmud
Yebam.	Yebamot
ZAC	*Journal of Ancient Christianity/Zeitschrift für Antikes Christentum*
ZAW	*Zeitschrift für die alttestamentliche Wissenschaft*
ZNW	*Zeitschrift für die neutestamentliche Wissenschaft und die Kunde der älteren Kirche*

INTRODUCTION

Is there anything that makes the four New Testament Gospels different from most of the "others"?[1] Are the four really different, or are they simply those Gospels that were later identified as a useful source of unity, or imposed through an act of suppressive power by the party that happened to emerge victorious? There is a strong majority of scholars now who disagree with the traditional Christian picture according to which there are sharp differences between the apocryphal Gospels, on the one hand, and the canonical, biblical Gospels, on the other.

The purpose of this book is to argue that there are in fact substantial differences of theological content between Matthew, Mark, Luke, and John, on the one hand, and most "noncanonical" early Christian Gospels, on the other. The book further argues that there is a reason for this commonality among the canonical Gospels: namely, that these four emerge from a context in which a particular understanding of the apostolic "good news" is preached, and so reflect that understanding of the good news in their literary productions.

This introduction will set the broader scholarly context of this book, and also clarify what it is about and what it is not. The first section here begins by presenting various ways in which scholars have debated the degrees of difference or similarity between canonical and noncanonical Gospels in order to paint a picture of this broader scholarly context. It then identifies *theological content* as the key point of differentiation to be explored in the first argument of this book. The latter section of this introduction identifies and clarifies the

---

1. In this book, "gospel" without a capital letter refers to the preached "good news"; "Gospel" with an initial capital letter is a written work, the Gospel of Mark or the Gospel of Marcion, etc. Apostles' names such as Philip refer to the person when not italicised, while *Philip, Judas*, etc., are sometimes used as shorthand for the Gospels attributed to them.

1

second argument of the book, namely that the four now-canonical Gospels follow an early Christian kerygma—that is, a preached gospel or message of "good news"—attested by Paul in 1 Cor 15 as apostolic.

1. Strategies for Differentiating Gospels

As noted, this first section will begin by setting the stage of current scholarship before focusing more narrowly on the first main thesis of the book.

1.1 *Circumstances of Composition*

Scholars often debate the comparative dates of the canonical and noncanonical Gospels, their authorship or pseudonymity, and their relative dependence. Traditionally, it has been common to distinguish between the canonical Gospels as handed down from the apostolic age, and apocryphal Gospels written "recently."[2] Going hand in hand with that is a judgment about authorship: the canonical Gospels were written by *apostoli* or *apostolici* (apostles or "apostolics"), while noncanonical Gospels were sectarian products of Gnostics or Valentinians or others.[3] As Cyril of Jerusalem says of the *Gospel of Thomas*, this Gospel must not be read "for it is not from one of the twelve apostles, but from one of the three evil disciples of Mani."[4] Additionally, as the "originals," the canonical Gospels have literary primacy, while the apocryphal Gospels are said to be dependent epiphenomena. As the *Synopsis scripturae sacrae* attributed to Athanasius puts it, in works like the *Gospel of Thomas* and the Pseudo-Clementines, "quite true and divinely inspired matters have been selected and paraphrased."[5] In modern scholarship, there have been ongoing battles over the relative dependence of *Thomas* and the Synoptics, on the one hand, and the *Egerton Gospel* and John, on the other.[6] A modern verdict on the apocryphal

---

2. E.g., Irenaeus, *Haer.* 3.11.9 on the *Gospel of Truth* originating *non olim* (see *OLD*, s.v. "olim").

3. E.g., Irenaeus, *Haer.* 1.31.1 on the *Gospel of Judas* as a Gnostic production, and *Haer.* 3.11.9 on the *Gospel of Truth* as a Valentinian composition.

4. Cyril of Jerusalem, *Catechesis* 6.31.

5. PG 28:432b. See Simon Gathercole, "Named Testimonia to the Gospel of Thomas: An Expanded Inventory and Analysis," *HTR* 105 (2012): 61, for text and English translation. For the judgment of apocryphal Gospels as epiphenomena, see further Markus Bockmuehl, *Ancient Apocryphal Gospels* (Louisville: Westminster John Knox, 2017).

6. See, e.g., the discussion of the literary relation of Thomas to the canonical Gospels,

Gospels as late, inauthentic, and dependent products can also appeal to the cultural distance from first-century Palestine that some apocryphal Gospels display. As F. F. Bruce remarked of the *Gospel of Thomas*: "the historical and geographical setting— Palestine under the Romans and the Herods around AD 30—has been almost entirely forgotten."[7]

By contrast, scholars in recent times have been reluctant to say that the canonical Gospels were composed in the "apostolic" age in the first century, with their apocryphal counterparts originating in a decadent *subapostolic* age in the second.[8] Relatedly, most deny that the canonical Gospels have any claim to apostolic authorship, even broadly defined to include an author with apostolic connections. For the majority of scholars now, canonical and noncanonical Gospels alike are all in the same anonymous, unapostolic boat. Nor is dependence a mark of apocryphal inferiority, given that Matthew, Luke, and John are all in varying degrees dependent upon Mark.

1.2 Attestation

Another criterion that has sometimes been used to distinguish between the canonicals and the noncanonicals has been the fact that the New Testament Gospels are those that were most frequently copied and quoted in the ancient world; in other words, they were the most popular. This argument has a long pedigree: Eusebius, after listing a number of apocryphal Gospels and Acts, remarks that "to them, no man from among those churchmen of the successions has thought it appropriate to make any reference in a work at all."[9]

Many argue that in early Christian writings the vast majority of quotation is of canonical Gospels. According to one tally, even as cosmopolitan a theo-

---

by Simon Gathercole, Mark Goodacre, Nicola Denzey Lewis, Stephen Patterson, and John Kloppenborg in *JSNT* 36 (2014), and on *Egerton*, e.g., Lorne Zelyck, *The Egerton Gospel (Egerton Papyrus 2 + Papyrus Köln VI 255): Introduction, Critical Edition, and Commentary* (Leiden: Brill, 2019), 5–13.

7. F. F. Bruce, "The Gospel of Thomas," in *Jesus and Christian Origins outside the New Testament* (London: Hodder and Stoughton, 1974), 155. Cf. also the discussion in Simon J. Gathercole, "Other Apocryphal Gospels and the Historical Jesus," in *The Oxford Handbook of Early Christian Apocrypha*, ed. Andrew Gregory and Christopher Tuckett (Oxford: Oxford University Press, 2015), 250–68, esp. 262–63.

8. The distinction between the first and second centuries is specious: as E. R. Dodds, *Pagan and Christian in an Age of Anxiety: Some Aspects of Religious Experience from Marcus Aurelius to Constantine* (Cambridge: Cambridge University Press, 1965), 3, points out, "strictly speaking there are no periods in history, only in historians."

9. Eusebius, *Hist. eccl.* 3.25.6.

logian as Clement of Alexandria overwhelmingly quotes the canonical rather than noncanonical Gospels:[10]

Matthew:	757×	Gospel of the Egyptians:	8×
Mark:	182×	Gospel according to the Hebrews:	3×
Luke:	402×	Gospel and Traditions of Matthias:	3×
John:	331×	Gospel of Thomas, et al.:	0×

In a different summary of ancient references to noncanonical Gospels, however, another scholar has concluded: "This survey shows clearly that about a dozen noncanonical gospels were known in the 2d century and that the evidence for these apocryphal writings compares quite well with the evidence for the canonical gospels. The attestations do not support a distinction between canonical and apocryphal gospels. Writings of both categories were used and are referred to quite early and often by the same writers."[11] On the other hand, again, more recently, Charlesworth has come to the opposite conclusion: "If non-canonical gospels had as much or indeed more currency than the canonical gospels, we should expect to find frequent citations or allusions in the Apostolic Fathers and 2nd-cent. writers."[12]

Moving from literary references on to extant manuscripts, figures for Greek Gospel manuscripts with a good probability of coming from the second and third centuries CE are as follows:[13]

10. Figures from Bernhard Mutschler, *Irenäus als johanneischer Theologe: Studien zur Schriftauslegung bei Irenäus von Lyon* (Tübingen: Mohr Siebeck, 2004), 101. Mutschler also refers to Irenaeus's citations of the New Testament: Matthew 478×, Mark 30×, Luke 310×, and John 237×. Among noncanonical Gospels, Irenaeus refers only to the *Gospel of Judas* (1×) and the *Gospel of Truth* (1×). There may be a few additional allusions to apocryphal works in Irenaeus, e.g., to IGT 6.3–5 (*Haer.* 1.20.1) and *Gos. Thom.* 38.1 (*Haer.* 1.20.2); cf. possibly *Gos. Thom.* 19.1 and *Dem.* 44.

11. Helmut Koester, "Apocryphal and Canonical Gospels," *HTR* 73 (1980): 110. Koester's sampling is rather tendentious: e.g., he refers to Clement of Alexandria as attesting equally to the canonical Gospels and to the *Gospel of the Egyptians*, the *Gospel according to the Hebrews*—and to the Secret Gospel of Mark.

12. Scott Charlesworth, "Indicators of 'Catholicity' in Early Gospel Manuscripts," in *The Early Text of the New Testament*, ed. C. E. Hill and M. J. Kruger (Oxford: Oxford University Press, 2012), 47 n. 40.

13. Figures for the canonical Gospels from Larry W. Hurtado, *The Earliest Christian Artifacts: Manuscripts and Christian Origins* (Grand Rapids: Eerdmans, 2007), 20, 22, updated with the additions of P. Oxy. LXXXIII 5345 (a fragment of Mark), the Willoughby papyrus (𝔓134, a fragment of John), and P. Oxy. LXXVI 5072. A question mark appears by the *Gospel of Peter* and P. Oxy. LX 4009, because some regard the latter as a fragment of the former.

Matthew:	12	*Gospel of Peter*:	1+?
Mark:	2	Fayyum Gospel:	1
Luke:	7	P.Ryl. 3.464:	1
John:	17	P. Oxy. II 210:	1
Gospel of Thomas:	3	P. Oxy. X 1224:	1
Protevangelium of James:	1	P. Oxy. LX 4009:	1?
Gospel of Mary:	2	P. Oxy. LXXVI 5072:	1
Egerton Gospel:	1		

Some have understood these figures to represent a great preponderance of manuscript attestation to the canonical Gospels.[14] Until recently, however, only one fragment of Mark was known, and so it could be concluded that a Gospel like the *Gospel of Peter* could be regarded as "arguably at least as popular" as Mark.[15] It is still the case that in terms of manuscript attestation in the first three centuries CE, the *Gospel of Thomas* has more than the Gospel of Mark. Hence the survival of these manuscripts demonstrates, it is said, that the noncanonical Gospels cannot be attributed merely to a lunatic fringe.

Related to this question of manuscript attestation is not the quantity of copying but the way in which canonical and noncanonical Gospels were copied. Hurtado has argued that certain features of the way canonical Gospels are copied indicate liturgical usage in contrast to the Greek fragments of *Thomas*, which seem to be designed for private study: this fact, Hurtado adds, comports

---

14. E.g., Charlesworth, "Indicators of 'Catholicity,'" 47 n. 41: "After excluding P7 and including P.Papyrus inv. 2, in terms of preservation the four canonical gospels outnumber the four non-canonical gospels by more than 4 to 1 (35 canonical gospel to 8 non-canonical gospel fragments). If P. Oxy. 41.2949 and 60.4009 are not early fragments of the Gospel of Peter, the ratio is 5.8 to 1." Charlesworth here, like many, assumes the lack of early manuscript attestation of Mark to be explicable, because of preference for Matthew.

15. Bart D. Ehrman, *Lost Christianities: The Battles for Scripture and the Faiths We Never Knew* (Oxford: Oxford University Press, 2003), 23: "Which Gospel was more popular in early Christianity, Mark or Peter? It is rather hard to say. But if the material remains are any gauge, one would have to give the palm to Peter, with three times as many surviving manuscript remains as Mark." It is questionable, too, whether all three of these fragments are part of the *Gospel of Peter*. Only P. Oxy. XLI 2949 has a strong claim. (Ehrman's statement was of course written before the publication of P. Oxy. LXXXIII 5345.) Cf. Christopher Tuckett, *The Gospel of Mary* (Oxford: Oxford University Press, 2007), 9–10, on Mary's attestation (two papyrus fragments to Mark's one): as a former mathematician, Tuckett expresses appropriate caution about such a statistical sample; similarly Larry Hurtado, "The Greek Fragments of the Gospel of Thomas as Artefacts: Papyrological Observations on Papyrus Oxyrhynchus 1, Papyrus Oxyrhynchus 654 and Papyrus Oxyrhynchus 655," in *Das Thomasevangelium: Entstehung— Rezeption—Theologie*, ed. J. Frey, J. Schröter, and E. E. Popkes (Berlin: de Gruyter, 2008), 29.

with the individualistic emphasis in the work itself.[16] Charlesworth has produced a series of more thoroughgoing studies with far-reaching conclusions:
he maintains that "early non-canonical gospel papyri are private manuscripts
without indications of catholicity,"[17] and that "scribal conventions in second-
and second/third-century gospel papyri are indicative of 'catholic' collabora-
tion and consensus, presumably among the 'orthodox.'"[18] On the other hand,
Luijendijk has noted that there may be some counterevidence to Hurtado's
position in that the fragments of *Thomas* evince clear writing and reading
aids, and so it is possible that they may have featured in worship settings.[19]

1.3 Literary Form

Some have pointed instead to the literary character of the four New Testament
Gospels by comparison with their competitors. One common judgment is a
literary distinction between canonical and apocryphal Gospels on the basis of
the *narrative character* of Matthew, Mark, Luke, and John. These Gospels, it is
said, are stories, biographical narratives fitting more or less into the conventions of how ancient authors wrote *Lives*; by contrast, the *Gospel of Judas* and
the *Gospel of the Egyptians*, for example, focus on the truths that Jesus reveals
in big discourses, rather than being narratives. The influential monograph of
Burridge can illustrate this view: "the canonical gospels form a subgenre of
βίοι Ἰησοῦ . . . but it is with the development of the non-canonical gospels and
commentaries on the canonical gospels that we have moved through the ter-
tiary stage into other related, but different, genres."[20] The apocryphal Gospels
are characterized by "lack of narrative, settings and chronological develop-

---

16. Hurtado, "Greek Fragments of the *Gospel of Thomas*," 31–32.

17. Charlesworth, "Indicators of 'Catholicity,'" 46. See further Scott Charlesworth, *Early
Christian Gospels: Their Production and Transmission* (Florence: Edizioni Gonnelli, 2016).

18. Charlesworth, "Indicators of 'Catholicity,'" 47, citing in the middle Birger A. Pearson, *Gnosticism and Christianity in Roman and Coptic Egypt* (London: T&T Clark, 2004),
13–14. See further Scott Charlesworth, "The Gospel Manuscript Tradition," in *The Content
and Setting of the Gospel Tradition*, ed. Mark Harding and Alanna Nobbs (Grand Rapids:
Eerdmans, 2010), 51–58.

19. See AnneMarie Luijendijk, "Reading the *Gospel of Thomas* in the Third Century:
Three Oxyrhynchus Papyri and Origen's *Homilies*," in *Reading New Testament Papyri in
Context*, ed. C. Clivaz and J. Zumstein (Leuven: Peeters, 2011), 241–67, arguing that P. Oxy. I 1
is a very clearly written text, and even P. Oxy. IV 654 has markings (line-dividers, coronides,
diaereses) to facilitate reading.

20. Richard Burridge, *What Are the Gospels? A Comparison with Graeco-Roman Biography*, 2nd ed. (Grand Rapids: Eerdmans, 2004), 243.

ment, the scale and focus on the ministry of Jesus and so on"; these "missing features" are present, by contrast, in Matthew, Mark, Luke, and John and "are the features which place the canonical gospels in the genre of βίος."[21] Adams similarly remarks that "none of the extant works, stemming from the early centuries of the church, that are designated 'gospels' either by themselves or by others, corresponds in literary shape to the four canonical Gospels."[22] (Burridge and Adams, however, do accept that some apocryphal Gospels, especially the "Jewish-Christian" Gospels, may have resembled the canonical ones.)[23] More recently, Markus Bockmuehl has made a case that what marks out the canonical Gospels is not only a narrative genre but a narrative with a particular extent—embracing the whole career of Jesus from baptism, including the ministry, through to his death and resurrection.[24] The canonical Gospels' narrative character also underpins Wright's judgment that the canonical Gospels contain "news," whereas "Thomas and the others are *advice*."[25]

To draw this kind of distinction between biblical Gospels, which are stories, and apocryphal Gospels, which are something else, does not work across the board, however. There are some particularly clear examples of full-length noncanonical Gospels. The *Diatessaron* of course covers everything in the canonical Gospels and was itself called a Gospel in some circles.[26] The *Gospel according to the Hebrews* appears to have been a full-length Gospel: we have an account of the baptism, and then various other episodes, culminating in a resurrection appearance to James.[27] Marcion's Gospel covers, with the exception of the baptism, the same career span as the canonical Gospels. Furthermore, the *Gospel of Peter* has a narrative form much like that of the New Testament Gospels, as (so far as we can tell) does the *Egerton Gospel*.[28] Of course, *Peter*

21. Burridge, *What Are the Gospels*, 243.

22. Edward Adams, *Parallel Lives of Jesus: Four Gospels—One Story* (London: SPCK, 2010), 3 n. 2.

23. Burridge, *What Are the Gospels*, 242; Adams, *Parallel Lives of Jesus*, 3 n. 2.

24. Bockmuehl, *Ancient Apocryphal Gospels*.

25. Tom Wright, *Judas and the Gospel of Jesus: Have We Missed the Truth about Christianity?* (Grand Rapids: Baker, 2006), 29. Italics original.

26. For the "Gospel" title, see Matthew Crawford, "Diatessaron, a Misnomer? The Evidence from Ephrem's Commentary," *EC* 4 (2013): 362–85.

27. The baptism is Gregory frag. 13 = Jerome, *Comm. Isa.* 11.1–3, and the resurrection Gregory frag. 11 = Jerome, *Vir. Ill.* 2. See Andrew F. Gregory, *The Gospel according to the Hebrews and the Gospel of the Ebionites* (Oxford: Oxford University Press, 2017).

28. See already H. Idris Bell and T. C. Skeat, *Fragments of an Unknown Gospel and Other Early Christian Papyri* (London: The British Museum, 1935), 30, because of how it looks back to Jesus's deeds (frag. 2r: "we know that you have come from God, for what you do testifies

and the *Egerton Papyrus* are fragmentary in their current state, but both are strongly suggestive of a longer narrative. And finally, however one might dispute whether *Thomas* and *Judas* represent *the* good news, they at least claim—and not without justification—that their revelatory content can be classified as "news": both claim to unveil what eye has not seen, ear has not heard, and what has never occurred to the human mind.[29]

1.4 Aesthetics

A different kind of literary evaluation is offered by distinguished papyrologist Peter Parsons, in what might be labeled an *aesthetic* judgment. Parsons offers a possible explanation of the great number of copies of Matthew and John by comparison with the quantity of apocryphal material in the Egyptian town of Oxyrhynchus as follows: "Gnostic texts turn up only in small numbers. Perhaps the Manichaean world-view was too depressing, or the neo-Platonic machinery too complicated. Certainly, there is a contrast between the plain speech of the [sc. NT] Gospels and (say) the cosmic rhetoric of the risen Christ in *The Wisdom of Jesus Christ*."[30] For Parsons, therefore, it is the aesthetic simplicity of the four New Testament Gospels that may have been part of their appeal, in contrast to the abstruse complexity of some of the others.

Naturally, however, there is some subjectivity involved here. Others present apocryphal Gospels as much more attractive—at least for the modern reader. For Elaine Pagels, for example, the orthodox view presupposes a "chasm separat[ing] humanity from its creator," with Jesus the unique Lord and Son of God announcing repentance from sin;[31] in the Gnostic Gospels, however, "the self and the divine are identical," and Jesus "comes as a guide who opens access to spiritual understanding," such that Jesus and his disciples become "equal—even identical," because ultimately "they have both received their be-

---

beyond all the prophets"), and points forward to the passion (frag. 1r: "they could not take him because the hour of his arrest had not yet come"). Hence the editors' conclusion that the fragments are "obviously part of a work designed on much the same lines as the canonical gospels. It may perhaps seem rash to affirm this so positively on the basis of two leaves and a small fragment; but the whole scale of the narrative, the variety of incidents recorded, the mixture of sayings and miracles, irresistibly suggest this conclusion; and it is strengthened by ll. 28–9, which seem to point forward to the Passion."

29. *Gos. Thom.* 17; *Gos. Jud.* 47.1–13.

30. Peter J. Parsons, *City of the Sharp-Nosed Fish: Greek Lives in Roman Egypt* (London: Weidenfeld & Nicholson, 2007), 198.

31. Elaine Pagels, *The Gnostic Gospels* (New York: Vintage Books, 1979), xx.

ing from the same source."[32] As Roger Bagnall has described such a view, "the gnostics are validated as a direction in which Christianity could have gone and which would have made it warmer and fuzzier, much nicer than this cold orthodoxy stuff."[33]

1.5 Theological Content

The presentation here of four sets of debates (in sec. 1.1–4) about the differences and similarities between canonical and noncanonical Gospels has set the wider scholarly context of this book. I have attempted to present the various approaches in a fairly evenhanded manner, because none of these is the main focus of attention in this book. The present study is interested neither in literary relations or form, nor questions of historical origin or usage per se, although naturally these will crop up in passing from time to time. The focus of study here is the *theological content* of canonical and noncanonical Gospels, and the present book is largely a comparison of their contents. This merits further elaboration.

As with the previous examples of circumstances of composition, attestation, and so on, many scholars in previous generations differentiated canonical from noncanonical Gospels on grounds of theological content. One ancient commentary sees the authors of apocryphal Gospels as all identical to the teachers referred to as "antichrists" in 1 John, "those who do not confess that the Lord has come in the flesh."[34] Moving to modern scholarship, J. Armitage Robinson prefaced one of the first discussions of the *Gospel of Peter* by printing in the front matter ἕτερον εὐαγγέλιον, ὃ οὐκ ἔστιν ἄλλο—"another gospel, which is not another" (Gal 1:6–7).[35] Moving forward to the twentieth century, two mainstream scholars of quite different theological views can serve as illustrations of how previous generations have drawn distinctions between canonical and noncanonical Gospels.

---

32. Pagels, *Gnostic Gospels*, xx.

33. Cited in Herb Krosney, *The Lost Gospel: The Quest for the Gospel of Judas Iscariot* (Washington, DC: National Geographic, 2006), 196. Bagnall is not here stating a view he endorses but specifically refers to Pagels in this regard.

34. *Quaestiones uel Glosae in euangelio nomine: Quaestiones euangelii 2* (late eighth century CE), in Robert E. McNally, ed., *Scriptores Hiberniae Minores. Pars I* (Turnhout: Brepols, 1973), 133 (text).

35. J. A. Robinson, "Lecture on the Gospel according to Peter," in J. A. Robinson and M. R. James, *The Gospel according to Peter and the Revelation of Peter* (London: C. J. Clay & Sons, 1892), 12.

First, F. F. Bruce states as follows: "The Jesus of the *Gospel of Thomas* is not the Jesus who came to serve others, not the Jesus who taught the law of love to one's neighbour in the way portrayed in the parable of the good Samaritan. . . . Unlike the Bible, the *Gospel of Thomas* sets forth the ideal of the 'solitary' believer. . . . No doubt there is a real concern for the blindness and ignorance of men . . . but on the whole it is the concern of one who has come to show them the true way rather than of one who has come to lay down his own life that true life may be theirs."[36] Here *Thomas* is therefore compared to the Jesus of "the Bible," alluding to the Synoptic language of Jesus as servant and of the love commandment; there is a comparison specifically with Luke 10, and a reference in the penultimate sentence to a Johannine idiom. Bruce concludes: "It is the absence of this self-sacrificing love more than anything else that puts the *Gospel of Thomas* and similar works into a class apart from the New Testament writings."[37] More expansively, in another article, Bruce comments on the *Gospel of Philip* and the *Gospel of Truth*, saying that the author of the latter marks a departure of a Gnostic sort "in his speculative treatment of the gospel."[38]

Second, American patristics scholar (and U-boat historian) Robert M. Grant offered a strident statement on the *Gospel of Thomas* at around the same time as Bruce, stating that *Thomas* is "our most significant witness to the early perversion of Christianity by those who wanted to create Jesus in their own image."[39] An explicit theological comparison with the canonical Gospels appeared elsewhere in the same year, in which Grant comments that while *Thomas* "is called a 'gospel' it is really not a gospel but a collection of sayings. The Church's gospels tell us what Jesus did as well as what he said. They are full of action. . . . In Thomas there is no action whatever. Everything is peace, unity, spirituality, and talk. The inevitable result of a collection of 'sayings of Jesus' is a distortion of the meaning of Jesus—and such a distortion is what Thomas intended to provide."[40] Applying similar theological criteria to the *Gospel of Philip*, Grant remarks—like Bruce on the *Gospel of Truth*—that it is "too obviously derived from speculation, largely Valentinian in nature, about the hidden significance of the titles given to Jesus in our gospels."[41] Overall, "the new gospels from Nag-Hammadi deserve a welcome because they will

36. F. F. Bruce, "The Gospel of Thomas," *Faith and Thought* 92 (1961): 21–22.

37. Bruce, "Gospel of Thomas," 23.

38. F. F. Bruce, "The Gospels and Some Recent Discoveries," *Faith and Thought* 92 (1962): 154.

39. Robert M. Grant and D. N. Freedman, *The Secret Sayings of Jesus* (New York: Doubleday, 1960), 20.

40. Robert M. Grant, "Two Gnostic Gospels," *JBL* 79 (1960): 3, the published version of the 1959 SBL presidential address.

41. Grant, "Two Gnostic Gospels," 6.

help show what Christianity is not, and what our canonical gospels are not. They may conceivably help us to see what our gospels are, but the differences will remain more important than the similarities."[42]

This kind of theological evaluation on the basis of comparing the contents of the Gospels is very much out of vogue in current scholarship. The quotations of Grant cited above are unimaginable in a Society of Biblical Literature presidential address today. It is customary now to read that there is nothing in the theology of the four New Testament Gospels that makes them especially worthy of canonical status over against the apocryphal Gospels, and no particular content that the four especially have in common that might differentiate them from the others.

Already in 1979, for example, Elaine Pagels's *Gnostic Gospels* had in some ways continued to endorse the divide between orthodox and Gnostic, but also seeks at points to undermine the distinction. She argues that the canonical Gospels do not always conform to the orthodox view, just as the apocrypha do not always take the "Gnostic" or heretical view. Aspects of the resurrection in Mark, Luke, and John, for example, comport better in Pagels's opinion with a Gnostic view of resurrection—where resurrection is spiritual not bodily.[43] At another point, she notes that some parts of Mark's Gospel are most strongly echoed in the *Gospel of Mary*.[44]

The difficulty of differentiating the four canonical Gospels on theological grounds has particularly been emphasized in connection with the *Gospel of Thomas*. Gregory Riley has commented that *Thomas* and John are near neighbors, with the Synoptics being more distant.[45] This position was endorsed by Dunderberg, who provides a list of theologoumena shared by the two Gospels, and concludes (quoting Riley): "Differences in literary style aside, John and *Thomas* do share many ideas that make their symbolic worlds look quite similar to each other. John and *Thomas* are, as Riley has correctly pointed out, 'much closer to each other in spirit than either is to the Synoptics.'"[46] This reflects the widely held view that there is no real theological distinction between canonical and noncanonical Gospels.[47]

---

42. Grant, "Two Gnostic Gospels," 10.

43. Pagels, *Gnostic Gospels*, 5–6: "Luke and Mark both relate that Jesus appeared 'in another form'—not his earlier form," referring to Mark 16:12 and Luke 24:13–32.

44. Pagels, *Gnostic Gospels*, 11: "This gnostic gospel recalls traditions recorded in Mark and John that Mary Magdalene was the first to see the risen Christ."

45. Gregory J. Riley, *Resurrection Reconsidered* (Minneapolis: Fortress, 1995), 3.

46. Ismo Dunderberg, *The Beloved Disciple in Conflict? Revisiting the Gospels of John and Thomas* (Oxford: Oxford University Press, 2006), 6, quoting Riley, *Resurrection Reconsidered*, 3.

47. At a general level, see also Tony Chartrand Burke, *Secret Scriptures Revealed: A New*

More recently, Watson has commented along similar lines. In reference specifically to the Gospel of John, the *Gospel of Thomas*, and the *Gospel of Peter*, he writes that "these gospels all claim apostolic authority, and they all present an image of Jesus rooted in early tradition and shaped by later interpretative developments."[48] And on *Thomas* in particular: "It would be difficult to argue on neutral exegetical grounds that differences between the Synoptics and Thomas are more fundamental than differences between the Synoptics and John."[49] Thus in the precanonical phase in which various early Christian Gospels emerge, Watson argues, one cannot pit supposedly *authentic* canonical Gospels against apocrypha, which can be dismissed as "free invention," for apocrypha too "are not fictions but renewed attempts to articulate the significance of an already inscribed tradition."[50]

Although this criterion of theological content has been criticized, however, it is this that will be taken up and defended in this book. This is not to return to the kind of value judgments made by Bruce and Grant. Nevertheless, it is to contend for the following, which constitutes the first thesis of this book: *The four New Testament Gospels share key elements of theological content that mark them out from most of the noncanonical Gospels.* My aim is that this becomes evident when the various Gospels are examined for what they say about the "kerygmatic" themes of Jesus's messiahship, his saving death and resurrection, and his fulfillment of scripture. In these respects, it is the four New Testament Gospels—including John—that are far closer to one another theologically than most of the noncanonical Gospels are to them.

2. The Gospels and the Kerygma

Related to this is a second point, namely: The reason why the four New Testament Gospels are theologically similar to one another is that they—unlike most others—follow a preexisting apostolic creed or preached gospel. In other words, the theological commonalities among Matthew, Mark, Luke, and John can be explained in part because they emerged from a setting in which many

---

Introduction to the Christian Apocrypha (London: SPCK, 2013), 141: "It should be made clear that non-canonical texts often incorporate material from canonical texts; so there is much in them that is 'orthodox.'"

48. Francis Watson, *Gospel Writing: A Canonical Perspective* (Grand Rapids: Eerdmans, 2013), 341.

49. Watson, *Gospel Writing*, 370.

50. Watson, *Gospel Writing*, 370.

Christians held to a particular preached gospel, or kerygma. As one scholar has commented, "Before an apostle put pen to papyrus a canonical authority already resided in apostolic teaching."[51] This cuts against some current tendencies in scholarship that tend to find the unity of the four canonical Gospels not in earliest Christian theology but in the theology of the proto-orthodox leaders of the third or fourth centuries.[52]

This tendency to focus on *retrospective* ecclesiastical judgments from a later period can be illustrated by the following statement:

> There were lots of gospels. . . . All of these gospels (and epistles, apocalypses, etc.) were connected with apostles, they all claimed to represent the true teachings of Jesus, and they were all revered—by one Christian group or another—as sacred scripture. As time went on, more and more started to appear. Given the enormous debates that were being waged over the proper interpretation of the religion, how were people to know which books to accept? In brief, one of the competing groups in Christianity succeeded in overwhelming all the others. . . . This group became "orthodox", and once it had sealed its victory over all of its opponents, it rewrote the history of the engagement—claiming that it had always been the majority opinion of Christianity, that its views had always been the views of the apostolic Churches and of the apostles, that its creeds were rooted directly in the teachings of Jesus. The books that it accepted as Scripture proved the point, for Matthew, Mark, Luke and John all tell the story as the proto-orthodox had grown accustomed to hearing it.[53]

I mention this statement of Ehrman to clarify the second step in the argument because it appears that he would agree with the first step, namely that there is a certain theological commonality among the canonical Gospels. The final sentence

---

51. Peter Head, *How the New Testament Came Together* (Cambridge: Grove Books, 2009), 6.

52. Bart D. Ehrman, "Christianity Turned on Its Head: The Alternative Vision of the Gospel of Judas," in *The Gospel of Judas*, ed. Rodolphe Kasser, Marvin Meyer, and Gregor Wurst (Washington, DC: National Geographic, 2006), 117–18. Or again, other scholars emphasize the malleability of earliest Christian tradition, with the result that the great variety of Gospels all have something of a legitimate hold in that tradition. Similarly, Pagels, *Gnostic Gospels*, 148, and Stephen J. Patterson, "The Gospel of Thomas and Historical Jesus Research," in *Coptica—Gnostica—Manichaica: Mélanges offerts à Wolf-Peter Funk*, ed. L. Painchaud and P.-H. Poirier (Leuven: Peeters, 2006), 683, though principally in reference to the teaching of Jesus. The focus of attention in this book is not on the Jesus tradition, however.

53. Ehrman, "Christianity Turned on Its Head," 117–18; cf. Ehrman, *Lost Christianities*, 248.

of the quotation above says as much. Where I would take issue with Ehrman is over the idea that the first and second centuries were simply a great melting pot of Gospel production and that any differentiation among Gospels can make sense only retrospectively, from a third- or fourth-century perspective. As we will see, differentiation among various Gospels is not just a bifurcation of orthodox canonical Gospels versus heretical others. Rather, just as one can classify the *Gospel of Truth* and the *Gospel of Philip* as reflective of Valentinian theology, and the Coptic *Gospel of the Egyptians* and the *Gospel of Judas* as reflective of "classic," or Sethian, Gnosis, so one can understand Matthew, Mark, Luke, and John as reflective of the "proto-orthodoxy" from which they emerged. The central theological tenets of the Valentinians, the Gnostics, and the proto-orthodox existed prior to the composition of their Gospels, although these texts naturally also went on in turn to shape and define the movements from which they emerged.

This present book is not about the canon and what political and social factors may have been involved in the construction of canon lists. I do want, however, to argue against the idea that "the history of the engagement"—the battle over what constituted the shape of early Christianity—had to be "rewritten" to justify the idea that Matthew, Mark, Luke, and John reflected what "had always been the views of the apostolic Churches" and were "rooted" in earliest Christian teaching.[54] It is of course true, from a fourth-century perspective, that "Matthew, Mark, Luke and John all tell the story as the proto-orthodox had grown accustomed to hearing it." The point of the present book is to argue that it is also the case that "Matthew, Mark, Luke and John all tell the story as the proto-orthodox had grown accustomed to hearing it" already when they were first composed. None of the Gospels emerged in a theological vacuum at the beginning, only subsequently in the late second or third or fourth centuries to enter a world of theological prejudice in which people developed criteria of orthodoxy.

The aim here, therefore, is to emphasize the point that there were theological criteria in operation, in the preached apostolic gospel or kerygma, *even before the compositions of any Gospels*. These theological criteria were embedded in the preaching of those who had been closest to the earthly Jesus, namely the apostles. All the written Gospels—canonical and apocryphal alike—emerged from a situation in which there were already established, though also developing, norms of what constituted authentic apostolic proclamation. Though it may sound odd to put it this way, in an important sense, a "canon"—in the sense of a widely held standard of teaching—*preceded* the composition of the Gospels, and the authors of Gospels, deliberately or unconsciously, reflected this preached gospel, or they did not.

---

54. This language comes from the quotation from Ehrman above.

CONCLUSION: OUTLINE AND THESES

The plan of the book is as follows.

Part I will outline the method to be used in the book. The method, especially in operation in the first argument of the book, is comparative, and so the central components of part I involve identifying the things to be compared (the "comparanda") and the tool of comparison (the "comparator"). Although this may sound arcane, it is merely an attempt to clarify the way people ordinarily compare different things all the time.

Part II, by far the longest part, consists of what comparativist scholars call "description," namely the process, prior to the comparison proper, in which the items being compared are outlined. This description is not of the items in some imaginary totality but in terms that enable the planned comparison to take place. This part, therefore, builds on part I's discussion of the comparanda and the comparator. The description of the comparanda in part II will therefore examine the relevant Gospels with respect to their treatments of the themes of the model, namely Jesus's messiahship, vicarious death for sins, resurrection, and fulfillment of scripture.

Part III begins, in chapter 15, with the actual work of comparison: explaining how, on the basis of the prior descriptions, work x resembles work y more than they resemble work z with respect to comparator p. Again, despite the jargon of "comparators" and the like, this is no different from any ordinary comparison, as, for example, where one might in the supermarket conclude that vegetable x resembles vegetable y more than they resemble vegetable z, with respect to their usefulness for a particular recipe. The second chapter of part III builds on the previous, contending for a second point, namely that Matthew, Mark, Luke, and John are united in reflecting the apostolic gospel that was known in the environments from which they emerged.

To repeat my contentions in the form of theses, then:

Thesis 1: *The four New Testament Gospels share key elements of theological content that mark them out from most of the noncanonical Gospels.*

Thesis 2: *The reason why the four New Testament Gospels are theologically similar to one another is that they—unlike most others—follow a preexisting apostolic "creed" or preached gospel.*

Part One

THE TOPICS OF COMPARISON

—

Chapter One

The Comparanda

A Selection of Early Christian Gospels

It is obvious that, in order to engage in a comparative study, the first field to define is the comparanda, the items that are going to be the objects of the comparison. The aim of this chapter is therefore to establish the range of which Gospels are to be compared in this study, and to offer some justification for that selection by outlining the criteria in use.

1. Listing the Comparanda

The primary sources that constitute the principal body of material investigated here is as follows. The four New Testament Gospels of Mark, Matthew, Luke, and John comprise one "half" of the collection of early Christian Gospels. The others are seven of the best-preserved and best-known apocryphal Gospels:

the *Gospel of Peter*,
Marcion's Gospel,
the *Gospel of Thomas*,
the *Gospel of Truth*,
the Coptic *Gospel of Philip*,
the *Gospel of Judas*, and
the Coptic *Gospel of the Egyptians*.

These Gospels, along with Matthew, Mark, Luke, and John, will therefore constitute the larger category of early Christian Gospels that are investigated here.[1] Although differentiations will be made later, at present the concern is to establish that they have sufficient similarity to make comparison possible.[2]

2. CRITERIA FOR SELECTION

The criteria for this selection are fivefold. In order to guarantee sufficient similarity, and also to keep the sample manageable, the works selected will satisfy all five conditions.

2.1 Date

First, dating is a factor. In order to limit the investigation to manageable proportions, we will not investigate all "forty other Gospels" (to cite one scholar's essay title) or the seventy or so works recently collected under the label of "Evangelien und Verwandtes."[3] The chronological span of the works covered here will be approximately the first two centuries CE: this is a rough period, since the dates especially of the *Gospel of Philip* and the *Egyptian Gospel* cannot be determined with any precision.

---

1. Margaret M. Mitchell, "On Comparing, and Calling the Question," in *The New Testament in Comparison*, ed. John Barclay and Benjamin White (London: Bloomsbury, 2020), 110, uses the term "category" to refer to the collection of things deemed sufficiently similar to be comparable.

2. As Poole notes in his often-cited statement, similarity makes comparison possible, while difference makes comparison interesting. See Fitz J. P. Poole, "Metaphor and Maps: Towards Comparison in the Anthropology of Religion," *JAAR* 54 (1986): 417. Similarly, Wendy Doniger, "Post-modern and -colonial -structural Comparisons," in *A Magic Still Dwells: Comparative Religion in the Postmodern Age*, ed. Kimberley C. Patton and Benjamin C. Ray (Berkeley: University of California Press, 2000), 65: "Even the most relentless of French deconstructionists could not, I think, compare the text of a Greek tragedy and, say, the text of an instruction manual for Word-Perfect for Windows, 1998; there is no common ground, no sameness."

3. Christopher M. Tuckett, "Forty Other Gospels," in *The Written Gospel*, ed. Markus Bockmuehl and Donald A. Hagner (Cambridge: Cambridge University Press, 2005), 238–53; Christoph Markschies and Jens Schröter, eds., *Evangelien und Verwandtes*, vol. 1 of *Antike christliche Apokryphen in deutscher Übersetzung* (Tübingen: Mohr Siebeck, 2012): even the vast list in that volume was already incomplete when published, since P. Oxy. LXXVI 5072 was published in volume 76 of the Oxyrhynchus papyri in 2011.

2.2 The Title "Gospel"

Second, a "nominalist" criterion can be applied. That is, one element taken into consideration will be whether the particular works are called Gospels in the ancient world.[4] This might seem an arbitrary criterion, but it is an important one, since those works that call themselves Gospels, or are called such by others, are ipso facto being related to preexisting Gospels. Authors who call their works "Gospel," therefore, for whatever reason align them with prior "Gospels"; or, scribes or commentators or detractors who refer to a work as a Gospel engage in the same kind of categorization.

Of those Gospels listed above, all are called Gospels in antiquity. To anticipate the treatment of the individual works in section 3 later in this chapter, the evidence for usage of "Gospel" as a title can be summarized as follows:

	in-text reference	ms. paratext title	external reference
Gospel of Mark		•	•
Gospel of Matthew		•	•
Gospel of Luke		•	•
Gospel of John		•	•
Gospel of Peter			•
Marcion's Gospel			•
Gospel of Thomas		•	•
Gospel of Philip		•	
Gospel of Judas		•	•
Gospel of Truth	•(?)		•
Gospel of the Egyptians		•	

Negatively, however, other texts have been categorized as Gospels only by modern scholars, although they attracted other sorts of titles in antiquity. The

4. See Andrew Gregory and Christopher Tuckett, "Series Preface," in *Gospel of Mary*, ed. Christopher Tuckett (Oxford: Oxford University Press, 2007), vi: "An alternative approach [sc. to deciding whether a work is a Gospel on the basis of its content] might be to accept as a 'gospel' anything which claims the name 'gospel' for itself, and/or perhaps is claimed by others to have such a name (a so-called nominalist approach). This would certainly provide a more extensive list than some 'essentialist' approaches; it would, however, come up against potential problems in cases where the text concerned is not extant in full and/or no third party refers to it: hence we do not have any claims, one way or the other, about what title the text claimed for itself or how others regarded it." Cf. also p. vii: "we have mostly accepted the claims—of either manuscripts themselves (e.g., in colophons) or of ancient authors talking about such texts—to identify some works as 'gospels.'" In the cases we are dealing with in this chapter, we do have references internally and/or externally.

Sophia of Jesus Christ, which is a postresurrection dialogue in similar form to the *Gospel of Mary*, could have been called a Gospel but happens not to have been as far as we know. The *Epistle of the Apostles* is part epistle, part Gospel, part polemical treatise, and part apocalypse. Of the various texts conventionally included in collections of Gospel material, only quite a small proportion were called as such in the ancient world.

2.3 Family Resemblance, or Gospels as a "Chain Complex"

A third criterion that one can apply is that of family resemblance. That is, apart from the first one to be written, a Gospel will presumably have some kind of similarity not just in name but also in form or content to its predecessors. This resemblance must be distinguished from identifying something like the "essence" of a Gospel—like "the life and teaching of Jesus" or some such criterion.[5] Not all early Christian groups in antiquity thought that the historical life of Jesus was especially good news: the *Gospel of Thomas* and the *Gospel of Judas*, for example, have little interest in it. On the other hand, the *Gospel of Philip* has only occasional, and the Coptic *Gospel of the Egyptians* has no reference to the teaching of Jesus. We need to be wary of judgments that "Gospel" is more a matter of literary form (and the canonical Gospels' literary form, at that) than of subject matter. A canonical bias may be in operation in supposing that a Gospel, and therefore a group's gospel message, should be cast in a particular mode. On the other hand, however, it would be surprising if a Gospel suddenly represented a total break from its predecessors. The key point here is that "Gospel" was an evolving category in antiquity.

Although, as far as I know, Wittgenstein did not himself illustrate his concept of family resemblance with a table, expositions of the idea commonly use such a table:[6]

---

5. Cf. the criterion of Gregory and Tuckett for a Gospel as a text claiming "to give direct reports of the life and/or teaching of Jesus" ("Series Preface," vii). This may be a criterion we might "instinctively" gravitate toward ("Series Preface," vi), but arguably reports of the saving activity of Jesus as constituting the content of the gospel message, such as are found in the *Gospel of Truth* and the *Gospel of the Egyptians*, might be equally important, as we shall see below. Although the criterion above is quite general, some of the texts called Gospels in antiquity still do not satisfy it.

6. E.g., Rodney Needham, "Polythetic Classification: Convergence and Consequences," *Man* NS 10 (1975): 349–69.

		characteristics A, B, C, etc.
members	1	A B D E G
1–6 of a	2	A C E F G
class	3	B C D F G
	4	B C E F G
	5	A B D E F
	6	A C D F G

This table illustrates the point of a class consisting of overlapping characteristics, but with no consistent defining characteristic that is a sine qua non. There is no single characteristic that all members possess, but at the same time, each characteristic is possessed by at least four of the six, and each member shares at least three characteristics with every other member.

A similar approach can be taken to the class of Gospels in antiquity:

	narrative	birth	ministry	death	resurrection	sayings/ dialogue	Jesus discourse	authorial discourse
Mark	•		•	•	(•)	•	•	
Matthew	•	•	•	•	•	•	•	
Luke	•	•	•	•	•	•	•	
John	•		•	•	•	•	•	•
Gos. Pet.	•	(?)	(?)	•	•	(?)	(?)	
Gos. Marcion	•		•	•	•	•	•	
Gos. Thom.			(•)	(•)		•		
Gos. Truth			•	•				•
Gos. Phil.			(•)	(•)	(•)	•		•
Gos. Jud.	•		(•)	(•)		•	•	
Gos. Eg.		•						•

(•) Referred to at least in some sense, but not described.
(?) Not in the extant text, but possibly in unattested portions.

With this in mind, we can perhaps be more precise than talking in terms of family resemblances and speak more precisely of a "chain complex." In this category, described by Vygotsky, there is no "nucleus," but rather, "the definitive attribute keeps changing from one link to the next."[7] If one compares, say, Mark and the *Gospel of the Egyptians*, it is difficult to find much similarity, just as Irenaeus found little in common between the canonical Gospels and the *Gospel of Truth*. If one adheres to a set-theory approach, identifying Gospels by essential defining features, it would be difficult to find many such features. If it is acknowledged, however, that instances of Gospel writing are instead a chain complex, one can see something of how development might take place. To speculate, it is easy to see how one can get from the canonical Gospels to the *Gospel of Mary* and the *Gospel of Judas*, which retain some Gospel framework and introduce myth; thereafter one can see how the myth becomes the principal interest and thus the *Gospel of Truth* and the *Gospel of the Egyptians* no longer feel the need to incorporate the old framework. Or again, it is a big leap to go from the Synoptics to the *Gospel of Philip*, but a journey via the *Gospel of Thomas* is much more comprehensible.

2.4 Subject Matter

A fourth criterion is related to the previous two, namely subject matter. This criterion is an important one because, unlike an epistle or even an apocalypse, a Gospel has a predetermined topic or theme, namely Jesus and his saving activity. The application of the title "Gospel" to these works is not so much a statement about literary form but much more an indication of subject matter: the application of the term here identifies the particular work within a tradition of discussions of *Heilsbotschaft* ("saving message"). Hence "epistles" (which can be about anything) or "revelations" (whose subject matters are not as unpredictable but still diverse) are not close analogies to "Gospels" (which do have a predictable subject matter).

I would suggest that a closer analogy to a Gospel might be, for example, the ancient tradition of writing books with titles identifying the topic of discussion.[8] In the case of works called *On the Soul* (Περὶ ψυχῆς or *De Anima*), for example, the title is defined not by genre but by the subject matter. This subject matter is so important that Plato wrote a book known to some by this title (usually called the *Phaedo*), as did Aristotle, Tertullian, and Alexander of Aphrodisias;

---

7. Lev Vygotsky, *Thought and Language*, rev. and exp. ed. (Cambridge: MIT Press, 2012), 124–25, describing the chain complex; cf. Needham, "Polythetic Classification," 350. Needham also talks in terms of "sporadic resemblances" (352).

8. See further Simon J. Gathercole, "The Nag Hammadi Gospels," in *Die Nag-Hammadi Schriften in der Literatur und Theologiegeschichte des frühen Christentums*, ed. J. Schröter and K. Schwarz (Tübingen: Mohr Siebeck, 2017), 199–218.

closer to home, there is also in Nag Hammadi Codex II the Exegesis on the Soul (ⲧⲉϨⲎⲄⲎⲤⲒⲤ ⲉⲧⲂⲉ ⲧⲉⳝⲨⲭⲎ). With the subject matter defined, the literary form—dialogue (the *Phaedo*), polemical treatise (in Tertullian's case), narrative (Exegesis on the Soul), or whatever—is a matter of choice. Or again one could take the case of works called *On Nature* (Περὶ φύσεως).[9] The work of Heraclitus known by this title consisted of oracular aphorisms, Parmenides's *On Nature* is a hexameter poem, while Melissus's work was a prose treatise;[10] Plato's *Timaeus* could also be called "On Nature."[11] To be clear, I am not saying that the Gospels are works about the soul or nature. Rather, just as there is a literary tradition of works *On the Soul* and *On Nature*, so it is also with the title *Gospel*. The subject matter is defined: the nature of salvation and how Jesus has effected it. Thereafter, as far as literary form is concerned, it is a case of chacun à son goût. As a result, form is not determinative for what makes a Gospel as much as is content, which in this case is Jesus's saving activity (εὐ-) being announced (-αγγέλιον).

2.5 Preservation

The final criterion is not important in the abstract but is relevant to the present investigation: there must be a substantial amount of the work preserved. This criterion is necessary because, in order to come to conclusion about the theological content of these works, we need to have enough of a sample. Unfortunately, this means excluding such well-known fragments as the *Egerton Gospel*, P. Oxy. V 840 (sometimes called the *Gospel of the Savior*), the Greek *Gospel of the Egyptians*, the *Gospel of Mary*, and the so-called Jewish-Christian Gospels. We cannot gain any detailed sense of their theological outlooks from the extant fragments of these works.[12] To give a sense of scale, the *Egerton Gospel*, for example, amounts to a quantity of text only slightly greater than

9. On the title *On Nature*, see G. S. Kirk, J. E. Raven, and M. Schofield, *The Presocratic Philosophers*, 2nd ed. (Cambridge: Cambridge University Press, 1983), 102–3, 184.

10. Admittedly, in these cases, the titles are probably later attributions (Kirk, Raven, and Schofield, *Presocratic Philosophers*, 102–3, 184, 391–92). See also Egidius Schmalzriedt, *Peri Physeos—Zur Frühgeschichte der Buchtitel* (Munich: Wilhelm Fink, 1970).

11. Diogenes Laertius, *Lives* 3.60. For discussion, see Jaap Mansfeld, *Prolegomena: Questions to Be Settled before the Study of an Author or a Text* (Leiden: Brill, 1994), 73.

12. See the meagre results presented in A. F. Gregory, *The Gospel according to the Hebrews and the Gospel of the Ebionites* (Oxford: Oxford University Press, 2017), 164–67, on the *Gospel according to the Hebrews*, where the theological themes identifiable in the surviving fragments are (1) the christological categories of king, prophet, Son of Man, teacher, miracle worker, as well as savior, which might suggest that the Gospel elsewhere dealt with soteriology (165), (2) the Spirit as mother of Jesus, and (3) the need for sibling solidarity; and also

that of the Johannine prologue, while P. Oxy. V 840 is about the same as the prologue.[13] More is preserved of the *Gospel of Mary*, but still only two short, disconnected sections. The *Gospel of Peter* also survives only in fragmentary form, but the fragments amount to a substantial and continuous portion of text in its original language. These two are the "limit" cases: the *Gospel of Mary* is the best-preserved work not discussed in this book, and the *Gospel of Peter* is the most poorly preserved text that is discussed here.

3. Application of the Criteria

These criteria will be applied in the order above to the various Gospels as follows, providing (1) a generally accepted date, (2) the evidence for the title, (3) family resemblances with other Gospels, (4) the work's subject matter, and (5) the state of preservation.

3.1 Mark, Matthew, Luke, John

Since it is generally agreed that the canonical Gospels count as Gospels, and because much of their manuscript tradition and patristic reception overlaps, we can treat these Gospels together. (1) The canonical Gospels are generally dated to the first century, though some take Luke and John in particular to come from the second century. In any case, they comfortably fit the criterion of arising within the first two centuries CE. (2) The canonical Gospels are widely called Gospels both in manuscripts and in patristic testimonia.[14] (3) If Mark was the earliest Gospel, then Matthew and Luke intentionally follow the form of Mark extremely closely. John also seems to know the Synoptic Gospels: he not only follows roughly the contents of his predecessors but writes a *bios*-like narrative of approximately the same length; John is about midway in length between Mark and Matthew.[15]

256–59 on the Gospel of the Ebionites, where the theological motifs seen are (1) Jesus as Son of God, (2) mission to Israel, (3) the role of John the Baptist, and (4) sacrifice and diet.

13. As an illustrative comparison, the NRSV of John 1:1–18 contains 304 words; Nicklas's English translation of the *Egerton Gospel* has 425 words, and Kruger's translation of P. Oxy. V 840 has 313 words.

14. On the former, see Simon Gathercole, "The Titles of the Gospels in the Earliest New Testament Manuscripts," *ZNW* 104 (2013): 33–76; and for the earliest instances of the latter, see Justin, *1 Apol.* 66.3 (referring to more than one of the canonical Gospels); Muratorian Fragment 2, 9; Irenaeus, *Haer.* 3.1.1; Clement, *Strom.* 1.21.147.5. See further Simon Gathercole, "The Alleged Anonymity of the Canonical Gospels," *JTS* 69 (2018): 447–76.

15. John has around fifty-nine thousand characters; cf. Mark (around forty-six thousand

(4) Despite their varying emphases, all are focused on the saving work of Jesus (e.g., Matt 1:21; Mark 8:35; 10:45; Luke 19:10; John 3:17; 12:47). (5) Although New Testament textual criticism is a vibrant discipline, it is generally agreed that the text of the Gospels is well preserved. This becomes even more evident when their preservation is compared with that of the noncanonical Gospels.

3.2 The Gospel of Peter

(1) The *Gospel of Peter* probably dates to around 150–190 CE.[16] (2) Although its principal textual witness does not have any title attached to it, there is a claim in the text that Peter is the author: "But I, Simon Peter (ἐγὼ δὲ Σίμων Πέτρος), and Andrew my brother, taking our nets went to the sea" (*Gos. Pet.* 14.60). There are also numerous patristic testimonia to a work called "the *Gospel of Peter*," beginning in the second century.[17] (3) The form of the surviving text is a narrative much like the passion narratives of the canonical Gospels. (4) Jesus is called "savior" by one of the criminals crucified with him; even though the dominant note surrounding the passion in the *Gospel of Peter* is one of judgment, there is (presumably) salvation in the preaching to the dead by the "cross." (5) Although it is a mere torso, beginning in medias res and breaking off before the end, the Akhmim text is a substantial excerpt, four times as long as the *Egerton Gospel* and five times as long as P. Oxy. V 840.

3.3 Marcion's Gospel

(1) Marcion's Gospel can be dated quite securely by the floruit of its author, to around 150 CE. (2) No manuscript of Marcion's Gospel survives, but on the positive side, it is the only apocryphal Gospel treated here for which we have a definitely known author. Although Marcion probably did not

---

characters) and Matthew (around seventy-four thousand characters). Luke is rather longer, consisting of around seventy-nine thousand characters.

16. Thus Paul Foster, *The Gospel of Peter: Introduction, Critical Edition and Commentary* (Leiden: Brill, 2010), 172.

17. According to Eusebius, Serapion of Antioch in the late second century was involved in a well-known controversy about the Gospel (Eusebius, *Hist. eccl.* 6.12.1–6) and wrote a book entitled "On the So-called Gospel of Peter" (Περὶ τοῦ λεγομένου κατὰ Πέτρον εὐαγγελίου). On the testimonia, see especially Foster, *Gospel of Peter*, 97–115. To the testimonia, a fragment of Philip of Side from the first half of the fifth century can be added: see C. de Boor, *Neue Fragmente des Papias, Hegesippus und Pierius in bisher unbekannten Excerpten aus der Kirchegeschichte des Philippus Sidetes* (Leipzig: Hinrichs, 1888), 169 (no. 4); there is also possible reference in Innocent I's letter to the bishop of Toulouse in 405 CE, though this may refer to an acts or apocalypse of Peter (*Epistula* 6.7 [PL 20.502a]).

affix his name to the text, there is general agreement that he referred to it as the "Gospel." Our principal sources for Marcion's Gospel, Tertullian and Epiphanius, both call it one, and they claim explicitly or implicitly that Marcion gave it this label.[18] (3) The text is clearly intended to be a rival to other Gospels as it has the same narrative structure as whichever canonical Gospel(s) Marcion may have known, and has almost identical content to Luke with certain omissions. (4) Enough can be reconstructed of the text to show that salvation by Jesus is a central theme: it surely contains, for example, Luke's saying that the Son of Man came to save what was lost (19:10).[19] (5) The latest edition of the text consists of about 2,400 Greek words in the categories of "secure" and "very likely," though it doubtless was considerably longer than that.[20]

3.4 The Gospel of Thomas

(1) The Gospel of Thomas was compiled around 140–180 CE.[21] (2) The Nag Hammadi text of Thomas refers to it as a Gospel in its colophon, as do various patristic authors.[22] The title is known in the third century by Hippolytus (or Pseudo-Hippolytus) and Origen.[23] (3) It is not as close in form to the canonical Gospels as are the Gospel of Peter and Marcion's Gospel, but it consists of a number of dialogues and sayings, about half of which are related to the Synoptic Gospels. (4) Its soteriological core is evident in that Jesus uniquely reveals the truth that must be understood in order to transcend death: this is stated in the programmatic first saying after the prologue (Gos. Thom. 1). (5) The Greek

---

18. See Tertullian, Marc. 3.17.5; 4.6.1 (Marcionis evangelium); cf. in evangelio . . . vestro, in Marc. 3.19.4; 3.24.8; cf. also Marc. 4.2.3, according to which Marcion apparently took "another gospel" in Gal 1 to refer to a corruption of the gospel, which was his impulse for attempting to restore it to its supposedly original form. Epiphanius also implies that Marcion called it "gospel," referring to τὸ . . . παρ᾽ αὐτῷ λεγόμενον εὐαγγέλιον (Pan. 42.10.2; cf. 42.11.17), and calling Marcion's text a Gospel "in name" (ὀνόματι) but not in reality (Pan. 42.11.7); also Epiphanius, Pan. 42.13.6, which says that Marcion "claimed to have something of the gospel and the apostle" (ἐπαγγειλάμενος ἔχειν τι τοῦ εὐαγγελίου καὶ τοῦ ἀποστόλου).

19. Cf. also Gos. Marcion 5.24, 31; 10.22; 18.18–22, 37–43.

20. See Dieter Roth, The Text of Marcion's Gospel (Leiden: Brill, 2016).

21. See Simon Gathercole, The Gospel of Thomas: Introduction and Commentary (Leiden: Brill, 2014), 112–27.

22. See Simon Gathercole, "Named Testimonia to the Gospel of Thomas: An Expanded Inventory and Analysis," HTR 105 (2012): 53–89, and Gathercole, Gospel of Thomas, 35–61, on named testimonia, and 617–18, on the subscriptio.

23. I am taking Origen as, to the best of my knowledge, writing without acquaintance with the (Pseudo-)Hippolytan Elenchos.

texts are highly fragmentary, but the text survives in an almost complete state (with only a few small lacunae) in the Coptic Nag Hammadi text.

3.5 The Gospel of Truth

(1) The *Gospel of Truth* was probably written around 140–170 CE. (2) A work with this title is known to Irenaeus, who calls it a Valentinian composition (*Haer.* 3.11.9), and the surviving Coptic text of the *Gospel of Truth*, though without an *inscriptio* or *subscriptio*, has as its opening words "The gospel of truth is. . . ." The title therefore probably came from this opening phrase, as often happened with opening words.[24] It would be an extraordinary coincidence if Irenaeus referred to a work by this title, and that there was also another Valentinian work that had the phrase as its opening line.[25] (The phrase "gospel of truth," as Nagel notes, is by no means a common one.)[26] The fact that there is not a title appended to the text in Nag Hammadi Codex I may well be a result of the scribal habits of the copyist of this codex rather than necessarily because the work did not have a title.[27] This work mentioned by Irenaeus, then, is very likely to be substantially the same as Nag Hammadi I,3. (3) It has certain liter-

---

24. See E. Nachmanson, *Der griechische Buchtitel: Einige Beobachtungen* (Darmstadt: Wissenschaftliche Buchgesellschaft, 1969), 37–52, for examples of titles derived from the opening words of works.

25. On the improbability of such a coincidence, see Peter Nagel, *Evangelien und Apostelgeschichten aus den Schriften von Nag Hammadi und verwandtes Kodizes: Koptisch und Deutsch*, vol. 1 of *Codex apocryphus gnosticus Novi Testamenti* (Tübingen: Mohr Siebeck, 2014), 31–32, contra Markschies in Markschies and Schröter, *Evangelien und Verwandtes*, 349. On the other hand, Nagel takes this Nag Hammadi work to be referring to and presupposing, rather than identifying itself as, the *Gospel of Truth* referred to by Irenaeus (*Evangelien und Apostelgeschichten*, 3). This seems to be an unnecessary multiplication of entities, however.

26. Nagel, *Evangelien und Apostelgeschichten*, 31.

27. Benoît Standaert, "'Evangelium Veritatis' et 'Veritatis Evangelium': La question du titre et les témoins patristiques," *VC* 30 (1976): 140: "il semble bien que la raison de l'absence de titre pour le second texte du Codex Jung est à chercher non pas dans le texte mais dans le Codex. . . . Ce resultat codicologique negatif ne permet cependant pas de conclure qu'à cette époque l'ouvrage n'avait pas encore de titre." Certainly, to look at the facsimile edition, one is struck by the erratic layout: see James M. Robinson, ed., *The Facsimile Edition of the Nag Hammadi Codices: Codex I* (Leiden: Brill, 1977). Only two works in Codex I have a title. The first (the Prayer of the Apostle Paul) is inscribed on the flyleaf, and because of the stylized nature of the script of the title, it is hard to tell whether it is in a different hand. The second, the *Treatise on the Resurrection*, is certainly written in a different hand from that of the rest of the codex (Standaert, "Evangelium Veritatis," 139), as can easily be seen from looking at the facsimile.

ary connections with preexisting Gospels, including a great number of small allusions as well as more substantial references to particular pericopes such as the parable of the lost sheep, and the question of rescuing a sheep on the Sabbath. (4) As we will see in more detail later, the soteriological center of the book is evident in the depiction of Jesus as the one who fills up deficiency and provides knowledge for the ignorant. (5) The text is extant in full in Coptic translation in Nag Hammadi Codex I, with only a few small gaps; another very fragmentary, and therefore not particularly useful, text also survives (if that is the right word) in Nag Hammadi Codex XII.

3.6 The Coptic Gospel of Philip

(1) The *Gospel of Philip* perhaps appeared around 200 CE. (2) Its title, also attached by Epiphanius to another work,[28] appears in the colophon of the work's only manuscript witness.[29] (3) It is probably closest in form to the *Gospel of Thomas* (consisting of theologically coherent, but discrete statements), and perhaps alludes to some of *Thomas*'s contents;[30] it also quotes some sayings from the canonical Gospels.[31] (4) Its subject matter is again Jesus and sote-

---

28. Epiphanius, *Pan.* 26.13.2–3 refers to a Gospel of Philip, but it differs from that attested in NHC II.

29. P. Nagel, "'Das (Buch) nach Philippus': Zur Titelnachschrift Nag Hammadi Codex II,3: p. 86,18–19," *ZNW* 99 (2008): 99–111, quite rightly points out the odd appearance of the title appended to the text of the *Gospel of Philip*: rather than a two-line title marked off at the end of the text, ΠΕΥΑΓΓΕΛΙΟΝ comes shortly after the end of the text with some spacing but on the same line, whereas ΠΚΑΤΑΦΙΛΙΠΠΟΣ appears after a line break in the normal way of a Gospel title. I would disagree with Nagel's conclusion that ΠΚΑΤΑΦΙΛΙΠΠΟΣ implies an original title other than "Gospel" however. In the first place, one could account for this as a scribal mistake. The ΠΕΥΑΓΓΕΛΙΟΝ is in the same hand as the rest of the text, suggesting an *in scribendo* correction. Alternatively, ΠΚΑΤΑΦΙΛΙΠΠΟΣ would be a perfectly acceptable abbreviation for ΠΕΥΑΓΓΕΛΙΟΝ ΠΚΑΤΑΦΙΛΙΠΠΟΣ, especially after a previous Gospel (Thomas precedes it): such abbreviation is not as unusual as Nagel makes out (110 n. 31), as the shorter form appears (though less commonly than the fuller form) in both initial titles, running headers and end titles in Gospel manuscripts. See Gathercole, "Titles of the Gospels," 72–76. We would then have in Codex II "the Gospel according to Thomas," followed by "that according to Philip." Finally, Nagel's alternative "Buch" is certainly no improvement on "Gospel," because the use of ΚΑΤΑ with "book" would be unusual, whereas ΚΑΤΑ with "Gospel" is widely established. There are also problems with the assumptions that Nagel begins with about what form a work ought to take to be called a Gospel (104), one of the issues that this discussion is addressing.

30. Gathercole, *Gospel of Thomas*, 76–77.

31. See Gos. Phil. 55.34 (cf. Matt 7:21; 15:13; 16:17; 18:10); Gos. Phil. 68.7–8 (Matt 8:12;

riology, as seen for example in the summary statement that "Christ came to purchase some, to save some, to redeem some."[32] (5) Again a continuous text from beginning to end survives, with occasional lacunae.

3.7 The Gospel of Judas

(1) The *Gospel of Judas* was probably written around 140–170 CE.[33] (2) A handful of patristic authors, beginning with Irenaeus at the end of the second century, refer to a "Gospel of Judas"—and it is notable that Irenaeus agrees with the title appended to the Coptic text.[34] This title is not "the *Gospel according to Judas*," with the usual κατά ("according to"), but the *Gospel of* (in the sense of *about*) *Judas*. (3) It has key points of contact with the passion narratives in the canonical Gospels. On the other hand, it has certain points in common with the *Gospel of Thomas*, and like the *Gospel of Mary* has quite conventional Synoptic-like settings into which the elaborate mythical material is interposed. This mythical material closely resembles the "classic" Gnostic myth also found in the *Gospel of the Egyptians*. (4) This myth is the revelation that Jesus announces, and his saving activity is also evident in the narrator's opening summary of Jesus's ministry: "when he appeared upon the earth, he performed signs and great wonders for the salvation of humanity" (*Gos. Jud.* 33.6–9). (5) We have a continuous text of the Gospel, with a large proportion of it surviving: now, with the publication of some new fragments in 2010, perhaps around 90 percent of the text is extant.[35]

3.8 The Coptic Gospel of the Egyptians

(1) The *Gospel of the Egyptians* perhaps was composed around 200 CE. (2) The title of the *Gospel of the Egyptians* is more complicated, because its *subscriptio* reads "the Holy Book of the Great Invisible Spirit." However, in its larger col-

---

22:13, and 25:30); Gos. Phil. 68.9–12 (cf. Matt 6:6); Gos. Phil. 68.26–27 (cf. Mark 15:34 // Matt 27:46); Gos. Phil. 72.29–73.1 (cf. Matt 3:15); Gos. Phil. 84.7–9 (cf. John 8:32).

32. Gos. Phil. 52.37–53.3.

33. For this date, see Simon Gathercole, *The Gospel of Judas* (Oxford: Oxford University Press, 2007), 133–40.

34. The *Gospel of Judas* in Codex Tchacos, unusually has the "genitive" ⲛ- prefix, rather than the more natural ⲕⲁⲧⲁ, and therefore matches the genitive form in Irenaeus (*Haer.* 1.31.1). This is consistent with the fact that Judas is not designated as the author or scribe in any sense. For other patristic testimonia, see Gathercole, *Gospel of Judas*, 114–31.

35. Herb Krosney, Marvin Meyer, and Gregor Wurst, "Preliminary Report on New Fragments of Codex Tchacos," *EC* 2 (2010): 282–94.

ophon, the title *Gospel of the Egyptians* is also present. This title *Gospel of the Egyptians* (or, strictly speaking, "the *Egyptian Gospel*"[36]) should therefore be considered to be *one* of the titles of NHC III,2 and IV,2 alongside "the Holy Book of the Great Invisible Spirit." Two different titles should occasion no surprise, given that double titles were very common in antiquity. Diogenes Laertius, for example, gives double titles for almost all of Plato's dialogues;[37] as already noted, Plato's *Phaedo* is known to some by this title (Aristotle, Celsus, Clement), while others call it the Περὶ ψυχῆς (Galen, Sextus Empiricus, Clement again).[38] Plautus's works have bilingual (though not synonymous) titles; the works of Varro and Lucian are also transmitted with multiple titles.[39] Diogenes Laertius even provides a triple title for the Pseudo-Platonic *Epinomis*, or *Nocturnal Gathering*, or *Philosopher*.[40] Although the *Gospel of the Egyptians* is often referred to as the "so-called" *Gospel of the Egyptians*,[41] Hedrick may well be correct that, in addition to the title "the Holy Book of the Great Invisible Spirit," the "Gospel title included in the colophon in Codex III attests to the fact that the document is 'gospel' in the sense of the proclamation of the early church."[42] (3) In terms of family resemblances to other Gospels, the *Gospel of*

---

36. This is preferred by Bentley Layton, *The Gnostic Scriptures* (London: SCM, 1987), 101. The text of the title in NHC III 69.6, ⲡⲉⲩⲁⲅⲅⲉⲗⲓⲟⲛ ⲛ̄ⲣⲙ̄ⲛ̄ⲕⲏⲙⲉ, suggests the sense "Egyptian Gospel." One might compare Jerome's title, "the Hebrew Gospel" (*Hebraicum euangelium*) in *Tract. Ps.* 135, in contrast to the more common "Gospel of the Hebrews": see Gregory, *Gospel according to the Hebrews*, 31–53, for the various testimonia. Because haplography of ⲛ̄ is very common in the Nag Hammadi Codices, however, the CGL supplies an additional ⲛ̄-, and so prints ⲡⲉⲩⲁⲅⲅⲉⲗⲓⲟⲛ <ⲛ̄>ⲣⲙ̄ⲛ̄ⲕⲏⲙⲉ, i.e., "Gospel of the Egyptians." See Alexander Böhlig and Frederik Wisse, eds., *Nag Hammadi Codices III, 2 and IV, 2: The Gospel of the Egyptians* (Leiden: Brill, 1975), 166 (III 69.6). I will generally refer to the work below as the *Gospel of the Egyptians*.

37. Diogenes Laertius, *Lives* 3.58–61. For discussion, see Mansfeld, *Prolegomena*, 71–74.

38. See also Diogenes Laertius, *Lives* 3.50 for the former, *Lives* 3.37 for the latter; together in *Lives* 3.58.

39. See A. P. Bitel, "Quis ille Asinus aureus? The Metamorphoses of Apuleius' Title," *Ancient Narrative* 1 (2000–2001): 208–44, which also has a helpful bibliography.

40. Diogenes Laertius, *Lives* 3.60.

41. See, e.g., Alexander Böhlig and Frederik Wisse, "Introduction," in *The Nag Hammadi Library in English*, ed. James M. Robinson (Leiden: Brill, 1977), 195; cf. John D. Turner's introduction to the work in *The Nag Hammadi Scriptures*, ed. Marvin Meyer (New York: HarperCollins, 2007), 247: "since the late 1940s it has become customary to refer to it inappropriately as the 'Gospel of the Egyptians,' a title based on the name given to it at the beginning of the colophon."

42. See C. H. Hedrick, "Christian Motifs in the 'Gospel of the Egyptians': Method and Motive," *NovT* 23 (1981): 259.

the Egyptians is probably at the extreme edge of the group considered here (hence the skepticism of some about it being labeled as a Gospel), although it contains a myth very similar to that of the *Gospel of Judas*. Unlike the *Gospel of Judas*, however, the *Gospel of the Egyptians* has abandoned the dialogical format involving Jesus and his disciples and concentrates exclusively on the myth. (4) In terms of subject matter, as we will explore in more detail later, the final act in the sequence of three saving events is accomplished by the union of the Great Seth with the living Jesus. (5) The text survives in two substantial manuscripts from Nag Hammadi.

Conclusion

The four canonical Gospels and these seven noncanonical Gospels are widely acknowledged by scholars to reflect a great variety of theological viewpoints (including those of Sethian Gnosticism, Valentinianism, as well as other unnamed movements). They therefore comprise a sufficiently large representative sample. They are only a sample: the aim of this chapter is not to set the canonical Gospels alongside an alternative apocryphal "corpus." The seven apocryphal Gospels selected here are, however, reasonably well known and accessible. Together with the canonical Gospels, they fit together in a larger category of early Christian Gospels and have sufficient similarities, in line with the criteria of selection above, to make comparison possible.

Chapter 2

THE COMPARATOR

The Early Kerygma and Its Components

The previous chapter identified the works that will be compared with each other. These comparanda that have been selected are not going to be compared with one another in their entireties, however, because a comparison of one whole with another whole is simply not possible. Claims of holistic comparison cannot be sustained. Jonathan Z. Smith, for example, says of the aim to compare religions in their entirety in Sanders's *Paul and Palestinian Judaism*: "I am baffled by what 'entire religion, parts and all' could possibly mean for Sanders";[1] Jacob Neusner, while agreeing with much of what Sanders says, pronounces the latter's attempt at systemic comparison to be "so profoundly flawed as to be hopeless."[2] The point here is not to have a dig at Sanders, but to clarify the point that holistic comparison is methodologically unsustainable. Even with single texts, it is impossible to compare, for example, every aspect of Matthew's Gospel with the *Gospel of Judas* in its entirety.

1. THE FUNCTION OF THE COMPARATOR

As most of those engaging in comparative religious study now recognize, what is necessary in any comparison is what Smith has called the "third term," or what I label here the comparator(s). That is, when one is comparing *A* with

---

1. Jonathan Z. Smith, "In Comparison a Magic Dwells," in *A Magic Still Dwells: Comparative Religion in the Postmodern Age*, ed. Kimberley C. Patton and Benjamin C. Ray (Berkeley: University of California Press, 2000), 39; reprinted from Smith, *Imagining Religion* (Chicago: University of Chicago Press, 1982), 19–35.

2. Jacob Neusner, "Comparing Judaisms," *HR* 18 (1978): 191. Cf. also p. 179, on the failure to compare, parts and all; p. 183 ("Sanders does not succeed in his systemic description"); and p. 189 ("we must ask ourselves what has gone wrong with Sanders' immense project").

B, one can never simply compare *A* and *B* in their totalities, but only make a comparison of them with respect to *x* (or x^1 and x^2 and x^3 etc.). On this point, Smith reflects the influence of an important article by Poole, who makes clear that comparison does not involve "phenomenologically whole entities" but rather "focused selection of significant aspects of the phenomena."[3] Or again, "comparison does not deal with phenomena *in toto* or in the round, but only with an aspectual characteristic of them."[4]

To ground this in a familiar example, those who have studied the New Testament will commonly find themselves thinking:

"Matthew is very much like Mark."

In fact, however, this is not really a meaningful statement; or, better, it is an incomplete statement—an ellipsis. What New Testament scholars mean when they say this is something like:

"[**comparanda:**] Matthew and Mark
resemble each other
[**comparator:**] with respect to verbal agreement and order."

My point here has nothing to with Matthew and Mark per se: this book is not about the Synoptic problem. The point is that essential in any comparison is this comparator, which is the criterion for determining similarity and difference.[5]

To refine the comparative process further, a richer comparison involves explaining how, with respect to *x*, *A* and *B* are more alike than either is like *C*. To continue our analogy of the Synoptic problem, scholars who say "Matthew is very much like Mark" probably mean not *only* "with respect to verbal agreement and order" but probably something more like this:

---

3. Fitz J. P. Poole, "Metaphors and Maps: Towards Comparison in the Anthropology of Religion," *JAAR* 54 (1986): 414–15.

4. Poole's point here is noted in, e.g., Jonathan Z. Smith, *Drudgery Divine: On the Comparison of Early Christianities and the Religions of Late Antiquity* (Chicago: University of Chicago Press, 1990), 50–53; Dale B. Martin, "The Possibility of Comparison, the Necessity of Anachronism and the Dangers of Purity," in *The New Testament in Comparison*, ed. John Barclay and Benjamin White (London: Bloomsbury, 2000), 64. Various contributors to the edited volume of Patton and Ray also refer to it (*Magic Still Dwells*, 10–11, 184, 188, 239).

5. Alluding to the words of William E. Paden, "Elements of a New Comparativism," in Patton and Ray, *Magic Still Dwells*, 184.

"[**comparanda:**] Matthew and Mark
resemble each other
[**comparators:**] with respect to (1) verbal agreement and (2) order
[**additional comparandum:**] more than either resembles John."

In this analogy, Matthew, Mark, and John are the *A*, *B*, and *C* above—the comparanda, the things being compared. Being clear about the comparators, or the criteria, in the comparison is essential here. An ancient scribe, who was paid by the line, might have regarded Mark and John as much more like each other: they are closer in length and so require about the same amount of papyrus and labor. *With respect to length*, Mark and John resemble each other more than either resembles Matthew.[6]

2. The Kerygma as Comparator

One of the distinctive features of this book is that it proposes the early Jewish-Christian message of the good news, or "kerygma," attributed to the apostles, as the comparator in operation. As has already been stated briefly in the introduction, the first aim of this book, and therefore the purpose of the comparison, is to evaluate the degree to which the various Gospels (the comparanda) follow or reflect the kerygma (the comparator). The choice of comparator therefore sets up the goal of the comparison.[7] The introduction also noted in passing that the components of the message or kerygma to be used were (1) Jesus's messiahship, (2) his death for sins, (3) his resurrection, and (4) his fulfillment of scripture. These components are drawn from Paul's summary in 1 Cor 15:3–4:

> For what I received I passed on to you as of first importance: that Christ died for our sins according to the Scriptures, that he was buried, that he was raised on the third day according to the Scriptures.

6. I am reminded of my former percussion teacher, whose favorite concerts to play in were those that involved the greatest range of percussion instruments—because they paid better.

7. Smith, *Drudgery Divine*, 51–54; Troels Engberg-Pederson, "The Past Is a Foreign Country: On the Shape and Purposes of Comparison in New Testament Scholarship," in Barclay and White, *New Testament in Comparison*, 55. Margaret M. Mitchell, "On Comparing, and Calling the Question," in Barclay and White, *New Testament in Comparison*, 110, notes the importance of defining the *skopos* or goal of the comparison.

A justification for the use of these particular components will be presented in chapter 3. The present chapter seeks to define as precisely as possible what the comparator to be used in this study is. This is to avoid overgeneralizing, as seen in how one more "radical" scholar can in nebulous terms state that John and *Thomas* are more similar to each other "in spirit" than each is to the Synoptics; another more conservative scholar can (equally vaguely) conclude a comparison of *Thomas* and the Synoptics by saying that in much of *Thomas* "the drift is completely different."[8] Rather than talking about the atmospherics of "spirit" or "drift," the aim here is to be as clear and precise as possible. As William E. Paden remarks, "the more . . . refinement one brings to the notions 'common factor,' 'similarity,' and 'difference,' and to the criteria for determining difference, the more systematically grounded comparativism becomes."[9]

As noted, the next chapter will offer justification for the proposed comparator (the kerygma) as a salient one. The account in this chapter of the comparator explains the four components of the kerygma attested in 1 Cor 15: (2.1) the identity of Jesus as the "Christ," (2.2) his saving death, (2.3) his resurrection, and (2.4) the work of Christ as fulfilling scripture. After this, (3) the form of the comparator will be clarified.

2.1 Jesus as Christ/Messiah

The comparator or criterion in operation in this study includes the specific identification of Jesus as messiah or Christ, including that particular terminology rather than understanding messiahship in a broad sense without necessary usage of the term. There is wide agreement that Jesus's messiahship or status as Christ was a fundamental component of earliest Christian preaching. To cite two quite different scholars on this point, Donald Juel noted of the formula in 1 Cor 15:3, "Presumably the confession could have stated that 'Jesus died for our sins.' It does not, however."[10] Paula Fredriksen similarly remarks, "This message of Jesus's crucifixion, death, resurrection, and impending return would have come together with a further affirmation, namely, that Jesus was ὁ χριστός, the messiah."[11] Here, then, a first key component of our comparator is the identity of Jesus as "Christ" or messiah. The early Jewish-Christian

8. Respectively, Gregory J. Riley, *Resurrection Reconsidered* (Minneapolis: Fortress, 1995), 3, and Riemer Roukema, *Jesus, Gnosis and Dogma* (London: Bloomsbury, 2010), 71.

9. Paden, "Elements of a New Comparativism," 184.

10. Donald Juel, *Messianic Exegesis: Christological Interpretation of the Old Testament in Early Christianity* (Philadelphia: Fortress, 1988), 9.

11. Paula Fredriksen, *Paul, the Pagans' Apostle* (New Haven: Yale University Press, 2017), 133.

kerygma draws the terminology of "messiah" from existing Jewish tradition and thus applies to Jesus a known descriptor.

In ancient Judaism, the term "messiah" is neither precisely defined nor endlessly applicable.[12] On the one hand, even though "anointed" could be a description of a variety of people, the term "messiah" could also be a manner of speaking about a particular figure. There was an exegetical tradition in Judaism that often talked of *the* "anointed" one (or perhaps in some cases, the *two* anointed ones). Horbury, for example, notes that certain passages imply a familiar sense of "messiah," as is shown from the way in which the term is used without explanation.[13] In the Qumran *Rule of the Congregation*, God is to engender *hmšyḥ*, "the messiah" (1QSa II, 11–12). In 2 Bar. 29, the messiah (*mšyḥ*) is introduced again with the implication that the term will be understood to refer to a particular figure, and the same is true of 4 Ezra 12.32 (*mšyḥ*, *unctus*). This usage is continued in the two instances in the Mishnah, implying an idiomatic usage that needs no explanation: referring to the "days of the messiah" (*ymwt hmšyḥ*) and the "footsteps of the messiah" (*ʿqbwt mšyḥ*).[14]

On the other hand, this is not to suggest that the contours of the figure are clearly defined. As Novenson has recently stated, Jewish (and Christian) messianic expressions are defined not by an essence but by a discursive field, namely that of scripture: "all ancient messiah texts, both Jewish and Christian, typically work," he remarks, by making use of "intelligible biblical imagery":[15]

12. In the only two uses of the term in classical literature, it means "salve" or "ointment," however, rather than referring to an anointed person: see Aeschylus, *Prom.* 480; Euripides, *Hipp.* 516.

13. Contra, e.g., Martin Karrer, who argues that sacral anointing of the sanctuary is the means for understanding the term "anointed," which means close to God or in connection/belonging to God: "Salbung besage Gotteszugehörigkeit." See Karrer, *Der Gesalbte: Die Grundlagen des Christustitels* (Göttingen: Vandenhoeck & Ruprecht, 1990), 213: "Die Betonung der Gottesnähe/Gottesverbindung im Gesalbtenbegriff wirkt sich terminologisch aus" (220). The strained translation of 1 Cor 15:3 (as "Gesalbter war er, der starb") reveals one of the flaws (Karrer, *Der Gesalbte*, 370). Novenson also correctly notes that one problem with Karrer's approach is that messiah language in early Jewish literature is deliberately archaizing, rather than corresponding to the contemporary realia of anointing: "Contra Karrer, as a rule, early Jewish 'anointing' language does not track with contemporary anointing practices, but rather adopts the outdated idiom of the scriptures." See Matthew Novenson, *The Grammar of Messianism: An Ancient Jewish Political Idiom and Its Users* (Oxford: Oxford University Press, 2017), 266. Similarly, William Horbury, *Jewish Messianism and the Cult of Christ* (London: SCM, 1998), 7. Novenson's point that messiah language is explicated in early Jewish and Christian texts in scriptural terms is crucial here.

14. m. Ber. 1.5; m. Soṭah 9.15.

15. Novenson, *Grammar of Messianism*, 2.

"they are all involved in negotiating a common set of social realities by using a common set of scriptural source texts."[16] Or again, "ancient messiah texts constitute one example—an excellent example—of the vast, sprawling ancient Jewish and Christian project of scriptural interpretation."[17] Making the point that Jewish and Christian messianic discourses operate in the same way, he comments that "all ancient messiah texts, Jewish or Christian, are the product of the reinterpretation of scriptural oracles in the light of the experience of their respective authors."[18] The "experience" point is relevant here, as it can encompass such varied experiences as, for example, the effects of the Hadrianic revolt on how Bar Kokhba was or was not interpreted as the messiah, or how experiences of Jesus shaped the ways in which Christian authors engaged in messianic exegesis.[19] Similarly, Bauckham has stated that "Jewish messianism was not so much a tradition of ideas as a tradition of exegesis" and depended a good deal on the way in which different scriptural passages were combined with each other.[20] Or again, as John Collins puts it, although we cannot measure the intensity or longevity of ancient Jewish hopes and expectations about the messiah, "when interest in messianic traditions arose, however, there was at hand a body of tradition which could be used to articulate it."[21] The first generation of Jewish adherents to Jesus tapped into that "body of tradition" or "tradition of exegesis." The earliest Christian kerygma, then, was an oral "ancient messiah text" and an example of "the vast, sprawling ancient and Jewish Christian project of scriptural interpretation."

Evaluation of how and to what extent the various Gospels reflect the Jewish-Christian kerygma, then, will first involve examination of whether or how certain Gospels can be classified as messianic literature; that is, alongside the specific usage of "messiah" and its translational equivalents, there will be an evaluation of

16. Novenson, *Grammar of Messianism*, 14.

17. Novenson, *Grammar of Messianism*, 17; cf. 213: "In this respect, messianism is just another instance of the vast ancient Jewish and Christian enterprise of biblical interpretation." Or again, 267: "there is nothing at all special about messianism. It is just a part . . . of the vast interpretive project of ancient Judaism"; cf. 274: "Exegesis, we might say, is the stuff messiah texts are made of."

18. Novenson, *Grammar of Messianism*, 184; cf. 1, which talks of "participation by ancient Jews and Christians in a common scriptural discourse in texts about their respective messiahs."

19. As Novenson, *Grammar of Messianism*, 184, goes on to say.

20. Richard J. Bauckham, *The Testimony of the Beloved Disciple* (Grand Rapids: Baker, 2007), 234.

21. J. J. Collins, *The Scepter and the Star: Messianism in Light of the Dead Sea Scrolls*, 2nd ed. (Grand Rapids: Eerdmans, 2010), 77.

the degree to which they employ or activate such a scripturally rooted discourse or body of messianic tradition to define their messiah or Christ figure. Put differently, we can exercise historical imagination in thinking about the extent to which calling Jesus the "Christ" in a particular Gospel reflects a tradition of messianic exegesis and could have been recognized by other Jews as participating in a similar discourse, however much there may have been disagreement about how legitimately that discourse was configured and about its application to Jesus.[22]

Second, in addition to exegesis of specific passages, there are *themes* in Jewish messianic discourse that are prominent—themes that themselves are often scriptural. One important example is the question of the messiah's paternity.[23] Jesse is the progenitor of the messiah in the Targum Isaiah (Tg. Isa. 11.1). More narrowly, in the Psalms of Solomon, the future king and "Lord's anointed" is the "son of David" (Pss. Sol. 17.21, 32); a Qumran Genesis commentary speaks similarly of the "messiah of righteousness, the branch of David" (4Q252). Another Qumran text designates the messiah as fathered by God (1QSa II, 11–12).[24] Simon ben Kosiba is restyled as Simon *bar Kokhba*, "son of the star"—again, an exegetical move, understanding Num 24:17 as referring to a known historical individual. In rabbinic literature and the targumim, these patronymic designations of the messiah are expanded to include, alongside existing designations, the "messiah son of Joseph" and "the messiah son of Ephraim."[25] The Jerusalem Talmud can talk of Hezekiah as the messiah's father (y. Ber. 2.4 [5a]). There can also be interest in the messiah's mother.[26] Other passages, however, speak of the more mysterious origins of the messiah.

These patronymics are one sort of collocation with the word "messiah." Another is what one might call "messiah + genitive" language.[27] The *Community*

---

22. Compare the disagreement evidenced in rabbinic literature over whether Simon Bar Kokhba was the messiah, as noted at the end of this section.

23. See Novenson, *Grammar of Messianism*, 65–113; Novenson, "Whose Son Is the Messiah?," in *Son of God: Divine Sonship in Jewish and Christian Antiquity*, ed. Allen et al. (Winona Lake, IN: Eisenbrauns, 2019), 72–84; the theme of the messiah's parentage is also surveyed at various points in Martha Himmelfarb, *Jewish Messiahs in a Christian Empire: A History of the Book of Zerubbabel* (Cambridge: Harvard University Press, 2017).

24. Cf. also, outside of passages with the specific terminology of "messiah," 4Q174 and 4Q246.

25. Messiah son of Joseph: b. Sukkah 52a; the messiah son of Ephraim: Tg. Ps.-J. Exod. 40.11; Tg. Song 4.5.

26. Himmelfarb, *Jewish Messiahs in a Christian Empire*, 35–59, discusses the anonymous mother of the messiah Menahem in y. Ber. 2.4 (5a), and Hephzibah in the Sefer Zerubbabel.

27. See further Matthew V. Novenson, *Christ among the Messiahs: Christ Language in*

Rule and the Damascus texts refer to the messiah of Aaron and the messiah of Israel,[28] for example, and 1 Enoch and 4Q521 talk of "his [i.e., God's] messiah."[29] Conversely, there are also phrases (as we have seen in the Mishnah) that take the form "of the messiah," such as "days" or "footsteps." Another sort of collocation is the linking of "messiah" with other titles, such as "king" or "lord."[30] Other, less distinctive themes that can be associated with the messiah include teaching, saving activity, and the messiah's predecessor or forerunner (cf., e.g., 1QS IX, 9–11; b. 'Erub. 43a–b).

The key aim here then is to evaluate the extent to which different Gospel texts activate this messianic, exegetical "body of tradition which could be used to articulate" the figure in question: as Collins notes by this language, there may or may not have been a febrile anticipation of the messiah's arrival in the first century CE, but there was certainly an available exegetical tradition that could be tapped. Again, the degree to which a Gospel not only uses the term "messiah" or "Christ" but also taps into that available tradition of exegesis is a useful guide to whether it would be recognized as messianic discourse in early Judaism, however much various people may have disagreed about the identification of Jesus as messiah. Such disagreement was an intra-Jewish debate, as the sharp disagreement about the messiahship of Bar Kokhba in the Yerushalmi illustrates: "When Rabbi Akiba saw Bar Koziba, he said, 'This is the king messiah.' Rabbi Yohanan ben Torta said to him, 'Akiba, grass will come up between your cheeks and still the son of David will not have come'" (y. Ta'an. 4.8).[31] The

---

Paul and Messiah Language in Ancient Judaism (Oxford: Oxford University Press, 2012), 98–136, on "Christ phrases."

28. 1QS IX, 11; CD XII, 23–XIII, 1. For the messiah of Israel, see also Tg. Isa. 16.1–5 and Tg. Mic. 4.8.

29. 1 En. 48.10; 52.4; 4Q521 2 II, 1.

30. See "king," e.g., in Tg. Neof. Gen. 49.11: "How beautiful is king messiah who is to arise from among those of the house of Judah." The collocation is common in the targumim and rabbinic literature: e.g., also Tg. Ps.-J. Gen. 3.15; 49.10–12; Tg. Ps.-J. Exod. 40.9. See Horbury, *Jewish Messianism and the Cult of Christ*, 9, and Philip S. Alexander, "The King Messiah in Rabbinic Judaism," in *King and Messiah in Israel and the Ancient Near East*, ed. J. Day (Sheffield: Sheffield Academic, 1998), 456–73. See "lord," e.g., in Pss. Sol. 17.32, as well as "lord messiah" in Midr. Ps. 2.9, on Ps 2:7–8 (Braude 1:41), and Midr. Ps. 18.29, on Ps 18:36 (Braude 1:261).

31. Matthew Novenson, "Why Does R. Akiba Acclaim Bar Kokhba as Messiah?," *JSJ* 40 (2009): 555. Or again, while one midrash portrays Rabbi Akiba as convinced of Simon's messiahship by his ability to catch Roman ballista shots, in the Talmud the rabbis execute him as a false pretender (Lam. Rab. 2.2; b. Sanh. 93b).

present book will seek to understand how different early Christian Gospels reflect the early Jewish-Christian messianism of the kerygma.

2.2 Jesus's Vicarious Death

There is a great multiplicity of terminology with which salvation through Jesus's death can be described. It can be called (and has been called) redemptive, soteriological, vicarious, cultic, necessary, substitutionary, atoning, cleansing, propitiatory, apotropaic, curse-bearing, or beneficiary; it can be a purchase, a liberation, a sacrifice (e.g., a sin offering or a guilt offering, or Passover sacrifice), a life-for-life exchange, a purgation or expiation or removal of sin, a ransom, a scapegoat (or *pharmakon*), or a death that brings suffering to a climactic end.[32] As a result of these multiple possibilities, it is very important to be clear about what is being affirmed and what is not.[33] It is also important to make "a careful distinction between the language of the sources and the language of description."[34]

First, this study will especially employ the analytical, or etic, categories of "effective death" and "vicarious death," as used in particular by the Dutch ancient historian Henk Versnel. These categories will be useful here because they are sufficiently precise to be helpful for the purposes of comparison, but are also not too narrow. The former (effective death) means "dying for" in a general sense that the death is beneficial. It can describe a person "dying for or instead of another or others—family, friends, the total community of city or fatherland."[35]

32. These terms and concepts are mainly drawn from the various essays in Jörg Frey and Jens Schröter, eds., *Deutungen des Todes Jesu im Neuen Testament*, 2nd ed. (Tübingen: Mohr Siebeck, 2012).

33. Clarifications of such terms in English-language New Testament scholarship are surprisingly rare. For two exceptions, see I. J. Du Plessis, "The Saving Significance of Jesus and His Death on the Cross in Luke's Gospel—Focussing on Luke 22:19b–20," *Neot* 28 (1994): 523, and F. G. Carpinelli, "'Do This as *My* Memorial' (Luke 22:19): Lucan Soteriology of Atonement," *CBQ* 61 (1999): 75.

34. See Frey and Schröter, "Einleitung," in *Deutungen des Todes Jesu*, xxii: "eine sorgsame Unterscheidung von Quellen- und Beschreibungssprache." Also Jens Schröter, "Sühne, Opfer, Stellvertretung: Zur Verwendung der analytischer Kategorien zur Deutung des Todes Jesu," in Frey and Schröter, *Deutungen des Todes Jesu*, 69, on how terms like "effective death" are abstractions.

35. Henk S. Versnel, "Making Sense of Jesus' Death: The Pagan Contribution," in Frey and Schröter, *Deutungen des Todes Jesu*, 230. See more generally Versnel, "Making Sense of Jesus' Death," 230–53, and Versnel, "Quid Athenis et Hierosolymis? Bemerkungen über die

By contrast, Versnel defines "vicarious death" as a particular kind of effective death that satisfies two further conditions: the death brings about salvation from some kind of doom, and it is the necessary condition of that salvation: "As I have observed considerable confusion on the question of what exactly may be understood by the term 'vicarious death' I here present my working definition: By vicarious or soteriological death I mean any deliberately sought or accepted death that is—or is a posteriori interpreted as—both unconditionally required and explicitly intended to guarantee the salvation of another or others from present or impending doom or death."[36] Thus vicarious death is glossed as "soteriological," as distinct both from "death for a conviction," which does not rescue others (though it may inspire them), and from a patriotic death, which may not guarantee victory—and indeed the soldier willing to die might well not be called upon to do so. According to the kerygma, the death of Jesus fits well within the broader category of an effective death, and into the narrower sense of a vicarious death that is necessary for the salvation of its beneficiaries.

Second, the kerygmatic formula specifies the particular saving benefit of Jesus's death, namely that it deals with sins ("Christ died *for sins*"). If we limit the possible meanings of "dealing with sins" to scriptural options, per the "according to the scriptures" of the kerygma, these possibilities include (1) *removal* of sins, that is, cleansing (by blood?), purgation, or the transference of sins to a scapegoat, or expiation in C. H. Dodd's sense of "purification" and cleansing from sin or defilement (e.g., Zech 3:1–4);[37] (2) *making amends* for sins, that is, using the metaphor of recompense or payment (Isa 40:1–2), or in the martyrological sense that sufficient suffering had taken place so as to bring God's wrath on Israel to an end (2 Macc 7–8);[38] (3) *forgiveness* of sins, for example, in the preaching of John the Baptist (Mark 1:4); (4) *as a result of the sins of others*, in a substitutionary manner, bearing their sins and death (cf. 1 Kgs 16:18–19 LXX), or (5) *protection from the future consequences* of sins, that is, construing the death as an apotropaic or propitiatory act, so that future condemnation will be averted (e.g., Lev 1–7). This is an illustrative rather than an exhaustive list of possibilities, and these examples are not intended

---

Herkunft von Aspekten des 'Effective Death,'" in *Die Entstehung der jüdischen Martyrologie*, ed. Jan Willem van Henten, B. A. G. M. Dehandschutter, and H. J. W. van der Klaauw (Leiden: Brill 1989), 162–96.

36. Versnel, "Making Sense of Jesus' Death," 226–27.

37. C. H. Dodd, "ΙΛΑΣΚΕΣΘΑΙ, Its Cognates, Derivatives and Synonyms in the Septuagint," *JTS* 32 (1931): 356.

38. Per the interpretation in Michael Wolter, "Der Heilstod Jesu als theologisches Argument," in Frey and Schröter, *Deutungen des Todes Jesu*, 298 n. 4.

as entirely different from and incompatible with one another; they could be combined. Exegesis of the particular passages will determine whether any such categories apply to the different Gospels.

2.3 Resurrection on the Third Day

The resurrection, as it is understood in the kerygma, appears to presuppose three points. First, the resurrection is an event distinct from Jesus's death. This is clear from the "third day" demarcation, which makes it clear that the resurrection is not a translation or assumption to God at death (Diodorus Siculus 4.38.4–5) or an alternative to death (cf., e.g., Livy 1.16; Plutarch, *Rom.* 27), though it has in common with such motifs that eventually Jesus is raised to heaven and thus disappears. Second, the risen Jesus is visible and at times recognizable in bodily form in his appearances. These appearances are treated where applicable in appendices to the subsequent chapters. Finally, the inclusion of the resurrection within the kerygma means that it is a "gospel" event, that is, that it is good news of soteriological significance. This component of the kerygma will therefore be used to determine whether an early Christian Gospel includes a resurrection of Jesus and the extent to which the work views this event as a saving "gospel" incident.

2.4 Fulfillment of the Scriptures

Finally, the formula in 1 Corinthians includes emphatically the common early Christian idea that the central events of salvation—the death and resurrection of Jesus—conformed to existing scripture. This presaging can take various forms, so that the fulfillment can consist of either a prediction coming true, or a symbolic "type" coming to fuller expression, or a foreshadowing being perfected. (These examples are merely illustrations, rather than a definitive list.) The plurality of scriptures in Paul's formula implies a diversity of modes of both promise and fulfillment. Similarly, "scriptures" does not specify any particular closed canon or open corpus of holy writ. The form that scriptural references might take is also left open here: there may be no explicit reference to scripture at all, or a Gospel may be studded with introductory formulae that mark quotations. Both programmatic statements and scriptural references (including quotations, allusions, echoes, etc.) will be taken into account. The final element of the comparator, then, will be applied to evaluate the extent to which different early Christian Gospels deem the saving activity of Jesus to be in accord or conformity with Israel's scripture.

3. THE FORM OF THE COMPARATOR

It may be helpful to clarify how these four elements combine to form a single comparator in operation in the comparative process. Smith remarks: "In the case of an academic comparison, the 'with respect to' is most frequently the scholar's interest, be this expressed in a question, a theory, or a model—recalling, in the case of the latter, that a model is useful precisely when it is different from that to which it is being applied."[39] The "with respect to," or comparator, used here matches most closely the last of these—a model (the kerygma) that differs from the comparanda (early Christian Gospels) to which it is applied. Here, "model" is understood in the sense of a *simplified description of a process or system*. Smith, for example, gives a vivid account of how the eighteenth-century polymath Joseph Priestley describes the "fall" of Christianity from its primitive purity, as follows: (1) philosophical Christians (2) adapted (3) religious ideas and practices taken from heathenism (4) thus contaminating (5) ancient doctrine (6) resulting in absurdities.[40] This six-part schema is what Smith calls "Priestley's model" in this same sense of a *simplified description of a process or system*.

As an analogy from New Testament scholarship, we can note Douglas Campbell's summary of the story of God and Jesus in Galatians and Romans:

> *Trajectory One: Descent.* (1) God the Father (2) sends, delivers up, and does not spare, (3) his own (4) Son, Jesus. (5) Jesus suffers (6) and dies, (7) in an act of identification. (8) This act also atones, or (in the most general terms) deals with humanity's problems, especially in relation to Sin. (9) This is also an act that speaks of the love of both the Father and the Son.

> *Trajectory Two: Ascent.* (10) The Spirit of God and Christ, (11) also the Spirit of life, (12) resurrects Jesus, that is, creates new life in and for him, (13) and glorifies him.[41]

Campbell calls this "schematis[ing] the key narrative" or "something of a template," the "basic story" or "fundamental outline."[42] It also corresponds to what Smith designates a "model."

39. Smith, *Drudgery Divine*, 51.
40. Smith, *Drudgery Divine*, 9–12.
41. Douglas Campbell, "The Story of Jesus in Romans and Galatians," in *Narrative Dynamics in Paul: A Critical Assessment*, ed. Bruce W. Longenecker (Louisville: Westminster John Knox, 2002), 108.
42. Campbell, "Story of Jesus," 108, 109.

In a similar way to how Smith and Campbell present their models, the model "with respect to" which the different Gospel comparanda are being compared in the present study is also a composite one—namely (1) Christ (2) died for our sins and (3) rose again on the third day (4) in fulfillment of scripture.

CONCLUSION

Here, then, the identity of the savior (Jesus, who is "Christ"), his actions (death for our sins, and resurrection), and their scriptural basis are the key elements of this model to be used as a comparator. One might naturally object that this definition of the comparandum is arbitrary, determined by Paul's construal of the gospel (and by one context-dependent expression of that gospel). Hence the next chapter will aim to justify the salience of this comparator.

Chapter Three

JUSTIFYING THE KERYGMA
AS A COMPARATOR

Jonathan Z. Smith, for many years the doyen of the comparative study of religion, commented extensively on comparators as a matter of scholarly choice: "comparison, in its strongest form, brings differences together within the space of the scholar's mind for the scholar's own intellectual reasons," and "in the case of an academic comparison, the 'with respect to' is most frequently the scholar's interest";[1] again, comparison tells a story in the "space of the scholar's mind,"[2] and "it is the scholar's intellectual purpose—whether explanatory or interpretative, whether generic or specific—which highlights that principled postulation of similarity."[3] Smith's statements along these lines have been widely cited.[4]

Smith is of course correct, but this should not make comparison a solipsistic enterprise. (Smith of course does not intend this.) Others have talked of how it is important to have rational rather than arbitrary comparators operative in the process of comparison: Poole talks, for example, of the "focused selection of *significant* aspects of the phenomena,"[5] and in the parallel field

---

1. Jonathan Z. Smith, *Drudgery Divine: On the Comparison of Early Christianities and the Religions of Late Antiquity* (Chicago: University of Chicago Press, 1990), 51.

2. Smith, *Drudgery Divine*, 115.

3. Smith, *Drudgery Divine*, 56.

4. In addition to various references in Kimberley C. Patton and Benjamin C. Ray, eds., *A Magic Still Dwells: Comparative Religion in the Postmodern Age* (Berkeley: University of California Press, 2000), and John Barclay and Benjamin White, eds., *The New Testament in Comparison: Validity, Method, and Purpose in Comparing Traditions* (London: Bloomsbury, 2020), see, e.g., Oda Wischmeyer, *Liebe als Agape: Das frühchristliche Konzept und der moderne Diskurs* (Tübingen: Mohr Siebeck, 2015), 58.

5. Fitz J. P. Poole, "Metaphors and Maps: Towards Comparison in the Anthropology of Religion," *JAAR* 54 (1986): 414–15.

of classification, Parsons notes that "it cannot be that *any* arbitrarily selected characteristics count as relevant."[6] She notes that for a category to be "interesting," a certain "relevance" is required.

Along similar lines, in a previous study of my own that was critical of the comparators operative in other scholars' work, I talked of the importance of both "salience" and "distinctiveness" as having the potential to satisfy these conditions of Poole and Parsons.[7] The previous chapter sought a degree of *precision* and *distinctiveness* in defining the comparator. This chapter focuses on salience. To have a salient comparator is to have a comparator that is an important theme, important either to the comparanda themselves or in their environment, or to our contemporary world. To return to the previous chapter's analogy of the Synoptic problem, Matthew and Luke both feature characters called Abijah. They are distinctive in this respect—no other book in the New Testament does. Abijah-reference is a (very!) precise comparator, but it is not a particularly *salient* one. The Abijahs are not the same person, as one is a king of Judah (that of Matt 1:7), and the other was the head of a priestly division (Luke 1:5). The similarity is therefore so unsalient as to be entirely coincidental.

This chapter seeks to argue for the salience of the kerygmatic model as a comparator on two grounds. First, it will seek to show that the four elements highlighted in the previous chapter were extremely early features of the kerygma: ergo the comparator's salience lies in part in the *antiquity* of the model's components. The second part of the chapter shows that the four components of the model are found together in other early Christian literature: ergo the model's salience lies also in its *wide distribution*. (The antiquity and distribution of the kerygma are of course related.) Part of the argument therefore consists in showing that the gospel articulated by Paul is not something invented by him but is something that he draws on: he draws on a preached message that has a considerable prehistory and that has influenced not only Paul but also other early Christian authors.

---

6. Kathryn Pyne Parsons, "Three Concepts of Clusters," *Philosophy and Phenomenological Research* 33 (1973): 517; italics original.

7. Simon Gathercole, "Resemblance and Relation: Comparing the Gospels of Mark, John and Thomas," in Barclay and White, *New Testament in Comparison*, 173–92.

1. Antiquity as Indicative of the Comparator's Salience

1.1 The Source and Its Significance

The summary of the gospel with the four elements noted appears in 1 Cor 15:1–11:

> [1]Brothers and sisters, let me remind you of the gospel I proclaimed to you, which you received and on which you have taken your stand. [2]By this gospel you are saved, if you hold firmly to the word I preached to you. Otherwise, you have believed in vain. [3]For what I received I passed on to you as of first importance: that Christ died for our sins according to the scriptures, [4]that he was buried, that he was raised on the third day according to the scriptures, [5]and that he appeared to Cephas, and then to the Twelve. [6]After that, he appeared to more than five hundred of the brothers and sisters on a single occasion, most of whom are still alive, although some have fallen asleep. [7]Then he appeared to James, and then to all the apostles. [8]Last of all he appeared to me as well, as to one abnormally born. [9]For I am the least of the apostles, not even deserving to be called an apostle, because I persecuted the church of God. [10]But by the grace of God I am what I am, and his grace to me was not without effect. No, I worked harder than all of them—yet not I, but the grace of God that was with me. [11]Therefore, whether it is I or they, this is what we preach, and this is what you believed.

Paul here defines the apostolic message in this passage as "the gospel" (15:1), which he preached and which the Corinthians believed, and he underlines its significance as the means by which the Corinthians are "saved" (15:2), and as "of first importance" (15:3).

It is clear that the gospel summary statement begins in the middle of verse 3, after the first "that" (ὅτι). The most likely end point is either the end of verse 5, or after the reference to Cephas. The additional material in verses 6–8 does not have a formulaic tone: verse 7 seems to go over some of the same ground as verse 5, since the "Twelve" and the "apostles" are hardly mutually exclusive groups, even if they are not identical. Everything in verses 8–9 is obviously ruled out since Paul would not have received tradition about himself.

This yields a formula as follows:

> A^1 *that* (ὅτι) *Christ died for our sins according to the scriptures,*
> A^2 *and that* (καὶ ὅτι) *he was buried;*

> B¹ *and that* (καὶ ὅτι) *he was raised on the third day according to*
> *the scriptures,*
> B² *and that* (καὶ ὅτι) *he appeared to Cephas [and then to*
> *the Twelve].*

On this view, we have a formula structured in two parts, focused on the death and resurrection. Each part is a couplet with a principal point (A¹, B¹) and an ancillary point (A², B²). Each of the four elements is introduced with a ὅτι, and after verse 5 the instances of ὅτι stop. In the former couplet (A), the burial is an auxiliary point to the main theme that Jesus died for our sins. In the latter couplet (B), the appearances are confirmation or testimony that Jesus rose on the third day. The priority of the first element in each part is confirmed by the fact that these principal points (A¹, B¹) are defined as "according to the scriptures," whereas the second elements (A², B²) are not given the heightened importance accorded by this prepositional phrase.

Paul's statement that the gospel is something that he "received" (1 Cor 15:3) is significant for the antiquity of his message: it has a considerable prehistory.[8] In its written form here, Paul's summary of the gospel in 1 Corinthians goes back to the mid-50s CE.[9] This gospel can be traced further back, however, to the time of Paul's proclamation, or "handing over," of the gospel to the Corinthians (1 Cor 15:3) around 50 CE. Indeed, it appears to go back earlier still, to when Paul himself "received" it (again, 15:3), presumably not long after his conversion sometime in the 30s CE. (Of course, the message may well not have existed then in exactly the same wording, or even in the same language.) In fact, one might trace this gospel back even further to before Paul's conversion: as he reports in Galatians, when he was converted, the churches of Judea rejoiced to hear that he was now proclaiming the good news of the very faith that he had previously sought to destroy (Gal 1:23).[10] Whatever the precise date of

---

8. The argument here does not depend on any putative Semitic source, per the mid-twentieth-century debate between Jeremias and Conzelmann over the original language and provenance of the formula. See Harvey K. McArthur, "'On the Third Day,'" *NTS* 18 (1971): 81 n. 1, for bibliography.

9. Anthony C. Thiselton, *The First Epistle to the Corinthians* (Grand Rapids: Eerdmans, 2000), 31: "the earlier part of AD 54 is widely accepted as the most likely date for the writing of 1 Corinthians."

10. On this, see Jeff Peterson, "The Extent of Christian Theological Diversity: Pauline Evidence," *ResQ* 47 (2005): 7.

origin, Paul's claim is that the gospel summarized in 1 Cor 15:3–5 is extremely old. There is further evidence to support this claim.

1.2 Paul's Reproduction of Tradition in 1 Corinthians 11

This supporting evidence consists in the fact that, where Paul elsewhere talks of having received tradition as he does here in 1 Cor 15, we can fact-check the details. His claim is externally verifiable. The key place here is Paul's account of the words of institution in 1 Cor 11, where he recounts the words used by Christians when they celebrated the Eucharist or Lord's Supper. The language that Paul uses to introduce the two sections is very similar:

1 Cor 11:23:	ἐγὼ γὰρ παρέλαβον ἀπὸ τοῦ κυρίου	ὃ καὶ	παρέδωκα ὑμῖν,	ὅτι . . .
1 Cor 15:3:		ὃ καὶ	παρέδωκα γὰρ ὑμῖν ἐν πρώτοις,	
	παρέλαβον,			ὅτι . . .

1 Cor 11:23:	For I received from the Lord	what also	I handed on to you,	that . . .
1 Cor 15:3:		what also	For I handed on to you as of first importance,	
	I received,			that . . .

There are clearly almost identical claims being made here: Paul states that he has received tradition (παρέλαβον 2×), which he also (ὃ καί 2×) passed on to the Corinthians (παρέδωκα ὑμῖν 2×), and he then introduces (ὅτι 2×) the content.

Moving to consider that content, we can compare Paul's words in 1 Cor 11 with the words of institution in the Gospels, and it is striking how much verbatim agreement there is either with all of the Synoptics or with Luke in particular. One could construct a very complicated tabulation of agreements and divergences across all three Synoptics and Paul (not to mention the versions in, e.g., the *Didache* and Justin's *First Apology*).[11] But the point about Paul's

11. Justin, *1 Apol.* 66.3; *Did.* 9.1–5. The relevant texts are all conveniently collected in

agreement with Synoptic tradition can easily be made by a comparison with Mark, where there is substantial similarity, and with Luke, where the agreement is uncanny. A few points particularly stand out in table 1.[12]

First, there is similarity in the opening reference to Jesus's actions in 1 Cor 11:23–24. Paul's verbs (λαμβάνω, εὐχαριστέω, κλάζω, λέγω) are all found in Luke, as is the only noun, "bread" (ἄρτος).

Second, in Jesus's statement, there is a string of thirty-three words (from the first τοῦτο to αἵματί μου), which 1 Corinthians preserves almost identically: the exceptions consist of one omission (διδόμενον), one addition (ἐστίν), one substitution (ἐμῷ for μου), and two changes of word order (the placements of μου and ὡσαύτως).[13] The similarities between Paul and Luke in particular doubtless reflect the two authors' memories of language used in liturgical practices in which they participated. After all, the whole point of the eucharistic practice is memorializing, ἀνάμνησις.[14]

Third, Paul and Luke do not simply share an esoteric "Pauline" tradition: Paul's report has much in common with Mark's (and Matthew's) account as well. As Pitre summarizes the theological content of the Synoptic and Pauline parallels: "in all four accounts of the Last Supper, Jesus identifies the wine of the meal with his own 'blood' that will establish a new 'covenant' between God and his people. . . . likewise, in all four accounts, Jesus uses the language of sacrifice to describe his blood as being offered for others."[15]

Kurt Aland's *Synopsis Quattuor Evangeliorum*, 5th ed. (Stuttgart: Deutsche Bibelgesellschaft, 2005), 437.

12. Cf. also the synopses of Paul, Mark, and Jewish tradition in Pitre, *Jesus and the Last Supper*, 428, and Wolter, *Luke*, 2:458.

13. Michael Wolter, *The Gospel according to Luke* (Waco, TX: Baylor University Press, 2017), 2:458, rightly comments: "From these findings one can draw the tradition-historical conclusion that Luke has combined Mark 14:22–24 with a pre-literary version of the text handed down in 1 Corinthians 11:23–25. A literary dependence on the Pauline text is unlikely."

14. A point ably discussed by Schröter, whose article is a very helpful treatment of a number of the key issues in 1 Cor 10–11. See Jens Schröter, "Die Funktion der Herrenmahlsüberlieferungen im 1. Korintherbrief: Zugleich ein Beitrag zur Rolle der 'Einsetzungsworte' in frühchristlichen Mahltexten," *ZNW* 100 (2009): 78–100.

15. Brant Pitre, *Jesus and the Last Supper* (Grand Rapids: Eerdmans, 2015), 12.

Table 1.

Mark 14:22–24	Luke 22:19–20	1 Cor 11:23–25	
A λαβὼν ἄρτον	καὶ λαβὼν	ἔλαβεν ἄρτον	
εὐλογήσας	ἄρτον	²⁴καὶ	
ἔκλασεν καὶ	εὐχαριστήσας	εὐχαριστήσας	String of thirty-three
ἔδωκεν	ἔκλασεν καὶ	ἔκλασεν καὶ	words identical in Luke
αὐτοῖς καὶ εἶπεν·	ἔδωκεν	εἶπεν·	and 1 Cor, except for:
λάβετε,	αὐτοῖς λέγων·		
τοῦτό ἐστιν τὸ	τοῦτό ἐστιν τὸ	τοῦτό μού ἐστιν	
σῶμά μου	σῶμά μου	τὸ σῶμα	← a transposition,
	τὸ ὑπὲρ ὑμῶν	τὸ ὑπὲρ ὑμῶν·	
	διδόμενον·		← an omission,
	τοῦτο ποιεῖτε	τοῦτο ποιεῖτε	
	εἰς τὴν ἐμὴν	εἰς τὴν ἐμὴν	
	ἀνάμνησιν.	ἀνάμνησιν.	
B ²³καὶ λαβὼν	²⁰καὶ τὸ	²⁵ὡσαύτως καὶ	← another
ποτήριον	ποτήριον	τὸ ποτήριον	transposition,
	ὡσαύτως		
	μετὰ τὸ	μετὰ τὸ	
	δειπνῆσαι	δειπνῆσαι	
C εὐχαριστήσας	λέγων·	λέγων·	
ἔδωκεν αὐτοῖς,	τοῦτο	τοῦτο	
καὶ	τὸ ποτήριον	τὸ ποτήριον	
ἔπιον ἐξ αὐτοῦ	ἡ καινὴ διαθήκη	ἡ καινὴ διαθήκη	
πάντες.		ἐστὶν	← one addition,
²⁴καὶ εἶπεν	ἐν τῷ αἵματί	ἐν τῷ ἐμῷ	← one substitution.
αὐτοῖς· τοῦτό	μου	αἵματι·	
ἐστιν			
τὸ αἷμά μου			
τῆς διαθήκης			
τὸ	τὸ ὑπὲρ ὑμῶν		
ἐκχυννόμενον	ἐκχυννόμενον.		
ὑπὲρ πολλῶν.			

Key:

Bold: agreement across Mark, Luke, and Paul
Underline: agreement between only Luke and Paul

In sum, the introductory "handing on what I received" formula in 1 Cor 11:23 is not merely casual preamble but seems to be something close to a citation formula. This is controlled reporting, not mere loose or free rehash. Given the similarity between the introductory formulae in 1 Cor 11:23 and 1 Cor 15:3, it is plausible to assume that Paul, at least, thought that in 1 Cor 15 he was giving an accurate rendition of the preexisting gospel that he had received. Additionally, we have here in 1 Cor 11 a place where Paul's claim to cite tradition can be checked, and he comes off very well under examination. In light of this, Paul's claim in 1 Cor 15—which cannot be checked by us in the same way—may be regarded as basically trustworthy. Paul is therefore very probably reporting in 1 Cor 15:3–5 a kerygma of some antiquity.

2. Wide Distribution as Indicative of the Comparator's Salience

Closely related to Paul's claim about the antiquity of his gospel is the fact that it is shared with the other apostles and more broadly across early Christianity. To his summary of the gospel and the list of resurrection witnesses, Paul appends the statement in 1 Cor 15:11: "Therefore, whether it is I or they, this is what we preach, and this is what you believed." It is striking that Paul defines the gospel here as the "ecumenical" gospel of all the apostles.[16] The point here is that the kerygma derives its salience for this study not only on the grounds of its antiquity (per sec. 1), but also from its wide distribution and usage. The following subsections seek to provide evidence that Paul's claim is credible, first because of the connections between the Corinthians and the Jerusalem church (sec. 2.1), but also because the distribution of the elements of the kerygma can be seen in other early Christian literature (sec. 2.2–4): Hebrews, 1 Peter, and Revelation will be called as witnesses to this.

---

16. See already C. H. Dodd, *The Apostolic Preaching and Its Developments* (London: Hodder, 1936), 12: "Paul himself at least believed that in essentials his gospel was that of the primitive apostles; for although in Gal. i. 11–18 he states with emphasis that he did not derive it from any human source, nevertheless in the same epistle (ii. 2) he says that he submitted 'the Gospel which I preach' to Peter, James and John at Jerusalem, and that they gave their approval. Not only so, but in the locus classicus, 1 Cor. xv. 1 sqq., he expressly declares that this summary of the Gospel is what he had 'received' as tradition; and after referring to other witnesses to the facts, including Peter, James, and 'all the apostles,' he adds with emphasis, 'Whether I or they, it was thus that we preached, and thus that you believed.'" See further Martin Hengel and Anna Maria Schwemer, *Paul between Damascus and Antioch: The Unknown Years* (London: SCM, 1997), 290–91.

2.1 Connections between Corinth and Jerusalem

First, there are the well-established connections between the Corinthian church and the Jerusalem church, which mean that it would be difficult for Paul to get away with misrepresenting what the other apostles preached.[17]

(1) One of Paul's circle who was with him when he first preached to the Corinthians was Silas (Acts 18:5; 2 Cor 1:19), a member of the Jerusalem church (Acts 15:22).[18] Titus has also visited both the Corinthian and Jerusalem churches.[19]

(2) Some of the Corinthians clearly associate themselves with Peter, who has exercised a good deal of influence (1 Cor 1:12, picked up in 1 Clem. 47.3).[20] It appears in 1 Corinthians 1 that Peter may have baptized some Corinthian converts; although this is not certain, Witetschek remarks that the most economical explanation is that the parallel of Peter, Paul, and Apollos in 1 Cor 1:12 indicates that those who belong to Cephas are no different in kind from those who belong to Paul or to Apollos.[21] Further, 1 Cor 3:22 ("whether Paul or Apollos or Cephas or the world or life or death or the present or the future— all are yours") implies personal acquaintance with Peter along with Paul and Apollos. If so, 1 Cor 9:5 might well imply that Peter visited Corinth with his wife, as Barrett and Witetschek argue.[22] In any case, the most natural explanation of Peter having adherents in Corinth is that he had been there.[23] Even on

17. Larry Hurtado, *Lord Jesus Christ: Devotion to Jesus in Earliest Christianity* (Grand Rapids: Eerdmans, 2003), 167–76, also notes that Paul attempted to foster among the Corinthian Christians beliefs (such as the gospel in 1 Cor 15) and practices (such as the *Maranatha* invocation) based on those in evidence in Jerusalem.

18. In addition to the other references to Silas in Acts, in 1 Peter he is presented as a member of the Petrine circle (5:12).

19. 2 Cor 7:6–7, 13–15; 8:6; 12:17–18; Gal 2:1–10.

20. See Thiselton, *1 Corinthians*, 110–11, for bibliography, and 128–29 for comment.

21. Stephan Witetschek, "Peter in Corinth? A Review of the Evidence from 1 Corinthians," *JTS* 69 (2018): 74–75.

22. C. K. Barrett, "Cephas and Corinth," in *Essays on Paul* (Philadelphia: Westminster, 1982), 32, makes the point that mention of Peter in this verse is redundant, given that Paul has just mentioned himself, Barnabas, and the other apostles: "Do we not have the right to take along a sister as a wife, just as do the other apostles and the brothers of the Lord and Cephas?" (9:5); similarly Witetschek, "Peter in Corinth?," 80–81.

23. C. K. Barrett, "Christianity at Corinth," *BJRL* (1964): 271: "Christian propagandists, other than, and some of them very different from, Paul had been at work in the city: Apollos certainly; Peter, with very great probability, and if not Peter himself disciples of his who made free with his name." The arguments of Manson, Barrett, and Bruce that Peter's influ-

the weaker hypothesis that Barrett suggests as an alternative ("and if not Peter himself disciples of his"), it would still be highly probable that the Corinthians were familiar with Peter's gospel.[24] As a result, Paul would not be in a strong position to make misleading claims about it.

(3) Even more than that, Paul cultivates and develops these connections between Corinth and Jerusalem.[25] In 1 Cor 16:3–4, he talks of the collection he has organized for the Christians in Jerusalem and says that the Corinthians can send whomever they like to take the collection there.[26] Paul seems remarkably relaxed about whether he himself should take part in this transprovincial visit or not (16:4). As Peterson remarks, "The whole procedure of the collection relies on the good standing of Paul with the Jerusalem church because the procedure assumes that visitors to Jerusalem from Corinth can rely on letters of introduction from Paul being effective (1 Cor 16:3)."[27] This deliberate attempt by Paul to foster further connections (to function independently from him) between Jerusalem and Corinth would be a strange—indeed, risky—thing to do if he was making a false claim about the gospel of the Jerusalem apostles.[28]

Paul acted along similar lines in other places as well. According to 2 Corinthians, Paul plans a second visit to Jerusalem for Titus.[29] At least according to Acts, Paul exposed several of his coworkers to Jerusalem, such as "Luke" and Trophimus (Acts 21:15, 17, 29). In sum, these actions are not the actions either of someone distancing himself from Jerusalem or of a man who thought that his claims about what Peter or James or other apostles preached could be open to challenge.

---

ence was of a nomistic kind, and that quite specific views of Peter can be seen to lurk in the background of 1 Corinthians, are more speculative, however. Cf. T. W. Manson, *Studies in the Gospels and Epistles* (Manchester: Manchester University Press, 1962), 190–224; Barrett, "Cephas and Corinth," 32–34; Barrett, "Christianity at Corinth," 273; F. F. Bruce, "Paul and Jerusalem," *TynBul* 19 (1968): 15.

24. The notion of a contingent of eastern Christians converted by Peter living in Corinth is a remote one, as Barrett rightly says ("Cephas and Corinth," 31).

25. On this point, see especially Peterson, "Extent of Christian Theological Diversity," 1–12, from which most of the observations below are derived.

26. See further Peterson, "Extent of Christian Theological Diversity," 10–11.

27. Peterson, "Extent of Christian Theological Diversity," 10–11.

28. Peterson's other justification is not so compelling, or at least would not be persuasive to some: "Second, in both 1 Corinthians and Galatians, Paul's authority is under some degree of challenge. In such circumstances, to claim an apostolic consensus that could be readily falsified would risk losing all credibility with these churches that Paul seeks to continue influencing. Paul's own self-interest, if not also higher motives, would suggest that his claims of agreement in essentials with the faith of Judean Messianists are substantially accurate" ("Extent of Christian Theological Diversity," 11).

29. 2 Cor 8:16–24; 9:3–5.

2.2 Hebrews

The elements of the apostolic kerygma in 1 Cor 15 are also reflected, as well as developed, in the diverse literature of the New Testament outside of Paul and the Gospels.[30] Some of the Catholic Epistles, as very short documents, do not incorporate all these elements: Jude, for example, explicitly states that the letter will not cover "our common salvation," because there is a pressing problem that needs to be addressed instead. Others, however, such as Hebrews, 1 Peter, and Revelation do. At the same time, each—while sticking with a certain rigidity to the basic elements—also adds new directions of interpretation. We will proceed to see how these three books both absorb and develop these aspects of the "common salvation," including for each book a paragraph on each of the four themes of Jesus's messiahship, vicarious death (dealing with sins), resurrection, and scriptural fulfillment.

Jesus's Messiahship

To begin with Hebrews, Jesus is here unquestionably Christ or messiah. The title appears twelve times. ("Son" is also prominent.) Psalms 2, 45, and 89 as well as 2 Samuel 7 are introduced as messianic "prooftexts." In addition, Ps 110, following early Christian tradition, is employed in the development of a priestly dimension to Jesus's messiahship in Hebrews.[31] For Hebrews, the priestly and royal dimensions are simply two sides of the same coin, as is seen in the author's combination of Ps 2:7 and Ps 110:4 in Heb 5:5–6: "In the same way, Christ did not take on himself the glory of becoming a high priest. But God said to him, 'You are my Son; today I have become your Father.' And he says in another place, 'You are a priest forever, in the order of Melchizedek.'"

Jesus's Saving Death

Christ's saving death is also a familiar feature of Hebrews. The effective and vicarious significance of Christ's death is clear in the language of his "tasting death for everyone" (Heb 2:9), "defeating, by death, the one who holds the

---

30. For the following (both in sec. 2.2 and sec. 2.3–4), I am very much indebted to the help of Dr. Robert Jamieson.

31. Deborah W. Rooke, "Jesus as Royal Priest: Reflections on the Interpretation of the Melchizedek Tradition in Heb 7," *Bib* 81 (2000): 81–94, does not see Hebrews's priestly emphasis as a development of or departure from traditional understandings of messiahship, but simply as bringing out the notion of sacral kingship that is inherent in it.

power of death, that is, the devil," thereby delivering humanity (2:14–15). Liberation is only one dimension of the cross in Hebrews. In Heb 9:14, there is purification of consciences; in 9:15, there is redemption from sins; in 9:16, there is the death's necessity. Reference to both Isa 53 and the imagery of the cult are included in Hebrews's depiction of Jesus as an offering to take away sins (9:28). Hebrews is thus also remarkably close to the kerygma reported by Paul in describing sins as a key aspect of the plight dealt with by the death of Christ.[32] The growing tendency in recent scholarship to see Christ's ordination to high priesthood and offering as taking place in the heavenly sanctuary does not detract from this. Rather, as Jamieson has shown, Hebrews sees Jesus's death on the cross and (via the resurrection) his heavenly offering as a sequential unity.[33] Or as Gäbel has put it, "The heavenly activity of Christ presupposes his earthly way; the earthly way of Christ comes into effect in his heavenly activity. It is in this way that the high-priestly Christology develops the soteriological significance of the traditional kerygma."[34]

Jesus's Resurrection

The resurrection of Jesus is not especially singled out for emphasis in Hebrews but is implied in the whole sequence of Jesus's career, which culminates in his activity in the heavenly tabernacle.[35] That this heavenly goal does not follow immediately upon Jesus's death is clear from certain places where reference is made to Jesus's resurrection. According to Heb 13:20, God "brought back from the dead the great shepherd of the sheep." This statement finds a counterpart in the reference to Jesus's prayer to the one who was able to accomplish this rescue from death (5:7). Resurrection is also implied by Jesus's ordination to high priesthood "on the basis of an indestructible life" (7:16).[36] A resurrection

32. ἁμαρτία appears in the plural 14×, and ἀγνόημα and παράβασις appear in the plural.

33. See Robert B. Jamieson, *Jesus' Death and Heavenly Offering in Hebrews* (Cambridge: Cambridge University Press, 2019), 97–179.

34. Georg Gäbel, *Die Kulttheologie des Hebräerbriefes: Eine exegetisch-religionsgeschichtliche Studie* (Tübingen: Mohr Siebeck, 2006), 17: "Das himmlische Wirken Christi setzt seinen irdischen Weg voraus; der irdische Weg Christi kommt in seinem himmlischen Wirken zur Geltung. So erschließt die Hohepriesterchristologie die soteriologische Bedeutsamkeit des überkommenen Kerygmas."

35. See David Moffitt, *Atonement and the Logic of Resurrection in the Epistle to the Hebrews* (Leiden: Brill, 2011), which sees resurrection as much more prominent than is usually appreciated in scholarship.

36. This is clearly postmortem, as Jesus's sufferings are a prerequisite to his appointment as high priest (see the parallel sequences in 2:17 and 2:18).

of Jesus also comports better than does a bodiless ascension with the general resurrection being part of the "elementary teaching" given to the Hebrews (6:2) and with the reference to a general resurrection of the faithful, clear in 11:35 (cf. 11:19), happening within the framework of a solidly material new creation (11:10; cf. 2:5; 11:14).[37] The sequence from Heb 11, where some of Jesus's predecessors are picked out as benefitting from resurrection, to Heb 12:1–2, where Jesus is the forerunner of the Christian faithful (who will, as we have seen, be raised), strongly implies Jesus's own resurrection. It would be an anomaly if both his predecessors (e.g., 11:35) and his followers (6:2) were raised from the dead, but Jesus, on whose life their destiny is patterned, was not. Moffitt admirably points out the potential further anomaly if Hebrews did not hold to a bodily resurrection of Jesus: "If he left the very constitutive elements of his humanity on earth to return to the heavenly realm as a spiritual being, a being like the angels who have no blood and flesh, he would have left behind the requisite qualifications he needed to be the one who could be elevated above the angels—his humanity."[38] In that sense, Jesus's resurrection is important to Hebrews (esp. in 5:7; 7:16; and 13:20), because it is the presupposition of his offering his blood in the heavenly sanctuary.[39]

Jesus's Fulfillment of Scripture

For Hebrews, Jesus's death and resurrection take place in fulfillment of scripture. Two passages are particularly important, Lev 16 and Ps 110. In line with the former, Jesus's whole career as sacrificial victim and eschatological high priest, encompassing both his death and heavenly offering, is patterned on Yom Kippur. The Levitical maxim "without the shedding of blood there is no forgiveness" (Heb 9:22) expresses negatively the positive truth that underlies both the Levitical cult and the work of Christ.[40] Psalm 110 is employed principally to cast Jesus's heavenly high priesthood as something qualitatively different from the Levitical priesthood (Ps 110:4).[41] Other scriptural passages

---

37. The reference to a *heavenly* country in 11:16 should not thereby necessarily be understood as an immaterial one.

38. Moffitt, *Atonement and the Logic of Resurrection*, 143.

39. As emphasized in both Moffitt, *Atonement and the Logic of Resurrection*, and Jamieson, *Jesus' Death and Heavenly Offering*.

40. See Jamieson, *Jesus' Death and Heavenly Offering*, 132–56, on Heb 9:22.

41. F. F. Bruce, "The Kerygma of Hebrews," *Int* 23 (1969): 7: "The two oracles [sc. Ps 110:1, 4] together, then, provide authority for regarding him as royal Messiah and priestly Messiah in his own person."

are important but referred to more sparely. The catena of citations in Heb 1 provides the scriptural attestation of Jesus's eschatological royal and priestly appointment(s). We have already noted that Jesus's sin-bearing death is cast in terms of Isa 53 (Heb 9:28). Resurrection is prefigured in Abraham's "only son" Isaac, who was "parabolically" (ἐν παραβολῇ) raised from the dead. Less enigmatically, the statement about resurrection in Heb 13:20 already noted is based on scripture. Hebrews's reference to "the God of peace, who brought up/back (ὁ ἀναγαγὼν) from the dead (ἐκ νεκρῶν), that great shepherd of the sheep (τὸν ποιμένα τῶν προβάτων τὸν μέγαν)" echoes the designation of God in Isaiah: "he who brought up/back (ὁ ἀναβιβάσας) from the ground (ἐκ τῆς γῆς) the shepherd of the sheep (τὸν ποιμένα τῶν προβάτων)" (Isa 63:11).[42]

Hebrews: Conclusion

In sum, all four elements of the kerygma in 1 Cor 15 are present in Hebrews but at the same time are not merely slavishly reproduced. Gäbel sums up nicely the way in which Hebrews interprets traditional categories: "Traditional christology and its declaration of Jesus' exaltation are interpreted in cultic and soteriological terms by means of a high-priestly christology: therein lies the key point of Hebrews."[43] Kraus similarly discusses both Hebrews's innovative features and the elements that the author presumes as foundational: on the latter, the author exhorts his readers, for example, "to pay more attention to what has been heard (τοῖς ἀκουσθεῖσιν) in order not to drift away" (2:1); "to hold on steadfastly to the original conviction (τὴν ἀρχὴν τῆς ὑποστάσεως) until the end" (3:14); to "hold on to the confession (τῆς ὁμολογίας)" (4:14); to "hold unswervingly (κατέχωμεν . . . ἀκλινῆ) to the confession (τὴν ὁμολογίαν) of hope" (10:23).[44] The author presumes the primitive kerygma in his exhorta-

42. The passage in Isa 63 LXX refers to God raising up Moses, but God doing this ἐκ τῆς γῆς is easily susceptible to being interpreted as a resurrection. Hence, Moses—like Jesus—being a "shepherd of the sheep" is understood typologically in Hebrews. The qualification added to the description of Jesus, in keeping with the theme of escalation in Hebrews, is that he is the *great* (μέγαν) shepherd.

43. Gäbel, *Kulttheologie*, 477: "Die traditionelle Christologie und ihre Erhöhungsaussage werden durch die Hohepriesterchristologie kulttheologisch und damit soteriologisch interpretiert: Eben darin besteht die Pointe des Hebr."

44. See Wolfgang Kraus, "Zur Aufnahme und Funktion von Gen 14,18–20 und Ps 109 LXX im Hebräerbrief," in *Text—Textgeschichte—Textwirkung: Festschrift zum 65. Geburtstag von Siegfried Kreuzer*, ed. Thomas Wagner, Jonathan Miles Robker, and Frank Ueberschaer (Münster: Ugarit-Verlag, 2014), 459, on the traditional elements, with reference to the passages cited above, and 463–74, on Hebrews's new themes.

tion to them not to drift from what they have heard, the message that originated from the Lord himself (Heb 2:1–4). He also reminds the Hebrews that they already possess a "foundation" (θεμέλιον)—consisting of the "elementary teaching about Christ" (τὸν τῆς ἀρχῆς τοῦ Χριστοῦ λόγον)—that they do not need to re-lay, and that they need to build on this elementary teaching and advance to maturity (6:1–3).

2.3 1 Peter

As William Wrede warned a long time ago, we must beware of making strong pronouncements about the theological character of 1 Peter.[45] But to all appearances, at least, it is perhaps theologically less adventurous than Hebrews, and more "elementary" in its teaching.

Jesus's Messiahship

In 1 Peter, "Christ" is clearly the dominant title for Jesus: it appears twenty-three times,[46] much more frequently than Jesus's personal name (9×), or the title "Lord" (8×); "Son of God" appears not at all, although God is clearly the father of Jesus (1:3). Among traditionally Jewish elements are the preexistence and chosenness of the messiah before his revelation (1:20; cf. 2:4), and the designation of the messiah as "lord" (3:15).[47]

Jesus's Saving Death

There is no dispute that Jesus's death in 1 Peter has a soteriological character. The letter's opening refers in cultic terms to the "the sprinkling of the blood of Jesus Christ" (1:2), and later in the same chapter, the blood is what redeems Christians from the foolish way of life handed down to them (1:18–19). In

---

45. W. Wrede, "The Task and Methods of New Testament Theology," in *The Nature of New Testament Theology*, ed. and trans. Robert Morgan (London: SCM, 1973), 75.

46. Not including the reference to χρηστός in 1 Pet 2:3. In some manuscripts, notably 𝔓72, the reading is Χ(ριστό)ς, but even if, as is probable, the original reading had χρηστός, a pun is very likely.

47. On "Christ" in 1 Peter, see especially David G. Horrell, "The Catholic Epistles and Hebrews," in *Redemption and Resistance: The Messianic Hopes of Jews and Christians in Antiquity*, ed. Markus Bockmuehl and James Carleton Paget (Cambridge: Cambridge University Press, 2009), 131–34. Horrell cites parallels to 1 Peter in the messianism of Pss. Sol. 18.5; 1 En. 46.1–4; 48.2–6; 4 Ezra 7.28–29; 12.31–34; 2 Bar. 30.1.

1 Pet 2, there is more of a focus on the event of Jesus's death: Christ "suffered for you" (2:21); therefore his death is effective in a broad sense. It is more clearly necessary and saving in the references to Jesus's removal of sin ("he himself bore our sins in his body on the tree"), in its liberative effect ("so that we might die to sins and live for righteousness")—and in its therapeutic function: "by his wound you are healed" (2:24). In 1 Pet 3:18, next, Christ "suffered for sins, the righteous for the unrighteous," making use again of cultic imagery in its statement that the death here brings access to God.[48] Moreover, scholars often comment that this verse in particular has a formulaic, creedal character.[49] In 1 Pet 4, the fact that believers who have suffered in the flesh have finished with sin is predicated upon Christ having suffered in the flesh (4:1–2).[50] The death of Jesus in 1 Peter is indisputably effective and vicarious.[51]

Jesus's Resurrection

There is dense reference to the resurrection in this epistle, although, as is usual in the New Testament epistles, there is no specification of the "third day."[52] The "resurrection of Jesus Christ from the dead" (1:3) is referred to at the outset as salvific in some sense:[53] it is connected most directly with the "living hope" and the "new birth" preceding in the same verse; in 3:21, the resurrection brings salvation through baptism. The plural "glories to come" in 1:11 certainly include, even if they do not exhaust, Jesus being raised from

48. See Otfried Hofius, "The Fourth Servant Song in the New Testament Letters," in *The Suffering Servant: Isaiah 53 in Jewish and Christian Sources*, ed. Bernd Janowski and Peter Stuhlmacher, trans. Daniel P. Bailey (Grand Rapids: Eerdmans, 2004), 185–88.

49. A number of scholars have identified credal formulae in 1 Peter. See, e.g., Rudolf Bultmann, "Bekenntnis- and Liedfragmente im ersten Petrusbrief," in *Coniectanea Neotestamentica XI: In honorem A. Fridrichsen* (Lund: Gleerup, 1947), 1–14, most of which (1–10) is taken up with the discussion of 1 Pet 3:18–22; also, more recently, David G. Horrell, "Jesus Remembered in 1 Peter? Early Jesus Traditions, Isaiah 53, and 1 Peter 2.21–25," in *James, 1 & 2 Peter, and Early Jesus Traditions*, ed. Alicia J. Batten and John S. Kloppenborg (London: Bloomsbury, 2014), 131, comments that "the headline phrase Χριστὸς ἔπαθεν ὑπὲρ ὑμῶν in 3:18 probably reflects an established creedal formulation."

50. On the identification of the one who has given up on sin, see the helpful argument in Paul J. Achtemeier, *1 Peter* (Minneapolis: Fortress, 1996), 278–79.

51. Cf. John H. Elliott, *1 Peter* (New York: Doubleday, 2000), 110: "his suffering and death were sacrificial, vicarious, atoning, and redemptive."

52. 1 Cor 15:4 is the exception.

53. See Elliott, *1 Peter*, 334–35, for a maximal account of the soteriological import of the resurrection.

the dead.[54] This resurrection is a divine action: God is "the one who raised him from the dead and gave him glory" (1:21), which fits with the fact that Christ, in his willingness to die, "committed himself to the one who judges justly" (2:23). In 3:18–22, he is also made alive in spirit or by the Spirit (3:18), after which he proclaimed his victory to the spirits in prison.[55] Like Hebrews, therefore, 1 Peter has a conception of resurrection that is more complex than simply a sequence of third-day raising followed by ascension to the right hand. Having said that, Jesus's resurrection does culminate in his heavenly session at the right hand of God (3:22).

Jesus's Fulfillment of Scripture

In addition to its individual references to Old Testament passages, 1 Peter also contains one of the New Testament's most striking programmatic statements about the christological meaning of scripture:[56]

Concerning this salvation, the prophets, who spoke of the grace that was to come to you, searched intently and with the greatest care, trying to find out the time and circumstances to which the Spirit of Christ in them was pointing when he predicted the sufferings of the messiah and the glories that would follow. It was revealed to them that they were not serving themselves but you, when they spoke of the things that have now been told you by those who have preached the gospel to you by the Holy Spirit sent from heaven. Even angels long to look into these things. (1 Pet 1:10–12)

1 Peter, then, (1) presupposes activity of the preexistent Christ (through the "Spirit of Christ") in the inspiration of prophets and (2) implies not so much

54. Achtemeier, e.g., sees resurrection here. See Paul J. Achtemeier, "The Christology of 1 Peter: Some Reflections," in *Who Do You Say That I Am? Essays on Christology in Honor of Jack Dean Kingsbury*, ed. Mark Allan Powell and David R. Bauer (Louisville: Westminster John Knox, 1999), 145. Compare 1:21, where the glory has been given to him, with 4:13, with its reference to the future revelation of his glory.

55. Elliott, *1 Peter*, 706; Horrell, "Hebrews and the Catholic Epistles," 133. Although frequently taken together with 3:19, 1 Pet 4:6 almost certainly refers to preaching to people, now dead, when they were alive. See David G. Horrell, "Who Are 'The Dead' and When Was the Gospel Preached to Them? The Interpretation of 1 Pet 4.6," *NTS* 48 (2003): 70–89.

56. For a brief overview of the use of scripture in 1 Peter, see, e.g., Richard J. Bauckham, "James, 1 and 2 Peter, Jude," in *It Is Written: Scripture Citing Scripture, Essays in Honour of Barnabas Lindars*, ed. D. A. Carson and H. G. M. Williamson (Cambridge: Cambridge University Press, 1988), 309–13.

the *continuity* between the prophetic message and the gospel but their *identity*.[57] Not only did the Spirit bear witness in advance, but the prophets "served up" the very things now proclaimed in the gospel (διηκόνουν αὐτά, ἃ νῦν ἀνηγγέλη ὑμῖν). This prophesied gospel in these verses contains *in nuce* all four elements of kerygma, namely "Christ," his death, his resurrection, and Scriptural testimony. There are also specific passages for which 1 Pet 1:10–12 provides the "hermeneutical key."[58] Horrell notes, for example, the various "stone" texts, as well as Passover, the sacrificial system, and Isa 53.[59] The last of these is one of the most prominent, there being a string of references to Isa 53 in 1 Pet 2:21–25. While the initial reason for the quotation is the example of Jesus forecast in Isaiah, by verses 24–25 the interest has shifted in the direction of Jesus's saving death. The advantage of the stone text of Ps 118 (117 LXX), by contrast, is that it can encompass not only rejection but also vindication, and 1 Peter like other New Testament authors cites the psalm as a reference to Jesus's resurrection: "the stone that the builders rejected has become the cornerstone" (Ps 118:22; 1 Pet 2:7).

1 Peter: Conclusion

Scholarship in recent years has moved away from seeing a dependence upon Paul in 1 Peter, and so it is all the more remarkable that there is such similarity on central topics between 1 Peter and the kerygma reported by Paul. In addition to what the author propounds himself, he assumes in 1 Pet 1:18–21 that his transprovincial readers (in Pontus, Galatia, Cappadocia, Asia, Bithynia) are aware of key elements of the gospel: he refers to these readers as "knowing that you were redeemed . . . by the precious blood . . . of Christ . . . because of you, who through him believe in God who raised him from the dead."[60]

2.4 Revelation

In many respects, Revelation closely reflects the same key elements of the apostolic gospel.

---

57. *Pace* Achtemeier, *1 Peter*, 110–11.

58. Horrell, "Catholic Epistles and Hebrews," 131, referring to Schutter and Achtemeier.

59. Horrell, "Catholic Epistles and Hebrews," 131; Horrell, "The Product of a Petrine Circle? A Reassessment of the Origin and Character of 1 Peter," *JSNT* 86 (2002): 40.

60. Martin Williams, *The Doctrine of Salvation in the First Letter of Peter* (Cambridge: Cambridge University Press, 2011), 82. Bultmann, "Bekenntnis- and Liedfragmente im ersten Petrusbrief," 10–12, notes the strongly traditional character of this language.

Jesus's Messiahship

It is perhaps not a coincidence that the title "Christ" occurs seven times in the book of Revelation.[61] Jesus is strongly identified as a Davidic messiah.[62] Four of the references to "his Christ" or simply "(the) Christ" come in contexts of reigning (11:15; 12:10; 20:4, 6), and the royal theme is also present in other places important in Revelation's messianism: Jesus has the "key of David" (3:7) and is depicted as the king in Ps 2 (who rules with an iron scepter) and as Ps 89's ruler above all other kings.[63] Revelation also alludes to several passages that Novenson lists as very frequently invoked in messianic contexts:[64]

- Rev 5:5: the "lion of Judah" (cf. Gen 49:9–10);
- Rev 5:5: "the root of David" (cf. Isa 11:10);
- Rev 1:7, 13: the one like a Son of Man coming on clouds (cf. Dan 7:13–14);
- Rev 22:16: "the bright morning star" (cf. perhaps Num 24:17).[65]

Jesus is both a human Christ, then, but also a supernatural figure, as these latter two examples suggest. John also employs the tradition of the messiah's victory over his enemies, though without bringing in the theme of a military victory in the earthly sphere. As Bauckham comments: "His [sc. John's] Messiah Jesus does not win his victory by military conquest, and those who share his victory and his rule are not national Israel, but the international people of God. But still it is a victory over evil, won not only in the spiritual but also in the political sphere against worldly powers in order to establish God's kingdom on earth. Insofar as the hope for the Davidic Messiah was for such victory of God over evil Revelation portrays Christ's work in continuity with that traditional Jewish hope."[66]

---

61. Paul Spilsbury, "The Apocalypse," in Bockmuehl and Carleton Paget, *Redemption and Resistance*, 138. "Son of God" appears only once (2:18), and Jesus is depicted as "one like a Son of Man" in two places (1:13; 14:14). Many of the instances of "Lord" are predicated of the Father as distinct from Jesus, though some apply to him.

62. As is emphasized in Richard Bauckham, *The Theology of the Book of Revelation* (Cambridge: Cambridge University Press, 1993), 68.

63. Ps 2:9; cf. Rev 12:5; 19:15. On Ps 89[88]:27 and Rev 1:5, see Spilsbury, "Apocalypse," 140.

64. Matthew Novenson, *Christ among the Messiahs: Christ Language in Paul and Messiah Language in Ancient Judaism* (Oxford: Oxford University Press, 2012), 57–58.

65. On the messianic interpretations of Num 24:17, see, among others, David E. Aune, *Revelation 17–22* (Grand Rapids: Zondervan, 1998), 1226–27.

66. Bauckham, *Theology*, 68.

Jesus's Saving Death

Jesus's death in Revelation is described as an earthly, temporal crucifixion (Rev 11:8),[67] and four explanations of the significance of that death can be drawn out in particular: *liberation, purchase, cleansing,* and *conquest.* (1) In Rev 1:5, Jesus is depicted as the one who loves us and "set us free from our sins by his blood." The "by his blood" probably implies that there is a cost involved in the liberation, suggesting perhaps that the "sins" had incurred an enslaving debt that needed to be repaid.[68] The language of "slaughter" (5:6, 9, 12; 13:8) in connection with Christ as the "lamb" may well echo the language of the guilt offering in Leviticus.[69] (2) Very similar, then, is the purchase motif.[70] In Rev 5:9, we hear the new song that Jesus is worthy "because you were slaughtered and by your blood *purchased* (ἠγόρασας) for God people from every tribe and language and people and nation." The language is picked up again later, when the 144,000 were *"purchased* (ἠγορασμένοι) from the earth" and *"bought* (ἠγοράσθησαν) from among people" (Rev 14:3-4). (3) The blood is also a detergent and a dye. About those who wear white robes and hold palm branches, it is said: "These are they who have come out of the great tribulation; they have washed their robes and made them white *in the blood of the Lamb* (ἐν τῷ αἵματι τοῦ ἀρνίου)" (7:14). The verb "wash" (πλύνω) is very commonly used in the Pentateuch for cultic washing, thus possibly drawing in the language of ritual purification into the work of Jesus, and purification or cleansing with blood appears elsewhere in the New Testament.[71] In addition, the theme of "whiteness" points in the direction of a *moral* purification of the saints (cf. Isa 1:18): white clothes are associated in Revelation with worthiness and not being "soiled" (3:4), and they cover up one's shame (3:18).[72] (4) Finally, there is the theme of conquest of the devil: "They overcame him by the blood of the

---

67. As should be clear, despite some drawn-out elaborations of the idea, Christ was not "slain from before the foundation of the world" in 13:8. As the parallel in Rev 17:8 makes clear, 13:8 should be translated (with, e.g., the NRSV against the AV) as referring to "everyone whose name has not been written from the foundation of the world in the book of life of the Lamb that was slaughtered."

68. As argued by, e.g., Leon Morris, *The Book of Revelation: An Introduction and Commentary* (Grand Rapids: Eerdmans, 1987), 48.

69. See, e.g., Lev 14:13, 25, where a lamb is slaughtered as a guilt offering: καὶ σφάξει τὸν ἀμνὸν τῆς πλημμελείας (14:25).

70. Cf. 1 Cor 6:20; 7:23; 2 Pet 2:1.

71. E.g., Heb 9:13-14; cf. 9:21-23; 1 John 1:7.

72. Robert H. Mounce, *The Book of Revelation,* rev. ed. (Grand Rapids: Eerdmans, 1998), 149: "In the book of Revelation . . . white robes are symbols of blessedness and purity."

Lamb and by the word of their testimony" (Rev 12:11).[73] As Mounce comments on this verse, "The primary cause of their victory is the blood of the Lamb. The great redemptive act that freed them from their sins (1:5) and established their right to reign (5:9) is the basis for their victory. Their share in the conquest stems from the testimony they have faithfully borne (cf. 6:9; 11:7)."[74] In short, the combined motifs of liberation, purchase, cleansing, and conquest lead the author of Revelation to depict Christ's death with a rich variety of imagery.

Jesus's Resurrection

Clear statements of the resurrection of Jesus are not frequent in Revelation, but they do appear. At the outset, Jesus is called "the faithful witness, the firstborn from the dead" (1:5).[75] Later in the chapter, the theme is elaborated: "I am the living one; I was dead, and behold I am alive for ever and ever! And I hold the keys of death and Hades" (1:18). Here Jesus is not just risen but has authority over death and hence—as firstborn—can ensure the resurrection of others. Elsewhere, the resurrection of Jesus is everywhere presupposed. He is the speaker whose words are reproduced by the prophet (e.g., Rev 22:16; cf. 1:1), and the dictator of the letters to the churches: the letter to the church in Smyrna, for example, consists of "the words of him who is the First and the Last, who died and came to life again" (2:8).

Jesus's Fulfillment of Scripture

It is impossible even to summarize effectively the different passages and uses of scripture featuring in Revelation. It is also not necessary, since there is a general scholarly consensus on the fact that John employs scripture at virtually every point to explicate what he has seen. Scholars express the detail of this differently. Moyise, for example, remarks that both the original biblical context and Revelation's new context of quotations and allusions mutually affect each other in the reading experience.[76] Beale places a greater emphasis

---

73. As Bauckham (*Theology*, 73) stresses: "Fundamental to Revelation's whole understanding of the way in which Christ establishes God's kingdom on earth is the conviction that in his death and resurrection Christ has already won his decisive victory over evil."

74. Mounce, *Revelation*, 239.

75. Cf. also Rev 2:8: "To the angel of the church in Smyrna write: These are the words of him who is the First and the Last, who died and came to life again."

76. Stephen Moyise, *The Old Testament in the Book of Revelation* (London: Bloomsbury, 1995), 82–83.

on fulfillment.[77] In terms of the general theme of discussion here, Bauckham's summary statement is apt: "John was writing what he understood to be a work of prophetic scripture, the climax of prophetic revelation, which gathered up the prophetic meaning of the Old Testament scriptures and disclosed the way in which it was being and was to be fulfilled in the last days."[78] There are also particular references to Jesus's death and resurrection fulfilling scripture. Jesus's crucifixion is taken as scriptural in, for example, the reference to Zech 12:10 in the opening doxology—"every eye will see him, even *those who pierced him*" (Rev 1:7)—and in the various references to the slaughter of the lamb (5:6, 12; 13:8) or "the blood of the lamb" (7:14; 12:11), implying a Passover or broader pentateuchal reference to sacrifice. Again, Revelation invokes Isaiah's language in Jesus's self-description as "the first and the last" to ground the fact that, despite having died, the living one is now alive forever (Rev 1:17–18; Isa 44:6; 48:12).

Revelation: Conclusion

In many ways, Revelation's genre and consequent *outré* imagery give it a very distinctive flavor, making it seem unusual in the New Testament and sub-Christian to some earlier interpreters.[79] In many other ways, however, and specifically in its depiction of Jesus's messiahship, death, resurrection, and fulfillment of scripture, it is not eccentric. At least two twentieth-century commentators took John to lie squarely in the mainstream of earliest Christian theology. Sweet commented as follows on his experience of studying Revelation: "Work on this commentary has brought awareness of a deep community of thinking and feeling between John and the other NT writers."[80] A little earlier, Farrer had written that "to a large extent Revelation merely colours in what was everywhere taken for granted."[81]

---

77. E.g., Gregory K. Beale, *The Book of Revelation: A Commentary on the Greek Text* (Grand Rapids: Eerdmans, 1998), 97; cf. also for an overview of his position, Beale, "Revelation," in Carson and Williamson, *It Is Written*, 318–36, which also has a valuable bibliography of material up to the time of its writing.

78. Richard J. Bauckham, *The Climax of Prophecy: Studies on the Book of Revelation* (Edinburgh: T&T Clark, 1993), xi.

79. See, e.g., the somewhat disparaging comments in R. H. Charles, *A Critical History of the Doctrine of a Future Life in Israel, in Judaism, and in Christianity* (London: A. & C. Black, 1899), 347, and Rudolf Bultmann *Theology of the New Testament* (London: SCM, 1955), 2:175.

80. John Sweet, *Revelation* (London: SCM, 1990), 51.

81. Austin Farrer, *The Revelation of St. John the Divine* (Oxford: Clarendon, 1964), 4.

2.5 Corinth and Jerusalem, Hebrews, 1 Peter, Revelation: Conclusion

This section has therefore taken in two different types of evidence for the credibility of Paul's claim that the gospel summarized in 1 Cor 15 was widely shared. Paul's assertion that the other witnesses to the resurrection proclaimed the same good news is partly confirmed by inner-Pauline evidence, namely the connections between the church at Corinth and the Jerusalem church: such connections mean that Paul could ill afford to make claims about what the Jerusalem apostles preached given the frequent traffic between Jerusalem and Corinth (sec. 2.1). The other strands of evidence, of a different nature, show that Paul's claim that the central components of his message were widely shared can be substantiated elsewhere from the literature of the New Testament, that is, in literature not by Paul and that has some degree of independence from Paul.[82] Hebrews (sec. 2.2), 1 Peter (sec. 2.3), and Revelation (sec. 2.4) all assign importance to the central kerygmatic features of Jesus's messiahship, his saving death (for sins), his resurrection, and his fulfillment of scripture in these events.

CONCLUSION: THE COMPARATOR AND ITS SALIENCE

The salience of the model proposed as a comparator in the previous chapter therefore lies both in its *antiquity* and in its *widespread use* and acceptance. Although the immediate source of the model for our purposes is Paul's formulation in 1 Cor 15, the kerygma Paul articulates neither originated with him nor was restricted to him. The kerygma's antiquity is evident from the chain of transmission prior to Paul's proclamation to the Corinthians: it was a gospel that Paul himself received. Its widespread use is evident not only from Paul's own claim in 1 Cor 15:11 but also in the prominence of the features of that kerygma in other literature such as Hebrews, 1 Peter, and Revelation. These claims of antiquity and widespread use are of course related. The existence of the kerygma at or near the beginning of the apostolic proclamation of the gospel is of course part of the reason for its wide diffusion across the literature of early Christianity, a diffusion that happened to bring it to Paul as well. In short, while I have chosen this model as a comparator for my own "intellec-

---

82. Of the three books considered, Hebrews is most likely to have some connection with the Pauline circle, as is evident both in Hebrews's theological content (N. B. Heb 11:12) and in the reference to Timothy in Heb 13:23.

tual reasons" and "intellectual purpose" (to use Jonathan Z. Smith's words), there are also, I would argue, good reasons for regarding this comparator as a historically "significant" and "relevant" one.[83]

Having established both the comparanda and the comparator, then, we can proceed (via a brief excursus) to the descriptive task of examining the relevant Gospels with respect to their treatments of the themes of Jesus's messiahship, vicarious death for sins, resurrection, and fulfillment of scripture.

---

83. Here echoing the stipulations of Poole and Parsons quoted at the beginning of this chapter.

THE KERYGMA AND
THE ACTS OF THE APOSTLES

One potential objection to the argument made in chapters 2 and 3 runs as follows: *the kerygma as reported and summarized in 1 Corinthians is not a universal one, because a quite different gospel message is presented in Acts, as is clear from the latter's lack of attention to the death of Jesus.*

One point to note at the outset is that the present book is not claiming that the kerygma as summarized in 1 Cor 15 was held universally. The argument made in chapters 2 and 3 is that it was a very old and widely adopted kerygma, not that it was adhered to strictly *semper ubique ab omnibus.*

Even so, to the extent that Acts is presenting the kerygma, the theology of Acts does not differ substantively from the kerygma summarized by Paul. This excursus will focus on factors in the interpretation of the death of Christ in Acts; Jesus's identity as messiah, the saving significance of the resurrection, and the Easter events as fulfillments of scripture are not in dispute in Acts scholarship. There are four observations to be made here, beginning with the question of whether or to what degree Acts, and the individual speeches within it, are presenting the kerygma. Naturally only a suggestive sketch, rather than a full treatment, is possible here.

THE SPEECHES IN ACTS

To begin with a negative observation, the speeches in Acts are not necessarily programmatic statements of the kerygma.[1] Soards has rightly argued that at-

---

1. Cf. Eduard Schweizer, "Concerning the Speeches in Acts," in *Studies in Luke-Acts,* ed. Leander Keck and J. Louis Martyn (Nashville: Abingdon, 1966), 210, who writes of the "far-reaching identity of structure" in the speeches. Wilckens writes of a "Schema" and

tempts to create a schema common to all the speeches are artificial, noting that "materials in the speeches must be juggled and rearranged, and frequently the critics are forced to admit that one (or more) of the regularly repeated elements simply does not occur in a particular speech."[2] He concludes that although there are repeated elements in various speeches, "one cannot think or speak of a single form that is repeated consistently."[3] It is important to reckon with the selectivity of the speeches. Those topics often thought to be integral to the soteriology of Acts (resurrection, exaltation, the Spirit, repentance, baptism) do not by any means appear in every case. The resurrection, for example, is absent from Stephen's speech in Acts 7. The exaltation is not mentioned in Peter's speech in Caesarea, or in Paul's lengthy proclamation in Antioch (10:34–43; 13:16–41). Summaries of the preaching of the apostles in certain places boil the message down to the kingdom of God, or to the identity of Jesus as the Christ.[4] The missionary speeches in Acts cannot be programmatic examples of Luke's kerygma because, although there are some frequently repeated themes, the sermons vary considerably.

To state the argument positively, Tannehill has noted in a study of Peter's speeches that "the speeches differ significantly in emphasis and function. These differences relate to the narrative setting in which each speech is found, and the setting influences the speech more profoundly than is commonly recognized. It is illuminating to think of each of the speeches as an action in the unfolding narrative plot."[5] As an example, he shows that the first two speeches focus on the guilt of the inhabitants of Jerusalem, in the context of the developing conflict between the disciples and the Jerusalem authorities. In Lystra, Paul speaks against idolatry (Acts 14:14–17), and in his Areopagus speech, he acknowledges his philosophical audience (17:22–31). Even Schweizer, who emphasizes the commonalities of the speeches, talks in terms of a "theologi-

---

Dibelius speaks of Luke preaching through the speeches. See Ulrich Wilckens, "Kerygma und Evangelium bei Lukas (Beobachtungen zu Acta 10.34–43)," *ZNW* 49 (1958): 223–37, and Martin Dibelius, *Studies in the Acts of the Apostles* (London: SCM, 1956), 165–66, 183. See more recently Carl R. Holladay, "Acts as Kerygma: λαλεῖν τὸν λόγον," *NTS* 63 (2017): 153–82.

2. Marion L. Soards, *The Speeches in Acts: Their Content, Context, and Concerns* (Louisville: Westminster John Knox, 1994), 11.

3. Soards, *Speeches in Acts*, 11; cf. also the comments on the phenomena of repetition and analogy, without there being a *template* (*Speeches in Acts*, 183).

4. Kingdom: Acts 19:8; 28:23, 31; Jesus as Christ: e.g., Acts 5:42; 9:22; 18:5, 28 (cf. Jesus as Son of God in 9:20). Cf. also 8:12 ("the kingdom of God and the name of Jesus Christ") and 20:21 (repentance to God and faith in Christ).

5. Robert C. Tannehill, "The Functions of Peter's Mission Speeches in the Narrative of Acts," *NTS* 37 (1991): 400.

cal kerygma" in Lystra and Athens as opposed to a "christological kerygma" elsewhere.[6] Again, the circumstances of Felix's and Drusilla's marriage probably shape the speech addressed to them, with the key elements of "faith in Christ Jesus" being "righteousness, self-control and the judgment to come" (24:24–25).[7] Marguerat notes that the speeches in Acts fit their audiences in language, subject matter, and theology.[8] Acts is not a collection of representative missionary sermons but a narrative in which the speeches are a part and play a narrative role.

The Necessity of Jesus's Death in Acts

Second, there is the question of to what degree the overall presentation of Jesus's death in Acts differs substantively from the "other" kerygma in any case. On one count, there are fourteen passages in Acts that mention Jesus's death: this excludes simple references to Jesus having been dead (e.g., Acts 2:24; 25:19) but includes the reference to his betrayal and arrest.[9] A minority of these passages focus exclusively on the human agency in Jesus's death and on the responsibility of the Jewish and gentile leaders and populace involved (Acts 2:36; 5:30–31). Two others have a more oblique relation between the statement about Jesus's death and prophecy of it (7:50–52; 10:39–43).

The majority (ten out of fourteen) supply a theological interpretation of Jesus's passion and death.[10] That is, they do not speak solely of the human execution of Jesus, but of God bringing his will to fulfillment in the events leading up to and including the crucifixion. Going through the events of the passion roughly in sequence, we can begin with Jesus's betrayal. The speech about the replacement of Judas (Acts 1:16–20) indicates that Jesus's betrayal and arrest were prefigured in the scripture that was spoken by the Holy Spirit and

6. Schweizer, "Concerning the Speeches in Acts," 212–13, 214.

7. Soon after her marriage to Gaius Julius Azizus, who converted to Judaism, Drusilla divorced him to marry the gentile Felix. Hence Josephus: "she was persuaded to transgress the ancestral laws (παραβῆναί τε τὰ πάτρια νόμιμα πείθεται) and to marry Felix" (*Ant.* 20.143).

8. Daniel Marguerat, *The First Christian Historian: Writing the "Acts of the Apostles"* (Cambridge: Cambridge University Press, 2004), 19. I am grateful to Monique Cuany for pointing me to Marguerat's very helpful discussion here.

9. Acts 1:16–20; 2:23, 36; 3:13–18; 4:10–11, 24–28; 5:30–31; 7:51–52; 8:27–35; 10:39; 13:27–29; 17:3; 20:28; 26:22–23.

10. Acts 1:16–20; 2:23; 3:13–18; 4:10–11, 24–28; 8:27–35; 13:27–29; 17:3; 20:28; 26:22–23. Acts 20:28 will be discussed in the subsequent section, "The Meaning of Jesus's Death in (Luke-)Acts."

"had to be fulfilled" (ἔδει πληρωθῆναι). In Jesus's trial, human responsibility is emphasized in Acts 3:13–15, though there is also an allusion to Isa 53.[11] In their judgment upon Jesus, the inhabitants of Jerusalem and their leaders unwittingly brought to fulfillment (ἐπλήρωσαν) the words of the prophets (Acts 13:27). The rulers (Herod and Pilate) with the Jews and gentiles in Jerusalem carried out what was prophesied in Ps 2, a prophecy that in turn was the result of God's action and will beforehand according to 4:28 (ὅσα ἡ χείρ σου καὶ ἡ βουλή σου προώρισεν γενέσθαι). In accord with Isa 53, Jesus remained silent and was led away to execution (Acts 8:27–35; cf. Luke 23:9). There is then strong emphasis on the divine instigation of Jesus's suffering in Acts 3:18: *God* brought to fulfillment what he had announced through the prophets in advance about the suffering of Christ (ὁ δὲ θεὸς ἃ προκατήγγειλεν διὰ στόματος πάντων τῶν προφητῶν παθεῖν τὸν χριστὸν αὐτοῦ ἐπλήρωσεν οὕτως). Paul explains from the scriptures that the messiah had to suffer (17:2–3), just as Moses and the prophets spoke of how the Christ was to suffer (παθητὸς ὁ χριστός [26:22–23]). In addition to the general language of suffering, Jesus's execution in particular took place "by God's determined plan and foreknowledge" (τῇ ὡρισμένῃ βουλῇ καὶ προγνώσει τοῦ θεοῦ) according to Acts 2:23. In Acts 4, there is an emphasis on human responsibility (ὃν ὑμεῖς ἐσταυρώσατε), followed immediately by an implication of prophecy in the reference to Ps 118 in the following verse (4:10–11).

In sum, God preordained Jesus's death by his will (τῇ ὡρισμένῃ βουλῇ [2:23]; ἡ βουλή σου προώρισεν [4:28]) and therefore foreknew it (καὶ προγνώσει [2:23]). It is clear, then, that the cross is a necessity (1:16–20; 17:2–3; 26:23). God announced it in advance (3:18; 17:2–3) through the spoken word of the prophets (e.g., 3:18; 4:25) and through the written word of scripture (e.g., 1:20; 8:27–35). The death of Jesus is then something brought about both by God fulfilling prophecy (ἐπλήρωσεν in 3:18) and by human beings fulfilling it (ἐπλήρωσαν in 13:27).

THE MEANING OF JESUS'S DEATH IN (LUKE-)ACTS

This demands explanation: *why*? It is obviously not sufficient to say that the cross was a *scriptural* necessity, as that simply begs the question: the cross was planned in the divine will, not just in scripture. As Barrett comments on

---

11. E.g., God ἐδόξασεν τὸν παῖδα αὐτοῦ (Acts 3:13); cf. Isa 52:13: ὁ παῖς μου καὶ ὑψωθήσεται καὶ δοξασθήσεται σφόδρα; Jesus is the one παρεδώκατε (Acts 3:13); cf. παραδίδωμι in Isa 53:6, 12 (bis); the servant is δίκαιος (Isa 53:11; Acts 3:14).

Acts 2:23, "What appeared to be a free concerted action by Jews and Gentiles was in fact done because God foreknew it, decided it, and planned it. Cf. 4.27, 28. Why he did this, and how the predetermined event was applied in the work of salvation, requires explanation."[12]

Before seeking an explanation in Acts, it is important to note that an answer has already been provided in Luke's Gospel. Theophilus was not a *tabula rasa* on encountering Acts: the Gospel, Luke's "former treatise" (Acts 1:1), is presumed. To anticipate the discussion in chapter 6 (esp. sec. 2), we will see there that it is tolerably clear that both the body and blood of Jesus are given "for" his disciples (Luke 22:19, 20)—hence it is clear that Jesus's death is an "effective" death; furthermore, Jesus's death inaugurates a new covenant (22:17–20)—hence in (re)establishing a framework of relation to God, that death is vicarious, or soteriological. It is probably also the case that Luke presents Jesus's death as a participation in divine judgment (Luke 12:49–50; 23:44–45a); that Luke sees Jesus's death in the light of the servant in Isa 53 (Luke 22:37); that Luke understands Jesus in his death as a substitute for Barabbas (23:13–25); that Jesus is presented as a Passover sacrifice (22:17–20); that the accumulation of soteriological pronouncements at the crucifixion reinforces the impression of Jesus's death as a saving event (23:34a, 35, 37, 39, 43); and that the (perhaps cosmic) significance of Jesus's death is evident in the darkness at noon and the tearing of the veil (23:44–45), the latter also signifying a new quality of access to God (23:45b). For the implied reader of Acts, who already knows the *prōtos logos* mentioned in Acts 1:1, this much is already in place at the outset, the first two points derived from the eucharistic words at the very least.

Coming to Acts, Barrett himself answers his "why" question with Paul's statement in Acts 20:28.[13] Here, Paul refers to "the church of God that he acquired [*or* he saved] through the blood of his own [*or* through his own blood]."[14] These alternative translations highlight two exegetical questions,

---

12. C. K. Barrett, *Acts 1–14* (Edinburgh: T&T Clark, 2004), 142 (on 2:23).

13. Barrett, *Acts 1–14*, 142. The observations of Michael Wolter, "Jesu Tod und Sündenvergebung bei Lukas und Paulus," in *The Reception of Paulinism in Acts*, ed. D. Marguerat (Leuven: Peeters, 2009), 19–20, 31, that Acts 20:28 (1) comes in an ecclesiological statement, not a christological or soteriological one, (2) is taken up primarily with God taking possession of his people, and (3) is addressed to an insider, Christian audience are all true but do not detract from the soteriological importance of the saying.

14. In addition to the exegetical questions seen in the translation alternatives above, there is the text-critical issue of whether one should read τὴν ἐκκλησίαν τοῦ θεοῦ or τὴν ἐκκλησίαν τοῦ κυρίου. The great majority of scholars take the former to be the *Ausgangstext*, and so that will be the reading taken here.

namely the meaning of the verb (περιποιέω) and the sense of the preposi-tional phrase (διὰ τοῦ αἵματος τοῦ ἰδίου). Neither of these needs detain us for long, because on any reading, there is a clear sense of vicarious death. The prepositional phrase probably means "through the blood of his own."[15] The verb in the middle voice can mean either "acquire" or "rescue," but the former sense is perhaps more likely: the verse is probably emphasizing the incalcu-lable cost of God acquiring his people (by his own son's blood) and therefore why the elders in Miletus should keep close watch over such a flock.[16] The closest New Testament parallel is the church being "a people as a possession" (λαὸς εἰς περιποίησιν) in 1 Pet 2:9, which also fits the motif of acquisition. The soteriological sense of Acts 20:28 is in any case implied, because—even on the "acquisition" reading—the statement belongs within the early Christian discourse of God purchasing his people or paying a ransom for the church.[17] We will see more of this in the expositions of the ransom sayings in Mark and Matthew in chapters 4 and 5. For now, in addition to the considerable amount of reference to Jesus's death in Luke's Gospel (which also contains a soteriological interpretation of the cross), we also have an account of Jesus's effective and vicarious death in Acts.

THE RARITY OF EXPLANATIONS OF SAVING EVENTS IN ACTS

A final, neglected, factor to consider is how rarely Acts explains the soteriologi-cal significance of any of the momentous salvation-historical events recounted. The exaltation, for example, is clearly assigned soteriological significance in only two places: in Acts 2, where it is identified as the precondition of Jesus giving the Spirit (2:32–33), and in Acts 5, in connection with Jesus granting repentance and the forgiveness of sins (5:31).[18] Furthermore, the resurrection

---

15. Steve Walton, *Leadership and Lifestyle: The Portrait of Paul in the Miletus Speech and 1 Thessalonians* (Cambridge: Cambridge University Press, 2000), 96, notes that the two options presented in the translation above are the most likely. The syntax favors "through the blood of his own," given that, in the case of "through his own blood," one would more normally expect διὰ τοῦ ἰδίου αἵματος, but that is a minor consideration. Walton, *Leadership and Lifestyle*, 97, offers a number of parallels to the substantival use of ἴδιος, to which one can add Josephus, *Ant.* 13.40, noted by Wolter, "Jesu Tod und Sündenvergebung," 19 n. 17.

16. Bernard Aubert, *The Shepherd-Flock Motif in the Miletus Discourse (Acts 20:17–38) against Its Historical Background* (New York: Lang, 2009), 288.

17. Purchase: 1 Cor 6:20; 7:23; and 2 Pet 2:1. Ransom: Mark 10:45 // Matt 20:28; 1 Tim 2:6; cf. also 1 Pet 1:18–19.

18. Green, e.g., sees "Jesus' exaltation (*i.e.*, resurrection and ascension) as *the* salvific

is not given much *direct* import as an instrument of salvation, though the provision of evidence of future judgment might fit into this category (17:31). More common than particular events being assigned salvific significance is the attribution of salvation to Jesus *tout simple* or to his "grace" or to his "name."[19] More frequent still are statements about the human actions required (faith, repentance, baptism) and their instrumentality in salvation.[20] In light of this, a single clear statement in Acts 20:28 about the redemptive significance of the death of Jesus looks less anomalous.

CONCLUSION

Overall, then, there is no great discrepancy between the kerygma as summarized in 1 Cor 15 and the theology of Acts. The missionary speeches in Acts are not sufficiently homogeneous to allow the conclusion that they are paradigms of the kerygma. They are selective and specific to their settings in the narrative of Acts, while also sometimes repeating certain key themes. Luke in fact lays considerable stress on the death of Jesus, emphasizing not only the human agency in Jesus's execution but also that God willed, planned, preannounced, and brought about the passion of Jesus. This death of Jesus was not just a necessary condition for the resurrection but itself an event of soteriological significance, as both Luke and Acts show. Moreover, Luke's clear statement in Acts 20:28 cannot be dismissed as a one-off, because Acts does not frequently offer explicitly soteriological explanations of any of the divinely willed events. Luke's overall message in Acts, therefore, is quite in keeping with what is summarized as the kerygma in Paul, and echoed in Hebrews, 1 Peter, and Revelation. As noted at the beginning, even if there were two divergent kerygmas here, this would not affect the overall argument, because the point made in chapters 2 and 3 concerns the antiquity and wide distribution of the message summarized by Paul, not its universal preeminence.

---

event." See Joel B. Green, "'Salvation to the End of the Earth' (Acts 13:47): God as Saviour in the Acts of the Apostles," in *Witness to the Gospel: The Theology of Acts*, ed. I. H. Marshall and D. Peterson (Grand Rapids: Eerdmans, 1998), 95.

19. Grace, e.g., in Acts 15:11; 20:32. For salvation by the name of Jesus, see Acts 4:12; 8:12; 10:43; 22:16. For healing by the name of Jesus, see Acts 3:6, 16; 4:7, 10; 4:30; 16:18; cf. also Acts 2:21, 38; 4:17–18; 5:28; 8:16; 9:14–16, 21, 27–28; 10:48; 15:14–17; 19:5, 13.

20. Acts 2:38; 3:19; 10:43; 11:18; 13:39; 15:9; 16:30–31; 22:16; 26:18; cf. 13:48; 19:5–6.

Part Two

DESCRIPTION

—

Having established both the comparanda and the comparator, then, we can proceed to the descriptive task of examining the relevant Gospels with respect to how they understand Jesus's messiahship, death, resurrection, and fulfillment of scripture.

Chapter Four

THE GOSPEL OF MARK

The aim of this chapter is to assess the degree to which Mark's Gospel reflects the apostolic kerygma. The argument will proceed in four parts, examining in turn each of the elements identified in part I as components of that kerygma, namely (1) the messiahship of Jesus, (2) his vicarious death, (3) his resurrection on the third day, and (4) the prior scriptural attestation of these events. These components will be the topics of sections 1–4 of the chapter, respectively, and the conclusion will summarize the extent to which Mark's Gospel is reflective of the kerygma in the round.

1. JESUS AS MESSIAH IN MARK'S GOSPEL

The aim in this first section is to show that the identification of Jesus as messiah participates in the wider discourse of Jewish messianism. In other words, like the early Christian kerygma, Mark's Gospel activates the tradition of messianic exegesis and presents Jesus as recognizably within that tradition. Mark's Gospel is another work illustrating Novenson's observation that "ancient messiah texts constitute one example—an excellent example—of the vast, sprawling ancient Jewish and Christian project of scriptural interpretation."[1] This first part of the chapter has three component subsections, and it aims (1.1) to summarize the evidence for Mark's identification of Jesus as messiah, (1.2) to argue that Mark engages in christological interpretation of scripture that shares points in common with non-Christian Jewish messianic exegesis, and (1.3) to show that

---

1. Matthew V. Novenson, *The Grammar of Messianism: An Ancient Jewish Political Idiom and Its Users* (Oxford: Oxford University Press, 2017), 17.

some of Mark's discussion of Jesus's messiahship stands in broader *thematic* continuity with existing messianic discourse.

1.1 The Identification of Jesus as Messiah in Mark

Of the New Testament's five-hundred-odd instances of χριστός, only seven appear in Mark. The title issues from the mouths of several different characters. The first occurrence is in the narrator's voice, in the opening verse: there is no question that Mark 1:1 unambiguously and without reservation applies the term χριστός to Jesus. Another comes in Peter's confession: again, this is a positive statement, even if Peter's understanding of the term may be deficient (Mark 8:29). Peter's confession employs the phrase ὁ χριστός without explanation, assuming that "messiah" is something recognizable. Near the end of the Gospel, the high priest asks Jesus, "Are you the Christ?" and Jesus answers with ἐγώ εἰμι (14:61–62). Then the chief priests and scribes taunt Jesus with the title on the cross (15:32). Χριστός also appears in three sayings of Jesus. In the dispute about the messiah's descent from David (12:35–37), what Jesus says does not in itself constitute a claim to be the messiah, although Mark's readers would naturally assume the identification. In Mark 9, however, there is an implied self-reference when Mark 9:41 is taken in its literary context.[2] Similarly, Mark 13's reference to a false messiah may also imply an identification with Jesus (13:21–22; cf. 13:5–6).[3] Even leaving aside the debatable examples in the sayings of Jesus, Mark unreservedly applies the designation χριστός to him.

---

2. The reference in Mark 9:41 to "whoever gives you a cup of water in the name of your belonging to messiah" (ὃς . . . ἂν ποτίσῃ ὑμᾶς ποτήριον ὕδατος ἐν ὀνόματι ὅτι Χριστοῦ ἐστέ) comes after a sequence of sayings of Jesus about doing things "in my name" (Mark 9:37, 38, 39). Therefore, when we come to 9:41 and hear a reference to someone donating a cup of water, literally, "in the name that you are of Christ" (ἐν ὀνόματι ὅτι Χριστοῦ ἐστε), we are predisposed to see the Christ-name as belonging to Jesus: so Joachim Gnilka, *Das Evangelium nach Markus*, 2nd ed. (Neukirchen: Neukirchener Verlag, 2015), 2:61. Rudolf Pesch, *Das Markusevangelium*, 3rd ed. (Freiburg: Herder, 1984), 2:111, and R. T. France, *The Gospel of Mark* (Grand Rapids: Eerdmans, 2002), 378, see it as unambiguous.

3. In Mark 13:6, Jesus has said that "many will come in my name, claiming 'I am he'" (πολλοὶ ἐλεύσονται ἐπὶ τῷ ὀνόματί μου λέγοντες ὅτι ἐγώ εἰμι). Jesus's warning in Mark 13:21–22 against those who say "Look, here is the messiah!" therefore may imply an identification of Jesus as the messiah in his own teaching. Alternatively, France, *Mark*, 378, 529, takes it as an objective reference, not a self-designation here.

1.2 Mark's Christological Exegesis and Jewish Messianic Tradition

We can group the scriptural passages used by Mark, and that are relevant to this study, into two broad categories: those that had already been employed messianically in Jewish literature, and those that had been used "only" eschatologically. In the first category are Dan 7:13–14, Zech 9–14 (esp. 13:7), and Ps 2. In the second category are Deut 18:15–18 (bridging the first and second groups of texts), Isa 40, and Ps 118. While these latter examples are not messianic prooftexts in early Judaism, they would make sense in a Jewish context as relevant to an eschatological scenario. Some of the evidence here predates Mark (e.g., the Qumran literature), and some is roughly contemporaneous with him (e.g., 4 Ezra and 2 Baruch); the rather later rabbinic and targumic evidence is adduced here more in an ancillary role.

Daniel 7:13–14

Mark has numerous references to Jesus as "Son of Man," and the term is not merely a free-floating one but retains its connection to Dan 7:13–14. In particular, Mark's usage of Dan 7 to refer to the parousia of Jesus is undeniable. The Son of Man is promised in Mark 13:26 as "coming in clouds with great power and glory" (ἐρχόμενον ἐν νεφέλαις μετὰ δυνάμεως πολλῆς καὶ δόξης), a clear reference to Dan 7, where "one like a son of man came on the clouds of heaven" (ἐπὶ τῶν νεφελῶν τοῦ οὐρανοῦ ὡς υἱὸς ἀνθρώπου ἤρχετο) and received all authority and glory (ἐξουσία . . . καὶ πᾶσα δόξα). The same is true of Jesus's claim in Mark 14, where he accepts the title messiah and promises that the high priest will see "the Son of Man sitting at the right hand of power (τῆς δυνάμεως) and coming with the clouds of heaven (ἐρχόμενον μετὰ τῶν νεφελῶν τοῦ οὐρανοῦ)" (Mark 14:61–62). Further applications of the passage, especially to the death and resurrection of Jesus, will be discussed below in section 4.

This messianic exegesis of Dan 7 is no Christian innovation, even if the evidence in non-Christian Jewish literature is not so much "pre-Christian" as roughly contemporaneous with Mark.[4] (4Q246 uses Dan 7 but is not "messianic" in the strict sense.) The influence of Dan 7 is evident in the *Parables of Enoch*'s depiction of the Ancient/Head of Days (1 En. 46.1; cf. 47.3) and the

---

4. For a thorough survey of Dan 7 and messiahship in a broad sense, see William Horbury, "The Messianic Associations of the 'Son of Man,'" *JTS* 36 (1985): 34–55.

overthrowing of kingdoms that persecute the righteous (1 En. 46.4–8). The "Head of Days" appears together with "that son of man" (1 En. 48.2), the latter also being called "the messiah of the Lord of Spirits" (1 En. 48.10; cf. 52.4). In 4 Ezra, the angel tells Ezra that he is bringing the interpretation of Daniel's vision, an interpretation that refers to "the messiah (*mšyḥ'*, *unctus*) whom the Most High has kept until the end of days" (4 Ezra 12.10–12, 32). This is apparently the "one like a man . . . on the clouds of heaven" (4 Ezra 13.2–3), therefore making clear the identification of the messiah and one like a son of man. There are also several allusions to Dan 7 in the vision referring to the anointed one in 2 Bar. 35–46.[5] Messianic usage of Dan 7 survives into the Talmud, where, for example, the glorious Danielic figure and Zech 9's picture of the lowly king on a donkey are two complementary depictions of the messiah (b. Sanh. 98a). The targumim also attest a surprising messianic interpretation of Dan 7: the name of Anani (*'nny*) son of Elioenai, a member of the royal line in 1 Chronicles (3:10–24), is spelled the same way as the "clouds" (*'nny*) of heaven in Dan 7, and therefore Anani must be the "king messiah."[6] Midrash Numbers attributes Dan 7's advent with the clouds of heaven to the "king messiah," a son of David as well.[7] Rather later, Midrash Psalms also uses Dan 7 specifically of the messiah.[8] This later usage continues what is already evident in the first century CE. Mark's use of Dan 7 would therefore contribute to an identification of Jesus as a recognizably messianic figure.

Zechariah 13:7

On the Mount of Olives, Jesus declares to the disciples that when he is condemned, they will desert him: "You will all fall away, for it is written: 'I will strike the shepherd, and the sheep will be scattered'" (Mark 14:27). The sheep are the disciples, and Jesus is obviously the shepherd who is about to be struck.[9]

---

5. Klijn's *OTP* translation notes, e.g., the four kingdoms in 2 Bar. 39.1–5, and an allusion to Dan 7:27 in 2 Bar. 40.3.

6. Tg. 1 Chr. 3.24. See Samson H. Levey, *The Messiah: An Aramaic Interpretation; The Messianic Exegesis of the Targum* (New York: Ktav, 1974), 140. This "Anani" exegesis also appears in Midr. Tanḥ. 6.14. See Samuel A. Berman, *Midrash Tanhuma-Yelammedenu: An English Translation of Genesis and Exodus from the Printed Version of Tanhuma-Yelammedenu with an Introduction, Notes, and Indexes* (Hoboken: Ktav, 1996), 182.

7. Num. Rab. 13.14, on Num 7:13 (Slotki 2:528).

8. Midr. Ps. 21.5, on Ps 21:7 (Braude 1:296).

9. The extent of the sheep may be broader, since Mark has earlier highlighted the plight

Mark's use of Zechariah's "strike the shepherd" oracle in Mark 14 has a parallel in the B text of the *Damascus Document*. In CD-B, the punishment of the wicked is seen as taking place in accordance with Zech 13:7: "'Awake, O sword, against my shepherd, and against the male who is my companion', says the Lord. 'Strike the shepherd, and the flock will scatter, and I shall turn my hand against the little ones.'" The *Damascus Document* interprets the "flock" (via Zech 11:11) as those who will escape judgment, "but those that remain shall be delivered up to the sword when the messiah of Aaron and Israel comes" (CD-B 19.7–11). The text is slightly obscure here, but the strong implication is that Zech 13:7 is taken to be expecting an eschatological fulfillment at the time of the messiah, even if the messiah may not himself wield the sword.[10] There is need for caution about seeing a pre-Christian messianic interpretation of this passage given the lateness of the manuscript and the lack of parallel in CD-A and in the Dead Sea Scrolls.[11] Nevertheless, White Crawford and Brooke have both argued for the originality of the Zechariah material to the Damascus Document.[12] Therefore, Mark and CD-B may attest to an existing association in certain circles of the messiah with the Zechariah oracle. Mark's passion narrative is full of allusions to Zech 9–14, and this larger framework will be treated later, in section 4.1.[13] Overall, the use of Zech 13 by both CD-B and Mark probably points to a shared tradition, although it could be coincidental.

---

of the people as a whole, who are "like sheep without a shepherd" (Mark 6:34). Cf. the idiom in Num 27:17; 2 Chr 18:16; Jdt 11:19.

10. George J. Brooke, "The Messiah of Aaron in the Damascus Document," *RevQ* 15 (1991): 223, notes that the implication of the passage may be that Belial exacts the punishment. Additionally, the messiah's appearance is used as "climactic chronological marker" (224).

11. Charlesworth introduces the discussion of CD-B by saying that it is hard to assess "because of the paucity of overlap with the extant portions of the Qumran manuscripts." See James H. Charlesworth, ed., *Damascus Document II*, vol. 3 of *The Dead Sea Scrolls: Hebrew, Aramaic, and Greek Texts with English Translations* (Tübingen: Mohr Siebeck, 2006), 1.

12. George Brooke, "The Amos-Numbers Midrash (CD 7.13b–8.1a) and Messianic Expectation," *ZAW* 92 (1980): 403: "Certainly A1 replaced the Zechariah material with the Amos-Numbers midrash and not the other way round, so A1 must be dated after the completion of A2 and B." Similarly, see Sidnie White (Crawford), "A Comparison of the A and B Manuscripts of the Damascus Document," *RevQ* 12 (1987): 541–46, and see 542–44 for a survey of conclusions about the originality or otherwise of the Zechariah reference. John J. Collins, *The Scepter and the Star: Messianism in the Light of the Dead Sea Scrolls*, 2nd ed. (Grand Rapids: Eerdmans, 2010), 87–90, sees the problem as impossible to resolve.

13. Some other constituent parts of this section of Zechariah are also later understood messianically. For Zech 9:1, see Sifre Deut. 1.14; on Zech 9:9, see, e.g., b. Sanh. 98a; on Zech 12:10–12, see b. Sukkah 52a and y. Sukkah 5.2 (55b); Tg. Yer. Zech. 12.10.

Psalm 2

A majority of scholars considers the pronouncement "You are my son" (σὺ εἶ ὁ υἱός μου [Mark 1:11]) at Jesus's baptism to refer to Ps 2 (υἱός μου εἶ σύ [Ps 2:7]).[14] The declaration "You are my son" appears only in Ps 2 in the Septuagint/Hebrew Bible. (There is also reference to Isa 42 later in the verse, but this will be treated in the next chapter on Matthew, where there is a clearer quotation.)[15] If so, the messianic exegesis of the psalm becomes relevant. This psalm as a whole receives a good deal of messianic interpretation in antiquity, beginning in the Second Temple period.[16]

In the Dead Sea Scrolls, there is probably an allusion to Ps 2:7's "You are my son; today I have begotten you" in the *Rule of the Congregation*'s statement that "God begets his messiah."[17] More obviously, the last two psalms in the Psalms of Solomon employ the Davidic psalm in their depictions of the messiah. Psalms of Solomon 17 refers to the canonical Ps 2 throughout its discussion of the Davidic messiah who will conquer the nations.[18] Additionally, Psalms of Solomon 18 alludes to Ps 2 in the collocation of "his anointed" (Pss. Sol. 18.5; cf. Ps 2:2) or the "Christ (of) the Lord" (Pss. Sol. 18.7; again cf. Ps 2:2) with the anointed one's "rod" (18.7; cf. Ps 2:9).[19] Fourth Ezra also employs the language of Ps 2, as will be discussed in the treatment of "Son of God" (in sec. 1.3) below.

---

14. E.g., Joel Marcus, *The Way of the Lord: Christological Exegesis of the Old Testament in the Gospel of Mark* (Louisville: Westminster John Knox, 2003), 52; Sharyn Dowd and Elizabeth Struthers Malbon, "The Significance of Jesus' Death in Mark," *JBL* 125 (2006): 273; France, *Mark*, 80; and Gnilka, *Markus*, 53. Indeed, Max Botner, *Jesus Christ as the Son of David in the Gospel of Mark* (Cambridge: Cambridge University Press, 2019), 37, remarks upon "the broad consensus that the evangelist alludes to Ps 2:7 and Isa 42:1 at Jesus's baptism," or, later only slightly more restrainedly, that it is "widely accepted in Markan scholarship" (52).

15. See Marcus, *Way of the Lord*, 1, 52–54, on Isa 42 in Mark 1:9–11.

16. See Marcus, *Way of the Lord*, 59–66; Sam Janse, *"You Are My Son": The Reception History of Psalm 2 in Early Judaism and the Early Church* (Leuven: Peeters, 2009); Susan Gillingham, *A Journey of Two Psalms: The Reception of Psalms 1 and 2 in Jewish and Christian Tradition* (Oxford: Oxford University Press, 2013).

17. 1Q28a II, 11–12. Rightly, William Horbury, *Messianism among Jews and Christians: Biblical and Historical Studies* (London: Bloomsbury, 2003), 18.

18. See, e.g., the list of parallels in Gillingham, *Journey of Two Psalms*, 35.

19. Indeed, the whole clause with the "rod" refers to submitting to the "rod of the discipline of the Lord's Christ, in fear" (ὑπὸ ῥάβδον παιδείας χριστοῦ κυρίου ἐν φόβῳ), echoing not only the second psalm's rod but also the disciplining of the kings of the earth (Ps 2:10, 12: παιδεύθητε, δράξασθε παιδείας) and their serving in fear (2:11: ἐν φόβῳ). See discussion in Janse, *You Are My Son*, 66. Cf. also the related depictions of God as ὁ κατοικῶν ἐν οὐρανοῖς (Ps 2:4) and ἔνδοξος ἐν ὑψίστοις κατοικῶν (Pss. Sol. 18.10).

Finally in the early period, 1 Enoch appears to allude to Ps 2 in its reference to the "kings of the earth" and their rebellion against "the Lord of Spirits and his anointed one" (1 En. 48.8–10 referring to Ps 2:2).

Midrash Psalms takes the "son" in Ps 2:7 to be the "king messiah" and also applies Isa 52:13, Dan 7, and Ps 110:1 to this figure.[20] The targum has a significant paraphrase of the psalm, in which the begetting is a creation, and the anointed one is *as dear to God as* a son is to a father (Tg. Ps. 2.7). The note of anointing is emphasized, however, being repeated in Tg. Ps. 2.6. In the Talmud, the request and the gift of the nations as an inheritance (Ps 2:8) are applied to "the messiah, son of David" (b. Sukkah 52a). Tractate ʿAbodah Zarah has an extended exegesis of Ps 2, covering verses 4, 2, 1, 3, and again verse 4, with the setting of the psalm imagined as the eschatological battle of Gog and Magog between the gentiles and "the Lord and his anointed one" during "the days of the messiah" (b. ʿAbod. Zar. 3b).[21] The use of Ps 2 messianically in early Judaism, even in the Second Temple period, is clear, as probably is Mark's own use.

Deuteronomy 18:15–18

Moving to passages for which there is evidence of existing eschatological, rather than messianic, interpretation, Joel Marcus notes that the concluding words of the voice from heaven in the transfiguration ("Listen to him!") are so close to the prophet-like-Moses passage in Deut 18 "that we may speak of a virtual citation" in Mark 9:7.[22] (The fact that Moses has just appeared perhaps encourages hearing such a reference.) There is also an allusion to Deut 18 in the *Rule of the Community*, where the reference to the prophet appears in a messianic context, though not identifying the prophet as a messiah: "they [sc. the men of holiness] shall be ruled by the primitive precepts in which the men of the community were first instructed *until there shall come the prophet* (*'d bw' nby'*) *and the messiahs of Aaron and Israel*."[23] The Qumran text known as Testimonia (4Q175) or the *Messianic Anthology* includes a citation of Deut 18:18–19 and Num 24:15–17 together, possibly suggesting a similar sequence or pairing of the Deuteronomic prophet and the messiah of Balaam's oracle, or a view

---

20. Midr. Ps. 2.9, on Ps 2:7 (Braude 1:41).

21. This is also a feature of the interpretation in Midrash Psalms.

22. Marcus, *Way of the Lord*, 81. Similarly, Dieter Lührmann, *Das Markusevangelium* (Tübingen: Mohr Siebeck, 1987), 156; Pesch, *Markusevangelium*, 2:76 ("frei zitiert"); Gnilka, *Markus*, 2:36; and France, *Mark*, 355 (an "echo").

23. 1QS IX, 10–11; trans. Vermes.

that the former "star" is the prophet and the latter "scepter" is the messiah. A possible allusion appears in 1 Maccabees, where Simon is appointed leader and high priest in perpetuity "until a trustworthy prophet should arise" (ἔως τοῦ ἀναστῆναι προφήτην πιστόν), with very similar language also in 4Q375.[24] The language here is very similar to that of the *Rule of the Community* and also echoes God's promise in Deuteronomy that he would raise up (ἀναστήσει) a prophet (προφήτην) whose words would come to pass (cf. Deut 34:10). Again, here the note is eschatological rather than messianic, although the conjunction of the prophet's and the messiah's comings in the *Rule of the Community* and *Testimonia* will be explored further below in section 1.3.

Isaiah 40:3

A very prominent place is accorded to Isa 40:3 in Mark, in a composite citation (with Exod 23:20 or Mal 3:1, or both) right at the beginning of the Gospel (Mark 1:2–3). John the Baptist is the one whose voice cries out in the wilderness, and the Lord for whom he prepares the way is Jesus. There is therefore a pesheristic interpretation in which characters in the quoted passage are identified as eschatological figures in Mark's narrative present. A similar approach is taken, as is widely recognized, in the *Rule of the Community*. Here the Qumran community is the preparatory agent, and the action by which they make the way ready is the study of the Torah (1QS VIII, 12–16; cf. IX, 17–20). The introductory formulae are mutatis mutandis the same in the Hebrew of 1QS (*k'šr ktwb*) and Mark's Greek (καθὼς γέγραπται). As Tzoref concludes, the common element between the two interpretations is the eschatological reading of Isa 40.[25] Indeed, this eschatological interpretation is further found elsewhere.[26]

Psalm 118

This psalm is important in the description of Jesus's entry into Jerusalem, and then again in the parable of the wicked tenants to refer to Jesus's death

---

24. For the interpretation of this figure as the prophet like Moses, see John J. Collins, "The Works of the Messiah," *DSD* 1 (1994): 104 and n. 25.

25. Shani Tzoref, "The Use of Scripture in the Community Rule," in *A Companion to Biblical Interpretation in Early Judaism*, ed. Matthias Henze (Grand Rapids: Eerdmans, 2012), 217, citing Lindars approvingly. See Tzoref's essay for a full interpretation of the 1QS passage.

26. See Klyne R. Snodgrass, "Streams of Tradition Emerging from Isaiah 40:1–5 and Their Adaptation in the New Testament," *JSNT* 8 (1980): 24–45, noting 4Q176, *As. Mos.* 10.1–5, and later rabbinic usage.

and resurrection (Mark 11:8–10; 12:10). Psalm 118 was not a messianic proof-text in early Jewish exegesis, but it is sometimes taken as eschatological in rabbinic literature.[27]

Conclusion

Overall, Mark's christological exegesis overlaps with other Jewish messianic and eschatological interpretation of scripture in its selection of passages.

1.3 Jewish Messianic Themes in Mark's Christology

In addition to Mark's choice of passages, there are also particular themes shared with non-Christian messianic discourse. One feature of Mark's usage is the pairing of "messiah," in almost every instance, with other titles such as "Son of God" (Mark 1:1), "Son of Man" (8:29–31), "Son of David" and "Lord" (12:35–36), "Son of the Blessed One" (14:61), and "king of Israel" (15:32).[28] We have covered "Son of Man" in the examination of the exegesis of Dan 7; the other supplements or explanatory glosses are an important part of how Mark taps into traditional messianic themes.

Son of God

As noted in chapter 2, a common feature of Jewish messianism is to propose the sonship or descent of the messiah from a particular ancestor—proposed fathers of the messiah include Jesse, David, Kokhba, Hezekiah, Ephraim, Joseph, and God.[29] In Mark, the phrase "Son of God" appears two or three times (Mark 3:11;

27. Marcus, *Way of the Lord*, 115, notes that Ps 118:10–12 is taken in Midrash Psalms to refer to the Gog Magog wars that are also the theme in the midrash to Ps 2, in which the messiah participates in the war. Hence, there may have been an exegetical link between the two. Andrew Brunson, *Psalm 118 in the Gospel of John: An Intertextual Study on the New Exodus Pattern in the Theology of John* (Tübingen: Mohr Siebeck, 2003), 90 n. 296, also notes that Ps 118 and Zech 9–14 are taken as mutually interpreting in the midrash.

28. Graham Stanton, *The Gospels and Jesus*, 2nd ed. (Oxford: Oxford University Press, 2002), 42, makes a typical, uncontroversial statement, that Mark's use of the messiah title "is usually qualified by other ways of spelling out the identity of Jesus." We could add here Mark 13:21–22, although the pairing of "false messiahs" and "false prophets" suggests a loose relation or analogy between "messiah" and "prophet" rather than identity.

29. See Novenson, *Grammar of Messianism*, 65–113; the theme of the messiah's parentage is also surveyed at various points in Martha Himmelfarb, *Jewish Messiahs in a Christian Empire: A History of the Book of Zerubbabel* (Cambridge: Harvard University Press, 2017).

15:39; cf. 1:1), along with cases of "Son of the Most High God" (5:7), "Son of the Blessed One" (14:61), and "the Son" *tout simple* (13:32).[30] The declaration of Jesus as Son of God by the centurion at the crucifixion (15:39) is undoubtedly a climactic revelatory moment. In addition, God twice acclaims Jesus as his Son (1:11; 9:7) and—in allegory—does so again in the parable of the wicked tenants (12:6). The titles "Son" and "Son of God" for Mark are clearly defined in scriptural terms, given the use of Ps 2 in the baptism scene, and the combination of "Son" with the distinctively Septuagintal/Jewish term "blessed" (εὐλογητός).

There has been abundant debate over the possible pre-Christian evidence for the messiah as son of God, especially between Fitzmyer, who has seen the New Testament as more exceptional, and Collins, who has seen early Christian exegesis as more in continuity with Jewish messianism on this point.[31] Partly under Collins's influence, the balance of scholarship has probably shifted in recent times toward more sympathy for seeing a tradition of "son of God" messianism in ancient Judaism. The earliest evidence comes in the Dead Sea Scrolls, with the *Rule of the Congregation* (1QSa), already mentioned, almost certainly referring to God's "begetting" of the messiah (1Q28a II, 11–12). Not to be neglected is the Florilegium (4Q174), which quotes 2 Sam 7. There, immediately after God's promise that he would count David's heir as his (God's) own son (2 Sam 7:14a), the Samuel passage is understood to refer to the "branch of David" who will save Israel (4Q174 I, 10–13). Notably, the work is selective in its quotation of 2 Sam 7, and so the reference to the adoption formula in 2 Sam 7:14a ("he shall be my son") is by no means an automatic function of the citation.[32] The "branch of David" figure here is messianic, as the identification of the branch of David as "the messiah of righteousness" in 4Q252 makes clear. Less directly messianic, in the strict sense of that word, is 4Q246 where there is a "son of God" and "son of the Most High" who is interpreted in terms of Dan 7.[33]

30. Whether "Son of God" should be judged to have been original to Mark 1:1 is uncertain, although on balance, the evidence probably favors its inclusion. It is not of great importance, however, since "the Messiah, the Son of the Blessed One" appears later, Jesus accepting in Mark 14:62 both parts of the designation ("I am"). For a recent study, see Tommy Wasserman, "The 'Son of God' Was in the Beginning (Mark 1:1)," *JTS* 62 (2011): 20–50.

31. See, e.g., Collins, *Scepter and the Star*, 171–90.

32. 4Q174 I, 10–13 quotes 2 Sam 7 as follows: "(7:11c) [And] the Lord [de]clares to you that he will build you a house . . . (v. 12b) and I will raise up your seed after you. . . . (v. 13b) and I will establish his royal throne [forev]er. (v. 14a) I wi[ll be] a father to him and he shall be my son."

33. More elusive but also possibly related is 4Q536 3 I, 10–11, which refers to the birth of "the elect [*or* chosen one] of God" and may allude to the standard messianic prooftext, Isa 11. Equally tantalizing is the Prayer of Enosh, which refers to a firstborn son as a ruler

The surviving versions of 4 Ezra make extensive use of the phrase "my son" as a designation of the messiah (4 Ezra 7.28, 29; 13.32, 37, 52; 14.9). Chester deems the phrase to be a "messianic designation" probably derived from Ps 2:7.[34] It is possible that the "son" language goes back via Greek to an original Hebrew referring to the *servant*, but the Latin and Syriac texts of these passages agree in referring to God's son (*filius meus, bry*).[35] The main skeptical influence on scholarship here is from Stone, although his approach appears not quite consistent, on one page noting that the textual evidence is "not unambiguous" (especially as both Latin and Syriac consistently have "son") yet later concluding that it is "compelling."[36] Knibb notes the lack of certainty, concluding that both "son" and "servant" remain possible as the original readings.[37] Helpfully, however, Collins notes how 4 Ezra 13.33–35 and the chapter as a whole show dependence on Ps 2: "nations" "gather together" (13.33–34; cf. Ps 2:1–2) against the anointed/messianic figure; but he stands on Mount Zion (13.35; cf. Ps 2:6) and rebukes these nations (13.37; cf. Ps 2:5) and ultimately destroys "the nations that gathered together" (13.49; cf. Ps 2:1–2).[38] This makes an original reading of the messiah as God's son (cf. Ps 2:7) much more likely, at least in 4 Ezra 13–14.

There is a further intriguing possibility of a reference to God's son in the Epistle of Enoch:

> "In those days," says the Lord, "they will summon and testify
>   against the sons of earth in their wisdom.
> Instruct them, for you are their leaders
>   and . . . rewards over all the earth.
> For I and my son will join ourselves with them forever

(4Q369 1 II, 6–10). Collins, following Kugel, however, notes that this is very unlikely to be a reference to a messiah (*Scepter and the Star*, 186). For further discussion of 4Q369 and 4Q536, see Craig A. Evans, "A Note on the 'First-Born Son' of 4Q369," *DSD* 2 (1995): 192.

34. Andrew Chester, *Messiah and Exaltation: Jewish Messianic and Visionary Traditions and New Testament Christology* (Tübingen: Mohr Siebeck, 2007), 346.

35. As argued by Marcus, *Way of the Lord*, 78, and Janse, *You Are My Son*, 69, both relying on Stone (see note below).

36. Michael E. Stone, *Fourth Ezra* (Minneapolis: Fortress, 1990), 207–8.

37. E.g., Richard J. Coggins and Michael A. Knibb, *The First and Second Books of Esdras* (Cambridge: Cambridge University Press, 1979), 169: "possibly because of a deliberate Christian alteration," noting also the messianic interpretation of Ps 2 as "a possible Jewish background for the use of this title."

38. Collins, *Scepter and the Star*, 186. Cf., e.g., Ps 2:2 (*convenerunt in unum*) with 4 Ezra 13.34 (*colligetur in unum*), and Ps 2:6 (*super Sion, montem sanctum eius*) with 4 Ezra 13.35 (*super cacumen montis Sion*).

in the paths of truth in their life.
And you will have peace.
Rejoice, O children of truth."
Amen. (1 En. 105.1–2; trans. Nickelsburg and VanderKam)[39]

The complication here is that some have argued that the original Aramaic could be understood not as an oracle of God but as Enoch speaking of himself and his son Methuselah.[40]

As noted in section 1.2 above, Mark's use of the theme of divine sonship is probably also indebted to Ps 2. In any case, Mark is clearly tapping into a tradition of the messiah's divine sonship, although he certainly emphasizes it more than previous authors.

Son of David

Also traditional is the connection between "messiah" and "son of David."[41] In Mark, the scribes refer to Davidic genealogy as a standard characteristic of the messiah (Mark 12:35), and, when Jesus himself is hailed as "Son of David" (10:47–48), there is not an implication that the blind man is *wrong* in his acclamation. Yet, in the Son of David controversy (Mark 12:35–37), Mark seems to qualify this association: there is something inadequate, though not inaccurate, about the designation "Son of David."[42] Nevertheless, Botner has shown

39. George W. E. Nickelsburg and James VanderKam, *1 Enoch: The Hermeneia Translation* (Minneapolis: Fortress, 2012), 162. The antecedent of "they" and "them" is "the righteous and pious and wise" (see 1 En. 104.12–13).

40. Thus Loren T. Stuckenbruck, *1 Enoch 91–108* (Berlin: de Gruyter, 2007), 603–4, while also rejecting the ideas of an interpolation or of insufficient room for the "I and my son" phrase. On the other hand, both Stuckenbruck and Nickelsburg and VanderKam translate 1 En. 105.2 as immediately following the explicit reference to the divine oracle. Nickelsburg allows for the possibility that the reference could be to Enoch and Methuselah. See George W. E. Nickelsburg, *1 Enoch 1: A Commentary on the Book of 1 Enoch, Chapters 1–36; 81–108* (Minneapolis: Fortress, 2001), 535.

41. On "Son of David" in Mark, see now Max Botner, *Jesus Christ as the Son of David in the Gospel of Mark* (Cambridge: Cambridge University Press, 2019). For an example of thinking Mark to be anti-Davidic, see William R. Telford, *The Theology of the Gospel of Mark* (Cambridge: Cambridge University Press, 1999), 113.

42. Donald H. Juel, *Messianic Exegesis: Christological Interpretation of the Old Testament in Early Christianity* (Minneapolis: Fortress, 1988), 144, is almost certainly correct that the apparent contradiction in Mark 12:35–37, of the messiah being both David's Son and David's Lord, is to be resolved eschatologically, when Jesus is exalted. Similarly, Martin Hengel, *Studies in Early Christology* (Edinburgh: T&T Clark, 1995), 56–57: "Mark 12:35–37 points out a messianic aporia that will only be resolved in the person of the Son of Man, Jesus." Cilliers

that in addition to the explicit references to David in Mark, there are further Davidic motifs that confirm the accuracy of the connection with David.[43]

Davidic descent is by no means a sine qua non in early Jewish constructions of the messiah: the anointed one in the *Parables of Enoch*, for example, has no connection with David (and perhaps no genealogy at all). Novenson also notes that 2 Baruch shows no interest in David.[44] Nevertheless, despite Karrer's marginalization of the theme, Davidic ancestry is a known feature.[45] In Pss. Sol. 17, the anticipated king of Israel is the Lord's messiah: God had sworn that David's descendants would never fail to sit on the throne over Israel (Pss. Sol. 17.3), but because of Israel's sin, her enemies overthrew that Davidic monarchy (17.6), hence the appeal to bring back the king, "the son of David" (17.21). Or again, the Qumran Commentary on Genesis (on Gen 49:10) refers to "the messiah of righteousness, the branch of David" (4Q252 I, 3–4), the latter epithet appearing five times in the Dead Sea Scrolls.[46] In 4 Ezra, the messiah—although a heavenly figure—will arise from the seed of David (4 Ezra 12.31–32). The David motif is a very common feature in the targumim.[47] The Talmud also has numerous instances.[48]

Breytenbach, "Das Markusevangelium, Psalm 110,1 und 118,22f.: Folgetext und Prätext," in *The Scriptures in the Gospels*, ed. Christopher M. Tuckett (Leuven: Leuven University Press, 1997), 208, rightly states that what Jesus denies is that his messiahship derives from his Davidic ancestry rather than his future exaltation to power. The contradiction is not resolved by denying that the messiah is the Son of David, *pace* Stephen P. Ahearne-Kroll, *The Psalms of Lament in Mark's Passion: Jesus' Davidic Suffering* (Cambridge: Cambridge University Press, 2007), 164; rightly, Richard B. Hays, *Echoes of Scripture in the Gospels* (Waco, TX: Baylor University Press, 2016), 54.

43. E.g., Botner, *Jesus Christ as the Son of David*, 60–61.

44. Novenson, *Grammar of Messianism*, 66.

45. Martin Karrer, *Der Gesalbte: Die Grundlagen des Christustitels* (Göttingen: Vandenhoeck & Ruprecht, 1990), 293: "Jüdische und christliche Entwicklung der Davidssohnvorstellung verlaufen teils vorsichtig anknüpfend, teils nebeneinander bis entgegengesetzt, nirgends jedoch in einem Verhältnis christlicher Entsprechung zu verbindlicher jüdisch-messianischer Vorgabe." Karrer is right that Davidic ancestry or associations are not *verbindlich*, but they are frequent. See the helpful summary table in Botner, *Jesus Christ as the Son of David*, 43, on Davidic ancestry, and the monograph as a whole on Davidic associations. The widespread use of Isa 11:1 in messianic texts is notable.

46. For a survey of the references, see Craig A. Evans, "Messiahs," in *Encyclopedia of the Dead Sea Scrolls*, ed. Lawrence H. Schiffman and James C. VanderKam (Oxford: Oxford University Press, 2000), 1:537–42.

47. See, e.g., the targumim to 1 Kgs 5:13; Jer 30:9; Hos 3:5; Ps 72; Song 4:5; 7:4 (two messiahs, one of whom is a son of David); see respectively, Levey, *Messiah*, 42, 71, 89, 115, 127–28, as well as Novenson, *Grammar of Messianism*, 180.

48. E.g., in the Jerusalem Talmud, Rabbi Akiba allegedly regarded Bar Kokhba as the messiah son of David (y. Ta'an. 4.8, 27). See Matthew Novenson, "Why Does R. Akiba

In conclusion, although Mark is clear on the limitations of the "Son of David" as a descriptor for the messiah, he does deem it a true designation of Jesus. In applying it to Jesus, Mark claims that he is aligning himself with Jewish scholarly opinion (Mark 12:35), no doubt stemming from passages like 2 Sam 7, Isa 11, and Jer 23:5. This opinion of Mark's γραμματεῖς is reflected in the Psalms of Solomon, Qumran, and 4 Ezra, as well as in later rabbinic and targumic literature. As Botner also concludes, "Markan language about Jesus Christ adheres to the linguistic conventions his contemporaries used to characterize their messiahs—whether messiahs *like* David or *descendants* of the Davidic line."[49]

King of Israel

Closely related to the Son of David title and the shepherd epithet is that of "king of Israel," although there is perhaps more reservation about this latter title: Jesus is called this only by the chief priests and the teachers of the law (Mark 15:31). The title "king of the Jews" also appears in Pilate's various questions (15:2, 9, 12), in the mockery from the soldiers (15:18) and in the *titulus* (15:26).

Mark's collocation of "messiah" and "king of Israel" is not frequent in non-Christian Jewish literature. The Psalms of Solomon do designate the messiah as the "king" who will "reign over Israel" (17.21, 23) and the "king of Israel" (17.42). Also attested are the overlapping idioms "messiah of (Aaron and) Israel" and "king messiah." The former features in the Dead Sea Scrolls and the latter in the targumim and the midrashim.[50]

The Messiah as "Lord"

This theme will be discussed further in the chapter on Luke's Gospel, where the conjunction of messiah and lord is closer than it is in Mark. Nevertheless, the connection in the Son of David controversy is a close one: Jesus questions the Davidic sonship of the messiah (Mark 12:35) by quoting Ps 110:1 (Mark 12:36). From this verse in the psalm, Jesus deduces that the messiah is "lord" or at

---

Acclaim Bar Kokhba as Messiah?," *JSJ* 40 (2009): 551–72. The Babylonian Talmud can also talk of the messiah son of David (e.g., b. Sukkah 52a).

49. Botner, *Jesus Christ as the Son of David*, 37.

50. "Messiah of (Aaron and) Israel": 1QS IX, 11; 1QSa II, 11–14, 20; CD XII, 22–XIII, 1; XIX, 10–11; XIX, 33–XX, 1; cf. the fragmentary CD XIV, 18–19; also Tg. Isa. 16.1, 5; "King Messiah": Tg. 1 Chr. 3.24; Tg. Neof. Gen. 49.10–12; Gen. Rab. 44.8, on 15:2 (Freedman 1:365) and Midr. Ps. 21.5, on Ps 21:7 (Braude 1:296).

least David's lord. In advance of the further discussion in chapter 6, it is worth merely noting at this point that the conjunction of messiah and lord appears also in the Psalms of Solomon and Midrash Psalms.[51]

The Messiah's Forerunner or Companion Figure

One final consideration is that both Mark's quotation of Isa 40 at the beginning of the Gospel (Mark 1:2–3) and the later reference to the scribes' belief that Elijah must come first (Mark 9:11–13) probably draw on a traditional understanding of a predecessor or companion figure to the messiah.[52] (Not all other texts are clear on a chronological sequence, hence the qualification "or companion figure.") In the *Rule of the Community*, "the prophet" is the first in the list of three figures coming, the others being the messiahs of Aaron and Israel (1QS IX, 9–11). In the *Damascus Document*, reference to the "Interpreter of the Law" precedes the "Prince of the Congregation,"[53] the messianic "branch of David" (CD VII, 18–21): these two figures are, respectively, the "star" and the "scepter" of Num 24:17. In 4Q174, the Interpreter of the Law is again described as accompanying the "branch of David."[54] Bar Kokhba's associate Eleazar the priest was prominent enough to be cited on a number of coins during the Hadrianic revolt.[55] Justin's Trypho claims that Elijah's advent before the messiah is a standard Jewish expectation (πάντες ἡμεῖς . . . προσδοκῶμεν).[56] Moreover in the passage in the Talmud in which the concept of Elijah as predecessor

---

51. Pss. Sol. 17.32; 18.7; Midr. Ps. 2.3, on 2:2 (Braude 1:37); 2.9, on 2:7 (Braude 1:41).

52. See now especially Anthony Ferguson, "The Elijah Forerunner Concept as an Authentic Jewish Expectation," *JBL* 13 (2018): 127–45, for thorough survey of evidence and previous literature, and also Anthony Giambrone, "'Why Do the Scribes Say' (Mark 9:11): Scribal Expectations of an Eschatological High Priest and the Implications of Jesus' Transfiguration," *RB* 128 (2021): 201–35.

53. For the "branch of David" and the "Prince of the Congregation," see further, e.g., 1Q28b V, 21; 4Q161 (4QIsaᵃ) 5–6 and 8–10; 4Q252 1 V, 1–7 and 4Q285 4–5. For a summary of the evidence, see Evans, "Messiahs," 1:537–42.

54. For other references, see 4QCatenaᵃ (4Q177) and CD VI, 7 (which refers to the Teacher of Righteousness). For discussion of the passages, see Michael Knibb, "Interpreter of the Law," in Schiffman and VanderKam, *Encyclopedia of the Dead Sea Scrolls*, 1:383–84.

55. See Ya'akov Meshorer, *A Treasury of Jewish Coins: From the Persian Period to Bar Kochba* (Jerusalem: Yad Ben-Zvi, 2001), 244–56 (sec. 219, 224–26, 234–35, 300–304).

56. Justin, *Dial.* 49.1: "For we all expect the Christ to be a man born of men, and that when Elijah comes, he [Elijah] will anoint him. If this man appears to be the Christ, he must certainly be known as man born of men; but from the circumstance that Elijah had not come (ἐληλυθέναι), I infer that this man is not the Christ." The pluperfect probably implies the expectation of Elijah's coming before the messiah.

to the messiah is explicitly set out (b. 'Erub. 43a–b), there is the additional statement that "it was promised long ago to Israel that Elijah would not come either on Sabbath eves or on festival eves owing to the trouble." Ferguson notes therefore that this belief is presented as a long-standing one, and Allison argues that it is unlikely rabbis would adopt a Christian idea: both scholars deduce from the circumstantial evidence a pre-Christian belief that Elijah would precede the messiah. The conclusion here is more modest, namely that Mark taps into a traditional understanding of a predecessor or companion figure to the messiah, a view that may have had its origins in connection with the reference to Elijah in Mal 3:1–4 and 4:5–6 (on which Mark 9:11 is dependent).[57] As was the case with the messiah's Davidic sonship, certainly Mark thinks he is in agreement with traditional messianic exegesis, as is seen in his assumption that the scribes also believe that Elijah comes before the messiah (Mark 9:11).

1.4 Interim Conclusion: Mark's Messiah and the Kerygma

Mark's messiah is recognizable as an instance of the scriptural, messianic discourse of early Judaism: he does not abandon or transform an existing messianic "concept." Taking section 1.3 first, we saw that Mark taps into common discourse of the messiah's paternity (Son of God, Son of David), and negotiates some traditional literary connections between "messiah" and other designations such as "king of Israel" and "Lord," as well as the assumption of a forerunner to the messiah. We saw in section 1.2 that Mark's exegesis of Dan 7, Zech 13, and Ps 2 reflects existing usage of those passages in discourse about a particular anointed figure, or messiah. Similarly, Mark's messianic applications of Isa 40, Ps 118, and Deut 18 have partial parallels in the eschatological use of the passages in early Judaism. In this respect, Mark's approach is quite in keeping with what happens elsewhere, as when early Jewish texts take an existing eschatological passage such as Dan 7 and make it explicitly messianic. Some of Mark's use of scripture is unprecedented as part of the characterization of an anointed figure (e.g., probably the use of Ps 110), but in that respect, Mark is doing the same thing as do other participants in the discourse of early Jewish messianism: no Jewish writer simply slavishly repeated what another had already said, and messianic exegesis was always shaped by experience. Oegema and Novenson have rightly emphasized how various different early Jewish and Christian writings draw on a range of scriptural passages to interpret

---

57. Gnilka, *Markus*, 2:41 n. 11, notes that Mark and Malachi both have Elijah and ἀποκαθιστάνω/ ἀποκαθίστημι.

messiah language.[58] *How* Mark depicts Jesus as messiah, then, is not through a revolutionary method.

In short, Mark applies the designation "messiah" to Jesus and explicates his Christology with reference to existing messianic and eschatological exegesis, as well as traditionally messianic themes. Mark's messianic discourse is a scripturally constituted one. Both the fact of calling Jesus messiah and Mark's method, then, are comprehensible within early Judaism, and more specifically within the Jewish-Christian setting of the early kerygma.

2. THE VICARIOUS DEATH OF JESUS IN MARK

Mark's Gospel threatens the death of Jesus early on in its narrative (Mark 3:6; cf. 2:20). Of the various passion predictions (8:31; 9:12, 31; 10:32–34, 38–39), the first specifies that the Son of Man "must" (δεῖ) suffer and be rejected, and Mark understands this necessity as scriptural and ultimately rooted in the Father's will.[59] When Mark cites the "striking of the shepherd" oracle (Mark 14:27; cf. Zech 13:7), he departs from the Hebrew and Greek of Zechariah: introducing the citation with the divine first person ("I will strike the shepherd"), he accentuates the fact that Jesus's death is not only subject to the divine "must" of the passion prediction but is even a divine action.[60]

Why this necessity and a death that is willed and even brought about by God? The two passages almost always invoked to explain the meaning of Jesus's death in Mark are Mark 10:45 and 14:22–25. The discussion here will proceed in three stages, dealing initially with these two passages (sec. 2.1–2), before examining the various narrative details of the passion narrative for what they may indicate about the significance of Jesus's death (sec. 2.3).

---

58. See especially Gerbern S. Oegema, *The Anointed and His People: Messianic Expectations from the Maccabees to Bar Kochba* (Sheffield: Sheffield Academic, 1994), 290–306, and Novenson, *Grammar of Messianism*, passim. Appendix 9, "List of Old Testament Passages Messianically Applied in Ancient Rabbinic Writings," in Alfred Edersheim, *The Life and Times of Jesus the Messiah*, 8th ed. (London: Longmans, 1907), 2:710–41 is also a valuable source.

59. W. J. Bennett, "The Son of Man Must . . . ," *NovT* 17 (1975): 118, notes (following Tödt) the parallel of the δεῖ in Mark 8:31 with the γέγραπται of Mark 9:12. In Gethsemane, it is implied that Jesus's death is his Father's will (Mark 14:36).

60. Cf. Ernest Best, *The Temptation and the Passion: The Markan Soteriology* (Cambridge: Cambridge University Press, 1965), 158: "Thus Mark sets forth Jesus as smitten by God in God's judgment over his people Israel."

2.1 The Ransom Saying and Vicarious Death (Mark 10:45)

"For even the Son of Man came not to be served, but to serve, and to give his life as a ransom for many." As France has commented of Mark 10:45, "Here is his answer to the puzzle of why Jesus had to die."[61] The key phrase to interpret is the "ransom for many" (λύτρον ἀντὶ πολλῶν). The backdrop to much contemporary discussion sees Mark 10:45 as an interpretation of Isa 53, and there are still numerous scholars who see the ransom saying in these terms.[62] Such an approach has attracted a number of criticisms, however.[63] While in broad terms Mark 10:45 has a good deal in common with Isa 53 thematically, especially if Mark's ransom saying is specifically seeking to invoke the scriptural necessity of Jesus's death, the verbal links are weak. Recently scholars have approached Mark 10:45 from various other angles.

Adela Yarbro Collins has argued that one key context for understanding Mark 10:45 is the ritual setting of Hellenistic cults. In the so-called confessional inscriptions, for example, there is a presupposed sequence of (1) an offense committed, (2) an ongoing misfortune understood as a divine penalty for the offense, and (3) a ransom paid by the punished offender in order to secure release from this misfortune. Hence in an inscription from 143 CE, Artemidorus and Amias dedicate a stele as a ransom (λύτρον) for an offense committed.[64] Against this sort of background, Mark 10:45 would then describe the death of Jesus metaphorically "as a ritual expiation of the offenses of the many."[65]

Cilliers Breytenbach emphasizes two aspects of the background to Mark 10:45, one internal to Mark, and another in the Septuagint.[66] On the former, he emphasizes Mark 8:34–38 with its ransom language (ἀντάλλαγμα)

---

61. France, *Mark*, 421.

62. E.g., Lührmann, *Markusevangelium*, 181; France, *Mark*, 419–21; David Garland, *A Theology of Mark's Gospel: Good News about Jesus the Messiah, the Son of God* (Grand Rapids: Zondervan, 2015), 475.

63. See, e.g., the summaries of criticisms in Morna D. Hooker, *The Gospel according to St. Mark* (London: A. & C. Black, 2001), 248–49; Cilliers Breytenbach, "Narrating the Death of Jesus in Mark," *ZNW* 105 (2014): 162–64; Matthew Thiessen, "The Many for One or One for the Many? Reading Mark 10:45 in the Roman Empire," *HTR* 109 (2016): 450–51.

64. Adela Yarbro Collins, "The Signification of Mark 10:45 among Gentile Christians," *HTR* 90 (1997): 375. See further Yarbro Collins, *Mark: A Commentary* (Minneapolis: Fortress, 2007), 500–502; Yarbro Collins, "Mark's Interpretation of the Death of Jesus," *JBL* 128 (2009): 546–49.

65. Yarbro Collins, "Signification of Mark 10:45," 382.

66. Breytenbach, "Narrating the Death of Jesus," 153–68.

equivalent to the ransom language in Mark 10, a point to which we will return. He also notes that the future tenses, "will lose" and "will save," in combination with the coming of the Son of Man in Mark 8:38, emphasize the horizon of eschatological judgment. The pessimistic question "what could anyone give as an exchange for their soul?" is in effect given an answer in Mark 10:45. The other horizon he emphasizes is the possible Septuagintal background in LXX Ps 48 and Isa 43.

Matthew Thiessen focuses on a Roman imperial context. Seeing Mark 10:45 as closely related to the preceding discussion of the rulers and authorities who lord it over others (10:42), Thiessen sees the most immediate parallel in the actions of Otho, who refuses to ransom many others for his own life, in contrast to Seneca's reassurances to Nero that it would be quite appropriate for many to give their lives as ransoms for his.[67] As a result, for Thiessen, Mark is tapping into contemporary ruler discourse in his presentation of a substitutionary understanding of Jesus's death.[68]

More recently, David du Toit has understood Mark 10:45 as describing Jesus as qualified, by his death, to be the eschatological Son of Man who will forgive sins at the parousia. He understands the "ransom for" (λύτρον ἀντί) specifically as a financial metaphor, referring in broad terms to a payment of compensation by someone who has caused another's loss or damage.[69] Notably, the Septuagint contains many of these usages, in both quotidian legal contexts and theological contexts where God demands payment for a life. Du Toit also takes account of the cultic evidence provided by Yarbro Collins and concludes: "the Son of Man has paid his life as compensation for many, to avert the punishment hanging over them. In the context of the soteriological conception of the Gospel (sc. of Mark), this can only mean to avert condemnation in the eschatological judgment."[70]

All of these recent studies have merit, and all agree in describing Jesus's death as a "vicarious death" in the sense assigned by Versnel. Three points in particular can make this soteriological meaning clear.

---

67. Thiessen, "Many for One," 447–66, referring especially to Plutarch, *Oth.* 15.3–4, Tacitus, *Ann.* 2.46, Dio Cassius 64.13 (on Otho), and Seneca, *Clem.* 1.3.3–4.

68. Thiessen, "Many for One," 453.

69. David S. du Toit, "Heil und Unheil: Die Soteriologie des Markusevangeliums," in *Sōtēria: Salvation in Early Christianity and Antiquity; Festschrift in Honour of Cilliers Breytenbach*, ed. David du Toit, Christine Gerber, and Christiane Zimmermann (Leiden: Brill, 2019), 203.

70. Du Toit, "Heil und Unheil," 204.

The Syntax of the Ransom Motif

First, the observation by du Toit that Mark 10:45 employs a financial meta-phor is correct. As noted, he refers to Septuagintal examples, and there are also various others. Du Toit and other scholars often refer to *lexical* aspects of ransom terminology (especially as it differs from the terminology of Isa 53), but perhaps less frequently discussed is the *syntax* of the ransom motif. The terminology and the syntax need to be discussed together. Expressed in full, maximal form, the ransom motif runs as follows:

(1) The payer (2) gives (3) to the recipient (4) a payment (5) as λύτρον/λύτρα (6) for (ἀντί, or simple genitive) the object held to ransom.[71]

Most statements do not refer to every component in this maximal account, but all the ingredients are in fact present in Exod 21 LXX. Here a negligent farmer, who has allowed an ox to kill a second time, is able to avoid the death penalty by paying a ransom:[72]

(1) The owner (κύριος) of the ox (2) is to give (δώσει) (3) to the victim's family (4) whatever they impose upon him (ὅσα ἐὰν ἐπιβάλωσιν αὐτῷ) (5) as a ransom (λύτρα) (6) for his life (τῆς ψυχῆς αὐτοῦ) (Exod 21:29–30).

In addition to this quotidian legal setting, the same motif appears in a theological context where an Israelite must pay the half-shekel poll tax as an offering to the Lord:

(1) Each (ἕκαστος) (2) is to pay (δώσουσιν) (3) to the Lord (τῷ κυρίῳ) (4) the half-shekel (5) as a ransom (λύτρα) (6) for his life (τῆς ψυχῆς αὐτοῦ) (Exod 30:12–13).

The other pentateuchal example comes in Numbers, in which Moses has to collect five shekels for each of the firstborn sons of Israel who exceed the tally of the Levites.[73] The Levites are a kind of ransom for their equivalent number

---

71. Conversely, a similar pattern is found in references to *receiving* a ransom payment, where (1) the recipient (2) takes (3) something (4) as a ransom (5) for the object held. See, e.g., Num 3:12; 35:31–32; 4 Macc 6:29.

72. The word order is modified in the examples below to illustrate the pattern more clearly.

73. Also closely related are Lev 19:20; 25:24–26; 25:51–52. Cf. also Lev 27:31 (financial payment made in lieu of tithed produce).

of firstborn Israelites, but the remainder of the firstborn need to be ransomed by a payment to the Lord, in the form of a donation to Aaron and his sons (Num 3:48, 51):

(1) Moses (2) is to pay (δώσεις) (3) to Aaron and his sons (i.e., to the Lord) (4) the money (τὸ ἀργύριον) (5) as a ransom (λύτρα) (6) for the surplus number among them (τῶν πλεοναζόντων ἐν αὐτοῖς) (Num 3:48).

(1) Moses (2) gave (ἔδωκεν) (3) to Aaron and his sons (4–5) the ransom (τὰ λύτρα) (6) for the surplus number (τῶν πλεοναζόντων) (Num 3:51).

Often cited as a background to Mark 10:45 is the statement of God's love for Israel in Isa 43, which has ἄλλαγμα rather than λύτρον/λύτρα:[74]

(1) "I, the Lord" (2) have appointed (ἐποίησα) (4) Egypt, Ethiopia, and Seba (5) as your ransom (σου ἄλλαγμα) (6) for you (ὑπὲρ σου).

(1) I (2) will give (δώσω) (4) many people (6) for you (ὑπὲρ σοῦ), and (4) rulers (6) for your life (ὑπὲρ τῆς κεφαλῆς σου) (Isa 43:3–4).

Outside of the Septuagint, Josephus reports that the priest Eleazar bargained with Crassus and offered him a massive beam of gold to take in place of all the temple decoration:

(1) Eleazar (2) handed over (παρέδωκε) (3) to him (αὐτῷ) (4) the beam (5) as a ransom (λύτρον) (6) for all the rest (ἀντὶ πάντων) (*Ant.* 14.107).

According to Plutarch, when the kidnappers of Bucephalus returned the horse to Alexander, he treated them with clemency, and even paid a ransom:

(1) He (2) gave (ἔδωκεν) (3) to the kidnappers (τοῖς λαβοῦσιν) (4–5) a ransom payment (λύτρα) (6) for the horse (τοῦ ἵππου) (*Alex.* 44.5).

In the inscriptions dedicated to the god Mēn, cited by Yarbro Collins, the expression is very elliptical:[75]

---

74. Emphasized by Werner Grimm, *Weil ich dich liebe: Die Verkündigung Jesu und Deuterojesaja* (Frankfurt am Main: Lang, 1976).
75. Yarbro Collins, "Signification of Mark 10:45," 373–76, citing from texts in Eugene N.

(1) Artemidorus and Amias [2: dedicate] (3) to Mēn and Zeus (Μηνὶ καὶ Διί) [4: this stele] (5) as a ransom (λύτρον) (*CMRDM* 61).

(1) A slave (παιδίσκη) [2: dedicates] (3) to Mēn Γαλλικῷ [4: this stele] (5) as a ransom (λύτρον) (6) for Diogenes (Διογένου) (*CMRDM* 90).[76]

Therefore, when we come to Mark 10:45, the syntax offers no surprise:

(1) The Son of Man came (2) to give (δοῦναι) (4) his life (τὴν ψυχὴν αὐτοῦ) (5) as a ransom (λύτρον) (6) for many (ἀντὶ πολλῶν).

The subject (1) obviously varies in each case. The terminology of (2) giving is present in a number of these examples. The recipient (3) of the ransom is left unstated in Mark 10:45, as in Isa 43.[77] The payment of (4) Jesus's own life is (5) the ransom, and the beneficiaries, the objects held to ransom, are (6) the many.

In sum, despite areas of ambiguity created by the absence of a recipient of the ransom, it is clear that the Son of Man's action conforms to the terminology and syntax of other ransom statements.[78] The Markan context will furnish the theological framework within which this ransom is to be understood.

The Markan Context

The epigraphic examples noted by Yarbro Collins and the Roman imperial parallels adduced by Thiessen are illustrative of the broader context of the

---

Lane, *The Monuments and Inscriptions*, vol. 1 of *Corpus Monumentorum Religionis Dei Menis* (Leiden: Brill 1971).

76. This is one reconstruction of the inscription, which has been much discussed (see Yarbro Collins, "Signification of Mark 10:45," 373–74). In particular, Γαλλικῷ may be the slave's name.

77. The payment may well—as in the theological example in Exod 30—be implied as given to God (cf. Heb 9:14).

78. As a result, Hooker's account (*Mark*, 249–51) is not sufficiently specific, arguing that the noun has "the more general sense of redemption" and the preposition means "for the sake of." See further Nathan Eubank, *Wages of Cross-Bearing and Debt of Sin: The Economy of Heaven in Matthew's Gospel* (Berlin: de Gruyter, 2013), 149–51, on the problems with a generalized interpretation of the noun. Similarly, it is inappropriate given Mark's language to pit substitution against the ethical significance of Jesus's death here and argue that he is "not a substitute but an exemplar." Thus Morna D. Hooker, *Not Ashamed of the Gospel: New Testament Interpretations of the Death of Christ* (Carlisle: Paternoster, 1994), 67.

ransom motif. The great benefit of Breytenbach's and du Toit's articles, however, is to draw attention to the more immediate background to Mark 10:45 in Mark's Gospel itself:

> [35]For whoever wants to save their life (ψυχήν) will lose (ἀπολέσει) it, but whoever loses their life (ψυχήν) for me and for the gospel will save (σώσει) it. [36]What good is it for someone to profit (κερδῆσαι) the whole world, yet lose (ζημιωθῆναι) their soul (ψυχήν)? [37]Or what could anyone give as an exchange for their soul (τί γὰρ δοῖ ἄνθρωπος ἀντάλλαγμα τῆς ψυχῆς αὐτοῦ;)? For if anyone is ashamed of me and my words in this adulterous and sinful generation, the Son of Man will be ashamed of him when he comes in his Father's glory with the holy angels. (Mark 8:35–38)

The first point that Breytenbach notes is the setting of future return of Christ, not only in the concluding saying in verse 38 but also in the future tenses "will lose" and "will save."[79] Second, he notes the ransom language, which follows the same pattern noted above:

> (1) A person (ἄνθρωπος) (2) might give (δοῖ) (4) what? (τί) (5) as a ransom (ἀντάλλαγμα) (6) for his soul (τῆς ψυχῆς αὐτοῦ)?

As in Mark 10:45, the third element, the recipient of the ransom, is suppressed.[80] Picking up on the point made by du Toit, that "ransom" (λύτρον) terminology is financial, the same is true here—not just in reference to a ransom (ἀντάλλαγμα) but also in the profit (κερδῆσαι) and loss (ζημιωθῆναι) mentioned in the previous verse.

In addition to the match in the use of the ransom formula, Mark 8 fits well as the theological background to Mark 10:45 for two reasons. First, Mark 10:45 implies a plight, a danger for which the ransom is the solution.[81] Mark 8:35–38 refers explicitly to the danger, namely the threat of a loss of life. As the passage makes clear, this threat is not merely physical death: loss of life in verse 35a is actually contrasted with physical death. Rather, the loss of life is apparently connected with the Son of Man's denial of the person at the judgment. Second,

---

79. Breytenbach, "Narrating the Death of Jesus," 160.

80. Gnilka, *Markus*, 2:104, notes that what is stressed instead is the free action of the Son of Man.

81. Pesch, *Markusevangelium*, 2:164: the life of the many, "ohne seine stellvertrende, ersatzweise Lebenshingabe im Endgericht dem Tod verfallen wäre."

the payment in Mark 10:45 corresponds exactly with the endangered object (hypothetically) held to ransom in Mark 8:35–37: in Mark 8, the ψυχή is in jeopardy, and in Mark 10, it is Jesus's ψυχή that he pays. There is thus, in certain respects, a like-for-like exchange.[82]

In sum, Breytenbach is right to conclude that Jesus gives a ransom for many "because at the final judgment men and women have nothing that they can give as an ἀντάλλαγμα for their lives," and thus Jesus's life "is best understood as an exchange, ransom for the doomed life of the many."[83] The death of Jesus in Mark 10:45 is thus a vicarious death, one that procures salvation for the jeopardized souls of the many. This is not just a preservation of ongoing life, but must for Mark be "eternal life" (Mark 10:17), as in the references to "entering life" (Mark 9:43, 45) and explained further in Mark 10:29–30 where Jesus contrasts "this age" and "the age to come" and eternal life in the latter for those who follow him.

Why Is Ransom Necessary?

If Breytenbach can (correctly) write of the ransom "for the doomed life of the many," why are the many doomed and in need of a ransom?[84] Although Mark does not answer this question directly, there are analogies that can be drawn.[85] The following sayings of Jesus in Mark address the question of why the life—not quotidian life, but the "soul-life" of Mark 8:35–38—is forfeit or in jeopardy, at least for some:

> [28]"Amen I tell you, all sins (τὰ ἁμαρτήματα) and whatever slanders they utter can be forgiven to people (τοῖς υἱοῖς τῶν ἀνθρώπων), but whoever blasphemes against the Holy Spirit can never be forgiven. [29]They are guilty of an everlasting sin (αἰωνίου ἁμαρτήματος)." (Mark 3:28–29)

> [42]"Whoever causes one of these little ones who believe [in me] to stumble— it would be better for them if a large millstone were hung around their neck and they were thrown into the sea. [43]If your hand causes you to stumble,

---

82. Pesch, *Markusevangelium*, 2:164, refers to "Äquivalenz" and "Substitution."

83. Breytenbach, "Narrating the Death of Jesus," 162, 166.

84. Breytenbach, "Narrating the Death of Jesus," 166.

85. The horizon of the final judgment in Mark 8 noted above makes it unlikely that the ransom is from the devil or God's enemies in the human sphere, *pace* Garland, *Theology*, 475, and Dowd and Malbon, "Significance of Jesus' Death in Mark," 281–84. See further the criticisms in Yarbro Collins, "Mark's Interpretation of the Death of Jesus," 545–50.

cut it off! It is better for you to enter life maimed than with two hands to go into gehenna, with its unquenchable fire. [45]And if your foot causes you to stumble, cut it off! It is better for you to enter life crippled than to have two feet and be thrown into gehenna. [47]And if your eye causes you to stumble, pluck it out! It is better for you to enter the kingdom of God with one eye than to have two eyes and be thrown into gehenna, [48]where 'their worms do not die, and the fire is not quenched.'" (Mark 9:42–48)

The common denominator in these two passages is that acting sinfully leads to everlasting guilt and gehenna, so the framework of eschatological judgment is the same as that in Mark 8:35–38. Two points need to be made. First, there are particularly heinous sins that merit such stark punishment: blaspheming the Spirit (Mark 3:29), which Mark glosses as ascribing Jesus's behavior to demonic forces (3:30), and causing little ones to stumble, which probably means leading the vulnerable astray on the path to hell (9:42).

Second, however, aside from those especially egregious sins, people also endanger themselves by sinful actions in general. Sins and slanders committed by people in general ("the sons of men") require forgiveness: the ἁμαρτήματα in Mark 3:28 that are not committed against the Holy Spirit need to be (and can be) forgiven and thus can potentially be "paid for" by the ransom. Jesus also challenges the disciples "if *your* hand or eye or foot causes *you* to stumble. . . ." In other words, it is not just the gross sins of Mark 3:29 and 9:42 that are so dangerous, but also the way in which people are endangered by their *own* hands, feet, and eyes. Mark's rigorist position here is that any sinful action that sets a person on the wrong path makes that sinner liable to punishment in hell. The alternative is "entering *life*" or "entering the kingdom of God" (9:45, 47). This appears to be what is gained by Jesus giving his life as a ransom, though not without the rigorous surgery required of discipleship in Mark 9 as well.

The sins and slanders of Mark 3:28a and the lives put in jeopardy by erring body parts therefore provide some context for how the lives of the "many" are forfeit and in need of a ransom. In any case, Mark 10 is unambiguous in providing evidence for a vicarious death, securing the eternal life of the many at the cost of Jesus's own life that is freely given. It also seems likely, however, that human sins are what have led to the endangering of those whom Jesus saves.

2.2 *The Eucharistic Words and Jesus's Vicarious Death (Mark 14:22–25)*

After Mark 10, the next important passage for understanding the meaning of Jesus's death is the report of the eucharistic words:

> [22]While they were eating, Jesus took bread, spoke a blessing, and broke the bread and gave it to them.
>
> "Take it," he said. "This is my body."
>
> [23]Then he took a cup, spoke a thanksgiving, and gave it to them, and they all drank from it.
>
> [24]"This is my blood of the covenant, which is poured out for many," he said. [25]"I tell you the truth, I will not drink again of the fruit of the vine until that day when I drink it anew in the kingdom of God." (Mark 14:22–25)

The identifications of the broken bread with Jesus's body and of the dispensed wine with Jesus's blood make it clear that these words are an interpretation of Jesus's impending death. Jesus's last statement in verse 25 shows that the death is the penultimate eschatological action of Christ before the arrival of the kingdom, thereby highlighting its significance. There are five soteriological themes or implications in these words that point to an effective and vicarious death.

First, Jesus's death is probably regarded as a covenant inauguration, because the "blood of the covenant" recalls the covenant inauguration with blood in Exod 24.[86] The fact that the Markan Jesus is inaugurating, or renewing, a *covenant* makes clear the substantial scope of his saving activity.[87]

Second, the blood here probably has connotations of purification.[88] Matthew takes Mark's words this way ("for the forgiveness of sins"), and Hebrews understands the sprinkling of the blood of the covenant in Exod 24 as cleansing (Heb 9:19–21). The thought of forgiveness follows on directly from this (9:22). Targum Onqelos and Targum Pseudo-Jonathan render Exod 24:8's "took the blood and sprinkled it on the people" as "took the blood and sprinkled it on *the altar to atone for* the people." In addition to the broader covenant motif, therefore, the "blood of the covenant" probably adds greater specificity to Jesus's death as bringing about purification.

Third, Jesus talks of his "blood" being "poured out for many" (Mark 14:24). This is probably an allusion to Isa 53:12, where the servant (1) "poured out" (niphal *'rh*) (2) his life ($\cong$ blood), (3) bearing "the sins of *many*" (*rbym*, πολλῶν).[89] This connection with Isa 53 draws further attention to the soteri-

---

86. Best, *Temptation and Passion*, 146–47, and many commentators.

87. Pesch, *Markusevangelium*, 2:358, overemphasizes the newness of the covenant here.

88. On Exod 24, Dozemann comments, "the parallel to Lev 8.22–30 underscores the purifying role of the ritual, preparing the people to live in proximity to holiness." See Thomas B. Dozemann, *Exodus* (Grand Rapids: Eerdmans, 2009), 566.

89. Douglas J. Moo, *The Old Testament in the Gospel Passion Narratives* (Sheffield: Almond, 1983), 127–32; Pesch, *Markusevangelium*, 2:360; Gnilka, *Markus*, 2:245–46; Marcus, *Way of the Lord*, 187; Craig A. Evans, "Zechariah in the Markan Passion Narrative," in *The*

ological dimensions of Jesus's words, especially in the sense of an expiation or removal of sins. An allusion to Isa 53 is more likely here than in Mark 10:45, although the eucharistic words probably pick up the similar reference to the "many" in 10:45.

Fourth, the Passover context further reinforces this soteriological note by implication.[90] If the blood is also understood as connected with the Passover ritual, there may also be an apotropaic dimension to it. There is in any case a conflation of Passover and covenant inauguration here.[91]

Finally, the eucharistic words imply that the disciples have a share in Jesus's death. It is a death that they do not go through but in which they nevertheless symbolically participate ("they all drank from it").

In sum, the evangelist is here consciously building on what was said in Mark 10:45, by picking up the motif of the "many" from there and developing additional reference to Jesus's death as vicarious. Here in the eucharistic words, Jesus is not said to give his life as a ransom-exchange for his people but is probably pictured as inaugurating a new covenant with them and applying his blood to them as a means of purification for their participation in that covenant. This inauguration takes place in anticipation of the consummation of the kingdom at the end.

2.3 Interpretative Motifs in the Passion Narrative (Mark 14–15)

It is not just the ransom and the eucharistic words that should be the focus. Other elements in Mark's passion narrative probably pick up the saving effects of Jesus's death, though these narrative elements are harder to evaluate.

The Cup (Mark 14:36)

Some have suggested that the cup, whose removal Jesus requests in Gethsemane, may be the cup specifically of God's judgment (cf., e.g., Jer 25:15). Thus Yarbro Collins states, "the image of drinking a cup in v. 36 suggests that Jesus,

---

Gospel of Mark, vol. 1 of *Biblical Interpretation in Early Christian Gospels*, ed. Thomas R. Hatina (London: T&T Clark, 2006), 76. Kelli S. O'Brien, *The Use of Scripture in the Markan Passion Narrative* (London: Bloomsbury, 2010), 84–85, notes that Hebrew *rab* is of course a very common word, but the characterization of a community as "the many" is certainly not frequent (Moo, *Old Testament in the Gospel Passion Narratives*, 131).

90. For Best, *Temptation and Passion*, 177, Mark 14:24 implies that death has paschal connotations. For Hooker, *Not Ashamed of the Gospel*, 58–59, the Markan Jesus replaces the Passover lamb, and through Jesus God redeems his people.

91. Rightly, Brant Pitre, *Jesus and the Last Supper* (Grand Rapids: Eerdmans, 2015), 415.

though innocent, will take upon himself the wrath that others deserve."[92] Others see the cup language as broader in scope, and perhaps the more immediate background is the cup of suffering in Mark 10:38–39.[93] Since (1) the cup that Jesus will drink in Mark 10:38–39 has been interpreted in Mark 10:45 and 14:22–25, and (2) the threatened cup causes such extreme, overwhelming grief in Mark 14:33–35, it may be something more specific than "merely" a suffering death, and perhaps the judgment and God-forsakenness in which Jesus participates on the cross. Certainty is not possible here, however, because the cup is not defined as the cup *of* something particular.[94]

Barabbas (Mark 15:6–15)

The crowd are offered the chance to release one of the people due to be executed, and they call for the release of a terrorist called Barabbas, rather than the innocent Jesus as Pilate suggests. Hence, Jesus dies in the place of Barabbas just as he dies for others, in place of others, more widely. Such an interpretation is perhaps likely, even if it is in the nature of the case unprovable.[95] As we shall see, such an interpretation will be made clearer by Luke and perhaps John. Even in Mark, however, Barabbas is apparently Jesus's counterpart, with his name "son of the father" and Jesus's execution with brigands bringing them together.[96]

Mockery (Mark 15:30–31)

Soon after Jesus is placed on the cross, those passing by utter taunts that Jesus should save himself and come down from the cross, and the chief priests and teachers mock his inability to save himself even though he saved others. In the light of the clearer soteriological statements earlier in the ransom saying and the eucharistic words, there is obviously irony at work here as well, in that it is precisely by not saving himself that he does save others.

---

92. Yarbro Collins, *Mark*, 680; similarly, Gnilka, *Markus*, 2:260.

93. Thus, e.g., Pesch, *Markusevangelium*, 2:390.

94. Cf., e.g., Job 21:20, Isa 51:17, and Jer 25:15, which define the cup as the cup of God's wrath. It is just possible, if the cup of wrath is in view in Mark, that Jesus falling to the ground (ἔπιπτεν [Mark 14:35]) is a consequence of the impending wrath: cf. Isa 51:17, 22, where the cup of wrath (ποτήριον τοῦ θυμοῦ) is a ποτήριον τῆς πτώσεως, and Jer 25:15, 27, where the nations who drink the cup of God's wrath will fall (πεσεῖσθε).

95. E.g., Gnilka, *Markus*, 2:300, is skeptical.

96. Joel Marcus, *Mark 8–16* (New Haven: Yale University Press, 2009), 1028–29.

The Darkness (Mark 15:33)

There is probably symbolism of judgment in the "darkness" here, echoing Amos 8:9–10, which, like Mark, refers to darkness at noon.[97] In the first instance, because of the stress on the darkness "over the *whole* land," the judgment hangs over Israel.[98] Since this darkness also overshadows Jesus's death on the cross, however, this judgment upon the land of Israel is one in which Jesus especially participates.[99] Especially in light of the fact that darkness is followed (*post hoc ergo propter hoc?*) by the cry of dereliction, Marcus concludes: "The judgment predicted by the Prophets has fallen on the crucified Jesus."[100] While the connection with the cry of dereliction is not straightforward to define, the darkness might indicate a judgment shared by Jesus; this aspect of the judgment at least could be one that Jesus endures in participatory solidarity with Israel.

The Cry of Dereliction (Mark 15:34)

"My God, my God, why have you forsaken me?" This cry is also not explained, and scholars have understood it variously as a supreme act of identification with human suffering,[101] or as having a soteriological and perhaps particularly a substitutionary sense, with Jesus bearing "the burden of the world's sin" that

---

97. See Marcus, *Mark 8–16*, 1062, for detailed explanation of the Old Testament background in Amos. Additionally, some scholars (e.g., Best, *Temptation and Passion*, 98) note Jer 15:9. Christoph Burchard, "Markus 15,34," *ZNW* 74 (1983): 7, and Lührmann, *Markusevangelium*, 262, add Mark 13:24–25 (cf. Isa 13:10–13; 34:4; Joel 2:10–31; 3:15–16) as a parallel to darkness as an apocalyptic sign. Best, *Temptation and Passion*, 177, also raises the possibility that this is paschal night darkness. Pesch, *Markusevangelium*, 2:494, is skeptical of judgment symbolism here.

98. "The darkness at midday symbolises the judgement that comes upon the land of Israel with the rejection of Israel's king" (Hooker, *Mark*, 376).

99. Yarbro Collins, *Mark*, 752, raises the possibility of Jesus taking the wrath upon himself being expressed in the darkness. So also Best, *Temptation and Passion*, 98.

100. Marcus, *Mark*, 1062.

101. Hooker, *Mark*, 375; Richard J. Bauckham, *Jesus and the God of Israel: God Crucified and Other Studies on the New Testament's Christology of Divine Identity* (Carlisle: Paternoster, 2008), 268. The interpretation in Burchard, "Markus 15,34," that the "why?" is answered in the tearing of the veil and the centurion's declaration is ingenious but probably overelaborate.

has caused the horror of the abandonment.[102] Or it may simply be a cry of dereliction, as the Davidic cry in Ps 22 is elicited by egregious misery.[103]

Clearly this is no ordinary human death, or even an "ordinary" crucifixion. It is worth taking note of the connotations of the divine abandonment. The language here implies a judgment of separation, with Jesus being cut off from God's people and put outside of the covenant. The verb "forsake" (ἐγκαταλείπω) often features in divine promises in which God takes an oath *not* to abandon his people, individuals, or the nation.[104] God gives a covenant assurance to Jacob: "I will never forsake (ἐγκαταλίπω) you" (Gen 28:15). Moses frequently passes on the divine promise to the people in Deuteronomy: "The Lord your God is merciful, and will not forsake you" (Deut 4:31); "The Lord your God goes ahead with you in your midst, and will not leave you or forsake you" (Deut 31:6; cf. 31:8); "I will never forsake you or overlook you" (Josh 1:5); "the Lord will never forsake him" (Ps 36:33 LXX); and so on. Elsewhere, however, the covenant stipulates that if the people forsake God, he will forsake them (2 Chr 12:5; 15:2; 24:20). Hence there may well be a substitutionary sense here, and there is at least the motif of divine judgment again.

The Tearing of the Curtain (Mark 15:38)

It is generally accepted that the tearing of the curtain is of the curtain in front of the holy of holies and, like the other events surrounding the crucifixion, is symbolic.[105] Various options for the significance of the tearing have been suggested.

First, some scholars have taken it as a foreshadowing of the destruction of the temple.[106] Despite Mark's interest in the fall of the temple and the mo-

---

102. Cranfield, *Mark*, 458–59. Marcus also understands it in terms of Mark's Pauline soteriology (*Mark 8–16*, 1064); similarly, Breytenbach remarks that Jesus is abandoned by God as he gives his life as a ransom for many ("Narrating the Death of Jesus," 167).

103. As implied in Yarbro Collins, *Mark*, 754–55, who offers no theological interpretation beyond Jesus's abandonment by God tinged with hope.

104. Translations here are of the Greek texts, with the English "forsake" always rendering ἐγκαταλείπω.

105. The καταπέτασμα is almost certainly the inner curtain here, in line with its theological significance in the Pentateuch and the early Christian interpretation in Hebrews.

106. For Best, *Temptation and Passion*, 99, the tearing of the veil is "in effect the destruction of the temple"; similarly, Pesch, *Markusevangelium*, 2:498–99; Burchard, "Mk 15.34"; Lührmann, *Markusevangelium*, 264; and Stephen Motyer, "The Rending of the Veil: A Markan Pentecost?," *NTS* 33 (1987): 155. See further Daniel M. Gurtner, "The Rending of the Veil and Markan Christology: 'Unveiling' the ΥΙΟΣ ΘΕΟΥ (Mark 15:38–39)," *BibInt* 15 (2007):

mentum of scholarly opinion, however, the tearing of the veil would be a very odd way to prefigure the temple's destruction. In particular, the function of the veil can hardly represent the overall function of the temple. It has been argued that Sir 50 might be evidence for this, but the argument is a non sequitur.[107] Similarly, the argument that *Lives of the Prophets* might attest this notion is also mistaken.[108]

Others, second, take the event especially in conjunction with the tearing of the heavens in Mark 1:10 as revelatory, prompting the centurion's recognition of Jesus immediately afterward as Son of God (15:39).[109] This revelatory interpretation is suggestive and is strengthened by a link between the use of the verb to "tear" or "split" (σχίζω) in both the baptism and the veil incident,

---

299, who notes various scholars taking this view. On the whole question, see John S. Kloppenborg, "*Evocatio Deorum* and the Date of Mark," *JBL* 124 (2005): 419–50, which contains a wealth of material that may be relevant to a view of the departure of God from the temple but is flawed because the *evocatio deorum*, in order to be an *evocatio*, necessitates a ritual act of prayer that asks the deity to leave the temple, as in the passages he cites: Livy 5.21.2–3 (*te simul, Iuno regina, quae nunc Veios colis, precor*); Pliny the Elder, *Nat.* 28.18–19 (*evocari deum*); Servius, *Aeneid* 12.841–842 (*exoratam Iunonem*); Macrobius, *Saturnalia* 3.9.7–9 (*numinibus evocatis*), etc. The belief merely that the deity has left the temple in question is not sufficient for an *evocatio deorum* but is simply an instance of "Ichabod," as in, e.g., Ezek 9–11 (and other passages in the OT and early Jewish literature cited in Kloppenborg, "Evocatio," 445–46 n. 81).

107. In any case, the Greek of Sir 50:3 is a word-for-word mistranslation, with apparently no subsequent footprint. On the *pars pro toto* argument here, Gurtner, "Rending of the Veil and Markan Christology," 300, argues that Greek Sirach's "house of the veil" (οἴκου καταπετάσματος) "would support the notion that the rending of the veil in Mark refers to the destruction of the temple, for if by saying 'veil' (καταπέτασμα) one could be expected to have the entire temple in mind, its rending more strongly suggests temple destruction." But the veil does not on its own suggest the entire temple; rather the temple is being defined by one of its principal components, as Gurtner does rightly note in "The 'House of the Veil' in Sirach 50," *JSP* 14 (2005): 200. One might compare Paul's description of Christian bodies as "temples of the Holy Spirit," where the Holy Spirit is highlighted as the most important contents of the body, but this is not to say that the reference to the Holy Spirit signifies the temple or the body.

108. In *Lives of the Prophets* 12, the "end of the sanctuary" is glossed as a time at which the veil (probably) will be torn to shreds and the capitals of the temple's pillars will be removed; this is clearly no justification for the idea that the veil can represent the temple in toto, contra the possibility raised in Gurtner, "'House of the Veil' in Sirach 50," 195 n. 41, which has become a certainty in Gurtner, "Rending of the Veil and Markan Christology," 300.

109. See Daniel M. Gurtner, *The Torn Veil: Matthew's Exposition of the Death of Jesus* (Cambridge: Cambridge University Press, 2007), 173. Best, *Temptation and Passion*, 99, is perhaps unusual in being unwilling to link the tearing of the veil with the baptism.

and on the theme in both passages of divine sonship.[110] Gurtner further adds the importance of the cosmological connotations of the veil, representing the firmament, since it was inlaid with images of the cherubim (Exod 26:31; 2 Chr 3:14). As Josephus puts it, "The curtain was inlaid with the entire heavenly spectacle, or at least its living creatures" (J. W. 5.214). On this view, Mark's passion narrative would be depicting the unveiling of God in heaven.

A third option is suggested by the main role of the veil in the cultic law, namely its separating function.[111] Normally, anyone unauthorized who went inside the curtain would die: apart from Aaron and his sons, "anyone else who approaches the sanctuary (ἔσω τοῦ καταπετάσματος) must be put to death" (Num 3:10; cf. 18:7). Even Aaron can come within the curtain (ἐσώτερον τοῦ καταπετάσματος) only at particular times, or he will also die (Lev 16:2). On this view, the tearing of the veil would imply no more separation from God, and the provision of general access into the holy of holies (normally accessible only once a year for the high priest), that is, general access into the presence of God.

The second and third options can perhaps be combined, since they can be regarded as two sides of the same coin: God breaking through the firmament to reveal himself to humanity, and people enabled to enter the presence of God in the most holy place.[112] The third element is clearer, however, since the centurion's confession is not the consequence specifically of the tearing of the veil but of his observing the manner and circumstances of Jesus's death in general. In short, the tearing of the veil on its own implies the removal of the separation from God, and the narrative juxtaposition of Mark 15:38 and 15:39 makes divine revelation a suggestive possibility.

2.4 Interim Conclusion: The Markan Death of Jesus and the Kerygma

In sum, in Mark's view, Jesus's execution is a human act of rebellion. At the same time, God brings about the death of his Son as an eschatological event, in accordance with his will expressed in scripture. Its purpose is to pay a ransom for God's people, the "many" (Mark 10:45). The death of Jesus is also an event that, in the eucharistic words, is interpreted with the aid of cultic imagery. The reference to the "blood of the covenant" being "poured out" probably indicates

---

110. In fairness to this view, there is also a possibility that the inner veil symbolizes heaven or the firmament. See Gurtner, Torn Veil, passim.

111. Exod 26:33; 35:12; 40:3, 21.

112. Gnilka, Markus, 2:324, sees all three elements as present.

the death of Jesus being understood as a covenant inauguration and an act of purification, as well as—given the chronological context—a Passover sacrifice (Mark 14:24).

The narrative details of Mark's passion narrative may also exemplify and elaborate these themes. Jesus's drinking the cup may perhaps suggest Jesus's vicarious bearing of the divine wrath (Mark 14:36). More clearly, being subject to the three-hour darkness, Jesus participates in a wider event of judgment on the land (15:33), as well as a Godforsakenness (15:34). His death opens up access to God through the curtain (15:38), offering a further cultic component to Mark's thought. It is precisely through not rescuing himself by coming down from the cross that he does in fact rescue the many. In the passion narrative, however, there is no apparent suggestion of the cross as a defeat of evil powers, which is perhaps surprising given the prominence of the demonic earlier in the Gospel.[113]

There is therefore not merely a negligible interest on Mark's part in the soteriological implications of Jesus's death. Morgan has remarked that "Mark attaches great importance to Jesus's death and sees it in theological terms but offers surprisingly little atonement theology."[114] Surprise of course depends on what one expects, and there is to be sure less dense concentration on soteriology than there is in, say, Galatians or 1 Peter.[115] For the case of Mark, which is a story, however, Gamel gives a fairer assessment in his attention to what is a standard feature of good narrative—"show, don't tell."[116] Mark only occasionally tells, in the ransom saying and in the words of institution. In the passion narrative, however, he also shows—not just illustrating what is expressed in more doctrinal mode in Mark 10:45 and 14:22–25 but offering further elaboration of it.

Mark's understanding of Jesus's death is therefore consistent with—and indeed overlaps considerably with—the kerygma according to which "Christ died for our sins." Although Mark does not use this particular language, Jesus's death manifestly deals with the plight of the "many" (Mark 10:45), a plight

---

113. Best, *Temptation and Passion*, 190. This still applies even if it is not the case, as Best puts it, that Satan is defeated at the temptation.

114. Robert Morgan, review of *Die Deutung des Todes Jesu im Markusevangelium*, by A. Weihs, *JTS* (2008): 274.

115. Indeed, Morgan may mean "atonement" in a cultic sense, in which case, there is not a heavy use of cultic imagery.

116. So Brian K. Gamel, "Salvation in a Sentence: Mark 15:39 as Markan Soteriology," *JTI* 6 (2012): 67. Similarly, Telford, *Theology of Mark*, 115, stresses that though Mark is a story, it is heavily theological in depicting Jesus's death.

that Mark may characterize as, inter alia, caused by sins (cf. 3:28–29; 9:42–48). Jesus's death and its benefits can also be elaborated through imagery derived from the cult, as the motifs of the "blood of the covenant"—implying covenant inauguration and atonement/purification—and of the tearing of the veil illustrate (14:24; 15:38). As a "vicarious death," therefore, Jesus's death in Mark can be seen as *gospel* in the kerygmatic sense of saving good news.

3. The Resurrection of Jesus in Mark's Gospel

Our understanding of Jesus's resurrection in Mark is complicated by the problem of the Gospel's ending. This section will begin by summarizing this issue (in sec. 3.1). It will then discuss (sec. 3.2) Mark's presentation of the resurrection and (sec. 3.3) its occurrence on the third day after the crucifixion, before finally addressing (sec. 3.4) the soteriological significance for Mark of Jesus rising from the dead.

3.1 The Problem of the Markan Ending

Mark's Gospel, as it stands, ends starkly and abruptly as follows:

> Trembling and bewildered, the women went out and fled from the tomb. They said nothing to anyone, for they were afraid. (Mark 16:8)

This peculiar conclusion has elicited two main options for assessing how Mark finishes, namely (1) that the ending is intentionally provocative, and (2) that the ending is lost.[117] The decision between these two options makes a modest difference to one's assessment of resurrection in Mark: if one thinks that Mark's

---

117. The views that (3) Mark's Gospel was unfinished or (4) the ending of Mark is one of those extant are not widely held. For the third option, see Matthew D. C. Larsen, *Gospels before the Book* (Oxford: Oxford University Press, 2018), arguing that it was an unfinished collection of notes. For a recent defense of the longer ending as original (4), see N. P. Lunn, *The Original Ending of Mark: A New Case for the Authenticity of Mark 16:9–20* (Cambridge: James Clarke, 2014). Against this view, see the studies of the style and date of the longer ending in J. K. Elliott, "The Last Twelve Verses of Mark: Original or Not?," in *Perspectives on the Ending of Mark: 4 Views*, ed. David A. Black (Nashville: Broadman & Holman, 2008), 80–102. The view of James A. Kelhoffer, *Miracle and Mission: The Authentication of Missionaries and Their Message in the Longer Ending of Mark* (Tübingen: Mohr Siebeck, 2000), 158, who dates it to 120–150 CE is widely accepted. For a very clear presentation of the variant forms of the end of Mark (six in all), see David C. Parker, *The Living Text of the Gospels* (Cambridge: Cambridge University Press, 1997), 124–28.

ending is lost, then claims about Mark's view of the resurrection perhaps need to be more provisional.[118] On the other hand, if the ending was and is Mark 16:8, one potential theological conclusion is that Mark's focus was more on the parousia than on the resurrection.[119]

The principal objection to Mark 16:8 as a suitable, or at least tolerable, ending of Mark raises this question: would a "Gospel," good news, end with "human failure, incomprehension, disobedience and fear"?[120] The women's fear cannot be read positively as awe, as Lincoln rightly notes.[121] Ending with the words "for they were afraid" (ἐφοβοῦντο γάρ) is linguistically possible,[122] but is it plausible in ancient (rather than modern or postmodern) narrative-theological terms?[123] Two factors mitigate the difficulty.

First, Magness's study succeeds in showing that taking Mark 16:8 as a "coherent closure" does not necessarily suffer from such charges of anachronism.[124] There are "suspended endings" in classical literature,[125] and incongruous endings perhaps of the same kind as Mark's can be found in, for example, Judges, Ezra, and 2 Kings. Jonah is a particularly good example of a suspended ending, because it concludes with a question about animals.[126]

---

118. N. Clayton Croy, *The Mutilation of Mark's Gospel* (Nashville: Abingdon, 2003), 170.

119. Andrew T. Lincoln, "The Promise and the Failure: Mark 16:7, 8," *JBL* 108 (1989): 297–98.

120. Morna D. Hooker, *Endings: Invitations to Discipleship* (London: SCM, 2003), 13.

121. For attempts to read the women's response in 16:8 in a less negative light, see, e.g., J. Lee Magness, *Sense and Absence: Structure and Suspension in the Ending of Mark's Gospel* (Atlanta: Scholars Press, 1986), 100–101. Lincoln's response to such attempts ("Promise and the Failure," 286, 288–89) is fairly devastating.

122. Against Croy, *Mutilation of Mark's Gospel*, 47–50, see Lincoln, "Promise and the Failure," 284, on γάρ as an ending, providing bibliography in 284 n. 4. Of the works noted there, Pieter W. van der Horst, "Can a Book End with γάρ? A Note on Mark xvi.8," *JTS* 23 (1972): 121–24, is probably the most widely cited by scholars. See also now, specifically against Croy's argument, Kelly Iverson, "A Further Word on Final γάρ," *CBQ* 68 (2006): 79–94. Nicholas Denyer, "Mark 16:8 and Plato, *Protagoras* 328d," *TynBul* 57 (2006): 149–50, is also relevant. The key passages are from Plotinus, noted by van der Horst, and Lucian, noted by Denyer.

123. W. L. Knox, "The Ending of St. Mark's Gospel," *HTR* 35 (1942): 23; N. T. Wright, "Early Traditions and the Origin of Christianity," *STRev* 41 (1998): 136; Croy, *Mutilation of Mark's Gospel*, 40, 171.

124. Magness, *Sense and Absence*; for the quotation, see p. 107.

125. Admittedly, in Magness, the quantity of suspended endings is probably exaggerated. The same is probably true of the remark of Hooker, *Endings*, 11, that all the Gospels conclude with suspended endings. The question of course depends on how one defines a suspended ending.

126. The examples of Ezra and Jonah as precedents for Mark are already noted in S. P. Tregelles, *Account of the Printed Text of the Greek New Testament* (London: Samuel Bagster, 1854), 257. I owe this reference to Croy, *Mutilation of Mark's Gospel*, 23.

Second, Lincoln emphasizes the need to see the ending not just in terms of the last verse but of the last two verses, with equal weight placed upon each:[127]

> [7]"But go, tell his disciples and Peter, 'He is going ahead of you into Galilee. There you will see him, just as he told you.'" [8]Trembling and bewildered, the women went out and fled from the tomb. They said nothing to anyone, because they were afraid. (Mark 16:7–8)

Taking these verses together, we do not merely have the Gospel ending in failure; we also have divine promise. Despite the failures of disciples both male and female, the reader knows—both from Mark's forecasts of mission (e.g., Mark 13:10; 14:9) and from the reader's own acquaintance with the good news—that the message of the resurrection has nevertheless gone forth.[128] The promise that the risen Jesus would go ahead of the disciples to Galilee (14:28; 16:7) is bound to be fulfilled.

In sum, although a lost ending is a good possibility, Mark 16:7–8 is far from implausible as a conclusion.[129] Hooker may be correct that Mark 16 as it stands is an apt conclusion for an evangelist whose focus was "the beginning of the good news" (Mark 1:1).[130] The present discussion of the resurrection in Mark will therefore proceed on the assumption that the Gospel ended at 16:8 but will also attempt not to rest too much on that assumption.

3.2 The Event of the Resurrection in Mark

Although Mark does not narrate any resurrection appearances, Jesus's resurrection from the dead is still clear from Mark 16:

---

127. Similarly, Andreas Lindemann, "Die Osterbotschaft des Markus: Zur theologischen Interpretation von Mk 16.1–8," NTS 26 (1979–1980): 310.

128. Lincoln, "Promise and the Failure," 291–92. Cf. Hooker, Endings, 21: "As for the promise that the disciples will see Jesus, that is apparently unfulfilled. But did it remain unfulfilled? Surely not." Similarly, N. T. Wright, The Resurrection of the Son of God (London: SPCK, 2003), 630.

129. The idea has certainly not been "refuted decisively," pace Yarbro Collins, Mark, 799. Pesch, Markusevangelium, 2:536, and Gnilka, Markus, 2:344–45, see Mark 16:8 as the intended ending, as does Lührmann, Markusevangelium, 268, who remarks that there is a "weitgehender Konsensus"—at least among German scholars in his time—on the matter.

130. Hooker, Endings, 17. Some scholars find it difficult to imagine how the Gospel could continue after the apparently conflicting verses 7 and 8. See, e.g., J. M. Creed, "The Conclusion of the Gospel according to Saint Mark," JTS 31 (1930): 177; France, Mark, 684.

[5]As they entered the tomb, they saw a young man dressed in a white robe sitting on the right side, and they were alarmed. [6]"Don't be alarmed," he said. "You are looking for Jesus the Nazarene, who was crucified. He has been raised! He is not here. See the place where they laid him. [7]But go, tell his disciples and Peter, 'He is going ahead of you into Galilee. There you will see him, just as he told you.'" (Mark 16:5-7)

Particularly important here are the two parts of the angel's announcement in verse 6.[131] The angel identifies the one who "has been raised" as the same Jesus who was crucified, and the rising receives some explanation from the supplementary statement "he is not here." The latter makes clear that the tomb is empty and that Jesus's resurrection is bodily. The women are invited to confirm this with an autopsy examination: "See the place where they laid him" (still 16:6). Even if the ἠγέρθη is not a divine passive, the point is clearly that God has raised Jesus. This reflects some interest in the historical veracity of the resurrection, since Mark was earlier concerned to point out that "Mary Magdalene and Mary the mother of Joseph saw where he was laid" (15:47).[132] Given that "he is not here," he must be somewhere else. But this is not a story of translation or assumption:[133] in the very ordinary-sounding depiction of Jesus's risen activity in Mark 16, Jesus is not in heaven but on his way to Galilee (16:7).

131. On the angelic identity of the young man, see Yarbro Collins, *Mark*, 795–96; cf. 2 Macc 3:24–28; Tob 5:5 (S); Josephus, *Ant.* 1.200; 5.277. *Pace* some interpreters, e.g., Neill Q. Hamilton, "Resurrection Tradition and the Composition of Mark," *JBL* 84 (1965): 419, there are no grounds for identifying or associating the νεανίσκος in Mark 16:5 with that in 14:51. In Mark 16:5, the noun is indefinite, whereas if the figure were already known, we might expect εἶδον τὸν νεανίσκον, or some other connection to Mark 14:51.

132. Nevertheless, Lindemann, "Osterbotschaft des Markus," 305, is right to note that the logic does not run rationalistically from the empty tomb to the resurrection, but vice versa.

133. Contra Hamilton, "Resurrection Tradition," 418; Smith argues a similar position but for the pre-Markan source. See Daniel A. Smith, "Revisiting the Empty Tomb: The Post-mortem Vindication of Jesus in Mark and Q," *NovT* 45 (2003): 133, while also suggesting that Mark 16 as it stands may indicate Jesus's return to the divine realm (136–37); Smith, *Revisiting the Empty Tomb: The Early History of Easter* (Minneapolis: Fortress, 2010), 99–100, however, talks of Mark using the category of resurrection while narrating the story as a "disappearance story"; cf. Helen Bond, "A Fitting End? Self-Denial and a Slave's Death in Mark's Life of Jesus," *NTS* 65 (2019): 441: "the disappearance of the body indicates the 'translation' of Jesus into heaven." Bond cites here R. C. Miller, "Mark's Empty Tomb and Other Translation Fables in Classical Antiquity," *JBL* 129 (2010): 759–76. One can note several weaknesses in Miller's attempt to style Mark's resurrection narrative as a translation. Perhaps the most grave is that Mark says not that Jesus has vanished and gone to heaven but that he is on his way to Galilee (Mark 16:7). There is also a problematic lack of linguistic

3.3 The Resurrection after Three Days

There are three blocks of material that emphasize the "third day" after the crucifixion as the time frame of the resurrection: the chronology noted in Mark 15–16, the passion-resurrection predictions, and the false accusations of Jesus's prophecy about the temple.

First, a chronological scheme is clearly laid out in the concluding chapters of Mark's narrative. All the events of Mark 15—including the appearance before Pilate very early in the morning, the crucifixion at the sixth hour, the death of Jesus at the ninth hour, and the burial as evening came—take place on the Friday, "Preparation Day, that is, the day before the Sabbath" (15:42). Nothing is narrated as happening on the Sabbath. The resurrection takes place on the Sunday, "when the Sabbath was over . . . on the first day of the week" (16:1–2). Hence, "on the third day," according to an inclusive reckoning.[134]

Second, there are the passion-resurrection predictions, where in all three cases there is a reference to Jesus being killed but then "after three days" (μετὰ τρεῖς ἡμέρας) rising again (Mark 8:31; 9:31; 10:33–34). There is no discrepancy between the expression "after three days" and the chronology of Mark 15–16. Josephus confirms the possible equivalence of "after three days" and "on the third day." In *Ant.* 7, for example, David appointed Amasa as general of his forces and commanded him to muster an army and come to him "after three days" (μεθ᾽ ἡμέρας τρεῖς); Amasa was delayed, however, and did not come on time, and so David acted with the forces he had "on the third day" (τῇ τρίτῃ

---

evidence. See, e.g., the remark: "the Gospel tradition appears to distinguish Jesus' theurgic acts of resuscitation (e.g., Lazarus, the son of the widow at Nain, and Jairus's daughter) from Jesus' own postmortem exaltation" (768). The difficulty with this view is that the same terminology is used for them. The usual verb in Mark to refer to Jesus's resurrection (ἀνίστημι) is used of Jairus's daughter (Mark 5:42). The supposed resurrection of John the Baptist employs the same verb as the account of Jesus's resurrection (Mark 6:14, 16; cf. 16:6). Miller makes considerable use of the connection between the flight of the women at Jesus's disappearance and the flight of the people (*populifugia*) at Romulus's disappearance, citing especially Dionysius of Halicarnassus, *Ant. rom.* 2.56.5 and Plutarch, *Rom.* 27.7 (p. 773). In Dionysius, however, the flight of the people is from the rain and the darkness in the assembly, leaving Romulus exposed, after which he was murdered. In Plutarch, similarly, the people flee the storm and only later believe the story put about by the nobles that Romulus has been deified. The gap between Jesus's death and resurrection also speaks against a translation, although a translation can appear at the funeral of a person, as in Suetonius's lives of Julius Caesar and Augustus.

134. Cf. Luke 13:32, where "on the third day" means "the day after tomorrow."

τῶν ἡμερῶν).[135] Similarly, in *Ant.* 8, Rehoboam tells the leaders of the people on his accession to the throne that they should return to him "after three days" (μετὰ τρεῖς ἡμέρας) for his decision about how he will rule, and they returned "on the third day" (τῇ τρίτῃ τῶν ἡμερῶν).[136] There are other similar cases.[137] There is even frequent equivalence of "on the third day" and "after three days and three nights," but this will be discussed in the next chapter on Matthew, where the latter phrase occurs.

Finally, in addition to Jesus's own predictions, there are also the reports of the false witnesses and the taunts of the onlookers. Here the claim is to have heard Jesus say that he would destroy the temple and then "within three days" (διὰ τριῶν ἡμερῶν) or "in three days" (ἐν τρισὶν ἡμέραις) build another (Mark 14:57–58; 15:29–30). These prepositional phrases with διά and ἐν have roughly the same sense. Josephus can use them interchangeably (*Ag. Ap.* 2.21–25). The former means something like "at the end of" or "within" three days, while the latter may have the sense of "over the course of."[138] They are therefore synonymous with Jesus's own predictions of resurrection "after three days" (μετὰ τρεῖς ἡμέρας). These passages seem to reflect knowledge of a resurrection prediction resembling John 2:19, 21.

In sum, all three sets of passages in Mark agree on Jesus's resurrection "on the third day," per the creed referred to by Paul, even though Mark does not actually use that particular phrase.[139]

3.4 The Soteriological Significance of the Resurrection in Mark

There are various theological implications of the resurrection. There is, for example, the narrative completion of Jesus's destiny as Son of Man, as well as

---

135. Josephus, *Ant.* 7.280–281.

136. Josephus, *Ant.* 8.214, 218.

137. E.g., probably 1 Sam 30:11–13; Luke 2:21 describes Jesus's circumcision as "when eight days had passed"; cf. John's circumcision "on the eighth day" (Luke 1:59). I owe this reference to James Bejon, who also notes y. Šabb. 59b. See France, *Mark*, 337 n. 54; John F. McHugh, *John 1–4: A Critical and Exegetical Commentary* (London: Bloomsbury, 2009), 207. Also see Harvey K. McArthur, "On the Third Day," *NTS* 17 (1971): 81–86, and Frederick Field, *Notes on Select Passages of the Greek Testament: Chiefly with Reference to Recent English Versions* (Oxford: Oxford University Press, 1881), 7–9; this was challenged by Norman Walker, "After Three Days," *NovT* 4 (1960): 261–62, whose distinction between the rejection of Jesus and his crucifixion probably is artificial. Walker also neglects the parallels outside the New Testament.

138. E.g., Judg 14:12; 2 Chr 7:8.

139. Interestingly, however, Mark in all three cases here uses the verb ἀνίστημι.

his vindication. Here the focus will be on those most directly soteriological, and which therefore most immediately relate to the resurrection being *gospel*. There are two principal components: first, the eschatological dimensions of Mark's resurrection narrative, and second, the missionary implication.

First, then, the eschatological dimension. Mark's narrative implies that the resurrection is a *new dawn*. When the Marys go to visit Jesus, they discover that Jesus is risen "very early on the first day of the week, when the sun had risen" (Mark 16:2). The combination implies "the time immediately after sunrise."[140] Both the day and the time are notable. Up to this point, as we have seen, Mark has emphasized that Jesus's resurrection will take place three days after his death. This has been stated five times. We might expect, therefore, a chronological marker at the beginning of Mark 16 indicating the third day (after his death), but we find instead that it is the *first* day (of the week) on which Jesus is found to have risen. The first day here is probably evocative of the first day of Gen 1. This reference to the day is probably reinforced by Mark's reference to the time, "when the sun had risen" (ἀνατείλαντος τοῦ ἡλίου), such that the beginning of the new week, as in Genesis, is accompanied by illumination (Gen 1:3–5). Just as Jesus's death had been accompanied by darkness, that is, judgment (Mark 15:33), so his resurrection is a moment of light, that is, salvation.[141] In Mark 1:15, the kingdom of God is near; now, surely, it is at least in some measure present. The new dawn motif perhaps suggests that Jesus's resurrection is an eschatological event in anticipation of the general resurrection of the dead (cf. 12:18–27).[142] Jesus's own prophecy is fulfilled (14:28; 16:7), as is the reversal of the builders' rejection in Ps 118. God has acted (παρὰ κυρίου ἐγένετο αὕτη) in Jesus's resurrection to make him the cornerstone (Mark 12:10–11). The language of the "cornerstone" is similar to Paul's "firstfruits," perhaps suggesting that Jesus is the harbinger of those who follow him.

Second, in addition to the eschatological dimensions of Jesus's death, there is the missionary motif, in which the disciples are restored so that they can preach the gospel. Jesus had predicted the disciples' dispersal: "You will all fall away, because it is written: 'I will strike the shepherd, and the sheep will be

---

140. Cranfield, *Mark*, 465.

141. G. Hebert, "The Resurrection-Narrative in St. Mark's Gospel," *SJT* 15 (1962): 67, however, goes too far in saying that the reference to the rising of the sun can have no temporal sense but is purely christological.

142. Cranfield, "St Mark 16.1–8 (Parts I and II)," *SJT* 5 (1952): 295, 414; he also uses the language of "first-fruits" (402).

scattered.'" (Mark 14:27). Then "all" of them did indeed desert Jesus (14:50), and their ringleader, Peter, denied Jesus three times (14:66–72).[143] Nevertheless, Jesus has already promised to see them again in Galilee (14:28).

Against this background of the disciples' failure, Jesus's promise gives the strong sense that the disciples are to be rehabilitated, especially Peter (Mark 14:28; 16:7).[144] The disciples are all to be reunited with Jesus in Galilee.[145] It is not merely a reunion, however. The mention of Galilee, although not in Mark suggestive of gentile symbolism, does nevertheless point back to where Jesus first commissioned his disciples.[146] Hence the regathering of the disciples in the sight of Jesus in Galilee is likely to be a "regrouping of the disciples" for mission.[147] After the events narrated in the Gospel comes the proclamation of that narrated good news. The postresurrection era is to contain the mission, begun by the disciples and continued by Mark's readers, when the gospel is preached "to all nations" and "throughout the world" (13:10; 14:9).[148]

This proclamation, after all, can begin only now, since Jesus's identity can be fully seen and proclaimed only from a postresurrection vantage point. The disciples were "not to tell anyone what they had seen until the Son of Man had risen from the dead" (Mark 9:9). Jesus's "narrative identity," as far as the message of the gospel is concerned, was incomplete without the crucial components of Jesus's crucifixion and resurrection. Hence the resurrection is of vital importance to Mark, however strange Mark 16:8 may appear as an ending.[149]

---

143. Cranfield, "St Mark 16.1–8," 288–89, rightly notes that it is Peter's restoration in view of his particularly heinous denial of Jesus that makes best sense of the order "the disciples and Peter," while Peter's primacy would have fitted better with the reverse order.

144. France, *Mark*, 681. The angel's repetition of Jesus's promise in Mark 16:7 contains a specific, indeed redundant mention of Peter ("go, tell his disciples and Peter, 'He is going ahead of you'"). Cf. 1 Cor 9:5, where Paul talks of the other apostles (i.e., other than Paul) *and Cephas*, and in 1 Cor 15:5 "to Cephas, and then to the Twelve."

145. C. F. Evans, "I Will Go before You into Galilee," *JTS* 5 (1954): 9. More specifically, it is "the re-assembly of the flock under the shepherd," after the scattering predicted in Mark 14:27: thus C. F. Evans, *Resurrection and the New Testament* (London: SCM, 1970), 81.

146. *Pace* Evans, "I Will Go before You," 13. Matthew, by contrast, has signaled an interest in the gentile connotation of Galilee by quoting Isa 9:1–2 in Matt 4:15–16.

147. Lincoln, "Promise and the Failure," 289.

148. This dawn of the era of gospel-proclamation in turn needs to be distinguished from the arrival of the age to come, which still lies in the future (Mark 10:30).

149. Lincoln also cautions, however, that the resurrection must not be seen as the definitive eschatological event, because of the importance of the parousia to come ("Promise and the Failure," 297–98).

3.5 Interim Conclusion: The Kerygma and the Markan Resurrection

When we compare the resurrection in Mark's Gospel with the resurrection's place in the earliest kerygma, then, there is a remarkable consistency. (This is the case on any view of Mark's ending.) The resurrection was of the Jesus who was crucified, and the chronological relation to the crucifixion is clear. The idiom "after three days" and other expressions like it are to be understood through the chronology of the Day of Preparation → Sabbath → First Day. In soteriological terms, the resurrection is not just a confirmation of the saving death of Jesus but is itself a saving event: it is an eschatological new dawn and is the event by which the disciples are reconstituted for mission, to proclaim the crucified and now risen Jesus.

Interestingly, there is no particularly close correlation of vocabulary between Mark and 1 Cor 15:4: Mark never uses the phrase "on the third day" but has "after," "within," and "in" three days. He uses, as does Paul's formula, the verb "raise" (ἐγείρω) but not with any consistency.[150] Nevertheless Mark is in agreement with the kerygma on (sec. 3.2) the event of Jesus's resurrection, (sec. 3.3) the third-day chronology, and (sec. 3.4) the soteriological significance of the event that makes it part of the evangel. Mark's account even accentuates the role of Peter, who is also marked out in 1 Cor 15 as the first (male) discile to see Jesus. The redundant mention of Peter in Mark 16:7 ("go, tell his disciples *and Peter*, 'He is going ahead of you'") invites comparison with the similarly redundant-sounding reference in 1 Cor 15:5: "he appeared to Cephas, *and then to the Twelve*."[151]

4. Fulfillment of Scripture in Mark's Gospel

This discussion will inevitably be a selective treatment. Whole monographs have, after all, been written about individual scriptural motifs or chapters in Mark.[152] There will be little interest in the text form of Mark's quotations, or general Old Testament references that Mark does not use specifically in con-

---

150. In the passion-resurrection predictions, the verb ἀνίστημι is used. But it is not at all clear that Mark differs from Paul in that the former speaks "of the resurrection of the Son of Man as his own act" in contrast to divine action in Paul. Cf. Ulrich Wilckens, "The Tradition-History of the Resurrection of Jesus," in *The Significance of the Message of the Resurrection for Faith in Jesus Christ*, ed. C. F. D. Moule (London: SCM, 1968), 51.

151. Cf. also in 1 Cor 9:5 where Paul talks of the other apostles (i.e., other than Paul) *and Cephas*.

152. E.g., Morna D. Hooker, *The Son of Man in Mark* (London: SPCK, 2007); Holly J.

nection with Christ's death and resurrection, such as the halakic discussions of divorce, the general resurrection, and which is the most important of the commandments (Mark 10:1–12; 12:18–27, 28–34).

In terms of Mark's exegesis of scripture, the focus here is narrowly on Jesus's death and resurrection, per the kerygma. The aim here will be to illustrate briefly what is actually an uncontroversial point, namely that Mark's use of scripture conforms to and develops the kerygmatic idea that the saving events of Jesus's death and resurrection took place "according to the scriptures."

4.1 Jesus's Death as Fulfillment of Scripture in Mark

As noted in section 2 above, Mark regards the death of Jesus as something that is bound to take place, by the personal purpose of God expressed in scripture:

> "It is written of the Son of Man that he will suffer greatly and be despised." (Mark 9:12)

> "The Son of Man will go just as it is written about him." (Mark 14:21)

> "Every day I was with you, teaching in the temple, and you did not arrest me. But may the scriptures be fulfilled!" (Mark 14:49)

It is clear, then, that Mark sees Jesus's passion as scripturally forecast, hence the lack of scholarly controversy on this point. Other passages go beyond statements about Jesus's passion or suffering in general and focus specifically on his death. The focus here will lie on the four specific blocks of scriptural material in the passion narrative also emphasized by Joel Marcus, namely Zech 9–14, the righteous-sufferer psalms, Dan 7, and Isa 53.

Zechariah 9–14

Zechariah can be seen not just as furnishing occasional prooftexts for details of the passion narrative but as providing a whole framework. One version of this framework, admittedly a maximalist account whose difficulties the author concedes, runs as follows:[153]

Carey, *Jesus' Cry from the Cross: Towards a First-Century Understanding of the Intertextual Relationship between Psalm 22 and the Narrative of Mark's Gospel* (London: Bloomsbury, 2009).
    153. Mark Black, "The Messianic Use of Zechariah 9–14 in Matthew, Mark, and Pre-

Event	Zechariah	Mark
1. The king enters Jerusalem	9:9–10	11:1–11
2. Blood of the covenant	9:11	14:24
3. The king rejected	11:4–17; 13:7	12–15
4. Desertion of the king	13:7	14:27, 50
5. Death of the king	12:10; 13:7	15:33–39
6. Mourning of people	12:11–14	15:39–45
7. Cleansing of people	13:1, 8–9	14:24
[8. Resurrection of saints	*14:3–5*	*Matt 27:51–53]*
9. Age of purified temple	14:21	11:15–17

Although there is not space here to examine the larger question of the Zechariah framework, a number of scholars rightly see Mark mirroring at least some aspects of the prophetic outline. What is especially clear is that—as we saw in section 1.2 above—Mark takes the shepherd oracle in Zech 13:7 as a prediction of Jesus's death:

> [26]And when they had sung a hymn, they went out to the Mount of Olives. [27]"You will all fall away," Jesus said to them, "for it is written: 'I will strike the shepherd, and the sheep will be scattered.' [28]But after I have risen, I will go ahead of you into Galilee." (Mark 14:26–28)

Indeed, πατάσσω in the Septuagint frequently means not just "hit" but "strike *down*" in the sense of "kill" (or "destroy" when a city is the object).[154] Here we have, therefore, a statement that Jesus's death in particular is a fulfillment of scripture. The introductory formula is also notable here. Jesus states that the disciples will abandon Jesus *because* it is written. The connection with the disciples' scattering is not just *analogous* to a scriptural passage but is actually *demanded* by scripture.

Markan Tradition," in *Scripture and Traditions: Essays on Early Judaism and Christianity in Honor of Carl Holladay*, ed. Patrick Gray and Gail R. O'Day (Leiden: Brill, 2008), 113–14. Black applies the framework to all four canonical Gospels, hence the Matthean reference in number 8. Cf. also Evans, "I Will Go before You," 8: "The parallels to Mark in Zech 9–14 which have been noted above seem to suggest something more than a number of isolated reminiscences. The sequence of events in the Marcan account of the last week in Jerusalem . . . reflects a similar presence, if not combination, of ideas in Zechariah." See also Craig A. Evans, "Zechariah in the Markan Passion Narrative," in Hatina, *Gospel of Mark* (London: Continuum, 2006), 64–80.

154. Pesch, *Markusevangelium*, 2:380.

The Psalms

A selection of the most important references to the Psalter will suffice here. These come principally from the so-called lament psalms. Hence, for example, "my soul is afflicted with deadly sorrow" (Mark 14:34) may echo Pss 42 and 43, although the echo is a faint one.[155] In the crucifixion scene, the bystanders offer him drinks (Mark 15:23, 36), episodes that echo Ps 69:21 (68:22 LXX).[156]

Psalm 22 in particular is probably reflected on three separate occasions in Mark's passion narrative.[157] First comes the soldiers' casting lots for Jesus's clothes (Ps 22:18 [21:19 LXX]; Mark 15:24), then their mockery in which they wag their heads and say "save yourself!" (Ps 22:8-9; Mark 15:29-30), and finally the cry of dereliction: "My God, my God, why have you forsaken me" (Ps 22:1; Mark 15:34). Apparently, Mark—or his source—knows the whole psalm. It is possible also that the noun ἐξουδένημα ("contempt") in Ps 21:7 LXX was an impulse for the cognate verb ἐξουδενέω in the prediction in Mark 9:12 that "the Son of Man would suffer greatly and *be treated with contempt*."[158]

Particularly important is Ps 118, since, as we shall see, it is also testimony to the resurrection for Mark: "The stone the builders rejected (ἀπεδοκίμασαν) has become the cornerstone" (Mark 12:10; Ps 118:22 [117:22 LXX]). Mark quotes both verses 22 and 23 in the appendix to the parable of the tenants. The passion prediction in Mark 8:31 also features the verb ἀποδοκιμάζω, which is not an especially common verb, appearing only in Ps 118 (117 LXX) and in Jeremiah in the canonical Greek Bible.

Finally, one implication of some of these uses of the Psalter is perhaps to make a link between Jesus and David. As Moo comments, "all the lament Psalms appropriated in the passion sayings have in their titles 'A Psalm of David.'"[159]

---

155. There is not quite the verbal correspondence that the Nestle-Aland marginal note implies.

156. S. P. Ahearne-Kroll, *The Psalms of Lament in Mark's Passion: Jesus' Davidic Suffering* (Cambridge: Cambridge University Press, 2007), 69-71, is skeptical of Mark 15:23 alluding to the psalm, but together with Mark 15:36 an allusion in Mark is convincing.

157. Indeed, Raymond E. Brown, *The Death of the Messiah: From Gethsemane to the Grave* (London: Geoffrey Chapman, 1994), 953, notes five possible connections between Mark and Ps 22.

158. Psalm 89 might also be a possibility here, however, since it connects the verb with "your anointed one" (τὸν χριστόν σου) in Ps 89:38 (88:39 LXX).

159. Moo, *Old Testament in the Gospel Passion Narratives*, 299. This excludes Pss 42-43, which he does not regard as used by Mark. See further, Botner, *Jesus Christ as the Son of David*, 174-88.

Daniel 7

As has already been noted earlier in this chapter (sec. 1.2), Dan 7 is a crucial passage for Mark, and the Son of Man title an important designation of Jesus.[160] The distribution of the Son of Man language is notable because in Mark, in contrast to the other Gospels, there is a rough pattern.[161] First, in Mark 2 near the beginning of the Gospel, we encounter the revelation of the Son of Man's authority, in his claims to forgive sins and to be lord of the Sabbath (2:10; 2:28). Second, in the middle of the Gospel, we see the rejection of that authority (8:31; 9:31; 10:33-34, 45). Finally, at the end, there is the vindication of that authority (13:26; 14:62). There are other passages that break the pattern, but broadly the usage of the Son of Man language follows the career of Jesus.

In these passages, the death of Jesus is clearly forecast, and the phrasing is modeled on the language of what happens to the one like a son of man or to the saints of the Most High in Dan 7: the vision of the son of man in Dan 7:13-14 is interpreted in terms of the destiny of the saints in Dan 7:25-27. In the course of the saints' suffering at the hands of the "different" king from the fourth kingdom, all "will be delivered into his hands (παραδοθήσεται . . . εἰς τὰς χεῖρας αὐτοῦ) for a time, times, and half a time" (Dan 7:25). Similarly, Mark's Son of Man "will be delivered into the hands of men" (παραδίδοται εἰς χεῖρας ἀνθρώπων [9:31]) and "delivered into the hands of sinners" (παραδίδοται . . . εἰς τὰς χεῖρας τῶν ἁμαρτωλῶν [14:41]), or elsewhere simply "delivered" (10:33; 14:21).[162] The consequence of this is the Son of Man being killed (8:31; 9:31; 10:33). In Mark 10:45, it is tolerably clear that Dan 7 is present, though with a view to being subverted: far from coming so that "all nations and peoples of every language worshiped him" (Dan 7:14), he came not to be served but to serve. In Mark, the Son of Man endures the suffering of the saints of the Most High and is delivered into hands that put him to death. Daniel 7 thus provides an important scriptural framework for Jesus's death.

Isaiah 50 and 53

Treatments of Isa 53 in the Gospels have, as is well known, often tended in either a maximalist or minimalist direction. The approaches of Moo and Marcus

---

160. As Marcus notes, whatever one thinks about the background of the Son of Man language, for Mark it is a messianic title (Way of the Lord, 110).

161. See Simon Gathercole, "Son of Man in Mark's Gospel," ExpTim 115 (2004): 366-72.

162. The fact that the "giving over" is both of the Son of Man and "into the hands" makes Dan 7 more likely than Isa 53 here at least, pace Darrell Bock, "The Function of Scripture in Mark 15.1-39," in Hatina, Gospel of Mark, 9-10.

are helpful, however, in identifying a relatively small core of highly probable references to the fourth servant song. As already noted in section 2.2 above, the most probable of these comes in the eucharistic words, where Jesus talks of his "blood" being "poured out for many" (Mark 14:24), which resembles Isa 53:12, where the servant "pours out" his life for "many."

Thereafter, Isaiah may have been an impetus for Mark's inclusion of the motifs of Jesus's silence and the amazement that ensues.[163] Like the silent sheep and the servant who, in the face of his mistreatment, did not open his mouth (Isa 53:7), Jesus on two occasions gives no reply to the accusations against him: before the high priest, "he was silent and made no reply" (Mark 14:61), and before Pilate, he "still made no reply" (15:5): with the repetition, the silence is thus accentuated. The consequence was Pilate's amazement (15:5; cf. 15:44), like the wonder of the nations before the servant (Isa 52:15).

In addition, the *slapping* and *spitting* and *whipping* in Isa 50 has clearly influenced the third passion-resurrection prediction (Mark 10:33–34) and the passion narrative (Mark 14:65 and 15:16–20).[164] These are not all common motifs in the Septuagint, as Moo points out.[165] Mark 14:65 records the ῥαπίσματα that Jesus receives; ῥάπισμα appears only once in the Septuagint, in Isa 50:6. The third passion-resurrection prediction foretells spitting; ἐμπτύω—used in the prediction in Mark 10:34 and in its fulfillment in Mark 15:19—and its cognate noun appear only three times in the Septuagint, one of which is ἔμπτυσμα in Isa 50:6. Finally, μάστιξ also appears in Isa 50:6, with which one can compare μαστιγώσουσιν in Mark 10:33–34.

Conclusion

Overall, then, Marcus is correct that these four blocks of material are especially important as scriptural attestation of Jesus's passion in Mark. Much of this material touches upon Jesus being treated with contempt and rejected, and suffering affliction. The use of Zechariah's "strike the shepherd" oracle, as well as the language drawn from Isa 53 (the blood poured out for many), focus particularly on the death of Jesus, although probably for Mark, the language of rejection (e.g., from Ps 118) is understood as referring to the cross as well.

---

163. See Bock, "Function of Scripture," 10–11.
164. See also O'Brien, *Use of Scripture*, 108, on the uncommon language.
165. Moo, *Old Testament in the Gospel Passion Narratives*, 88–89, 139.

4.2 Jesus's Resurrection as Fulfillment of Scripture in Mark

Returning to the passion-resurrection predictions for a moment, it is important to remember that the "it is necessary" (δεῖ) stands over both, that is, over the resurrection as well. Jesus's rising, too, is a scriptural necessity. We will see here three fairly clear cases of particular passages taken to prefigure the resurrection, as well as two more speculative suggestions. Some have suggested rather tenuous scriptural allusions to the vindication of Jesus, principally on the basis of the wider contexts of the Old Testament passages; with one exception, these will not be a focus here.[166]

Psalm 118: The Chief Stone

There is a slight dissonance between the gruesome pessimism of the parable of the wicked tenants, on the one hand, and the optimism of the quotation from the Psalter that follows it, on the other: "The stone the builders rejected has become the cornerstone; the Lord has done this, and it is marvelous in our eyes" (Ps 118:22–23 [117:22–23 LXX]; Mark 12:10–11). The clear sense of this quotation is that Jesus will be vindicated after his rejection. Moreover, this vindication does not appear to be deferred to the parousia. The past tenses would probably make best sense to Mark and his readers as referring to an event already accomplished in their own day. The uses of the same verses from Ps 118 in Acts 4:11 and 1 Pet 2:7 clearly point to an event that has already taken place. The language of Jesus as the cornerstone may also imply an ecclesiological sense in which Jesus's vindication is the foundation of a new community. Juel may be right that the false witnesses' accusations that Jesus would "after three days build another temple not made with hands" turn out ironically to be correct (Mark 14:58; 15:29), and that "the house for all nations" could also be an extension of this ecclesiological motif (Mark 11:17; Isa 56:7).[167] Whatever the truth of these ecclesiological possibilities, Ps 118 clearly functions for Mark as a forecast of Jesus's vindication, taking place most probably at the resurrection.

The language of Palm Sunday is also shaped by Ps 118. For Mark, Jesus's death and resurrection constituted the arrival of salvation, the coming one, and the Davidic kingdom (Ps 118:25–26 [117:25–26 LXX]; Mark 11:9–10). In short,

166. O'Brien's study of the use of the Old Testament in the passion narrative suggests, e.g., Isa 50:6 (*Use of Scripture*, 138–41), Ps 37:32 (pp. 128–33), and Pss 42–43 (pp. 125–28), because in their wider contexts they contain notes of vindication.

167. Donald H. Juel, *Messiah and Temple: The Trial of Jesus in the Gospel of Mark* (Atlanta: Society of Biblical Literature, 1977), 213, referring to the "birth of a new community"; Marcus, *Way of the Lord*, 121.

Ps 118:22–23 provides in very brief compass a proof for both Jesus's rejection and vindication: it offers a "preview of the passion and resurrection of Jesus."[168]

Psalm 110: The Seat at the Right Hand

At his appearance before the high priest in Mark 14:62, Jesus alludes to Ps 110: "you will see the Son of Man seated at the right hand of power." Especially given the widespread interpretation of Ps 110:1 in early Christianity as testimony to Jesus's resurrection and exaltation (understood together), Mark's understanding may well have followed similar lines.[169] The allusion to Ps 110 is unlikely to refer to the very end of all things, given that "sit at my right hand" is distinct from and prior to the parousia: "you will see the Son of Man seated at the right hand of power, and coming with the clouds of heaven."[170] The "sitting" is "the definitive first act" in the eschatological drama.[171] As Mark's fuller quotation in Mark 12:35–37 makes clear, in the psalm the act of sitting is *preliminary* to the subjugation of the enemies: "Sit at my right hand, until I put your enemies under your feet." Mark therefore probably understood the session at the right hand to apply to the resurrection/exaltation prior to the parousia. Hay rightly notes that the *vision* in Mark 14:62 is a unity, while there is a distinction of events: "Probably, then, Mark concurred in the general opinion that Jesus sat down beside God with, or directly after his resurrection. The evangelist's interest, however, was concentrated on the parousia revelation, when Jesus's claims will be proven true."[172]

Daniel 7: The Vindication of the Son of Man

Picking up from where we left off in the earlier mention of Dan 7, in that chapter, the saints of the Most High suffer terribly, but this suffering is temporary,

---

168. Breytenbach, "Markusevangelium, Psalm 110,1 und 118,22f.," 220; similarly Lührmann, *Markusevangelium*, 199.

169. See Hengel, *Studies in Early Christology*, 220, referring to "the resurrection of Jesus and—inseparable from that—his enthronement as companion on the throne of God"; similarly, 222, noting that in the early period, "resurrection and ascension are one act." See also Jürgen Becker, *Die Auferstehung Jesu Christi nach dem Neuen Testament: Ostererfahrung und Osterverständnis im Urchristentum* (Tübingen: Mohr Siebeck, 2007), 9–10.

170. Breytenbach, "Markusevangelium, Psalm 110,1 und 118,22f.," 213.

171. Marcus, *Way of the Lord*, 135, as well as 136, on the periodization of fulfillments in Jesus's ministry ("anticipation"), resurrection ("realization"), and the parousia ("complete fulfillment").

172. David Hay, *Glory at the Right Hand: Psalm 110 in Early Christianity* (Atlanta: Society of Biblical Literature, 1973), 66; similarly, Juel, *Messianic Exegesis*, 145.

for "a time, times, and half a time" (Dan 7:25). Similarly, Mark's Son of Man is temporarily dead, after which, mutatis mutandis, the court sits (Dan 7:26), and "the sovereignty, power, and greatness of all the kingdoms under heaven will be handed over" so that "his kingdom will be an everlasting kingdom, and all rulers will worship and obey him" (Dan 7:27). This vindication is, for Mark, partly deferred to the parousia (Mark 13:26; 14:62). Only partly deferred, however. The verdict of reversal comes already in the resurrection, as the passion-resurrection predictions (and Mark's use of the "cornerstone" oracle) make clear. It is specifically Jesus qua Son of Man who is the focus of these predictions in Mark 8, 9, and 10. Moreover, as noted already, the resurrection just as much as the death is a matter of scriptural necessity (δεῖ) in these predictions.

Psalm 22?

Among the debatable Old Testament texts for resurrection, the case with the highest probability is Ps 22. As we have seen, Mark's passion narrative clearly refers to different parts of Ps 22 on three occasions, which is likely to indicate that Mark has the whole psalm in mind.[173] As a result, since the psalm so clearly moves from misery to hope to redemption, Mark may have this movement in mind as he refers to the psalm. After the woes that Mark cites from Ps 22:1, 7-8, 18, the psalmist pleads "save my life from the sword" (ῥῦσαι ἀπὸ ῥομφαίας τὴν ψυχήν μου) (Ps 22:20 [21:21 LXX]), and this prayer is answered as the speaker declares "my soul lives to him" (ἡ ψυχή μου αὐτῷ ζῇ) (Ps 22:29 [21:30 LXX]). One might imagine Mark seeing in these words the vindication of the messiah.[174]

Zechariah 14?

Joel Marcus's consideration of the Zecharian framework of Mark also includes a possible prophecy of resurrection. Mark immediately follows his quotation of Zech 13:7 with a reference to resurrection: "'You will all fall away,' Jesus said to them, 'for it is written: "I will strike the shepherd, and the sheep will be scattered." But after I have risen, I will go ahead of you into Galilee'" (Mark 14:27-28). Notably, Zech 14:1-5—which follows three verses after 13:7—

173. Strongly emphasized in Carey, *Jesus' Cry from the Cross*, where Mark's knowledge of the whole psalm is argued for.

174. Hays, *Echoes of Scripture in the Gospels*, 85.

is often interpreted eschatologically. The Masoretic Text has a reference to the Lord coming with his holy ones and the splitting of the Mount of Olives, while in Jewish interpretation, this opening of the Mount of Olives gives rise to the resurrection of the "holy ones" or "saints." This interpretation can be found in the Dura-Europos synagogue, the Targum Zechariah, and the Targum Song of Songs; additionally, some midrashic passages take the "holy ones" accompanying the Lord to be resurrected prophets.[175] Jesus appears to be perched on the Mount of Olives, or at least on his way up it, when he utters the quotation of Zechariah and the subsequent reference to resurrection (Mark 14:26, 27–28). If that exegetical tradition was already live in the first century, then Mark's use of it seems very plausible.

We can conclude this discussion of resurrection and scripture in Mark. Whatever rags of academic respectability the last two or three possibilities may wear, the first three have a very good claim to be seen in Mark as scriptural testimony to the resurrection. Some, therefore, may have unduly underplayed the motif of resurrection according to the scriptures in Mark.[176]

4.3 Interim Conclusion: Mark's Use of Scripture and the Kerygma

Mark's Gospel is shot through with scriptural imagery. As Hooker remarks in a study of Mark, "Jesus' words and activities constantly echo OT scenes and language."[177] It also exhibits considerable variety. Mark can employ larger scriptural frameworks (such as that of Zech 9–14) as the backdrop to his scenes. On the smaller scale, Mark's allusion to Job in the reference to Jesus intending

---

175. For discussion of the primary sources, see Marcus, *Way of the Lord*, 155; Robert P. Gordon, "Targumists as Eschatologists," in *Congress Volume: Göttingen 1977*, ed. John Emerton (Leiden: Brill, 1978), 117–20. The principal sources are Tg. Zech. 14.3–5 (v.l.); Tg. Song 8.5. On Dura, see Erwin R. Goodenough, *Symbolism in the Dura Synagogue II*, vol. 10 in *Jewish Symbols in the Greco-Roman Period* (New York: Pantheon, 1964). On the whole issue, see especially Dale C. Allison, "The Scriptural Background of a Matthean Legend: Ezekiel 37, Zechariah 14, and Matthew 27," in *Life beyond Death in Matthew's Gospel: Religious Metaphor or Bodily Reality?*, ed. Wim Weren, Huub van de Sandt, and Joseph Verheyden (Leuven: Peeters 2011), 162–73.

176. Lidija Novakovic, *Raised from the Dead according to Scripture* (London: Bloomsbury, 2012), contains surprisingly little on Mark.

177. Morna D. Hooker, "Mark," in *It Is Written: Scripture Citing Scripture; Essays in Honour of Barnabas Lindars, SSF*, ed. D. A. Carson and H. G. M. Williamson (Cambridge: Cambridge University Press, 1988), 220. Similarly, Mark Proctor, "'After Three Days He Will Rise': The (Dis)Appropriation of Hosea 6.2 in the Markan Passion Predictions," in Hatina, *Gospel of Mark* (London: T&T Clark, 2006), 141.

to pass by the disciples, for example, is an allusive prefiguring (Mark 6:45–51).[178] As well as retrospective allusion, many recent scholars have also argued for promise and fulfillment in Mark: events in Mark occur in direct correspondence to or as determined by what is taken to be promised scripture.[179] There is a scriptural *necessity* for certain events to happen. This is expressed in phrases such as "Have you not read the scripture?" (Mark 12:10), or "so that the scriptures would be fulfilled" (14:49), which respectively imply an expected fulfillment and an orchestration of fulfillment. The dispersion of the disciples (14:27) also happens as a necessity because of a prospective prophecy in Zech 13:7 (ὅτι γέγραπται). God's purpose includes a predetermined eschatological scenario, and so the divine will necessitates (δεῖ) the fulfillment of his plan.[180] The action of God is also clear in bringing about the death and resurrection of Jesus: the phrasing of the Zechariah quotation "I will strike" makes God an agent in the crucifixion of Jesus, and the passives of ἐγείρω (Mark 14:28; 16:6) may make a similar point for the resurrection.

In terms of Mark's relation to the model of the kerygma, scholars regularly observe that Mark embodies the "primitive Christian idea that the kerygma as presently announced fulfils the past prophetic scriptures (e.g., in 1 Cor. 15:3ff)" or that Mark's narrative "reflects the primitive Christian conviction that Christ died and was raised on the third day in accordance with the scriptures (see 1 Cor. 15:3–4)."[181] The scriptural prefiguring of the cross and resurrection, for Mark, is part of what makes them *gospel* events, good news. For example, the death of Jesus is the pouring out of "the blood of the covenant," echoes the history of God's covenantal dealings with Israel, and points to the institution of a covenant through the cross. Or again, one aspect of the scriptural character of the resurrection of Christ is that it reverses the human verdict and establishes

---

178. For this language, see, e.g., Richard B. Hays, *Reading Backwards: Figural Christology and the Fourfold Gospel* (Waco, TX: Baylor University Press, 2014), 17, and Hays, *Echoes of Scripture in the Gospels*, 19–20, 98.

179. Slightly older scholarship particularly reacted against the work of Suhl on this point. See, e.g., Hugh Anderson, "The Old Testament in Mark's Gospel," in *The Use of the Old Testament in the New and Other Essays: Studies in Honor of William Franklin Stinespring*, ed. J. M. Efird (Durham, NC: Duke University Press, 1972), 299; Marcus, *Way of the Lord*; Rikki E. Watts, *Isaiah's New Exodus and Mark* (Tübingen: Mohr Siebeck, 1997), 16–17.

180. I take this to be the argument of Adela Yarbro Collins, "The Appropriation of the Psalms of Individual Lament by Mark," in Tuckett, *Scriptures in the Gospels*, 231–32; cf. also Juel, *Messianic Exegesis*, 96.

181. D. Moody Smith, "The Use of the Old Testament in the New," in Efird, *Use of the Old Testament in the New*, 42; Marcus, *Way of the Lord*, 153.

God's verdict, vindicating Jesus; there may, moreover, be an ecclesiological sense in the use of Ps 118 as well. There may also be other passages underlying Mark's understanding of the scriptural character of the resurrection. Some have suggested that Hos 6:2, with its reference to third-day resurrection, was in Mark's mind, though this is more speculative.[182] Psalms 110 and 118, along with Dan 7, are the most obvious passages that are important to Mark as the scriptural backdrop to Jesus's resurrection and—closely related to it—his exaltation.

CONCLUSION: MARK'S GOSPEL AND THE KERYGMA

It remains merely to summarize the ways in which Mark reflects the apostolic kerygma reported in 1 Cor 15:3–5 and whose elements can be traced more widely in earliest Christian literature.

In the first place, Jesus is clearly identified as messiah in Mark, and the ways in which this identification is made fit recognizably within early Jewish messianic discourse. Mark engages with passages of scripture that had already been part of the reservoir of Jewish messianic exegesis, such as Ps 2, Zech 13, and Dan 7. He also employs epithets, such as Son of God, Son of David, and Son of Man, which had already been drawn into messianic tradition, and further picks up the theme of a forerunner or companion of the messiah. Mark not only attaches the label of "messiah" to Jesus, then, but also presents Jesus in comprehensibly messianic terms, however much such a presentation might have been contested.

Second, in line with the kerygma's proclamation of a vicarious death of Jesus, Mark presents Jesus's death in soteriological terms. The clearest statements of this are in Mark 10:45 and 14:22–25. Mark also appears to assume that the jeopardy of a forfeit life is the result of human sin. Mark's narration of the death of Jesus has a "show, don't tell" technique, however. As a result, the various features of the passion narrative, in particular the cup, the Barabbas exchange, the mockery, the darkness, the cry of dereliction, and the tearing of

---

182. Proctor's argument that Mark's use of ἀνίστημι reflects Hos 6:2 is implausible and requires the argument that Mark changes it to "three days" in deliberate contrast to "on the third day" ("After Three Days He Will Rise," 131–50). The argument there (149–50)—that since we do not know either way whether Mark had Hos 6:2 in mind, we should think he did for "the practical effect of promoting scholarly dialogue" (150)—is rather baffling.

the veil are—especially together—highly suggestive of a soteriological meaning for Jesus's death. At the same time, these elements allude to different aspects of the saving activity of Jesus in brief, undeveloped mentions. Irrespective of how this or that particular detail of the passion narrative is to be understood, however, Mark's Gospel displays a sufficiently clear understanding of Jesus's death as effective and vicarious, an intentional and necessary death with saving significance.

Third, even if the picture of the resurrection in Mark is complicated by the question of the Gospel's ending, there is clear reference to Jesus's rising ("he has been raised"), to an empty tomb ("he is not here"), and to a resurrection appearance ("you will see him"). (The fact that the angel promises that Jesus is going ahead of the disciples to Galilee, where they will see him, means that Mark cannot intend an assumption or a translation of Jesus as opposed to a resurrection.) Both in Jesus's passion-resurrection predictions and in the chronological construction of Mark 15–16, there is an obvious resurrection "on the third day." The resurrection's "good news" credentials are evident from the Gospel narrative's implications of the vindication of Jesus and his reconstitution of the disciples for mission, and are also suggested by the imagery of a new dawn in Mark 16.

Finally, and as is the majority view at present, Mark's Gospel has a clear sense of scriptural fulfillment, especially as regards Jesus's death. The fact that scholars such as Crossan have even believed that the passion narrative could have been spun entirely from scripture, as "prophecy historicized," attests to the rich intertextual character of the crucifixion narrative in particular.[183] The resurrection is also the subject of scriptural fulfillment, as Mark's use of Dan 7, Ps 110, and Ps 118 makes clear, and as may be suggested (albeit less straightforwardly) by the evangelist's use of Ps 22 and a possible allusion to Zech 14.

In sum, Mark's Gospel reflects closely the early Christian kerygma summarized in 1 Cor 15. The word "reflects" is deliberate here. It is not that Mark is repackaging specifically *Pauline* theology.[184] Nor did Mark set out merely to

---

183. See, e.g., J. D. Crossan, *The Birth of Christianity* (Edinburgh: T&T Clark, 1998), where he contrasts "prophecy historicized" with "history remembered." See further Mark Goodacre, "Prophecy Historicized or Tradition Scripturalized? Reflections on the Origin of the Passion Narratives," in *The New Testament and the Church: Essays in Honour of John Muddiman*, ed. John Barton and Peter Groves (London: Bloomsbury, 2015), 37–51.

184. Rightly, Michael Kok, "Does Mark Narrate the Pauline Kerygma of 'Christ Crucified'? Challenging an Emerging Consensus on Mark as a Pauline Gospel," *JSNT* 37 (2014): 146. In addition to the points made by Kok, there is a lack of correspondence in terminology between Mark and Paul in their descriptions of the death and resurrection of Jesus.

cast the kerygma in narrative form; if he had, his Gospel would probably have been considerably shorter.[185] Nevertheless, there is a high degree of correspondence between Mark's Gospel and the model (set out in chapter 2) consisting of the four kerygmatic elements.[186]

APPENDIX 1: THE BURIAL OF JESUS IN MARK'S GOSPEL

In conformity with Paul's report of the kerygma in 1 Cor 15:4, there is a clear account in Mark's Gospel of Jesus's burial:

> [42]It was Friday, the day before the Sabbath. So as evening approached, [43]Joseph of Arimathea, a prominent member of the Council, who was himself waiting for the kingdom of God, went boldly to Pilate and asked for Jesus's body. [44]Pilate was surprised to hear that Jesus was already dead. Summoning the centurion, he asked him if Jesus had already died. [45]When he learned from the centurion that it was so, he gave the body to Joseph. [46]So Joseph bought some linen cloth, took down the body, wrapped it in the linen, and placed it in a tomb cut out of rock. Then he rolled a stone against the entrance of the tomb. [47]Mary Magdalene and Mary the mother of Joseph saw where he was laid. (Mark 15:42–47)

There is no need, for the purposes of the present argument, to examine this passage in any detail. The actual statement of Jesus's burial is a rather lapidary one: only verse 46 refers to the burial proper. Mark 16 only contributes the additional detail that the stone rolled against the entrance was "very large" (16:4). Leaving aside the historical question of whether we should expect a victim of crucifixion to have been buried, it is entirely expected within Mark's narrative given what was said of the woman at the house of Simon the Leper, who "poured perfume on my body beforehand to prepare for my burial. Truly I tell you, wherever the gospel is preached throughout the world, what she has done will also be told, in memory of her" (Mark 14:8–9). The reader, then, like Jesus according to this passage, is ready for the burial in Mark 15. It may

---

185. The presence, e.g., of warnings against impostors (Mark 13:21–22) reveals concerns that go beyond the content of the kerygma.

186. In addition to the remarks of Smith and Marcus earlier, Best comments that "what Mark hereby preaches is not the kerugma of Phil ii.5–11; it lies nearer that of I Cor xv.3,4" (*Temptation and Passion*, 191).

be that Mark assumed that the burial was part of the kerygma proper, given his juxtaposition of the reference to burial in 14:8 with what he says about the proclamation of the gospel in 14:9. Possibly he is thinking narrowly of the circulation of his own Gospel account, but possibly he has in mind the preaching of the gospel in general—with the burial like the other gospel events being foretold by Jesus in advance.

APPENDIX 2: THE RESURRECTION APPEARANCE IN MARK'S GOSPEL

The working assumption in this chapter has been the (perhaps marginal) probability that Mark's Gospel originally ended with Mark 16:7-8. If it does not, then any absence of resurrection appearances is mere papyrological happenstance rather than theologically significant. For those who think that the ending is lost, it is a foregone conclusion that there would have originally been resurrection appearances. But even supposing that Mark did end at verse 8, there is still clear reference to (but not narration of) at least one resurrection appearance.

In the midst of the passion predictions is the transfiguration, at the end of which Mark's Jesus "gave them orders not to tell anyone what they had seen until the Son of Man had risen from the dead" (Mark 9:9). Jesus's instruction here implies that the resurrection must be something witnessed by the disciples; otherwise, they would not know when they would be permitted to speak of the transfiguration.

The appearance of Jesus after his resurrection is strongly implied in the last resurrection prediction: "But after I have risen, I will go ahead of you into Galilee" (Mark 14:28). This makes it clear that Mark is not uninterested in the idea of resurrection appearances, even if he does not narrate them.[187] The most important reference to resurrection appearance in Mark comes, in fulfillment of that promise in Mark 14, in the angel's instruction to Mary:

> [7]But go, tell his disciples and Peter, "He is going ahead of you into Galilee. There you will see him, just as he told you." [8]Trembling and bewildered, the women went out and fled from the tomb. They said nothing to anyone, because they were afraid. (Mark 16:7–8)

---

187. Croy, *Mutilation of Mark's Gospel*, 168–69: "The suggestion that the evangelist was indifferent to resurrection appearances is belied by 14:28 and 16:7." As suggested above, Mark 9:9 can be added to these two references.

Jesus visits Galilee, then, in order to make a resurrection appearance: "There you will see him."[188] Hence, even without a narrated appearance, we have a statement of the event. Often neglected here is the fact that Jesus's appearance does not depend on the women's report to the disciples taking place. They were commanded to tell the disciples what was going to happen, but the appearance would happen in any case, and so we are to assume that the disciples did see Jesus.

There is a strong connection with the statement of the resurrection appearance in Mark and Paul's kerygma in 1 Cor 15. The interesting point of correspondence is that the redundant mention of Peter ("go, tell his disciples and Peter, 'He is going ahead of you'") resembles the other apparently superfluous reference to him in 1 Cor 9:5, where Paul talks of the other apostles (i.e., other than Paul) *and Cephas*, and especially in 1 Cor 15:5 "to Cephas, and then to the Twelve." Hamilton has remarked, "The reference to Peter in 16 7 shows that he is aware of the tradition of I Cor 15 3–5 and that he feels he ought to make Peter the first witness to Jesus' resurrection."[189] This is probably going beyond the evidence, but attention is certainly drawn to Peter.

188. The reference is not to the parousia. See Lincoln, "Promise and the Failure," 285: "ὄψομαι is also the natural verb to use for experiencing a resurrection appearance (see 1 Cor 9:1; Matt 28:17; John 20:18, 25, 29)." It is probably safe to assume that the appearance in Galilee is intended by Mark to refer to a postresurrection appearance and not to the parousia. See Evans, "I Will Go before You," 12; Lindemann, "Osterbotschaft," 307–8; Lincoln, "Promise and the Failure," 285; Yarbro Collins, *Mark*, 659–60, 671, 797, and the bibliography on the subject in France, *Mark*, 680 n. 30.

189. Hamilton, "Resurrection Tradition," 417.

Chapter Five

THE GOSPEL OF MATTHEW

The pattern of this chapter will be very similar to that of the chapter on Mark, proceeding through the four different elements of the kerygma: Jesus's identity as the messiah, his vicarious death, his resurrection on the third day, and the scriptural foretelling of these events. The individual sections of the chapter will discuss Matthew's treatment of these themes. As one would expect in a discussion of Matthew, there is a good deal of overlap with Mark. Where this is the case, material will not be repeated from the previous chapter but will be briefly summarized. In some places, the overlap is very considerable, for example in the scriptural attestation of the death of Jesus, which will therefore be discussed very briefly. On the other hand, there are areas of significant difference or expansion, such as the themes of messiahship and resurrection.

1. JESUS AS MESSIAH IN MATTHEW'S GOSPEL

The aim in this first section, then, is to show that Matthew's presentation of Jesus as messiah continues to activate the existing scriptural discourse of Jewish messianism. He both absorbs the conventional early Christian claim that Jesus is the messiah, and develops it further.

1.1 The Identification of Jesus as Messiah in Matthew

There is no sense of doubt or reservation about Jesus's identity as messiah in Matthew's Gospel. Putting the point positively, Matthew opens his Gospel with a reference to "Jesus the messiah" or "Jesus Christ" (Matt 1:1). Matthew has a commendation of Peter's confession in the middle of the Gospel additional to Mark's account:

"But who do you say I am?" Jesus asked.

"You are the messiah, the Son of the living God," Simon Peter answered.

"Blessed are you, Simon bar Jonah," Jesus replied, "for this was not revealed to you by flesh and blood, but by my Father in heaven." (Matt 16:15–17)

Matthew frequently—as here—refers to "*the* messiah," showing that he does not regard *Christos* simply as a personal name. Here again, "the messiah" is presented as a recognizable designation to be applied to one particular individual. As in Mark, the identity and characteristics of "the messiah" can be discussed in the abstract, as in Herod's question about where the messiah was to be born (Matt 2:4–6), or in the David's son question (22:41–46).

1.2 Matthew's Christological Exegesis and Jewish Messianic Tradition

Matthew follows almost all Mark's messianic use of scripture. Important for Matthew's Christology—as for Mark's—are Pss 22 and 110, though these (the psalms in particular) are not commonly used messianically in contemporaneous Judaism. What are attested outside of Matthew's and Mark's messianic exegesis are Dan 7 and Zech 13:7, and to these can be added the passages seen as eschatological (though not explicitly messianic) in non-Christian Jewish exegesis: Deut 18:15–18, Isa 40, and Ps 118. (See chapter 4 on Mark above.) Matthew also expands upon the Markan repertoire of messianic exegesis. Here we can note Isa 42 and Isa 53, as well as Mic 5 and Zech 9.

Isaiah 42

In Matt 12, the evangelist unmistakably employs an excerpt from Isa 42:

Isa 42:1–4 (MT)	Matt 12:17–21
	This was to fulfill what was spoken through the prophet Isaiah:
"Here is my servant, whom I uphold,	"Here is my servant whom I have chosen,
my chosen one in whom my soul delights;	the one I love, in whom my soul delights;
I will set my Spirit upon him,	I will set my Spirit upon him,
and he will bring justice to the nations.	and he will proclaim justice to the nations.
He will not shout or cry out,	He will not quarrel or cry out;
or raise his voice in the streets.	no one will hear his voice in the streets.
A bruised reed he will not break,	A bruised reed he will not break,
nor a smoldering wick will he snuff out . . .	nor a smoldering wick will he snuff out,
till he establishes justice on earth.	till he has brought justice through to victory.
And in him the nations will hope."	And in his name the nations will hope."

The *Parables of Enoch* probably also use Isa 42 messianically: the messiah is "the chosen one" (1 En. 39.6; cf. Isa 42:1), "the light for the gentiles" (1 En. 48.4; cf. Isa 42:6) and the one to whom God grants the Spirit (1 En. 62.2–3; cf. Isa 42:1). The chapter is also interpreted in some manuscripts of the targum in a clearly messianic way:

> Behold my servant [the messiah], I *will bring* him *near*, my chosen one in whom my *Memra is pleased*; I will put my *Holy* Spirit upon him, he will reveal *my* judgment to the *peoples*. (Tg. Isa. 42.1)[1]

Tantalizingly, it is hard to know which is the most ancient reading here,[2] but even if the term "messiah" is not to be read in this particular targumic verse, there is a reference to the messiah nonetheless. Shortly after this, Tg. Isa. 43.10 refers to "my servant *the messiah*, with whom I *am pleased*": the Hebrew text of Isa 43:10 echoes 42:1, and the targum reinforces the connection with the "pleased" motif. At Tg. Isa. 52.13 as well, the servant is equated with the messiah.[3] The same Aramaic phrase from Tg. Isa. 43.10, "my servant the messiah" (*'bdy mšyḥ'*), also appears in 2 Baruch (70.9) and in Targum Zechariah (3.8).

Isaiah 53

In addition to Isa 42, Matthew further cites from Isa 53, with his characteristic introductory formula:

> [16]When evening came, many who were demon-possessed were brought to him, and he drove out the spirits with a word and healed all the sick. [17]This was to fulfill what was spoken through the prophet Isaiah:

> > "He took up our infirmities
> > and bore our diseases." (Matt 8:16–17)

1. Bruce D. Chilton, *The Isaiah Targum* (Edinburgh: T&T Clark, 1987), 81.
2. Samson H. Levey, *The Messiah: An Aramaic Interpretation; The Messianic Exegesis of the Targum* (New York: Ktav, 1974), 155 n. 66: so Lagarde's text and the Rabbinic Bible; Chilton, *Isaiah Targum*, 80 n. 42:1 cites also the Antwerp Polyglot, Reuchlinianus, and MS Jews' College.
3. See Jostein Ådna, "The Servant of Isaiah 53 as Triumphant and Interceding Messiah," in *The Suffering Servant: Isaiah 53 in Jewish and Christian Sources*, ed. Bernd Janowski and Peter Stuhlmacher, trans. Daniel P. Bailey (Grand Rapids: Eerdmans, 2004), 198.

Although there is little evidence for the pre-Christian idea of a suffering messiah, it has recently been more widely recognized that Isa 53 was a subject of Jewish messianic exegesis. The *Parables of Enoch* are the earliest, most important evidence. (The text of 4QIsa[a] also refers to God's anointing of the servant.)[4] George Nickelsburg in particular, drawing on previous scholarship, has made a detailed case for a shared interpretation of Isa 53 by the Wisdom of Solomon and 1 Enoch.[5] The former uses Isa 53 in its depiction of the archetypal righteous person who is persecuted by the wicked. More relevant than the use of Wisdom in the present argument is the use in 1 Enoch, because we are dealing there with a messianic usage. The figure interpreted by Isa 53 is labeled "his anointed," that is, the messiah of the Lord of Spirits in 1 En. 48.10 and 52.4, as well as "the elect one" or "the chosen one," which is how he is styled in the relevant passage from 1 En. 62–63. This passage, like Isa 53 (and Wis 5), might be called a drama of delayed recognition.[6] That in itself is not remarkable, as this motif is widespread in ancient literature, from the Joseph story to Euripides's *Electra*. The details, however, make the connection more compelling. This schema adapts that of Nickelsburg:[7]

	Isa 52–53	1 En. 62–63
1. God's address presenting his "chosen one":	"Behold, my servant" (52:13); cf. "chosen servant" in Isa 41:8–9; 42:1; 43:10; 44:1–2; 45:4; 49:7.	"And thus the Lord commanded the kings and the mighty and the exalted and those who possess the land, and he said, 'Open your eyes and lift up your horns, if you are able to recognize the chosen one'" (62.1).[8]
2. God exalts the chosen one:	"my servant . . . will be raised and lifted up and highly exalted" (52:13).	"And the Lord of Spirits <seated him> upon the throne of His glory" (62.2).

4. See Eugene Ulrich, ed., *Isaiah–Twelve Minor Prophets*, vol. 2 of *The Qumran Biblical Scrolls: Transcriptions and Textual Variations* (Leiden: Brill, 2013), 434, on Isa 52:14 where 4QIsa[a] has *mšḥty* ("I have anointed") while 4QIsa[b] and MT have *mšḥt* ("disfigurement").

5. See the whole discussion in George W. E. Nickelsburg, *Resurrection, Immortality, and Eternal Life in Intertestamental Judaism and Early Christianity*, exp. ed. (Cambridge: Harvard University Press, 2006), 67–118.

6. See Bernd Janowski, "He Bore Our Sins: Isaiah 53 and the Drama of Taking Another's Place," in Janowski and Stuhlmacher, *Suffering Servant*, 48–74.

7. See Nickelsburg, *Resurrection, Immortality, and Eternal Life*, 94; George Nickelsburg and James VanderKam, *1 Enoch 2: A Commentary on the Book of 1 Enoch, Chapters 37–82* (Minneapolis: Fortress, 2011), 258.

8. Nickelsburg and VanderKam, *1 Enoch: A New Translation* (Minneapolis: Fortress, 2004), 79–83.

	Isa 52–53	1 En. 62–63
3. Rulers as spectators:	"kings . . . will see" (52:15).	"all the kings and the mighty, and the exalted and those who possess the earth . . . will see" (62.3)
4. Recognition of the chosen one's identity:	Isa 53 passim.	"And they will see and recognize that he sits on the throne of his glory" (62.3).
5. Shaming of the rulers:	"kings will shut their mouths because of him" (52:15).	"And one group of them [sc. the kings etc.] will look at the other; and they will be terrified, and will cast down their faces . . . when they see that son of man" (62.5). "And after that their faces will be filled with darkness and shame in the presence of that son of man" (63.11).
6. Confession:	"We all, like sheep, have gone astray, each of us has turned to our own way" (53:6), and passim.	"the mighty and the kings who possess the land will beseech (him) that from the angels of punishment, to whom they have been delivered, he might give them a little respite, that they might fall down and worship in the presence of the Lord of Spirits, and that they might confess their sins in his presence" (63.1). "For in his presence we did not make confession, nor did we glorify the name of the Lord of kings" (63.7). "Now they will say to themselves: 'Our souls are full of ill-gotten wealth'" (63.10).
7. Acclamation of the chosen one:	"Therefore, I will allot him a portion with the great, and he shall divide the spoil with the strong" (53:12), and elsewhere.	"And all the kings and the mighty and the exalted and those who rule the earth shall fall down before him on their faces, and worship and set their hope upon that son of man" (62.9). "Now we know that we should glorify and bless the Lord of kings, and him who reigns over all kings" (63.4).

Other factors can be mentioned: the chosen one in the Similitudes, for example, is described as the "light to the gentiles" (1 En. 48.4), which is obviously reminiscent of Isaiah's servant (Isa 49:6).[9] Of course, 1 Enoch is employing a varied palette of scriptural imagery, especially Dan 7. There

9. Catrin H. Williams, "Johannine Christology and Prophetic Traditions: The Case of

are also significant differences between the *Parables of Enoch*, where the chosen one is a merciless judge of the kings of the earth, and the citation in Matthew, which identifies him as a healer. Nevertheless, as others besides Nickelsburg have argued, Isa 52–53 appears to stand behind the dramatic sequence in 1 En. 62–63.[10]

Another element of Isa 52–53's history of interpretation is less controversial in sense, though more uncertain in its antiquity.[11] Targum Isaiah has a kind of bifurcating exegesis, applying statements of triumph and glorification to the messiah but taking negative statements to refer either to Israel's sin and suffering or to the punishment of the nations. A selection will illustrate this:[12]

Servant-messiah	Israel
52:13 Behold, my servant the messiah shall prosper. He shall be exalted and increase, and shall be very strong.	52:14 Just as the house of Israel hoped for him many days—their appearances were so dark among the peoples, and their aspect beyond that of the sons of men—
52:15 so he shall scatter many peoples; kings shall be silent because of him; they shall place their hands upon their mouths, for things that have not been told to them they have seen: and that which they have not heard they have understood.	

Here the disfigured appearance of the servant is transferred to Israel, and the following section of Isa 53 continues by rehabilitating the appearance of the servant and contrasting him with the gentiles:

Isaiah," in *Reading the Gospel of John's Christology as Jewish Messianism*, ed. Benjamin Reynolds and Gabriele Boccaccini (Leiden: Brill, 2018), 115.

10. In addition to Nickelsburg and those he cites, see also Martin Hengel with Daniel P. Bailey, "The Effective History of Isaiah 53 in the Pre-Christian Period," in Janowski and Stuhlmacher, *Suffering Servant*, 99–101 (cautiously); Williams, "Johannine Christology and Prophetic Traditions," 114.

11. The general view, however, seems to favor a dating of the core of the targum in the early second century CE. See Ådna, "Servant of Isaiah 53," 197 and n. 24, citing previous scholarship.

12. Translation from Chilton, *Isaiah Targum*.

Servant-messiah

53:2 His appearance is not a common appearance, and his fearfulness is not an ordinary fearfulness, and his brilliance will be holy brilliance, that everyone who looks at him will consider him.

53:6–7 (All we like sheep have gone astray)
And before the Lord it was a pleasure to forgive the sins of us all for his sake. He beseeches, and he is answered, and before he opens his mouth he is accepted;

The nations

53:3 Then the glory of all the kingdoms will be for contempt, and cease; they will be faint and mournful, behold, as a man of sorrows and appointed for sicknesses; and as when the face of the Shekinah was taken up from us, they are despised and not esteemed.

53:7 The strong ones of the peoples he will hand over like a lamb to the sacrifice, and like a ewe that before its shearers is dumb, so there is not before him one who opens his mouth or speaks a saying.

The man of sorrows, then, is an image for the defeated gentiles, and it is they who are led like a lamb to the slaughter and are silent. Far from being silent, the servant is vocal in his intercession. In sum, Matthew (with, as we will see, Luke and John) is not without precedent in his application of Isa 53 to the messiah.

Zechariah 9:9

Another important messianic prooftext for Matthew is his use of Zech 9:9 in the narrative of the triumphal entry into Jerusalem. Here Matthew makes explicit the scriptural reference that is implicit in Mark 11:7. Matthew 21:5 is in fact a conflated citation:[13]

Isa 62:11b LXX + Zech 9:9 LXX

"Say to Daughter Zion" (Isa 62:11b)
"See, your king comes to you,
gentle and riding on a donkey,
and on a colt, the foal of a donkey" (Zech 9:9).

Matt 21:4–5
This took place to fulfill what was spoken through the prophet:
"Say to Daughter Zion,
'See, your king comes to you,
gentle and riding on a donkey,
and on a colt, the foal of a donkey.'"

There is a possibility of some Second Temple period interpretation of Zech 9:9–10 in messianic terms, though it is by no means certain.[14] There may be

---

13. For examples of conflated citations in Judaism, see W. D. Davies and D. C. Allison, *The Gospel according to St Matthew* (Edinburgh: T&T Clark, 1988–1997), 3:118. On the related phenomenon of composite citations, see Sean A. Adams and Seth M. Ehorn, *Composite Citations in Antiquity* (London: Bloomsbury, 2018).

14. See Kelly D. Liebengood, *The Eschatology of 1 Peter: Considering the Influence of Zechariah 9–14* (Cambridge: Cambridge University Press, 2014), 55–57, who also refers to

resonances in Pss. Sol. 17. The humble "king" in Zechariah is "righteous" and "will destroy" the "horse" and "bow" of the enemy, leading to peace for the "nations" (Zech 9:9–10), and the "righteous" and anointed "king" in Pss. Sol. 17 will not hope in the "horse" or the "bow" but will still "destroy" the ungodly and bring mercy to the "nations" (Pss. Sol. 17.24, 31–34).

Perhaps more promising are the *Testaments of the Twelve Patriarchs*, where a star arises "in peace," coming in "meekness" (πραότητι) and "righteousness," from whom a "scepter" will shine forth and who will "save" (T. Jud. 24.1–6). This is similar to the "ruler" who will come, "righteous" and "meek" and "saving," bringing "peace" (Zech 9:9). Additionally, in the *Testament of Dan*, God's "savior" figure is "meek" (πρᾶος) (T. Dan 6.9). With the *Testaments of the Twelve Patriarchs*, however, there is the danger that this is simply Christian interpretation that is contaminated with interference from the Gospel of Matthew (or John).

In rabbinic literature, however, such interpretation is widespread. One passage in Genesis Rabbah understands the Judah oracle in terms of Zechariah: "*His foal and his colt* [Gen 49:11] intimate: when he will come of whom it is written, *Lowly, and riding on a donkey, even upon a colt, the foal of a donkey* [Zech 9:9]."[15] A further passage understands the donkey reference in Gen 32:5/6 in a similar manner: "*Donkey* refers to the king messiah, for it says of him 'Lowly, and riding on a donkey'" (Zech 9:9).[16] In addition to this passage cited above, the Zechariah passage is also taken messianically in various places in the Talmud (e.g., b. Sanh. 98a, 99a). The donkey motif appears also in the Midrash Tanḥuma-Yelammedenu,[17] and Pesiqta Rabbati quotes Zech 9:9 in a larger discussion of the messiah.[18]

Micah 5:2 (5:1 LXX)

Another passage with a claim to be the subject of existing messianic exegesis is Mic 5, which refers to "one who will be ruler over Israel" arising from Beth-

---

an unpublished dissertation by M. C. Black (1990). For other Christian texts, see John 12:15 and Sib. Or. 8.324–326. There is a bare soteriological understanding in b. Ber. 56b.

15. Gen. Rab. 98.8–9, on Gen 49:10–11 (Freedman 2:956–57).

16. Gen. Rab. 75.6, on Gen 32:6 (Freedman 2:698).

17. Midr. Tanḥ. 1.1; see Samuel A. Berman, *Midrash Tanhuma-Yelammedenu: An English Translation of Genesis and Exodus from the Printed Version of Tanhuma-Yelammedenu with an Introduction, Notes, and Indexes* (Hoboken: Ktav, 1996), 7. The interpretation here is very similar to that in Gen. Rab. 75.6, on Gen 32:6 (Freedman 2:698). Also Eccl. Rab. 1.9 (§1), on Eccl 1:9 (Cohen 31), states that just as Moses, the first redeemer, rode a donkey (Exod 4:20), so will the last (Zech 9:9).

18. Pesiq. Rab. 34.2 (Braude 2:665).

lehem. Matthew's own use of the relevant verse is an interesting one in its own right: the evangelist modifies the description of Bethlehem from "*small* among the clans of Judah" to "*no means least* among the rulers of Judah" (Matt 2:6), presumably because Bethlehem "AD" is now celebrated as the place of the birth of Jesus, who has brought greatness to the town.[19]

The targum, whose origins—like the ruler over Israel—might be old,[20] takes an explicitly messianic interpretation of Micah's oracle:

> And you, O Bethlehem Ephrathah, you who were too small to be numbered among the thousands of the house of Judah, from you shall come forth before me *the anointed one*, to exercise dominion over Israel, he whose name was mentioned from of old, from ancient times. (Tg. Mic. 5.1)[21]

This interpretation of Mic 5:1 may also lie behind the interpretation of Ruth in the targum, where there is a possible exegetical identification of Elimelek as (or as foreshadowing) the messiah.[22] It may also underlie the idea in Targum Pseudo-Jonathan that the king messiah reveals himself at Migdal-Eder, which is close to Bethlehem.[23] The same messianic interpretation of Micah is implied in the Jerusalem Talmud, where in a dialogue between an Arab and a Jew about the birth of the messiah, the messiah's name is Menachem son of Hezekiah, and he is from the "royal fort (*byrt mlk'*) of Bethlehem of Judah" (y. Ber. 2.4). Rather later, Bethlehem features in the Pirqe Rabbi Eliezer, but the Micah citation is adduced as proof of the messiah's preexistence rather than of his birthplace.[24] The reply of the chief priests and scribes to Herod's question about the messiah's birth in Matt 2:4-6 is therefore not too fanciful as reflective of an existing exegetical tradition. Some of the people in John 7:42

---

19. Davies and Allison, *Matthew*, 1:242; R. T. France, *The Gospel of Matthew* (Grand Rapids: Eerdmans, 2007), 73.

20. See Kevin Cathcart and Robert Gordon, *The Targum of the Minor Prophets* (Edinburgh: T&T Clark, 1990), 18, referring to "the period after A. D. 70 as that when the significant work of composition or editing of *Tg.* Prophets was carried out."

21. Trans. Cathcart and Gordon, *Targum of the Minor Prophets*, 122.

22. See Levey, *Messiah*, 133. In Ruth 1:1, "there was a famine in the land, and a man from Bethlehem in Judah, together with his wife and two sons, went. . . ." The targum enumerates the various famines from creation to the time of the messiah and notes after the final case: "And when that famine was mighty in the land of Israel, a great man (*gbr' rb'*) went out of Bethlehem of Judah and went. . . ."

23. Tg. Ps.-J. Gen. 35.21.

24. Pirqe R. El. 3; see Gerald Friedlander, *Pirkê de Rabbi Eliezer (The Chapters of Rabbi Eliezer the Great)* (London: Kegan Paul, 1916), 12.

ask, "Does not scripture say that the messiah will come . . . from Bethlehem?"; this also presupposes Micah and is not necessarily dependent on Matthew at this point.[25] Matthew may well have incorporated a reference to Bethlehem as the place of Jesus's birth to conform precisely to this particular strand of messianic expectation.

Summary

Be that as it may, although Zech 9:9 and Mic 5:1/2 are not straightforward evidence for Matthew tapping into existing exegetical traditions, other passages are. Matthew shares with Mark (along with 1 Enoch, 4 Ezra, 2 Baruch and a host of rabbinic passages) a messianic exegesis of Dan 7. He also takes over Mark's exegesis of Zech 13:7, which has a messianic point of contact with the interpretation in the B text of the *Damascus Document*. (See the previous chapter on Mark.) Matthew also expands upon the Markan usage of traditional messianic exegesis in the case of Isa 42 and Isa 53. The cases of Mic 5 and Zech 9 are potentially useful supplementary evidence.

1.3 Jewish Messianic Themes in Matthew's Christology

As in the discussion of Mark above, the explicit use of scriptural passages can be supplemented with shorter biblical epithets and other themes associated with presentations of messiah figures in Jewish literature.

Throne of Glory

One of the most compelling links between Matthew and the *Parables of Enoch* has been their shared reference to the messiah sitting on a "throne of glory" or "glorious throne."[26] In particular, it is the messiah qua son of man, in Matthew as well as in 1 En. 62 and 69, who sits on it. The glorious throne, in both books, is the place from which the Son of Man pronounces judgment. It may well also be the case that the "throne of glory" is the seat of the messiah in 4Q161 (4QpIsaa) 8–10 III, 11–24 where the exegesis of Isa 11 talks of the branch of

---

25. Justin, *1 Apol.* 34 and *Dial.* 78, along with *Prot. Jas.* 21.2, are clearly dependent on Matthew.

26. Matt 19:28; 25:31; 1 En. 45.3; 55.4; 61.8; 62.2–3, 5; 69.27–29. Cf. Isa 63:15; Jer 14:21; 17:12, where the throne is God's; similarly in the other instances in 1 En. 37–71. In Pesiq. Rab. 36.1 (Braude 2:677), the messiah lives *under* God's throne of glory.

David (introduced in line 17) and then of the throne of glory (in line 19). The passage is fragmentary, however.[27]

The Expected Arrival of the Messiah

Matthew apparently employs "the coming one" as a title, in John's embassy to Jesus: "Are you the coming one (ὁ ἐρχόμενος), or should we expect someone else?" (Matt 11:2–3). The messiah is thus an awaited figure, whose arrival is anticipated. While the "coming one" designation is not known from Jewish literature, the anticipation of the messiah's coming is a standard feature of Jewish idiom. In the Dead Sea Scrolls, for example, 4Q252 refers to the time "until the messiah of righteousness comes" (4Q252 V, 3), and the *Damascus Document* looks forward to the moment "when there comes the messiah of Aaron and Israel" (CD-B XIX, 10–11). The triple expectation of the prophet and the two messiahs is voiced in the *Rule of the Community*: "until there shall come the prophet and the messiahs of Aaron and Israel" (1QS IX, 11). It is not just that Jesus the messiah *has* come in Matthew (e.g., Matt 5:17). For John the Baptist, as for the authors of these Qumran texts, the messiah's arrival has been expected.

The Deeds of the Messiah

Matthew glosses the coming one, moreover, as a messiah with identifying "deeds." It is hearing about "the deeds of the messiah" that prompts John the Baptist to send his inquiry to Jesus (Matt 11:2). The response to John's question implies that Jesus is the messiah, and his miraculous activity is the evidence: "Go and report to John what you see and hear" (11:4). It is true that "the Messiah was hardly expected to be a wonder-worker,"[28] if that is understood as a general statement. There were strands of expectation along these lines, however, especially tied to Isa 11 where the shoot of Jesse is endowed with supernatural wisdom enabling him to judge apparently without the aid of witnesses and slay the wicked with a mere utterance (11:1–4). Chapter 7 (sec. 1.3) of this book, on John, further catalogs evidence for the messiah as characterized by certain actions. In particular, however, Matt 11 here combines scriptural passages that are also used (though not as straightforwardly in connection with the messiah) in 4Q521:

27. The idea might go back to Ben Sira, where David has a throne of glory (Sir 47:11).
28. Davies and Allison, *Matthew*, 2:241.

Isa 35; Ps 146; Isa 61	4Q521 2 II	Matt 11:5
Isa 35:5–6 Then will the eyes of the blind be opened and the ears of the deaf unstopped. Then will the lame leap like a deer, and the mute tongue shout for joy.		The blind can see again, the lame walk, those who have leprosy are cleansed, the deaf hear,
Ps 146:7–8 The Lord frees prisoners, the Lord gives sight to the blind, the Lord lifts up those bowed down.	. . . he who frees the prisoners, restores sight to the blind, straightens the b[ent].	
	[10] And the Lord will accomplish glorious things that have never been as [He . . .] For he will heal	
Isa 61:1 The Spirit of the Sovereign Lord is on me, because the Lord has anointed me to proclaim good news to the poor.	the wounded, and revive the dead and bring good news to the poor.	the dead are raised, and good news is preached to the poor.

Some have, probably correctly, surmised that there was an exegetical tradition linking Isa 61 with resurrection.[29] However the relationship between Matthew and the Qumran fragment is construed, Matt 11:2–5 is similar to 4Q521 in that both derive eschatological miracles from scripture and apply them to the messiah or to the messianic age.[30]

The Messiah as Teacher

Matthew's Jesus refers to the crowds' and disciples' "one instructor, the messiah" (Matt 23:10), thereby clearly talking about himself in Matthew's eyes. This is certainly borne out in Matthew's emphasis on Jesus's teaching especially in the five well-known blocks of teaching material. There is some evidence for the messiah having a role of teacher in Jewish messianic ex-

29. E.g., John J. Collins, "The Works of the Messiah," *DSD* 1 (1994): 107. Similarly, Paul Foster, "Paul and Matthew: Two Strands of the Early Jesus Movement," in *Paul and the Gospels: Christologies, Conflicts and Convergences*, ed. Michael Bird and Joel Willitts (London: Bloomsbury, 2011), 91–92.

30. For the latter, less controversial conclusion, see Matthias Konradt, *Das Evangelium nach Matthäus* (Göttingen: Vandenhoeck & Ruprecht, 2015), 179.

pectation. In the Psalms of Solomon, God will raise up the messiah "over the house of Israel to educate (παιδεῦσαι) them" (17.47). The meaning of the verb here could be "discipline" or "correct," however. Similarly, in the *Parables of Enoch*: "the elect one shall in those days sit on my throne, and his mouth shall pour forth all the secrets of wisdom and counsel, for the Lord of Spirits has given them to him and has glorified him" (1 En. 51.3). In rabbinic literature, Isa 11's statement about the nations seeking the anointed one can be understood as the messiah teaching them: in Midrash Psalms, the messiah will "teach the nations of the earth thirty precepts," whereas Israel will be taught by God;[31] Judah washing his garments in wine (Gen 49:11) is taken to mean that "he [the messiah] will compose for them [the nations] words of Torah," Rabbi Chanin repeating the idea that Israel will not need instruction from the messiah.[32]

The Messiah as Son of David

Matthew's Gospel is probably the most enthusiastic about a messiahship rooted in Jesus's Davidic lineage.[33] (On the messiah's Davidic ancestry in some early Jewish texts, see the previous chapter.) Statistically, Matthew refers to David more often than the other evangelists (Matthew 17×; Mark 7×; Luke 13×; John 1×), and there is depth as well as quantity to David's significance in Matthew.[34] Importantly for Matthew, Jesus is not "naturally" a descendant of David. Konradt makes the helpful observation that traditionally the king of Israel was by birth a descendant of David but adopted as God's son (Ps 2:7); in the case of Jesus, however, he is naturally God's Son (Matt 1:18, 20) but adopted into the Davidic line through his adoption by Joseph.[35] Even this adoption has a supernatural cause, however, because left to his own devices Joseph would have divorced Mary; after the intervention of the angel of the Lord, however, Joseph marries Mary and names Jesus.[36]

---

31. Midr. Ps. 21.1, on Ps 21:1–2 (Braude 1:293).

32. Gen. Rab. 98.8–9, on Gen 49:10–11 (Freedman 2:956–57).

33. See, e.g., Peter Fiedler, *Das Matthäusevangelium* (Stuttgart: Kohlhammer, 2006), 342, for an example of a standard comment that, while Mark may relativize the title "Son of David," Matthew does not have such reserve.

34. See, e.g., Matthias Konradt, *Israel, Church, and the Gentiles in the Gospel of Matthew* (Waco, TX: Baylor, 2014), 25–26.

35. Konradt, *Israel, Church, and the Gentiles*, 28.

36. According to Ulrich Luz, *Studies in Matthew* (Grand Rapids: Eerdmans, 2005), 86, it is by "divine intervention" that he becomes part of the Davidic line.

The function of Son of David messiahship in Matthew has sometimes been confined to Jesus's healing activity,[37] but Konradt does better justice to Matthew's Christology in seeing healing as part of the motif of Jesus as the eschatological, Davidic shepherd.[38] Part of the shepherd's role is care for the sheep, which includes healing in Ezekiel.[39] Similarly, in Pss. Sol. 17, the messiah who shepherds (ποιμαίνων) God's people "does not allow them to fall sick" (οὐκ ἀφήσει ἀσθενῆσαι) in their pasture (Pss. Sol. 17.40). The note of compassion, which is characteristic of the shepherd, is introduced by Matthew into the healing episodes (Matt 14:14; 20:34).[40]

As the Davidic shepherd, Jesus focuses his work on the people of Israel. They are "like sheep without a shepherd" (Matt 9:36), though not because they lack leaders; rather, "because Israel's leaders are arrogant (9:11), heartless (9:13), fickle (11:16–19), unbelieving (12:38–39) and hypocritical (23:13–36), the nation has been de facto orphaned."[41] These sheep without a shepherd, then, are the "lost sheep," to whom Jesus is sent.[42] Jesus is already in the birth narrative introduced as the "ruler who will shepherd my people Israel," and at the end of the Gospel is the shepherd who not only judges but also is struck on the cross.[43] As shepherd, he has compassion on these lost sheep (Matt 9:36). In sum, in the depiction of Jesus as Son of David in Matthew, there is "a concentrated expression of the essential Matthean focus on the merciful care God brings through Jesus to his people standing in need of salvation."[44]

The Messiah as Son of God

As we saw in the discussion on Mark above, "son" appears as a title for the messiah figure in 4 Ezra, and the *Rule of the Congregation* refers to God begetting

37. E.g., Luz, *Studies in Matthew*, 86.

38. In particular, the healings by the "Son of David" are healings of blindness, and this may well not only denote physical healing but also connote proper understanding, by comparison with the leaders who are repeatedly called "blind." See Matt 23:16, 17, 19, 24, 26.

39. See Ezek 34:4, 16, contrasting what the wicked shepherds have not done and what God will do through the true shepherd. Konradt, *Israel, Church, and the Gentiles*, 44, further notes Zech 10:2 LXX. On the Ezekiel passage, see Wayne Baxter, "Healing and the 'Son of David': Matthew's Warrant," *NovT* 48 (2006): 41–43, and Baxter, *Israel's Only Shepherd: Matthew's Shepherd Motif and His Social Setting* (London: Bloomsbury, 2012), 137–50.

40. Konradt, *Israel, Church, and the Gentiles*, 39–40.

41. Baxter, "Healing and the 'Son of David,'" 39.

42. Matt 10:6; 15:24.

43. Matt 2:6; 25:32; 26:31.

44. Konradt, *Israel, Church, and the Gentiles*, 48–49.

his messiah. Matthew has a number of references to Jesus as Son of God. Having been conceived by the Holy Spirit, Jesus is not just Son of David (Matt 1:18, 20). He fulfills his destiny as Son of God through his obedience to his Father, in his reenactment of the history of Israel in the temptation narrative (4:1–11).[45] The "Son of God" epithet is therefore defined in scriptural terms. In contrast to Jesus's more exclusive focus, qua Son of David, on Israel, his divine sonship is further reaching. As servant or child of God (παῖς), he will proclaim justice to the nations, and those nations will put their hope in him (12:17–21), and this receives a kind of preliminary fulfillment already in Matthew's narrative. Those guarding Jesus at the crucifixion confess him as Son of God, and they are gentiles (27:54). The fulfillment proper will come when the gospel goes to all the nations, and new disciples are baptized into the name of the Father, the Son (of God), and the Holy Spirit (28:18–20). Notably, however, this occurs *through* the Israelite disciples first confessing him as Son. Matthew's narrative proceeds from the devil and his minions recognizing Jesus as Son (4:3, 6; 8:29) in the first instance. Then after a fleeting recognition of Jesus as Son in the boat (14:33), Peter makes a more formal confession that Jesus is Son of God on behalf of all the disciples—it is in response to the question "who do you [*plural*] say that I am?" (16:15–16). After the resurrection this confession is available to the gentiles (though cf. 27:54).[46]

1.4 Interim Conclusion: Matthew's Messiah and the Kerygma

Matthew's Gospel is therefore clearly recognizable as a Jewish messianic work. Matthew has no reservations about applying the term "messiah" to Jesus. From the opening verse, the Gospel participates in the discourse of messianic genealogy, with Jesus the *Christos*, "Son of David" and "son of Abraham." To this are added the filial epithets "Son of God" and "Son of Man," which, because of the early Jewish interpretations of Ps 2 and Dan 7, echo existing messianic exegesis. There is also the collocation of Christ with "coming" language, a standard feature of messianic idiom. The Gospel answers the question of what the messiah is to be called (Matt 1:21), per the rabbinic debate about the name

---

45. Luz, *Studies in Matthew*, 93. On this theme in the temptation narrative, see Thomas Söding, "Der Gehorsam des Gottessohnes: Zur Christologie der matthäischen Versuchungserzählung (4,1–11)," in *Jesus Christus als die Mitte der Schrift: Studien zur Hermeneutik des Evangeliums*, ed. Christof Landmesser, Hans-Joachim Eckstein, and Hermann Lichtenberger (Berlin: de Gruyter, 1997), 711–49; also Richard B. Hays, *Echoes of Scripture in the Gospels* (Waco, TX: Baylor University Press, 2016), 140.

46. See further Konradt, *Israel, Church, and the Gentiles*, 307–11.

of the messiah (b. Sanh. 98b). The place of the messiah's birth, according to some strands of targumic and talmudic interpretation of Mic 5, is Bethlehem. Matthew also sees the messiah as marked out by particular deeds, a theme we will explore particularly in the analysis below of John's Gospel.

Matthew populates his Gospel portrait of the messiah with extensive scriptural discourse. He reuses the messianic prooftexts already present in Mark, including Dan 7 and Zech 13:7. (As we will see later, there is some extension of Mark's use of Dan 7.) He makes explicit a scriptural reference implied in Mark's narrative, namely the oracle in Zech 9:9 about the humble king seated on a donkey. He also introduces other passages that are a familiar part of the messianic exegetical landscape. He uses Isa 42 and 53 and—as noted already—Mic 5's prophecy as a forecast of the messiah's birth. All these passages are already used to varying degrees in the messianic discourse of early Judaism. This is not to say that Matthew is staunchly conservative in this respect. He also, for example, uses Isa 7:14, which was to become a highly contentious passage. There is plenty in Matthew's exegesis, however, that is recognizably messianic. Matthew's messianism is an example of what Novenson regards as typical of messianic discourse: the evangelist's picture of Jesus as messiah emerges out of the combination of scripture and experience—in the latter case, the particular knowledge of the outline of Jesus's earthly biography. In terms of his presentation of Jesus as messiah, then, he reflects the earliest kerygmatic claims made within a Jewish context.

2. The Vicarious Death of Jesus in Matthew's Gospel

Matthew's absorption of almost everything in Mark means that a good deal of this section can be quickly summarized as similar to Mark's view of the death of Jesus. Matthew, however, both structures his soteriological narrative differently and adds further material. In Matthew's birth narrative, the son of Mary is named "Jesus" in Matt 1:21 "because he will save his people from their sins." How exactly this will occur remains unexplained for a number of chapters. In Matt 12:14, the Pharisees are conspiring to kill Jesus (cf. Mark 3:6). Shortly after this, there is an implicit passion prediction in the comparison with Jonah (Matt 12:40):[47] this verse "is the first prelude of the Matthean passion and Easter story and also a first response of Jesus to the decision of the

---

47. Matt 17:9 also implies Jesus's death and resurrection.

Pharisees in 12:14 to kill Jesus."[48] In the second half of the Gospel, we begin to see explicit passion predictions (16:21; 17:22–23; 20:18–19), and as in Mark, so here in Matthew, the necessity of Jesus's death is not yet explained.

2.1 The Ransom Saying and Life-for-Life Exchange (Matt 20:28)

Again as in Mark, Matthew explains this necessity in the first instance by means of the ransom saying: "just as the Son of Man did not come to be served, but to serve, and to give his life as a ransom for many" (Matt 20:28).[49] As in Mark, the term "ransom" is correct here; the reference is not to redemption in a more generalized sense.[50] Here, too, we have a life-for-life exchange, where Jesus takes the place of the many in his death. First, Matthew has almost exactly the same wording as Mark (only the introductory particles differ) and so evokes the same terminology and syntax of the ransom motif. Second, Matthew also includes the other "ransom" passage, concerned with saving one's soul at the eschaton (16:25–27; cf. Mark 8:35–38). Third, in terms of explicating why ransom is necessary, Matthew is actually a good deal clearer than Mark that the plight is human sin: this is established as the plight, as noted above, in Jesus being so named "because he will save his people from their sins" (Matt 1:21).[51] More specifically, sins in Matthew's Gospel incur a debt, and so the ransom language takes on additional meaning in Matthean redaction.[52]

2.2 The Eucharistic Words (Matt 26:26–29)

There is further illumination of Jesus saving his people from their sins (Matt 1:21). In the eucharistic words, we find the closest parallel to this statement in Matthew's significant addition to Mark:

48. Ulrich Luz, *Matthew: A Commentary* (Minneapolis: Fortress, 2001–2007), 2:218.

49. Luz sees redemption at a price here, rather than a reference to Isa 53 (*Matthew*, 2:546). Overall, like Hooker's interpretation of Mark 10:45 noted in the previous chapter, the sense given by Luz to the λύτρον is too vague. Joachim Gnilka, *Das Matthäusevangelium* (Freiburg: Herder, 1986–1988), 2:190, is one example of a commentator who sees Isa 53 as essential to the interpretation of Matt 20:28, but see the comments on Mark 10:45 in the previous chapter; he also, however, does pay attention to the λύτρον terminology.

50. See further Nathan Eubank, *Wages of Cross-Bearing and Debt of Sin: The Economy of Heaven in Matthew's Gospel* (Berlin: de Gruyter, 2013), 149–51.

51. France, *Matthew*, 54, 763; Konradt, *Matthäus*, 318.

52. See Eubank, *Wages of Cross-Bearing*, 53–67, 148–62.

Mark 14:22–24	Matt 26:26–28
While they were eating, he took bread, said a blessing, and broke it, and gave it to them, saying, "Take it; this is my body." Then he took the cup, gave thanks, and offered it to them, and they all drank from it. And he said to them, "This is my blood of the covenant, which is poured out for many."	While they were eating, Jesus took bread, and having said a blessing, broke it, and gave it to his disciples, saying, "Take it and eat; this is my body." Then he took a cup, and gave thanks, and offered it to them, saying, "Drink from it, all of you. This is my blood of the covenant, which is poured out for many *for the forgiveness of sins.*"

The features of Mark's wording are all included, thereby picking up on the themes laid out in the previous chapter (sec. 2.2): (1) Jesus's death is probably a covenant inauguration, through the "blood of the covenant";[53] (2) Jesus's talk of his "blood" being "poured out for many" is probably an allusion to Isa 53:12;[54] (3) Matthew, like Mark, also presupposes the Passover context, thereby conflating Passover and covenant inauguration here;[55] (4) the words "they all drank from it" imply that the disciples symbolically participate in Jesus's death.

In addition to all this, Matthew makes explicit what is only implied in Mark: that Jesus sheds his blood "for the forgiveness of sins" (Matt 26:28).[56] Indeed, Senior comments that as a result of this statement about forgiveness of sins, "no other Gospel presents the salvific impact of Jesus' passion in such explicit terms."[57] As well as the undetermined promise of Jesus's salvation from sins in Matt 1:21, we have heard in the meantime that Jesus has the authority to forgive sins (9:2, 5, 6), and that people can be forgiven for all manner of sins (12:31), without specifying how this takes place.[58] Matthew not only char-

---

53. Gnilka, *Matthäusevangelium*, 2:401, and Luz, *Matthew*, 3:380, are clear that for Matthew the covenant is "new," as in Luke and Paul.

54. With Gnilka, *Matthäusevangelium*, 2:401–2; D. A. Carson, *Matthew* (Grand Rapids: Zondervan, 1995), 538–39; Donald A. Hagner, *Matthew* (Waco, TX: Word, 1993–1995), 2:773, and Konradt, *Matthäus*, 406; contra Luz, *Matthew*, 3:380.

55. See the acute observations on the Passover setting in Matthew in Konradt, *Matthäus*, 403.

56. Catherine Sider Hamilton, *The Death of Jesus in Matthew: Innocent Blood and the End of Exile* (Cambridge: Cambridge University Press, 2017), 222 n. 97.

57. Donald P. Senior, *The Passion of Jesus in the Gospel of Matthew* (Collegeville, MN: Liturgical, 1990), 167.

58. Thomas R. Blanton IV, "Saved by Obedience: Matthew 1:21 in Light of Jesus' Teaching on the Torah," *JBL* 132 (2013): 393–413, provides a strong challenge to what he calls

acterizes the death of Christ as an act of ransom but also draws on the cultic imagery of atonement and purification: blood accomplishing forgiveness of sins here recalls most clearly Levitical offerings such as the guilt offering or the sin offering (cf. Lev 17:11).[59] The conjunction of covenant and forgiveness of sins perhaps also evokes Jer 31.[60] Such forgiveness would normally have been attributed to divine action through the temple cult, but for Matthew now "something greater than the temple is here" (Matt 12:6).[61]

---

the conventional view, according to which the death of Jesus is what primarily or even exclusively resolves the issue raised in Matt 1:21. He is right to emphasize the importance of law observance in Matthew's Gospel, of course, but neglects the connections among the references to "sins" in the Gospel. (Blanton also speaks too much of "sin" in general.) He comments, "Although the Gospel never indicates explicitly that Jesus saves people from their sins by advocating Torah observance, the logic of Matthew's narrative demands it" (411). As noted above, however, the closest Matthew comes to talking about Jesus saving people from their sins is precisely in Matt 26:26–28. Herein lies the difficulty with Blanton's conclusion: "The standard view, as should by now be quite plain, suffers from severe shortcomings: it completely overlooks the most significant means by which Jesus saves people from sin in Matthew's narrative, his advocacy of Torah observance, and focuses almost exclusively on the least developed—and therefore the least significant—means by which Jesus saves in the Gospel, his death on the cross" (413). Eubank, *Wages of Cross-Bearing*, 159, however, does see Matt 20:28 as deeply connected with a number of Matthean themes in the wider narrative, especially the debt of sin, and therefore unwittingly responds to Blanton's objection here. (Both pieces were published in 2013 and so are independent.) The treatment in this present chapter is in any case not seeking to disconnect salvation-from-sins from the wider themes of Matthew's Gospel, although it is for the purposes of the present argument focusing on the saving significance of the death of Jesus. I do see significant merit, however, in Blanton's important criticisms of the conclusions of Carter and Repschinski.

59. Hamilton, *Death of Jesus in Matthew*, esp. 181–228, is convincing in showing Matthew's emphasis on Jesus's "innocent blood" (27:4; cf. 27:19, 24) as connected to the innocent blood of Abel and Zechariah (23:35), and bringing defilement and destruction to the temple and judgment upon Israel. Less convincing is the argument that Jesus's death qua innocent blood effects purgation and that this purgation goes beyond forgiveness.

60. So Carson, *Matthew*, 538, and Konradt, *Matthäus*, 406.

61. As Luz (*Matthew*, 3:381) notes: "The passages in Matthew that summon to the forgiveness of sins (18.21–22, 23–35; cf. 6.12) receive their depth from the Lord's supper."

2.3 Interpretative Motifs in the Passion Narrative (Matt 26–27)

The other elements in Matthew's passion narrative—the cup (Matt 26:39, 42),[62] the Barabbas exchange (27:15–26),[63] the darkness (27:45),[64] the cry of dereliction (27:46),[65] and the rending of the curtain (27:51)—probably function in ways similar to their effects in the Markan passion narrative, though there may be additional nuances. In the case of Barabbas, there is some manuscript support for his name being "Jesus Barabbas" in Matthew (Matt 27:16–17): Barabbas being called both Jesus and "son of the father" (*br 'b*') would strengthen the idea of him being a kind of counterpart to Christ.[66] Some have seen the rending of the curtain in the Matthean context as relating more clearly to the destruction of the temple, especially given Matt 24:2 and the very recent 27:40.[67] But the problem of how or why the tearing of the veil might prefigure

62. In the Matthean context, Carson (*Matthew*, 543–44) and Hagner (*Matthew*, 2:783) take the cup as the cup of wrath (Gnilka, *Matthäusevangelium*, 2:412, also sees a secondary martyrological sense); Luz (*Matthew*, 3:396) and Konradt (*Matthäus*, 412) are more skeptical.

63. For this interpretation, see, e.g., Gnilka, *Matthäusevangelium*, 2:459: "Jesus stirbt anstelle des Übeltäters (vgl. Is 53, 5)."

64. Davies and Allison catalog a number of different interpretations (*Matthew*, 3:621–23), but Amos must be kept in mind, as they acknowledge; see further the brilliant survey of interpretation in Dale C. Allison, "Darkness at Noon," in *Studies in Matthew: Interpretation Past and Present* (Grand Rapids: Baker, 2005), 79–105. Carson, *Matthew*, 578, holds together judgment upon the nation but that is also experienced by Jesus and that elicits the cry of dereliction. Luz, *Matthew*, 3:544, combines judgment and heavenly sorrow; Gnilka, *Matthäusevangelium*, 2:474, prefers the latter.

65. Hagner (*Matthew*, 844) and Carson (*Matthew*, 578–79) interpret the cry in a soteriological manner. Davies and Allison note the culmination of abandonments of Jesus—by his own country in ch. 13, then by the disciples (ch. 26), then by the crowds (27:15–26), and finally by God (*Matthew*, 3:625). Gnilka, *Matthäusevangelium*, 2:475, emphasizes that the whole psalm (esp. verse 25) needs to be kept in mind.

66. As Davies and Allison say of the inclusion of the name "Jesus" with Barabbas (*Matthew*, 3:584), "most commentators now accept its originality." Since their commentary, see also, e.g., France, *Matthew*, 1053; Luz, *Matthew*, 3:496–97 (though cf. 491–92 n. 3); Charles L. Quarles, *Matthew* (Nashville: Broadman & Holman, 2017), 334, and Konradt, *Matthäus*, 433. Fiedler also includes a statement of the general view that is almost a translation of the comment of Davies and Allison (*Matthäusevangelium*, 409 n. 107).

67. Davies and Allison, *Matthew*, 3:630–31. While Luz, *Matthew*, 3:566, takes the tearing as symbolizing judgment on the temple, Carson rightly sees the access theme as primary, with the impending destruction a necessary consequence of access to God now coming through Jesus (*Matthew*, 580–81). Gnilka, *Matthäusevangelium*, 2:476, sees both inseparably present.

the destruction of the temple remains. Gurtner suggests that the heightened apocalyptic content in the neighborhood of the tearing of the veil implies an identification of the veil with the heavenly firmament: this would mean that heaven is opened, and the identity of Jesus revealed to, not deduced by, the soldiers; the veil's separating function also comes to an end.[68] Herzer also asserts that the addition of "Jesus" to the titulus (Matt 27:37) connects the death of Jesus to the interpretation of Jesus's name in Matt 1:21, which is a possibility.[69] Finally, there are two unique features of Matthew's passion narrative that merit more extended comment.

First, in response to Pilate's protestation of innocence, there is the chilling cry of the crowd: "his blood be upon us and upon our children" (Matt 27:25). Some have seen here an ironic statement that Jesus's blood "covers" sinful Israel in an atoning sense. But Davies and Allison are probably correct that this is "excessively subtle."[70] The language is more strongly suggestive of responsibility, with the reference to the "children" of the contemporaries of Jesus pointing to those alive when the sacking of Jerusalem takes place.[71] An ironic reading remains a possibility but not more than that.[72]

Second, a perhaps neglected feature in discussion of Matthew's understanding of the cross is the contribution of Matt 27:52–53 (to be discussed further in sec. 3.4 below).[73] After Jesus's resurrection, the resurrected saints appear in Jerusalem (27:53). Before that, however, irrespective of how one punctuates and interprets this very difficult passage, already on the day of Jesus's death, "the tombs broke open."[74] There is thus a sense that (1) the death of Jesus brings new life, and (2) a new age has dawned with an element of the general resurrection being

68. See Daniel M. Gurtner, *The Torn Veil: Matthew's Exposition of the Death of Jesus* (Cambridge: Cambridge University Press, 2007), 138–98, esp. 172, 178, 182–83, 189.

69. Jens Herzer, "The Riddle of the Holy Ones in Matthew 27:51b–53: A New Proposal for a Crux Interpretum," in *The Synoptic Gospels*, vol. 1 of *"What Does the Scripture Say?" Studies in the Function of Scripture in Early Judaism and Christianity*, ed. Craig A. Evans and H. Daniel Zacharias (London: Bloomsbury, 2012), 155.

70. Davies and Allison, *Matthew*, 3:592.

71. Fiedler, *Matthäusevangelium*, 411; Konradt, *Matthäus*, 436–37.

72. For "blood upon" meaning responsibility for death, see Jer 2:34; 26:15 (33:15 LXX); 51:35 (28:35 LXX); Ezek 18:13; 33:4–5; Acts 5:28; 18:6.

73. As the Old Testament background, commentators often note Isa 26:19, Ezek 37:13, and Dan 12:2.

74. See Davies and Allison, *Matthew*, 3:634–35, for an interpretation that (by excising μετὰ τὴν ἔγερσιν αὐτοῦ as a later gloss) takes all the events of the episode happening at the crucifixion; Carson, *Matthew*, 581–82, following John W. Wenham, "When Were the Saints Raised? A Note on the Punctuation of Matthew xxvii.51-3," *JTS* 32 (1981): 150–52,

anticipated. Ezekiel 37, where God announces that he is going to open the graves (Ezek 37:12–13), lies in particular in the background.[75] It is disputed whether the revivification accompanies the death of Jesus (rather than, as one might expect, the resurrection), but this is the more natural reading. Hence, Davies and Allison are correct: "Jesus' death is a resurrecting death: the dead are revived by his dying. As he passes from life to death they pass from death to life."[76]

2.4 Interim Conclusion: The Matthean Death of Jesus and the Kerygma

Like Mark, then, Matthew shares the view that Jesus's death is a ransom, a covenant inauguration, and an event that takes place at the Passover. It is thus clearly an effective and vicarious death. There are, however, some significant ways in which Matthew's understanding of Jesus's death is a development of Mark. The eucharistic words are much more strongly indicative of a saving death for sins, both in themselves and in the way they link back to the language of salvation from sins and forgiveness earlier in the Gospel. In this sense, there is a clear link to the language of Christ's death "for sins" in the kerygmatic formula in 1 Cor 15. Matthew probably shares with Mark an understanding of the narrative features of chapters 26–27, although his addition of Matt 27:52–53 adds the significant additional dimension of the tombs opening during the crucifixion narrative, implying that Jesus's death plays an important part in the liberation from, or conquest of, death.

3. THE RESURRECTION OF JESUS IN MATTHEW'S GOSPEL

We move to Jesus's resurrection. The discussion here will cover first Matthew's understanding of the event of the resurrection, and the fact that the resurrection took place on the third day (sec. 3.1–2). Thereafter, the subsequent sections will explore the theological implications of Jesus's resurrection, as an eschatological event inaugurating a new dawn (sec. 3.3) that brings the defeat of death (sec. 3.4); Jesus is also installed as authoritative messiah (sec. 3.5), as a result of which, he commissions his disciples to extend his dominion (sec. 3.6).

---

understands the opening of the tombs as taking place on Good Friday but dates both the resurrections and the appearances to after Jesus's resurrection.

75. Cf. especially Ezek 37:12a (ἐγὼ ἀνοίγω ὑμῶν τὰ μνήματα) and Matt 27:52a (καὶ τὰ μνημεῖα ἀνεῴχθησαν).

76. Davies and Allison, *Matthew*, 3:633; this aspect of their view is not dependent on emending the text.

3.1 The Event of the Resurrection in Matthew

At risk of beginning with what Bryan refers to as a subplot, we can start by examining what Matthew says is a Jewish account of what happened, namely that the disciples came in the night and stole the body while the guards were asleep (Matt 28:11–15).[77] By responding to this Jewish counter-narrative, Matthew makes especially clear what he sees as the historicity of the resurrection:

> [62]The next day, the one after the Day of Preparation, the chief priests and the Pharisees went to Pilate. [63]"Master," they said, "we remember that while he was still alive that deceiver said, 'After three days I will rise again.' [64]So give the order for the tomb to be made secure until the third day. Otherwise, his disciples may come and steal the body and tell the people that he has been raised from the dead. This last deception will be worse than the first." [65]"Take a guard," Pilate answered. "Go and make the tomb as secure as you know how." [66]So they went and made the tomb secure by putting a seal on the stone and posting the guard. (Matt 27:62–66)

Despite these precautions, the angel announces on the following day that Jesus has been raised and has gone (Matt 28:6). The three portents—the earthquake, the luminescent angel, and the miraculous rolling of the stone—make abundantly clear that the disappearance of Jesus's body from the tomb is the result of the action of God, not of the disciples.[78] The securing of the tomb in Matt 27:62–66 and the resurrection account in chapter 28 are clearly intended to

---

77. Christopher Bryan, *The Resurrection of the Messiah* (Oxford: Oxford University Press, 2011), 88. On the other hand, Giblin makes a good case for seeing the burial and resurrection narratives as a unit. See Charles H. Giblin, "Structural and Thematic Correlations in the Matthean Burial-Resurrection Narrative (Matt. XXVII.57–XXVIII.20)," *NTS* 21 (1974–1975): 406–20. On the Jewish account, see Justin, *Dial.* 108.2, where the narrator attributes the story of the stolen body to Trypho; *Gos. Pet.* 30 is also very close to Matthew. In Origen, *Cels.* 2.55, Celsus's Jew attributes the resurrection appearances to hallucinations.

78. Possibly echoed in the ἠγέρθη (Matt 28:6) if that is meant to imply divine passive; so, e.g., Wim Weren, "Matthew's Stories about Jesus' Burial and Resurrection (27:55–28:20) as the Climax of His Gospel," in *Life beyond Death in Matthew's Gospel: Religious Metaphor or Bodily Reality?*, ed. Wim Weren, Huub van de Sandt, and Joseph Verheyden (Leuven: Peeters, 2011), 197.

portray the resurrection as a supernatural event, but also as a historical one.[79] It has happened just as Jesus said it would (28:6).[80]

Matthew's account also clearly implies a bodily resurrection. The mention of the empty tomb in combination with standard resurrection terminology (ἠγέρθη [Matt 28:6]), and especially resurrection "from the dead" (ἠγέρθη ἀπὸ τῶν νεκρῶν [28:7]), makes the point clear. Matthew can distinguish between a "ghost" (φάντασμα [14:26]), an "angel" (1:20, 24, etc.), and people resurrected whether in the present or on the last day.[81] Those resurrected are consistently predicated, in Matthew, with the verb "raise" (ἐγείρω).[82] Matthew's terminology both in the passion predictions and in chapter 28 places what happens to Jesus clearly in the (admittedly broad) resurrection category: describing the resurrection of Jesus specifically, Matthew again uses the language of being "raised" (passive of ἐγείρω), along with the noun "raising" (ἔγερσις in 27:53).

The category of translation or assumption therefore does not fit the resurrection in Matthew. We have already noted how Jesus is described in the same terms (ἐγείρω etc.) as other raised figures in Matthew (and, in chapter 4, in Mark). Syreeni notes several additional ways in which Matt 28 fits the category of resurrection rather than assumption: (1) Jesus's appearance to the women in Matt 28:9–10 in its context is clearly a resurrection appearance; (2) there is no hint that a possible Moses typology in Matt 28:16–20 taps into a story of Moses's translation to heaven; and (3) Matthew presents Jesus as enduringly *present* not absent (28:20).[83] Syreeni concludes: "The evangelist and his community may have been aware of a variety of resurrection or translation beliefs,

---

79. Davies and Allison, *Matthew*, 3:671, list a series of ironies here, including the fact that it is the guards and the chief priests who end up perpetrating a deception (cf. Matt 27:64). Similarly, Bryan, *Resurrection*, 92.

80. As Giblin, "Structural and Thematic Correlations," 413, notes: "Matthew evidences his concern for the fulfilment of Jesus' prediction regarding his resurrection (xxviii. 6): '. . . he is risen as he said.'"

81. In Matt 22:30, those resurrected are "like angels" (ὡς ἄγγελοι), but Matthew leaves unspecified in what senses.

82. The exception in Matthew to the use of ἐγείρω is the men of Nineveh who ἀναστήσονται ἐν τῇ κρίσει (Matt 12:41): this clearly means the same as the singular ἐγερθήσεται ἐν τῇ κρίσει in the following verse. The verb ἐγείρω is used of those raised by Jesus (νεκροὶ ἐγείρονται [11:5; cf. 9:25]) or by the disciples (νεκροὺς ἐγείρετε [10:8]), or of John supposedly raised (ἠγέρθη ἀπὸ τῶν νεκρῶν [14:1–2]), or of the miraculously resuscitated saints (ἠγέρθησαν [27:52]). Cf. the noun in the phrase "at the resurrection . . . of the dead" (ἐν τῇ ἀναστάσει. . . . τῶν νεκρῶν [22:23–33]).

83. Kari Syreeni, "Resurrection or Assumption? Matthew's View of the Post-mortem

but the Gospel text is quite clear about Jesus' bodily resurrection on the third day."[84] On the one hand, as in Luke and John, the body of Jesus is no ordinary body, as is evident from the fact that Jesus has already escaped from the tomb and set off for Galilee before the stone is removed; in this sense, he is different from the saints revivified in Matt 27.[85] On the other, there is continuity in Jesus's nature, in his being visible (Matt 28:7, 17), that he can be recognized and touched (28:9) and can speak apparently as a human being (28:9-10, 18-20). Gnilka may also be correct to see the reference to Galilee in Matt 28:16 securing the identity of the risen Christ with the earthly Jesus.[86]

3.2 Resurrection in Three Days

Matthew also lays a particular emphasis on the resurrection taking place after three days or on the third day, and this is evident in four areas: in the analogy between Jesus and Jonah, in the passion predictions, in the testimony of the false witnesses, and in the narrative chronology of Matt 27-28.

Jesus and Jonah (Matt 12:38-40)

The first indication of the third-day resurrection is the analogy between Jesus and Jonah.[87] This passage will be discussed further below (sec. 4.2). At this point, we need merely note the analogy: "For as 'Jonah was three days and three nights in the belly of a sea monster,' so the Son of Man will be three days and three nights in the heart of the earth" (Matt 12:40). The description of the interval between Jesus's death and resurrection as three days *and three*

Vindication of Jesus," in Weren, van de Sandt, and Verheyden, *Life beyond Death in Matthew's Gospel*, 70, 73-75, and 75, respectively.

84. Syreeni, "Resurrection or Assumption?," 76.

85. Rightly, Jürgen Zangenberg, "'Bodily Resurrection' of Jesus in Matthew?," in Weren, van de Sandt, and Verheyden, *Life beyond Death in Matthew's Gospel*, 230.

86. As Setzer notes, "the details of the apologetic speak only about a body and its whereabouts." See Claudia Setzer, "Resurrection in the Gospel of Matthew: Reality and Symbol," in Weren, van de Sandt, and Verheyden, *Life beyond Death in Matthew's Gospel*, 43. Similarly, in the same volume, Syreeni, "Resurrection or Assumption?," 76; Weren, "Matthew's Stories about Jesus' Burial and Resurrection," 185-200, esp. 197, 199-200. *Pace* Zangenberg, "'Bodily Resurrection' of Jesus in Matthew," 223, one cannot really draw any conclusion from the absence of the word σῶμα in Matt 28. See also Gnilka, *Matthäusevangelium*, 2:506.

87. For discussion and extensive bibliography, see Lidija Novakovic, *Raised from the Dead according to Scripture: The Role of the Old Testament in the Early Christian Interpretations of Jesus' Resurrection* (London: Bloomsbury, 2012), 175-84.

nights is distinctive to Matthew and might appear to contradict the narrative chronology of Matt 27–28 (outlined below).

The discrepancy between Jesus being in the earth "for three days and three nights" and the chronology of the passion and resurrection, however, is more apparent than real.[88] "Three days and three nights" can be idiomatic. Esther, for example, says the Jews in Susa should fast "for three days, night and day" (ἐπὶ ἡμέρας τρεῖς νύκτα καὶ ἡμέραν), and says she will do the same; then "on the third day" (ἐν τῇ ἡμέρᾳ τῇ τρίτῃ), she ventured to see the king (Esth 4:16; 5:1). The second Esther targum renders 4:16 with the more straightforward phrase "for three days and three nights," followed by "the third day" in 5:1. Moreover, the midrash connects this passage with Jonah 2:1 and Hos 6:2: "Israel are never left in dire distress more than three days. . . . Of Jonah it says, *And Jonah was in the belly of the fish three days and three nights.* The dead also will come to life only *after three days*, as it says, *On the third day he will raise us up, that we may live in his presence.*"[89] Here, as in Matthew, the time frame in Jonah is equated with rescue "on the third day." Elsewhere, in the Midrash on Genesis, the events in Esther and Jonah are again described as taking place on the third day (in connection with Hos 6).[90] The Hosea and Jonah passages are taken as synonymous again in Midrash Psalms and Yalqut Shimeoni.[91] Having referred to all these passages, McArthur concludes: "the tension between these two formulations which modern scholars find puzzling would not have troubled first-century Jewish exegetes."[92] Similarly, going backwards, the Egyptian in 1 Sam 30 had not eaten or drunk "for three days and three nights," because his master had left him behind "the third day today" (1 Sam 30:11, 13); this example is not clear, however, as it depends on whether the counting is inclusive or exclusive.[93] What is likely is that the superinclusive reckoning in the midrashim is dependent on the doctrine of the *onah* (*'wnh*); definitions of the *onah* ("time span" or "stage") vary, but according to Rabbi Eleazar ben Azariah, "A day and a night constitute an *onah*, and part of an *onah* is equivalent to the whole of it" (y. Šabb. 9.3). The possibility of saying that the third

---

88. *Pace* Giblin, "Structural and Thematic Correlations," 416, see Harvey K. McArthur, "On the Third Day," *NTS* 18 (1971): 83–85 and 85 n. 1.

89. Esth. Rab. 9.2, on Esth 5:1 (Simon 112).

90. Gen. Rab. 56.1, on Gen 22:4 (Freedman 1:491).

91. Midr. Ps. 22.5, on Ps 22:1 (Braude 1:302); Yalqut Shimeoni to Josh 2:16: see Beat Zuber, *Jalkut Schimoni zu Josua* (Berlin: de Gruyter, 2017), 50.

92. McArthur, "On the Third Day," 85 (and see sec. 5, 7, 11, and 12 for the quotations, on pp. 83–85). Cf. also *Prot. Jas.* 24.3–4.

93. The meaning of the unusual expression *hywm šlšh* in 1 Sam 30:13 is unclear.

day comes after "three days and nights," however, is probably already evident in canonical Esther.

The Passion Predictions (Matt 16:21; 17:22–23; 20:18–19)

The Jonah material is distinctive to Matthew, but Matthew also absorbs much of the Markan material about the resurrection. In the so-called passion predictions (which are of course also concerned with the resurrection), Matthew follows Mark's language closely but prefers "on the third day" (τῇ τρίτῃ ἡμέρᾳ) to Mark's "after three days" (μετὰ τρεῖς ἡμέρας). Matthew also has "to be raised" (passive of ἐγείρω) in place of Mark's use of the verb "to rise" (ἀνίστημι).[94] These "third day" passion predictions are also reflected in the concern of the authorities to have Jesus's tomb guarded until the third day (Matt 27:63).

The Ironic Testimony of the False Witnesses (Matt 26:60–61; 27:39–40)

Matthew also contains a reflection of the Johannine statement, "Destroy this temple, and I will raise it again in three days," with the temple probably being Jesus's body (cf. John 2:19, 21), though perhaps there is (also) an ecclesiological sense.[95] Matthew, like Mark, twice states the allegation that Jesus plans to destroy the temple and rebuild it "in three days" (Matt 26:60–61; 27:39–40). This testimony is perhaps ironic: while Jesus will not save himself from the cross, there will be a "rebuilding" in three days.[96]

The Narrative Chronology (Matt 27–28)

Matthew shares with Mark, again, the clear indication of a Friday-Saturday-Sunday death and resurrection narrative:

> *The day before the day after Friday (cf. Matt 27:62):*
>   Early in the morning. . . . (27:1)
>   From noon until three in the afternoon. . . . (27:45)
>   At about three in the afternoon. . . . (27:46)

---

94. Cf. also Matt 17:9, drawing on Mark 9:9.

95. See the discussion of this question in the treatment of Mark in the previous chapter.

96. Matthew does not have an explicit temple Christology; indeed, Jesus and what he brings are supertemplar (Matt 12:6). But there may be an implicit idea of Jesus as a new temple in statements such as Jesus being Emmanuel, "God with us."

When evening came. . . . (27:57)

Holy Saturday:
The next day, which was after Friday [or after Preparation Day],[97] *the chief priests and the Pharisees went to Pilate. "Master," they said, "we remember that while he was still alive that deceiver said, 'After three days I will rise again.' So give the order for the tomb to be made secure until the third day." (Matt 27:62–64)*

Resurrection Sunday:
After the Sabbath, at dawn on the first day of the week, Mary Magdalene and the other Mary went to look at the tomb. And there was a violent earthquake! For an angel of the Lord came down from heaven. (Matt 28:1–2)

Some have argued that Matt 28:1a (Ὀψὲ δὲ σαββάτων, τῇ ἐπιφωσκούσῃ εἰς μίαν σαββάτων) means late on the Sabbath, in the afternoon, as the first day of the week approaches at sunset.[98] This cannot possibly be correct, however, because of the chronology of the guarding. At some point on Saturday, the guard is posted (27:62–66). When Jesus rises from the dead (28:1–10), the chief priests tell the guards to say that the disciples must have stolen the body during the night while they were asleep (28:11–15). On Saturday afternoon, as sunset approaches, however, the guards have not yet been there a night. Therefore, the time signaled in Matt 28:1 must be the Sunday morning.[99]

97. *Pace* Giblin, "Structural and Thematic Correlations," 412, "Preparation" is not ambiguous, as its reference to the day before the Sabbath was well established. For "Preparation" meaning Friday, see, e.g., Josephus, *Ant.* 16.163; *Did.* 8.1; *Mart. Pol.* 7.1.

98. See Keith H. Reeves, *The Resurrection Narrative in Matthew: A Literary-Critical Examination* (Lewiston, NY: Mellen, 1993), 54; J. Michael Winger, "When Did the Women Visit the Tomb: Sources for Some Temporal Clauses in the Synoptic Gospels," *NTS* 40 (1994): 284–88; Daniel Boyarin, "'After the Sabbath' (Matt. 28:1)—Once More into the Crux," *JTS* 52 (2001): 678–88.

99. Additionally, a three-day chronology in Matthew would then be impossible (the translation "after the Sabbath" is not just a harmonization with the other Gospels). Furthermore, as Davies and Allison, *Matthew,* 3:663, note, it would not make sense for the women to go to see the tomb as it was getting dark. Finally, it is perfectly possible for ὀψέ to mean "after," as note, s.v., LSJ, BDAG, and Franco Montanari, ed., *The Brill Dictionary of Ancient Greek* (Leiden: Brill, 2015); however, of BDAG's examples, the parallels from Philostratus's *Life of Apollonius* (4.18.5; 6.10.24) are much stronger than those of Aelian and Polyaenus, which do not support such a meaning.

The day of the week on which the crucifixion takes place, therefore, can be deduced, retrospectively, from Matt 27:62. There is clear, immediate linkage of the three days in Matt 27:62 and 28:1. The foregoing predictions, by both Jesus and the false witnesses, are confirmed in the course of events in Matt 27–28.[100]

3.3 A New Dawn

As in Mark, the language of resurrection on the "third day," so emphatic in Matthew so far, shifts in chapter 28 to "on the first day": "After the Sabbath, at dawn on the first day of the week" (Matt 28:1). Matthew's awkward Greek here emphasizes both the time (dawn) and the day (the first of the week). As Davies and Allison note, it is probably the case that "the literal dawning of a new day signals a new period of history."[101] There is possibly even an echo of Haggai's eschatological prophecy of the shaking of the heavens and the earth (σείω), since the quake (σεισμός) is caused by an angel coming down from heaven (Matt 28:2), though such a fulfillment is by no means certain.[102] Although Matthew maintains a considerable eschatological reserve,[103] the echoes of a new dawn are probably present, and this new eschatological scenario is extended further by Matthew in his depiction of Jesus's conquest of death (sec. 3.4) and his messianic appointment (sec. 3.5).

3.4 Jesus's Triumph over Death

Jesus's own resurrection is clearly a triumph over the Roman power that had attempted to secure and seal a tomb already closed with a "great stone" (Matt 27:60). When Jesus rises from the dead, then, there is perhaps a nice, comic touch in the statement that the angel rolled the stone away and sat on it:

---

100. Hence the "as he said" (Matt 28:6) may perhaps hint at the chronological element, as suggested by Reeves, *Resurrection Narrative*, 18.

101. Davies and Allison, *Matthew*, 3:664. Cf. Luz, *Matthew*, 3:594–95, who sees it simply as a chronological marker (which remains a possibility).

102. Cf. Hag 2:6, 21; Heb 12:26. Possibly Matt 28:2 represents the shaking of heaven, paired with the shaking of the earth (ἡ γῆ ἐσείσθη) when Jesus died (Matt 27:51).

103. For Matthew, as for the other evangelists, the resurrection does not instantly produce a utopia of unalloyed certainty, a situation that can come only after the parousia. See, e.g., the outstanding fear (Matt 28:8; cf. 28:9–10) and the doubts of some of the disciples (28:17): on the translation of Matt 28:17 ("they [or some of them] worshiped him; but some doubted"), see Pieter W. van der Horst, "Once More: The Translation of οἱ δέ in Matthew 28.17," *JSNT* 27 (1986): 27–30; so Davies and Allison, *Matthew*, 3:681–82. It is possible that Jesus's approach in 28:18 removes the doubt.

"That hefty rock (*lithon megan*), which was meant to *contain* the Christ, turns out to be nothing more than a perch for God's angel, who sits on it—possibly with a mocking grin?—inviting all who will to join him in the Easter joke."[104] The sitting here indicates divine triumph, with a hint of gloating mockery.

The moment of Jesus's resurrection is also the occasion for the resurrection of the saints whom we considered above in the discussion of the crucifixion. With Jesus's death and the tearing of the veil, the tombs broke open, but the holy people appear only after Jesus rises:

> [51]At that moment the curtain of the temple was torn in two from top to bottom. The earth shook, the rocks split [52]and the tombs broke open. The bodies of many holy people who had died were raised to life, [53]and, having come out of the tombs after Jesus's resurrection, they went into the holy city and appeared to many people. (Matt 27:51–53)

As noted above, this is a difficult passage to translate, but the rendering above is more probable, despite the holy people apparently being left alive in the tombs for three days. Although Wenham and Carson object to the oddity of "living saints cooped up for days in tombs around the city,"[105] the passage is sufficiently peculiar that an additional peculiarity of this sort is not such a problem; Wenham has to concede that, on his interpretation, Matthew has written "clumsily."[106] Hence (1) at the crucifixion the tombs break open, and the saints are revivified, and (2) after Jesus's resurrection they come forth. The crucifixion therefore already marks the conquest of death, but for Matthew the resurrection decisively demonstrates this to be the case.[107]

3.5 Jesus's Messianic Appointment (Matt 28:18)

The resurrection of Jesus in Matthew goes beyond simply being a vindication of Jesus, though that is a motif.[108] The Great Commission highlights a more far-reaching implication of the resurrection for Christology: "Then Jesus came

104. Bryan, *Resurrection*, 93.

105. So Wenham, "When Were the Saints Raised," 151.

106. Again, Wenham, "When Were the Saints Raised," 151.

107. Herzer, "Riddle of the Holy Ones," 152–55, pays attention to the Matthean intertexts, but it is not clear that these are the right intertexts. For example, the claim that those who see the risen saints are the guilty is far-fetched.

108. E.g., in the parallel between Jesus's resurrection to life and the transformation of the guards into ὡς νεκροί (Matt 28:4).

to them and said, 'All authority in heaven and on earth has been given to me'" (Matt 28:18). The foundation of the Great Commission in verses 19–20 is the fulfillment of Jesus's messianic appointment.[109] The invitation of Ps 2:8, "Ask me, and I will make the nations your inheritance, the ends of the earth your possession," is taken up by Jesus. Closer to the language and thought of Matthew in verse 18 is Dan 7:13–14, as we shall see in section 4.2 below.[110] In Matthew 28, then, we have the fulfillment of Jesus's messianic appointment and the fulfillment of Jesus's destiny as the Son of Man of Dan 7. (For Matthew at least, the Son of Man obviously has messianic associations.) In Matt 11:27, all things were revealed to Jesus, whereas now with the resurrection, all things have been granted to him and placed under his authority.[111] In the first mention of the Son of Man in Matthew, he had nowhere (οὐκ ἔχει ποῦ) to lay his head (Matt 8:20); now he has all authority in heaven and on earth and dwells wherever his disciples go (28:18, 20). "The risen Jesus now has all the power in the entire cosmos."[112]

3.6 The Great Commission: Mission and Salvation (Matt 28:16–20)

Jesus has already reconciled the disciples to himself, by calling them "brothers" (Matt 28:10) despite Peter's denial and the scattering of the others. Just before the Great Commission, Jesus expresses his intention to be reunited with his disciples in Galilee (28:10; cf. 26:32). This comes to pass: "The eleven disciples went into Galilee, to the mountain about which Jesus had instructed them" (28:16).[113] They

---

109. Bryan, *Resurrection*, 97: "The word therefore makes clear that what follows, that is, the work to which Jesus sends them, is dependent on what has been named, that is, his *exousia*, and is dependent on nothing else." Of course, some ancient readers might understand this fulfillment as an apotheosis: thus Wendy Cotter, "Greco-Roman Apotheosis Traditions and the Resurrection Appearances in Matthew," in *The Gospel of Matthew in Current Study*, ed. David E. Aune (Grand Rapids: Eerdmans, 2001), 127–53, with a survey of the primary sources. It is unlikely that this is a *good* reading, however, since Matthew has already signaled Jesus's divine identity.

110. For a comprehensive listing of the similarities between the two passages, see Davies and Allison, *Matthew*, 3:682–83. See further Konradt, *Matthäus*, 461. Cf. also the contrast with what is offered by Satan in Matt 4, on which see Bryan, *Resurrection*, 96–97. More distant is the parallel with Moses: what Jesus does here is a bit like what Moses does, but little more. See the discussion in Syreeni, "Resurrection or Assumption?," 73–74.

111. As Davies and Allison, *Matthew*, 2:279–80, rightly observe, the note in Matt 11:27 is not authority but revelation (ἐπιγινώσκει, ἀποκαλύψαι); cf. ἀπεκάλυψας in Matt 11:25.

112. Luz, *Matthew*, 3:624.

113. On the interpretation of the "mountain," see Luz, *Matthew*, 3:621–22.

then see Jesus there. The reason for the meeting taking place in Galilee cannot merely be that Jesus promised it: that would simply be to beg the question.

The meeting in Galilee where Jesus first calls his disciples evokes their initial callings. The disciples are in effect reappointed by Jesus as "fishers of men," but not merely as a return to the past status quo. It is here in Matt 28 that we see a more comprehensive fulfillment of the passage in Isaiah that Matthew cited much earlier: "Galilee *of the gentiles*—the people living in darkness have seen a great light; on those living in the land of the shadow of death a light has dawned" (Matt 4:15–16; Isa 9:1–2).[114] Now the recommissioning of the disciples to go to *all nations* (Matt 28:19) brings out the *gentile* dimension of the Isaian prophecy.[115]

The Great Commission lays out the soteriological ramifications of Jesus's messianic appointment:

> [18]Then Jesus came to them and said, "All authority in heaven and on earth has been given to me. [19]Therefore, go and make disciples of all nations, baptizing them in the name of the Father and of the Son and of the Holy Spirit, [20]and teaching them to obey everything I have commanded you. And surely I am with you always, to the very end of the age." (Matt 28:18–20)

The "therefore" (οὖν) in verse 19 is important. The disciples here are extending the ministry of Jesus himself:[116] by teaching additional disciples everything that Jesus taught, Jesus's authority is put into effect. The circles of these new disciples reach into the whole world, beyond Israel to include the gentiles as well. Second, the new baptism, "in the name of the Father and of the Son and of the Holy Spirit," is also significant. John's baptism was a mark of repentance, but the baptism of Jesus's disciples, while doubtless including repentance, has a rather wider scope and means being marked with the threefold divine name. Third, Jesus's presence, while promised to the Twelve, presumably extends to the wider circles of disciples, as in Matt 18:20 ("where two or three are gathered in my name, I am there among them"). As a result, the presence of Jesus, promised at the beginning of the Gospel in the designation of Jesus as Emmanuel, "God with us" (1:23), extends to all nations and to the end of the age (28:20).

---

114. See, e.g., Carson, *Matthew*, 460; Konradt, *Matthäus*, 460, and most commentators.

115. Hence Matthew does not have a Jewish mental geography with Jerusalem at the center (cf. Acts 1:8); indeed, there may even be, in addition to the positive prophetic associations of Galilee, negative reasons for Jesus leading the disciples away from Jerusalem. So Davies and Allison, *Matthew*, 3:667–68: "away from the corruption of Jerusalem."

116. Davies and Allison, *Matthew*, 3:686.

3.7 Interim Conclusion: The Kerygma and the Matthean Resurrection

Matthew adopts, and also articulates his own view of, the traditional kerygma of resurrection. One particularly noticeable feature of it is that he explicitly seeks to rebut a Jewish objection to the resurrection. He also expands upon Mark's interest in the three-day chronology of the death and resurrection with the Jonah analogy. Matthew prefers "on the third day" (τῇ τρίτῃ ἡμέρᾳ) to Mark's "after three days" (μετὰ τρεῖς ἡμέρας), and Matthew has "to be raised" (passive of ἐγείρω) in place of Mark's use of the verb "to rise" (ἀνίστημι). This means that Matthew conforms more closely to Paul's language in 1 Cor 15:4 (ἐγήγερται τῇ ἡμέρᾳ τῇ τρίτῃ). Matthew's use of "raising" language (ἐγείρω, ἔγερσις), describing Jesus as raised from the dead (e.g., in Matt 28:7), puts Jesus in a broad category of people already mentioned in the Gospel (Jairus's daughter, John the Baptist supposedly, the revivified saints, etc.). The similarities between Matthew's and Paul's language, Matthew's use of "raising" language of others earlier in the Gospel, and Matthew's presentation of the resurrection narrative all mean that the evangelist does not envisage an assumption rather than a resurrection.

Matthew's account of the soteriological significance of the resurrection incorporates some elements of Mark, such as the implication of a new dawn and a reconstitution of the disciples, but the much fuller resurrection narrative in Matt 28 has further implications, not least the defeat of death—albeit a defeat that awaits its final fulfillment at the parousia. There is also an emphasis on God installing Jesus as messiah, which in turn entails the reconstitution of the disciples for mission: this does not merely remain implied in Matthew as it is in Mark. Matthew 28 fleshes out the mission to make in every nation new disciples, who are marked by a new baptism and who will know Jesus's uninterrupted presence. Alkier's remark is only a slight exaggeration: "It is principally the narrative of the resurrection that makes the book of Matthew become a gospel."[117]

4. Fulfillment of Scripture in Matthew's Gospel

We have already considered how Matthew reuses certain messianic prooftexts already present in Mark, including Dan 7 and Zech 13:7. He makes explicit a

---

117. Stefan Alkier, *The Reality of the Resurrection: The New Testament Witness* (Waco, TX: Baylor University Press, 2013), 105. This is a little one-sided given the importance of salvation through the cross (Matt 20:28; 26:28).

scriptural reference implied in Mark's narrative, namely the oracle in Zech 9:9 about the humble king seated on a donkey. Additionally, we have seen in section 1 how Matthew uses certain new messianic prooftexts, especially a number from Isaiah, along with Zech 9:9 and Mic 5:2 (5:1 LXX). In the following discussion, the focus will be on the scriptural material particularly associated with the death and resurrection of Jesus, concluding with an assessment of Matthew's overall view of scripture.

4.1 Jesus's Death as Fulfillment of Scripture in Matthew

Again, Matthew takes over much of the Markan material associated with the death of Jesus. Zechariah 9–14, the Psalms, Dan 7, and Isa 50 and 53 all play a role in Matthew much as they do in Mark. Some of the Markan material is taken over holus-bolus, as in the case of the rejected stone of Ps 118: Mark copies the oracle of the rejected stone (so it would seem) verbatim from Ps 118:22–23 (117:22–23 LXX); Matthew in turn reproduces the wording from Mark (Matt 21:42). Similarly, as in Mark, Zechariah's "strike the shepherd" oracle is important in Matthew as focusing specifically on Jesus being killed. On the other hand, Mark's unacknowledged reference to the humble king of Zech 9:9 is made into an explicit quotation, with Zechariah's content expanded (Matt 21:1–9). In general, however, Matthew's additions to Mark are minor. Matthew perhaps amplifies Mark's allusion to Isa 50 by making it clear that the spitting Jesus endures is in his face (Matt 26:67).[118] There is a possible allusion to 2 Sam 1:16 in "his blood be upon us" (Matt 27:25), because David pronounces that the killer of the Lord's anointed has his (the killer's own) blood on his head.[119] In addition to the "strike the shepherd" oracle, there is only one other explicit fulfillment quotation in the passion narrative, in the pericope about Judas's death:

> [9]Then was fulfilled what was spoken by Jeremiah the prophet: "They took the thirty silver coins, the price set on him by the sons of Israel, [10]and they used them to buy Potter's Field, as the Lord commanded me." (Matt 27:9–10)

---

118. So Hays, *Echoes of Scripture in the Gospels*, 161, tentatively.

119. Hays, *Echoes of Scripture in the Gospels*, 133, while also seeing the possibility of a more optimistic reading of the passage (135).

Although presented as a quotation, it is more of a collage of allusions.[120] In addition to this, there is an obvious, though unmarked, quotation of Ps 22:8 (21:9 LXX) later in Matthew 27:

"He hoped in the Lord.	"He trusts in God.
Let the Lord rescue him!	Let God rescue him now
Let him save him,	
since he delights in him!" (Ps 21:9 LXX)	if he delights in him!" (Matt 27:43)

Beyond that, however, there is not much Matthean expansion of Mark.[121] Hays's conclusion is accurate here: "Matthew retains the scriptural allusions present in Mark's passion story and, as we have seen, sharpens and amplifies a few of the Markan allusions to the psalms of suffering. . . . On the whole, however, it is striking how little Matthew has done to create new correspondences between Jesus's death and its scriptural foreshadowing."[122] It is of course not the case that Matthew is uninterested in scriptural fulfillment. What is striking is how closely he sticks to Mark.

4.2 Jesus's Resurrection as Fulfillment of Scripture in Matthew

As noted in the previous chapter, Mark's principal scriptural evidence for the resurrection comes from Ps 110, Ps 118, and Dan 7. Matthew takes over most of this material.

Psalm 118

Most similar to Mark is Matthew's quotation of Ps 118, which appears in a similar context with apparently the same sense:

120. The main reference is to Zech 11:13, but this makes no reference to a field, which is the focus in Matt 27:10. Therefore, there are probably allusions to Jer 19:1–11 (which refers to a clay jar, the "elders of the people" and the priests, "innocent blood," and a place of burial) and Jer 32:6–15, which refers to the purchase of a field. Jeremiah 18:1–12 is also perhaps in view. See Konradt, *Matthäus*, 430, for an interesting explanation of the attribution to Jeremiah, not as a slip but as signaling the opposition to Jesus associated with Jeremiah earlier in the Gospel.

121. Donald Senior, "The Lure of the Formula Quotations: Re-assessing Matthew's Use of the Old Testament with the Passion Narrative as a Test Case," in *The Scriptures in the Gospels*, ed. Christopher M. Tuckett (Leuven: Peeters, 1997), 110–11, provides a list of the small expansions and additions to Mark's use of scripture in the passion narrative.

122. Hays, *Echoes of Scripture in the Gospels*, 160.

Jesus said to them, "Have you never read in the scriptures: 'The stone the builders rejected has become the cornerstone; this (cornerstone) is from the Lord, and it is marvelous in our eyes'?" (Matt 21:42, citing Ps 118:22–23 [117:22–23 LXX])

Here again, then, the cornerstone is vindicated after its rejection. Indeed, more than that, it is given prime position, just as is the case with Jesus in his resurrection and his reception of all authority in heaven and on earth.[123]

Psalm 110

On the other hand, in connection with Ps 110, Matthew incorporates a surprising change to Jesus's declaration to the high priest and the rest of the Sanhedrin:

Mark 14:62	Matt 26:64
"I am," said Jesus. "And you will see the Son of Man seated at the right hand of power and coming with the clouds of heaven."	"You have said so," Jesus said. "But I say to you all: From now on (ἀπαρτι) you will see the Son of Man seated at the right hand of power and coming on the clouds of heaven."

Matthew's "from now on" is intriguing here. Among the possible meanings, Davies and Allison conclude judiciously that two are most likely.[124] Either the Greek should be taken to mean "certainly" (ἀπαρτί) and refers solely to the parousia, or the Greek means "in the future" (ἀπ' ἄρτι), and the reference is both to the parousia and to the more immediate events surrounding the crucifixion and resurrection. The reference to the session of Jesus at the right hand from Ps 110 is more likely to include Jesus's victory already in evidence at his crucifixion (27:52–53) and his lordship fulfilled at the resurrection (28:18).[125] As elsewhere in the New Testament, Ps 110 refers to Jesus's enthronement.[126] The subsequent reference to Dan 7 points beyond that, to the parousia.

---

123. Gnilka, *Matthäusevangelium*, 2:230, identifies both the resurrection and Jesus's exaltation as implied in the citation.

124. Davies and Allison, *Matthew*, 3:530.

125. Davies and Allison, *Matthew*, 3:530. Similarly, Konradt, *Matthäus*, 422, speaks of Jesus's death and resurrection seen as a single complex of events here.

126. Matthew's use of Ps 110 is a conscious one, as he has conformed the wording more closely to the Greek text of the psalm. See Davies and Allison, *Matthew*, 3:529, noting the same with Matthew's use of Dan 7.

Daniel 7

Although Dan 7 is used to depict the parousia, Daniel's vision also receives some fulfillment in the Great Commission (Matt 28:18–20). As already noted (see sec. 3.5 above), the Great Commission begins with a statement of the authority given to Jesus, in terms strongly reminiscent of Dan 7:

- in Daniel, "authority" (ἐξουσία), along with "all the nations of the earth" (πάντα τὰ ἔθνη τῆς γῆς), "is given" (ἐδόθη), and that authority is an "everlasting authority" (ἐξουσία αἰώνιος);
- in Matthew, "all authority" (πᾶσα ἐξουσία) "is given" (ἐδόθη) in heaven and on "earth" (γῆς) to Jesus, who commissions the disciples to go to "all the nations" (πάντα τὰ ἔθνη), and he will be with them "forever" (ἕως τῆς συντελείας τοῦ αἰῶνος).

Matthew 28 therefore represents an extension of Mark's existing use of Dan 7.

Jonah 1:17 (2:1 LXX)

Moving into territory where the evangelist introduces new scriptural material, the most significant addition to Matthew's evidence for the resurrection is Jonah (see further sec. 3.2 above), where Jesus quotes from the book:[127]

> [38]Then some of the Pharisees and teachers of the law said to him, "Teacher, we want to see a sign from you." [39]He answered, "A wicked and adulterous generation asks for a sign! But none will be given it except the sign of the prophet Jonah. [40]For as 'Jonah was three days and three nights in the belly of the sea monster,' so the Son of Man will be three days and three nights in the heart of the earth." (Matt 12:38–40)

Unlike Luke, Matthew focuses in on Jonah's sojourn in the sea monster's innards. This episode in Jonah is understood as an appropriate analogy for death, burial, and resurrection, not unreasonably given that Jonah itself makes this connection: Jonah's prayer is heard from Sheol (ἐκ κοιλίας ᾅδου) in Jonah 2:3 LXX, he

---

127. Though not usually marked in English versions, there is a quotation here: Matt 12:40 draws the words ἦν Ἰωνᾶς ἐν τῇ κοιλίᾳ τοῦ κήτους τρεῖς ἡμέρας καὶ τρεῖς νύκτας verbatim from Jonah 2:1 LXX.

"descended into the earth (εἰς γῆν)" (2:7), and he asks for what is left of his life to ascend (ἀναβήτω φθορὰ ζωῆς μου, 2:7). As discussed earlier, Jesus's analogy specifies the interval of "three days and three nights" during which Jonah was in the sea monster, and the Son of Man will be in the heart of the earth; thereafter comes deliverance. The "sign of the prophet Jonah," therefore, is the resurrection,[128] or perhaps Jesus's death, burial, and resurrection in toto.

In sum, the use of Jonah in Matt 12, then, reflects the early kerygma of (1) raised (2) on the third day (3) according to the scriptures. The sign of Jonah is picked up again in Matt 16: "A wicked and adulterous generation looks for a sign, but none except the sign of Jonah will be given to it" (Matt 16:4).

4.3 Matthew's View of Scripture

We can summarize how Matthew saw the relation between Jesus and scripture in a series of theses.

1. *Central to Matthew is Jesus's fulfillment of scripture.* It is hardly possible to read any scholarship on Matthew's Gospel without encountering the importance of the theme of fulfillment. The fulfillment of scripture is one way of talking about the purpose of Jesus's advent (Matt 5:17).[129] Often, in the so-called fulfillment quotations, a particular prediction is highlighted as having come to pass. Jesus's birth from a virgin, for example, is predicted in Isa 7:14, while Jesus's birth in Bethlehem is the fulfillment of Mic 5:2, and so on. The rejection and death of Jesus is not just the fulfillment of one passage, however, but rather connects with multiple passages, or perhaps the entirety of scripture:

   > [53]"Do you not realize that I can call on my Father, and he will at once put at my disposal more than twelve legions of angels? [54]But how then would the scriptures be fulfilled that say it must happen in this way?" [55]In that hour Jesus said to the crowd, "Am I leading a rebellion, that you have come out with swords and clubs to capture me? Every day I sat in the temple courts teaching, and you did not arrest me. [56]But this has all taken place that the writings of the prophets might be fulfilled." Then all the disciples deserted him and fled. (Matt 26:53–56)

128. Gnilka, *Matthäusevangelium*, 1:466.
129. On this, see the helpful discussion in Carson, *Matthew*, 141–45.

For Matthew, then, fulfillment takes place at both the microlevel and the macrolevel.

2. *Matthew's phrasing of the fulfillment quotations indicates that scripture exerts a pressure on history.* Scripture, for the evangelist, dictates what *must* take place. The virgin could not have failed to give birth to the son, because it was determined by scripture. Matthew's focus in the quotations is on the one-way track from prophecy to its realization.[130]

3. *Scripture, for Matthew, is divine speech.* The reason for this pressure is not merely an apologetic or a legitimating strategy but is a consequence of Matthew's view of scripture. When Jesus says in the temptation narrative that man lives on every word that proceeds from the mouth of God, he is characterizing scripture as the divine voice (Matt 4:4). Similarly, when Jesus says that David in Ps 110 was "speaking by the Spirit," he signals the inspiration of David's words (Matt 22:43). At the same time, it is really David speaking, and the words of the prophets were really spoken and written down by the prophets. The "by the Lord, through the prophet" (ὑπὸ κυρίου διὰ τοῦ προφήτου) formula expresses neatly the primary and secondary speakers or authors of scripture (Matt 1:22; 2:15). Scripture therefore carries with it the authority of God for Matthew.

4. *Fulfillment also consists in Matthew taking up typological figures and events.*[131] Just as important as the explicit fulfillment of particular promises are the ways in which Jesus is depicted by means of recapitulating or completing narrative patterns in scripture. Jesus's ministry is an extension of the narrative of Israel's history and recapitulates it: a particularly obvious example is Jesus's forty days of testing in the wilderness, reenacting Israel's forty years of testing in the wilderness. Jesus is also the new Moses, the rejected prophet like Jeremiah, and so on.[132] His activity on the cross is a covenant inauguration ("my blood of the covenant").

5. *Behind scripture lies what is ordained by God.*[133] This is an obvious point, but it is important that the will of God precedes even scripture.

---

130. In this respect, I am not quite sure that the relation is "dialogic rather than linear," as Senior, "Lure of the Formula Quotations," 104, remarks.

131. Hays, *Echoes of Scripture in the Gospels*, 351, maintains a good balance between "the coming true of prophetic utterances" and "the narrative enactment of figural correspondences."

132. I note Moses and Jeremiah here because Dale C. Allison, *The New Moses: A Matthean Typology* (Edinburgh: T&T Clark, 1993), and Michael P. Knowles, *Jeremiah in Matthew's Gospel: The Rejected Prophet Motif in Matthean Redaction* (Sheffield: JSOT Press, 1993), are particularly helpful studies of Matthean typology.

133. D. Moody Smith, "The Use of the Old Testament in the New," in *The Use of the Old*

In short, in both Matthew's programmatic statements (like Matt 5:17), his direct quotations (e.g., in 1:22; 2:15), the various allusions (e.g., in 28:18), and his use of typology (Moses, Zechariah, etc.), there is a common thread of Jesus bringing scripture to fulfillment. Matthew has a varied and extensive account of how Jesus's activity is "in accordance with the scriptures."[134]

Conclusion: Matthew's Gospel and the Kerygma

Scholars have frequently pitted Matthew against Paul, but there is certainly no quibble on Matthew's side with the kerygma as preserved in 1 Cor 15.[135] Matthew is an enthusiastic advocate of Jesus's messiahship, from the announcement of "Jesus Christ the Son of David" in the first verse, to his receiving "all authority" (per Daniel's vision) at the resurrection. Jesus's lineage in the genealogy and his birth in Bethlehem are incorporated to make him recognizable early on as the messiah in line with certain traditions of Jewish expectation. Matthew also includes reference to Isa 42 and 53, as well as Zech 9. Matthew's attribution of particular miracles to Jesus qua "coming one" also overlaps strikingly with 4Q521, one of the few messianic texts from Qumran—although the fragmentary nature of the text makes positing a close similarity to Matthew difficult. Overall, however, Matthew is not just eager to endorse Jesus as messiah, but, like Mark, wants to do so in ways that are familiar from existing Jewish messianic exegesis.

Second, Matthew makes explicit that Jesus's death is "for sins." While only obvious on a second reading, Matthew's announcement that the name "Jesus" is given "because he will save his people from their sins" foreshadows Jesus's vicarious death (Matt 1:21). The connection is made clearly in the eucharistic words, in which Jesus states: "This is my blood of the covenant, which is poured out for many *for the forgiveness of sins.*" Jesus's death is therefore marked as a pouring out of blood for the purpose of expiation. Furthermore, alongside the familiar ransom saying from Mark, Matthew's peculiar reference to tombs opening at the time of Jesus's crucifixion strongly implies a crushing blow

---

Testament in the New and Other Essays: Studies in Honor of William Franklin Stinespring, ed. J. M. Efird (Durham, NC: Duke University Press, 1972), 47.

134. This taxonomy comes from the helpful summary in Senior, "Lure of the Formula Quotations," 115.

135. A good balance is struck in the conclusion to Joel Willitts, "Paul and Matthew: A Descriptive Approach from a Post–New Perspective Interpretive Framework," in Bird and Willitts, *Paul and the Gospels,* 84–85.

being delivered to death even before the resurrection. Jesus's death addresses the twofold plight of transgressions and the power of death. The crucifixion therefore clearly fits into the category of a vicarious death, being both beneficial and necessary for salvation.

Third, an area of considerable expansion of Mark is Matthew's account of the resurrection of Jesus. On the fact of Jesus's resurrection, Matthew is responding to criticism in Jewish circles of this element of the kerygma.[136] The language that Matthew uses in Jesus's passion-resurrection predictions (ἐγείρω, τῇ τρίτῃ ἡμέρᾳ) is closer to that of Paul's formula in 1 Cor 15 than it is to Mark. Matthew also expands upon Mark in his narration of resurrection appearances and in the theological significance he attaches to the resurrection. For Matthew, Jesus's rising is an eschatological event probably inaugurating a new dawn and a triumph over death: with Jesus's resurrection, the resuscitated saints come out of the previously opened tombs. The Great Commission is significant in particular as marking Jesus's investiture with "all authority," as a result of which he also reconstitutes the disciples for mission to all the nations. This mission extends that authority of Jesus as new disciples are taught his full course of instruction and baptized in his name (the name also of the Father and the Spirit). The resurrection is therefore not just a bare event but an event that counts as gospel.

Finally, Matthew's attitude to scripture is both conservative and innovative. His use of scripture both to justify and to elucidate the death of Jesus (and its circumstances) remains almost entirely within the territory already marked out in Matthew's primary source.[137] On the other hand, "the sign of Jonah" is a key piece of scriptural testimony to the resurrection. Daniel 7 receives partial fulfillment at the resurrection, even if Jesus's coming on the clouds will not happen till later. Overall, Matthew's understanding of the death and resurrection fits within his larger understanding of how Christ fulfills scripture, whether that scripture is understood as predictive prophecy or narrative prefiguring. Jesus's whole activity in Matthew, from his birth to his resurrection, takes place "according to the scriptures."

Overall, far from resisting a "Pauline" gospel, Matthew, if anything, conforms more closely or more explicitly than Mark to the kerygmatic formula. Matthew makes explicit a death of Jesus "for sins" and also narrates the resur-

---

136. Robert Vorholt, *Das Osterevangelium: Erinnerung und Erzählung* (Freiburg: Herder, 2013), 202.

137. Senior, "Lure of the Formula Quotations," 89, notes that Matthew never omits a Markan quotation from scripture.

rection appearance in Galilee to which Mark only refers, as well as having an appearance of Jesus to the two Marys. This is not to say that Matthew writes his Gospel under the shadow of Paul but simply that he reflects the widely dispersed early Christian kerygma.[138]

APPENDIX 1: THE BURIAL OF JESUS IN MATTHEW'S GOSPEL

Before narrating Jesus's burial, Matthew alludes to the event both in the "sign of Jonah" pericope (Matt 12:38–40) and—as in Mark—when the sinful woman "anoints" Jesus in preparation for his burial (26:12). The description of the burial itself, however, is very brief:

> [57]When evening fell, a rich man from Arimathea came, named Joseph, who had himself become a disciple of Jesus. [58]He approached Pilate and asked for Jesus's body. So Pilate ordered that it be given to him. [59]Joseph took the body, wrapped it in clean linen, [60]and placed it in his own new tomb that he had had cut out of the rock. He rolled a great stone at the entrance to the tomb and went away. [61]Mary Magdalene and the other Mary were sitting there opposite the tomb. (Matt 27:57–61)

There are only a few notable additions to Mark: Joseph is a disciple of Jesus (as in John), and the linen is clean. Matthew truncates the passage about Pilate's consent to Joseph's request, summarizing the twenty-six words of Mark 15:44–45 in five words in Matt 27:58c. Overall, then, Matthew's account is briefer, perhaps making space for the account of the placing of the guard and the sealing of the tomb. The burial of Jesus is still an integral part of the story for Matthew, however.

APPENDIX 2: THE RESURRECTION APPEARANCES IN MATTHEW'S GOSPEL

Matthew 28 consists of three parts, with Jesus appearing to the male disciples only in the final third. In Matt 28:1–10, the female disciples, Mary Magdalene

---

138. Foster, "Paul and Matthew," 114, notes the similarities between Paul and Matthew, concluding that "this is primarily due to both sharing some of the core commitments, beliefs and affirmations in common with the wider early Jesus movement."

and (presumably) Mary the mother of James and Joseph, go to the tomb. They see Jesus only at the end of the episode (28:9–10). The second portion of the chapter is devoted to the conspiracy of the priests and the soldiers (28:11–15). The final scene harks back to Matt 26:32 where, as in Mark, Jesus promises to go ahead of the disciples into Galilee. None of the Eleven are named in Matt 28:16–20, and there is thus neither agreement nor disagreement with the kerygma on whether Peter is the first of the Twelve to see the risen Jesus. The primacy of Peter in Matthew in other respects is clear, however. Peter is the first disciple listed of the two brothers in Matt 4:18, the first of the Twelve in 10:2, the respondent among the disciples in the Caesarea Philippi episode (16:16), and the rock on which Jesus promises to build his church (16:18). Therefore, Matthew may merely assume that Peter is the first of the Twelve to see Jesus, though he does not say so. In Matthew, the two Marys are the witnesses to the first resurrection appearance.

Chapter Six

THE GOSPEL OF LUKE

The question here remains the same as in the previous chapters. This study of Luke will therefore inquire into how reflective his gospel is of the early Christian kerygma, assessing the extent to which and the ways in which Luke (1) understands Jesus as messiah, (2) considers Jesus's death and (3) resurrection to be saving gospel events, and (4) thinks of these gospel events as taking place "in accordance with the scriptures."

There is one way in which this discussion of Luke will need to differ from that of Matthew and Mark. Luke, after all, is not the only product of its author, because we also have Acts. Luke's Gospel will nevertheless be treated here largely on its own, as it is a complete literary work in its own right, comprehensible without Acts. It is not quite true to say that Luke's Gospel is "unfinished" and therefore requires Acts.[1] As Luke himself puts it, his Gospel is a single *logos* in its own right, and the book of Acts a subsequent *logos* (Acts 1:1). It is an early Christian Gospel, in scope modeled very closely on Mark (and probably Matthew). In terms of their early reception, Luke and Acts are by no means treated as a single work.[2] On the other hand, however, there is a certain artificiality in keeping Acts out of the picture altogether, since it can of course shed light on Luke's thought. Nonetheless, given the points just made about the self-contained character of Luke's Gospel, I will use Acts as the drunk uses the lamppost—more for support than for illumination.

---

1. Richard B. Hays, *Echoes of Scripture in the Gospels* (Waco, TX: Baylor University Press, 2016), 195.

2. See Andrew F. Gregory and C. Kavin Rowe, eds., *Rethinking the Unity and Reception of Luke and Acts* (Columbia: University of South Carolina Press, 2010).

1. Jesus as Messiah in Luke's Gospel

As in previous chapters, the intention of this first section is to assess the degree to which Luke's identification of Jesus as messiah participates in the wider discourse of Jewish messianism. Again, this first part of the chapter has three subsections that aim respectively (sec. 1.1) to summarize the evidence for Luke's identification of Jesus as messiah, (sec. 1.2) to demonstrate that Luke's christological interpretation of scripture shares points in common with non-Christian Jewish messianic exegesis, and (sec. 1.3) to show that elements of Luke's messianic themes and idioms are in continuity with existing messianic discourse.

1.1 The Identification of Jesus as Messiah in Luke

The term Χριστός/χριστός is roughly as frequent in Luke as it is in Mark, though not so common as in Matthew and John, or for that matter as in Acts (Matthew 16×; Mark 7×; Luke 12×; John 19×; Acts 25×). There are three characters in the narrative who are witnesses to the fact of Jesus's messiahship. First, in the countryside around Bethlehem, an angel announces that "Christ the Lord" is born (Luke 2:11).[3] Second, Peter declares that Jesus is the "Christ of God" (9:20). Finally, after the resurrection, Jesus refers to himself as messiah (24:25–27, 44–47). There are also various editorial references that make it obvious that Luke has no reservations about applying the title to Jesus. The term needs to be understood correctly, but that is not the same as regarding the title as a kind of necessary evil or a mere relic of tradition.[4] Nor, as we have seen in previous chapters, is it necessarily helpful to talk in terms of Luke *redefining* messiahship, as if there were previously a set definition.[5] In fact, we will shortly see that Luke contains recognizable features of traditional messianic discourse.

---

3. On the pairing here and in the Psalms of Solomon, see C. Kavin Rowe, *Early Narrative Christology: The Lord in the Gospel of Luke* (Berlin: de Gruyter, 2006), 50–51.

4. This is rather the idea in Brendan Byrne, "Jesus as Messiah in the Gospel of Luke: Discerning a Pattern of Correction," *CBQ* 65 (2003): 80–95. More positively, Christopher M. Tuckett, "The Christology of Luke-Acts," in *The Unity of Luke-Acts*, ed. Joseph Verheyden (Leuven: Leuven University Press, 1999), 151: "Luke nowhere gives any explicit hint that χριστός itself is inadequate as a term for Jesus." Or again, 161: "If one wishes to try to pin Luke down to a single Christological title, then probably Jesus as the χριστός would have to be the most likely candidate."

5. Rightly, Matthew V. Novenson, *The Grammar of Messianism: An Ancient Jewish Political Idiom and Its Users* (Oxford: Oxford University Press, 2017), e.g., 213.

1.2 Luke's Christological Exegesis and Jewish Messianic Tradition

There is no need here to repeat discussion of the material that Luke takes over from Mark. Like his primary source, Luke makes considerable use of Dan 7 to explicate Jesus's destiny. Although Luke's trial contains a more muted allusion to the coming of the Son of Man (Luke 22:68), the reference in the eschatological discourse is unmistakable (21:27). Like Mark, Luke also alludes more clearly than Matthew to Ps 2 in the baptism scene (3:22). There is also usage of passages that, while not messianic before early Christian exegesis, were used in Jewish texts for their eschatological potential: these include Deut 18 (cf. Luke 9:35), Isa 40 (Luke 3:3-6, with reference to John the Baptist), and Ps 118 (Luke 13:35; 19:38; 20:17). Luke also shares with Matthew the cluster of allusions in his response to John the Baptist's inquiry, which resembles the list in 4Q521. To these can be added three more distinctive passages interpreted messianically by Luke: Ps 89, Isa 53, and Isa 61.

Psalm 89

While Strauss is correct that there is no explicit citation of a messianic proof-text in the infancy narrative, he is also right to emphasize the function of Ps 89 in Luke 1.[6] There is a particularly loud and clear allusion to the psalm in the middle of the Magnificat:[7]

Ps 89:2, 11 LXX	Luke 1:50-51
[2]Your *mercies* (ἐλέη), O Lord, I will sing forever, *from generation to generation* (εἰς γενεὰν καὶ γενεάν). . . . [11]You have turned the *proud* (ὑπερήφανον) into humble victims, and with your powerful *arm* (ἐν τῷ βραχίονι) you have *scattered* (διεσκόρπισας) your enemies.	His *mercy* (ἔλεος) is from generation to generation (εἰς γενεὰς καὶ γενεάς) for those who fear him. He has shown his strength *in his arm* (ἐν βραχίονι αὐτοῦ). He has *scattered* (διεσκόρπισεν) the *proud* (ὑπερηφάνους) in the devices of their hearts.

---

6. Mark L. Strauss, *The Davidic Messiah in Luke-Acts: The Promise and Its Fulfillment in Lukan Christology* (Sheffield: Sheffield Academic, 1995), 88. Dietrich Rusam, *Das Alte Testament bei Lukas* (Berlin: de Gruyter, 2003), 67, sees an "Anspielung" to Ps 89:11, and also allusions to Ps 89 in the angel's words in Luke 1:32-35 (64-65). Similarly, see the helpful synopsis of Luke 1:32-33; 2 Sam 7; Ps 89 in Strauss, *Davidic Messiah*, 88-89.

7. Helmer Ringgren, "Luke's Use of the Old Testament," *HTR* 79 (1986): 231, says that Luke 1:51b is "almost a quotation from Ps 89:11."

In addition to these more substantial connections, there are numerous other smaller links between the Magnificat and Ps 89 LXX:[8]

Ps 89:8: μέγας	Luke 1:46, 49: μεγαλύνει, μεγάλα
Ps 89:13, 17: ἀγαλλιάσονται	Luke 1:47: ἠγαλλίασεν
Ps 89:27: σωτηρίας	Luke 1:47: σωτῆρι
Ps 89:11: ἐταπείνωσας	Luke 1:48, 52: ταπείνωσιν, ταπεινούς
Ps 89:16: μακάριος	Luke 1:48: μακαριοῦσιν
Ps 89:14: δυναστείας	Luke 1:49, 52: ὁ δυνατός, δυνάστας
Ps 89:36: τῷ ἁγίῳ μου	Luke 1:49: ἅγιον
Ps 89:13, 17, 25: ἐν τῷ ὀνόματί σου	Luke 1:49: τὸ ὄνομα αὐτοῦ
	[verses 50–51: see above]
Ps 89:10: τοῦ κράτους	Luke 1:51: κράτος
Ps 89:14 etc.: ὑψ- verb forms	Luke 1:52: ὕψωσεν
Ps 89:5: θρόνον	Luke 1:52: θρόνων
Ps 89:12: πλήρωμα	Luke 1:53: ἐνέπλησεν
Ps 89:19, 22, 27: ἀντίλημψις, συναντιλήμψεται, ἀντιλήμπτωρ	Luke 1:54: ἀντελάβετο
Ps 89:51: μνήσθητι	Luke 1:54: μνησθῆναι
Ps 89:5, 30, 37: σπέρμα	Luke 1:55: σπέρματι
Ps 89:2: εἰς τὸν αἰῶνα	Luke 1:55: εἰς τὸν αἰῶνα

Caveat lector: a number of these words are obviously very common in Greek, and many of these connections are between words that are used in different contexts in the Magnificat and the psalm, and of course Ps 89 is long and therefore the danger exists of coincidental agreement. In the light of the very clear link between the psalm and Luke 1:50–51, however, the further echoes between the two passages should be taken seriously.

The use of Ps 89 is relevant to this discussion because it is clearly used messianically in early Jewish literature.[9] Chester has argued that it is significant in Qumran messianism, indeed "Psalm 89 is very much more important here than is usually allowed," although the passages discussed do not use "messiah" language per se.[10] Perhaps more clear is the influence of Ps 89

---

8. Rusam, *Das Alte Testament*, 49–50, like most interpreters, also sees close affinities between the Magnificat and 1 Sam 2:1–10.

9. See, e.g., Donald Juel, *Messianic Exegesis: Christological Interpretation of the Old Testament in Early Christianity* (Philadelphia: Fortress, 1988), 105–7.

10. Andrew Chester, *Messiah and Exaltation: Jewish Messianic and Visionary Traditions and New Testament Christology* (Tübingen: Mohr Siebeck, 2007), 273. He suggests that it is influential upon 4Q381, 4Q471b+4Q491, and—with Zimmermann—4Q521 (frag. 9). See

upon Pss. Sol. 17,[11] and beyond the overlap in language, Knibb also avers that the influence is more extensive, in that "Psalm of Solomon 17 follows a structure comparable to that of Psalm 89."[12] In a more explicit reference to Ps 89, the Mishnah interprets the motif of the "footsteps" or "footprints" of the messiah eschatologically: "With *the footprints of the Messiah* (Ps 89:51) presumption shall increase and dearth reach its height" (m. Soṭah 9.15; trans. Danby). There is also further development of this interpretation in the Babylonian Talmud (b. Sanh. 97a). Additionally, the targum takes the passage as referring to an eschatological messiah figure rather than alluding to a past king: the reference to "*the delay of* the footsteps of your Messiah" shows that the anointed one is a future figure (Tg. Ps. 89.51–52).[13] The same motif of the footsteps of the messiah also features in Midrash Psalms and Midrash Song of Songs.[14]

Other midrashim give messianic interpretations of other parts of the psalm. Genesis Rabbah discusses the royal messiah by combining some of the most frequent messianic prooftexts: Isa 11:10, Gen 49:10, and 2 Sam 7:16, alongside Ps 89:28 ("forever will I keep him for my mercy"), and Ps 89:37 ("this throne is like the sun before me").[15] Exodus Rabbah draws an analogy between Israel's status as firstborn in Exod 13:2, and that of the messiah, to whom God says in Ps 89:27: "I also will appoint him firstborn."[16] Pesiqta

---

Chester, *Messiah and Exaltation*, 241, 247, 254; Johannes Zimmermann, *Messianische Texte aus Qumran: Königliche, priesterliche und prophetische Messiasvorstellungen in den Schriften von Qumran* (Tübingen: Mohr Siebeck, 1998), 376.

11. See further Sam Janse, '*You Are My Son.*' *The Reception History of Psalm 2 in Early Judaism and the Early Church* (Leuven: Peeters, 2009), 57–60, on the links between Ps 89 and Pss. Sol. 17. N. B. especially:

Ps 89:4 (88:5 LXX): ἕως τοῦ αἰῶνος ἑτοιμάσω τὸ σπέρμα σου καὶ οἰκοδομήσω εἰς γενεὰν καὶ γενεὰν τὸν θρόνον σου.

Pss. Sol. 17.4: σύ κύριε ἡρετίσω τὸν Δαυιδ βασιλέα ἐπὶ Ισραηλ καὶ σὺ ὤμοσας αὐτῷ περὶ τοῦ σπέρματος αὐτοῦ εἰς τὸν αἰῶνα τοῦ μὴ ἐκλείπειν ἀπέναντί σου βασίλειον αὐτοῦ.

12. Michael Knibb, *Essays on the Book of Enoch and Other Early Jewish Texts and Traditions* (Leiden: Brill, 2008), 308.

13. See, e.g., Samson H. Levey, *The Messiah: An Aramaic Interpretation; The Messianic Exegesis of the Targum* (New York: Ktav, 1974), 121.

14. Midr. Ps. 18.5, on Ps 18:1 (Braude, 1:233); Song Rab. 2.13 §4, on Song 2:13 (Simon, 127); cf. Pesiq. Rab. 15.14–15 (Braude, 1:328); Pesiq. Rab Kah. 5.9 (Braude and Kapstein, 149).

15. Gen. Rab. 97 (var.), on Gen 49:8 (Freedman, 2:901). Juel, *Messianic Exegesis*, 106, also quotes Gen. Rab. 66.8, on Gen 22:11 (Freedman, 1:498), as a possible messianic use of Ps 89, though this is less clear.

16. Exod. Rab. 19.7, on Exod 13:1 (Lehrman, 237–38).

Rabbati derives the power and indestructibility of the messiah from other parts of the psalm: "The enemy shall not do him violence, nor the son of wickedness afflict him" (Ps 89:22); "I will beat to pieces his adversaries before him" (89:23); and "I will set his hand also on the sea, and his right hand on the rivers" (89:25).[17]

Clearly, then, the messianic interpretation of Ps 89 is a long-standing one, going back at least as far as the Mishnah, but probably already evident in the Psalms of Solomon.

Isaiah 53

Luke, like Matthew, also cites from Isa 53, but Luke's quotation deserves separate treatment because it refers to a different part of the suffering servant passage in a quite different context. As we saw in the previous chapter, there is evidence for the messianic interpretation of Isaiah prior to, or at least independent of, the Synoptic Gospels. Luke's interpretation relates not to Jesus's healing activity as in Matthew, but to the passion:

> "For I say to you that what is written must find its completion in me: 'And he was numbered with the transgressors.' And indeed this matter about me is coming to its completion." (Luke 22:37, citing Isa 53:12)

This quotation will be treated in more detail in section 4.1 below. Here we can merely note that Luke, like 1 Enoch and Targum Isaiah (and Matthew), applies a section of Isa 52:13–53:12 to Jesus.

Isaiah 61:1–2

The aptly named Nazareth Manifesto in Luke 4 also quotes a traditionally messianic prooftext, in its almost verbatim reference to Isa 61, with one line interpolated from Isa 58:[18]

---

17. Pesiq. Rab. 36.1 (Braude, 2:678).

18. Luke also stops the quotation of Isa 61:1–2 short, omitting reference to divine vengeance. In the context, this is probably deliberate, as Ringgren ("Luke's Use of the Old Testament," 229) rightly says.

Isa 61:1–2	Luke 4:18–19
"The Spirit of the Lord is on me,	"The Spirit of the Lord is on me,
because he has anointed (ἔχρισεν) me	because he has anointed (ἔχρισεν) me
to proclaim good news to the poor.	to proclaim good news to the poor.
He has sent me	He has sent me
to heal the afflicted,	
to proclaim freedom for the captives	to proclaim freedom for the captives
and recovery of sight for the blind,	and recovery of sight for the blind,
[58:6: "Set the oppressed free!"]	*to set the oppressed free,*
to *invoke* the year of the Lord's favor."	to *proclaim* the year of the Lord's favor."

Luke's quotation here is not limited to proclamation and prophetic messiahship, because the words in Luke 4:18–19 also refer to the Spirit-anointed figure in fact *effecting* liberation: the inclusion of Isa 58:6 here means that the Lord has anointed the messiah not only to proclaim freedom but also *to set the oppressed free.*[19]

This last point is reinforced in Luke 7, which picks up the Nazareth Manifesto:[20]

> [21] At that very time, Jesus cured many who had diseases, illnesses, and evil spirits, and gave sight to many who were blind. [22] So he replied to the messengers, "Go back and report to John what you have seen and heard: *the blind receive sight*, the lame walk, those who have leprosy are cleansed, the deaf hear, the dead are raised, *and the good news is proclaimed to the poor.*" (Luke 7:21–22)

The main point of overlap with Luke 4 appears in the first and last items, namely the healing of the blind and the preaching of the good news to the poor, which also appear in Isa 61.[21] These are not merely eschatological events *accompanying* the arrival of the coming one but are surely to be understood as Jesus's own activity, as the editorial introduction to verse 21 preceding Jesus's reply makes clear. There is also considerable overlap with what Luke actually narrates in the course of the Gospel.[22]

19. Strauss, *Davidic Messiah*, 231.
20. Tuckett, "Christology of Luke-Acts," 143.
21. Other elements can be derived in particular from Isa 35 (e.g., the healing of the blind, deaf, and lame in 35:5).
22. The blind receive sight: Luke 18:35–43
    The lame walk: x (but cf. Luke 5:22–26)

Luke's messianic use of Isa 61 is not an innovation, however, and there are two places in particular where the chapter is used apparently messianically prior to Luke.

First, there is clear reference to Isa 61 in 4Q521. This Qumran passage is often thought simply to refer exclusively to the actions of God, and not to include activity on the part of the "his messiah" (*mšyḥw*) mentioned at the beginning of fragment 2:

> [11]And the Lord will accomplish glorious things that have never been as [he
> ...]. [12]For he will heal the wounded and revive the dead. He will preach good
> news to the poor ('*nwym ybsr*). (4Q521 2 II, 11–12; trans. Vermes, adapted)

As is noted in the previous chapter on Matthew, however, the item "preaching good news to the poor" makes better sense as something done by or through a human herald, as is indeed the case in Isa 61.

Second, in the Qumran Melchizedek text (11Q13), the mysterious figure of the title is, among other things, the Danielic anointed prince, and the details of Isa 61 are applied to him and his activity. There is extensive discussion of the parallels by Miller, and more recently by Michael Cover.[23] The first passage from column II is very lacunose, but there is unmistakable reference to Isa 61:

> [4][And it will be proclaimed at] the end of days concerning the captives
> ('*l hšbwyym*) [cf. Isa 61:1] as [. . .] will assign them to [5]the sons of heaven
> and to the inheritance of Melchizedek; f[or he will cast] their [lot] amid the
> po[rtions of Melchize]dek, who [6]will return them there and will proclaim to
> them liberty (*wqr' lhmh drwr*) [Isa 61:1], forgiving them [the wrongdoings]
> of all their iniquities. And this will [7][occur] in the first week of the Jubilee
> that follows the nine Jubilees. And the Day of Atonement is the e[nd of the]
> tenth [Ju]bilee, [8]when all the sons of [light] and the men of the lot of Mel[-
> chi]zedek will be atoned for. [And] a statute concerns them [to prov]ide

---

Those with leprosy cleansed:	Luke 5:12–16; 17:11–19
The deaf hear:	x
The dead are raised:	Luke 7:11–17; 8:40–56
The good news preached:	Luke 4:43; 8:1; 20:1; "for the poor": 6:20; 14:13, 21

23. Merrill P. Miller, "The Function of Isa 61:1–2 in 11Q Melchizedek," *JBL* 88 (1969): 467–69; Michael Cover, *Lifting the Veil: 2 Corinthians 3:7–18 in Light of Jewish Homiletic and Commentary Traditions* (Berlin: de Gruyter, 2015), 154–56; notable also is Chester, *Messiah and Exaltation*, 259–61.

them with their rewards. For [9]this is the moment of the year of favor for (*šnt ḥrṣwn l-*) [Isa 61:2] Melchizedek.

. . .

[13]And Melchizedek will execute the vengeance (*nqm*) [cf. Isa 61:2] of his judgments of [. . .] Belial, and from the hand of all [. . .] [14]And for his aid are all the gods of [. . .] all the sons of God [. . .] [15]This is the day of [. . .] about which [God] spoke [through Isa]iah the prophet, who said, "[How] beautiful [16]upon the mountains are the feet of the messenger who proclaims peace, who brings good news, who proclaims salvation, who says to Zion: Your God [reigns]" [Isa 52:7]. [17]Its interpretation: the mountains are the prophets . . . [18]and the messenger is the anointed one of the spirit (*mšyḥ hrw[ḥ]*) [cf. Isa 61:1], concerning whom Dan[iel] said, [. . .] [19]good [. . .], who proclaims [salvation]: it is concerning him that it is written [. . .] [20]"To comfort (*lnḥ[m]*) those [. . .]" [Isa 61:2]. (11Q13 II, 4–9, 13–20; trans. Vermes, adapted)

Here the messianic figure is pictured as standing atop the prophets as he proclaims the good news that connects Isa 52 and 61. To conclude, there is clear precedent at Qumran for Luke's usage of a powerful anointed figure who fulfills Isa 61.[24]

Conclusion to 1.2

As well as absorbing Mark's christological exegesis (of Ps 2 and Dan 7), Luke therefore also contributes some of his own, which is unique among the Four Gospels. He shares with the Psalms of Solomon and later rabbinic exegesis a messianic interpretation of Ps 89, with 1 Enoch and the targum a messianic exegesis of Isa 53, and with 4Q521 and 11Q13 a messianic understanding of Isa 61. That the first and last of these passages are understood messianically is not surprising, given their references to anointing—as is also the case in one Qumran manuscript of Isa 52:13–53:12 (1QIsa[a]).

1.3 Jewish Messianic Themes in Luke's Christology

In addition to clear allusions to particular scriptural passages, there are other themes that embrace a number of passages or are simply associated with the

---

24. The targum appears not to interpret Isa 61 messianically, introducing the chapter with the words "the prophet said."

messiah. We can begin with more widespread themes before highlighting particular messianic phraseology that Luke shares with Jewish authors.

Jesus as Messiah Son of David

The Davidic ancestry of the messiah is stated more frequently and strongly in Luke than in any of the other Gospels. Indeed, by the albeit narrow margin of six to five, David is named more frequently than Joseph in Luke 1–2. In this birth narrative alone, David is Jesus's "father" (Luke 1:32), and Jesus comes from David's house (1:69), because Joseph belongs to the "house and line of David" in Luke 2:4. Jesus is born "in the town of David," Bethlehem.[25] God, furthermore, gives Jesus "the throne of his father David" (Luke 1:32). Jesus is therefore David's son (via Joseph who is from David's line), born in David's town, in David's house, to reign from David's throne.[26] The constant distinctions drawn in Luke 1–2 between Jesus and John, along with the emphasis on Jesus's royal status, probably mean that Jesus is not best characterized as a *prophetic* messiah in Luke.[27] The qualitative difference between Jesus and John is reinforced shortly after the infancy narrative, where the question of whether John is messiah is answered by the Baptist's distinction between himself, a mere water-baptizer, and the coming one who will bring the Holy Spirit and fire (Luke 3:15–16).[28]

The Son of David motif is also apparent in the exegesis of Ps 110 in Luke 20:

[41]Then Jesus said to them, "How can people say that the messiah is the Son of David? [42]For David himself declares in the book of Psalms:

'The Lord said to my Lord:
"Sit at my right hand
[43]until I make your enemies
a footstool for your feet."'

---

25. On the messianic associations of Bethlehem, see the discussion of Mic 5 in the previous chapter. John Nolland, *Luke* (Waco, TX: Word, 1989–1993), 1:98, and François Bovon, *Luke* (Minneapolis: Fortress, 2002–2012), 1:88, see an allusion to Mic 5 in Luke's references to Bethlehem as the city of David and the birthplace of Jesus, but Luke is not explicit on this.

26. Jens Schröter, *From Jesus to the New Testament: Early Christian Theology and the Origin of the New Testament Canon* (Waco, TX: Baylor University Press, 2013), 231: "The view of Jesus as the one with whom the Davidic promises are fulfilled is therefore a way of interpreting the χριστός designation that is central for Lukan Christology."

27. *Pace*, e.g., Luke Timothy Johnson, "The Christology of Luke-Acts," in *Contested Issues in Christian Origins and the New Testament* (Leiden: Brill, 2013), 145–61. The royal motif is also very prominent in the depiction of Jesus on the cross. See, e.g., Luke 23:2–3, 35–39, 42.

28. Although scholars sometimes understand Luke 12:49 in terms of Elijah, there is a difference between Elijah's request to God to send fire and Jesus himself casting fire on the earth.

> [44]"David calls him Lord, so how can he be David's son?"
> (Luke 20:41–44)

Although in one sense, the implied answer to this final question is "he cannot," there is in Luke—as in Matthew and Mark—another dimension. Especially in a Lukan context, there can be no question of the messiah's Davidic ancestry being denied. The paradox can be resolved in the person and career of Jesus.[29]

Jesus as Messiah Son of God

The infancy narrative and the account of Jesus's baptism combine Davidic kingship (in the reference to Ps 2) with divine paternity. In Luke 1:32, 35 Jesus's father is David, but he is also Son of the Most High (υἱὸς ὑψίστου) and Son of God (υἱὸς θεοῦ). In the baptism—like Mark but not Matthew—Luke has the heavenly declaration "You are my Son" (Luke 3:22; Ps 2:7).[30] Jesus's sonship is therefore defined in the scriptural terms of Ps 2 (cf. also Ps 89:26–27). The idea that the divine sonship of Jesus is communicated only by supernatural beings is continued in the temptation narrative (Luke 4:3, 9) and in the references to exorcisms (4:41; 8:28). However, in the trial narrative, the Sanhedrin ask Jesus whether he is the Son of God, and Jesus himself gives a coy acceptance (22:70).

Jesus as Messianic Savior

There is also the close identification of Jesus with salvation, especially in the infancy narrative. Jesus's role as savior receives considerable emphasis in the early chapters, though of course at this point, how this salvation will be accomplished remains undeveloped; indeed for the reader, there is a jarring move in first referring to Jesus as messiah and savior, and in the next breath as a baby (Luke 2:11–12). Zechariah's Benedictus announces that God has raised up a horn of *salvation* (1:69), which is first described as Israel's "salvation from our enemies" and subsequently as "salvation through the forgiveness of their sins" (1:71, 77).[31] (See further sec. 2.2 below.) The narrator refers to this as "the

---

29. Rightly, Michael Wolter, *The Gospel according to Luke* (Waco, TX: Baylor University Press, 2016–2017), 2:407.

30. Rusam, *Das Alte Testament*, 168: "Mit Sicherheit alludiert Lk 3,22 bzw. Mk 1,11 die Worte aus Ps 2,7." Cf. Acts 4:25–26; 13:33.

31. Gregory Lanier, *Old Testament Conceptual Metaphors and the Christology of Luke's Gospel* (London: Bloomsbury, 2018), 35–79, argues convincingly here that the horn metaphor shows Jesus to be a messiah figure not so much from the prior usage of horn imagery but through the Lukan context.

redemption of Jerusalem" (2:38). The salvation in view is therefore defined in strongly scriptural terms. In fact, Jesus is referred to not just as savior but also as the personification of salvation. In his Nunc Dimittis, Simeon states that he has actually seen God's salvation (2:30), probably echoing Isa 40:5, which is quoted in the following chapter.[32] Further references to Jesus's saving activity in the passion narrative will be discussed in section 2.4. This naturally taps into the widespread sense in early Jewish tradition that the messiah was a redeemer figure, as in Pss. Sol. 17–18, 4 Ezra 13, and the various messianic interpretations of Num 24 and Isa 11.

Messianic Idiom

There are also a number of stereotyped phrases that to varying degrees reinforce the connection between Luke's messianism and that of early Jewish tradition.

Christ of the Lord (Luke 2:26). The combination of messiah language with the title "lord" is also important in Luke and appears in two distinct ways. First, the record of Simeon's revelation is that he would not die before seeing "the Lord's messiah" or "the Lord's anointed," a phrase strongly redolent of how kings in the Old Testament are described.[33] The phrase itself appears in various places in the Old Testament, as well as in eschatological contexts in Targum Isaiah and perhaps the Psalms of Solomon.[34]

Christ the Lord (Luke 2:11). While the previous formula distinguishes between Christ and Lord, Luke can also identify the Christ as Lord (χριστὸς κύριος).[35] This is also a feature of Jewish messianic discourse, with the phrase "Lord messiah" appearing in rabbinic literature, and probably also already in the Psalms of Solomon.[36] It is significant that this "Lord messiah" desig-

---

32. Isa 40:5 LXX: καὶ ὀφθήσεται ἡ δόξα κυρίου καὶ ὄψεται πᾶσα σὰρξ τὸ σωτήριον τοῦ θεοῦ. See Luke 3:4–6, where Luke extends the quotation beyond where the other evangelists stop.

33. In addition to several passages in 1–2 Samuel, see also Lam 4:20.

34. Possibly Pss. Sol. 17.32, although this is dependent on an emendation; Tg. Isa. 4.2 and 28.5 ("the Lord's messiah"). These are messianic instances; "the Lord's anointed" is common in other contexts as well.

35. See Wolter, *Luke*, 1:127, for careful enumeration of the possible senses, concluding in favor of "the anointed [i.e., the Messiah], the Lord." See further Rowe, *Early Narrative Christology*, on this theme.

36. Again, Pss. Sol. 17.32 (though the text is usually emended); also Pss. Sol. 18.7. On the readings in the Psalms of Solomon, see Robert R. Hann, "Christos Kyrios in PsSol 17.32: 'The Lord's Anointed' Reconsidered," *NTS* 31 (1985): 620–27. In rabbinic literature, see, e.g.,

nation is applied to Jesus on the first occasion that the messiah title appears in Luke.[37]

God's messiah (Luke 9:20). In the Caesarea-Philippi episode, Peter here uses the designation "God's messiah," as the people do in the crucifixion narrative (23:35). This is not common in the New Testament (Luke is the only evangelist to include the phrase), but the Psalms of Solomon and the Qumran *Messianic Apocalypse* refer to God or the Lord and "his messiah."[38]

King messiah (Luke 23:2). Luke also employs the collocation of "Christ" and "king" (χριστὸς βασιλεύς): "king messiah" or "anointed king" or "messiah, a king."[39] This is redolent of the common targumic and rabbinic formula "king messiah."[40]

The chosen one (Luke 9:35; 23:35). Additionally, Luke refers to Jesus as God's son "the chosen one" (ὁ ἐκλελεγμένος) in chapter 9 and as God's messiah "the chosen one" (ὁ ἐκλεκτός) in chapter 23; this is a messianic epithet also in 1 En. 49–62.[41]

The messiah's/Son of Man's "day(s)." Luke's distinctive phrase "the days of the Son of Man" (Luke 17:22, 26) may also be compared to the idiom "the days of the messiah" common in rabbinic literature beginning with the Mishnah.[42] Some texts of Luke also have the Son of Man's singular "day" (17:24): compare the messianic son's "day" in 4 Ezra 13.52.[43] How closely Luke's usage here is to be connected with the rabbinic language is not clear, however.[44]

Messianic Idiom: Conclusion. Luke does not simply trot out such messianic idioms from his Markan source; some of his phrasing is unique to him among

---

Midrash Psalms 2.3, on Ps 2:2 (Braude 1:37). Cf. Rom 16:18; Col 3:24. The two of course occur frequently elsewhere in the New Testament but usually with the name "Jesus" intervening.

37. Rowe, *Early Narrative Christology*, 54.

38. Pss. Sol. 18.5; 4Q521 2 and 4 II, 1.

39. Nolland, *Luke*, 3:1118 ("Christ, a king"); Bovon, *Luke*, 3:254 ("Christ king"); Wolter, *Luke*, 2:503 ("anointed king").

40. See, e.g., Tg. 1 Chr. 3.24; Tg. Neof. Gen. 49.10–12; Gen. Rab. 44.8, on Gen 15:2 (Freedman, 1:365–66); Num. Rab. 13.14, on Num 7:13 (Slotki, 2:528).

41. The messiah-like figure in *Apoc. Ab.* 31.1 is "the elect one."

42. Rabbinic references include m. Ber. 1.5; y. Meg. 2.1 (73a); b. Ber. 34b; b. Šabb. 63a, 113b; b. Sukkah 2b; b. Yebam. 24b; b. Sanh. 91b, 97a–b, 99a; Gen. Rab. 44.23 (Freedman, 378). There are numerous references to "the days of the messiah" in Sifre Deuteronomy (e.g., 318.5, 6; 322.3).

43. On the text-critical question, see Wolter, *Luke*, 2:307–8.

44. Caution is needed given that the "days of x" formula is widely applied. See Wolter, *Luke*, 2:306.

the evangelists. Only Luke has the traditional collocation "the Christ of God" or "God's messiah" (Luke 9:20; 23:35). Similarly, Luke alone has the "Lord's messiah [*or* anointed]" (2:26; cf. Rev 11:15) and the combination of the two titles, "the Lord messiah" (2:11). Also distinctive is the juxtaposition of "Christ" and "king" in Luke 23:2.[45]

1.4 Interim Conclusion: Luke's Messiah and the Kerygma

We can summarize Jesus's messianic identity in Luke. The evangelist's interpretation of Jesus's life, death, and resurrection has clearly shaped his understanding of what it means to be messiah. It is these particular specifics of the career of Jesus that are labeled as messianic that lead some to the *interpretatio Christiana* view. Tuckett comments: "It is Jesus who determines what messiahship means; it is not messiahship that determines Jesus."[46] Indeed, he goes further in stating that "Luke's Jesus seems to be at most a Christ figure in name only."[47] In two important respects beyond the mere usage of the term, however, Luke's Christology is recognizably Jewish messianism.

First (sec. 1.3), there is continuity in the usage of messianic themes and language that are already familiar from Jewish literature, such as Davidic sonship, which is a particular focus for Luke. No less important is divine sonship. Luke therefore taps into two known messianic paternity tropes. Additionally, Luke uses traditional messianic epithets such as "the chosen one" (Luke 9:35; 23:35), "the Christ of God" or "God's messiah" (9:20; 23:35), and both "messiah, the Lord" (2:11) and "the Lord's messiah" (2:26), as well as "king messiah" or "anointed king" (23:2).

Second (sec. 1.2), there is continuity with existing scriptural usage in messianic contexts. Luke's birth narrative makes use of Ps 89, understood in the same way in Pss. Sol. 17 and common in the messianism of the Talmud and midrashim. The baptism alludes to Ps 2, which already featured in early Jewish messianic exegesis.[48] Jesus's ministry is characterized by the miraculous activity of Isa 61, also used of the eschatological anointed figure in 11Q13 and probably 4Q521. The death and resurrection of Jesus in Luke (as in Mark and

---

45. The closest parallel is "the messiah, the king of Israel" in Mark 15:32.

46. Tuckett, "Christology of Luke-Acts," 164.

47. Tuckett, "Christology of Luke-Acts," 163. Byrne, "Jesus as Messiah in Luke," 95, endorses the former, though not the latter.

48. See the discussion in the chapter on Mark's Gospel above (sec. 1.2).

Matthew) is elucidated through Isa 53, as well as Dan 7's son of man, a phrase used of the messiah in the *Parables of Enoch*, with the wider passage important in characterizations of the messiah in 4 Ezra, 2 Baruch, the targumim, the Talmud, and the midrashim. Luke therefore illuminates all the key parts of his narrative through the use of passages traditionally seen as messianic.

In sum, there is ample evidence that Luke portrays Jesus in ways that root him in traditional messianic exegesis and in other features of the linguistic world of the messiah. Luke's Gospel therefore not only shares with the kerygma an identification of Jesus as the messiah but also depicts him in ways that would make that identification a recognizable part of Jewish messianic discourse.

2. The Vicarious Death of Jesus in Luke

Luke notoriously is often thought to neglect or deliberately downplay a prior early Christian understanding of the saving significance of Jesus's death.[49] One recent treatment summarizes the evidence adduced for this as follows:

> (1) emphasis on the ignorance and sinfulness of those who crucified Jesus, (2) omission of Mark 10:45, (3) avoidance of vicarious suffering passages in quotations from Isa 53, (4) shorter form of the Lord's Supper text (if taken to be authentic), (5) movement of the rending of the temple veil prior to Jesus' death, (6) lack of an explicit statement connecting the death of Christ to the forgiveness of sins, and (7) emphasis on the saving significance of the resurrection.[50]

Such a barrage of evidence might seem to be compelling. Certain strands of scholarship, however, have taken a quite different view (as we saw above in the discussion of Acts), with two recent monographs in particular contending

---

49. For scholars skeptical of a saving death of Jesus in Luke, see the bibliographies of the various essays in Dennis D. Sylva, ed., *Reimaging the Death of the Lukan Jesus* (Frankfurt am Main: Hain, 1990), especially John T. Carroll, "Luke's Crucifixion Scene," 194 n. 1; Earl Richard, "Jesus' Passion and Death in Acts," 204 n. 3, and Dennis D. Sylva, "Death and Life at the Center of the World," 211 n. 1.

50. John Kimbell, *The Atonement in Lukan Theology* (Newcastle: Cambridge Scholars, 2014), 7 n. 15. For a similar account, see Hermie C. van Zyl, "The Soteriological Meaning of Jesus' Death in Luke-Acts: A Survey of Possibilities," *Verbum et Ecclesia* 23 (2002): 533–36.

strongly for a saving death in Luke's Gospel.[51] The question of the meaning of Jesus's death in Luke does force itself upon the reader because Luke perhaps more than the other evangelists thematizes the inevitability of the crucifixion.[52] Beyond what is said in Mark and Matthew, Luke adds reference to the necessity of the cross in his special material,[53] as well as the distinctive statement that Jesus's death was "in accord with what is ordained" (κατὰ τὸ ὡρισμένον [Luke 22:22; cf. Acts 2:23]). In addition to its inevitability, however, there are also indications in Luke that it has soteriological significance.

2.1 Jesus's Death as Terminus (Luke 13:31–33), Exodus (9:31), and Baptism (12:49–50)

We will first deal with three places prior to the passion narrative that assign theological significance to the cross, in ascending order of their significance.

In the last of these, in Luke 13, the surprising intervention of the Pharisees elicits an interpretation of Jesus's destiny:

> [31]At that time some Pharisees approached Jesus and said to him, "Get away from here, because Herod wants to kill you." [32]He replied, "Go and tell that fox, 'I am going to cast out demons and bring healing today and tomorrow, and on the third day I will be finished.' [33]In any case, I must press on today and tomorrow and the next day, for it is impossible for a prophet to die outside Jerusalem!" (Luke 13:31–33)

Jesus states in verse 32 that after his exorcisms and healings, he will be "finished" (τελειοῦμαι). The verb "be finished" here includes Jesus's death (explicit in verse 33's ἀπολέσθαι) but does not focus on it, highlighting rather Jesus's completion of his work.[54] It is noteworthy that Luke can regard Jesus's work

---

51. Kimbell, *Atonement in Lukan Theology*, and Benjamin Wilson, *The Saving Cross of the Suffering Christ: The Death of Jesus in Lukan Soteriology* (Berlin: de Gruyter, 2016); cf. the heavily maximalist articles by Francis G. Carpinelli, "Do This as My Memorial" (Luke 22:19): Lucan Soteriology of Atonement," *CBQ* 61 (1999): 74–91, and van Zyl, "Soteriological Meaning."

52. So Richard Zehnle, "The Salvific Character of Jesus' Death in Lucan Soteriology," *Theological Studies* 30 (1969): 427.

53. Luke 17:25; 22:37; 24:7, 26, 44.

54. The passive of τελειόω does not normally seem to mean "to die." Franco Montanari, ed., *The Brill Dictionary of Ancient Greek* (Leiden: Brill, 2015), s.v. "τελειόω" (2095a), has no gloss of anything like "die" for middle or passive uses; the same is true of James Diggle et al., eds., *The Cambridge Greek Lexicon* (Cambridge: Cambridge University Press, 2021), 1366.

as in some sense complete at his death (cf. John's τετέλεσται), before the resurrection and ascension.

In this connection, Jesus's exodus should also be noted:

> [30]Just then, two men—Moses and Elijah—appeared in glorious splendor, talking with Jesus. [31]They spoke about his departure (τὴν ἔξοδον αὐτοῦ), which he was about to fulfill (πληροῦν) in Jerusalem. (Luke 9:30–31)

While the Greek word ἔξοδος is not a rare one, it may well also have a theological, indeed soteriological, significance, especially given the reference to it being fulfilled.[55] Luke's use of the term probably conjures up the event of the Israelite exodus (and possibly also the book of Exodus).[56] For Luke, the exodus here may refer specifically to the death of Jesus, or it may be the larger complex of the Easter events. As we will see further in the exploration of the eucharistic words, Luke refers to the Passover in his discussion of Jesus's death, but here in Luke 9 Jesus's death could already be presented as an event suggestive (but only suggestive) of soteriological significance.

Another relatively neglected passage in Luke's understanding of the death of Jesus also refers to Jesus's activity coming to completion:

> [49]"I have come to cast fire on the earth, and how I wish it were already kindled! [50]I have a baptism to undergo, and how bound I am until it is completed (τελεσθῇ)!" (Luke 12:49–50)

LSJ, s.v. "τελειόω," II.4, gives the gloss "die," but the evidence is a Christian funerary inscription dated by the editors to "AD 490?" and could in any case mean "she was perfected"; cf. "the spirits of the righteous made perfect" in Heb 12:23; also 11:40. Similarly, Lampe provides a number of examples of the passive of τελειόω in the sense of "die," but the examples concern the perfecting death of Christians, especially martyrs (*PGL*, s.v. "τελειόω"). Wolter, *Luke*, 2:202, notes Wis 4:13 as a parallel: this could have the sense of perfecting, though might be a poetic reference simply to death.

55. The word is therefore not here merely a euphemism for "death," *pace* Bovon, *Luke*, 1:376. The reference to Jesus's ἔξοδος here can be paired with his εἴσοδος in Acts 13:24.

56. So John T. Carroll, *Luke: A Commentary* (Louisville: Westminster John Knox, 2012), 217, also noting other scholars. For the use of the term to describe the event, see, e.g., Exod 19:1; Num 33:38; 1 Kgs 6:1; Ps 114:1 (113:1 LXX), with the phrase ἡ ἔξοδος υἱῶν Ισραηλ ἐξ Αἰγύπτου appearing repeatedly in the Septuagint. The time of origin as a book title is unclear. Although the manuscript evidence is inconsistent, Philo probably has the title as Ἐξαγωγή in all cases (as Ezekiel Tragicus's poem is similarly called). The earliest extant uses of the Ἔξοδος title are in Justin, *Dial.* 59.1–2; 75.1; 126.2; Melito, *Pasch.* 1, and Melito frag. 3 in Eusebius, *Hist. eccl.* 4.26.13–14.

Jesus probably refers in verse 49 to his bringing the fire of God's wrath with him.[57] The passage continues with a quotation of Mic 7:6, where divisions among families are some of the woes that Jesus's coming brings.[58] Verse 50 refers to Jesus's death, and the link between the two verses may well indicate that Jesus himself will be immersed in the wrath of verse 49. The two sayings are closely connected: Jesus longs for his suffering to come to an end, the suffering that will take place "when darkness reigns" (Luke 22:53). The baptism language refers to his downward movement into death.[59] Though the saying is a difficult one, it is plausible that here in Luke 12 Jesus speaks of his immersion in divine judgment, although no soteriological implications are drawn from this.

Overall, then, while Luke does not have a version of Mark 10:45, he nevertheless assigns theological significance to Jesus's death as (1) the terminus of his ministry in Luke 13:32, (2) possibly an exodus suggestive of saving activity in Luke 9:31, and (3) a baptism according to Luke 12:49–50 whereby he perhaps shares in the divine wrath he has brought.[60]

2.2 The Eucharistic Words (Luke 22:17–20)

The clearest piece of evidence for Luke's interest in the saving effects of Jesus's death appears in his eucharistic discourse.[61] Luke begins with Jesus

57. See the discussion in Simon Gathercole, *The Preexistent Son: Recovering the Christologies of Matthew, Mark, and Luke* (Grand Rapids: Eerdmans, 2006), 161–63. While Wolter, *Luke*, 2:168–69, recognizes the problems with the various interpretations, his proposal that the fire is the Holy Spirit is unlikely, because of the sense of anguish in verses 49–50.

58. In connection with Ps 89, the Mishnah cites the same verse from Micah to illustrate the events foreshadowing the messiah's coming (m. Soṭah 9.15). Song Rab. 2.13 §4, on Song 2:13 (Simon, 127), also quotes Ps 89 and Mic 7:6 together in a messianic context.

59. *Pace* the tentative suggestion, in Wolter, *Luke*, 2:169, and Wilson, *Saving Cross*, 47, that resurrection might be included in Luke 12:50: first, normal Greek usage generally covers only being plunged into water; second, Paul's discussions in Romans and Colossians associate baptism with death and burial (Rom 6:3–4; Col 2:12); third, Matthew distinguishes between baptism and the subsequent coming up out of the water (Matt 3:16).

60. Cf. perhaps Luke 23:44–45a where the darkness covering the earth, in which Jesus is also included, may symbolize wrath.

61. Some remarks on the text of Luke 22:17–20 are in order here. It is probably true to say now that the longer reading is favored by the majority of textual critics. The data and the principal arguments for the longer version are summed up in Bruce M. Metzger, *A Textual Commentary on the Greek New Testament*, 2nd ed. (Stuttgart: Deutsche Bibelgesellschaft, 1994), 148–50: (1) There is the "overwhelming preponderance of external evidence supporting the longer form," including some Western evidence; only part of the Western tradition

stating his desire to eat the Passover and his offer of the cup (22:15, 17), after each of which comes a statement of his abstinence from eating the Passover and drinking wine until their fulfillment in the coming kingdom (22:16, 18). Then comes Luke's version of the eucharistic words known in Matthew, Mark, and Paul:

Mark 14:22–24	**Matt 26:26–28**	**Luke 22:19–20**
While they were eating,	While they were eating,	
Jesus took bread,	Jesus took bread,	And he took bread,
gave thanks	gave thanks	gave thanks
and broke it,	and broke it,	and broke it,
and gave it	and gave it	and gave it
to his disciples, saying,	to his disciples, saying,	to them, saying,
"Take it;	"Take and eat;	
this is my body."	this is my body."	"This is my body given for you; do this in remembrance of me."
Then he took the cup,	Then he took a cup, and gave	
gave thanks, and offered it	thanks, and offered it	In the same way, after sup-
to them,	to them, saying,	per he took the cup,
and they all drank from it.	"Drink from it, all of you.	saying,
"This is my blood of the	This is my blood of the	"This cup is the new cov-
covenant,	covenant,	enant in my blood,
which is poured out for	which is poured out for many	which is poured out for
many."	for the forgiveness of sins."	you."

---

supports the shorter reading; the shorter reading is represented by only a single *Greek* manuscript; (2) the shorter reading is easier to explain as a smoothing out of the text by removing the second reference to the cup, whereas seeing the longer reading as secondary requires that the scribe brings in a second mention of the cup from Paul but leaves the first untouched; (3) the shorter reading essentially represents a misunderstanding of the first reference to the cup, which belongs as part of 22:15–18, rather than 22:17–20 being the primary unit; verses 19–20 belong more closely together (verse 19, ὡσαύτως verse 20); a misunderstanding is more likely than the attempt to preserve secrecy about the institution. Additionally, (4) it is attested in Marcion (see Dieter T. Roth, *The Text of Marcion's Gospel* [Leiden: Brill, 2015], 433) and in Justin Martyr, whose version resembles Luke's more than it does the other forms (*1 Apol.* 66.3). The discussion in Joachim Jeremias, *The Eucharistic Words of Jesus* (Oxford: Basil Blackwell, 1955), 87–106, is still valuable, and see also the extensive bibliography on the question in Nolland, *Luke*, 3:1040, and for more recent bibliography, Bradley S. Billings, *Do This in Remembrance of Me: The Disputed Words in the Lukan Institution Narrative (Luke 22.19b–20); An Historico-Exegetical, Theological and Sociological Analysis* (London: Bloomsbury, 2006).

There are three elements in the Lukan version that are illuminating for Luke's understanding of the death of Jesus. These will be treated in turn, after which there will be a response to three objections.

First, Luke has Jesus inaugurating a "new covenant in my blood."[62] We have seen in the previous two chapters above on Mark and Matthew that the connection between covenant and blood probably evokes the covenant inauguration ritual in Exod 24. Here in Luke, the language of the "*new* covenant" also recalls Jeremiah's prophecy, the only place in the Old Testament where the phrase appears. As Wilson has observed, "Jesus declares the institution of this eschatological covenant in his blood, drawing together the promise of a reconstituted people of God with the imagery of the cultic blood ritual that instituted the covenant at Sinai."[63] Luke thus echoes both Exod 24 and Jer 31, and the latter allusion may carry with it the promise of forgiveness of sins (Jer 31:34).[64] The scope of the Lukan Jesus's claim is noteworthy here. Du Plessis has remarked that "it seems as if Luke purposely limits Jesus's death to its covenantal effect."[65] This is a surprising statement, because—if anything—the statement that Jesus's death brings about a new covenant is a very sweeping one: a biblical covenant is hardly a narrowly defined entity but rather a whole framework within which divine-human relations are navigated.

There is therefore a considerable soteriological component to Jesus's death included here. This is especially the case since Luke, unlike Mark or Matthew, describes Jesus's death as bringing a *new* covenant and therefore a (re)new(ed) state of affairs in the relations between God and his people.[66] Luke may not tie the death of Jesus explicitly to the forgiveness of sins, as Matthew does. However, Jesus's death does inaugurate a covenant, and traditionally the covenant is the whole framework within which salvation (including forgiveness) takes place. In Acts, the covenant includes the promise that all nations would be blessed through Abraham (Acts 3:25; cf. 7:8). Luke's Gospel, as is

---

62. There is some strong textual evidence for the reading "new" (καινή) in Mark 14:24 and Matt 26:28 as well, but in Luke it is clear.

63. Wilson, *Saving Cross*, 83.

64. Wolter, *Luke*, 2:463, is probably unduly cautious in not connecting Luke's phraseology with Jer 31. Luke's redaction, of Mark's (and perhaps Matthew's) "covenant" *tout simple*, is presumably purposeful here.

65. Isak J. Du Plessis, "The Saving Significance of Jesus and His Death on the Cross in Luke's Gospel," *Neot* 28 (1994): 535.

66. Carroll, *Luke*, 435, understands "new" in the sense of "renewed," which is partly correct, although Jer 31:31–34 itself focuses just as much on discontinuity.

clear from the Benedictus, understands God remembering the covenant in the first instance as his deliverance of his people from their enemies so they can worship him:

> [68]"Blessed be the Lord, the God of Israel,
>   because he has visited his people and brought redemption
>   to them.
>   [69]He has raised up a horn of salvation for us
>   in the house of his servant David
>   [70]just as he said through the mouths of his holy prophets
>   of old—
>   [71]salvation from our enemies
>   and from the hand of all who hate us,
>   [72]to show mercy to our ancestors
>   and to remember his holy covenant,
>   [73]the oath he swore to our father Abraham:
>   [74]to rescue us from the hand of our enemies,
>   and to enable us to serve him without fear
>   [75]in holiness and righteousness before him all our days."
>   (Luke 1:68–75)

The "horn of salvation" thus far, then, rescues Israel from her adversaries, and that is how it fulfills God's covenant promises. Latterly, however, after introducing this covenantal "salvation" (1:69, 71, 72) in these terms, Luke in the second half of the hymn then reframes it:

> [76]"And you, my child, will be called a prophet of the Most High;
>   for you will go ahead before the Lord to prepare his ways,
>   [77]to give knowledge of salvation to his people
>   through the forgiveness of their sins." (Luke 1:76–77)

Therefore, here salvation is recast from rescue from enemies into "salvation in the forgiveness of their [sc. the people's] sins," which will also be brought about by Jesus (1:77).[67] Luke, therefore, probably understands the new covenant in-

---

67. Carroll, *Luke*, 59, comments on the first half: "Luke will have more to say about this matter, beginning with the singer's own later reframing of sōtēria (salvation) as forgiveness (v. 77)."

augurated in Jesus's death as including forgiveness, which is an entirely natural component of a biblical covenant (cf., e.g., Isa 59:20–21; Jer 31:31–34).

Second, Luke makes it explicit that it is not just the blood that is poured out "for" others (as in Mark and Matthew) but that his body is "given for" the disciples as well.[68] The "for you" (ὑπὲρ ὑμῶν) is therefore repeated in Luke 22:19–20, by comparison with Mark and Matthew—and 1 Cor 11.[69] The benefit to the disciples from Jesus's death is thus emphasized.

Third, Luke understands Jesus's death in terms of the Passover. The Lukan Jesus emphasizes, more than Mark and Matthew, that this meal with the disciples is unambiguously a Passover meal. The Passover approached (Luke 22:1); the day of the slaughter of the Passover lambs came (22:7); Jesus told the disciples to prepare the Passover meal (22:8); the disciples made the preparations for the Passover (22:13); when the hour came, Jesus stated: "I have eagerly desired to eat this Passover with you before I suffer" (22:15). For Luke, therefore, Jesus inaugurated the commemoration ("do this in remembrance of me") of a new or eschatological Passover. Against that background, the blood may represent the protection of God's people from judgment. More clearly, the mention of both bread and blood signifies that Jesus sums up in himself the whole apparatus of Passover, which is of course a strongly soteriological motif: perhaps both the Israelites' protection from judgment and their deliverance from bondage are being figuratively applied to Jesus here, though it is difficult to be certain. However, in addition to the emphasis Luke places on the meal being a Passover, the reference to Jesus's death as an exodus (ἔξοδος) back in Luke 9 may anticipate and emphasize this understanding of Jesus's death as a Passover event (cf. 1 Cor 5:7).

Finally, we can take the recent monograph of Jantsch as a representative of an opposing view and attempt to respond to some of his objections.

(1) Jantsch emphasizes that the language of the eucharistic words is not Luke's own and therefore concludes that it does not reflect Luke's theology.[70]

---

68. Wolter *Luke*, 2:460: "It therefore deserves attention that Luke (and only Luke!) uses the verb διδόναι twice here and in this way relates the 'giving' of the bread to the disciples (αὐτοῖς) and the 'giving' of the body 'for' the disciples. The body that is represented by the bread 'given' to the disciples is for this reason always only the 'given-for-you (sc. the disciples)' body."

69. Martin Hengel and Anna Maria Schwemer, *Jesus und das Judentum* (Tübingen: Mohr Siebeck, 2007), 232–33.

70. Torsten Jantsch, *Jesus, der Retter: Die Soteriologie des lukanischen Doppelwerks* (Tübingen: Mohr Siebeck, 2017), 113: "Das bedeutet nun, dass Lukas, wenn er selbständig formuliert, die Hingabe- und Sterbenformulierungen ausdrücklich nicht auf Jesus bezieht. Das

This view that only redactional material (rather than sources) reflects an author's theology is methodologically indefensible, however. Where Luke incorporates his sources entirely or almost unchanged, it is presumably because he agrees with them and values them highly.[71] In any case, it is notable that—as was seen in chapter 3 (sec. 1.2) above—Luke's formulation of the eucharistic words agrees to a striking extent with that of Paul in 1 Cor 11.[72] This probably means that Luke is giving from memory the version of the eucharistic words with which he was familiar from a liturgical context.[73] If that is the case, then it is the wording that he has known over some length of time and has absorbed. Far from being merely absentminded regurgitation, then, where Luke diverges from Mark's wording here, he is using the language in which he has been immersed in his religious practice. He would then have had ample time to reflect deeply on these words. (It is perhaps a peculiarly modern Protestant idea that ritual liturgical language is not really assimilated by the participant.) Additionally, Luke's careful framing of the Last Supper as a Passover meal makes it unlikely that he is indifferent to a large chunk of what Jesus says there. Finally, we do not know for certain that Luke leaves his liturgical tradition unchanged, because the end of verse 20 has "poured out for you," which corresponds neither to Mark nor to the parallel in 1 Corinthians.[74] The conclusion, then, that Luke 22:19–20 constitutes a "Fremdkörper" is therefore untenable.[75]

(2) The fact that Luke 22:19–20 is a one-off explanation of the soteriological significance of Jesus's death is no reason to relativize it.[76] One clear state-

---

bedeutet im Umkehrschluss für den einzigen Beleg, an dem eine solche Formulierung auf Jesus bezogen ist, dass wir hier keine lukanische Theologie finden, sondern dass Lukas hier traditionelles Gut aufgenommen hat, das er aber sonst in keiner Weise positiv aufnimmt oder auswertet. Lukas selbst deutet den Tod Jesu nicht als ein Geschehen, das für ein personales Objekt geschieht." Cf. Joel B. Green, "The Death of Jesus, God's Servant," in Sylva, *Reimaging the Death of the Lukan Jesus*, 4, refers to "the more or less mechanical copying of the ancient eucharistic liturgy by Luke. That is, Luke has neither exploited the redemptive themes of the Last Supper nor made this material his own by integrating it more fully into his narrative."

71. For criticism of this kind of redaction-critical approach, see Graham N. Stanton, *The Gospels and Jesus*, 2nd ed. (Oxford: Oxford University Press, 2002), 29–30, and Simon Gathercole, *Defending Substitution: An Essay on Atonement in Paul* (Grand Rapids: Baker, 2015), 51–52.

72. As well as the synopsis in chapter 3 (sec. 1.2), see also those in Wolter, *Luke*, 2:458, and Wilson, *Saving Cross*, 92.

73. So, e.g., Bovon, *Luke*, 3:158.

74. See the discussion of the details of the different versions in Wilson, *Saving Cross*, 91–93.

75. Jantsch, *Jesus, der Retter*, 111, uses this term.

76. Pace Jantsch, *Jesus, der Retter*, 112–13.

ment ought to be sufficient. In any case, we have already seen in section 2.1 two or three passages that do assign theological significance to Jesus's death. Additionally, Luke, like the other Synoptic evangelists, locates this particular explanation of Jesus's death in a strategic location, just before that death takes place. Jantsch remarks that it is noticeable how much less frequently Luke uses the soteriological "for" language than Paul does.[77] But is this really "ein auffälliger Befund," "a striking discovery"? Fitzmyer's words are appropriate here:

> Luke also offers an interpretation of the Christ-event, but it seems unfair to compare Luke and Paul and to expect, as is often done, that Luke should put things the way Paul does. He [sc. Luke] has not proposed his interpretation of the ministry, passion, death and resurrection of Jesus in essay-like letters. . . . Luke has rather chosen the narrative form for his proclamation of the Christ-event.[78]

With the difference in genre, one has to take other factors into account, such as narrative placement. The narrative location of the eucharistic words just before Jesus's death gives them a certain importance. In addition, there is the physical location: the last supper in Luke is "the climactic meal scene within a gospel that uniquely locates much of Jesus's ministry and teaching at the table."[79] On one count, it is the seventh meal in the Gospel.[80]

(3) Jantsch concludes that Luke 22:19–20 and Acts 20:28 cannot bear the weight of the argument that the center and the starting point of Luke's soteriology are the death of Jesus.[81] This is clearly true, though I am not sure how many scholars have affirmed the position that is being opposed here. Certainly, the present study seeks to do justice to the fact that Jesus's resurrection is also extremely important as good news, and a study of Acts would yield additional key soteriological themes.

In conclusion, the eucharistic words here make it abundantly clear that the death of Jesus has saving significance. The cross is not a "mediate" part of the

---

77. Jantsch, *Jesus, der Retter*, 112: "Es ist ein auffälliger Befund, dass Lukas zwar auch solche Formulierungen verwendet, aber sehr viel seltener als dies bei Paulus der Fall ist."

78. Joseph A. Fitzmyer, *Luke the Theologian: Aspects of His Teaching* (New York: Paulist, 1989), 211–12.

79. Wilson, *Saving Cross*, 93.

80. See the discussion of Gen 3 in sec. 4.2 below.

81. Jantsch, *Jesus, der Retter*, 125: "Die beiden immer zum Thema der Deutung des Todes Jesu im lukanischen Doppelwerk herangezogenen Stellen (Lk 22,19f.; Apg 20,28) können also den Beweis nicht tragen, dass der Tod Jesu für Lukas das Zentrum und der Ausgangspunkt seiner Soteriologie sind."

plan of salvation in the sense that it is prefatory to the more important saving events. Rather, it has "intrinsic soteriological value" even if it is not the only saving event in Luke.[82]

2.3 The Role of Isaiah 53 in the Passion Narrative

Shortly after the last supper, Jesus quotes Isa 53:12 with a very clear indication of its scriptural status and imminent fulfillment:[83]

"For I say to you that what is written must find its completion in me: '*And he was numbered with the transgressors.*' And indeed this matter about me is coming to its completion." (Luke 22:37)

This statement has already been touched on in section 1.2 and will be noted further in section 4.1. The first point to note is that it is highly probable that the ultimate fulfillment of Isaiah's oracle is Jesus's death between two criminals.[84] The language of completion (both τελεσθῆναι and τέλος ἔχει) is highly emphatic, recalling the metaphorical baptism whose completion (τελεσθῇ) Jesus anticipates (Luke 12:50) and his own "completion" (τελειοῦμαι), which is paralleled by a reference to his death (13:32–33).[85] Jesus's execution between the criminals (23:33) is both a more salient fulfillment than his arrest in Luke 22:52, and also a more clear one, with Jesus on the cross really being counted "with" (μετά) transgressors, not just as one.

Second, the placement of the quotation is significant. Jesus quotes Isa 53 on the eve of his death, and so—like the eucharistic words—this citation directs us to understand Jesus's death in the light of the servant of that chapter.[86]

It is highly probable, therefore, that Luke understands Isa 53 as a background to Jesus's death. Whether he thinks of Jesus's death in terms of the

---

82. Zehnle, "Salvific Character," 420–44, makes this distinction. Similarly, Carroll, "Luke's Crucifixion Scene," 124, noting that the death of Jesus is "not merely the necessary prelude to resurrection and glory."

83. C. K. Barrett, "Luke/Acts," in *It Is Written: Scripture Citing Scripture; Essays in Honour of Barnabas Lindars, SSF*, ed. D. A. Carson and H. G. M. Williamson (Cambridge: Cambridge University Press, 1988), 236: "the citation formula is unique and calls for special consideration."

84. There may be an initial fulfillment also in Luke 22:52.

85. Barrett, "Luke/Acts," 236–37: "The verb τελέω occurs not at all in Mark, several times in Matthew, but never in relation to Scripture."

86. R. T. France, *Jesus and the Old Testament* (London: Tyndale, 1971), 115. France is dealing with the historical Jesus, whereas the present argument is dealing with the Lukan Jesus, but mutatis mutandis his point still applies. More specifically in connection with Luke, the same point is made in Green, "Death of Jesus," 23.

substitutionary place-taking of the servant in Isa 53 is less clear. There is no problem with the idea, as in his eucharistic words Jesus describes his death in terms similar to the death of the servant in Isaiah. On the other hand, however, there are no obvious linguistic cues that indicate that Luke is picking up this aspect of the servant.[87] It may be that this is an overly atomistic approach to Isa 53, but the burden of proof especially in current scholarship rests heavily upon anyone arguing for the specifically soteriological features of Isa 53 having an impact on Luke.[88]

2.4 Interpretative Motifs in the Passion Narrative (Luke 22–23)

Luke has a similar set of circumstances accompanying the death of Jesus as do Matthew and Mark, with the important exception that there is no cry of dereliction. The cup, the Barabbas exchange, the darkness, and the rending of the veil are drawn into Luke's account from Mark, although he does not always follow Mark's order. In some cases, there are particular Lukan nuances that must be noted, and there is also special Lukan material. Given that these are features of the narrative, rather than dogmatic statements, conclusions about their significance must be drawn tentatively.

The Cup (Luke 22:42)

On its own, without further description, the cup—as in Matthew and Mark—is ambiguous. Some gloss it too confidently as the "cup of wrath."[89] Wilson rightly cautions against overreading the motif, although Wolter is undoubtedly correct that at the very least, the cup functions in this particular context as a metaphor for a tragic destiny assigned by God.[90]

---

87. For example, ὑπέρ in the eucharistic words is, perhaps surprisingly, not found in Isa 53.

88. E.g., U. Mittmann-Richert, *Der Sühnetod des Gottesknechts: Jesaja 53 im Lukasevangelium* (Tübingen: Mohr Siebeck, 2008).

89. *Pace* David P. Moessner, "Suffering, Intercession and Eschatological Atonement: An Uncommon View in the Testament of Moses and in Luke-Acts," in *The Pseudepigrapha and Early Biblical Interpretation*, ed. James H. Charlesworth and Craig A. Evans (Sheffield: Sheffield Academic, 1993), 217, and Darrell Bock, *Luke* (Leicester: Inter-Varsity, 1994), 356, who gloss it too confidently as the "cup of wrath."

90. Wilson, *Saving Cross*, 102–3; Michael Wolter, *Lukasevangelium* (Tübingen: Mohr Siebeck, 2008), 722 ("das von Gott zugeteilte Unheilsgeschick"). Bovon, *Luke*, 3:200–201, sees suffering, death, and martyrdom; Carroll, *Luke*, 445, combines destiny and judgment.

The Barabbas Exchange (Luke 23:13–25)

One of the most important reworkings of Markan material is the Barabbas exchange. An astute study of Luke's version of this pericope by Cuany argues that what other scholars have taken to be a clunky account is actually a carefully constructed piece.[91] In particular, Luke has no reference to a Passover amnesty but does have a clear declaration by Pilate of Jesus's innocence—both points at which Luke differs from the other Synoptics. As a result, the release of Jesus is not a matter of special custom but of law, and therefore the release of Barabbas "is causally linked to the verdict of innocence pronounced upon Jesus.... Pilate's *decision* to release Jesus is based on a verdict: Jesus is innocent and there is no reason to put him to death. At this point, the crowds bring up the name of Barabbas."[92] In consequence, for Luke, of all of the Synoptic evangelists, Jesus is most clearly an "exchange" or "substitute" for Barabbas.[93] Moreover, in a final stage in the argument, Barabbas might also be a representative of the people of Jerusalem: he is their Barabbas ("release Barabbas *to us*" [23:18]); therefore in siding with a murderer and wanting to kill the innocent Jesus, they are just like the Barabbas who had been "in prison for sedition and murder" (Luke 23:25). As Cuany concludes, "the third evangelist has crafted his climactic account to depict the very *cause* of Jesus's death to be a substitution with his people's seditious and murderous representative."[94]

The Plea for Forgiveness (Luke 23:34a)

Unique to Luke is Jesus's prayer to God: "Father, forgive them, for they do not know what they are doing" (Luke 23:34a; cf. Acts 7:60).[95] Wilson suggests tentatively that this could be an illustration of the "remembering sins no more"

---

91. Monique Cuany, "Jesus, Barabbas and the People: The Climax of Luke's Trial Narrative and Lukan Christology (Luke 23.13–25)," *JSNT* 39 (2017): 442.

92. Cuany, "Jesus, Barabbas and the People," 447; see also Wilson, *Saving Cross*, 113.

93. Cuany, "Jesus, Barabbas and the People," 449, 454.

94. Cuany, "Jesus, Barabbas and the People," 455; similarly Wilson, *Saving Cross*, 113.

95. When one takes account of both manuscripts and patristic citations, the external evidence is perhaps fairly evenly divided for the question of whether Luke 23:34a is original. In favor of retaining the logion is that it is probably easier to see how a plea for forgiving those who crucified Jesus, especially given the explanation that they were committing an unintentional sin, would be omitted rather than added. See Nathan Eubank, "A Disconcerting Prayer: On the Originality of Luke 23:34a," *JBL* 129 (2010): 521–36, who also emphasizes helpfully the fit with Luke's theology of ignorance, and the fact that the prayer was usually understood in the patristic period as a prayer for the Jews.

of Jer 31, picking up the new covenant motif from Luke 22:19–20.[96] Even if this is not the case, the pronouncement of forgiveness on the cross is certainly suggestive, perhaps implying a connection between Jesus's death and forgiveness. A firm conclusion is not possible, however.

The Mockery (Luke 23:35–39)

In this scene, the authorities (ἄρχοντες), soldiers, and the unrepentant criminal in turn taunt Jesus. Fitzmyer has observed that Luke, a little more than the other evangelists, has a concentration of "save" language in connection with Jesus in this passage: "In the course of five verses, Luke uses it [sc. the verb σῴζω] four times with reference to the crucified Jesus."[97] It may well be the case that there is irony here, in that through his crucifixion, Jesus is precisely doing for others what he is taunted to do for himself.[98]

The Promise to the Penitent Criminal (Luke 23:43)

Also unique to Luke's passion narrative is the saying: "Truly I tell you, today you will be with me in paradise." Here we have a promise of a saving event uttered at the cross, perhaps—especially given that the man is a criminal—implying forgiveness. Alkier suspects that whereas the criminal was asking that Jesus would be an advocate for him at the final judgment, Jesus in fact promises him immediate salvation.[99]

The Darkness (23:44–45a) and the Tearing of the Veil (23:45b)

Since the darkness of the eclipse here may cover the whole earth rather than just the land, there could be a sense that the death of Jesus "is significant for the whole world."[100] This is probably correct, but either way there is a clear sense of divine judgment—echoing the darkness at noon prophesied in Joel 2:31. In this

---

96. Wilson, *Saving Cross*, 117.

97. Fitzmyer, *Luke the Theologian*, 212.

98. Bock, *Luke*, 374: "Ironically, by accepting the way of the cross, saving is exactly what Jesus is doing."

99. Stefan Alkier, *The Reality of the Resurrection: The New Testament Witness* (Waco, TX: Baylor University Press, 2013), 129.

100. Wolter, *Luke*, 2:531; similarly, Bovon, *Luke*, 3:324. Nolland, *Luke*, 3:1156, sees the focus of the judgment on God's people, and Carroll, *Luke*, 468, sees τὴν γῆν as the land.

darkness and judgment, Jesus himself is included.[101] The power of darkness, of which Jesus spoke in Luke 22:53, is at work.

As in the other Synoptic Gospels, the interpretation of the tearing of the veil as portending the destruction of the temple does not convince.[102] The part-for-whole understanding of the veil as representing the temple is not intuitive. Again, the tearing is more likely to signify access to God.[103]

In any case, both events are portents pregnant with significance. This is notable because the resurrection is not accompanied by such portents in Luke; Matthew has an earthquake (Matt 28:2), and the Fourth Gospel a miraculous catch of fish (John 21:1–14). Luke's signs here are connected to Jesus's death, which immediately follows. Such signs, then, clearly mark out the crucifixion as an event pregnant with meaning.

The Remorse of the People (Luke 23:48)

One of the last elements of the scene is the reaction of the crowds: "When all the people who had gathered to witness this sight saw what took place, they beat their breasts and went away" (Luke 23:48). The reference to the beating of their breasts has led Matera to conclude that the death of Jesus elicits repentance.[104] On the other hand, some scholars have understood this action as falling short of real repentance, on the grounds that the Jerusalem multitude only truly repents in Acts 2.[105] The other place, however, where Luke uses this phrase is in the description of the tax collector's plea for mercy (Luke 18:14), which seems to be a full repentance especially since he is "justified" (δεδικαιωμένος) as a result. If the action of the crowd is reflective more

---

101. Frank J. Matera, "The Death of Jesus according to Luke: A Question of Sources," *CBQ* 47 (1985): 485: "Thus, by explaining the darkness as a failure of the sun's light, Luke makes a connection between the darkness at Jesus's death and the darkness foretold by Joel. With the death of Jesus the last days have begun."

102. *Pace*, for Luke, e.g., Carroll, *Luke*, 469–70; Wolter, *Luke*, 2:532.

103. Rightly, Bovon, *Luke*, 3:326, and Wilson, *Saving Cross*, 124. Nolland (*Luke*, 3:1157) distinguishes between "new access to God opened up for all" (his view in iv) and "the means by which close contact is established between the divine and human sphere" (his view in vi), but it is hard to see how different these are.

104. Matera, "Death of Jesus according to Luke," 484, commenting that Luke 23:48 indicates that "the death of Jesus should and does lead to repentance."

105. Carroll, "Luke's Crucifixion Scene," 112; also Wolter, *Luke*, 2:533.

of remorse than repentance, the death of Jesus should at least be understood here to be eliciting something that *anticipates* true repentance.[106]

Conclusion

"Luke, in fact, illustrates in his crucifixion narrative the saving effect of his death."[107] Since we have already been told of Luke's understanding of the cross in the eucharistic words, several features of the crucifixion narrative may well be illustrating or elaborating such an interpretation. The Barabbas episode suggests a substitution of Jesus and Barabbas. In the crucifixion scene, two unique Lukan sayings (Luke 23:34, 43) either side of the mockery accentuate salvation. The mockery scene itself (23:35–39) contains a dense concentration of salvation terminology. Two portents indicate the significance of Jesus's death, one probably implying access to God. In sum, there is considerable illustration in the crucifixion narrative of the saving significance of the death of Jesus more straightforwardly articulated in the eucharistic words of Luke 22:19–20.

2.5 *"The Pattern of Proclamation within a Jewish Context"*

Finally, we can consider Wilson's argument that the juxtaposition of the Easter events and forgiveness should be understood against the background of the Levitical cult, in which the offering makes atonement for sin.[108] The relevant passage comes from the end of the Gospel:

> [46]He said to them, "Thus it is written:
> [1] the messiah will suffer (παθεῖν),
> [2] and rise (ἀναστῆναι) from the dead on the third day,
> [3] [47]and repentance for the forgiveness of sins will be preached
> (κηρυχθῆναι) in his name to all nations." (Luke 24:46–47)

The argument has two components. First, Wilson makes the neglected point that "the proclamation outlined in 24:47 is conceived as but another link in

---

106. Bovon, *Luke*, 3:328, sees a "movement of repentance" rather than repentance per se; similarly, Carroll, *Luke*, 472.

107. Carroll, "Luke's Crucifixion Scene," 120.

108. This section is indebted to the chapter of this title in Wilson, *Saving Cross*, 157–90.

the chain of scripturally mandated elements."[109] In Luke 24 on its own, however, the relation between the death and resurrection, on the one hand, and repentance and forgiveness, on the other, is unclear.

The second step in the argument, then, is "the inter-dependence of the concepts of repentance, divine forgiveness, and cultic atonement in a Jewish context."[110] The basis of this is found in Leviticus, where certain cultic offerings, often accompanied by the confession of sin, obtain forgiveness. Hence, for example:

> [5]When anyone becomes aware that they are guilty in any of these matters, they must confess the sin they have committed. [6]They are to bring to the Lord a penalty for the sin they have committed, a female lamb or goat from the flock as a sin offering; and the priest shall make atonement for them for their sin. (Lev 5:5–6)

The refrain "the priest will make atonement for them, and they will be forgiven" runs through Leviticus, concluding the treatments of the sin offering (e.g., Lev 4:20, 26) and the guilt offering (Lev 5:16, 18; 6:7; 19:22); it also explains the combination of burnt offering, grain offering, drink offering, and sin offering in Num 15:22–26.

Wilson's conclusion is therefore that the proclamation of repentance for the forgiveness of sins is not merely a preview of Acts with little connection to the death of Jesus. Negatively, he remarks: "If the Lukan understanding of repentance and divine forgiveness is completely divorced from any conception of cultic atonement, then Lukan soteriology truly is a strange anomaly, a *Fremdkörper*, within the [sc. Jewish] religious context of Luke's day."[111] While certainty is not possible here, Luke's "pattern of proclamation in a Jewish context" is at least suggestive.

2.6 Interim Conclusion: The Lukan Death of Jesus and the Kerygma

The foregoing discussion has reached some fairly confident conclusions, while others contain liberal sprinklings of "probably" and "perhaps." It may be useful to tabulate these conclusions:

109. Wilson, *Saving Cross*, 183.
110. Wilson, *Saving Cross*, 158.
111. Wilson, *Saving Cross*, 177–78.

Clear
- Luke presents the crucifixion as ordained or decreed by God (Luke 22:22).[112]
- Jesus's death is in one (albeit restricted) sense the completion of his work (13:31–33; cf. 12:50).
- The death of Jesus is an effective death, since his body and blood are both given "for" his disciples (22:19, 20).
- Luke knew, from the liturgy in his own church circle, the idea that the death of Jesus is saving in a wide-ranging covenantal sense. In the Gospel, he therefore explains Jesus's death as inaugurating a new covenant (22:17–20). For Luke, the covenant is a means of blessing, probably including forgiveness of sins.

Probable
- Luke presents Jesus's death as a participation in divine judgment (Luke 12:49–50; 23:44–45a).
- Luke understands Jesus's death in the light of the servant in Isa 53 (22:37).
- Luke emphasizes that Jesus in his death is a substitute for Barabbas (23:13–25).
- Jesus is presented by Luke as a Passover sacrifice (22:17–20).
- The impression of Jesus's death as a saving act is reinforced through the accumulation of soteriological pronouncements at the crucifixion (23:34a, 35, 37, 39, 43).
- The tearing of the veil and the darkness at noon are portents illustrating the (perhaps cosmic) significance of Jesus's death (23:44–45).
- The tearing of the veil signifies a new quality of access to God (23:45b).

Possible
- The pattern of proclamation outlined presumes the importance of the death of Jesus for the forgiveness of sins (Luke 24:46–47).
- Jesus's death is likened to the exodus (9:31).
- The death of Jesus is saving insofar as it is portrayed as eliciting repentance (23:48).

Support from Acts
- Acts clearly portrays Jesus's death as having saving significance (Acts 20:28), as noted in the excursus following chapter 3 above.

---

112. See the further references in the excursus on Acts above.

When these various aspects of the death of Jesus are seen together in this way, it becomes apparent that Jesus's death (1) is intended by him (sec. 2.1), (2) reflects the divine decree and necessity, and (3) makes possible a whole new covenantal framework of salvation. His death is "for" his disciples (Luke 22:17–20). The covenant in Luke is one of "salvation" and "deliverance" (1:71, 74), a salvation that Luke reframes not as deliverance from human enemies (cf. 1:74) but as forgiveness of sins (1:77).[113] There are various other likely passages that add to the picture of the eucharistic words (N. B. the "probable" instances above). In these respects, Luke understands the cross as a *vicarious* death of Jesus, per Versnel's definition: "any deliberately sought or accepted death that is—or is a posteriori interpreted as—both unconditionally required and explicitly intended to guarantee the salvation of another or others from present or impending doom or death."[114] It is not accurate to say that "nothing is said of the saving significance of the cross of Christ" in Luke.[115]

In fact, it is often neglected that there is a considerable body of scholarship arguing, in various ways, for a soteriological understanding of Jesus's death, including in particular a distinguished contingent of Catholic scholars such as Fitzmyer, Karris, and Neyrey.[116] Leading commentators on Luke note the point, with varying levels of emphasis. Michael Wolter concludes: "one should speak only in a very reserved manner of a 'receding of the conception of atonement' in Luke."[117] More strongly, François Bovon states that "the cross does not represent the unavoidable cursing of the Son. . . . Nevertheless, the shed blood of Jesus seals the new covenant of God with humankind (Luke 22:19–20) and the founding of the church (Acts 20:28)"; or again, that "Luke discreetly suggests that Jesus's death, as much as it may be the suffering of a martyr, also belongs to the category of the expiatory sacrifice for the sins of the people."[118]

There are a number of important soteriological actions of God in Luke-Acts. We can begin with predestination (Luke 18:7; Acts 13:48; cf. Acts 18:10), which is presumably not accomplished by any event other than God's decree. The res-

---

113. Carroll, *Luke*, 59–60.

114. Versnel, "Making Sense of Jesus' Death," 226–27.

115. Philipp Vielhauer, "On the Paulinism of Acts," in *Studies in Luke-Acts: Essays Presented in Honor of Paul Schubert*, ed. Leander E. Keck and J. Louis Martyn (Nashville: Abingdon, 1966), 45.

116. Fitzmyer, *Luke the Theologian*, 203–22; Robert J. Karris, *Luke, Artist and Theologian: Luke's Passion Account as Literature* (New York: Paulist, 1985); Jerome Neyrey, *The Passion according to Luke: A Redaction Study of Luke's Soteriology* (New York: Paulist, 1985).

117. Wolter, *Luke*, 2:461, responding to Schnelle.

118. Respectively, Bovon, *Luke*, 1:11 and 3:184.

urrection and exaltation of Christ are also vital to salvation. Christ also pours out, and baptizes in, the Holy Spirit (e.g., Acts 2:38; Luke 3:16). Luke can also talk of justification (Luke 18:14; Acts 13:38) and eschatological resurrection (Luke 20:35–38; Acts 24:15). It is important that these different themes are not seen in some kind of competitive relationship with one another, as is the case for some scholars who prioritize the resurrection as the *real* saving event to the exclusion of Christ's death. What we see in Luke 22 is that the cross is singled out as the specific means of covenant inauguration, which is a strikingly wide-ranging soteriological function. It also needs to be recognized that in an important sense, the death and resurrection of Jesus cannot be separated but are "of a piece."[119] It is necessary to emphasize, as Jantsch does, that the death of Jesus should be understood as significant alongside other significant events in Luke's theology.[120] Hence we now turn to the other climactic event in Luke's Gospel, the resurrection.

3. The Resurrection of Jesus in Luke's Gospel

The account of the resurrection in Luke is quite different from that in Mark and Matthew. There is some overlap between Luke 24:1–12 and the other Synoptics, but thereafter Luke apparently has an entirely different set of sources and goes his own way. There is nevertheless considerable overlap in how the nature of the event is reported. The focus here will first be on the character of the resurrection in Luke and its occurrence on the third day (sec. 3.1–2), and second on the soteriological significance of the resurrection—in other words, its gospel status (sec. 3.3–6).

3.1 The Character of the Resurrection on the Third Day in Luke

Luke is clear on the character of the resurrection, which is not understood as an assumption;[121] his use of ἐγείρω (Luke 24:6, 34) and ἀνίστημι, with or without ἐκ νεκρῶν (24:7, 46), to denote the event speaks against such an idea. In particular, Luke's report that Jesus was to "rise from the dead" (ἀναστῆναι ἐκ νεκρῶν [24:46]) clearly parallels the phrase ἀνάστασις ἐκ νεκρῶν (20:35), which refers to the general resurrection.[122] Luke makes a distinction between

---

119. Sylva, "Death and Life," 215 n. 34; cf. Alkier, *Reality of the Resurrection*, 123: "the death and resurrection of Jesus are events that have brought salvation to the entire cosmos."

120. Jantsch, *Jesus, der Retter*, 125.

121. Contra Paul B. Decock, "The Breaking of Bread in Luke 24," *Neot* 36 (2002): 42.

122. Cf. Luke has used the phrase ἐγείρω ἐκ νεκρῶν in reporting the suspicions that John

resurrection and assumption, through using different vocabulary for each. The resurrection is described with one set of terms (ἐγείρω, ἀνίστημι, ἀνάστασις, ἐκ νεκρῶν). Jesus's assumption or ascension to heaven is described with another set: in Luke 24:51, "he was carried up" (ἀνεφέρετο); in Acts 1:9, "he was lifted up" (ἐπήρθη), and in both Luke and Acts, there is especially the language of Jesus being "taken up" (ἀνάλημψις in Luke 9:51; ἀνελήμφθη in Acts 1:2, 22; ἀναλημφθείς in Acts 1:11).[123]

The resurrection is, moreover, bodily, although, as in John's Gospel, Jesus's body may not be exactly the same in nature as his preresurrection body: while Jesus eats fish and shows off his flesh and bones as evidence that he is not a ghost, he can be recognized only by revelation (Luke 24:16, 31) and can vanish or appear at will (24:31, 36).[124]

As in the other Gospels, the event takes place on the third day. This is evident not only from these resurrection predictions (Luke 9:22; 18:33; cf. 24:7) but also from the chronology of Luke 22–24.[125] When Jesus was crucified and buried, "it was Preparation Day/Friday" (23:54). On the following day, there is rest on the Sabbath (23:56). Then, third, Jesus rose again "on the first day of the week" (24:1). These clear chronological markers seem again to reflect a concern for the traditional "on the third day" motif.

3.2 Resurrection on the Third Day as a Fulfillment

The resurrection is a fulfillment of Jesus's own promise.[126] The angelic figures declare: "He is not here, but is risen! Remember how he told you while he was still with you in Galilee: 'The Son of Man must be delivered into the hands of sinners, be crucified and on the third day rise again'" (Luke 24:6-7). The resurrection therefore corresponds to Jesus's own pre-Easter predictions that

---

the Baptist has risen from the dead (Luke 9:7).

123. For discussion of the ἀνάλημψις/ἀναλαμβάνω terminology, see chapter 8 on the *Gospel of Peter* below.

124. See, e.g., Jürgen Becker, *Die Auferstehung Jesu Christi nach dem Neuen Testament: Ostererfahrung und Osterverständnis im Urchristentum* (Tübingen: Mohr Siebeck, 2007), 62; N. T. Wright, *The Resurrection of the Son of God* (London: SPCK, 2003), 657–58; and Alkier, *Reality of the Resurrection*, 132, on Luke's concern with the physicality of the resurrection. Christopher Bryan, *Resurrection of the Messiah* (Oxford: Oxford University Press, 2011), 115, emphasizes both sides. Before his resurrection, however, Jesus's escape from the hostile crowd in Luke 4:30 also seems miraculous (Alkier, *Reality of the Resurrection*, 121).

125. Richard J. Dillon, *From Eye-Witnesses to Ministers of the Word: Tradition and Composition in Luke 24* (Rome: Pontificio Istituto Biblico, 1978), 47–48.

126. Becker, *Die Auferstehung Jesu Christi*, 44.

he would rise "on the third day" (9:22; 18:31–33).[127] The resurrection, then, is for Luke a vindication of Jesus's own words.[128]

Additionally, Jesus's own promises of his resurrection are in turn rooted in scriptural promises. The passion-resurrection prediction in Luke 18 refers to the resurrection on the third day (καὶ τῇ ἡμέρᾳ τῇ τρίτῃ ἀναστήσεται) as part of "everything that is written by the prophets about the Son of Man to be fulfilled" (Luke 18:31–33). According to Luke 24 in particular, "this is what is written: the messiah will suffer and rise from the dead on the third day" (24:45–46; cf. 24:25–27). There is little doubt here that not only resurrection per se but resurrection on the third day in particular is envisaged as part of what is forecast in scripture. The specific scriptural backdrop to Luke's understanding of the resurrection will be considered in section 4 below. For the present, it is sufficient to note that there is little exaggeration in Schubert's remark that "Luke's proof-from-prophecy theology is the heart of his concern in chapter 24."[129] At the same time, since "all the scriptures" (Luke 24:27) are about Jesus for Luke, the resurrection unlocks for believers the meaning of scripture.

Beyond Luke's report of the resurrection and his narration of the appearances "on the third day," we can also identify aspects of its soteriological importance. Luke views the resurrection as a gospel event of saving significance in four ways (sec. 3.3–6).

3.3 Revelation and Recognition in Luke's Resurrection Narrative

The resurrection for Luke is the moment when the true identity of Jesus is revealed. Carroll comments that the resurrection is the occasion for "(1) the disciples' misperception and lack of understanding, which (2) is overcome by Jesus's interpreting Scripture in the light of the (apparently disconfirming) events of the passion, and interpreting those events in the light of the Scriptures; (3) revelation-bearing hospitality at table."[130]

---

127. Curiously, it is not clear that either of these prophecies was uttered in Galilee: in the latter case, Jesus is just about to approach Jericho (Luke 18:35), and in the former, while Luke does not name Caesarea Philippi, that is where Jesus speaks the words of Luke 9:22 according to Matthew and Mark.

128. There is also a thinly veiled hint at Jesus's resurrection in his conclusion to the parable of the rich man and Lazarus, as Abraham says to the rich man: "If they do not listen to Moses and the Prophets, they will not be persuaded even if someone were to rise from the dead" (Luke 16:31). Alkier, probably correctly, takes this as an "ironic commentary" on those in Luke's day who do not believe (*Reality of the Resurrection*, 126).

129. Paul Schubert, "The Structure and Significance of Luke 24," in *Neutestamentliche Studien für Rudolf Bultmann*, ed. Walther Eltester (Berlin: Alfred Töpelmann, 1954), 176.

130. Carroll, *Luke*, 474.

In both of the key recognition scenes (Luke 24:28–31, 36–49) the revelation of the risen Jesus is emphatically the revelation of the crucified and risen Jesus.[131] First, in the Emmaus meal scene (24:28–31), it is as Jesus breaks bread that he is recognized, with the breaking of bread language in Luke 24 echoing for readers the eucharistic words in Luke 22.[132] Second, in the scene with the Eleven (24:36–49), Jesus initially proves that he is truly risen by inviting the disciples to look at his hands and feet: "le Ressuscité ne dit pas: 'Regardez mon visage,' mais bien 'regardez mes mains et mes pieds; c'est bien moi' (v. 39)."[133] Then he opened their minds to enable them to understand the scriptures, which in turn illuminate the identity of the crucified and risen Jesus. In sum, true knowledge of Jesus's narrative identity is not complete until the cross and resurrection.[134] With the resurrection, Jesus's identity as not just living, but "the living one" (24:5) is apparent.[135] It is through his death and resurrection that he accedes to his position of triumphant rule, "seated at the right hand of God's power" (22:69).[136] The reminiscences of Jesus's death in these recognition scenes show that the two events are "of a piece," as noted earlier.

3.4 Resurrection and Judgment

Briefly, the resurrection in Luke also entails judgment. Just as in Acts 17, the resurrection is the proof that judgment will take place (Acts 17:31), so there is a hint of this already in Luke:

131. Many take these episodes as "recognition scenes." Dillon, *Eye-Witnesses*, 146, notes the scholarly majority on this point of identifying the scenes in this way, at least as scholarship stood in 1978.

132. See, inter alia, Robert Vorholt, *Das Osterevangelium: Erinnerung und Erzählung* (Freiburg: Herder, 2013), 246. Compare the statements:

Luke 22:19: λαβὼν ἄρτον εὐχαριστήσας ἔκλασεν καὶ ἔδωκεν αὐτοῖς.

Luke 24:30: λαβὼν τὸν ἄρτον εὐλόγησεν καὶ κλάσας ἐπεδίδου αὐτοῖς.

133. Odette Mainville, "De Jésus à l'Église: Étude rédactionelle de Luc 24," *NTS* (2005): 205.

134. There are, however, connections with the resurrection in the earlier narratives: scholars often point to Luke 2:41–52 and 7:11–16.

135. On the importance of this designation, see Mainville, "De Jésus à l'Église," 195, and the article more generally.

136. Whether there is a polemical political edge to the resurrection already in the Gospel of Luke (so Wright, *Resurrection of the Son of God*, 653) is unclear. Similar to Wright, see Paul-Gerhardt Klumbies, "Himmelfahrt und Apotheose Jesu in Lk 24,50–53," *Klio* 89 (2007): 147–60, adding the idea that Jerusalem for Luke is the alternative to Rome (157). Perhaps Jesus's resurrection and ascension together have "inescapable political significance," though this is more likely in Acts than already in the Gospel (cf. Wright, *Resurrection of the Son of God*, 656).

¹⁷Jesus looked directly at them and asked, "What then is the meaning of that which is written: 'The stone the builders rejected has become the cornerstone'? ¹⁸Everyone who falls on that stone will be broken to pieces; anyone on whom it falls will be crushed." (Luke 20:17-18)

The identification of Jesus as the stone is clear, and it is notable that the vindicated cornerstone (i.e., the *risen* Jesus) is the same entity ("*that* stone") that will break and crush. In other words, it is the risen Jesus who will inevitably bring judgment from which "there is no possibility of escaping."[137] The connection with the resurrection is apparent here in Luke 20, whereas in other passages in Luke, there are more general references to Jesus's judgment (Luke 9:26; 12:8-9; 18:8).

3.5 From Sorrow and Doubt to Joy and Worship

Luke's concluding chapters catalog a wide range of emotions experienced by Jesus's followers before the happy resolution at the end of the Gospel.[138] Immediately prior to Jesus's death, all the disciples were "exhausted from sorrow," apparently because by this stage, they were aware of what was about to happen (Luke 22:45). Peter in particular wept bitterly after his denial (22:62). While Jesus was on his way to be crucified, the "daughters of Jerusalem" were mourning and wailing (23:27). After the crucifixion, all those who knew Jesus stood at a distance, eerily silent (23:49; cf. 22:54).

When Jesus is risen, but before he is revealed, the initial reaction of the women to the empty tomb and the angels is "fright" (Luke 24:5), and the two on the road to Emmaus are downcast (σκυθρωποί [24:17]). When Jesus first appears to the Twelve, they are aflutter with fear, disturbed, and doubtful (24:37).

---

137. See Wolter, *Luke*, 2:391, on how the antithetical structure of the proverb makes clear the "no-win situation."

138. On the progression in Luke 24, see, e.g., Vorholt, *Osterevangelium*, 243; similarly, Schubert, "Structure and Significance of Luke 24," 176-77. See the list of emotions of the characters in Vorholt, *Osterevangelium*, 266: concern (24:1), destroyed hope (24:21), sadness (24:17), perplexity (24:4, 12), shock (24:5), unbelief (24:11), amazement (24:22), urgency (24:9, 22-23), consternation (24:38), burning hearts (24:32), great joy (24:41, 52), and faith (24:52-53). See also Decock, "Breaking of Bread in Luke 24," 54-55, and Luke Timothy Johnson, "Luke 24:1-11: The Not-So-Empty Tomb," *Int* 46 (1992): 58: "Luke shows an impressive display of purely human emotional responses to the events: The women at the tomb are puzzled (24:4); men are 'amazed' (24:12, 22) or 'disbelieve because of their joy' (24:41). The disciples are shown to be in need of correction (24:5, 25-27, 39; Acts 1:7-8). Yet their incredulity (24:11), discussions (24:14), recitations (24:19-24), and doubts (24:41) are all part of the process by which the human experience of Jesus' resurrection is shaped."

There is a transitional stage. The women, having been terrified, do not appear to doubt the angels' proclamation but go and report it to the disciples (Luke 24:9).[139] The Emmaus disciples had already been "astonished" at the women's report, but whether this reaction is positive or negative or neither is unclear.[140] Jesus's exposition of scripture to the two disciples on the road to Emmaus elicits some positive emotion: they were gripped with excitement even while being unaware who their fellow traveler was ("our hearts burning within us," in 24:32).[141] Similarly, the disciples have an interim experience of joy and amazement, even while they do not yet believe (24:12, 41).

The climax, however, comes in the last two verses of the Gospel (Luke 24:52–53).[142] At this point, the assembled group is a broad one, encompassing Cleopas and his companion, the Eleven, and those with the Eleven (24:33), presumably including the women.[143] Finally, then, all these disciples are characterized by "great joy," with their attitudes now rightly ordered both in "worship" to Jesus and in "praise" to God.[144]

3.6 The Commissioning of the Disciples (Luke 24:48–49)

The disciples are gathered together in one place at the end of the Gospel narrative for the work to which Jesus has called them (Luke 24:36).[145] Jesus appoints them as "witnesses" (24:48) and is "sending" them (24:49), but first they must

---

139. Joseph Plevnik, "The Eyewitnesses of the Risen Jesus in Luke 24," *CBQ* 49 (1986): 90–103.

140. Vorholt, *Osterevangelium*, 243, noting that astonishment, or in his German, that the disciples were "irritiert," is neither unbelief nor faith.

141. *Pace* Vorholt, *Osterevangelium*, 247; rightly Wolter, *Luke*, 2:559, noting that "hearts burning" is "an old metaphor for being seized by excitement."

142. Metzger, *Textual Commentary*, 163, notes that the longer reading of Luke 24:52 is more probable, homoiarcton probably being the best explanation of the omission (αὐτοὶ προσκυνήσαντες αὐτὸν ὑπέστρεψαν).

143. There is no indication that the women have left the Eleven, and Acts 1:14 implies that they were part of the wider group.

144. Luke 24:52–53: Καὶ αὐτοὶ προσκυνήσαντες αὐτὸν ὑπέστρεψαν εἰς Ἰερουσαλὴμ μετὰ χαρᾶς μεγάλης καὶ ἦσαν διὰ παντὸς ἐν τῷ ἱερῷ εὐλογοῦντες τὸν θεόν. Bryan, *Resurrection of the Messiah*, 110, comments that the humor of 24:5b paves the way for this joy. Plevnik, "Eyewitnesses of the Risen Jesus," 102–3, rightly notes the worship of Jesus "in the strict sense," contra Mainville, "De Jésus à l'Église," 210. Klumbies, "Himmelfahrt und Apotheose Jesu," 157, is not correct to say that the ascension is the apotheosis of Jesus; the change in Luke vis-à-vis Jesus's divine identity lies in the understanding of the disciples, not in Jesus himself.

145. Carroll, *Luke*, 474, rightly talks of the "rehabilitation of the disciples" alongside the inauguration of mission.

wait for the Holy Spirit. With the resurrection and the sending of the Spirit by the exalted Jesus, a new phase in salvation history begins, while there is some continuity in how the disciples' mission extends Jesus's prior activity of granting forgiveness.[146]

3.7 Interim Conclusion: The Kerygma and the Lukan Resurrection

First, then, we have seen that the resurrection is the vindication of Jesus's own words. It is not merely evidence of Jesus's truthfulness, however, but is a fulfillment of scripture, bringing to a climax a whole phase in history and inaugurating a new one. Jesus had taught that there was a certain dispensation in operation "until John," since which time the kingdom of God has been proclaimed (Luke 16:16); now the arrival of the new covenant with Jesus's death has brought this kingdom to a new realization. The resurrection also has an important epistemological function, revealing the true nature of Jesus's work, as well as who he is. This revelation contributes to the transformation of the disciples from misery to joyful worship, and the resurrection is the occasion for their commission to proclaim the good news.

As far as the kerygma is concerned, scholars often note that Luke's descriptions and account of the resurrection are a very close fit with 1 Cor 15:4-5a: indeed sometimes Luke is said to show knowledge of something very close to Paul's formulation. Certainly, the key ingredients—the fact of the resurrection, the third-day chronology, the scriptural attestation, and the saving significance of the resurrection—are integral to Luke's narrative. The "protophany" to Peter is also accentuated, and this is touched upon in this chapter's appendix 2.

4. Fulfillment of Scripture in Luke's Gospel

As has already been noted in the discussion of Jesus's messiahship in Luke, there are important citations of scripture at every point in the narrative. John the Baptist's preparatory ministry is, as in other Gospels, explained by way of Isa 40. Psalm 89 is referred to in the birth narrative, there is an allusion to Ps 2 at the baptism, and Jesus's ministry is inaugurated with a quotation of Isa 61. Other

---

146. On the former, Wright, *Resurrection of the Son of God*, 649; on the latter, Carroll, *Luke*, 474.

usage could be mentioned.[147] The focus now will be on how Luke uses scripture to interpret the necessity and meaning of Jesus's death and resurrection.

4.1 Jesus's Death as Fulfillment of Scripture in Luke

We have already seen how, considered in general terms, Jesus's death was necessary (δεῖ) because for Luke it was ordained (κατὰ τὸ ὡρισμένον) by God.[148] Since this divine will for Jesus is encapsulated in scripture, that scripture must be fulfilled in him (τοῦτο τὸ γεγραμμένον δεῖ τελεσθῆναι ἐν ἐμοί). The Lukan Jesus describes in general terms how his destiny of suffering is mapped out in "all the scriptures" or in "everything written about me in the Law of Moses and in the Prophets and the Psalms" (Luke 24:27, 44). There are also, however, *particular* scriptures that can be identified.[149]

As we have seen in previous chapters, the material in Zech 9–14, the Psalms (especially lament psalms), Dan 7, and Isa 53 were especially important for the passion narratives of Mark and Matthew. In Luke, Zechariah is not so central: there is no clear reference in Luke's triumphal entry to Zech 9:9 and the foal oracle, and no quotation of the "strike the shepherd" prophecy (Zech 13:7) prefacing Jesus's arrest and crucifixion. On the other hand, the other blocks of scriptural material are important for Luke. Daniel 7 and Ps 118 play a similar role to their usage in Mark and Matthew. More distinctive is Luke's use of the Psalms and of Isa 53.

The Davidic Psalms

Jipp observes that "Luke peppers his passion narrative not only with an abundance of royal imagery but also with frequent quotations of and allusions to explicit Davidic psalms."[150]

> [34]Jesus said, "Father, forgive them, for they do not know what they are doing." As they divided up his clothes, they cast lots for them [Ps 21:18 LXX].

147. See above all the comprehensive analysis in Rusam, *Das Alte Testament*.

148. Respectively, Luke 9:22; 13:33; 17:25; 22:37; 24:7, 44; 22:22.

149. See on this still Douglas J. Moo, *The Old Testament in the Gospel Passion Narratives* (Sheffield: Almond, 1983).

150. Joshua W. Jipp, "Luke's Scriptural Suffering Messiah: A Search for Precedent, a Search for Identity," *CBQ* 73 (2010): 260. On this theme, see also Hays, *Echoes of Scripture in the Gospels*, 234–37.

> [35]The people stood watching, and the rulers too were mocking him [cf. Ps 21:7–8 LXX]. "He saved others!" they said. "He should save himself if he is God's messiah, the chosen one!" [36]The soldiers also came up and made fun of him as they offered him wine vinegar [cf. Ps 68:22 LXX]. (Luke 23:34–36)

> [46]Jesus called out with a loud voice, "Father, into your hands I commit my spirit" [Ps 30:6 LXX]. . . . [49]All those who knew him, including the women who had followed him from Galilee and were watching these things, stood at a distance [cf. Ps 37:12; 88:8–9 LXX]. (Luke 23:46, 49)

Although there is overlap with Mark and Matthew in the use of Pss 22 (21 LXX) and 69 (68 LXX), Luke's use of the Psalter is more wide-ranging. These psalms are therefore regarded as prefiguring Jesus's experience of suffering in general, and—in the case of Ps 30 LXX—his death in particular. Since those noted above (with the exception of Ps 88) are all traditionally Davidic psalms, there is presumably a sense that Jesus's suffering is specifically a Davidic fulfillment.[151]

Isaiah 53

Isaiah 52:13–53:12 is also an important passage for Luke's passion narrative. There is no problem with Luke using the chapter in principle: it is clearly referred to in Acts on two occasions (Acts 3:13–14; 8:32–33).[152] Moreover, in the lead-up to the passion narrative, Jesus himself quotes Isa 53:12, "And he was numbered with the transgressors" (Luke 22:37), encased in a convolutedly emphatic quotation formula:[153]

---

151. Jipp's conclusion on Jesus's messiahship in Luke is inevitable, especially in terms of the passion narrative: "Luke . . . found in the psalms exactly that combination of royalty and righteous suffering that had been embodied in the crucified Jesus of Nazareth" ("Luke's Scriptural Suffering Messiah," 274).

152. Acts 8:32–33 is a straightforward citation of Isa 53:7–8. Acts 3:13–14 is more complicated but still has a clear combination of allusions: God ἐδόξασεν τὸν παῖδα αὐτοῦ (Acts 3:13); cf. Isa 52:13: ὁ παῖς μου καὶ ὑψωθήσεται καὶ δοξασθήσεται σφόδρα; Jesus is the one παρεδώκατε (Acts 3:13); cf. παραδίδωμι in Isa 53:6, 12 (bis); the servant is δίκαιος (Isa 53:11; Acts 3:14). So Green, "Death of Jesus," 20.

153. Barrett, "Luke/Acts," 236: "the citation formula is unique and calls for special consideration."

"For I say to you that what is written must find its completion (τελεσθῆναι) in me: '*And he was numbered with the transgressors.*' And indeed this matter about me is coming to its completion (τέλος ἔχει)." (Luke 22:37)

We have already discussed this quotation in section 2.3 above. There are four main points relevant to the fulfillment of Isa 53.

First, as discussed in section 2.3, the emphatic "completion" language here indicates that an important event is finding its fulfillment, and this is most likely to refer to Jesus's death and/or the events surrounding it. As noted above, Jesus's arrest is one possible, perhaps preliminary, fulfillment; Jesus asks in Luke 22:52 whether he is being treated as a brigand or revolutionary (λῃστής). The ultimate fulfillment is most likely to be the crucifixion.

Second, as France notes, the placement of the quotation from Isa 53 on the night before Jesus dies indicates that his death should be understood in the light of Isaiah's servant.[154]

Additionally, more tentatively, it could be argued that the Gethsemane scene also echoes Isa 53, with the distinctive emphasis on God's will that the servant/Jesus should go through suffering (Luke 22:39–46).[155]

Finally, and again tentatively, Jesus's prayer for those who "know not what they do" may echo the servant's intercession for transgressors (Isa 53:12; Luke 23:34).[156]

Even if these last two points are more speculative, the importance of Luke 22:37 cannot be downplayed. Luke clearly understands Isa 53 as a key passage fulfilled in Jesus's death.

Summary

Overall, Luke draws from Mark's use of Ps 118 and Dan 7 and develops additional reference to the Davidic psalms and Isa 53 in his portrayal and interpretation of the death of Jesus: Luke understands Ps 30 LXX and (probably) Isa 53 in particular as highlighting Jesus's death. As well as individual scriptural passages, there are programmatic statements in Luke 24 about scripture dic-

---

154. France, *Jesus and the Old Testament*, 115. France is dealing with the historical Jesus, whereas the present argument is dealing with the Lukan Jesus, but mutatis mutandis his point still applies. More specifically in connection with Luke, the same point is made in Green, "Death of Jesus," 23.

155. Green, "Death of Jesus," 21–22. Cf. βούλομαι in Isa 53:10 with βούλομαι, θέλημα in Luke 22:42, though they are of course common words.

156. Wilson, *Saving Cross*, 116.

tating the messiah's suffering followed by glory (24:25–27), or his suffering and resurrection (24:44–47). To these we can add those passages, noted in section 2.2, that supply a broader framework for the understanding of the crucifixion, namely Exod 24 and Jer 31 as well as the theme of the Passover.

4.2 Jesus's Resurrection as Fulfillment of Scripture in Luke

The points just made about the divine determination, necessity, and scriptural inevitability of the cross also apply to the resurrection (e.g., Luke 24:26, 46). This much is a matter of scholarly agreement.[157] As with the other Gospels, what is more difficult is determining which particular scriptures Luke might have had in mind. Five particular candidates have been proposed.[158]

Genesis 3

First, Wright suggests that there are deliberate links between the recognition scene of Luke 24:31 and Gen 3:

> Then the eyes of them both were opened (διηνοίχθησαν οἱ ὀφθαλμοί), and they recognized (καὶ ἔγνωσαν) that they were naked. (Gen 3:7)

> Then their eyes were opened (διηνοίχθησαν οἱ ὀφθαλμοί) and they recognized (καὶ ἐπέγνωσαν) him. (Luke 24:31)

Wright here contrasts the "new and unwelcome knowledge" in Genesis with the "new and deeply welcome knowledge" in Luke.[159] There are also possible indications that this has wider implications of a "start of the new creation." Wright notes that on the most likely count of meals in Luke, this is the eighth meal.[160] The fact that Luke, like the other evangelists, also identifies Easter

---

157. See, e.g., Bryan, *Resurrection of the Messiah*, 112–13; Alkier, *Reality of the Resurrection*, 131.

158. There are others in Acts. In Acts 2:25–31, Luke takes Ps 16 to be speaking of Jesus's resurrection. Barrett, "Luke/Acts," 244, also suggests the possibility that the rebuilding of the tent of David in Acts 15:16 (citing Amos 9:11) might refer to the resurrection.

159. Wright, *Resurrection of the Son of God*, 652, followed by Lidija Novakovic, *Raised from the Dead according to Scripture: The Role of the Old Testament in the Early Christian Interpretations of Jesus' Resurrection* (London: Bloomsbury, 2014), 173, 190.

160. Following Ellis, Wright counts Emmaus as the eighth meal in the Gospel of Luke, after Luke 5:29; 7:36; 9:16; 10:38–40; 11:37; 14:1; 22:14.

Sunday not as the *third* day but as the first day of the week (Luke 24:1) may also signal an interest in the theme of (new) creation. This is certainly an intriguing suggestion.

Psalm 110

Like Mark and Matthew, Luke employs Ps 110:1 in the trial scene before the high priest: "In the future the Son of Man will be *seated at the right hand* of the power of God" (Luke 22:69).[161] This signals the imminent fulfillment of the passion-resurrection predictions in which the Son of Man is the subject. There are two differences between Luke's version and those of his Synoptic predecessors. In Luke, there is perhaps a stronger sense of reference to the risen Jesus, as Luke's wording (ἀπὸ τοῦ νῦν) probably refers to an event close at hand. Additionally, the focus is on Jesus's heavenly installation, with Luke removing the reference—present in Matthew and Mark—to the parousia. Like his predecessors, the centrality of Luke's knowledge of Ps 110 is apparent from the use of it in the "Son of David" question in Luke 20:41–44. Luke's application of Ps 110 to Jesus's resurrection is quite in keeping with other early Christian usage, in Acts 4 and 1 Pet 2, for example.

Psalm 118

Again, as in Mark and Matthew, Luke has Ps 118:22 (as well as an additional aphorism) appended to the parable of the wicked tenants:

> [17]Jesus looked directly at them and asked, "What then is the meaning of that which is written: 'The stone the builders rejected has become the cornerstone'? [18] Everyone who falls on that stone will be broken to pieces; anyone on whom it falls will be crushed." (Luke 20:17–18)

Here again, as in the other Synoptic Gospels, there is a fairly clear indication of a specific scriptural source being taken to refer to Jesus's vindication.[162] Jesus's becoming the cornerstone is taken to refer to his vindication in the resurrection (and perhaps exaltation).[163]

---

161. See Wolter, *Luke*, 2:499, on the meaning of ἀπὸ τοῦ νῦν in Luke.

162. See the helpful remarks in Bovon, *Luke*, 3:42–43.

163. It is not clear to me how the omission of Mark 12:11 by Luke makes a great deal of difference here, *pace* Rusam, *Das Alte Testament*, 232.

Hosea 6

Dillon and Novakovic see Hosea behind Luke's language of resurrection specifically on the third day:[164]

"After two days he will revive us; on the third day we will rise again (ἐν τῇ ἡμέρᾳ τῇ τρίτῃ ἀναστησόμεθα) and we will live in his presence." (Hos 6:2)

"On the third day he will rise again (τῇ ἡμέρᾳ τῇ τρίτῃ ἀναστήσεται)." (Luke 18:33)

"The Son of Man must be delivered over to the hands of sinners, be crucified, and on the third day be raised again (τῇ τρίτῃ ἡμέρᾳ ἀναστῆναι)." (Luke 24:7)

"The messiah will suffer and rise from the dead on the third day (ἀναστῆναι ἐκ νεκρῶν τῇ τρίτῃ ἡμέρᾳ)." (Luke 24:46)

Unlike Mark, Luke refers to resurrection "on the third day" rather than "after" or "within" three days.[165] Influence from Hosea seems very likely here. The only question is whether Luke is directly dependent upon Hos 6 or influenced indirectly via some form of the kerygma. The latter is highly probable, but this would not preclude the possibility of Luke also knowing Hos 6 independently.

Jonah 1–2

We have seen already in the discussion of Matthew in the previous chapter that Jonah in that Gospel is significant as a type of Jesus and his burial and resurrection. In Luke, however, the situation is more complex:[166]

[29] As the crowds increased, Jesus said, "This generation is a wicked generation. It seeks a sign, but no sign will be granted to it except the sign of Jonah. [30] For just as Jonah was a sign for the Ninevites, so also will the Son of Man be to this generation. [31] The queen of the South will rise at the judgment with the men

---

164. Dillon, *Eye-Witnesses*, 48, followed by Novakovic, *Raised from the Dead*, 173.
165. Cf. also Luke 9:22, which uses the verb ἐγερθῆναι.
166. See Novakovic, *Raised from the Dead*, 177 n. 19, for the various scholarly proposals for the meaning of the sign of Jonah.

of this generation and will condemn them, because she came from the ends of the earth to hear the wisdom of Solomon—and now something greater than Solomon is here! ³²The men of Nineveh will rise up at the judgment with this generation and condemn it, because they repented at the preaching of Jonah—and now something greater than Jonah is here!" (Luke 11:29–32)

The initial impression here is that the "sign of Jonah" is his proclamation of repentance to Nineveh, and therefore the corresponding (καθώς . . . οὕτως) sign that Jesus provides is his proclamation.[167] Or perhaps the "something greater than Jonah" is itself the sign. However, there are also indications in the passage that the sign may be something different. A "sign" is an odd (though not impossible) way of referring to preaching.[168] Jonah's sojourn in the sea monster followed by his regurgitation was certainly an iconic motif in ancient Judaism.[169]

More importantly, however, the sign is something *future*: "no sign will be granted (δοθήσεται) to it except the sign of Jonah." The contrast is not between Jonah in the past and Jesus in his present ministry in Luke 11 but between what Jonah was and what the Son of Man *will be* (ἔσται) to this generation.[170] This would appear to point decisively away from Jesus's preaching of repentance during his ministry as the sign. The risen Jesus is therefore more likely to be the "sign of Jonah."[171] Perhaps the focus of the sign is not so much on the risen Jesus per se, however: the point of contact could well be that Jonah pronounced judgment on Nineveh, just as the Son of Man at the eschaton (or in 70 CE?) will pronounce judgment on this generation.[172]

Summary

Overall, it is highly likely that Luke envisages Pss 110 and 118 as among the scriptures that testify to the necessity of Jesus's resurrection. Perhaps in the second

167. So, e.g., Rusam, *Das Alte Testament*, 219.

168. See Anthony Le Donne, "Greater Than Solomon: Orality, Mnemonics and Scriptural Narrativization in Luke," in *The Gospel of Luke*, vol. 3 of *Biblical Interpretation in Early Christian Gospels*, ed. Thomas Hatina (London: Bloomsbury, 2010), 99, noting Vögtle as making this objection.

169. See, e.g., 3 Macc 6:8; Josephus, *Ant.* 9.213; cf. Celsus's reference to "Jonah with his gourd" (Origen, *Cels.* 7.53).

170. The importance of the future tense is emphasized in James Swetnam, "No Sign of Jonah," *Bib* 66 (1985): 127, but ignored by Nolland, *Luke*, 2:653, Bock, *Luke*, 264, and Carroll, *Luke*, 257.

171. Swetnam, "No Sign of Jonah," 128.

172. See Wolter, *Luke*, 2:113–14.

division of certainty are Jonah and Hosea, the former because it is hard to be sure of the identity of the "sign of Jonah," and the latter because it is impossible to know whether Luke's knowledge of the language of Hos 6 is direct or only indirect. Finally, Luke's possible use of Gen 3 is certainly an intriguing suggestion.

4.3 Luke's Relation to Scripture

As in other chapters, we can assess Luke's overall attitude to scripture through a series of interconnected theses:[173]

1. *God's will stands behind scriptural history.* What is "ordained" (τὸ ὡρισμένον [Luke 22:22; cf. Acts 2:23]) by God lies behind history.

2. *God's will and purpose are enscripturated in Moses and the Prophets.* Luke does not have Matthew's statement referring to scripture as containing "every word that comes from the mouth of God" (Matt 4:4). He does, however, see "Moses and the Prophets" as providing sufficient evidence for knowing God and for salvation, so that even "someone" rising from the dead will not be able to add anything more to convince the skeptical (Luke 16:29, 31).[174] Similarly, in the Son of David question, the scriptural debate over the nuances of the phraseology of Ps 110 means that both sides in the discussion assume "the belief that every word of Scripture is significant."[175] Luke, like his predecessors, has a similar mixture of patience and impatience about the urgency of understanding scripture. On the one hand, instead of Mark's liking for the question "have you not read?" (Mark 12:10, 26), Luke has the perhaps more dialogical "then what is the meaning of that which is written?" (Luke 20:17) and the less polemical "Moses indicated" (Luke 20:37).[176] At the same time, Jesus assumes, in line with the sufficiency of scripture mentioned in Luke 16, that those who do not grasp its christological meaning are "foolish and slow of heart to believe all that the prophets have spoken" (Luke 24:25).

3. *Since scripture contains the will of God that is guaranteed to come to pass, the*

---

173. See also Rusam, *Das Alte Testament*, 492–96, who also has three concluding summary theses: "Die γραφή als Handlungsanweisung," "Die γραφή als Illustration," and "Die γραφή als Vorankündigung des Jesus- und Missionsgeschehens."

174. Hays, *Echoes of Scripture in the Gospels*, 207.

175. Barrett, "Luke/Acts," 234.

176. It is perhaps not quite true (*pace* Barrett, "Luke/Acts," 233) that "there is no essential difference between Mark's οὐδὲ τὴν γραφὴν ταύτην ἀνέγνωτε; and Luke's τί οὖν ἐστιν τὸ γεγραμμένον τοῦτο;" in Mark 12:10 and Luke 20:17. At the very least, the tone is slightly different.

events foretold are bound to take place. The binding character of scripture is expressed in a number of places, especially where the verb "it is necessary" (δεῖ) is used to describe the inevitability of the central gospel events.[177] The events are therefore no accident. Rather, their inevitability is proved by scripture. As Schubert remarked some decades ago in the statement cited earlier (sec. 3.2): "this proof-from-prophecy theology is Luke's central theological idea throughout the two-volume work."[178]

4. *These events promised in scripture therefore mark the fulfillment of scripture.* This is not a fatalistic result of astrological destiny but the fruits of God keeping his self-involving promises.[179] There is, moreover, a great variety of ways in which Luke appropriates scripture, rather than there being a simple promise-fulfillment formula.[180]

5. *Conversely, the events enable the meaning of scripture to be truly grasped.* As Bryan puts it, "The Scriptures gave to the early church a vocabulary and symbols with which to comprehend the life, death, and resurrection of Jesus, while the life, death, and resurrection of Jesus gave them a new way of understanding the Scriptures."[181] Hence, for example, Isa 61 explains the events of Jesus's ministry as functions of an anointed, Spirit-empowered servant, and therefore—conversely—Jesus illuminates the true meaning of Isa 61. In addition to the citations, there are numerous subtle allusions:[182] for Hays, Luke occupies a position on the spectrum between the elusiveness of Mark, on the one hand, and the Matthean sledgehammer, on the other.[183]

6. *The gospel events are for Luke in basic continuity with the history of Israel.* Do the gospel events relate to the history of Israel "seamlessly"?[184] In one sense, there are discontinuity and rupture: for Luke's Jesus, there was an epoch of the law and the prophets that culminated in John the Baptist (Luke 16:16),

---

177. Luke 9:22; 13:33; 17:25; 21:9; 22:37; 24:7, 44.

178. Schubert, "Structure and Significance of Luke 24," 176, and Barrett, "Luke/Acts," 237, rightly note that "the question whether his use of the OT should be described as proof from prophecy or apologetic" is really a false dichotomy.

179. Hays, *Echoes of Scripture in the Gospels*, 191–92.

180. Rowe, *Early Narrative Christology*, 33 n. 8, on Luke's "varied and multi-faceted use of the Old Testament."

181. Bryan, *Resurrection of the Messiah*, 112–13. Similarly, Rusam, *Das Alte Testament* 495–96: "Intertextualität im lk Doppelwerk heißt aber nicht nur, dass γραφαί als prophetisch auf das Jesus- und Missionsgeschehen hinweisend gelesen bzw. abgehört werden sollen (vgl. Lk 24,44), sondern zugleich erscheint der Posttext dem impliziten Leser in einem neuen Licht."

182. Hays, *Echoes of Scripture in the Gospels*, 243.

183. Hays, *Echoes of Scripture in the Gospels*, 273.

184. Hays, *Echoes of Scripture in the Gospels*, 191, 277.

followed by the epoch of the kingdom, the new covenant, and the coming of the Spirit. On the other hand, the new covenant and the Holy Spirit's advent are themselves foretold in passages quoted by Luke (Jer 31; Joel 2), and so there is continuity even in the discontinuity. It is continuity through fulfillment that is stressed by Luke.[185]

4.4 Interim Conclusion: Luke's Use of Scripture and the Kerygma

Overall, there is clearly a close accordance between the events of the death and resurrection of Jesus, on the one hand, and scripture, on the other—as is the case in the kerygma. Just as we saw that Luke's portrayal of Jesus as messiah draws copiously upon scripture, so also Jesus's death and resurrection are emphatically seen as fulfillments of scripture, as Luke 24 especially insists. Nor is this merely an assertive tour de force. Luke's passion narrative is full of quotations, allusions, and echoes.[186] While biblical allusions are not quite as strong in Luke's resurrection account, they are not absent: there may well be echoes of Gen 3 in the "eye-opening" recognition scene with Jesus and the two Emmaus disciples, and Hos 6 may have exerted an influence on Luke's phrasing of the "third day" chronology, which differs from that of Mark. Additionally, Luke takes Pss 110 and 118 (and perhaps Jonah 1–2) as presaging the fact of the resurrection.

CONCLUSION: LUKE'S GOSPEL AND THE KERYGMA

As far as the kerygma is concerned, there is a tension in some currents of scholarship on Luke. On the one hand, he is sometimes considered sub-Pauline in his view of the cross, but on the other, he is almost super-Pauline in adherence to the kerygma's presentation of a resurrection on the third day with an accompanying protophany to Peter. Drawing on what has been argued so far in this chapter, we can conclude by revisiting briefly the four themes that have been examined.

First, Luke's portrayal of Jesus as Christ is not a sham marriage of convenience between the Gospel's *bios* of Jesus and Jewish messianism. From the

---

185. Similarly, Rowe, *Early Narrative Christology*, 32–33, where Rowe, with Dahl, queries Brown's analogy of Luke 1–2 as a "bridge," on the grounds that there is no gulf to bridge.

186. Again, see the surveys in Rusam, *Das Alte Testament*, and Hays, *Echoes of Scripture in the Gospels*, 193–280.

scriptural atmosphere of Luke 1–2, Luke has a rich tapestry both of scripture and of Jewish messianic language. Isaiah 53 and 61, along with Pss 2 and 89, play important roles in interpreting the identity of Jesus. He is identified first of all as "Lord messiah," as well as—soon after—"the Lord's messiah" and then "the chosen one," all phraseology for which there is precedent in Jewish messianic discourse. Luke's Jesus recognizably wears the garb of a Jewish messianic figure.

Second, far from downplaying the soteriological function of the death of Jesus, Luke clearly affirms it, especially in the eucharistic words. (There is also a clear indication of this in Acts 20:28.) The discourse at the Last Supper stresses that Jesus's life is "given for" the disciples and that Jesus's death inaugurates a new covenant: the covenant is also a framework within which, according to the Benedictus, forgiveness probably operates for Luke. One passage even talks of Jesus's death as (from one point of view) the terminus of his work (Luke 13:31–33; cf. 12:50; 22:37). Luke may well also be depicting Jesus's death as a participation in divine judgment (12:49–50; 23:44–45a), and perhaps more than the other evangelists, he presents Jesus as a substitute for Barabbas. The crucifixion narrative probably illustrates Jesus's saving activity in various ways, perhaps especially through the tearing of the veil. In these respects, then, the Lukan portrait of the death of Jesus is scarcely indifferent to the soteriological concerns of the wider early Christian kerygma but like other New Testament books presents the cross as the vicarious death of Jesus.

Third, Luke's understanding of the resurrection aligns very closely with the way Paul describes the apostolic preaching in 1 Cor 15:3–5: Jesus is raised, the event takes place on the third day, and he appears to Peter and to various others. Luke 24 is not a mere afterword, with the resurrection just offering confirmation of the cross. The resurrection itself is "gospel," that is, it has saving significance: it is the vindication of Jesus, it reveals who he is, and it transforms the disciples from sorrow to joy, reconstituting them for the proclamation of the good news.

Fourth, the events of Jesus's death and resurrection (inter alia) are emphasized by Luke as taking place "according to the scriptures." This is especially stressed in two places in Luke 24, but these are merely climactic expressions of what has been said on a number of occasions before Easter.

In sum, Bryan's conclusion to his discussion of Luke can stand here as well. The manner in which Luke portrays the scripturally anticipated death and resurrection of Jesus the messiah "is essentially what the apostolic formula implied by its claim that the death and resurrection of Christ were 'according to the Scriptures.'"[187]

187. Bryan, *Resurrection of the Messiah*, 112–13.

Appendix 1: The Burial of Jesus in Luke's Gospel

Luke's narration of the burial of Jesus is clearly similar to its parallels in Mark and Matthew:

> [50]Now a man named Joseph from the Judean town of Arimathea was a member of the council. [51]He had not consented to their decision and action; he was a good and righteous man who was waiting for the kingdom of God. [52]He went to Pilate, and asked for Jesus's body. [53]He took it down, wrapped it in linen cloth and placed it in a tomb cut in the rock, one in which no one had yet been laid. [54]It was Preparation Day, and the Sabbath was about to begin. [55]The women who had come with Jesus from Galilee followed Joseph and saw the tomb and how his body was laid in it. [56]Then they returned home and prepared spices and perfumes. But they rested on the Sabbath in obedience to the commandment. (Luke 23:50–56)

Luke has a few differences from Mark's version, especially in the removal of some Markan details.[188] Outside of this narrative, there are not many other hints at a burial in Luke. The tomb is of course mentioned at the beginning of Luke 24, but there is no reference to any anointing of Jesus for burial by the sinful woman in Luke 7:36–50.[189] Nor does the reference to the sign of Jonah in Luke bring out the burial motif as Matthew does. Curiously, in Acts 13, "the inhabitants of Jerusalem and their leaders . . . laid him in a tomb" (Acts 13:27–29); the fact that Joseph was a member of the council presumably makes sense of the statement in Acts. The differences between Luke 23 and Acts 13 may suggest that Luke is not especially interested in the details of Jesus's burial, except for its location (Luke 23:55); the witnesses to where Jesus was buried thereby ensure that it was really Jesus's tomb that was open and empty (24:2–3). Whatever the level of agreement between Luke and Acts, there is nevertheless a clear correspondence between Luke-Acts and the subsidiary claim (ὅτι ἐτάφη) in the kerygma as Paul expresses it in 1 Cor 15:4a.[190]

---

188. Bryan, *Resurrection of the Messiah*, 108: "Even more than Matthew, Luke simplifies Mark's account, omitting the hesitations of Pilate and the mention of the stone in the mouth of the tomb."

189. This pericope appears to be a rather different story from the accounts, which in certain respects resemble it, in Mark 14:3–9 // Matt 26:6–13 // John 12:1–8.

190. Bovon, *Luke*, 3:335, connects Luke's account of the burial with 1 Cor 15:4, remarking that "the placing of the body in the tomb is the signature to the crucifixion."

Appendix 2: The Resurrection Appearances in Luke's Gospel

The exact order of the appearances is difficult to derive from Luke 24. Jesus appears to Cleopas and his companion on the road to Emmaus (Luke 24:13–32). These two then set off to Jerusalem where they discover that the Lord has already appeared to Peter (24:33–35). Whether Jesus appeared to Cleopas and friend before he appeared to Peter is therefore not clear.

At the very least, Peter is the first of the Eleven to see Jesus: in verse 34, he has seen Jesus, but the others have not. Eckstein notes that this reflects the kerygma that assigns a primacy to Peter.[191] Even Robinson states: "There is relatively strong attestation to the fact that the first appearance to a male was to Peter (1 Cor 15:5; Luke 24:34)."[192] At the same time, there is a prominence in the role of the women in Luke's resurrection narrative; although they are not identified as those who first see the risen Jesus, they are the first to report the angel's proclamation.[193] Luke 24:34 is striking for its resemblance to Paul's language: the disciples report that the Lord has appeared (ὤφθη), just as Paul reports on the appearance to Peter with the same word (ὤφθη).[194] Some have posited a near relation: Becker, for example, states that Luke formulates 24:34 in the language of the kerygma, although not from 1 Cor 15 directly but from tradition common to both.[195]

Both in form and content, then, the protophany to Peter is very similar in both Luke and the Pauline formulation of the kerygma.

---

191. Hans-Joachim Eckstein, "Die Wirklichkeit der Auferstehung Jesu," in *Die Wirklichkeit der Auferstehung*, ed. Hans-Joachim Eckstein and Michael Welker (Neukirchen-Vluyn: Neukirchener, 2002), 3–4; cf. Bryan, *Resurrection of the Messiah*, 114.

192. James M. Robinson, "Jesus from Easter to Valentinus (or to the Apostles Creed)," *JBL* 101 (1982): 8.

193. See Luke 24:1–12; N. B. the reference to the women also in 24:22–24.

194. Alkier, *Reality of the Resurrection*, 132, on 24:34: "That the resurrected Crucified One was seen by Simon Peter is formulated in the exact same way as Paul hands it down in 1 Corinthians 15." Similarly, also Bovon, *Luke*, 3:376; Eckstein, "Die Wirklichkeit der Auferstehung Jesu," 12. Compare:

Luke 24:34: ὅτι ὄντως ἠγέρθη ὁ κύριος καὶ ὤφθη Σίμωνι.

1 Cor 15:4–5: ὅτι ἐγήγερται τῇ ἡμέρᾳ τῇ τρίτῃ κατὰ τὰς γραφὰς καὶ ὅτι ὤφθη Κηφᾷ.

195. Becker, *Die Auferstehung Jesu Christi*, 50.

Chapter Seven

THE GOSPEL OF JOHN

The present discussion does not treat John's Gospel as a *tell* whose archaeological layers can be neatly excavated and dated. This chapter will approach the Gospel in its final form, importantly including John 21, there (still) being no evidence that the Fourth Gospel circulated widely without it.[1]

The pattern of the present chapter will be similar to that of the previous three, namely proceeding through each of the four elements of the kerygma—Jesus's messiahship, his saving death and resurrection, and their "accordance with the scriptures"—to assess the degree to which John's Gospel reflects the kerygma discussed in chapters 2–3. As before, this chapter will not only identify the presence of the elements of the kerygma but also show (naturally to a very limited extent) how John treats them. As in the case of Luke where the use of Acts was discussed, here the question arises whether the Johannine epistles should contribute to our understanding of the Gospel: there is only one point at which this becomes an important issue, and the epistles will play an illustrative rather than a substantive role.

---

1. Rightly, Hartwig Thyen, *Das Johannesevangelium*, 2nd ed. (Tübingen: Mohr Siebeck, 2015), 771; Jörg Frey, *The Glory of the Crucified One: Christology and Theology in the Gospel of John* (Waco, TX: Baylor University Press, 2018), 21. Christian Askeland, "A Coptic Papyrus without John 21?," in *The New Testament in Antiquity and Byzantium: Traditional and Digital Approaches to Its Texts and Editing: A Festschrift for Klaus Wachtel*, ed. H. A. G. Houghton, David C. Parker, and Holger Strutwolf (Berlin: de Gruyter, 2020), 93–108, has shown that MS Copt.e.150(P) in Oxford provides no evidence for the circulation of John 1–20 alone. Similarly, a paper by Ryan Kaufman ("Does 𝔓66 Suggest a Vorlage Lacking John 21?," Academia, https://independent.academia.edu/RyanKaufman1), has shown the same for P. Bodmer 2, and Brent Nongbri has very commendably retracted—as far as I can tell—the conclusion of his "P. Bodmer 2 as Possible Evidence for the Circulation of the Gospel according to John without Chapter 21," *EC* 9 (2018): 345–60.

1. JESUS THE MESSIAH IN JOHN'S GOSPEL

There is an interesting irregularity in John's treatment of the messiahship of Jesus. On the one hand, the prologue in John 1:1–18 makes only passing reference to Jesus as "anointed," χριστός, in the reference to grace and truth coming "through Jesus Christ" (John 1:17). The focus in John 1:1–18 lies much more on Jesus as the incarnation of the Word. On the other hand, the end of the Gospel highlights perception of Jesus's messianic identity as key to the very purpose of John's writing: "Jesus performed many other signs in the presence of his disciples that are not recorded in this book. But these are written about so you may believe that Jesus is the messiah, the Son of God, and by believing this have life in his name." (20:30–31).[2]

These two facets of John's Christology, however, are not given equal treatment in the Gospel. Of the most striking christological designations in the prologue, "Word" disappears entirely after John 1:14, and "only begotten" (John 1:14, 18) appears only twice again and never after John 3:18; the predication of Jesus as "God," bookending the prologue (1:1, 18), appears again only once as a description of Christ (20:28). By contrast, messiah language is used twenty-one times in the Gospel and is a subject of explicit discussion in connection with both John the Baptist (1:19–28) and Jesus (7:37–43).[3]

The present discussion will focus initially on the identification of Jesus as messiah (sec. 1.1). The second subsection homes in on how John's portrayal of Jesus—contra some strands of Johannine scholarship—draws on biblical passages that have traditionally been associated with the messiah (sec. 1.2). Finally, the discussion will focus on other traditionally messianic themes that are not tied to one particular scriptural passage (sec. 1.3).

1.1. The Identification of Jesus as Messiah in John

The most obvious point to make about Jesus's identity as the Christ in the Fourth Gospel is that John 20:30–31 presents an unambiguous affirmation of Jesus's identity as the messiah. In fact, John may put it the other way around,

---

2. On the tension, see Judith Lieu, "Messiah and Resistance in the Gospel and Epistles of John," in *Redemption and Resistance: The Messianic Hopes of Jews and Christians in Antiquity*, ed. Markus Bockmuehl and James Carleton Paget (London: Bloomsbury, 2007), 97, and Matthew Novenson, "Jesus the Messiah: Conservatism and Radicalism in Johannine Christology," in *Portraits of Jesus in John*, ed. Craig Koester (London: Bloomsbury, 2018), 110.

3. χριστός appears 19× and μεσσίας 2×. In the interests of space, this chapter will not address the question of Jesus's identity as prophet.

namely that the messiah is Jesus.[4] As in Matthew and Mark, Jesus is introduced in the Gospel as "Jesus Christ" from the beginning (John 1:17). He is contrasted with Moses and then implicitly with John the Baptist, who denies being the messiah (1:19–27). Distinctive in John is the very early confession of Jesus as the Christ by a character in the narrative, when Andrew speaks of Jesus's messiahship already in John's first chapter (1:41). A saying from Martha, because it correlates so closely with John 20:30–31, seems to be framed as a kind of ideal confession: "I believe that you are the messiah, the Son of God, who comes into the world" (11:27). Hence there is no doubt about Jesus's identity as messiah. This messiah is clearly a Jewish messiah: the dialogue with the Samaritan woman connects Jesus's messiahship with salvation coming from the Jews (4:21–26).[5]

Nor does John have reservations about the term.[6] It is not quite true to speak, as does de Jonge, of the "inadequacy" of "messiah" as a designation for Jesus merely because it is supplemented with "Son of God."[7] Similarly, to say that Jesus "gives his own interpretation of the term," and takes up with it the Samaritan's statement "he will show us all things," is hardly to dilute Jesus's acceptance of the title.[8] To say that it needs to be interpreted correctly is true of almost anything.[9]

1.2. John's Christological Exegesis and Jewish Messianic Interpretation

As is well known, John's use of scripture prefers allusion to quotation. Therefore, after addressing three fairly clear-cut references, we will examine two other more implicit allusions to traditionally messianic passages.

---

4. D. A. Carson, *The Gospel according to John* (Grand Rapids: Eerdmans, 1991), 662–63.

5. Lieu, "Messiah and Resistance," 103.

6. Cf. C. K. Barrett, "The Old Testament in the Fourth Gospel," *JTS* 48 (1947): 155–69, who implies that John reluctantly or half-heartedly retained elements of the title: "His basic assertion was not, Jesus is the Messiah (though he did not wholly abandon this belief), but, The Word became flesh" (168).

7. Marinus de Jonge, "Jewish Expectations about the 'Messiah' according to the Fourth Gospel," *NTS* 19 (1973): 251.

8. *Pace* de Jonge, "Jewish Expectations about the 'Messiah,'" 268.

9. Loader is a good example of balance here. He notes the importance of the messiah category, while concluding that for John "to acclaim [Jesus] as Messiah is to acknowledge that he is the one sent from the Father to make him known." See William Loader, *Jesus in John's Gospel: Structure and Issues in Johannine Christology* (Grand Rapids: Eerdmans, 2017), 436 (on the importance of "messiah"), 438 (for the quotation).

Isaiah 52–53

John's use of Isa 53 (or, more precisely, Isa 52:13–53:12) is most apparent in John 12, where the evangelist states that "Isaiah saw his glory and spoke about him," with reference to both Isa 6 and 53. John therefore not only identifies a vision of God as a vision of Jesus but also appropriates Isaiah's depictions of the servant: the servant is the light of the nations, the lamb to the slaughter, and possibly "the chosen one."[10] Most importantly, it is not just God in Isa 6 who is "high and lifted up"; the servant is also "lifted up and glorified" (Isa 52:13). Therefore, when John talks about Jesus being "lifted up" (especially in connection with his death) and "glorified," the servant is just as much in view as the Lord, if not more so.[11] As we will see in section 2 below, there may also be an allusion to Isa 53 in the Baptist's declaration that Jesus is "the lamb of God who takes away the sin of the world" (John 1:29). Chapter 5 discussed the evidence for the messianic interpretation of Isa 53 in non-Christian Jewish exegesis, and we can see that John also makes use of this chapter, though in ways different from Matthew and Luke.

Zechariah 9:9 (with Gen 49:11?)

One of John's few actual quotations of scripture appears in John 12:15, where the evangelist has the wording: "Do not fear, daughter (of) Zion: behold, your king is coming, seated on the foal of a donkey." This is an explicit quotation, introduced by a citation formula ("as is written"). The most obvious reference point is Zech 9:9, John's "do not fear, daughter Zion" echoing the prophet's "rejoice greatly, daughter Zion," with the phrase "behold your king is coming" cited verbatim (ἰδοὺ ὁ βασιλεύς σου ἔρχεται). Thereafter, John modifies Greek Zechariah's "mounted upon a pack-animal and a young foal" to "seated on the foal of a donkey." This may have its roots in the Hebrew text of Zechariah, or John could be drawing on the language of Gen 49, where Judah is foreseen as tethering his "foal of a donkey" to the tendril of a vine (Gen 49:11).

As discussed above in chapter 5 on Matthew, Zech 9:9 is frequently used in early Jewish depictions of the messiah. Psalms of Solomon 17 has one potential

10. "Light of the nations" (Isa 42:6–7) and "light of the world" (John 8:12; 9:5); "lamb" (John 1:29; cf. Isa 53:7); "the chosen one" (Isa 42:1; 43:10; John 1:34 ℵ*). On these, see Catrin Williams, "Johannine Christology and Prophetic Traditions: The Case of Isaiah," in *Reading the Gospel of John's Christology as Jewish Messianism*, ed. Benjamin Reynolds and Gabriele Boccaccini (Leiden: Brill, 2018), 93–94.

11. Lifted up: John 3:14; 8:28; 12:32, 34. Glorified: 7:39; 8:54; etc.

application of Zech 9 to the messiah, and the *Testaments of the Twelve Patriarchs* another.[12] Less in doubt is the frequent use in rabbinic literature.[13]

Also in no doubt is the extensive messianic exegesis of Gen 49, especially of verse 10: "The scepter shall not depart from Judah, nor the ruler's staff from between his feet, until tribute comes to him [*or* until Shiloh comes]; and the obedience of the peoples is his." The Commentary on Genesis A (4Q252) has an exegesis of Gen 49:10, which is understood as about "the messiah of righteousness, the branch of David" (4Q252 V, 1–5). This is the general understanding in the targumim: Onqelos, Neofiti, the Fragment Targums, and Pseudo-Jonathan all refer to the "messiah" in Gen 49:10, and Neofiti, the fragmentary Targum V, and Pseudo-Jonathan have additional references to the "king messiah" in their renderings of verses 11 and 12.[14] Such an approach is also common in rabbinic interpretation: "Shiloh" is one of the proposed names of the messiah, for example (b. Sanh. 98b).[15]

Daniel 7

In John 12, the crowd associates the messiah directly with the Son of Man, moving from the premise that the messiah will remain forever to the question of how it would be possible for the Son of Man to be "lifted up" (John 12:34). In another passage, the Johannine Jesus uses the title with a clear sense of a scriptural source that is traditionally messianic:

Dan 7:13b–14		John 5:27
"as a son of man came . . . and authority was given to him."	⋈	"and he gave to him authority . . . because he is the Son of Man."[16]

The similarities here (υἱὸς ἀνθρώπου, ἐξουσία, δίδωμι αὐτῷ) are striking.[17] Like the Synoptic Gospels, along with the *Parables of Enoch*, 4 Ezra, and 2 Baruch—

---

12. Pss. Sol. 17.24, 31–34; T. Jud. 24.1–6.

13. E.g., b. Sanh. 98a, 99a; Gen. Rab. 75.6, on Gen 32:6 (Freedman, 2:698); Gen. Rab. 98.8–9, on Gen 49:10 (Freedman, 2:956–57); Eccl. Rab. 1.9 §1, on Eccl 1:9 (Cohen, 33); Midr. Tanḥ. 1.1; Pesiq. Rab. 34.2 (Braude, 2:665).

14. The Geniza fragments are lacunose in the relevant places.

15. Cf. also, e.g., the various interpretations in Gen. Rab. 98.8–9, on Gen 49:10 (Freedman, 2:956–57), and Gen. Rab. 99.8, on Gen 49:10 (Freedman, 2:982); as Freedman notes (p. 977 n. 2), the latter originates in the Tanḥuma.

16. Cf. John 5:27 (καὶ ἐξουσίαν ἔδωκεν αὐτῷ κρίσιν ποιεῖν, ὅτι υἱὸς ἀνθρώπου ἐστίν) and Dan 7:13–14 (ὡς υἱὸς ἀνθρώπου ἤρχετο . . . καὶ ἐδόθη αὐτῷ ἐξουσία).

17. Thyen, *Johannesevangelium*, 314, takes the reference here to be to the Semitic idiom for a human being. Against those who take this view, and against those who see the absence

as well as the Talmud and Midrash—John's Gospel also defines the messiah further as the son of man figure of Dan 7.[18] (See the discussion in chapter 4, sec. 1.2, above for the non-Christian Jewish parallels.) Here again, John taps into traditional scriptural discourse to construct his picture of the messiah. Passages such as John 5:27 show that the apocalyptic Son of Man of 1 Enoch and the Synoptic Gospels has not evolved in John into something quite different—synonymous with son of God, or focusing on Jesus's humanity, for example.[19]

Ezekiel 34 and 37

The "good shepherd" imagery in John 10 probably also evokes the Davidic language of Ezek 34 and 37, especially the gathering of the "one" community under "one shepherd," which is common to both. In Ezek 37, the prophetic action of combining two sticks into one (εἰς ῥάβδον μίαν) represents God's promise to make the Israelites like one single stick (εἰς ῥάβδον μίαν), and this means that the Israelites will be "one nation" (ἔθνος ἕν) with "one prince" (ἄρχων εἷς) over them (37:17–22). Back in Ezek 34, God had promised to provide "one shepherd (ποιμένα ἕνα), my servant David" (34:23), and following the stick imagery in Ezek 37:24 he renews this promise that David would be their singular shepherd (ποιμὴν εἷς). The statement by John's Jesus that "there shall be one flock and one shepherd (μία ποίμνη, εἷς ποιμήν)" in John 10:16 appears to allude to these promises in Ezekiel, especially given the similar literary settings of the "scattered" sheep (Ezek 34:5; John 10:12) and the false shepherds who abandon those sheep to wild animals (Ezek 34:5, 8; John 10:12–13).[20]

Various places in non-Christian literature share a similar messianic interpretation of Ezekiel.[21] Psalms of Solomon 17 probably echoes the depiction in Ezek 34 and 37 of the eschatological David shepherding his flock, not allowing any of them to languish (Pss. Sol. 17.40; cf. Ezek 34:16), as well as sharing more predictable (though not common) language of "pasture" (νομή in Pss. Sol. 17.40; cf. Ezek 34:14 [bis], 18 [bis]). There is a possible messianic use of this section of Ezekiel in

---

of the articles as further evidence for a connection to Dan 7, one would not expect υἱὸς ἀνθρώπου to have the article(s) here, because it is a predicate.

18. See Benjamin Reynolds, *The Apocalyptic Son of Man in the Gospel of John* (Tübingen: Mohr Siebeck, 2008), passim, for further connections between John and the use of Dan 7.

19. Andrew Lincoln, *The Gospel according to St John* (London: Continuum, 2005), 204, comments that John follows the Synoptics in connecting the Son of Man with final judgment.

20. See Johannes Beutler, *A Commentary on the Gospel of John* (Grand Rapids: Eerdmans, 2017), 277–78.

21. Notably, Targum Ezekiel does not have a single reference to the messiah.

4Q504 1–2 IV, 5–8.[22] Very widespread in the Qumran literature is the designation for the messiah as "the prince" (*nsy'*; cf. *nsy'* in Ezek 34:24; 37:25): the phrase "the prince of the (whole) congregation" appears numerous times.[23] Ezekiel 37 is also interpreted messianically in the Talmud (b. Sanh. 98b), as well as among later rabbis.[24] It is notable that the good shepherd pericope (John 10:1–21) is followed immediately by the question of Jesus's messianic identity (10:22–24).[25]

Zechariah 3:8–10

An allusion of a more suggestive kind is found in John 1, where Jesus says that he saw Nathaniel under the fig tree (ὑπὸ τὴν συκῆν) before Philip called him (John 1:48; cf. also 1:50).[26] Various scholars have suggested here an allusion to Zechariah, where God announces in Zech 3:8 that he is going to bring his servant, the "Branch" or "Shoot" (*Ṣemaḥ*).[27] When this happens, "each of you will invite your neighbor to sit under your vine and fig tree" (Zech 3:10). Notably, after Jesus refers to Nathanael being under the fig tree, Nathanael immediately concludes that Jesus is the king of Israel, and Jesus then again refers to the fig tree (John 1:48–50).

This Zechariah passage (along with Zech 6:12, which also refers to the Branch figure) is interpreted messianically in a number of places. The Dead Sea Scrolls may not pick up Zechariah in their messianic references to the "branch of David," but messianic interpretation is widespread in the targumim and rabbinic literature. The Targum Zechariah interprets the Branch in explicitly messianic terms in both Zech 3:8 (*'bdy mšyḥ'*) and 6:12 (*mšyḥ' šmyh*).[28]

---

22. Willitts also argues for 11Q5 XXVIII, 3–14. See Joel Willitts, *Matthew's Messianic Shepherd-King: In Search of 'The Lost Sheep of the House of Israel'* (Berlin: de Gruyter, 2007), 72–75, and 4Q504 (*Matthew's Messianic Shepherd-King*, 75–78).

23. CD VII, 19–20; 4Q266 3 III, 21; 1Q28b III, 20; 1QM V, 1; 4Q285 6 and 4 II, VI, X; 5 IV; 4Q376 1 III, 1.

24. Samson H. Levey, "The Targum to Ezekiel," *HUCA* 46 (1975): 144 n. 20.

25. Klaus Wengst, *Das Johannesevangelium: Neuausgabe in einem Band* (Stuttgart: Kohlhammer, 2019), 317.

26. There is also reference in the wider pericope to Zeph 3. See, e.g., Thyen, *Johannesevangelium*, 140.

27. See especially Craig R. Koester, "Messianic Exegesis and the Call of Nathanael (John 1:45–51)," *JSNT* 39 (1990): 23–34, and Richard J. Bauckham, *Gospel of Glory: Major Themes in Johannine Theology* (Grand Rapids: Baker 2015), 157–58. Lincoln (*John*, 120–21) is more skeptical.

28. See translation and notes in Kevin Cathcart and Robert P. Gordon, *The Targum of*

Ṣemaḥ is one of the proposed names of the messiah, along with David and Menachem, in the Jerusalem Talmud (y. Ber. 2.4; 17a): R. Joshua ben Levi's claim "Ṣemaḥ is his name" is a quotation from Zech 6:12. Zechariah's "Branch" is also identified as messiah in Lam. Rab. 1.51 in another discussion of what the messiah's name will be. To these can be added the later references in Num. Rab. 18.21 and Pirqe R. El. 48. It is very curious that John 1 talks about Jesus seeing Nathaniel "under *the* fig tree," as if the statement implies reference to something definite. Nothing of this sort has been mentioned thus far in John 1, but it is possible that the definite reference to the fig tree implies an Old Testament reference ("under *that* fig tree"—that you know about from Zechariah).[29] Because there is no clear quotation of Zechariah in John 1, however, this case must remain tentative.

Conclusion

Overall, though one hesitates to disagree with the mighty Barrett, it is difficult to conclude that there is a divergence between "John's new use of the O. T." and "the esoteric speech of Jewish Messianism."[30] There is evidence that John's use of scripture could have been recognized as messianic, as including various points of contact with existing Jewish exegesis.

1.3 Jewish Messianic Themes in John's Christology

This is equally the case with John's use of particular themes that are often based on a cluster of various scriptural sources. We will look first at perhaps the two most important aspects of John's messianism, namely his understanding of Jesus as messiah Son of God and his attribution of signs to Jesus.

---

the Minor Prophets (Edinburgh: T&T Clark, 1990), 192, 198. The reference to the messiah building the temple in Tg. Isa. 53.5 probably is influenced by Zech 6:12.

29. There are other scriptural references to being "under the fig tree," but only Zechariah has a plausible messianic connection.

30. Barrett, "Old Testament in the Fourth Gospel," 168. Similarly, Jocelyn McWhirter, "Messianic Exegesis in the Fourth Gospel," in Reynolds and Boccaccini, *Reading the Gospel of John's Christology*, 124–48, comments that the Old Testament passages quoted by John "bear little resemblance to passages used to support Jewish messianism in the Second Temple Period" (125); further, "None of them contains the word משיח or coheres with generally accepted messianic prophecies" (145).

Jesus as Messiah, Son of God

The evangelist's aim in writing expressed in John 20:30–31 picks up another theme that we have seen in previous Gospels, namely the *kind* of messiah that Jesus is.[31] John's emphasis is clearly on the fact that Jesus is the "messiah Son of God" (ὁ χριστὸς ὁ υἱὸς τοῦ θεοῦ in John 20:31), with the latter title of vital importance to John's Christology. In addition to this passage, we have already noted Martha's confession of Jesus as "the messiah, the son of God" (11:27). The "son" title—either simply "the son" or as "son of God"—is extremely common in John, and "Son" is paired with "Father" much more commonly than is the case in the Synoptics. Already at the beginning of the Gospel, Jesus is the "only begotten from the Father" (1:14; cf. 1:18), and shortly afterward, Nathanael says to Jesus, "You are the son of God; you are the king of Israel" (1:49). John shares with 4 Ezra, then, the notion that the messiah was to be designated as "son of God" (cf. also 4Q246), and with 1QSa that the messiah is begotten by God. Probably the primary connotations of Jesus as divine son in John are twofold: intimacy or reciprocity with the Father is crucial in John, more so than in the Synoptics; second, Jesus's mission from the Father is an important dimension, with Jesus referring to himself as "the messiah whom you have sent" (John 17:3).[32] There is a great deal more that could be said about divine sonship in John, but the point here is to note the close connection between Jesus as messiah and Jesus as son of God.

Jesus as a Sign Messiah

The other main distinctive in John is the emphasis on Jesus's signs: he is qualified to be messiah by virtue of his deeds, or perhaps better, can be identified as messiah by those deeds (John 7:31; 20:30–31; cf. 4:29).[33] It is possible that a messiah identified by particular deeds is something John inherited merely from existing Christian ideas of messiahship. As we have seen, Matt 11 in particular refers to "the deeds of the messiah," and Jesus's healing in Matthew is associated

---

31. Among the mountain of literature on "Son of God" in John, see the elegant summary in Craig Koester, *The Word of Life: A Theology of John's Gospel* (Grand Rapids: Eerdmans, 2008), 96–107, as well as Loader, *Jesus in John's Gospel*, 315–64, and the mass of secondary literature cited there.

32. See Lieu, "Messiah and Resistance," 100, 107, on these two themes.

33. On this theme, see John Painter, *The Quest for the Messiah: The History, Literature and Theology of the Johannine Community*, 2nd ed. (Edinburgh: T&T Clark, 1993), 10–16.

on four occasions with his being son of David.[34] In the eschatological discourse, Jesus warns of the signs that will be performed by *false* messiahs (Mark 13:22; Matt 24:24). Similarly, as we saw in the previous chapter on Luke, the activities set out in the Nazareth Manifesto are vital to Jesus's messianic identity.

On the other hand, the identification of the messiah by signs either that he will perform or that will accompany him is not a particularly Christian novelty, as several places attest:

- In the messianic exegesis of Isa 11:4 in various Jewish works, the messiah is not merely a mighty warrior but a miraculously powerful one, defeating whole groups or nations apparently single-handedly (1 En. 62.2; Pss. Sol. 17.24; 2 Bar. 72; cf. Isa 11:4).[35] Later, in Tg. Isa. 10.27 and Tg. Ps.-J. to Num 24:17, the conquest of Israel's enemies is again not merely impressive but extraordinary: again, the messiah appears to conquer whole nations by himself.[36]

- Although 4Q521 is often taken to refer to mighty *divine* acts *accompanying* the coming of the messiah, they might also be taken to be the works of God performed through the messiah: as we have already noted, the proclamation of good news to the poor, for example, fits much better as coming from a human herald than from a heavenly voice.[37] If the messiah is not doing these works, then they are at least signs accompanying his coming.

- In Tg. Isa. 53, the logic runs accordingly: "the wonders that will be done in his days, who will be able to recount? *For he* [sc. the messiah] will take away the rule of the gentiles." In other words, the messiah is the one who accomplishes the wonders.[38]

---

34. See, respectively, Matt 11:2 and Matt 9:27; 12:22–23; 15:22; 20:30–31.

35. There is perhaps an allusion to Isa 11:2 in John 1:32–33. See Bauckham, *Gospel of Glory*, 166–71.

36. See further comment in Samson Levey, *The Messiah: An Aramaic Interpretation; The Messianic Exegesis of the Targum* (Cincinnati: Hebrew Union College, 1974), 23–24, 47, noting the contrast between Onqelos and Pseudo-Jonathan. Similarly, Tg. Neof. Gen. 49.10–12: "How beautiful is king messiah who is to arise from among those of the house of Judah. He girds his loins and goes forth to battle against those that hate him; and he kills kings with rulers, and makes the mountains red from the blood of their slain and makes the valleys white from the fat of their warriors. His garments are rolled in blood; he is like a presser of grapes."

37. John J. Collins, "The Works of the Messiah," *DSD* 1 (1994): 100: "It is surprising, however, to find God as the subject of preaching good news. This is the work of a herald or messenger."

38. Translation from Bruce Chilton, *The Isaiah Targum* (Edinburgh: T&T Clark, 1987), 104.

- In a slightly more indirect manner, where the agency of God and the messiah are linked, we can cite a targumic formula that resembles the motif in John that the works of the Son come from the Father.[39] The targumim in several places refer to "the miracle/sign (Aramaic: *nys'*) and deliverance that you [i.e., God] will perform for your messiah."[40]
- In one early midrash, the reason Rabbi Akiba understood Bar Kokhba to be the messiah was that the latter had superhuman abilities: "And what is it that Ben Koziba used to do? He used to catch the ballistas from the enemy's catapults on one of his legs and throw them back, killing many men. For this reason R. Akiba spoke thus [sc. that Simon was the messiah]" (Lam. Rab. 2.2 §4).[41] Conversely, in the Talmud, Bar Kokhba's messianic credentials are imagined as testable precisely on the basis of what he can *do*: "Bar Koziba reigned two and a half years. He said to the rabbis, 'I am the messiah.' They said to him, 'Of the messiah it is written, *He smells and judges* (Isa 11:3–4). Let us see whether he can judge by smell.' When they saw that he was unable to judge by smell, they killed him" (b. Sanh. 93b).[42]
- Also in the Bavli, R. Joshua ben Levi asks: "What is his mark (*symnyh*; cf. John's σημεῖον) that indicates who the messiah is?" In reply, Elijah identifies the messiah as the one who sits at the gate of the city replacing the bandages of the poor (b. Sanh. 98a). This section of Sanhedrin discusses other identifiable features, such as coming with clouds (per Dan 7) or coming on a donkey (Zech 9)—even a miraculous donkey of a thousand colors according to R. Samuel.
- Van Belle also notes that combining the messiah (who in his view may not have been expected to perform signs) with an/the eschatological prophet (who was) is a quite natural exegetical move, and Barrett observes that it is plausible that this connection may well have already been made in Judaism.[43]

39. John 5:19–20, 36; 10:25, 32, 37–38; 14:10–11. Leon Morris, *Gospel according to John* (Grand Rapids: Eerdmans, 1971), 686, notes John 3:2 and 9:16, understanding them together to imply that "the signs then take their origin from God."

40. Tg. 2 Sam. 22.32; Tg. Ps. 18.32; Tg. Hab. 3.18. Levey, *Messiah*, 95, has "miracle"; Cathcart and Gordon, *Targum of the Minor Prophets*, 161 (on Tg. Hab. 3.18), have "sign."

41. Matthew Novenson, "Why Does R. Akiba Acclaim Bar Kokhba as Messiah?," *JSJ* 40 (2009): 552; Haim Weiss, "A Double Edged Sword—The Power of Bar-Kosibah: From Rabbinic Literature to Popular Culture," in *The Reception of Ancient Virtues and Vices in Modern Popular Culture: Beauty, Bravery, Blood and Glory*, ed. Eran Almagor and Lisa Maurice (Leiden: Brill, 2017), 342–43.

42. For the translation and discussion, see Matthew Novenson, *The Grammar of Messianism: An Ancient Jewish Political Idiom and Its Users* (Oxford: Oxford University Press, 2017), 93–95.

43. Gilbert Van Belle, "The Signs of the Messiah in the Fourth Gospel: The Problem of

On several grounds, then, the common view that a messiah identified by and/ or accomplishing signs is a Christian innovation may not be as obvious as many assume.[44]

Jesus as Davidic Messiah?

A further potential source of a traditional messianic theme is the use of Davidic traditions in John. Reference to the messiah's Davidic lineage appears in John 7, though not as applied to Jesus but as one of the popular opinions cited. Jesus, it is alleged by some of his hearers, cannot be the messiah because he is a Galilean and does not hail—as the messiah should—either from David's town of Bethlehem or from the Davidic line (John 7:41–42). By attributing these assumptions to skeptics, however, John is not necessarily criticizing this traditional account of the messiah's origins.[45] Indeed, Lincoln poses the question: "how likely is it that the evangelist would raise an objection based on a specific scripture, in this case Mic. 5:2, if he did not think that the objection could be met and that Jesus had actually fulfilled this scripture?"[46] There may well be a double irony here. The crowds, after all, make apparently incompatible demands: for some, the messiah is from Bethlehem, but for others his origin is unknown (John 7:42, 27). However, as in the Synoptic Son of David question (Mark 12:35–37; and parr.), Jesus may be able to fulfill both these requirements if he is both Davidic messiah and eternal Word.[47]

A point potentially supporting some kind of association with David is the frequent use of the Psalter in John. Among the clear references to

---

a 'Wonder-Working Messiah,'" in *The Scriptures of Israel in Jewish and Christian Tradition: Essays in Honour of Maarten J. J. Menken*, ed. Bart J. Koet, Steve Moyise, and Joseph Verheyden (Leiden: Brill, 2013), 159–78, and C. K. Barrett, *The Gospel according to St. John*, 2nd ed. (London: SPCK, 1978), 323.

44. See, e.g., de Jonge, "Jewish Expectations about the 'Messiah,'" 257–58, and Lieu, "Messiah and Resistance," 98. Van Belle, "Signs of the Messiah in the Fourth Gospel," 160–63, refers to a number of scholars taking this view, noting the influence especially of J. Louis Martyn in this direction. At the same time, what Martyn emphasized was that although "the Davidic Messiah was not expected to perform signs, that is precisely what was expected of the Mosaic Prophet-Messiah." See J. Louis Martyn, *History and Theology in the Fourth Gospel* (Louisville: Westminster John Knox, 2003), 108.

45. *Pace* de Jonge, "Jewish Expectations about the 'Messiah,'" 263. Against a similar claim by another scholar, rightly Novenson, "Jesus the Messiah," 116.

46. Lincoln, *John*, 258.

47. Koester, *Word of Life*, 94.

scripture in John are the following (noting also where relevant the psalms' superscriptions):

Psalmist's (David's) experience ascribed to Jesus:
- Ps 6 ("Psalm of David"): Ps 6:4 in John 12:27
- Ps 22 ("Psalm of David"): Ps 22:18 (21:19 LXX) in John 19:24
- Ps 34 ("of David"): Ps 34:20 (33:21 LXX) in John 19:36
- Ps 35 ("of David"): Ps 35:19 (34:19 LXX) in John 15:25
- Ps 69 ("of David"): Ps 69:9 (68:10 LXX) in John 2:17
- Ps 69 ("of David"): Ps 69:21 (68:22 LXX) in John 19:28-30

Other christological references to Jesus in the Psalter:
- Ps 78:24 (77:24 LXX) in John 6:31
- Ps 82:6 (81:6 LXX) in John 10:34
- Ps 118:25-26 (Ps 117:25-26 LXX) in John 12:13

This list is perhaps striking, and others have sought to identify even more Davidic allusions of christological significance for John.[48] The allusions to Ezek 34 and 37 (and possibly those to Zech 3) noted above also associate Jesus with David.[49] In his comment on the use of the Davidic psalms (esp. Pss 22 and 69), Hays concludes cautiously: "There is an implicit suggestion here that Jesus paradoxically fulfills the role of Davidic kingship precisely through his conformity to the extreme suffering portrayed in the Davidic lament Psalms."[50] As Hays also notes, however, John often resists heavy-handed one-to-one identifications but instead generates associations by "evoking images and figures

---

48. See Sanghee M. Ahn, *The Christological Witness Function of the Old Testament Characters in the Gospel of John* (Milton Keynes: Paternoster, 2014), 128-72, for a long discussion of scholarly views of the Davidic messiahship in or not in John. Above all, there is a "witness function of David for the messianic qualification of Jesus," and David "foreshadows the characteristics of the messiah" (172). See also Margaret Daly-Denton, *David in the Fourth Gospel: The Johannine Reception of the Psalms* (Leiden: Brill 2000), and Daly-Denton, "The Psalms in John's Gospel," in *The Psalms in the New Testament*, ed. Steve Moyise and Maarten J. J. Menken (London: T&T Clark, 2004), 119-37.

49. Cf. the scholars who see John as dissociating Jesus from David, noted in Joel Willitts, "David's Sublation of Moses: A Davidic Explanation for the Mosaic Christology of the Fourth Gospel," in Reynolds and Boccaccini, *Reading the Gospel of John's Christology*, 203-25.

50. Richard B. Hays, *Echoes of Scripture in the Gospels* (Waco, TX: Baylor University Press, 2016), 326.

from Israel's Scriptures."[51] Daly-Denton emphasizes how Jesus is not so much a genealogically son of David messiah in John but is nevertheless prefigured in the experience of David qua psalmist.[52] Jesus is therefore *Davidic* (or David-ish!) but not *Davidide* by dynastic genealogy: he is clearly a king, as is evident from Nathanael's confession (John 1:49) and the acclamation in the triumphal entry (12:13–15)—to which the evangelist gives his seal of approval (12:16).[53] The use of the Psalms and of the shepherd imagery shows that John's Gospel does take up Davidic imagery as part of its portrayal of Jesus's reign.[54] This is only one aspect of John's use of scriptural figures, however; David is another foreshadowing figure alongside Abraham, Moses, and others, rather than being a definitive template for Jesus.

1.4 Interim Conclusion: John's Messiah and the Kerygma

In conclusion, Moody Smith presents the tension that many scholars sense in John's Gospel. On the one hand, Smith can say that "John knows the traditional expectation that the Messiah would be born in Bethlehem of Davidic lineage (7:42; cf. 2 Sam 7:12–13; Mic 5:2), although he makes nothing of it and never refers to Jesus as the Son or progeny of David," and Jesus can be said to be "far removed from traditional messianic expectation."[55] After all, the Jesus of John's Gospel "defies and shatters traditional criteria or expectations."[56] Lieu similarly states that "few would challenge the assertion that John has redefined 'Messiah.'"[57] At the same time, Smith can also say that "as far removed from traditional messianic expectation as John may seem, the Gospel makes contact with such expectation in a significant way."[58] Similarly, "the pieces of such tra-

---

51. Richard B. Hays, *Reading Backwards: Figural Christology and the Fourfold Gospel Witness* (Waco, TX: Baylor University Press, 2014), 78.

52. Daly-Denton, "Psalms in John's Gospel," 120.

53. For Jesus as "king" in John, see 1:49; 6:15; 12:13, 15; 18:33, 37, 39; 19:3, 12, 14, 15, 19, 21. For discussion, see Novenson, "Jesus the Messiah," 115, and the balanced treatments in Koester, *Word of Life*, 93, and Adele Reinhartz, "'And the Word Was God': John's Christology and Jesus's Discourse in Jewish Context," in Reynolds and Boccaccini, *Reading the Gospel of John's Christology*, 71–72.

54. See Hays, *Echoes of Scripture in the Gospels*, 323–27, on king of Israel and Davidic kingship.

55. D. Moody Smith, *The Theology of the Gospel of John* (Cambridge: Cambridge University Press, 2010), 87.

56. Smith, *Theology of the Gospel of John*, 94.

57. Lieu, "Messiah and Resistance," 100.

58. Smith, *Theology of the Gospel of John*, 87.

ditions can be reassembled in a new way. The pieces will remain recognizable, but the new configuration will not be."[59]

This section has attempted to demonstrate that there are indeed "recognizable pieces" of Jewish messianic exegesis in John. At the same time, John's "new configuration" is not an outlier, because, as Novenson has shown, there is no fixed messianic expectation with which John's christological exegesis can be contrasted. To say that John "redefines" messianism presupposes an established definition, which does not exist.[60] What is common to all construals of the messiah in early Judaism is simply the interplay of scripture and experience, and the "new configuration" of messiahship is never identical from one work to the next. Some texts evince an expectation that the messiah has a distinguished (especially Davidic) genealogy; others (e.g., Similitudes of Enoch, 2 Baruch) display no such interest. Some Jews—corresponding to Davidic expectation—assumed that the messiah would come from Bethlehem (e.g., y. Ber. 2.4), while others saw his origins as more mysterious (e.g., 4 Ezra 13.52). As Bauckham has similarly noted, "Jewish messianism was not so much a tradition of ideas as a tradition of exegesis."[61]

The discussion here has undoubtedly been selectively one-sided, as one could easily show ways in which John's Christology diverges from certain other contemporaneous portrayals of the messiah. John's messianism, however, is also recognizable as not only drawn around a particular individual but also as rooted in scriptural discourse. We saw in sections 1.2–3 several points of contact with existing messianic uses of scripture. John's use of Isa 52:13–53:12 is paralleled to some extent in the messianic exegesis of 1 Enoch and the Isaiah Targum. Daniel 7, for example, is already used in the Similitudes of Enoch, 4 Ezra, and 2 Baruch. John's allusions to Ezekiel's "one shepherd" and Zech 9, as well as perhaps to Zech 3 and Gen 49, evoke existing messianic exegesis.[62] John also draws extensively on existing christological exegesis evident in the Synoptic Gospels, in his use of Ps 118 on Palm Sunday, and Pss 22 and 69 in the passion. Additionally, certain traditionally messianic scriptural *themes* that are not tied to one particular passage are evident in John, such as the messiah's identity as Son of God or association with David. One could poten-

---

59. Smith, *Theology of the Gospel of John*, 94.

60. Cf. Lieu, "Messiah and Resistance," 100. Lieu's review of Novenson's *Grammar of Messianism*, in *Theology* 121 (2018): 294–95, seems to admit as much.

61. Richard Bauckham, *The Testimony of the Beloved Disciple* (Grand Rapids: Baker, 2007), 234.

62. See also John's use of Zech 12:10 and its use (in addition to Rev 1:7) in b. Sukkah 52a, where the Zechariah oracle foretells the death of the messiah ben Joseph.

tially add others, such as the messiah as bridegroom,[63] or the Spirit's resting on the messiah.[64] Even John's innovative use of scripture has contact with existing messianic expectation, as in his frequent use of Davidic psalms. John not only identifies Jesus clearly as messiah, then. The Gospel also does so in a way that is identifiable within the wider tradition of Jewish and Christian messianic exegesis.[65]

2. The Vicarious Death of Jesus in John's Gospel

There are two contrasting temptations in treating the death of Jesus in John. One is to say, with Käsemann, that for John (unlike the Synoptics) the account of the death of Christ "was more an embarrassment to the evangelist than the natural conclusion"; the other is "to see the four [canonical Gospels] blending harmlessly together and so to miss the singularity of John's vision."[66] Here— in a similar vein to the messianic discussion above—we will see that John's Gospel does maintain a strong attachment to the traditional understanding of the death of Christ as a saving act but also adds its own singular vision. As Moody Smith has remarked, "The early traditional and Pauline theological theme of the crucifixion of Christ as the point and means of God's redemption of humanity is then not lost in John. Rather, it becomes an underpinning of his distinctive view and presentation of Jesus's whole ministry as the revelation of God's judgment and of his gift of eschatological life."[67] Certainly the glorification of the Son in his death on the cross is unusually prominent in the soteriology of John's Gospel.[68] It is not just in the Johannine "expansion" of the

63. Ruben Zimmermann, "Jesus—the Divine Bridegroom? John 2–4 and Its Christological Implications," in Reynolds and Boccaccini, *Reading the Gospel of John's Christology*, 358–86.

64. Again, see Bauckham, *Gospel of Glory*, 166–71.

65. See the nicely balanced statement in Novenson, "Jesus the Messiah," 123: "We find an unlikely trove of messiah traditions in the Gospel of John because the author (or redactor), for all his theological bravura, also has a strong conservative streak, an impulse to preserve and to lay claim to the venerable old category of messiah."

66. John Ashton, *Understanding the Fourth Gospel* (Oxford: Oxford University Press, 2007), 460, 461. On Bultmann's and Käsemann's views of the death, see Martinus C. de Boer, *Johannine Perspectives on the Death of Jesus* (Kampen: Kok Pharos, 1996), 20–29.

67. Smith, *Theology of the Gospel of John*, 120.

68. See, e.g., J. Terence Forestell, *The Word of the Cross: Salvation as Revelation in the Fourth Gospel* (Rome: Biblical Institute Press, 1974), who provides some discussion of his various predecessors. For Bultmann, of course, Jesus's death is subordinated to the incarna-

scope of the cross to include the revelation of the glorious crucified Jesus that we see John's distinctive angle of vision, however. John's different approach is also evident in the fact that he has no ransom saying or eucharistic words but a host of various images that elucidate Jesus's death as a saving event. The focus here on Jesus's vicarious death is naturally a narrow one, and so other important elements of Jesus's death will have to be ignored here.[69]

2.1 The Necessity of Jesus's Death for Salvation

After a deliberately vague reference to the rejection of Jesus (John 1:10–11) and the allusions to Jesus as the lamb of God (1:29, 36), clear indications of Jesus's death come in John 2–3, with Jesus's challenge to his interlocutors to destroy his bodily temple (2:18–21). This is presented not merely as a hypothetical challenge; rather Jesus's death and *postmortem* resurrection will be a definite "sign" (2:18).

Again, in John 3, Jesus's "lifting up" is necessary. Like the Synoptic evangelists, John uses the verb δεῖ ("it is necessary" [John 3:14–15]); in the Fourth Gospel, it appears in the analogy between Jesus's elevation and that of the bronze serpent.[70] The bronze serpent was God's provision of a remedy for a death threatened as a result of sin (Num 21:6–7). There was the promise of life for looking at the serpent, and those who did look lived (Num 21:8–9). Similarly, believing in the lifted-up Jesus (like looking upon the serpent on the pole) means that one does not perish but will live (John 3:15–16). The connection between John 3:15 and 3:16 here probably points to the lifting up, as in this instance,[71] referring particularly to the death of Jesus: the Son of Man lifted up brings life (3:15), for God *gave* his Son for them to have life (3:16). A further hint at the crucifixion comes from the fact that the snake is lifted up on a standard in the Numbers narrative (Num 21:9), an image suggestive of crucifixion, which is also a hanging on a pole.[72] In sum, John 3:14–16 together show that the death of Jesus is necessary for bringing eternal life.

Other statements of the soteriological necessity of the cross appear later in the Gospel. As his public ministry reaches its conclusion in John 12, Jesus has

tion but is still his exaltation at which Jesus acts as revealer. See Rudolf Bultmann, *Theology of the New Testament* (New York: Scribner, 1951), 2:52–53.

69. For a broader treatment, see, e.g., Frey, *Glory of the Crucified One*, 171–97.

70. Num 21:5–9; cf. Wis 16:5–7.

71. Similarly, also in John 8:28; 12:32–33.

72. Cf. the common phrase κρεμάννυμι ἐπὶ ξύλου. Interestingly in a Johannine context, the pole in Num 21:9 LXX is called a "sign" (σημεῖον).

already been anointed for burial (John 12:1–8) and announces that "the hour has come for the Son of Man to be glorified" (12:23). Integral to this glorification is a vicarious death. As Jesus goes on to explain in the following verse, "Very truly I tell you, unless a kernel of wheat falls to the ground and dies, it remains only a single seed. But if it dies, it produces many seeds" (12:24). That is, if Jesus had not died, he would have been alone in the sense that he would not have received the gift of the disciples from the Father.[73] Hence his death is necessary to procure their life.

2.2 Jesus's Death as Life-for-Life Exchange

With the grain image in John 12 we therefore begin to see the motif that Jesus's death somehow procures life: that is, that he gives up his life to preserve life, indeed more than that—to bring *new* life to others. This is apparent in a number of places in John.

Jesus Gives His Flesh and Blood for the Life of the World (John 6:22–58)

The bread of life discourse in John 6:22–58 offers further grounds for seeing the soteriological function of Jesus's death. Jesus declares that he is the bread (John 6:35, 48) "that gives life to the world" (6:33). Like the bronze serpent, the provision of this bread is to snatch life from an otherwise inevitable death, "so that one might eat of it and not die" (6:50):[74] Jesus's flesh is the bread that is "for (ὑπέρ) the life of the world" (6:51). There is no substitutionary sense intrinsic to the preposition ὑπέρ here—it means "for the provision of," "for the sake of"—but the preposition does appear frequently in soteriological contexts in John.[75] The implication, however, is that Jesus gives his flesh (in death) so that life comes to the world: there is a life-for-life exchange. This is probably suggested in particular by the drinking of Jesus's blood, given that "the life is

---

73. *Pace* Christian Dietzfelbinger, *Das Evangelium nach Johannes* (Zurich: Theologischer Verlag Zürich, 2001), 1:390, the point here is not that Jesus would be alone by being without his Father. The contrast is between remaining alone in the sense of being fruitless and being fruitful by producing many other seeds.

74. As Thyen notes (*Johannesevangelium*, 362), this is not merely death as the natural end of life but "death as the wages of sin" (noting Rom 6:23).

75. Though not always in a sacrificial context, *pace* D. A. Carson, *The Gospel according to John* (Grand Rapids: Eerdmans, 1991), 386 (see 1:30; 11:4). The formulation "repeatedly found in a sacrificial context" (*John*, 295) is more accurate.

in the blood,"[76] and Jesus states that drinking his blood is the precondition for having life (6:53). The grizzly language of eating flesh and drinking blood obviously presupposes the death of the victim.[77] Again, participation is key (6:53-58): eating and drinking the flesh and blood of Jesus correspond to believing (cf. 3:14-16).

The Good Shepherd Lays Down His Life for the Sheep (John 10:10-11)

John 10 changes the image and portrays Jesus as the good shepherd who lays down his life for his flock (John 10:11, 15). This is "the most extensive presentation of Jesus's death as a vicarious sacrifice"[78] and there is clearly a life-for-life exchange involved here:

> [10]"The thief comes only to steal and kill and destroy; I have come that they may have life, and have it in abundance. [11]I am the good shepherd. The good shepherd lays down his life for the sheep." (John 10:10-11)

In contrast to the thief who kills for what he supposes to be his own benefit, Jesus lays down his life so that his sheep might have life.[79] The point is clear: "the assumption is that the sheep are in mortal danger; that in their defence the shepherd loses his life; that by his death they are saved."[80] More than that, life is not just *preserved* but *enhanced* according to John 10:10 ("life in abundance"). Some speak of "sacrifice" here, and of course—in the everyday sense of that term—the theme is present, though not in the sense of a cultic sacrifice.[81]

---

76. Lev 17:11, 14; cf. also Deut 12:23.

77. Lincoln, *John*, 232; Wengst, *Johannesevangelium*, 214.

78. Smith, *Theology of the Gospel of John*, 118.

79. σῴζω in John 10:9 is there not mere preservation but rescue from death for heightened life (cf. John 10:10); rightly, Jörg Frey, "Edler Tod—wirksamer Tod—stellvertretender Tod—heilschaffender Tod: Zur narrativen und theologischen Deutung des Todes Jesu im Johannesevangelium," in *The Death of Jesus in the Fourth Gospel*, ed. Gilbert Van Belle (Leuven: Leuven University Press, 2007), 85.

80. Carson, *John*, 386.

81. E.g., Lincoln, *John*, 297, refers to "sacrifice." Cf. Jens Schröter, "Sterben für die Freunde: Überlegungen zur Deutung des Todes Jesu im Johannesevangelium," in *Religionsgeschichte des Neuen Testaments: Festschrift für Klaus Berger zum 60. Geburtstag*, ed. Axel von Dobbeler, Kurt Erlemann, and Roman Heiligenthal (Tübingen: Francke, 2000), 270, on the absence of atonement for sins.

One Man Dying for the People (John 11:49–52)

In the following chapter, Caiaphas also unwittingly, yet prophetically, describes the effects of Jesus's death:

> [49]One of them, Caiaphas who was high priest that year, spoke. "You know nothing!" he said. [50]"You do not realize that it is better for you that one man die for the people than that the whole nation perish."
>
> [51]He did not say this on his own, but as high priest that year he prophesied that Jesus would die for the nation, [52]and not only for that nation but also to gather the scattered children of God and make them one. (John 11:49–52)

Carson rightly comments that "Johannine irony reaches its apogee here."[82] Caiaphas is obviously depicted as making a political calculation, but also as unwittingly speaking the divine truth about Jesus's death. Here, in one man dying rather than the whole (Jewish) nation perishing, Jesus's death has a substitutionary, soteriological function: "Jesus dies 'for' the people (λαός)—in place of the people and for its benefit."[83] This death also has the ecclesiological implication of uniting the scattered—that is, gentile—children of God (John 11:49–52; cf. 18:14). Like the good shepherd discourse, this passage has both salvation and ingathering (cf. 10:16). Von Wahlde rightly notes the intrinsic value of Jesus's death in passages such as John 10:11–15 and 11:49–52, rather than it being a logical prelude to something else.[84]

Laying Down Life for One's Friends (John 15:13)

Similar language to that of John 10 and 11 appears in the Farewell Discourse, where Jesus states that he dies not for his sheep or for the nation but for friends:

---

82. Carson, *John*, 421. Cf. also 422: "Both Caiaphas and John understand Jesus' death to be substitutionary: either Jesus dies or the nation dies." See further Tobias Nicklas, "Die Prophetie des Kajaphas: Im Netz johanneischer Ironie," *NTS* 46 (2000): 589–94, who remarks on further irony in the accusation "do you know nothing?" (591); see further 592–93 on 11:50, and the astute point (derived from Beutler) on the subtle *inclusio* in the uses of συνάγω in 11:47 and 11:52 (594).

83. Frey, *Glory of the Crucified One*, 186.

84. Urban C. von Wahlde, "The Interpretation of the Death of Jesus in John against the Background of First-Century Jewish Eschatological Expectations," in Van Belle, *Death of Jesus in the Fourth Gospel*, 560.

"Greater love has no one than this: to lay down one's life for one's friends" (John 15:13). Since this is followed up by the gloss that Jesus's disciples are his friends, there is clearly an allusion to his death for the disciples. The motif of vicarious death for a friend is a very common one in the ancient world. In philosophical literature, the good, even the necessity, of dying for a friend is found across Pythagorean, Stoic, and Epicurean schools.[85] The point in John, as in those classical texts, is clearly a substitutionary death in the place of another.

Narrative Substitutions (John 18:8–9; 18:38–40; 19:25–27?)

Finally, there are the cases of what Frey groups together as three narrative substitutions, scenes in the drama of the passion that may suggest Jesus's substitutionary or vicarious death.[86]

First, Jesus commands his aggressors to leave the disciples alone so that none are lost:

> [8]Jesus answered, "I told you that I am he. If you are looking for me, then let these men go." [9]This happened so that the words he had spoken would be fulfilled: "I have not lost one of those you gave me." (John 18:8–9)

Dietzfelbinger raises the question of whether the external protection is a symbol of eschatological salvation but does not answer it.[87] The use of ἀπόλλυμι here for "lose" is suggestive of a two-level meaning (cf., e.g., John 3:16), especially given that John 18 here is quoting Jesus's prediction in John 6:39, where the "losing none" is given an eschatological interpretation: "I shall lose none of all those he has given me, but raise them up at the last day." Smith is therefore right to comment on 18:8–9 as follows: "The vicarious nature of Jesus' death, in the sense that he died for, and instead of, his followers, is more than once made clear. At his arrest Jesus identifies himself to the arresting party and tells them to let the others, his disciples, go (18:8). Presumably he will die in their stead."[88]

---

85. Simon Gathercole, *Defending Substitution: An Essay on Atonement in Paul* (Grand Rapids: Baker, 2015), 97–102. In addition to references there, see Seneca, *Ben.* 1.10.5: "A worthy person I would defend even at the cost of my blood and share in his peril; as for an unworthy person, if I can save him from robbers by raising a cry, I would not hold back from speech to save the man."

86. Frey, *Glory of the Crucified One*, 192.

87. Dietzfelbinger, *Evangelium nach Johannes*, 1:255: "Soll die von den Jüngern in V. 8f. erlebte äussere Bewahrung Symbol für die eschatologische Bewahrung sein?"

88. Smith, *Theology of the Gospel of John*, 118; similarly, Wengst, *Johannesevangelium*, 486 (Jesus acting "stellvertretend"); also Carson, *John*, 579.

Second, there is the Barabbas episode:

[38]"What is truth?" retorted Pilate. With this he went out again to the Jews gathered there and said, "I find no basis for a charge against him. [39]But it is your custom for me to release to you one prisoner at the time of the Passover. Do you want me to release 'the king of the Jews'?" [40]They shouted back, "No, not him! Give us Barabbas!" (Barabbas was an insurgent.) (John 18:38–40)

There is a clear contrast here between Jesus, the "king of the Jews," and Barabbas, the polar opposite of a king, namely an insurgent. Thyen further points out that the characterization of Barabbas as a λῃστής evokes the *bad* shepherds (John 10:1, 8) with whom Jesus is contrasted. Therefore, as in Luke, though by different means, Barabbas is a kind of counterpart to Jesus.[89] The question in the pericope is who is going to be set free. The default position, the only option proposed by Pilate, is that Jesus should be released (John 18:39); indeed Jesus has two reasons for being released: first, he should not be in prison in the first place, and second, he has the chance for release through the Passover amnesty. The crowd's verdict is the opposite. Given John's propensity for irony of this kind (cf. John 11:49–52), and his theological interest in life-for-life exchange elsewhere, it is highly likely that the substitutionary motif is being reinforced here.[90]

Frey notes these two examples as illustrating the substitutionary nature of the death of Jesus, adding a third more speculative or "less developed" example—the exchange of roles between Jesus and the beloved disciple at the foot of the cross.[91] In John 19:25–27, Jesus and the disciple change places in the sense that Mary becomes the mother of the beloved disciple, and the disciple becomes the son of Mary.[92]

Conclusion

Overall, then, the notion of Jesus's death as vicarious, in the sense that he dies to secure or rescue the lives of others, is embedded in John's narrative at

---

89. Thyen, *Johannesevangelium*, 720.

90. Contra Dietzfelbinger, *Evangelium nach Johannes*, 280.

91. Frey, *Glory of the Crucified One*, 192.

92. Frey, "Edler Tod—wirksamer Tod," 88. John's language in 19:30 suggests that in his death, Jesus is "passing on" (rather than simply *giving up*) his spirit, perhaps especially to the nucleus of the new family of God (Mary and the beloved disciple) at the foot of the cross: so Jean Zumstein, "The Purpose of the Ministry and Death of Jesus in the Gospel of John," in *The Oxford Handbook of Johannine Studies*, ed. Judith Lieu and Martinus C. de Boer (Oxford: Oxford University Press, 2018), 343–44; similarly Thyen, *Johannesevangelium*, 737.

a number of points. He "lays down his life for his friends," evoking the widespread motif of vicarious death in philosophical literature; he dies instead of the people, both in Caiaphas's intended meaning and in a theological sense; he dies to protect the lives of his sheep and to preserve the lives of those the Father has given him and give them life in abundance. The Barabbas episode probably provides a further narrative illustration of the idea.

2.3 The Death of Jesus as Attraction

In John 12, Jesus's lifting up draws the elect:

> [30]Jesus said, "This voice was for your benefit, not mine. [31]Now is the time for judgment on this world; now the prince of this world will be driven out. [32]And I, when I am lifted up from the earth, will draw all people to myself." [33]He said this to show the kind of death he was going to die. [34]The crowd spoke up, "We have heard from the law that the messiah will remain forever, so how can you say, 'The Son of Man must be lifted up'? Who is this 'Son of Man'?" (John 12:30–34)

In this dialogue, John glosses Jesus's "lifting up" as his death (John 12:33), an interpretation also assumed by the crowd (12:34). The "drawing" that Jesus talks about is a divine action, to which corresponds the more frequent Johannine language, emphasizing the human agency, of "coming" to Jesus.[93] The "all" here in the context probably has an ethnically universal point, since the pericope begins with the arrival of some Greeks (12:20).[94] The cross, then, brings to Jesus those whom the Father has given him. The agency of the Father, Son, and believer are all real, so that the Father gives, the Son draws, and the believer comes.

2.4 Jesus as Passover Sacrifice?

In John's passion narrative, there may be a suggestion that Jesus is identified in some sense with the Passover lamb.[95] First, commentators often remark that Jesus is killed on the Preparation Day of Passover, at noon (John 19:14), when the

93. This is roughly synonymous with "believing" (esp. 6:44; cf. also John 6:35, 37, 65; 7:37; [negatively] 5:40).

94. Carson, *John*, 444.

95. For the primary sources, see Raymond E. Brown, *The Death of the Messiah: From Gethsemane to the Grave* (London: Geoffrey Chapman, 1994), 847–48. Thyen, *Johannesevangelium*, 118, is confident on the point.

lambs are sacrificed.[96] Second, Jesus is presented with hyssop on the cross (19:29), the plant used to daub the lintel in the Passover. Third, not one of Jesus's bones is broken (19:36), which may echo the fact that the Passover lamb had to be without defect (Exod 12:5). None of these points is particularly decisive, however.

In the first place, the time for the sacrificing the Passover lambs is not clearly noon: Jubilees is insistent on twilight; the Mishnah states that the sacrifice takes place subsequent to the afternoon daily offering, which on a Friday was slaughtered at 12:30 p.m. and offered at 1:30 p.m., noting that the Passover sacrifice was invalid if it took place before noon; Philo states in one place that it did not take place before three o'clock in the afternoon, the ninth hour, and in another place that the sacrifices did begin at noon; Josephus reports that the sacrifices took place between the ninth and eleventh hours, that is, between 3:00 p.m. and 5:00 p.m. in the afternoon.[97] In sum, then, there is no consensus at all about the exact timing of the Passover sacrifice. In the second and third cases, there are other associations to hyssop and the unbroken bones. Hyssop is involved as a component in other rituals in the Pentateuch, and its association in Ps 51 is with cleansing, not Passover. The unharmed bones could signal divine protection, as in Ps 34:20 (33:21 LXX).

It is possible, however, that this series of "not necessarily" objections is overcautious. John 1:29 (Jesus as "lamb of God") may have Passover associations as well. It is hard to make a decision either way, and so the best conclusion may simply be *non liquet* and not to rule out the possibility. If there was an association of Jesus with the Passover lamb, the implication could be that Jesus's death has an apotropaic function.[98] Koester emphasizes that the sense would be deliverance from death and divine sparing.[99] As was noted in discussion of John 18:8–9, a key theme in John's Gospel is Jesus's preservation and protection of his disciples, in which context an apotropaic sense of his death would work well.

2.5 The Death of Jesus as Cleansing

Perhaps the most controversial matter in the discussion of the soteriological character of the death of Christ in John concerns whether John believes that

96. E.g., John Marsh, *Saint John* (London: Penguin, 1968), 610.

97. Respectively, Jub. 49.12; m. Pesaḥ. 5.1, 3; Philo, *QE* 1.11; *Spec. Laws* 2.145; Josephus, *J. W.* 6.423.

98. Ashton, *Understanding the Fourth Gospel*, 466.

99. Koester, *Symbolism in the Fourth Gospel*, 220–21.

Jesus's death is sacrificial and expiatory, that is, *atoning* in the sense that John draws upon cultic imagery. Eminent Johannine scholars line up on both sides of the debate. On the one hand, Jean Zumstein can claim that "the themes of sacrifice and blood" and "expiation" are absent.[100] However, Martinus de Boer states that salvation comes not only through baptism but also "by a cleansing with Jesus's blood, shed in his death," which is therefore "an act of expiation."[101] Even John Ashton can say that "Bultmann's judgement that 'the thought of Jesus' death as atonement for sin has no place in John' is far too sweeping."[102] It needs to be borne in mind here that the debate among scholars is often not just a straightforward exegetical dispute but is shaped by various "metaissues," such as whether scholars should use the Johannine epistles as an aid to the interpretation of the Gospel, or what the criteria are for identifying Old Testament allusions, especially allusions to Isa 53. A case will be made here for a partially cultic or expiatory dimension to Jesus's death, in the sense that Jesus's death cleanses from sin or sins. Regardless of whether John's understanding is cultic in a strong sense (e.g., understanding Jesus's death as replicating or replacing the functions of the temple), John's depiction of Jesus's death probably *draws on cultic language* at points. The focus here, however, is on Jesus's death as removing or cleansing from sin.

John 1:29 and the Removal of Sin

First, we can note John the Baptist's introductory announcement. Like Matthew, the Gospel of John provides an early statement about the identity of Jesus in which soteriology is integral: "Behold the lamb of God who takes away the sin of the world" (John 1:29). And as with Matt 1:21, John's statement gives no indication at this early point in the narrative of how this is going to take place. The effect, however, is likely to be that Jesus "takes away sin" in the sense of removing guilt: αἴρω τὴν ἁμαρτίαν is a calque of the Hebrew idiom *ns' 't-'wn* (or

---

100. Jean Zumstein, "L'interprétation de la mort de Jésus dans les discours d'adieu," in Van Belle, *Death of Jesus in the Fourth Gospel*, 117–18.

101. De Boer, *Johannine Perspectives*, 290, 291. Craig R. Koester, "The Death of Jesus and the Human Condition: Exploring the Theology of John's Gospel," in *Life in Abundance: Studies of John's Gospel in Tribute to Raymond E. Brown*, ed. John Donahue (Collegeville, MN: Liturgical, 2005), 148, also talks of Jesus's death as a purgation. De Boer takes this to be the removal of postbaptismal sin.

102. Ashton, *Understanding the Fourth Gospel*, 466, citing Bultmann, *Theology of the New Testament*, 2:54.

ns' 't-ḥṭ't), which means to forgive sin or remove guilt.[103] Additionally the Johannine αἴρω τὴν ἁμαρτίαν is very close to the Septuagintal αἴρω τὸ ἁμάρτημα (← *ns' 't-ḥṭ't* [1 Sam 15:25]), meaning *forgive a sin*, or ἐξαίρω τὰ ἁμαρτήματα (← *ns' 't-ʿwn* [Exod 28:38]), meaning *take away sins*,[104] and to αἴρω ἁμαρτίας plural in 1 John 3:5. For what it may be worth, a similar idiom comes in the Testament of Job.[105] Moreover, the Greek is perfectly capable of this interpretation even without a Semitic background. John frequently defines guilt as "having sin" (ἁμαρτίαν ἔχω).[106] If someone has ἁμαρτία, which someone else takes away (αἴρω), the sense of removal of sin would make good sense even to a biblically illiterate Greek speaker.[107] There may well be other nuances in John 1:29, such as Jesus being depicted as the Passover lamb or suffering servant, and the removal of sin as purification as well as forgiveness, but at this point in John's Gospel, such aspects are underdetermined, and even a reference to the death of Jesus is not yet necessary.[108] Still, this announcement from John the Baptist about Jesus is an important one, as it comes "at the moment he [Jesus] first enters public view."[109] At this point, we have a tolerably clear reference to the removal of sin.[110] In the case of the good shepherd discourse, I expressed reservations about the term "sacrifice"; on John 1:29, some use the language of "atoning sacrifice."[111] Again, certainly the quotidian sense of "atonement," that is, reconciliation, is implied here, but the extent to which John is here thinking of something like cultic atonement is unclear.[112]

There may, additionally, be a particular background to John's use of αἴρω here. Although the Old Greek text of Isa 53:12e reads "and he took up (ἀνήνεγκεν) the sins of many," Aquila's text has "and he took away (ἦρεν) the

---

103. Barrett, *John*, 176–77. The Hebrew phrase *ns' 't-ʿwn* can also mean to bear guilt, or carry the consequence of sins, but the Greek is less amenable to this sense.

104. At least in the Greek; in the Hebrew the sense is rather "bear the guilt."

105. In T. Job 43.17, Eliphaz sings ἦρται τὰ ἁμαρτήματα ἡμῶν, κεκαθάρισται ἡμῶν ἡ ἀνομία.

106. John 9:41; 15:22, 24; 19:11; cf. also sin "remaining" in 9:41.

107. E.g., Euripides, *El.* 942 (following the manuscript reading, not any of the conjectures). Cf. Matt 13:12; 25:28, 29; Mark 4:25; Luke 8:18; 19:24–26. E.g., Mark 4:25: ὃς γὰρ ἔχει, δοθήσεται αὐτῷ· καὶ ὃς οὐκ ἔχει, καὶ ὃ ἔχει ἀρθήσεται ἀπ᾽ αὐτοῦ.

108. See the appropriately cautious remarks in Carson, *John*, 150–51; Frey, *Glory of the Crucified*, 191, is more confident of a clear reference forward to the cross.

109. Koester, "Death of Jesus and the Human Condition," 145.

110. Frey, *Glory of the Crucified*, 190.

111. E.g., Carson, *John*, 150.

112. Rightly, Frey, *Glory of the Crucified*, 195.

sins of many," using the verb αἴρω, which John employs.[113] Therefore, John 1:29 may have been influenced by a Greek text resembling one of the predecessors of Aquila. The presence in John of what were to become Aquilan readings is paralleled elsewhere as well.[114] Many of course see Isa 53 behind John the Baptist's announcement here: the grounds for this lie in (1) the removal of sin just noted, (2) the reference to the "lamb"/"sheep," (3) the evangelist's reference to Isa 53 elsewhere, in John 12:38, and (4) that the statement "this is the chosen one of God" (1:34) is more easily understood in this connection.[115] We will return to this question later.

The Footwashing (John 13:3–15)

A second passage relevant to the question of cleansing is the scene in which Jesus washes the disciples' feet. This event is obviously to be understood symbolically, because Jesus stresses that, as it was happening, Peter did not understand it (John 13:7). Jesus makes it clear that the event both points to salvation (13:4–10) and is an example to be followed (13:12–15).[116] Here John emphasizes that unless the disciples are washed, they can have no part in Jesus (13:8): this scene probably suggests that the cross accomplishes or completes the disciples' purification (13:10). "Probably the basic, salvific meaning of Jesus' washing of his disciples' feet is that it symbolizes his vicarious death for them."[117] De Boer rightly emphasizes that in various places in the Pentateuch, cleansing and atoning are analogous in sin-removal contexts, although the extent to which we can understand the footwashing in a cultic sense depends on what one means by "cultic."[118] Forestell also usefully notes that "the question of purification appears with greater prominence in the fourth gospel than in the

---

113. Frederick Field, *Origen: Hexapla* (Oxford: Clarendon, 1875), 2:535.

114. On John 1:23, see M. J. J. Menken, "The Quotation from Isa 40,3 in John 1,23," *Bib* 66 (1985): 194; in the quotation from Zech 12:10 in John 19:37, John and Aquila (as well as Theodotion) have ἐξεκέντησαν instead of the Septuagint's κατωρχήσαντο. Maarten Menken, *Old Testament Quotations in the Fourth Gospel: Studies in Textual Form* (Leuven: Peeters, 1996), 130–31, also notes that the quotation of Ps 41 in John 13:18, with Aquila and Theodotion against the Septuagint, has πτέρνα (rather than πτερνισμός as in Ps 40:10 LXX [Heb 41:9]); see also pp. 24, 176.

115. Beutler, *John*, 59. Cf. the chosen servant in Isa 41:8–9; 42:1; 43:10; 44:1–2; 45:4; 49:7.

116. De Boer, *Johannine Perspectives*, 284.

117. Smith, *Theology of the Gospel of John*, 118; similarly Wengst, *Johannesevangelium*, 397, who also notes that the consequence is forgiveness of sins.

118. De Boer, *Johannine Perspectives*, 273–74.

synoptics."[119] Rather than the footwashing symbolizing Jesus dealing with postbaptismal sins, however, it is probably better to see the death of Jesus as completing the process of purification, or describing it from a different point of view.[120] Here again we have a clear sense of a cleansing or purifying death of Jesus; what is less certain, but possible, is whether this points to an atoning or sacrificial or cultic sense of the cross: again, this depends on what one means by these terms.

Jesus's Consecration for and of the Disciples (John 17:19)

Third, we have another potentially cultic statement in John 17:19: "For them I sanctify myself (ὑπὲρ αὐτῶν ἐγὼ ἁγιάζω ἐμαυτόν), that they too may be truly sanctified." Three points can be made here. (1) The reference is almost certainly to Jesus's death.[121] Although the verb can be used in a variety of contexts, the *self*-consecration of Jesus probably refers to his dedication of himself to death.[122] (2) The combination of the reference to Jesus's death with the ὑπέρ language strongly implies a sense of a soteriological death "for them."[123] (3) It is certainly notable that here we have a rare instance of John's employment of cultic terminology; on the other hand, whether it is right to speak of atonement or sacrifice on the basis of the use of cultic terminology depends on one's definition. ἁγιάζω can mean "sanctify" or "consecrate" in a broad sense, although when referring to a victim being given over to death, as here, John is probably drawing on the language of a sacrificial offering for sins.[124]

---

119. Forestell, *Word of the Cross*, 155.

120. *Pace* de Boer, *Johannine Perspectives*, 290–91. The language 13:8 (ἐὰν μὴ νίψω σε, οὐκ ἔχεις μέρος μετ᾽ ἐμοῦ) seems too definite and decisive to be concerned with an ongoing plight of postbaptismal sin.

121. Rightly, Frey, *Glory of the Crucified*, 189; Wengst, *Johannesevangelium*, 474.

122. So most interpreters, *pace* de Boer, *Johannine Perspectives*.

123. Thyen, *Johannesevangelium*, 695: Here Thyen understands the self-consecration of Jesus, on the basis of the use of the verb in passages such as Exod 13:2 and Deut 15:19, and the related ὑπέρ language in John, to relate to sacrifice for sins. Wengst, *Johannesevangelium*, 475, refers to "[die] positive Wirkung seines Todes."

124. E.g., Thyen, *Johannesevangelium*, 695, connects John 17:19 here with 1:29; 10:11; and 15:13. Brown surmises that we have here a Hebrews-like portrayal of Christ as both priest and victim. See Raymond E. Brown, *The Gospel according to John* (New York: Doubleday, 1966–1970), 2:767: Jesus is "a priest offering himself as a victim for those whom God has given him."

The Blood and the Water (John 19:34–35)

Fourth, there is the flow of blood and water from Jesus's body:[125]

> [34]Instead, one of the soldiers pierced Jesus's side with a spear, bringing a sudden flow of blood and water. [35]The man who saw it has given testimony, and his testimony is true. He knows that he tells the truth, and he testifies so that you also may believe. (John 19:34–35)

What is not in dispute among scholars is the considerable importance of verse 34, as is accentuated by the insistence on its veracity in verse 35.[126] Beyond that, there is disagreement. Leaving aside here debates about the statement's antidocetic character, scholars have struggled to find an interpretation that can account for both the water *and* the blood.[127] Overall, it is probably not necessary to be unduly restrictive in interpreting the blood and water. The evangelist probably did not want to focus merely on *either* baptism/washing/cleansing *or* the life-giving properties of water.[128] Similarly, there is probably a constructive ambiguity in the reference to blood as suggesting both life/death and cleansing. Life-giving and cleansing are therefore probably common both to the water and the blood.[129]

Illumination from 1 John?

Finally, although some would prefer to keep 1 John out of the discussion, it probably is relevant. In my view at least, it was written by the same author and was intended precisely to clarify the meaning of the Gospel. The reference in

---

125. This is perhaps related to the theme of Jesus as the new temple in John. See Frey, "Edler Tod—wirksamer Tod," 92–93; Carson, *John*, 182. Frey notes John 1:51; 2:21; 7:38–39; and 19:34 in this regard.

126. De Boer, *Johannine Perspectives*, 293; Lincoln, *John*, 479.

127. See the criticisms made in de Boer, *Johannine Perspectives*, 294–97.

128. Thyen, *Johannesevangelium*, 749, is probably correct that the water symbolizes the Spirit, linking John 19:34 to 7:37–39.

129. Craig R. Koester, *Symbolism in the Fourth Gospel: Meaning, Mystery, Community* (Minneapolis: Fortress, 2003), 201, notes a possible nice irony in that the leaders were concerned about defilement from Jesus's body (John 19:31; Deut 21:22–23), whereas for John, Jesus's body is a source of cleansing. De Boer, *Johannine Perspectives*, 297–98, comments that cleansing from sin (in a baptismal sense) is crucial here, in that the water gives the blood its cleansing significance. He points further to 1 John 1:7–2:2 and 5:6–8 in this regard. Lincoln, *John*, 479, sees the focus, in both the water and the blood, on life.

1 John to the testimony of the blood, water, and Spirit seems to concern the three elements that proceed from the body of Jesus at his death (1 John 5:7–8; John 19:30, 34). In the epistle, there is unambiguous language of expiation in what is normally regarded as cultic language: purification from sin (καθαρίζει ἡμᾶς ἀπὸ πάσης ἁμαρτίας) and from all unrighteousness (καθαρίσῃ ἡμᾶς ἀπὸ πάσης ἀδικίας), forgiveness of sins (ἀφῇ ἡμῖν τὰς ἁμαρτίας), and atoning sacrifice for sins (ἱλασμός ἐστιν περὶ τῶν ἁμαρτιῶν ἡμῶν) are presented analogously as rough equivalents (1 John 1:7, 9; 2:2; cf. 4:10). According to 1 John 1, these are accomplished by Jesus through his blood, or death.

Concluding Synthesis

In conclusion, how should one join the dots in this diverse but related material in John 1:29; 13:1–10; 17:19; 19:34–35; and 1 John? It seems to me that, even if one *both* is skeptical about the influence of Isa 53 on John 1:29 *and* brackets 1 John from the discussion, there are still strong grounds for seeing Jesus's death as cleansing from sin. On the one hand, John 1:29 refers to a removal of sin but does not explain how this occurs; on the other, John 13 and 19:34 refer to a cleansing, strongly implying that it takes place in Jesus's death, but do not clarify what the cleansing is from: they do state, however, that this cleansing is essential for fellowship with Jesus (John 13:8) and that the flow of blood and water is reported to elicit belief in Jesus (19:35). The two parts therefore complement each other neatly: John 1:29 notes what the cleansing is from but not how it happens; John 13 and 19 do not say what the cleansing is from but do imply how it happens. Jesus's self-consecration ὑπέρ the disciples (John 17:19) amplifies the sense of Jesus's death for others as a purification or sanctification for and of the disciples (ἵνα ὦσιν καὶ αὐτοὶ ἡγιασμένοι ἐν ἀληθείᾳ).[130]

If, in addition, Isa 53 is seen in the background to John 1:29, the point is strengthened further. Many, such as Frey, take this to be the case even without reference to the Aquilan reading of Isa 53:12 with ἦρεν.[131] The question here is whether the agreement between John 1:29 and this text form of Isa 53:12 is mere coincidence, which is of course possible. Perhaps more importantly, 1 John probably should be taken into account. The epistle is a prosaic explanation

---

130. Sanctification through the death of Jesus should not be understood as in competition with sanctification through other means (cf. John 17:17).

131. Frey, "Edler Tod—wirksamer Tod," 86–87; also Michel Gourgues, "'Mort pour nos péchés selon les Écritures': Que reste-t-il chez Jean du Credo des origines? John 1,29, chaînon unique de continuité," in Van Belle, *Death of Jesus in the Fourth Gospel*, 193–94.

in theological mode of what appears in hints and implications in the Gospel: writing the letter, the author is, one might say, writing "no longer in figures, but plainly." If this is the case, then the epistle can be seen to agree with the joining of the dots above. The epistle attributes to the "blood" of Jesus (John 19:34) "purification" (John 13:10–11) from "sin" (John 1:29) through Jesus's death when it declares that "the blood of Jesus his son cleanses us from all sin" (1 John 1:7). As noted earlier, 1 John 3 employs the same collocation of αἴρω + ἁμαρτία as does John 1:29, the epistle highlighting this as the reason for the incarnation (1 John 3:5). The epistle can still speak elliptically, simply referring to Jesus giving his life on our behalf (1 John 3:16), or it can speak more expansively, of Jesus as an atoning sacrifice (4:10).

2.6 Interim Conclusion: The Johannine Jesus's Death and the Kerygma

The difficulty in assessing John's view of the death of Christ is not that there is so little to go on but that there is so much. The cross has revelatory and ecclesiological functions in John, and these are an integral part of salvation, just as Jesus's death removes sin and gives life in a life-for-life exchange, not only snatching others from death and preserving the lives of others but also providing life "in abundance" (John 10:10). I am unpersuaded by Ashton's view that the soteriological function of Jesus's death in John is marginal.[132] As we have seen, references to the death of Jesus and its soteriological interpretation are scattered throughout the Gospel.[133] As another commentator has summarized the evidence in John: "the cross is not *merely* a revelatory moment . . . it is the death of the shepherd for his sheep, the sacrifice of one man for his nation, the life that is given for the world."[134] In John, certain passages present the crucifixion as a vicarious "death for friends," or perhaps as a Passover lamb. There is evidently a sense of cleansing from sin as well, perhaps with cultic connotations.

Smith provides a helpful comment on John's relation to kerygmatic tradition:

132. Ashton, *Understanding the Fourth Gospel*, 466.

133. Cf. Zumstein, "Purpose of the Ministry and Death," 339, according to whom the death of Jesus is "the constant horizon of the story."

134. Carson, *John*, 97; see too the similar remark in C. H. Dodd, *The Interpretation of the Fourth Gospel* (Cambridge: Cambridge University Press, 1968), 369. The procrustean nature of Forestell's theory of revelation as salvation is evident from its inability to cope with passages such as John 13:10 ("necessarily secondary") or John 20:23 ("completely foreign to the Johannine theology"). See Forestell, *Word of the Cross*, 157, for these judgments.

Paul, in citing an early kerygmatic formula, says that Christ *died for our sins* according to the scriptures (1 Corinthians 15:3). Mark's account of the eucharistic words of institution, followed by Matthew and Luke, portrays Jesus speaking of his blood as poured out for many (or for his disciples), an obvious allusion to his death upon the cross, understood in cultic sacrificial terms (Mark 14:24). . . . Therefore, it is all the more surprising that such an understanding and interpretation of Jesus' death does not find a larger place in the Gospel of John. Yet several passages in the Gospel clearly allude to the primitive Christian interpretation of Jesus' death as a vicarious sacrifice: he is greeted as the lamb of God who takes away the sin of the world (1:29; cf. verse 34); out of his love God *gave* him (3:16; cf. Romans 5:8); Jesus gives his flesh for the life of the world (6:51); Jesus is said to die for the people (*hyper tou laou*), that the nation (*ethnos*) not perish (11:51). Moreover, the eucharistic language in 6:52–58 strongly suggests the participants' partaking of the redemptive benefits of Christ's death, and thus of his real humanity.[135]

Smith's conclusion is helpfully balanced here. John probably does make use of some cultic imagery: the self-sanctification of Jesus in the Gospel has the goal of the disciples' sanctification, and 1 John makes explicit what may already be implicit in John 1, 13, and 19. The concern to "let John be John" should not blind us to the sense of Jesus's death as cleansing (even perhaps cleansing in a "sacrificial" sense), although this facet of the death of Jesus is not stressed in John in the way it is elsewhere.[136] Even so, John agrees with the kerygma in strongly attributing saving significance to Jesus's vicarious death.[137]

3. The Resurrection of Jesus in John's Gospel

The significance of Jesus's resurrection in John's Gospel has often been underestimated. Some have averred that the cross in John is essentially co-extensive with Jesus's glorification, and so the resurrection at best enabled

---

135. Smith, *Theology of the Gospel of John*, 115, 116. Gourgues's essay, "Mort pour nos péchés selon les Écritures," is useful here, in that it reflects on how John uses the same words as the kerygma to describe a different reality and vice versa, while also using the same words to describe the same reality.

136. Frey, "Edler Tod—wirksamer Tod," 90, notes that the concern to maintain John's distinctive character underlies anxiety about atoning sacrifice in John.

137. Wengst, *Johannesevangelium*, 355, connects Caiaphas's prophetic word with 1 Cor 15:3.

the possibility of understanding the really significant events that had taken place already.[138] Or, more radically, in Bultmann's frequently cited words, "If Jesus' death on the cross is already his exaltation and glorification, *his resurrection* cannot be an event of special significance. No resurrection is needed to destroy the triumph which death might be supposed to have gained in the crucifixion."[139]

Certainly, there is a finality to the cross in John that makes understanding the resurrection a challenge. Lincoln rightly notes that in his death, Jesus has fulfilled the Father's commission to reveal God, to display his glory, to testify to the truth, and to give his life, so that Jesus's cry, "It is finished" (τετέλεσται), in John 19:30 is entirely appropriate.[140] As a result, the chapters narrating the resurrection appearances have been described by Attridge as "something of an anomaly."[141] There are some significant difficulties with such a claim, however. Quantitatively, there is extensive reference to the resurrection in the public ministry and in the Farewell Discourse, and John, in its final form, has a resurrection narrative both longer than and containing more copious appearances than the other canonical Gospels.[142] Qualitatively, John's particular interpretation of the tradition of Jesus's third-day resurrection *adds* to that tradition, as we shall see, rather than diminishing it. After noting two important aspects of the resurrection to begin with (sec. 3.1), the focus will be on the gospel significance of the resurrection, as the occasion of (sec. 3.2) the vindication of Jesus, (sec. 3.3) revelation, and especially (sec. 3.4) the transformation of the disciples.

138. Smith, *Theology of the Gospel of John*, 123.

139. Bultmann, *Theology of the New Testament*, 2:56. For citations of this passage, see, e.g., Smith, *Theology of the Gospel of John*, 123, and Craig R. Koester and Reimund Bieringer, eds., *The Resurrection of Jesus in the Gospel of John* (Tübingen: Mohr Siebeck, 2008), 15 n. 46 (Harold Attridge, "From Discord Rises Meaning"), 155 (Sandra Schneiders, "Touching the Risen Jesus"), and Andrew Lincoln, "'I Am the Resurrection and the Life': The Resurrection Message of the Fourth Gospel," in *Life in the Face of Death: The Resurrection Message of the New Testament*, ed. Richard N. Longenecker (Grand Rapids: Eerdmans, 1998), 124.

140. Lincoln, "I Am the Resurrection," 123.

141. Attridge, "From Discord Rises Meaning," 15.

142. Matthew 28 has twenty verses; Mark 16 has eight (though it may have had more); Luke 24 has fifty-three verses; and John 20–21 has fifty-six. (Even these verse numbers make Luke 24 and John 20–21 seem closer in length than they actually are: compare Luke 24's 818 words with John's 1,162 words.) John's Gospel has four appearances: the reference to the "third" appearance to the disciples (plural) in John 21:14 excludes the first appearance, to Mary.

3.1 The Event of the Resurrection

Two characteristics of the resurrection in John are notable at the outset. First, the resurrection is an act performed by Jesus himself, and second, John describes this as happening on the third day.

Jesus as Agent of the Resurrection

First, then, we also see already near the beginning of the Gospel a distinctive theme in John, namely that Jesus himself is the agent of the resurrection:

> [19]Jesus answered them, "Destroy this temple, and I will raise it again in three days." [20]They replied, "It has taken forty-six years to build this temple, and you are going to raise it in three days?" [21]But the temple he was speaking of was his body. (John 2:19–21)

This point is developed further in the less symbol-laden statement in John 10:17–18:

> [17]The reason my Father loves me is that I lay down my life—only to take it up again. [18]No one takes it from me, but I lay it down of my own accord. I have authority to lay it down and authority to take it up again. This command I received from my Father.

John 2 and 10 here mark a strong contrast with the language elsewhere in early Christian writings about the resurrection. Invariably, elsewhere in the New Testament, *God* raised Jesus from the dead. Sometimes Jesus is the subject of the active verb "rise" (ἀνίστημι), but then only intransitively and not reflexively.[143] More usually, we find God as the (sometimes implied) subject of the verb "raise" (ἐγείρω) with Jesus as the object,[144] or Jesus "raised" (by God) with the passive of the same verb.[145] On a few occasions in Acts, God is the subject, and Jesus the object, of "raise up" (ἀνίστημι) used transitively.[146] John can reflect this traditional variety, with Jesus as the subject of the active

---

143. Mark 9:9; Luke 24:7; 1 Thess 4:14; cf. Luke 16:31.

144. Acts 3:15; 4:10; 5:30; 10:40; 13:30, 37; Rom 4:24; 8:11; 10:9; 1 Cor 6:14; 15:15; 2 Cor 4:14; Gal 1:1; Eph 1:20; Col 2:12; 1 Thess 1:10; 1 Pet 1:21. Cf. ἀνάγω in Heb 13:20.

145. Matt 16:21; 17:9, 23; 20:19; 26:32; 27:64; 28:6–7; Mark 14:28; 16:6; Luke 9:22; 24:6, 34; Rom 4:25; 6:4, 9; 7:4; 8:34; 1 Cor 15:4, 12, 13, 14, 16, 17, 20; 2 Cor 5:15; 2 Tim 2:8.

146. Acts 2:24, 32; 3:26; 13:33–34; 17:31.

verb "rise" (ἀνίστημι), used intransitively (John 20:9), as well as describing the resurrection with the passive of "raise" (ἐγείρω in John 2:22; 21:14).[147] The assertion in John 2:19 that Jesus will raise up his own body, on the one hand, and the justification of the claim in his explanation that he has the authority to take up his life (John 10:18),[148] on the other, are striking against the wider Christian backdrop. Having said that, John also states in John 10:18 that Jesus's authority to rise again is a command from the Father.

Resurrection "on the Third Day"

Second, the anticipation of the resurrection in John 2 illustrates not only John's difference from the rest of the New Testament but also his traditionalism. As just noted, Jesus issues the challenge: "Destroy this temple, and I will raise it again in three days" (John 2:19; cf. 2:20). Immediately we see here John's absorption of an existing claim about the resurrection, and this reference to the "three days" is followed in the passion and resurrection narratives of John 19–20, with their sequence of days:

- Preparation/Friday (death and burial): John 19:31 and 19:42 refer to the day on which Jesus was crucified as Friday (Παρασκευή)[149] and note the onset of the Sabbath late in that day.
- Saturday (special Sabbath): "Now it was the Day of Preparation, and the next day was to be a special Sabbath. Because the Jewish leaders did not want the bodies left on the crosses during the Sabbath, they asked Pilate to have the legs broken and the bodies taken down" (John 19:31).
- Sunday: the first day of the week (John 20:1).

Overall, then, John reflects a traditional interest in the third-day resurrection, as well as designating Jesus as the agent of the resurrection in line with his high Christology.

---

147. In John's usage of ἐγείρω, as more widely with verbs in Koine, the passive form can denote a middle meaning, however, as is clear in John 11:29.

148. Lincoln, "I Am the Resurrection," 129, rightly notes that the use of ψυχή here refers to Jesus's human life, whereas ζωή in John refers to the divine life in Jesus.

149. For Παρασκευή ("Preparation") meaning Friday, i.e., the day before any Sabbath, see, e.g., Josephus, *Ant.* 16.163; Mark 15:42; Luke 23:54; *Did.* 8.1; *Mart. Pol.* 7.1; cf. προσάββατον in Jdt 8:6; cf. 2 Macc 8:26 and again Mark 15:42.

3.2 The Resurrection as the Vindication of Jesus

In John 2, the threat or challenge that Jesus issues (2:19) gives further content to the significance of the resurrection. As Jesus casts it there, the resurrection becomes in the first instance a reversal and frustration of the human attempt to get rid of Jesus. More than that, however, it is also a (delayed) vindication of Jesus.[150] The resurrection is the ultimate response to the question: "What sign can you show us to prove your authority to do all this?" Having performed in John 2:1–11 his first sign, Jesus shortly thereafter points forward to his last one.[151] As Moody Smith comments, "Already in 2:19–21 the Gospel points us forward to the resurrection, understood as Jesus' assertion of his own authority and mission."[152]

3.3 Resurrection, Revelation, and Faith

Further significance of the resurrection can be seen in its revelatory function. This can be discussed in dialogue with a statement by Moody Smith:

> In fact, the resurrection of Jesus adds nothing theologically to what has already been accomplished through his deeds, words, and death. At the same time, none of it would count as revelation and deliverance apart from Jesus' resurrection from the dead. The resurrection allows Jesus' ministry and message to be seen for what they were, and are.[153]

For the purposes of the argument here, we can leave aside the initial statement about whether nothing substantive is added. Smith suggests here that the resurrection "activates" for human beings the ministry and death of Jesus: without the resurrection, "none of it would count." But this activation is itself a work of Jesus and a part of or an aspect of revelation. Enabling "Jesus' ministry and

---

150. With Lincoln, "I Am the Resurrection," 134–35, *pace* Schneiders, "Touching the Risen Jesus," 155.

151. Craig R. Koester, "Jesus' Resurrection, the Signs, and the Dynamics of Faith in the Gospel of John," in Koester and Bieringer, *Resurrection of Jesus in the Gospel of John*, 47–74, distinguishes between the signs and the resurrection but talks of their similar functions; Barrett, *John*, 78, insists that the resurrection is not a sign, because it is the subject matter to which the signs point. It is identified fairly clearly as a sign in John 2, however.

152. Smith, *Theology of the Gospel of John*, 123.

153. Smith, *Theology of the Gospel of John*, 123.

message to be seen for what they were and are" is therefore far from "nothing theologically" in a Gospel where revelation is a central feature.

It is certainly true that the resurrection is a turning point for understanding Jesus's activity in his pre-Easter ministry:

> After he was raised from the dead, his disciples recalled what he had said. Then they believed the scripture and the words that Jesus had spoken. (John 2:22)

> At first his disciples did not understand all this. Only after Jesus was glorified did they realize that these things had been written about him and that these things had been done to him. (John 12:16)

The new understanding comes not just chronologically after the resurrection but follows it logically and theologically. The disciples' reminiscence comes as a result of the risen Jesus sending the Spirit (14:26; cf. 20:22). In addition to the blessing of understanding, however, there are more gifts that come as a consequence of the resurrection, to which we now turn.

3.4 The Transformation of the Disciples

The resurrection has a dramatic effect on the disciples. After the cross, we first see them locked in a house in fear (John 20:19). John 19:38–42 also makes clear that Joseph and Nicodemus were not expecting a resurrection: one does not place a hundred *litrai* of myrrh and aloes next to a body expected soon to rise from death.[154] In a number of places in the Farewell Discourse, Jesus highlights the woeful existence of the disciples both in the dramatic present and immediately upon Jesus's death, and draws a stark contrast with the condition of those disciples *after* Jesus's resurrection.[155]

Just before he is crucified, Jesus tells the disciples that "in a little while" he will depart; but he will also return again "a little while" after that (John 16:16).

---

154. Koester, *Word of Life*, 124.

155. See especially on this Jean Zumstein, "Jesus' Resurrection in the Farewell Discourses," in Koester and Bieringer, *Resurrection of Jesus in the Gospel of John*, 103–26. For his argument for the interval of the "little while" marking the space between death and resurrection in both 14:18–24 and 16:16–22, see 108–11 and 116–20; similarly, Thyen, *Johannesevangelium*, 630. For further bibliography on the correspondences between the Farewell Discourse and the Easter narratives, see Hans-Ulrich Weidemann, "Eschatology as Liturgy: Jesus' Resurrection and Johannine Eschatology," in Koester and Bieringer, *Resurrection of Jesus in the Gospel of John*, 286 n. 32.

Without doubt, there are complexities in the Farewell Discourse that make it impossible to sift through the passages and identify some as referring simply to the risen Jesus and some as referring to the ascended Jesus. The strong impression is that the resurrection and ascension are sometimes telescoped together, or regarded as a continuum (with perhaps the resurrection marking a stage in Jesus's return to the Father). This exploration here in section 3.4 of the disciples' transformation will avoid some of these difficulties by seeking to highlight very specific ways in which the resurrection narratives (at least partially) fulfill the promises of the Farewell Discourse.

Zumstein identifies a series of effects accompanying Jesus's resurrection when he traces a growing intensity in what Jesus promises in John 14:18–21:

> [18]I will not leave you as orphans; *I will come to you.* [19]Before long, the world will not see me anymore, but *you will see me.* Because I live, you also will live. [20]On that day *you will know* that I am in my Father, and you are in me, and I am in you. [21]Whoever has my commands and keeps them loves me. *The one who loves me will be loved by my Father,* and I too will love them and *I will show myself to them.* (John 14:18–21)

Zumstein helpfully notes here that the "restoration of the relationship between the disciple and his master is expressed by referring to different semantic fields."[156] He sees in particular a sequence of four different kinds of imagery: *spatial* (14:18), *seeing* (14:19), *knowing* (14:20), and finally *love* (14:21).

First, then, there is spatial imagery (John 14:18). The separation implied in the orphaned state is remedied in the first instance by Jesus's promise to come to the disciples (ἔρχομαι πρὸς ὑμᾶς). This happens in all three resurrection appearances to the disciples. In John 20:19, despite the locked doors, Jesus came (ἦλθεν ὁ Ἰησοῦς) into the midst of the disciples. Thomas was not there on that occasion "when Jesus came" (ὅτε ἦλθεν Ἰησοῦς) according to John 20:24, so—again, locked doors notwithstanding—Jesus came (ἔρχεται ὁ Ἰησοῦς) a second time into the disciples' midst (20:26).[157] In the third appearance, in John 21:13, there is a syntactically redundant reference to Jesus's coming (ἔρχεται Ἰησοῦς).[158] Hence it may be no accident that all three of the appearances to the disciples include instances of his coming to them. The spatial imagery is extended from Jesus's coming in the midst of the disciples to

---

156. Zumstein, "Jesus' Resurrection in the Farewell Discourses," 111.

157. Carson, *John*, 501, and Beutler, *John*, 383, both relate John 14:18 to the resurrection appearances.

158. Barrett, *John*, 582: the ἔρχεται "seems pleonastic."

their following him. The disciples were initially not able to follow Jesus where he went (13:33, 36–37), but after the resurrection, Jesus commands Peter twice, "Follow me!" (21:19, 22).[159] We might perhaps also connect Jesus's promise not to leave the disciples as orphans in John 14:18 with his address to them as (implicitly his?) "children" (παιδία) by the lake (21:5; cf. 13:33).[160]

Second, there is seeing (John 14:19): Jesus promises that in the immediate future (i.e., with his death), they will not see him, but afterward they will see him again.[161] This is realized in the resurrection narrative when Mary (20:14) and then the disciples (20:20) saw him.[162]

Third, the intensity is raised further when the disciples *know*: "On that day you will know that I am in my Father, and you are in me, and I am in you" (John 14:20). The verbal links with the resurrection accounts are not as close as those in the first two cases, but corresponding to what the disciples are to know is perhaps the content of Jesus's announcement to Mary, that "I am ascending to my Father and your Father, to my God and your God" (20:17). The triadic relationship of the disciples, Jesus, and the Father appears in both Jesus's promise in John 14:20 and his declaration in John 20:17.

Fourth, there is love: "The one who loves me will be loved by my Father, and I too will love them and show myself to them" (John 14:21). Peter's love for Jesus, expressed three times in John 21:15–17, makes Peter an example of "the one" spoken of in John 14:21, and so we are perhaps to understand that if Peter loves Jesus, then Peter is therefore loved by Jesus and the Father. Jesus's promise of love in John 14 is connected in some way to his self-revelation: "I too will love them and show myself (ἐμφανίσω . . . ἐμαυτόν) to them" (14:21). The latter certainly takes place in John 21, when Jesus "showed himself" (ἐφανέρωσεν ἑαυτόν) by the Sea of Galilee (21:1) on the third occasion on which "he was revealed" (ἐφανερώθη) in John 21:14.

There are further aspects of transformation that can be highlighted. Jesus promises in John 16:20–22 a change from grief to joy (cf. John 15:11; 16:24; 17:13). This comes to pass in John 20, where Mary's tears give way to her acclamation of Jesus and her journey to bring news to the disciples (20:11–18), and where "the disciples rejoiced (ἐχάρησαν) when they saw the Lord" (20:20). Similarly, the risen Jesus's appearance to the disciples is accompanied by him

---

159. Martin Hasitschka, "The Significance of the Resurrection Appearance in John 21," in Koester and Bieringer, *Resurrection of Jesus in the Gospel of John*, 324.

160. So Thyen, *Johannesevangelium*, 630.

161. Cf. John 16:16–19. Jesus will also see them (John 16:22).

162. Zumstein, "Jesus' Resurrection in the Farewell Discourses," 109, 118.

saying three times, "Peace be with you!" (20:19, 21, 26). Like "joy," peace was promised in the Farewell Discourse (14:27; 16:33) and is brought in the resurrection narrative.[163]

Finally, these transformed disciples can themselves be sent out. This is what Jesus had declared in John 17:18 ("As you sent me into the world, I have sent them into the world"), and he brings it about in John 20:21: "As the Father has sent me, I am sending you."[164] Beutler writes helpfully that the double mission of Jesus in which he proclaims the saving message and confronts unbelief is reflected in the disciples' mission as they proclaim both forgiveness of sins and judgment when sins are "retained" (20:23).[165] Recognizing the risen Jesus is a condition of this mission: before the recognition scene in John 21, the disciples cannot draw the fish to shore; it is only after Peter has recognized Jesus that he is able to bring in the perfect number of Christian fish (21:11).

In sum, the transformation that Jesus effects upon the disciples is not merely a return to the status quo before his death; the alteration is more profound.[166] Jesus's departure at his death is "not a loss but a gain."[167] As Jesus said, "It is for your good that I am going away" (John 16:7): the believer will do "greater things" even than Jesus, precisely because Jesus is going to the Father (14:12).[168] As Zumstein has put it, "the announced post-Easter period, which was presented in 14:12 as qualitatively superior and in 14:22–24 as inaccessible for the world, is now realized in chapter 20: The disciples are taking part in a new situation from which the world is excluded."[169] The fulfillment of Jesus's

163. Another possible contrast lies in the difference between them being "scattered" (16:32) and then "together" (21:2). So Hasitschka, "Significance of the Resurrection Appearance," 313.

164. Zumstein, "Jesus' Resurrection in the Farewell Discourses," 106.

165. Johannes Beutler, "Resurrection and the Remission of Sins: John 20:23 against Its Traditional Background," in Koester and Bieringer, *Resurrection of Jesus in the Gospel of John*, 237–51 (242 and 251 on the link between John 20:23 and John 1:29). The formulation above also reflects the helpful explanation in Lincoln, "I Am the Resurrection," 136: "So as the disciples in their witness announce God's verdict of Jesus, they will be pronouncing forgiveness for those who receive their witness.... God stands behind the disciples' witness," and their activity "reflects God's forgiveness or retention."

166. Koester, *Word of Life*, 128.

167. Zumstein, "Jesus' Resurrection in the Farewell Discourses," 118 n. 39.

168. Zumstein, "Jesus' Resurrection in the Farewell Discourses," 118 n. 39. Jesus's manifestation in 21:1, and indeed the appearances in general, may also correspond to the "greater things" that Nathanael is to see when heaven is opened (1:50–51); so Hasitschka, "Significance of the Resurrection Appearance," 312–14.

169. Zumstein, "Jesus' Resurrection in the Farewell Discourses," 106 n. 7.

promises may not be *entirely* realized until the parousia, but there are certainly substantial ways in which the postresurrection period is not just a reversal of Jesus's death or a return to the pre-Easter status quo for the disciples. There is, rather, an escalation beyond that pre-Easter reality.

3.5 Interim Conclusion: The Johannine Resurrection and the Kerygma

It is clear from this brief survey that the resurrection is of major significance for John.[170] It is the vindication of Jesus (John 2:19–21). It is also transformative in a number of ways, with a reversal—or better, an escalation—of the disciples' fortunes coming with the resurrection. In the first place, there is relationship with Jesus as a living savior, rather than the Christian life simply being recollection of Jesus's pre-Easter ministry and death. The life of the believer consists of dwelling with, and being loved by, Jesus and the Father (John 14:21, 23), and it is therefore a life of joy and peace. Believers have the gift of the Spirit infused in them by the risen Jesus, as we will see in section 4.2 below, and the disciples are granted "an authorization in respect of the forgiveness and retention of sins."[171]

John's resurrection narrative is in line with broader early Christian claims about the resurrection, rather than having a prickly, sectarian edge. There is no trace here of competing communities or polemic against other Christians. As Barrett wittily remarks on the arrival of the other disciple before Peter, "We must however be careful not to suggest that John identified fleetness of foot with apostolic pre-eminence."[172] Similarly, attempts to show that John's portrayal of "doubting Thomas" is intended as a slight upon "Thomas Christianity" have not won wide acceptance.[173]

In connection with the more widely held early Christian kerygma, John both accepts the fact of the resurrection of Jesus "on the third day" and assigns

---

170. The conclusion of Michael Theobald, "Der johanneische Osterglaube und die Grenzen seiner narrativen Vermittlung (Joh 20)," in *Von Jesus zum Christus. FS P. Hoffmann*, ed. R. Hoppe and U. Busse (Berlin: de Gruyter, 1998), 123, that Jesus's resurrection appearances are only clues that point to the "wholly other" of his ascension seems reductive. The argument that John 20:17 is the hermeneutical key to John and thereby relativizes the resurrection appearances (112) does not give due weight to the fact that resurrection appearances are so abundant in John 20 and 21.

171. David R. Catchpole, *Resurrection People: Studies in the Resurrection Narratives of the Gospels* (London: Darton, Longman & Todd, 2000), 175–76.

172. Barrett, *John*, 563.

173. See the main books and articles in the discussion in Simon Gathercole, *The Gospel of Thomas: Introduction and Commentary* (Leiden: Brill, 2014), 62 n. 4, especially the excellent discussion in Ismo Dunderberg, *The Beloved Disciple in Conflict? Revisiting the Gospels of John and Thomas* (Oxford: Oxford University Press, 2006).

the event considerable soteriological significance. Of course, the way in which John casts the resurrection has various distinctive, indeed unique, features, not least Jesus's own agency in the event. Nevertheless, the integral requirement of Jesus's "resurrection on the third day" finds an important place in John's Gospel. In qualification of a more radical sounding claim, Moody Smith remarks that "the reality of Jesus' resurrection is affirmed, through and with tradition, in distinctively Johannine ways."[174] In addition to the resurrection's reality, John is noticeably interested in its gospel significance.

4. Fulfillment of Scripture in John's Gospel

The aim of this section is to examine the extent to which scripture furnishes a substructure for John's presentation of Jesus, especially Jesus's death and resurrection. A great deal will not be covered here. There will be no extended treatment of characters such as Moses or David, or of festivals. There will be no attention to possible sources and putative differences between John's and these sources' views of scripture.[175] If one scholar can write a whole monograph on Zech 12:10 in John 19:37, then of course the aim of a section covering scripture in John as a whole must be limited.[176]

This is helped by the fact that John's use of scripture is more selective than that in the Synoptics.[177] According to one count, there are thirteen quotations of the Old Testament prefaced by introductory formulae, two citations without introduction, and four references to particular passages but without citation.[178] In addition to individual citations, there are also general statements that scripture speaks of Jesus. The focus here will be on fairly clear references; it is difficult to be more ambitious than that, given that in John "scriptural echoes

---

174. Smith, *Theology of the Gospel of John*, 124.

175. As discussed in, e.g., de Boer, *Johannine Perspectives on the Death of Jesus*, 92–94. Catrin H. Williams, "'He Saw His Glory and Spoke about Him': The Testimony of Isaiah," in *Honouring the Past and Shaping the Future: Religious and Biblical Studies in Wales; Essays in Honour of Gareth Lloyd Jones*, ed. Robert Pope (Leominster: Gracewing, 2003), 55–56, by contrast sees the difference in formulae arising because the fulfillment quotations proper appear only after the announcement of Jesus's hour.

176. See William R. Bynum, *The Fourth Gospel and the Scriptures: Illuminating the Form and Meaning of Scriptural Citation in John 19:37* (Leiden: Brill, 2012).

177. Hays, *Echoes of Scripture in the Gospels*, 284, cites figures of references as follows: Matthew, 124; Mark, 70; Luke, 109; John, 27.

178. D. A. Carson, "John and the Johannine Epistles," in *It Is Written: Scripture Citing Scripture; Essays in Honour of Barnabas Lindars, SSF*, ed. D. A. Carson and H. G. M. Williamson (Cambridge: Cambridge University Press, 1988), 246.

are to found everywhere."[179] Here, as in previous chapters, this section will confine itself to the function of scripture in John's accounts of Jesus's death and resurrection and then to the evangelist's overall view of scripture.

4.1 Jesus's Death as Fulfillment of Scripture in John

In John's Gospel, various analogies from all over the Old Testament are employed to explain the saving death of Jesus, and only a brief whistle-stop tour can be conducted here. Although there are occasional fulfillments of straight-forwardly predictive promises or prophecies (e.g., John 6:45; cf. Isa 54:13), many are fulfillments of different kinds.

The lamb of God who takes away the sin of the world (John 1:29; Isa 53:12). We have already seen in section 2 of this chapter the possibility that there is allusion to Isa 53 in John the Baptist's acclamation of Jesus as the lamb of God, especially if the evangelist knew the Greek of Isaiah in something like an Aquilan text form. If that is the case, then the likelihood is that John interprets Jesus's death through the lens of Isa 53. This may also be combined with Passover imagery as was discussed earlier, though this is also uncertain.[180]

"Zeal for your house will consume me" (John 2:17; Ps 69:9). The first clear reference to Jesus's death in John is a scriptural one: "His disciples remembered that it is written: 'Zeal for your house will consume me,'" a quotation of Ps 69:9 (68:10 LXX). The "consumption" ultimately refers to Jesus's death.[181] The zeal itself is ambiguous, perhaps referring to Jesus's zeal for the temple's purity but more probably meaning the zeal (in the sense of hostile envy) of the opponents.[182]

---

179. Judith M. Lieu, "Narrative Analysis and Scripture in John," in *The Old Testament in the New Testament: Essays in Honour of J. L. North*, ed. Steven Moyise (Sheffield: Sheffield Academic, 2000), 148.

180. *Pace* Reimund Bieringer, "Das Lamm Gottes, das die Sünde der Welt hinwegnimmt (Joh 1,29): Eine kontextorientierte und redaktionsgeschichtliche Untersuchung auf dem Hintergrund der Passatradition als Deutung des Todes Jesu im Johannesevangelium," in Van Belle, *Death of Jesus in the Fourth Gospel*, 199–232, with the chiasm on 220. I am not convinced that the best explanation of "lamb of God" in John 1:29 is that it parallels "Son of God" in 1:34. (Specifically, the chiasm looks unbalanced, with a very short B' and C' answering to the rather long B and C.)

181. Benjamin Lappenga, "Whose Zeal Is It Anyway? The Citation of Psalm 69:9 in John 2:17 as a Double Entendre," in *Abiding Words: The Use of Scripture in the Gospel of John*, ed. Alicia D. Myers and Bruce G. Schuchard (Atlanta: SBL Press, 2015), 141–60, on reference to both unbelief and the death of Jesus (see esp. the summary on 157).

182. See Steven M. Bryan, "Consumed by Zeal: John's Use of Psalm 69:9 and the Action in the Temple," *BBR* 21 (2011): 459–74.

The serpent on the pole (John 3:14; Num 21:6–9). John 3 recalls Moses lifting up the serpent in the desert. This serpent that saved the Israelites in the wilderness when it was lifted up is like Jesus who saves his people when he is "lifted up," presumably a reference especially to the cross here. (See further sec. 2.1 and sec. 2.3 above on "lifting up.") Here John's Gospel sees Jesus fulfilling a prefiguring episode from the book of Numbers.

The bread from heaven (John 6:48–58; Exod 16; Num 11:1–9). Similarly, in John 6, Jesus as the true bread from heaven is presented as a perfect instance of what was imperfectly foreshadowed in the manna in the wilderness (6:49, 58). The consumption of this bread takes place because Jesus has come from heaven to give his life for the world.

The entry into Jerusalem (John 12:12–19; Zech 9:9–10). Here John uses Zechariah along with Ps 118:25–26 (and possibly Gen 49:11) to show that Jesus is "the peaceful king of Zech 9:9–10."[183]

The rejection of Jesus (John 12:38–41; Isa 53:1; 6:10). Scripture also explains the obduracy of Jesus's opponents.[184] These particular quotations are structurally significant for John, because they mark the end of Jesus's public ministry.[185]

Judas's betrayal of Jesus (John 13:18; Ps 41:9). After the footwashing, Jesus speaks of the blessedness of the disciples but adds, "I am not referring to all of you; I know those I have chosen. But this is to fulfill this passage of scripture: 'He who shared my bread has turned against me'" (John 13:18). This reference to Ps 41 highlights even the betrayal as forecast in scripture, as is perhaps implied very subtly in the Synoptic Gospels (Mark 14:21 and parr.) and is explicit in citations of different psalms in Acts.[186] A further possible reference to the betrayal as being prophesied comes at John 17:12.[187]

Jesus's lifting up and glorification (Isa 52:12–15). The motif of Jesus being "lifted up" appears in three places in John, probably with exclusive reference to Jesus's death on the cross (John 3:14; 8:28; 12:32–34). The glorification motif is more widely dispersed through John's narrative. There is a clear preglorification phase: in the first half of John, Jesus has definitely not yet been glorified

---

183. Maarten J. J. Menken, "The Minor Prophets in John," in *The Minor Prophets in the New Testament*, ed. Maarten J. J. Menken and Steve Moyise (London: Bloomsbury, 2009), 84.

184. For helpful overviews of the subject, see Carson, "John and the Johannine Epistles," and Hays, *Echoes of Scripture in the Gospels*, 305–8.

185. Barrett, "Old Testament in the Fourth Gospel," 167.

186. Pss 69:25 and 109:8 in Acts 1:20.

187. John 17:12b could in theory mean *either* "None of them has been lost (except the one doomed to destruction) so that scripture would be fulfilled" *or* "None of them has been lost—except the one doomed to destruction so that scripture would be fulfilled." All the commentators I have seen take the sentence in the latter sense.

(7:39; 12:16). Then, with the commencement of the final week, the time for Jesus's glorification is announced as having arrived (12:23). The theme then abounds in Jesus's farewell discourse and high-priestly prayer (14–17). The glorification is also focused especially in Jesus's death (12:23–24). Notably, Isa 52:13 LXX combines both verbs: "Behold, my servant will understand and will be lifted up (ὑψωθήσεται) and glorified (δοξασθήσεται) greatly." The Hebrew text then continues to recount the servant's ignominious death before this great glory. In John, the glory and the death are combined into one.[188] Indeed, Williams proposes that the "'humiliation-as-exaltation' pattern is in fact already established in the Septuagint version of the oracle" in Isa 52:13–15.[189]

The soldiers and Jesus's clothes (John 19:24; Ps 22:18). "They divided my clothes among them and cast lots for my garment." This quotation is introduced with the fulfillment formula "so that the scripture would be fulfilled" (ἵνα ἡ γραφὴ πληρωθῇ), and the marking of the quotation is particular to John, even though the language of the Synoptic evangelists describing this event is also strongly resonant of that of the psalm.[190] Whether the wholeness of the garment should be interpreted ecclesiologically, speaking of "something precious that belongs to Jesus whose unity must be maintained," is more speculative.[191]

Jesus's statement of thirst (John 19:28; cf. Ps 22:15; 69:21). "So that scripture would be fulfilled, Jesus said, 'I am thirsty.'" Neither of the two psalm references matches the statement of thirst in John very closely.[192] This means that it is likely that, according to John, it is not the thirst per se that fulfills scripture.[193] Jesus's statement does, however, prompt the soldiers to bring vinegar; the "I thirst" is not the fulfillment itself but rather the trigger for it. The action of the soldiers constitutes the fulfillment: this is the link between John and

---

188. See further Williams, "He Saw His Glory and Spoke about Him," 72–73, and Williams, "Johannine Christology and Prophetic Traditions."

189. Williams, "Johannine Christology and Prophetic Traditions," 100.

190. Wengst, *Johannesevangelium*, 529; Marianne Meye Thompson, *John: A Commentary* (Louisville: Westminster John Knox, 2015), 399.

191. Francis J. Moloney, *The Gospel of John* (Collegeville MN: Liturgical, 1998), 503, who tentatively takes this view. On the priestly interpretation of the χιτών, see Thyen, *Johannesevangelium*, 735; Wengst, *Johannesevangelium*, 529. See Carson, *John*, 614–15, for other views of a possible symbolism.

192. In addition, others have less plausibly suggested Pss 42 and 63, which talk of a thirsting for God. See the views taken by different scholars in the overview in Thompson, *John*, 400 n. 109.

193. Thyen, *Johannesevangelium*, 741; also Carson, *John*, 619, citing correspondence from Moule to this effect.

Ps 69, according to which others bring the suffering psalmist vinegar in order to slake his thirst. The sovereign control of Jesus is therefore apparent in his determination to fulfill scripture.[194]

The preservation of Jesus's bones (John 19:31–33, 36).[195] Unlike those crucified with him, Jesus's bones were not broken, because he was already dead: this was the case so that the scripture, "no bone is to be broken," would be fulfilled. Thompson rightly notes that Ps 34 is the closest intertext; whether John includes with the psalm the implication of divine protection and eventual raising is unlikely.[196] John's fulfillment quotations generally refer to events that are fulfillments there and then. A pentateuchal connection is also plausible, however: there may well be a connotation, harking back to the "lamb of God" in John 1:29, that Jesus is "the perfect Paschal lamb."[197]

The piercing of Jesus's body (John 19:37; Zech 12:10). "They will look on the one they have pierced." John's quotation here resembles the Hebrew of Zechariah, or a translation like that of Aquila or Theodotion, rather than the Septuagint; there is not a single word in common between the Septuagint and John. Notably, in Zech 12, the speaker of the words and the one pierced is the Lord. Scholars have debated who "they" who look are, what kind of look it is, and when the looking takes place.[198] John's focus is on the fulfillment of the piercing.[199]

In sum, there is a wealth of christological interpretation in scripture in John's references to, and account of, the passion. Some of these passages are concerned with the circumstances around Jesus's death, such as the casting of lots for his garments, or his thirst. Others focus on the death per se, such as the zeal that "consumes" Jesus or his "lifting up." Sometimes the focus is on Jesus's own agency, and at other times, the death is instigated by the Father: the "lifting up" is initially explained as God giving his son (John 3:14–16). In

194. Wengst, *Johannesevangelium,* 531.

195. Cf. Ps 34:20; Exod 12:10, 46; Num 9:12.

196. Thompson, *John,* 404. Compare John's ὀστοῦν οὐ συντριβήσεται αὐτοῦ (John 19:36) with κύριος φυλάσσει πάντα τὰ ὀστᾶ αὐτῶν, ἓν ἐξ αὐτῶν οὐ συντριβήσεται (Ps 33:21 LXX).

197. Moloney, *John,* 506; cf. also Barrett, *John,* 558; Carson, *John,* 627; Wengst, *Johannesevangelium,* 538, and numerous other interpreters.

198. Menken, "Minor Prophets in John," 88–89, draws a parallel with, e.g., John 3:14–15, arguing for a salvific "looking," especially at the resurrection. See Ruth Sheridan, "They Shall Look upon the One They Have Pierced: Intertextuality, Intra-textuality and Anti-Judaism in John 19:37," in *Searching the Scriptures: Studies in Context and Intertextuality,* ed. Craig A. Evans and Jeremiah J. Johnston (London: Bloomsbury, 2015), 191–210, on the identity of the piercers and the lookers.

199. Barrett, *John,* 559.

the first half of the Gospel, the quotations are introduced by more general references to prefiguring, while in the final week as the hour approaches, there is an increased stress particularly on fulfillment.[200]

4.2 Jesus's Resurrection as Fulfillment of Scripture in John

Although John does not specify particular portions of the Old Testament that he has in mind, he is clear that the resurrection is a fulfillment of scripture:

> [6]Then Simon Peter followed along and went into the tomb. He saw the strips of linen lying there, [7]along with the cloth that had been on Jesus's head: it was not lying with the linen, but was on its own, rolled up. [8]Finally the other disciple, who behind him had reached the tomb first, also went inside. He saw and believed. [9](They had not yet understood from scripture that Jesus had to rise from the dead.) (John 20:6–9)

Presumably the point here is not that, having seen the grave, the disciples still did not understand. Rather, it is more likely that up until that point, they had not understood Jesus's fulfillment of scripture, but thereafter the other disciple was the first to grasp the truth.[201] This ambiguity does not affect the main point that resurrection is foretold in scripture, however.

Which scriptures John has in mind is another question. Carson notes that suggestions have included Ps 16:10 (which is cited in Acts), Lev 23:11, and Hos 6:2, any of which is theoretically possible.[202] As noted earlier, Thompson makes the suggestive comment that the quotations in John 19:36–37, although included in the passion narrative, in fact foreshadow the resurrection. For her, the citation that "not one of his bones will be broken" (John 19:36) highlights the divine protection promised in Ps 33:21 LXX, and Zechariah's oracle that "they will look on the one they have pierced" (19:37) may foreshadow the vision of the pierced Jesus by Thomas.[203] We have queried this view already (in

---

200. Carson, "John and the Johannine Epistles," 248, Hays, *Echoes of Scripture in the Gospels*, 286, Bynum, "Quotations of Zechariah in the Fourth Gospel," 54, and Williams, "He Saw His Glory and Spoke about Him," 55–56, take the differences in the formulae to be a result of the fulfillment quotations coming after the statement that Jesus's hour has come. See the helpful table in Bruce G. Schuchard, "Form versus Function: Citation Technique and Authorial Intention in the Gospel of John," in Myers and Schuchard, *Abiding Words*, 45.

201. Hence my pluperfect in verse 9.

202. Carson, *John*, 639.

203. Moloney's claim (*John*, 520) that the Johannine narrative itself is the γραφή in question here is extremely unlikely in view of John's usage of the word elsewhere in the Gospel.

sec. 4.1 above). Others have proposed that John is thinking less of particular passages than of scripture as a whole.[204] There are, however, two particular sets of passages that should also be borne in mind.

The first possibility is the set of passages that foresee a new temple. As we saw in section 2 above, Jesus issues the challenge: "Destroy this temple, and in three days I will raise it up" (John 2:19). John provides a gloss, giving a clear interpretation of the temple as Jesus's body.[205] There are various scriptural passages about temple building that could be adduced, and there is no need to choose a particular one. Second Samuel 7 refers to the Davidic heir who will raise up a house for God's name (2 Sam 7:13). Psalm 118, as quoted in the Synoptics (though not in John), refers to the rejected stone becoming the cornerstone. Amos 9:11 contains the prophecy that God will restore David's fallen tent. Zechariah 6 refers to the branch who will build the temple of the Lord (Zech 6:12). In Second Temple Jewish literature, there is abundant prophecy of the rebuilding of the temple (metaphorical or literal), sometimes connected with particular passages: 2 Sam 7 and Amos 9, for example, are interpreted eschatologically in 4Q174 (Florilegium); Tg. Isa. 53.5 includes a reference to the messiah rebuilding the temple.[206] It is easy to see how John could connect Jesus's promise to raise up the temple of his body with the tradition of eschatological temple exegesis.

A second possibility that should be considered is that the resurrection is a recapitulation of creation. The correspondence between John's Gospel and Genesis is established very early; it is no great scholarly insight to note that John 1:1 must be echoing Gen 1:1. John's prologue then introduces the themes of light and dark that continue the association. Thereafter, there are two significant weeks in the Gospel: the first, less important one, covers John 1:19–2:11, and the second covers John 12–19 or John 12:1–20:18.[207] In this second week, Jesus's crucifixion takes place at the sixth hour on the sixth day of the week

---

204. Carson, *John*, 639.

205. Lidija Novakovic, *Raised from the Dead according to Scripture: The Role of Israel's Scripture in the Early Christian Interpretations of Jesus' Resurrection* (London: Bloomsbury, 2012), 192, argues that the reference to scripture in John 2:21 is connected to John 2:19, not 2:17. The point above would be strengthened if this is the case, but it is hard to be sure.

206. See details of the primary sources in Andrew Chester, "The Sibyl and the Temple," in *Templum Amicitiae: Essays on the Second Temple Presented to Ernst Bammel*, ed. William Horbury (Sheffield: Sheffield Academic, 1991), 47–54; William Horbury, "Herod's Temple and 'Herod's Days,'" in Horbury, *Templum Amicitiae*, 112–13, and most recently Novakovic, *Raised from the Dead*, 187.

207. Bauckham, *Gospel of Glory*, 131–84; Schuchard, "Form versus Function," 39–42.

(John 19:14), which is also the sixth day of the Passover festival, which is itself the sixth festival in John's Gospel.[208]

On this sixth day, Jesus completed his work. The Father had given him work to complete: "I have brought you glory on earth by finishing the work (τὸ ἔργον τελειώσας) you gave me to do" (John 17:3). The very end of Jesus's work comes on the cross, and he effects its completion by declaring "I thirst" (19:28). This he did "knowing that everything had now been finished (ἤδη πάντα τετέλεσται), and so that scripture would be fulfilled (τελειωθῇ)." The double use of τελέω/τελειόω, coupled with the fact that this is the only time that John uses these verbs to refer to scriptural fulfillment, is telling. It is followed further by Jesus's famous "it is finished" (τετέλεσται) in John 19:30. The point here is that these sixth-day, sixth-hour events probably reflect God's *completing* of his *works* on the *sixth day* in Gen 2:2 (καὶ <u>συνετέλεσεν</u> ὁ θεὸς <u>ἐν τῇ ἡμέρᾳ τῇ ἕκτῃ</u> τὰ ἔργα αὐτοῦ ἃ ἐποίησεν).[209] After Jesus's quasi-rest on "the Great Sabbath" (John 19:31), he appears again on two successive first days of the week. When he rises, Mary thinks he is the gardener, which—against an Edenic background—may for John be ironically true.[210]

After completing this divine work of creation on the sixth day, his work continues in a new week. On the first day of the new week, Jesus infuses the Spirit in the disciples: "he breathed on (ἐνεφύσησεν) them and said, 'Receive the Holy Spirit'" (John 20:22). This verb appears only once in the New Testament and probably recalls the first of only a few Old Testament instances: "the Lord God formed a man from the dust of the ground and breathed into (ἐνεφύσησεν) his nostrils the breath of life" (Gen 2:7).[211] The two passages share not only the same verb but also the same form.[212]

---

208. See further Schuchard, "Form versus Function," 38 n. 67. See John 2:13; 5:1; 6:4; 7:2; 10:22; 11:55.

209. Martin Hengel, "The Old Testament in the Fourth Gospel," in *The Gospels and the Scriptures of Israel*, ed. Craig A. Evans and W. R. Stegner (Sheffield: Sheffield Academic, 1994), 394; Michael A. Daise, "Quotations with 'Remembrance' Formulae in the Fourth Gospel," in Myers and Schuchard, *Abiding Words*, 89.

210. John Painter, "The Light Shines in the Darkness," in Bieringer and Koester, *Resurrection of Jesus in the Gospel of John*, 44, e.g., points to the reference to the gardener (κηπουρός) and Jesus's burial in a κῆπος; similarly Beutler, *John*, 495. See Carlos Siliezar, *Creation Imagery in the Gospel of John* (London: Bloomsbury, 2015), 174–79, for discussion of the various scholars who take such a view.

211. Hengel, "Old Testament in the Fourth Gospel," 391. See, e.g., Painter, "Light Shines in the Darkness," 45. The word is not especially common and appears echoing creational context also in 1 Kgs 17:21, Ezek 37:9, and Wis 15:11.

212. Beutler ("Resurrection and the Remission of Sins," 249) also links the coming of

In the end, John does not specify explicitly—as he does for the death—which scriptures he has in mind for Jesus's resurrection. John 20:9 makes it clear that the resurrection is foretold in scripture. Two neglected but promising candidates for at least part of this "scripture" are the creation narrative, especially Gen 1:1–2:7, and prophecies of a rebuilt temple.[213]

4.3 John's Relation to Scripture

The overall assessment of John's relation to scripture, because of its complexity, will be treated here in two parts. A later section (sec. 4.4) will consider the problem of the Johannine Jesus's references to "your law." Initially as in previous chapters, however, we will express the essential points of John's relation to scripture through a series of theses.

1. *John sees scripture as incontrovertible.* As Jesus puts it in John 10, scripture cannot be broken (10:35). That is, in the particular context of the debate, it cannot be invalidated because it is unfailingly correct. One might take John 10:35 as follows: "If it calls those to whom God's word came 'gods'—and scripture cannot be overridden (καὶ οὐ δύναται λυθῆναι ἡ γραφή)." Like John the Baptist, scripture is not the light, but as we have seen in sections 4.1–2 it does bear witness to the light.

2. *In one sense, John's editorial use of scripture is retrospective.* Although many scholars argue that the preresurrection and postresurrection boundary is a porous one for John, he does sometimes clearly distinguish between the terms applied to Jesus during his ministry and later reflection. Hence after Jesus cleanses the temple, John adds: "After he was raised from the dead, his disciples recalled what he had said. Then they believed the scripture and the words that Jesus had spoken" (John 2:22). This motif of recollection and understanding after Jesus rises from the dead is reflected throughout the Gospel (John 12:16; 14:26; 20:9).[214] From the point of view of the Gospel's composition, some of the scriptural attestation is seen or understood only with Spirit-inspired hindsight.

3. *While some scriptural institutions are replaced, other correspondences are more figural.* Various scholars note, for example, that for John, the temple and

---

the Spirit and forgiveness in John 20:22–23 to the new covenant in Ezek 36:25–27, where the indwelling of the Spirit and cleansing from sins are adjacent.

213. They are neglected, e.g., in Novakovic, *Raised from the Dead.*

214. On this theme of recollection, see Lieu, "Narrative Analysis and Scripture in John," 152–55.

festivals are replaced.[215] Jesus is the sole locus of the presence of God for John. On the other hand, typology or "figural correspondence" might be a more appropriate category for other scriptural figures or events or institutions.[216] Moses, for example, is not replaced by Jesus but continues to serve as a witness to him.[217]

4. *Scripture maps out the course of events in the Gospel.* John's statement that scripture cannot be overturned is illustrated by the numerous places where events take place *because* scripture demands fulfillment. Hence, for example, people failed to believe "*so that* the word of Isaiah the prophet would be fulfilled" (ἵνα ὁ λόγος Ἡσαΐου τοῦ προφήτου πληρωθῇ [12:38]). Judas betrays Jesus *so that* scripture would be fulfilled (ἵνα ἡ γραφὴ πληρωθῇ [13:18]), and so on. The same formula, or wording very like it, appears frequently in John 12–19, meaning that there is a predetermined script for the passion that needs to be acted out.

Sometimes the providential hand of God is guiding the unwitting actors behind the scenes, as in the rejection and betrayal of Jesus, or in the casting of lots for his clothes, all of which take place *in order to* (ἵνα) fulfill scripture (John 12:38; 15:24–25; 19:24). But the same language also illustrates Jesus's own orchestration of scriptural fulfillment: Jesus declares that he is thirsty so that scripture would be fulfilled (ἵνα τελειωθῇ ἡ γραφή) in 19:28. The same is probably true of Jesus's transportation on Palm Sunday: "Jesus found a young donkey and sat on it, as it is written: 'Do not be afraid, Daughter Zion; see, your king is coming, seated on a donkey's colt'" (12:14–15).[218] As well as Jesus's death, his resurrection takes place because scripture dictates that "it is necessary" (δεῖ) according to John 20:9.

---

215. Carson, "John and the Johannine Epistles," 253–56, uses this language. Similar, though without perhaps negative overtones, is the language of Hays, who talks of Jesus embodying "that which the temple had signified" and "everything to which Israel's feasts and cultic observances had pointed" (Hays, *Echoes of Scripture in the Gospels*, 314). The "everything" here implies a lack of remainder and therefore replacement.

216. Hays, *Echoes of Scripture in the Gospels*, 313. See also 290–94 on the relation between Jesus and the patriarchs and prophets.

217. *Pace* Ashton, *Understanding the Fourth Gospel*, 446. See Catrin Williams, "Patriarchs and Prophets Remembered: Framing Israel's Past in the Gospel of John," in Myers and Schuchard, *Abiding Words*, 192–201, for a more balanced view.

218. Some could be the result of either the unseen hand of God, or Jesus's deliberate action. Jesus's bones were unbroken by divine providence, but also because Jesus had already given up his spirit and voluntarily died (John 19:30, 36). The betrayal by Judas is (1) providential, (2) the result of Satanic agency (13:2), and (3) a consequence of Jesus's own action because he has in some sense not chosen Judas (13:18; cf. 6:70).

In sum, for John, the gospel events do not comport with scripture in a loose sense, nor is it simply the discerning reader who can see retrospectively that biblical motifs prefigure Jesus's ministry: rather, scripture prospectively maps out the course of events for John. In John's conception of the gospel in accordance with the scriptures, the "accordance" is a very strong one.

5. *Scripture was always about Jesus.* John therefore does not think that scripture bears witness to Jesus in a secondary sense, or has a christological sensus plenior. For John, much more than the other evangelists, scripture speaks directly about Jesus (τὰς γραφάς . . . ἐκεῖναί εἰσιν αἱ μαρτυροῦσαι περὶ ἐμοῦ [John 5:39]). Already Philip says without qualification, "We have found the one Moses wrote about in the law, and about whom the prophets also wrote—Jesus of Nazareth, the son of Joseph" (1:45).

For John, Abraham had had a vision of Jesus. Roughly contemporaneously with John, 4 Ezra contains an address to God about Abraham: "to him alone you have shown the end of times, secretly by night."[219] Similarly, in John, Abraham not only rejoiced at the thought of seeing Jesus's day but did actually see it, presumably as in 4 Ezra by divine revelation: "Your father Abraham rejoiced at the thought of seeing my day; he saw it and was glad" (John 8:56). Moses also wrote *about* Jesus (περὶ γὰρ ἐμοῦ ἐκεῖνος ἔγραψεν [5:46]). Similarly, Isaiah had actually seen Christ crucified and so could speak of Jesus's rejection in advance. This is the logic of the connection between Isaiah and John 12:40–41: the prophet declared Isa 6's hardening oracle (John 12:40), and he did so (according to John 12:41) because he had had a vision of the future glory of Jesus, presumably on the cross (ταῦτα εἶπεν Ἡσαΐας ὅτι εἶδεν τὴν δόξαν αὐτοῦ).[220]

6. *Understanding scripture christologically is therefore obligatory for John.* Because of John's understanding of scripture as directly about Jesus, it is a culpable mistake to read scripture without reference to him. In two passages, Jesus condemns his hearers for their combined misapprehension of both himself and scripture:

"You study the scriptures diligently because you think that in them you have eternal life. These are the very scriptures that testify about me, yet you refuse to come to me to have life." (John 5:39–40)

219. 4 Ezra 3.14: *demonstrasti ei temporum finem solo secrete noctu*; John 8:56: Ἀβραὰμ ὁ πατὴρ ὑμῶν ἠγαλλιάσατο ἵνα ἴδῃ τὴν ἡμέραν τὴν ἐμήν, καὶ εἶδεν καὶ ἐχάρη. Carson, *John*, 356–57, also notes Gen. Rab. 44.22, on Gen 15:18 (Freedman, 1:376) on this tradition.

220. Ashton, *Understanding the Fourth Gospel*, 299; Williams, "Johannine Christology and Prophetic Traditions," 98. For Isaiah's vision of the future, see Sir 48:22–25; Josephus, *Ant.* 10.35.

"But do not think I will accuse you before the Father. Your accuser is Moses, on whom your hopes are set. If you believed Moses, you would believe me, for he wrote about me." (John 5:45-46)

In the former passage, the problem is the audience's disbelief in Jesus; in the latter, he accuses them of disbelieving Moses as well. John therefore not only interprets scripture christologically but also asserts that such a hermeneutic is "a moral obligation."[221] For John, part of understanding the Gospel is learning to read scripture correctly.[222]

4.4 "Your" and "Their" Law: A Non-Jewish Distance from Scripture?

In apparent tension with what has just been said are the statements where Jesus appears to distance himself from scripture:[223]

"*In your law* it is written that the testimony of two witnesses is true." (John 8:17)

Jesus answered them, "Is it not written *in your law*, 'I have said you are "gods"'? If he called them 'gods,' to whom the word of God came—and scripture cannot be set aside. . . ." (John 10:34-35)

"If I had not done among them the works no one else did, they would not be guilty of sin. As it is, they have seen, and yet they have hated both me and my Father. But this is to fulfill what is written *in their law*: 'They hated me without reason.'" (John 15:24-25)

Augenstein remarks that there is—or was in 1997—a "scholarly consensus" that "'your law' in the mouth of the Johannine Jesus reflects the distance of the so-called Johannine community from Judaism."[224] He cites Bultmann and an ar-

---

221. Carson, "John and the Johannine Epistles," 246, 257. See also Hays, *Echoes of Scripture in the Gospels*, 283, on the hermeneutical point; he, like some other commentators, adduces the parallel with Luke 24.

222. As emphasized especially by Hays, *Echoes of Scripture in the Gospels* (see esp. 312, 322).

223. Similar to these references is the statement in John 7:22 that "Moses gave you circumcision."

224. See Jörg Augenstein, "'Euer Gesetz'—Ein Pronomen und die johanneische Haltung zum Gesetz," *ZNW* 88 (1997): 311: the "Forschungskonsens" that "'Euer Gesetz' im Munde

ray of more recent German scholars to this effect.[225] English-language scholarship is not so consistent, although Brown is a powerful voice arguing that these statements reflect Jesus speaking "like a non-Jew" (cf. John 18:31).[226] A number of challenges to this view have been mounted, not least Augenstein's own.

First, Augenstein observes that there is indeed a degree of distance from the law. This arises not out of a gentile perspective, however, but from the fact that Jesus stands in the same relation to the law as does the Father. Jesus asks his audience, "Has not Moses given *you* the law?" (John 7:19). Jesus, on the other hand, is not straightforwardly a recipient of the law, because he preexists it, is himself the law's subject matter, and has direct knowledge of God (7:16–17). The law is subordinate to him, not the other way around.[227]

Second, Augenstein refers to a number of Old Testament uses of "your," which have some similarities to those in John. Moses, for example, speaks to Israel of "your God," and the phrase "the Lord your God" is formulaic in addresses of Moses and Joshua. Moses can also speak of "your towns" (Deut 31:12), "your brothers" (18:15), and "your tribes and officials" (31:28). Such an address need not be confined to a paraenetic context, however. To these passages cited by Augenstein, we can add one from Josephus. In his entreaty to the Jews to surrender to the Romans (*J. W.* 5.362–419), he highlights the sins of his own people, not least against the temple. On the other hand, he says in *J. W.* 5.402, "the Romans reverenced it from afar, *setting aside many of their own customs to give place to your law* (πολλὰ τῶν ἰδίων ἐθῶν εἰς τὸν ὑμέτερον παραλύοντες νόμον)."[228] Josephus's reference to "your law" here comes—like

---

des johanneischen Jesus spiegelt die Distanz der sogenannten johanneischen Gemeinde zum Judentum wider." Augenstein's own study draws on Hugo Odeberg, *The Fourth Gospel: Interpreted in Its Relation to Contemporaneous Religious Currents in Palestine and the Hellenistic-Oriental World* (Uppsala: Almqvist & Wiksell, 1929), 292.

225. Citing, e.g., Rudolf Bultmann, *Das Evangelium des Johannes* (Göttingen: Vandenhoeck & Ruprecht, 1986), 59: "Jesus selbst redet zu ihnen wie ein Fremder." For a recent example, see Hermut Löhr, "Jesus and the Ten Words," in *Handbook to the Study of the Historical Jesus*, ed. Tom Holmén and Stanley Porter (Leiden: Brill, 2010), 3151, referring to a "remarkable distance."

226. Raymond E. Brown, *The Gospel and Epistles of John: A Concise Commentary* (Collegeville, MN: Liturgical, 1988), 10. In commentaries published before Augenstein's article, see Barrett, *John*, 339, and Carson, *John*, 340, who see distance but not straightforwardly so; additionally, Smith, *Theology of the Gospel of John*, 76, and Ruth Sheridan, "The Testimony of Two Witnesses: John 8:17," in Myers and Schuchard, *Abiding Words*, 162.

227. Lincoln, *John*, 76.

228. There are textual variants here, so that not all manuscripts read ὑμέτερον. See Benedikt Niese, ed., *Flavii Iosephi Opera* (Berlin: Weidmann, 1894), 6:490.

the instances in John—in a frustratedly polemical speech addressed by Josephus to his fellow countrymen.

"In your law it is written . . ." (John 8:17). In terms of the specific passages, Augenstein notes that the description "your law" appears in the specific contexts of Jesus defending himself against accusations and should not be taken out of that context. He argues that, in this case, "your law" does not reflect distance but highlights the common basis from which Jesus's opponents have departed. Here Jesus replies to the Pharisees' objection that he is simply uttering false testimony about himself (John 8:14–18). Even on the Pharisees' own terms, Jesus argues, they ought to accept the truth of what he says. As Charlier concludes, the "your," on the one hand, underscores that this element of the argument is irrefutable, because the premise must a priori be accepted by Jesus's interlocutors; on the other hand, it puts the Jews in self-contradiction.[229]

"Is it not written in your law . . . ?" (John 10:34–35).[230] This second case is very similar. Here Jesus is defending himself against the direct charge of blasphemy. His reply again appeals to common ground, namely "the word of God" and "scripture," which "cannot be set aside," and which his opponents must accept as authoritative.[231]

"This is to fulfill what is written in their law: 'They hated me without reason'" (John 15:24–25). This final case is different but no more problematic. This is, first, because the citation is of Ps 35:19 or 69:4, and the Psalter is, again, a most unlikely corpus for any early Christian community to jettison; John in

---

229. J.-F. Charlier, "L'exégèse johannique d'un précepte légal: Jean VIII 17," *RB* 67 (1960): 506. Similarly, Colin Kruse, *The Gospel according to John: An Introduction and Commentary* (Grand Rapids: Eerdmans, 2004), 243 (on "your law"): "Jesus was not denigrating or distancing himself from the law, but reminding his opponents that his appeal was to what they too held as sacrosanct." Further from the mark is Smith, *Theology of the Gospel of John*, 290: "It is not called 'their law,' because John and his community reject it (cf. 10:35) but this way of talking is an indication of the tension between the community. Perhaps this is the equivalent of saying in 'the law as they [the Jews] read it' (cf. 8:17)."

230. John 10:34 is potentially easily disposed of because the textual evidence for and against the "your" (ὑμῶν) is quite evenly divided. It is present in 𝔓66, 𝔓75, Codex Alexandrinus, and Codex Ephraemi Rescriptus and is inserted by the first corrector of Sinaiticus, but it is not present in 𝔓45 and the original text of Sinaiticus. It is easy to imagine a scribe inserting it, under the influence of the recent John 8:17, and it is perhaps more difficult to account for its omission.

231. Barrett, *John*, 384: As Barrett comments, "his purpose in using the word ὑμῶν (if he used it) was not to disavow the Old Testament but to press upon the Jews the fact that the truth of the Christian position was substantiated by their own authoritative documents."

particular has a strong positive interest in the Psalms.[232] Second, just as Ps 82 above contains divine speech ("the word of God"), so the putative speaker in the psalm in John 15 is Jesus himself: the statement "they hated *me* without reason" pictures Christ as uttering the words.[233] Third, recalling John 5:45 where Moses is the accuser of "the Jews," the point is the polemical one that scripture itself is testimony against Jesus's opponents.[234]

In conclusion, these utterances of Jesus do not reflect a gentile perspective, in which Jesus regards scripture as a foreign body. Rather, they arise partly out of a divine perspective on Jesus's part, and partly from a polemical viewpoint. On the former point, Jesus is eternal and therefore transcends the law rather than being a recipient of it like his Jewish contemporaries (John 7:19). In the latter case, Jesus appeals to the law as a concession. The first thesis of section 4.3, namely that for John scripture is incontrovertible, still stands.

4.5 Interim Conclusion: John's Use of Scripture and the Kerygma

In sum, Old Testament scripture is the "encyclopedia" presupposed in John's narrative.[235] It provides preliminary definition for the language, even if that language is then christologically reshaped. It also determines the course of the narrative, whose events take place *so that* scripture is fulfilled. Hence the "accordance" with the scriptures is a very strong one. Moreover, scripture is not used merely as a vehicle for John's theology but exerts a pressure of its own. Williams notes the fact that Isaiah's framework impacts upon John's thinking,[236] even as John can exert "mnemonic control" over scripture, especially Moses.[237] As Barrett states, "It may finally be observed that the Johannine Passion narrative contains several testimonies . . . which seem to have no close relation with specifically Johannine theology, and which therefore give a distinctly primitive air to the story. Here John seems to be working quite in the manner of the primitive argument from Scripture."[238] John's Gospel sees Jesus's death (with its circumstances) and resurrection not as coming out of

---

232. Hays, *Echoes of Scripture in the Gospels*, 286, notes that "more than 60 percent of John's quotations come from the Psalter."

233. Cf. also John 2:17, where "Jesus himself is the speaker of Psalm 69:9" (Hays, *Echoes of Scripture in the Gospels*, 312).

234. Barrett, *John*, 482.

235. Hays, *Echoes of Scripture in the Gospels*, 289.

236. Williams, "Johannine Christology and Prophetic Traditions."

237. Williams, "Patriarchs and Prophets Remembered," 197.

238. Barrett, "Old Testament in the Fourth Gospel," 168.

a clear blue sky but rather as forecast or anticipated in the Old Testament. In conclusion, as in the kerygma, scripture is the "foundation" and "witness" and "backdrop," as well as the "indispensable reference point and scaffolding . . . it is scripture that makes the gospel 'work.'"[239]

CONCLUSION: JOHN'S GOSPEL AND THE KERYGMA

The summary statement in John 20:30–31, in which John states his reason for writing, makes clear that the Gospel of John is itself a proclamation of the good news even if the word "gospel" is not mentioned in the body of the work. Whatever the intended audience, the Fourth Gospel aimed to inculcate or strengthen belief in Jesus as the messiah and son of God. Hence, as already noted, there can be no real dispute about whether John regarded the term "messiah" positively. He unequivocally endorses the designation and—alongside "son of God"—regards it as the feature of Jesus's identity that readers must most grasp. John's Christology has often been seen as a radical departure from Judaism—witness, for example, the title of Maurice Casey's book, *From Jewish Prophet to Gentile God*, where the Johannine Jesus is regarded as the latter.[240] However, John's messianism has a number of traditional features, using the son of God and Son of Man titles, applying Davidic language from the Psalms, shepherd imagery from Ezekiel, and the portrait of the servant from Isa 52–53. Even the association of Jesus's messiahship with signs is not as unexpected as many scholars have suggested. As is the case with the other canonical Gospels, John's use of the term "messiah" is not mere artifice but taps into the traditional discourse of messianic exegesis to ensure that Jesus was recognizably messianic. More promising than Casey's title is that of the recent edited volume of Boccaccini and Reynolds: *Reading the Gospel of John's Christology as Jewish Messianism*.

John's understanding of the death of Jesus also overlaps with the kerygma, which states that "Christ died for our sins." Although John never uses that particular language, certain passages obviously speak of the vicarious death of Jesus. There is a clear sense that Jesus's death saves, and John employs a large number of motifs to show that: the lamb who takes away sin, the elevation of

239. Respectively, Myers, "Introduction," in Myers and Schuchard, *Abiding Words*, 1, 21, and Lieu, "Narrative Analysis and Scripture in John," 144.

240. P. Maurice Casey, *From Jewish Prophet to Gentile God* (Cambridge: James Clarke, 1991).

the Son of Man like the elevation of the serpent in the wilderness, Jesus's gift of his flesh that is the bread of life, the love of the shepherd for his sheep, the ironic Realpolitik of Caiaphas, the necessary death of the seed, Jesus's drawing of all through his elevation, the cleansing in the footwashing, the vicarious death for friends, Jesus's self-sanctification for the sanctification of the disciples, and so on. There is a clear vicarious and indeed substitutionary death of Jesus. Moreover, the sense of Jesus's death as a quasi-cultic atoning sacrifice is probable, given that the cleansing envisaged is described in the language of "sanctification" and removal of sin even within the Gospel; even leaving aside a cultic dimension, Jesus effects the removal of sin and cleansing of his disciples through his death. Hence Jesus can be said in John to have died "for sins" in the sense that his death is a purificatory removal of sin. If one employs 1 John as an interpretative aid, then the sense of cleansing or forgiveness is stronger still.

As with John's messianism and his understanding of Christ's death, the resurrection is characterized both by Johannine distinctives and by traditionalism. For all the surprise there is in John's language of Jesus's ability to raise himself, there is also the very familiar fare of a bodily resurrection of the crucified Jesus on the third day, who appears on several occasions to Mary Magdalene and then the apostles. The resurrection is also "gospel" in the sense that it does not merely return the situation of the disciples to how it was before Jesus's death. The situation of the disciples is escalated, in terms of their understanding (e.g., John 2:22), their promised joy and peace (partially) fulfilled in the course of the resurrection appearances, and in their commissioning and sending—also anticipated in the Farewell Discourse and brought about in John 20–21.

Finally, in John's understanding of the events of his narrative, there is again a very strong "accordance with the scriptures." This is seen in a range of different usages—allusions such as the reference to the lamb who takes away sin, analogies such as the elevation of the serpent in the wilderness, as well as more direct "this is that" fulfillments, as, for example, when Isaiah sees Jesus's glory; similarly, Abraham did not see typological anticipations of Jesus but actually did see "Jesus's day" (John 8:56), and Moses did not narrate foreshadowings of Jesus but in fact wrote about him (5:46). Notably, the passion and death of Jesus are a particular focus of scriptural fulfillment in John. Moreover, John is also insistent on the fact that to understand scripture is to know that "it was necessary for Jesus to rise from the dead" (John 20:9).

Overall, there is a high level of correlation with the primitive kerygma even in John. For all John's theological innovation in, for example, introducing into a Gospel the motif of Jesus as the eternal Word through whom all things were made (John 1:1–3), he remains committed to the traditional elements of the kerygma. And he remains committed to them not just in theory, or as foundations to remain below the surface of a more interesting superstructure. Rather, John repeatedly focuses attention on Jesus's messiahship, his saving death and resurrection on the third day, and their scriptural forecasting. In these respects at least, John's Gospel is no sectarian document.

APPENDIX 1: THE BURIAL OF JESUS IN JOHN'S GOSPEL

As an ancillary element of the kerygma, but an element nonetheless, the burial (John 19:38–42) features as an integral part of the plot of John's Gospel.[241] The main events are the same as in the Synoptics: Joseph of Arimathea asked Pilate for the body and went and took it away for burial (19:38). A new element in John is the presence of Nicodemus, who accompanies Joseph and carries the spices (19:39); both Joseph and Nicodemus are depicted as rather surreptitious disciples: Joseph was a secret disciple, and Nicodemus was the one who had initially come to Jesus "by night" (19:38–39). There is also a specific reference to the vast quantity of spices (about a hundred *litrai*, or approximately seventy-five pounds/thirty-three kilograms) and to Joseph's and Nicodemus's adherence to Jewish burial custom (19:39–40).[242] John refers to the burial in a "garden," paralleled only in the *Gospel of Peter*, and conflates two details from Matthew and Luke: Jesus is buried in a "new" tomb (also Matt 27:60), "in which no one had ever been laid" (also Luke 23:53). A stone was apparently placed over the entrance to the tomb (John 20:1). As in the Synoptics, Jesus is buried on the Friday (19:42). John does not use the standard word for "bury" (θάπτω), which also appears in 1 Cor 15:4, but employs the less common cognate ἐνταφιάζω ("prepare for burial") in reference to the Jewish burial customs and the simple verb "place" (τίθημι) for the act itself. There is additionally a reference to Jesus's burial earlier in the Gospel (John 12:1–8), where Mary of Bethany anoints Jesus with a very valuable quantity of nard (worth three hundred denarii): Judas objects to this, but Jesus responds, "Leave her alone, so that she may keep it *for the day of my burial* (εἰς τὴν ἡμέραν τοῦ ἐνταφιασμοῦ μου)."

---

241. Lincoln, *John*, 486–87, connects John 19:38–42 with 1 Cor 15:4.

242. Cf. the burials of Asa (2 Chr 16:14) and Herod the Great (Josephus, *Ant.* 17.199), both of which refer to spices: in the latter case, five hundred of Herod's attendants carried them. Lincoln, *John*, 487, sees Jesus's kingship reflected in the grandeur of his burial.

APPENDIX 2: THE RESURRECTION APPEARANCES IN JOHN'S GOSPEL

John's account of the appearances of the risen Jesus is carefully crafted. Jesus is not seen until verse 14 of the resurrection narrative, and even there Mary unwittingly sees Jesus (John 20:14); only in verse 16 does she recognize him. There is then an appearance to the ten disciples, that is, excluding Judas and Thomas (20:19–23) and then to Thomas with the other disciples (20:26–29). In John 21, some of the disciples who are fishing are named, in this order: Peter—Thomas—Nathanael, followed by the sons of Zebedee and "two other disciples" (21:2). Picking up on the visit to the tomb by Peter and the beloved disciple (20:3–10), John 21 also names Peter first among the disciples, as John 20 names him first of the Twelve. But the other, beloved disciple is the first in John 20:8 to believe and the first in John 21 to recognize Jesus (21:7). Peter does receive a special commission in the third resurrection appearance in John 21:15–19, and the final episode in the drama is a dialogue between Jesus and Peter about the destiny of the beloved disciple (21:20–23). Peter therefore occupies an important role in John 20–21, though none of the disciples is singled out as the first recipient of an appearance.

Chapter Eight

THE GOSPEL OF PETER

The *Gospel of Peter* has attracted considerable scholarly attention, not only for its literary relation to the canonical Gospels but also for its themes. It is those themes that will be the focus here, and again a specific subset of them, namely Jesus's identity as the Christ, his death and resurrection, and the extent to which these events are brought about "according to the scriptures."

A particular difficulty arises in any analysis of the theology of the *Gospel of Peter*, namely that our surviving text is a fragment—or more accurately, a deliberate excerpt.[1] It is likely that the original *Gospel of Peter* was roughly comparable in length to the canonical Gospels, because according to Origen it refers to Jesus's siblings.[2] Its fragmentary nature makes wide-ranging generalizations about the *Gospel of Peter*'s theology extremely hard. Serapion's discussion of the *Gospel of Peter* cannot be invoked, since it is both incomplete and indirectly attested.[3] A further difficulty is that there may be a number of differences between the text of the passion in the Akhmim Codex and the earliest form of the second-century text. A comparison of the Akhmim extract with the only early papyrus having a strong claim to being a fragment of the *Gospel of Peter* (P. Oxy. XLI 2949) reveals some fluidity in the text.[4]

---

1. See discussion of the codex in Peter van Minnen, "The Akhmim Gospel of Peter," in *Das Evangelium nach Petrus: Text, Kontexte, Intertexte*, ed. Thomas J. Kraus and Tobias Nicklas (Berlin: de Gruyter, 2007), 53–60.

2. See Origen, *Comm. in Matt.* 10.17 (on Matt 13:53). Although some dispute the relation of this testimonium to the work from which the Akhmim text was excerpted, there is no reason to doubt Origen here. For such skepticism, see, e.g., T. A. Wayment, "A Reexamination of the Text of POxy. 2949," *JBL* 128 (2009): 380.

3. Jerry McCant, "The Gospel of Peter: Docetism Reconsidered," *NTS* 30 (1984): 259.

4. See the careful treatment in David F. Wright, "Apocryphal Gospels: The 'Unknown Gospel' (Pap. Egerton 2) and the Gospel of Peter," in *The Jesus Tradition outside the Gospels,*

Nevertheless, the Akhmim fragment is a fairly substantial one. Although it has less material than any of the other texts covered in the present study, it is a great deal longer than any of the texts usually included in collections of "Gospel fragments," and is about 50 percent longer than the surviving text of the *Gospel of Mary*. The extant fragment also covers ground that is central to the interest of this book, namely the death and resurrection of Jesus. All the same, to a greater degree than with other works covered in this study, conclusions will need to be tentative.

1. Jesus as Messiah in the Gospel of Peter?

The reason for the interrogative title above is that the *Gospel of Peter*, at least in the fragment that has come down to us, makes no use of the terms Χριστός or Μεσσίας. This is not so remarkable, because in the overlapping passages in the canonical Gospel narratives, there are also few references to "messiah" language.[5] Oddly enough, the name "Jesus" does not appear either.[6] The *Gospel of Peter* does, however, employ several titles for Jesus.[7] The predominant one is "Lord," which the narrator invariably uses to refer to Jesus. One of the criminals crucified by his side calls him "savior." There are two titles in the *Gospel of Peter* that could have messianic resonances: "son of God" and "king of Israel." We will first consider the usage of these titles by Jews and Romans in the narrative, before proceeding to assess how the author might understand the titles in relation to messiahship.

1.1 *The Jewish Perspective*

This first passage portrays the maltreatment of Jesus by "the people" who mock the idea that Jesus is the son of God or king of Israel:

---

vol. 5 of *Gospel Perspectives*, ed. David Wenham (Sheffield: JSOT Press, 1985), 221–27, and the recent reedition and discussion in Wayment, "Reexamination."

5. Mark 15:32 and Luke 23:35, 39 appear to be the only cases.

6. Paul Foster, "Passion Traditions in the Gospel of Peter," in *Gelitten—Gestorben—Auferstanden*, ed. T. Nicklas, A. Merkt, and J. Verheyden (Tübingen: Mohr Siebeck, 2010), 59–60.

7. See Paul Foster, *The Gospel of Peter: Introduction, Critical Edition and Commentary* (Leiden: Brill, 2010), 148–57, on the christological titles in the *Gospel of Peter*.

⁶Those who were taking the Lord ran along pushing him, and said, "Let's drag this 'son of God' along, since we're in charge of him!" ⁷They dressed him in purple, and sat him on the seat of judgment saying, "Judge righteously, O king of Israel!" ⁸And one of them brought a crown of thorns and fastened it on the Lord's head. ⁹Some standing by were spitting in his eyes, others slapped his cheeks, and still others were stabbing him with reeds. Some also whipped him and said, "This is the way to honor the 'son of God'!"

¹⁰And they brought two criminals, and crucified them, with the Lord between them. He was silent, as if he were not in pain at all. ¹¹And when they lifted up the cross, they inscribed on it, THIS MAN IS THE KING OF ISRAEL. ¹²And laying out his clothes in front of him, they divided them up and cast lots for them. (*Gos. Pet.* 3.6–4.12)

The Jewish mockery here combines the titles "son of God" with "king of Israel," along with the other imagery of "judging justly" on "the judgment seat," the crown, and the clothing of Jesus in royal or imperial purple. In the *Gospel of Peter*'s depiction, the people speak in biblical idiom in calling on Jesus as king of Israel to "judge righteously" (*Gos. Pet.* 3.7; Deut 1:16; Prov 31:9; 1 Pet 2:23). In the second case, the inscription (in the *Gospel of Peter*, by the people, not the Romans) provides a permanent official verdict.

1.2 *The Roman Perspective*

The next two instances of "son of God," in contrast, are probably both expressions by the Roman soldiers of Jesus's true identity:

⁴³The soldiers were considering whether to go off and report this to Pilate. ⁴⁴And while they were still pondering, again the heavens looked as though they were open, and a man came down and went into the tomb. ⁴⁵When the centurion's men saw this, they hurried to Pilate, even though it was night. They left the grave they were guarding to explain everything they had seen. They were in turmoil as they told him, "Truly this man was the son of God (υἱὸς ἦν θεοῦ)!"

⁴⁶"I am innocent of this son of God's blood (τοῦ αἵματος τοῦ υἱοῦ τοῦ θεοῦ)," Pilate replied. "This was your doing." (*Gos. Pet.* 11.43–46)

This passage sees the centurion's men convinced that Jesus is a (or *the*) son of God because they have witnessed the portentous descent of an angel-like figure into Jesus's tomb, and, even more startlingly, the prior exit from it of Jesus, the enormous angels, and the talking cross.[8] These portents are evidence for the soldiers of a son of God, but at least within the drama, one imagines these Roman soldiers thinking in terms of the apotheosis of an august human figure rather than of a vindicated Jewish messiah. In Pilate's statement in 11.46, the tone is also noteworthy, in that he disavows any responsibility for the crucifixion. This is probably indicative of Pilate being conscious of Jesus's true identity and anxious to distance himself from any wrongdoing against this son of God.

1.3 The Authorial Perspective

As has been noted, in the course of the narration the author invariably refers to Jesus as "the Lord." This can hardly be the happenstance of the fragment that has survived, since the author uses the term of Jesus thirteen times (with two references to "the Lord's Day"), employing no other editorial title and not even Jesus's name. The author clearly has an overwhelming preference for this designation of Jesus.

The "son of God" is presumably regarded positively, and the Jewish mocking of Jesus is presumably in a sense ironic because the title is reaffirmed by the Roman soldiers and Pilate. It is difficult to say, however, what content the author would assign to the title. It may be a metaphysical affirmation of Jesus's nature and relation to God, or it may have more royal or imperial overtones. It is hard to conclude categorically that the author gives voice to a messianic understanding of Jesus through this title.[9] There is no sign that the author is tapping into a messianic exegesis of Ps 2 or Ps 89, for example.[10]

In the descriptions of Jesus as "king of Israel," there is even more ambiguity. The "son of God" title seems fairly clearly to be affirmed by the author, as it is voiced by Petronius's men after a realization of Jesus's resurrection and the

---

8. N. B. *Gos. Pet.* 9.36–11.45: εἶδον, ἰδόντες, εἶδον, πάλιν ὁρῶσιν, ἤκουον, ἠκούετο, ἰδόντες. On the emphasis on sense perception, see Tobias Nicklas, "Resurrection in the Gospels of Matthew and Peter: Some Developments," in *Life beyond Death in Matthew's Gospel: Religious Metaphor or Bodily Reality?*, ed. Wim Weren, Huub van de Sandt, and Joseph Verheyden (Leuven: Peeters, 2011), 30–31.

9. Cf. Tobias Nicklas, "Die 'Juden' im Petrusevangelium (PCair 10759): Ein Testfall," *NTS* 47 (2001): 216, who argues for a messianic sense.

10. Some have seen allusion to Ps 2 in the *Gospel of Peter*, but this relies in the end on the common usage of the single word συνεσκέπτοντο (*Gos. Pet.* 11.43), as a parallel to συσκέπτονται in Symmachus's text of Ps 2:1. See, e.g., Foster, *Gospel of Peter*, 437–38.

events surrounding it. By contrast, it is less clear that "king of Israel" is valued positively by the author.[11] Some interpreters have sought to explain the "king of Israel" title by way of comparison with the canonical Gospels. On this view, in contrast to the mockery of Jesus as "king of the Jews" and the appearance of the same phrase (ὁ βασιλεὺς τῶν Ἰουδαίων) in the *titulus* in all four Gospels,[12] the *Gospel of Peter* seeks to replace the reference to "Jews" with a more positive reference to historic Israel.[13]

One difficulty with this view is that, at least in the case of the mockery, Jesus is also ridiculed in the *Gospel of Peter*'s sources as a spurious "king of Israel" (Mark 15:32; Matt 27:42). This kind of redactional hypothesis, second, may also assume an overly scribal approach to the *Gospel of Peter*'s editing: it would require at least a very clear memory of textual detail or an open copy of one or more of the canonical Gospels for this redaction to be conscious. Finally, we have no sense from elsewhere in the *Gospel of Peter* that the author had a positive view of "historic Israel" over against the negatively valued Jewish contemporaries of Jesus: this seems to be an imposition from other early Christian writings. The *Gospel of Peter*'s author may have taken this view, or he may have taken a view like that in the *Epistle of Barnabas*, a work that is not particularly positive about historic Israel either. Since the *Gospel of Peter* shows no attachment to the law ("written *for them*" [5.15]) or Passover ("*their* festival" [2.5])—on which more later—such evidence as there is in the Gospel suggests little if any distinction between Jesus's Jewish contemporaries and historic Israel.

1.4 Interim Conclusion: Messiahship in the Gospel of Peter and the Kerygma

As a result, it is not clear that "king of Israel" is a rehabilitated messianic title, evoking the historic people of God and regarded as positive in the *Gospel of Peter*. The author of the *Gospel of Peter* may have thought in terms of Jesus's messianic kingship, or alternatively may have regarded messiahship as somehow suspicious. Certainly, our fragment's overwhelming, indeed exclusive,

11. Heike Omerzu, "'My Power, Power, You Have Left Me': Christology in the *Gospel of Peter*," in *Connecting Gospels: Beyond the Canonical/Non-canonical Divide*, ed. Francis Watson and Sarah Parkhouse (Oxford: Oxford University Press, 2018), 174–75, takes both as normative for the author, though taking Israel here to be the new Israel.

12. Mockery: Mark 15:18; Matt 27:29; Luke 23:37; John 19:3; *titulus*: Mark 15:26; Matt 27:37; Luke 23:38; John 19:19.

13. Foster, *Gospel of Peter*, 155, and Foster, "Passion Traditions," 57, 60.

preference for the title "Lord" is striking. While we should be cautious of drawing conclusions about the work as a whole, the surviving evidence is at best ambiguous as support for the *Gospel of Peter* reflecting the messianic language of the kerygma. Nor does the *Gospel of Peter*'s passion and resurrection narrative make use of scriptural passages previously used in Jewish messianic exegesis.

2. Jesus's Death in the Gospel of Peter

One point to note at the beginning of a discussion of Jesus's crucifixion in the *Gospel of Peter* is that, even if there may be other elements in Jesus's nature, we do have a real human death at some point in the narrative. This is made clear in *Gos. Pet.* 6.21–24 where the nails are extracted from the "hands of the Lord," and the body is buried by Joseph of Arimathea.[14] Features of that death can be explored initially through the *Gospel of Peter*'s account of the crucifixion:

> [15]It was midday, but darkness engulfed the whole of Judea. And the people were in uproar, distressed at the thought that the sun had already set while he was alive. (It is written for them, "The sun must not set over a murdered man.") [16]And one of them said, "Give him a drink of gall with vinegar." So they mixed it and gave it to him to drink. [17]And so they brought everything to fulfillment, heaping upon themselves the full measure of their sins. [18]Many people, thinking it was night, were stumbling around with lamps.
>
> [19]Then the Lord cried out, "My power, O power, you have abandoned me." As he said this, he was taken up. [20]And at the same hour, the curtain of the temple in Jerusalem was ripped in two.
>
> [21]Then they removed the nails from the hands of the Lord and placed him on the ground. The whole land was shaken, and great fear came upon them. [22]Then the sun shone again, and it was discovered to be the ninth hour. (*Gos. Pet.* 5.15–6.22)

14. Whichever way one takes the ὡς μηδὲν πόνον ἔχων ("as not suffering at all"), it is still the case that the Lord qua human being dies. On the interpretation of the statement, see Peter M. Head, "On the Christology of the Gospel of Peter," *VC* 46 (1992): 213, and Tobias Nicklas, "Die Leiblichkeit der Gepeinigten: Das Petrusevangelium und frühchristliche Märtyrerakten," in *Martyrdom and Persecution in Late Ancient Christianity*, ed. J. Leemans (Leuven: Peeters, 2011), 208–9. The latter article rightly emphasizes that "das Petrusevangelium ist durchaus an der Körperlichkeit des 'Herrn' interessiert," referring to his head, face, cheeks, and perhaps legs (217). Nicklas explores fully the possible connections between the *Gospel of Peter* and the Acts of the Martyrs.

In this scene, there are the two elements directly connected with the death of Jesus himself, namely his cry of dereliction and the reference to him being taken up (5.19). In addition, there are the accompanying signs: the darkness (5.15; 6.22), the tearing of the curtain (5.20), and the shaking of the land (6.21).

2.1 The Cry and the Ascension

We can begin with the two elements directly connected with the death of Jesus himself.

The Cry of Dereliction (Gos. Pet. 5.19a)

The cry of dereliction (ἡ δύναμίς μου, ἡ δύναμις κατέλειψάς με) differs markedly from the corresponding language in the canonical Gospels: in the *Gospel of Peter*, the cry is turned from a question into a statement and is addressed to "my power" rather than "my God." There are three main types of interpretation.

First, some have taken the cry to mean simply that Jesus's life is ebbing away.[15] The difficulty with this is that it assigns a rather banal meaning to the saying. Does Jesus break the silence he has maintained during the crucifixion to say something so pedestrian? The tone of such a grandiose saying seems rather too flamboyant simply to refer to a process of dying. Additionally, Jesus "cried out" (ἀνεβόησε) the statement rather than gasping it out.

Second, it is possible that the *Gospel of Peter* means "power" as a circumlocution for God.[16] On this view, the meaning is—apart from the shift from question to statement—in essence the same as that of the cry of dereliction in Matthew and Mark. Evidence for such a circumlocution can be seen in Jesus's challenge to the high priest in the Synoptics, where he declares that he will be seated "at the right hand of power" (Mark 14:62; Matt 26:64; cf. Luke 22:69). Against the idea of a mere circumlocution, however, is the fact that *Peter*'s version of the saying seems to reflect a background of linguistic speculation. A passage in Justin explains the origins of this substitution: "So the word 'Israel' means this: *Man conquering a power*. The 'Isra' means *man conquering*, and the 'el' means *power*."[17] Moreover, Myllykoski poses the question of

---

15. L. Vaganay, *L'Évangile de Pierre* (Paris: Gabalda, 1930), 256, attributes this view first to Jouissard. See Foster, *Gospel of Peter*, 163, and Omerzu, "My Power, Power," 181, 187.

16. See the helpful criticisms of Brown's adoption of this view in Foster, *Gospel of Peter*, 328–29. A more reasonable case is made in Head, "Christology," 214.

17. Justin, *Dial.* 125.3: καὶ τὸ οὖν Ἰσραὴλ ὄνομα τοῦτο σημαίνει· ἄνθρωπος νικῶν δύναμιν· τὸ γὰρ "ἴσρα" ἄνθρωπος νικῶν ἐστι, τὸ δὲ "ἢλ" δύναμις.

whether the author of the *Gospel of Peter* would really use such a circumlocution for no particular reason.[18] Jesus's cry is rather striking and enigmatic.

Third is the idea that a divine power that accompanied Jesus during the course of his ministry leaves him.[19] This itself covers a broad spectrum of opinion. At one extreme is the old "docetic" or "Gnostic" view, which appealed to the Valentinian views expressed in Irenaeus (according to which the savior came upon Christ at his baptism, preserved him from suffering, and departed when he came before Pilate),[20] or the similar statements in Clement's account of Theodotus's teaching.[21] A more modest interpretation, that of Vaganay, proposes that we have here a "popular" Christian view that the miracle-working power of Jesus, which also enabled his silence and survival, had left him.[22] There is also the argument of Myllykoski that the adoptionist power, which came upon Jesus perhaps at his conception, is departing. This would imply a separationist Christology but not of a Gnostic or docetic kind.[23]

If it is hard to know exactly what the *Gospel of Peter* means by Jesus's "power," it is more difficult still to imagine the departure of the power merely meaning expiring. The first two views expressed, the expiration and circumlocution views, clearly reflect part of the reaction in recent times against a docetic understanding of the *Gospel of Peter* and seek to provide a more tame or conventional interpretation for the cry of dereliction. But it need not follow that doing justice to the flamboyant cry entails a docetic Christology, as Myllykoski has shown. Although *Peter* may not be docetic, Painchaud is almost

18. Matti Myllykoski, "Die Kraft des Herrn: Erwägungen zur Christologie des Petrusevangeliums," in Kraus and Nicklas, *Evangelium nach Petrus*, 319.

19. Vaganay, *Évangile de Pierre*, 236. See also Thomas Hieke, "Das Petrusevangelium vom Alten Testament her gelesen: Gewinnbringende Lektüre eines nicht-kanonischen Textes vom christlichen Kanon her," in Kraus and Nicklas, *Evangelium nach Petrus*, 106, who is followed by Tobias Nicklas, "Angels in Early Christian Narratives on the Resurrection of Jesus: Canonical and Apocryphal Texts," in *Angels: The Concept of Celestial Beings—Origins, Development and Reception*, ed. F. V. Reiterer, T. Nicklas, and K. Schöpflin (Berlin: de Gruyter, 2007), 307–8.

20. See, e.g., Irenaeus, *Haer.* 1.7.2.

21. See Clement, *Exc.* 61, on the spirit that came at baptism and left Jesus as he died.

22. Cf., e.g., Mark 5:30 (when the woman touched him, "Jesus realized that power had gone forth from him"); Luke 5:17 ("the power of the Lord was present for him to heal"); Luke 6:19 ("power came forth from him and healed").

23. See Myllykoski's discussion of "Spuren adoptianistischer Christologie" ("Die Kraft des Herrn," 313–25): at the departure, "die übernatürliche Kraft ist von ihm bei seinem Tod geschieden" (324). Myllykoski appeals to the views of Cerinthus and the Ebionites in support of the view that this is a Jewish-Christian idea.

certainly correct to conclude that the choice of "my power" is not innocent.[24] The evidence from Justin for the idea that "el" can be taken to mean "power" also supports this. Therefore, some form of the third view above is most likely to be correct, even if we do not know whether the power in question is Jesus's supernatural spirit or an adoptionist power.

The Ascent: "He Was Taken up" (Gos. Pet. 5.19b)

Partially corresponding to these approaches to the cry of dereliction are particular interpretations of the statement immediately following: "As he said this, he was taken up (ἀνελήφθη)."

First, some understand the statement to be a simple reference to Jesus's death without any special theological point. Being "taken up" is sometimes described as a euphemism (like English "taken").[25] A second option is that there is a lack of theological sophistication here,[26] and that there is "some confusion between the language of death and ascension" that arises "from lack of authorial skill."[27]

The main difficulty with both these other positions is that ἀνελή(μ)φθη and its cognates are such standard terms for an ascension or translation. The verb and the related noun are used only very rarely to refer merely to death but feature in accounts of a number of biblical figures with reference to an ascent:[28]

24. Louis Painchaud, "Le Christ vainqueur de la mort dans l'Évangile selon Philippe: Une exégèse valentinienne de Matt. 27:46," NovT 38 (1996): 390.

25. Pace Timothy P. Henderson, The Gospel of Peter and Early Christian Apologetics: Rewriting the Story of Jesus' Death, Burial, and Resurrection (Tübingen: Mohr Siebeck, 2011), 102, and Omerzu, "My Power, Power," 182, who take the euphemistic view. Head suggests euphemism as the possible origin of the meaning "die" (Head, "Christology," 215). But the reference in Pss. Sol. 4.18 to ἀνάλημψις in the sense of death concerns the death of the wicked, as Myllykoski, "Die Kraft des Herrn," 320, points out.

26. Robert G. T. Edwards, "The Theological Gospel of Peter?," NTS 65 (2019): 496–510, helpfully opposes such a characterization of the Gospel of Peter's theology.

27. Foster, Gospel of Peter, 331. Head, "Christology," 215, attributes confusion to other thinkers in the second century, e.g., among those opposed by Justin and Irenaeus. It is not quite true, however, that the parallels in Justin and Irenaeus are references to confusion between death and ascension: they are references to views that Christ (in Irenaeus) and believers (in Justin) ascend at death instead of rising bodily.

28. See A. Denaux, Studies in the Gospel of Luke: Structure, Language and Theology (Münster: LIT Verlag, 2010), 17–22; J. Dupont, "ΑΝΕΛΗΜΦΘΗ (Act. 1.2)," NTS 8 (1962): 154–57; Michael Wolter, The Gospel according to Luke (Waco, TX: Baylor University Press,

- The ambiguity of Enoch's disappearance in Genesis is clarified in Ben Sira, who takes it that he was assumed alive into heaven: καὶ γὰρ αὐτὸς ἀνελήμφθη ἀπὸ τῆς γῆς (Sir 49:14).

- Abraham is told that he will be taken up into heaven (ἀναλαμβανέσαι εἰς τοὺς οὐρανούς), while his body is left behind, but he tells Michael that he wants to be taken up bodily (σωματικῶς ἤθελον ἀναληφθῆναι) (T. Ab. B 7).

- Michael returns to heaven (ἀνελήφθη εἰς τοὺς οὐρανούς) after visiting Abraham and Sarah in T. Ab. B 4.

- Philo describes the consumption of Nadab and Abihu as their being dispatched to the circuits of heaven (ἄχρι τῶν οὐρανοῦ περιόδων παραπεμφθέντες [Somn. 2.67]). Elsewhere this is described as a translation to God (ἀναληφθέντων Ναδὰβ καὶ Ἀβιούδ [Leg. 2.58])—presumably for judgment.

- Moses's transcendence of death and assumption into heaven are noted by Philo (Mos. 2.291; cf. 2.288): in Deut 34, Moses is just being or is on the point of being translated (ἤδη γὰρ ἀναλαμβανόμενος) as he is ready "to steer his flight on course for heaven" (ἵνα τὸν εἰς οὐρανὸν δρόμον διιπτάμενος εὐθύνῃ). The verb here is not a reference simply to death.[29]

- Job's children disappeared, "for they were taken up (ἀνελήφθησαν) into heaven by their maker" (T. Job 39.12).

- When carried in his chariot of fire, "Elijah was taken up (ἀνελήμφθη) into heaven in a whirlwind" (2 Kgs 2:11; cf. 2:9–10). In Ben Sira's apostrophe to Elijah, the passive of ἀναλαμβάνω is again used (Sir 48:9). When 1 Maccabees recounts Elijah's zeal, the same language (ἀνελήμφθη εἰς τὸν οὐρανόν) is employed (1 Macc 2:58).

- Jesus's ascension is described using this language. Before the event, Luke refers to Jesus's ἀνάλημψις without specifying its character (Luke 9:51). Thereafter, we find the meaning clarified through the use of the verb in Acts 1:2 (ἀνελήμφθη), 11 (ἀναλημφθεὶς ἀφ᾽ ὑμῶν εἰς τὸν οὐρανόν), 22 (ἀνελήμφθη ἀφ᾽ ἡμῶν). It is also found in the longer ending of Mark (ἀνελήμφθη εἰς τὸν οὐρανόν [16:19]) and in 1 Tim 3:16 (ἀνελήμφθη ἐν δόξῃ). The Lord is taken up (ἀνελήμφθη) after speaking to John in Acts of John 102. The noun ἀνάλημψις is used of Jesus's ascension in Clement, Strom. 6.15.122.1 and T. Levi 18.3.[30]

2017), 2:46; cf. P. A. van Stempvoort, "The Interpretation of the Ascension in Luke and Acts," NTS 5 (1958–1959): 30–42.

29. Pace Stempvoort, "Interpretation of the Ascension," 32.

30. Again, pace Stempvoort, "Interpretation of the Ascension," 32, T. Levi does not refer

- At the end of Paul's life, according to 1 Clement (5.7), he was transported and taken up "to the holy place" (εἰς τὸν ἅγιον τόπον ἀνελήμφθη).
- In addition to biblical characters, in the apocalypse at the beginning of Hermas, Rhodē announces that she has been taken up (ἀνελήμφθην) to heaven (1.1.5); the sheet that is lowered down to Peter in Acts 10 returns again to heaven (εὐθὺς ἀνελήμφθη τὸ σκεῦος εἰς τὸν οὐρανόν [Acts 10:16]); in *Dial.* 80.4, Justin criticizes pseudo-Christians who say that there is no resurrection but that their souls go up to heaven (τὰς ψυχὰς αὐτῶν ἀναλαμβάνεσθαι εἰς τὸν οὐρανόν).
- The seer is taken up in the visionary ascent in the Apocalypse of Ezra (ἀνελήφθην οὖν εἰς τὸν οὐρανόν).[31]

It is evident here that there is a strong tendency, not least in connection with Jesus, of using this term to refer to ascent (i.e., assumption or translation); nor is the commonly disambiguating "to heaven" required, as we saw in several cases.[32] In only one or two places is there clear reference to this language being used straightforwardly of death.[33] It is also not quite true that the two usages get conflated or confused, as noted above. As a result, an unsophisticated confusion here is probably unlikely.

Third, is it possible to take the *Gospel of Peter* to be referring to an ascension here? Two problems immediately present themselves.

For one, Jesus's body remains on the cross, whereas other references to Jesus's ascension seem clearly to be bodily. However, the semantic potential of the language can easily be put to use to refer to an ascension of some other, nonbodily element of Jesus.[34] Hence, among the examples cited above, Abraham is told that his soul will be "taken up," although he requests a bodily "taking up" (*T. Ab.* B 7). Paul's ἀνάλημψις in 1 Clement is presumably an ascent of the soul or spirit, like the psychic ascent of Justin's heretics. Similarly,

---

to death here, because the reference is to Jesus being on earth until he is no longer on earth: καὶ μεγαλυνθήσεται ἐν τῇ οἰκουμένῃ ἕως ἀναλήψεως αὐτοῦ.

31. C. von Tischendorf, ed., *Apocalypses Apocryphae: Moses, Esdrae, Pauli, Iohannis item Mariae Dormitio* (Leipzig: H. Mendelssohn, 1851), 24.

32. Luke 9:51 would only later (in Acts) be disambiguated, if that were necessary. Note also the examples of Enoch, Nadab and Abihu, and Elijah in Ben Sira, where no specification of heaven is added.

33. In Pss. Sol. 4.18, ἀνάλημψις means death, clearly by divine action, and in Ps.-Clem., *Hom.* 3.47, ἀνάλημψις probably refers to the death of Moses.

34. There are perhaps three aspects or elements of Jesus's nature: the power that has gone, the Jesus who speaks, and the body remaining after death.

according to some accounts, Julius Caesar's soul (*anima*) was translated to heaven, and the same happened to Augustus's "image" (*effigies*).[35] Against this background, the ἀνάλημψις of Jesus in the *Gospel of Peter* could easily be a disembodied departure of "my power." As we will see in the discussion of the *Gospel of Philip* below (chapter 12, sec. 2.1), other works contemporaneous with the *Gospel of Peter* can talk in terms of the ascent of Jesus's soul or spirit.

A consequent difficulty with this, however, is that one would expect to see the order reversed: *He was taken up, then he said, "My power, O power you have left me."* As the text stands, it looks on the surface as though we have the cry and after that (καὶ εἰπών) the ascent. However, Greek grammarians have long noted that when the main verb is aorist (in this case ἀνελήφθη), an aorist participle (here εἰπών) can mark an event simultaneous with, or even (rarely) subsequent to, the action in the finite verb.[36] Indeed, more recently some scholars have argued (perhaps exaggerating) that in fact the majority of aorist participles in the New Testament do not refer to antecedent actions.[37] As Robertson puts it elegantly, if a little mystically, "The aorist participle of simultaneous action is in perfect accord with the genius and history of the Greek participle."[38] He cites ἥμαρτον παραδοὺς αἷμα ἀθῷον ("I have sinned by betraying innocent blood"), ὑπολαβὼν ὁ Ἰησοῦς εἶπεν ("replying, Jesus said"), and τοῦτον . . . προσπήξαντες ἀνείλατε ("put him to death, nailing him to the cross") as examples of simultaneous or identical action expressed by the aorist participle.[39] In light of this, it is not difficult to see the "taking up" as effectively simultaneous with the departure of the power and the cry of dereliction.[40] Hence my rendering above: *"As he said this*, he was taken up." It therefore solves a number of problems to take Jesus's ἀνάλημψις in *Gos. Pet.* 5.19 as the

---

35. Julius Caesar: Ovid, *Metam.* 15.843–848; Suetonius, *Jul.* 88. Augustus: Suetonius, *Aug.* 100.4.

36. A. T. Robertson, *A Grammar of the Greek New Testament in the Light of Historical Research*, 3rd ed. (London: Hodder & Stoughton, 1919), 1112, citing predecessors. More recently, see Daniel B. Wallace, *Greek Grammar beyond the Basics: An Exegetical Syntax of the New Testament* (Grand Rapids: Zondervan, 1997), 614.

37. Charles A. Anderson, "'Time, Time, Time. See What's Become of It': Factors on the Temporal Relation of Aorist Participles and Verbs in the New Testament" (paper presented at the annual meeting of the Society of Biblical Literature, Washington DC, 19 November 2006).

38. Robertson, *Grammar of the Greek New Testament*, 1113.

39. Matt 27:4; Luke 10:30; Acts 2:23.

40. Painchaud, "Le Christ Vainqueur," 389–90 n. 22, noting a possible contrast between the κατά- prefix in the cry of dereliction and ἀνά- in the reference to the ascension.

departure of his power; hence there is an ascension in the *Gospel of Peter*, though not a bodily one.[41]

Synthesis: The Cry and the Ascension in 5.19

The biggest difficulty here is again that our Akhmim fragment is a mere torso without beginning or end. We have no larger narrative context from which to interpret the passion. This means that any detailed theological assessment is very difficult. On the one hand, minimalist arguments of the "not necessarily" kind, especially when multiplied (e.g., in combining conservative interpretations of both the cry and the ἀνάλημψις), have the effect of producing lowest-common-denominator results, which are not merely cautious but can be misleading. On the other hand, we do not have the annunciation or baptism scenes that might be able to add ballast to separationist accounts of the *Gospel of Peter*'s Christology.[42] Even so, the most likely interpretation of the cry and the ἀνάλημψις is that they refer to a departure to heaven of Jesus's power.

From the cry and the ascent, then, we cannot deduce a soteriological significance in the death of Jesus. There is no hint in the cry of dereliction—as far as we can see—that Jesus is bearing judgment on behalf of others. Nor does the ascent appear to mean—as in some systems—that humanity's soul-stuff or spirit-material is being redeemed and returned to its heavenly source. Perhaps more promising are the signs that accompany the death of Jesus in the *Gospel of Peter*.

2.2 The Signs

Myllykoski notes suggestively that although Jesus is silent apart from the cry of dereliction, the divine signs ("these awesome signs" [8.28]) do speak.[43]

---

41. A further potential difficulty that has not been noted in scholarship is a possible textual problem in *Gos. Pet.* 5.19. The statement καὶ εἰπὼν ἀνελήφθη might well betray an omission between εἰπὼν and ἀνελήφθη. The bare καὶ εἰπὼν without an object is a tad peculiar.

42. Cf. Myllykoski, "Die Kraft des Herrn," 324–25, with speculations about the annunciation and end of the *Gospel of Peter*.

43. Myllykoski, "Die Kraft des Herrn," 318. See also the helpful discussion of Henderson, *Gospel of Peter*, 107–12. *Pace* Henderson, however, I do not take the destruction of Jerusalem (7.25) to be a sign of the same kind as the other three. It lies, at least from the dramatic setting of the narrative, in the future and so is a different kind of event. Perhaps it would best be described as the confirmation for the post-70 reader of what was threatened in the signs that accompanied the crucifixion in the *Gospel of Peter*.

The Darkness (Gos. Pet. 5.19–6.22)

The scene with the darkness is much more elaborate than in the Synoptic Gospels, where the references are confined to single sentences (Mark 15:33; Matt 27:45; Luke 23:44–45a). In the *Gospel of Peter*, the darkness covers eight verses:

> ¹⁵It was midday, but darkness engulfed the whole of Judea. And the people were in tumult, distressed at the thought that the sun had already set while he was alive. (It is written for them, "The sun must not set over a murdered man.") . . . ¹⁸Many people, thinking it was night, were stumbling around with lamps. . . . ²²Then the sun shone again, and it was discovered to be the ninth hour. (*Gos. Pet.* 5.15–6.22)

For a number of scholars, the reference to "midday" reinforces an intertextual link with Amos 8:9, which would in turn emphasize the note of judgment in the event. (This will be discussed further in sec. 4.1.) Be that as it may, the note of judgment sounds clearly enough without it. First, darkness not only "came," as in the canonical Gospels, but engulfed or seized or gripped (κατέσχεν) the territory. Second, the arrival of the darkness automatically brings a curse, because the people are thereby made guilty of contravening the law "written for them" forbidding exposure of a murdered man when the sun has set. Third, there is the tumult brought upon the people at the prospect of this guilt, and the (real and symbolic) stumbling in the dark. The overall picture is clear that this scene announces judgment upon Judea and its denizens.

A final point to note is that, unlike in the canonical Gospels, the darkness in the *Gospel of Peter* enfolds not only Judea but also the other two signs. In the Synoptic Gospels, nothing happens between the sixth and ninth hours, and the portents take place when it has become light again. In the *Gospel of Peter*, however, the other signs occur within the framing of the dark judgment, a point that may assist in their interpretation.

The Tearing of the Curtain (Gos. Pet. 5.19–20)

It is notable that the tearing of the curtain is tied more closely to Jesus's death/ἀνάλημψις than in the canonical Gospels.[44] In the *Gospel of Peter*, it happens "at the same hour":

44. Head, "Christology," 216.

[19]And the Lord cried out, "My power, O power, you have abandoned me." As he said this, he was taken up. [20]And at the same hour the curtain of the temple in Jerusalem was ripped (διεράγη) in two. (*Gos. Pet.* 5.19–20)

Vaganay interpreted this in much the same positive manner as the scene in the canonical Gospels is sometimes approached, namely as introducing a new and universal covenant.[45] Foster and Omerzu are more cautious about assigning a meaning.[46]

Two points, however, assist in the interpretation of the tearing of the curtain. First, the use of the verb διαρρήγνυμι connotes quite violent, destructive ripping (cf. σχίζω in the Synoptics). The verb is commonly used to refer to the rending of garments by those in distress, and indeed the Pseudo-Clementine *Recognitions*, which may well be influenced by the *Gospel of Peter*, understand the event to mean that "the curtain of the temple was split, for it was wailing as if in mourning" (*Recogn.* 1.41.3).[47] Melito takes it similarly, as "the angel" tearing his clothes (*Pasch.* 98, line 727). This along with the fact, noted above, that the ripping takes place while darkness is covering Judea renders unlikely the optimistic interpretation of the event that Vaganay proposes. The darkness provides a context for understanding the tearing as a negative event of some sort, like a divine lament (cf. Melito), or a figurative lament of the temple (cf. *Recognitions*) at the flagrant violation of the sunset commandment quoted.

The Shaking of the Earth (Gos. Pet. 6.21)

The earthquake, again, has a different sense from its counterpart in Matthew, where it is the occasion for the opening of graves. In the *Gospel of Peter* by contrast, the scene is apparently a much more menacing one:

Then they removed the nails from the hands of the Lord and placed him on the ground. And the whole land/earth (γῆ) was shaken, and great fear came upon them. (*Gos. Pet.* 6.21)

45. Vaganay, *Évangile de Pierre*, 258–59.

46. Foster, *Gospel of Peter*, 332; Omerzu, "My Power, Power," 183. Also Maria Grazia Mara, *Évangile de Pierre: Introduction, texte critique, traduction, commentaire et index* (Paris: Cerf, 2006), 141.

47. See Joel Marcus, "The Gospel of Peter as a Jewish Christian Document," *NTS* 64 (2018): 482–84.

The motif of the earth shaking is common in the Bible, as a way in which God indicates his power, especially in judgment, and that brings fear to mortals.[48] This is exactly the sense here—"great fear came upon them." The fact that the tremor occurs (again, it must be remembered) in the dark adds to its menacing character.

Synthesis: The Trio of Signs

In short, the trio of signs—the darkness, the veil tearing, and the earthquake—are instructive, but they constitute a sequence of unremitting negativity. There is a strong note of divine disapproval, and the extensive darkness that enfolds the other two signs communicates a strong note of judgment, as recognized in *Gos. Pet.* 7.25: "The judgment and end of Jerusalem is looming!"

2.3 Interim Conclusion: Jesus's Death in the Gospel of Peter and the Kerygma

Taking *Gos. Pet.* 5.19 first, this scene in which Jesus dies in the *Gospel of Peter* raises as many questions as it answers. This is no doubt in part because it is an extract from a larger narrative that might have offered context for interpreting the cry of dereliction and the ἀνάλημψις. As noted, some scholars have interpreted these items as meaning almost the same thing as the corresponding narrative elements in the canonical Gospels. On the other hand, as other scholars have suggested, the two events can be understood as meaning something quite different. Overall, the divergence from the canonical portrayal of Jesus's death appears significant, with a probable reference in the *Gospel of Peter* to the departure to heaven of Jesus's supernatural power (in some unknown sense) from his body.

More instructive are the darkness, the tearing of the curtain, and the shaking of the earth. It is tolerably clear that they are a sequence of signs of divine displeasure toward the land of Judea and its inhabitants.[49] To this extent, they are divine "reactions" to Jesus's death rather than interpretations of its significance. The signs also constitute a vindication of Jesus's innocence and of his

---

48. Cf. Job 9:5–6; Ps 82:5; 99:1; Isa 2:19–21; 13:13; 24:17–21; Joel 2:1–11; Hag 2:6–7, 21–22; Heb 12:26–28.

49. Rightly, Henderson, *Gospel of Peter*, 107, 110; Edwards, "Theological Gospel of Peter," 505, is also correct, however, that they lead to repentance.

positive righteousness: the Pharisees and elders conclude in *Gos. Pet.* 8.28: "See what a righteous man he must be!" (ἴδετε ὅτι πόσον δίκαιός ἐστιν).

In terms of the overall subject of this study, it is very hard to extract from the surviving fragments (the Akhmim Codex and P. Oxy. XLI 2949) any suggestion of a soteriological significance to the death of Jesus, or even of an effective death in a broader sense. The most that can be said is that the signs are a trigger for the people's repentance (cf. Luke 23:48). Jesus is often called "savior" in the *Gospel of Peter*, but it is difficult to see how his death or ἀνάλημψις might in some sense be redemptive.[50] As we will see in our analysis of the resurrection, however, there is clearer indication there of a saving event taking place after Jesus's death.[51]

3. Jesus's Resurrection in the Gospel of Peter

The *Gospel of Peter*'s version of the resurrection scene is its most remarkable and well-known feature. None of the canonical Gospels' resurrection accounts actually contains a narration of the resurrection. The *Gospel of Peter*, however, after the burial, and the lamentation of the Jews over their guilt, does come close to narrating the event:[52]

> [35]But in the night in which the Lord's Day dawned, as the soldiers were guarding two by two on duty, there was a great voice in the sky. [36]And they saw the heavens opened and two men coming down from there, in brilliant light, approaching the tomb. [37]That stone that had been placed at the entrance rolled away by itself and made some space for them to enter. So the tomb was opened and both the young men went in.

50. Contra Edwards, "Theological Gospel of Peter," 509, who argues that the crucifixion saves through eliciting repentance and demonstrating Jesus's innocence, and that the cross and resurrection are coordinated as saving events by the shared use of (ὑπ)ορθόω. It is really the signs rather than the crucifixion that lead to repentance and show Jesus to be righteous.

51. Rightly, Jürgen Denker, *Die theologiegeschichtliche Stellung des Petrusevangeliums: Ein Beitrag zur Frühgeschichte des Doketismus* (Frankfurt: Herbert Lang, 1975), 97, on the absence of a soteriological sense of the cross.

52. As David F. Wright, "Apologetic and Apocalyptic: The Miraculous in the Gospel of Peter," in *Miracles of Jesus*, vol. 6 of *Gospel Perspectives*, ed. David Wenham and Craig L. Blomberg (Sheffield: JSOT Press, 1986), 410, correctly notes, even the *Gospel of Peter* stops short of describing what happens in the tomb.

[38]When the soldiers saw this, they woke the centurion and the elders. (They were also on guard there.) [39]As they were explaining what they had seen, again they now saw coming out from the tomb three men, two of them holding the other one aloft, and a cross following behind them. [40]The heads of the two reached up to heaven, but the head of the one carried along by them went up beyond the heavens. [41]And they heard a voice from the heavens saying, "Have you preached to those who are asleep?" [42]And an answer was heard from the cross, "Yes!" (*Gos. Pet.* 9.35–10.42)

3.1 Jesus's Bodily Resurrection on the Third Day

We see here the resurrection of Jesus's crucified but now transfigured body. Although different in appearance, the risen body is also continuous with the buried body, as can be seen from the fact that later the angelic figure announces that the corpse is no longer where it had been laid (*Gos. Pet.* 13.56).[53] The gigantic Jesus and accompanying walking cross can be seen to be a hendiadys for the crucified but risen Jesus. There is clearly a strong christological dimension to the resurrection scene. Where previously Jesus was the silent victim of battering and crucifixion, he now emerges triumphant and exalted. The accompanying angels are not needed to support Jesus because he gave up his power on the cross; rather, he must be escorted by the greatest possible angels, to bolster what is quite literally a very high Christology.[54] Edo notes a parallel in the Martyrdom and Ascension of Isaiah that specifies the nature of the escort that may also be in view in the *Gospel of Peter*: "the angel of the Holy Spirit and Michael, the chief of the holy angels, will open his grave on the third day, and the Beloved, sitting upon their shoulders, will come forth and send out his twelve disciples."[55] If this sort of scene is in view, the note is clearly one of triumph.

---

53. For parallels to the massive size of Jesus here, see Jeremiah J. Johnston, *The Resurrection of Jesus in the Gospel of Peter: A Tradition-Historical Study of the Akhmim Gospel Fragment* (Bloomsbury: T&T Clark, 2015), 157–58.

54. Nicklas, "Angels," 307–8. Similarly, Pablo M. Edo, "A Revision of the Origin and Role of the Supporting Angels in the Gospel of Peter (10:39b)," *VC* 68 (2014): 223–24, takes the action of the angels to be a servile one (so also Foster, *Gospel of Peter*, 421). On the height of Jesus, see Nicklas, "Angels," 308; see also Nicklas, "Resurrection in the Gospels of Matthew and Peter," 36–37, on the massive dimensions of Jesus in the Revelation of Elchasai (Epiphanius, *Pan.* 19.4.1).

55. *Mart. Ascen. Isa.* 3.15–17; trans. Knibb.

Jesus's resurrection also takes place "on the third day," as is clear from the chronology of the *Gospel of Peter*.[56] Jesus is crucified on the Friday. Then Antipas comments—oddly, given that it is not yet midday—that even as Jesus is about to be crucified, the Sabbath was approaching (2.5). Then, with no intervening days, the Sabbath comes (9.34), followed by the Lord's Day (9.35–end). In these two respects, the resurrection of Jesus in the *Gospel of Peter* is similar to its presentation in the canonical Gospels: Jesus rises from the dead with a body that is both continuous and discontinuous with his previous physicality, and he does so on the third day.

3.2 Preaching to the Dead

Moving on to the soteriology of the scene, in *Gos. Pet.* 10.41–42, we have a dialogue between the heavenly voice and the cross. The cross is the speaker here as an accompanying symbol of the crucified Christ,[57] perhaps, as Combs has suggested, in the same way that in epiphanies of Greek gods, those gods are accompanied by symbolic tokens.[58] The content of the dialogue makes it clear that a soteriological event has taken place, namely the proclamation to those who are asleep (ἐκήρυξας τοῖς κοιμωμένοις; ναί). Here we have an allusion to the idea, quite young at the point at which the *Gospel of Peter* was written, that after his death and burial, Christ descended into the underworld and announced the good news to the dead.

To illustrate this from the second century, an "elder" cited by Irenaeus recounts that the Lord descended and preached to those who had hoped in him—the righteous, the prophets, and the patriarchs.[59] Justin also has an apocryphal quotation from "Jeremiah": "The Lord God remembered his dead from Israel, those who have fallen asleep in the dusty earth, and he went down to them to preach to them the good news of his salvation."[60] The Shepherd of

---

56. See further J. A. Robinson and M. R. James, *The Gospel according to Peter, and the Revelation of Peter: Two Lectures on the Newly Discovered Fragments together with the Greek Texts* (London: Clay, 1892), 35–36.

57. Cf. also *Ep. Apos.* 16 and *Apoc. Pet.* 1 (Ethiopic), where the cross accompanies Jesus at this second coming.

58. J. R. Combs, "A Walking, Talking Cross: The Polymorphic Christology of the Gospel of Peter," *EC* 5 (2014): 200: "The animated cross in the Gospel of Peter is best understood as both the sign of the resurrected Lord and one of his divine manifestations." He gives the example of Athene being accompanied by her aegis and Asclepius being accompanied by serpents. The cross is thus a "metonymy epiphany" in this view.

59. Irenaeus, *Haer.* 4.27.2.

60. Justin, *Dial.* 72.4: καὶ ἀπὸ τῶν λόγων τοῦ αὐτοῦ Ἰερεμίου ὁμοίως ταῦτα περιέκοψαν·

Hermas has the harrowing of hell extended further by the preaching of the good news by dead apostles as well, and the recipients of their preaching were saved as a result.[61] Irenaeus himself cites an apocryphal prophecy, like Justin's Jeremiah quotation, that the Lord "remembered his own dead ones who had formerly fallen asleep, and came down to them in order to deliver them,"[62] and can even give the harrowing of hell as the reason for Christ's suffering.[63]

The *Gospel of Peter*, being roughly contemporaneous with Justin, Hermas, and Irenaeus, probably had a similar understanding of the preaching of the gospel to the dead and of its effects. Not much detail about the *Gospel of Peter*'s particular understanding can be gleaned from the bare question (ἐκήρυξας τοῖς κοιμωμένοις) and its affirmative answer (ναί), but three points can be made.

(1) Unlike 1 Pet 3:18–20, which places proclamation by Jesus to imprisoned spirits *after* his resurrection, the *Gospel of Peter* has it prior to the appearance of the risen Jesus.[64] The fact that it is the cross that acknowledges the preaching may mean that Jesus accomplished it after his crucifixion (e.g., on Holy Saturday), although it may have been the first act of the risen Jesus before his appearance.

(2) The scope of the audience of the kerygma is not defined. It may have comprised patriarchs and prophets,[65] and/or, given the outlook of the *Gospel of Peter*, righteous gentiles.[66] However, some of the ambiguity in 1 Pet 3 about whether the proclamation is beneficial to the spirits is removed in the *Gospel of Peter*;[67] the reference to those "asleep" probably implies temporary death from which they will wake up. They have "fallen asleep" (κοιμάομαι) rather than "per-

---

Ἐμνήσθη δὲ κύριος ὁ θεὸς ἀπὸ Ἰσραὴλ τῶν νεκρῶν αὐτοῦ, τῶν κεκοιμημένων εἰς γῆν χώματος, καὶ κατέβη πρὸς αὐτοὺς εὐαγγελίσασθαι αὐτοῖς τὸ σωτήριον αὐτοῦ. The passage does not appear in any known manuscript of Jeremiah.

61. Herm. Sim. 9.16.5.

62. Irenaeus, *Haer.* 4.33.1; cf. 3.22.4.

63. Irenaeus, *Haer.* 4.33.12.

64. First Peter 4:6 is not a reference to the same event. Whether Eph 4:8–10 or 5:14 refers to an event between (or after) the death and resurrection is very unclear (cf. Foster, *Gospel of Peter*, 246, with Robinson and James, *Gospel according to Peter*, 25). *Quest. Barth.* 1 places Jesus's descent to hell during the darkness on Good Friday.

65. So Tertullian, *An.* 55.

66. The audience of the dead apostles' preaching, in contrast to Jews, to whom Christ preached, according to Clement, *Strom.* 6.6.45.5.

67. For the ambiguity of 1 Pet 3:18–20, reflected in modern discussion, see Paul J. Achtemeier, *1 Peter: A Commentary on First Peter* (Minneapolis: Fortress, 1996), 259–62, where there is a survey of different scholars on either side.

ished" (ἀπόλλυμι). This is the conventional understanding of Christ's descent in the second century—that Jesus makes a positive, saving proclamation.

(3) Clearly the divine question is not voiced because God was unsure of the answer. The dialogue is recounted so that the event can be publicly announced. It was a step too far even for the *Gospel of Peter* to narrate the harrowing of hell. The purpose of the resurrection appearance, then, is in large measure to announce that Jesus has brought about the salvation of the sleepers.

The reference in the *Gospel of Peter*, therefore, to the harrowing of hell is the clearest statement in the Gospel of how Jesus is "the savior of mankind" (4.13). As Robinson remarked, "No subject had a greater fascination for the early Christian mind than the descent of Christ into Hades and the Harrowing of Hell."[68] This is certainly true for the *Gospel of Peter*. While the death and resurrection of Jesus do not appear to be themselves straightforwardly soteriological events, the resurrection is in the *Gospel of Peter* the occasion for the public announcement that this missionary journey has indeed taken place.

3.3 Interim Conclusion:
Jesus's Resurrection in the Gospel of Peter and the Kerygma

In spite of its bizarre account of the risen Jesus and the cross, and the anti-Jewish emphasis, in some other ways the resurrection narrative in the *Gospel of Peter* is quite conventional. The resurrection is bodily, even if Jesus's bodily form is unusual (as is also true in the canonical Gospels). The resurrection also takes place on the third day, in accord with the same chronology as the canonical Gospels and the statements in Acts 10:40 and 1 Cor 15:4. There is no restored fellowship between Jesus and the disciples, although this may have followed our extant fragment: the final sentence in which Peter says that he and some of the other disciples went fishing might suggest a continuing narrative akin to John 21. (See further appendix 2 below.)

68. Robinson and James, *Gospel according to Peter*, 25. For a survey of early literature, see J. B. Lightfoot, *St. Ignatius, St. Polycarp*, part 2 of vol. 2 of *The Apostolic Fathers* (London: Macmillan, 1889), 131–33 (on Ign. *Magn.* 9); Jean Daniélou, *The Theology of Jewish Christianity: A History of Early Christian Doctrine before the Council of Nicaea* (London: Darton, Longman & Todd, 1964), 233–48; Denker, *Die theologiegeschichtliche Stellung*, 93–96; Henderson, *Gospel of Peter*, 167 n. 28. In the view ascribed to Marcion in Irenaeus, *Haer.* 1.27.3, it is still a positive proclamation even if the patriarchs do not accept it; the authenticity of the ascription to Marcion of this view is doubted, however, in Judith M. Lieu, *Marcion and the Making of a Heretic: God and Scripture in the Second Century* (Cambridge: Cambridge University Press, 2015), 45–46.

The soteriological focus in *Peter*'s resurrection narrative is not so much on the death or resurrection of Jesus per se but on what happened (presumably) in between them, namely the harrowing of hell. Perhaps the main narrative and theological function of the resurrection in the *Gospel of Peter* is to bear witness to this event. Again, we are considerably hampered by the selectivity of our fragment of the *Gospel of Peter*, but this harrowing of hell is the only surviving reference in the Akhmim Codex to a saving event. It is probable that before and/or after the surviving passion and resurrection account, there is further soteriological material, since Jesus is described by the (probably reliable) criminal as "the savior of mankind" (*Gos. Pet.* 4.13). But we can only speculate about the character of other spheres of salvation. In any case, the resurrection in the *Gospel of Peter* resembles the position of the resurrection in the kerygma, given that the event of Jesus rising from the dead has significance as "good news."

4. FULFILLMENT OF SCRIPTURE IN THE GOSPEL OF PETER?

The use of scripture in the *Gospel of Peter* is another theme that has attracted considerable scholarly attention. Some scholars have attempted to identify affinities with particular recensions of the Greek Old Testament.[69] Dibelius sought to show that the use of scripture in the *Gospel of Peter* is in certain respects more primitive than that of the Synoptics, and Denker emphasizes the independence of the *Gospel of Peter*'s biblical usage in general.[70] Nicklas has examined the use of scripture for the light it sheds on the characterization of the Jews.[71] Various scholars have also noted the *Gospel of Peter*'s inclusion of a

---

69. Foster, *Gospel of Peter*, 118: "At a number of points the text shows affinities with readings preserved from Symmachus' recension of the LXX Psalms." He notes Ps 43:19 LXX (44:18 MT) and *Gos. Pet.* 10.39, and Ps 2:2; 30:14 LXX and *Gos. Pet.* 11.43. I am skeptical about whether one can identify a particular text type of the Septuagint to which the *Gospel of Peter* is indebted. Some of the terminology identified as potentially Symmachan is not particularly rare. See, e.g., Edo, "Origin and Role of the Supporting Angels," 210 n. 15, on the exaggeration by Vaganay of the rarity of ὑπορθόω.

70. Martin Dibelius, "Die alttestamentlichen Motive in der Leidensgeschichte des Petrus- und des Johannes-Evangeliums," in *Abhandlungen zur semitischen Religionskunde und Sprachwissenschaft: FS Wolf Wilhelm Grafen von Baudissin*, ed. W. Frankenberg and F. Küchler (Giessen: Töpelmann, 1918), 125–50; Denker, *Die theologiegeschichtliche Stellung*, 93.

71. Nicklas, "Die 'Juden' im Petrusevangelium."

wealth of biblical themes and scriptural idioms.[72] For the purposes of our in-quiry into whether the death and resurrection of Jesus take place "according to the scriptures," this section will treat (sec. 4.1) the use of scripture in the *Gospel of Peter's* presentation of Jesus's passion, (sec. 4.2) an alleged biblical allusion in the account of the resurrection, (sec. 4.3) the *Gospel of Peter's* broader relation to scripture, before drawing tentative conclusions about (sec. 4.4) the extent to which the *Gospel of Peter's* attitude to scripture and fulfillment reflects or resembles that of the kerygma.

4.1 Jesus's Death as Fulfillment of Scripture?

The challenge in assessing the *Gospel of Peter's* use of scripture is evaluating the degree to which the Gospel is simply drawing on existing Christian texts, or whether the author might know particular scriptural passages directly. A few passages give possible evidence for independent knowledge of scripture on the part of the *Gospel of Peter*.

The first of these is the reference to maltreatment of the servant in Isa 50:

Isa 50:6	Gos. Pet. 3.9a (N. B. order changed)
I yielded my back to their whips (μάστιγας), and my cheeks to their slaps (τὰς δὲ σιαγόνας μου εἰς ῥαπίσματα); my face I did not turn away from the shame of their spitting (ἀπὸ αἰσχύνης ἐμπτυσμάτων).	(αδ) some also whipped (μάστιζον) him, (αβ) others slapped his cheeks (τὰς σιαγόνας αὐτοῦ ἐράπισαν), (αα) some standing by were spitting (ἐνέπτυον) in his eyes; (αγ) others were stabbing him with reeds.

---

72. Hieke, "Petrusevangelium," 99, notes numerous thematic links—e.g., resurrection after three days (cf. Hos 6:2); the silence of Jesus (cf. Isa 53:7) might be connected with the servant in Isaiah. See also Philipp Augustin, *Die Juden im Petrusevangelium: Narratologische Analyse und theologiegeschichtliche Kontextualisierung* (Berlin: de Gruyter, 2015), 179: the *Gospel of Peter's* αὐτὸς δὲ ἐσιώπα is more likely to be indebted to Mark 14:61 or Matt 26:63; there are also ritual and moral dimensions of handwashing in the Old Testament perhaps reflected in the opening lines of the *Gospel of Peter* (Augustin, *Die Juden im Petrusevange-lium*, 156–58). These connections are very loose, however, and certainly need not imply any intentional allusion to scripture. On biblical idioms in the *Gospel of Peter*, see especially Hieke, "Petrusevangelium." E.g., "judge justly!" (*Gos. Pet.* 3.7) has its closest parallel in Prov 31:9 but is natural Greek: see Deut 1:16; Josephus, *Ant.* 19.82; 1 Pet 2:23; *Did.* 4.3; *Barn.* 19.11; Melito, *Apol.* frag. 1*.6 (Hall); Theophilus, *Autol.* 1.11, as well as Demosthenes, *Aristocr.* 2; Epictetus, *Diatr.* 3.7.21; Plutarch, *Cor.* 39.3[5]; for the contrast between "sinning" and "falling into the hands of" (*Gos. Pet.* 11.48), cf. LXX Dan 13:23; 2 Sam 24:14/1 Chr 21:13; Sir 2:18; cf. John 11:50 (Hieke, "Petrusevangelium," 112); similarly, compare ταύτῃ τῇ τιμῇ τιμήσωμεν τὸν υἱὸν τοῦ θεοῦ (*Gos. Pet.* 3.9) with Zech 11:13 Aquila; 4 Macc 17:20; Matt 27:9; Acts 28:10.

The degree of agreement here is striking.[73] Although the *Gospel of Peter* consistently has verbs where the Septuagint has nouns, there are two cognate verbs (in 3.9aα and 3.9aδ) and one longer phrase (in 3.9aβ). On the other hand, one could also argue that the primary or even exclusive reference point is the canonical Gospels. The sequence—scarlet or purple clothing, crown of thorns, and beating or spitting—is the same across the *Gospel of Peter* and Matthew and Mark:

Gos. Pet. 3.7:	clothing in purple	cf. Matt 27:28	Mark 15:17a
Gos. Pet. 3.8:	crown of thorns	Matt 27:29	Mark 15:17b
Gos. Pet. 3.9:	beating or spitting	Matt 27:30	Mark 15:19

Hence the episode in *Gos. Pet.* 3.9 comes in a Synoptic sequence. There is no necessity for the events to happen in this order, as John's Gospel shows (where the order runs John 19:13 → 19:2, 5 → 19:1). Additionally, the vocabulary in the *Gospel of Peter* is all found in the canonical Gospels. However, since the reference to cheek-slapping occurs not in the passion narrative of the canonical Gospels but in the Sermon on the Mount (Matt 5:39; cf. Luke 6:29), this may well indicate that the *Gospel of Peter* has independent knowledge of Isaiah here. The degree of agreement here is striking, and the *Gospel of Peter* shares with Isaiah the compression of all these elements into a short verse.

The second case is the midday darkness (*Gos. Pet.* 5.15; cf. Amos 8:9).[74] Here the *Gospel of Peter* displays two points in common with Amos over against the Synoptic Gospels: first, the word for "noon" (μεσημβρία); and second, a form of the verb "to set" (δύω). This seems like telling evidence. But it should be noted that the *Gospel of Peter*'s ὁ ἥλιος ἔδυ is derived from his form of the burial law discussed above (ἥλιον μὴ δῦναι ἐπὶ πεφονευμένῳ). The *Gospel of Peter* states "the sun set" (ὁ ἥλιος ἔδυ) in that context: the people were in anxious uproar because "the sun set" while Jesus was still alive. This leaves

---

73. See, e.g., Denker, *Die theologiegeschichtliche Stellung*, 62; Augustin, *Die Juden im Petrusevangelium*, 176. Omerzu, "My Power, Power," 175, sees a "conscious allusion" here. Additionally, she takes Jesus's silence in the *Gospel of Peter* to echo Isa 53:7.

74. Denker, *Die theologiegeschichtliche Stellung*, 70. Foster, *Gospel of Peter*, 313, states: "Thus, while Amos 8.9 may have shaped the Markan narrative, it appears that the imagery from Amos has been exploited to a greater extent and to a more readily identifiable degree in the *Gospel of Peter*. It is no longer possible to determine if the author was responsible for this increased correspondence, or whether he utilised a tradition that had aligned this aspect of the Passion more closely with Amos 8.9."

μεσημβρία, and it is noticeable that at this point, the *Gospel of Peter* is following the Synoptic sentence structure, not that of Amos:

Amos 8:9	Luke 23:44	Gos. Pet. 5.15
And the sun will set	It was	It was
(δύσεται ὁ ἥλιος)	now about the sixth hour,	noon (μεσημβρία)
at noon (μεσημβρίας),	and darkness came	and darkness seized
and darkened	over the whole land/earth	all Judea.
over the earth	until the ninth hour	They were in uproar, distressed
in day will the light be.	by an eclipse of the sun	that the sun had set (ὁ ἥλιος ἔδυ)
	(τοῦ ἡλίου ἐκλιπόντος).	while he was still alive.

Here the *Gospel of Peter*'s statement is close in structure and in content to that of Luke, while treating the individual components with a certain freedom. Working backward, he specifies the ambiguous τὴν γῆν ("land" or "world"?) as τὴν Ἰουδαίαν, uses the more vivid "seized" (κατέσχεν) for "came over" or "came upon" (ἐγένετο ἐπί), and initially replaces the reference to the sixth hour with the more common "noon" (μεσημβρία).[75] This is not a surprising substitution. The word appears nearly five thousand times in Greek literature according to TLG, and I am therefore rather baffled that it can be described as "uncommon."[76] It remains a possibility that the *Gospel of Peter* or its source had access, either visual or in memory, to the text of Amos, but it is by no means as certain as scholars have assumed.

A third possibility is the presentation of the gall and vinegar to Jesus:[77]

---

75. My description here of course implies that the process is more mechanically scribal than was no doubt the case.

76. Deane Galbraith, "Whence the Giant Jesus and His Talking Cross? The Resurrection in Gospel of Peter 10.39–42 as Prophetic Fulfilment of LXX Psalm 18," *NTS* 63 (2017): 477–78. He refers to Foster, *Gospel of Peter*, 323, at this point, but Foster merely states that μεσημβρία is less common than πίπτω. A similar redaction appears where Marcion changes "the second or third watch" to the "evening watch." See Epiphanius, *Pan.* 42.11.6 (§35): Ἀντὶ τοῦ "δευτέρᾳ ἢ τρίτῃ φυλακῇ" εἶχεν "ἑσπερινῇ φυλακῇ." Cf. Luke 12:38.

77. H. B. Swete, *The Akhmîm Fragment of the Apocryphal Gospel of St. Peter* (London: Macmillan, 1893), 8, comments that it is "possibly" because of Amos 8:9; Nicklas, "Die 'Juden' im Petrusevangelium," 18, sees an allusion as much clearer.

Ps 68:22 LXX	Gos. Pet. 5.16	Matt 27:34, 48	Mark 15:23, 36	Luke 23:36
And they gave me gall (χολήν) for a meal, and for my thirst gave me a drink of vinegar (ἐπότισάν με ὄξος).	"Give him a drink (ποτίσατε) of gall with vinegar (χολὴν μετὰ ὄξους)!" So they mixed them (κεράσαντες) and gave it to him to drink (ἐπότισαν).	[34]They gave him a drink of wine mixed with gall (οἶνον μετὰ χολῆς μεμιγμένον). . . . [48]Immediately one of them, who had filled a sponge with vinegar (ὄξους) and put it on a stick, ran up and gave him the drink (ἐπότιζεν).	[23]They gave him perfumed wine (ἐσμυρνισμένον οἶνον). . . . [36]One of them filled a sponge with vinegar (ὄξους) and put it on a stick. He ran up and gave him the drink (ἐπότιζεν).	The soldiers mocked him, and approached him and offered him vinegar (ὄξος).

Here again, as in the possible Isaiah reference, Ps 68 and *Gos. Pet.* 16 have very similar language compressed together. On the other hand, it is hard to tell whether the text of the *Gospel of Peter* here has come directly from the Old Testament or from a conflation of the canonical accounts. The *Gospel of Peter*, with Matthew but against Ps 68, has the vinegar and gall mixed together: Matthew and the *Gospel of Peter* have both the preposition μετά and the "mixed" participles κεράσαντες (*Gospel of Peter*) and μεμιγμένον (Matthew).[78] These commonalities between the *Gospel of Peter* and Matthew mean that the *Gospel of Peter* is almost certainly influenced by one or more of the canonical accounts here. Not only does all the vocabulary appear in Matthew, but so does the agreement—against the Septuagint—on the mixing.[79]

These latter two cases (Amos 8 and Ps 68) are just some of the biblical references in the *Gospel of Peter* that are probably derived from the canonical Gospels and appear more distant from their scriptural sources. The cry of dereliction becomes a statement rather than a question and comes in a form reflecting an exegetical tradition attested in Justin.[80] In its reworded form, and without

78. Mark's ἐσμυρνισμένον οἶνον also implies a mixture, hence the many English translations that have "wine mixed with myrrh" (NIV, ESV, NRSV; cf. KJV: "wine mingled with myrrh").

79. Foster concludes, rightly, that "it is unnecessary to postulate that the combination was an intentional allusion to the LXX Ps 68:22 on the part of the author of the Gospel of Peter" (*Gospel of Peter*, 317). Hieke, "Petrusevangelium," 104, sees reference to both the canonical Gospels and the psalm.

80. Denker, *Die theologiegeschichtliche Stellung*, 74, also notes Aquila's translation of *eli* as ἰσχυρέ μου, though this is not so directly relevant.

the Aramaic or Hebrew provided by Mark and Matthew, the formulation in the *Gospel of Peter* ignores its scriptural origin. (See further sec. 2.1 above.)

Additionally, the casting of lots for Jesus's clothing (*Gos. Pet.* 4.12) has nothing distinctive in common with Ps 21:19 LXX, and can be accounted for solely from the Gospels.[81]

Further, in transferring the leg-breaking reference from Jesus to the penitent thief, the *Gospel of Peter* distances Jesus from this scriptural motif (4.13–14). He also uses terminology shaped by the Gospel episode (σκελοκόπτω specifically referring to legs being broken) rather than the scriptural language used by John, which refers to bones not being broken (ὀστέον + οὐ + συντρίβω), and John's reference to scriptural fulfillment.[82]

Finally, when we come to the death of Jesus itself, the *Gospel of Peter* presents the event as actually *contrary* to scripture rather than in accordance with it: against the one explicit "quotation" of scripture in the *Gospel of Peter*—"The sun is not to set over a murdered man" (ἥλιον μὴ δῦναι ἐπὶ πεφονευμένῳ [2.5; 5.15])—the sun *does* set over a murdered man. We will explore this further in section 4.3 below.

It is not the case that the *Gospel of Peter* has derived all his knowledge of scripture from the Synoptic Gospels: clearly, he had knowledge of Deuteronomy's law of burial from somewhere else, even if that knowledge was very imprecise. (See further sec. 4.3 below on the *Gospel of Peter*'s version of the Deuteronomy law.) In the instances surveyed here, it is possible that the *Gospel of Peter* shows particular knowledge of passages relating to Jesus's passion: his maltreatment (Isa 50), the darkness (Amos 8), and the presentation of the vinegar and gall (Ps 68); in the case of Isa 50, there is a good probability.[83] He does not acknowledge his indebtedness to scripture at these points, however, and so, if they do reflect these Old Testament passages independently of the canonical Gospels, we do not know if the allusions were deliberate or whether this knowledge was direct or indirect. Hieke rightly comments that with the exception of the two allusions to Deuteronomy, "it is not certainly obvious whether there is an underlying literary dependence or whether the reference is intended."[84]

---

81. Rightly, Foster, *Gospel of Peter*, 300: "It appears that both Justin and the *Gospel of Peter* have drawn on gospel tradition independently to fashion their own accounts" (noting *Dial.* 97.3). Cf. Augustin, *Die Juden im Petrusevangelium*, 182, who sees a more conscious allusion to the psalm.

82. *Pace* Hieke's suggestion ("Petrusevangelium," 100–101) that there is christological reference to the suffering righteous here.

83. Augustin takes an allusion to be "zweifelsfrei" (*Die Juden im Petrusevangelium*, 177).

84. Hieke, "Petrusevangelium," 113: "es ist nicht sicher erkennbar, ob eine literarische Abhängigkeit vorliegt und ob der Bezug . . . intendiert ist."

4.2 The Resurrection and Scriptural Fulfillment?

The most interesting proposal for scriptural reference in the *Gospel of Peter* is that of Galbraith, who, following a lead from Harris and Vaganay, argues that the resurrection narrative is modeled on Ps 18: "all of the seemly innovative elements of the resurrection scene in *GPet* 10.39–42 have been constructed on the basis of a christocentric interpretation of LXX Ps 18:1–7."[85] The thought is that, first, the psalm's depiction of a giant in heaven is the basis for Jesus's stratospheric height, and second, the speech of the heavens and the firmament (Ps 18:2) is the basis for the dialogue between the heavenly voice and the cross:

Ps 18 LXX (19 MT)	Gos. Pet. 10.40–42
[5c]He pitched his tent in the sun; [6]like a groom coming forth from the bridal chamber, like a giant he will rejoice to run his course. [7]From height of heaven (ἀπ᾿ ἄκρου τοῦ οὐρανοῦ) he departs, his goal the height of heaven (ἕως ἄκρου τοῦ οὐρανοῦ); and nothing will be hidden from his heat.	[40]The heads of the two reached up to heaven (μέχρι τοῦ οὐρανοῦ), but the head of the one carried along by them went up beyond the heavens (ὑπερβαίνουσαν τοὺς οὐρανούς).
[2a]The heavens (οὐρανοί) declare the glory of God,	[41]They heard a voice from the heavens (οὐρανῶν) saying, "Have you preached to those who are asleep?"
[2b]and the firmament (στερέωμα) announces the work of his hands.	[42]And an answer was heard from the cross, "Yes!"

This has an initial attraction, but overall the argument does not convince. The first difficulty is a lack of verbal linkage that is usually thought to be a necessary condition of allusion. As far as I can see, the only verbal link between the cited verses in Ps 18 (19 MT) and *Gos. Pet.* 39–42 (besides trivial words such as καί, αὐτός, etc.) is οὐρανός.[86] Moreover, the *Gospel of Peter's* reference to the voice from heaven is much closer to the instances of voices from heaven in the New Testament than to Ps 18.[87]

The first parallel, between Ps 18:5–7 and *Gos. Pet.* 10.40, is very rough: the figure in the psalm goes to the summit of heaven but not *above* heaven, like Jesus in the *Gospel of Peter*. In Ps 18:2a, "the heavens *declare* (διηγοῦνται),"

85. Galbraith, "Whence the Giant Jesus," 480.

86. φωνή appears in Ps 18:4 and in *Gos. Pet.* 10.41.

87. Cf. *Gos. Pet.* 10.41's φωνὴ . . . ἐκ τῶν οὐρανῶν with the identical wording in Matt 3:17 and Mark 1:11 (φωνὴ ἐκ τῶν οὐρανῶν); Luke 3:22, John 12:28, and Acts 11:9 have φωνὴ ἐκ τοῦ οὐρανοῦ.

rather than posing a question as in the *Gospel of Peter*. Moreover, as Denker notes, in the *Gospel of Peter*, it is not the heavens per se that are speaking, but presumably someone in heaven.[88]

As far as Ps 18:2b ("the firmament announces the work of his hands") is concerned, there is a lack of sufficient connection between the cross and the firmament—a link that is central to Galbraith's argument. The first piece of evidence provided for a link is the description of the cross as "wide as the firmament" in Pseudo-Hippolytus, *Can. pasch.* 3. However, the term for "wide as the firmament" is οὐρανομήκης, which is a problem because the distinction between heaven language (οὐρανός) and firmament language (στερέωμα) is crucial to Galbraith's argument: "heaven" in the psalm must represent the question from heaven in the *Gospel of Peter* so that the voice of the "firmament" is then the cross's reply. Or again, for Galbraith, Melito says that Jesus is fastened to a tree, where the verb is ἐστήρικται, which is cognate with στήριγμα, which could refer to the pillar that supports the firmament.[89] This form of argument by free association is hardly convincing. The passages "in which the cross is identified primarily or even exclusively with the firmament" may perhaps relate the cross indirectly to the firmament, if at all, but this is never actually said. It is not clear to me that we ever have any explicit identification or relation of the cross with firmament terminology (στερέωμα and cognates) in second-century literature.[90] It is thus a considerable stretch to say that "the interpretation of the firmament as a prophetic type is well attested in Christian literature from the second century onwards."[91] As a result, the case for Ps 18 LXX as a backdrop to the *Gospel of Peter*'s resurrection account is an intriguing one, but unconvincing. In fact, there may be other more plausible options for a source.[92]

---

88. Denker, *Die theologiegeschichtliche Stellung*, 98, although he goes too far in saying that the cross does not speak either, with ἀπό merely meaning "from the direction of" the cross (97).

89. Galbraith, "Whence the Giant Jesus," 488–89.

90. Galbraith, "Whence the Giant Jesus," 488–89, cites Daniélou in support at two points (esp. at 489 n. 64), but in all Daniélou's discussion of the Old Testament typology of the cross and the cross's cosmic scope, there is never any specific mention, as far as I can see, of the firmament (*Theology of Jewish Christianity*, 270–92, on the "typology of the cross"). Rightly, Denker, *Die theologiegeschichtliche Stellung*, 97, on the absence of a cosmological sense of the cross in the *Gospel of Peter*.

91. Galbraith, "Whence the Giant Jesus," 489.

92. For another intriguing suggestion for the origin of the account, see Edo, "Origin and Role of the Supporting Angels," 213. He considers the possibility of Luke's transfiguration narrative, in which there are two figures in glory alongside Jesus, a voice from heaven, a

4.3 The Gospel of Peter's Relation to Scripture

To sum up, we see in the *Gospel of Peter* a distance from the text of scripture, but also a degree of reluctance to associate with scripture. For the author, scripture was written for, belongs to, and is witness against the Jews in the *Gospel of Peter*.

We can begin with the first "citation" of scripture and its repetition later in the narrative:

> And Herod said, "Brother Pilate, even if no one had asked for him, we would have buried him since now the Sabbath is beginning. For it is written in the law: 'The sun is not to set over a murdered man (γέγραπται γὰρ ἐν τῷ νόμῳ ἥλιον μὴ δῦναι ἐπὶ πεφονευμένῳ).'" And he handed him over to the people the day before the Passover, their feast. (*Gos. Pet.* 2.5)

> It was midday, but darkness gripped the whole of Judea. And they were in anxious uproar in case the sun should set when he was still alive: it was written for them, "The sun is not to set over a murdered man." (*Gos. Pet.* 5.15)

The first point to note here is a degree of distance from the text of scripture. The quotation shows knowledge of the law in Deut 21:23 that a body should not be left hanging overnight. This knowledge is independent of the New Testament, for in the canonical Gospels, one finds a sense of urgency that Jesus's body should be buried before nightfall (Mark 15:42; John 19:31) but not enough detail to deduce the law from that.[93] While the *Gospel of Peter* clearly knows about the burial law here and presents Herod Antipas as a Jew concerned to fulfill it, there is no knowledge of its wording in the Septuagint. As Foster points out, "Even a cursory comparison shows a lack of close verbal correspondence between the text of Deut 21:23 and the stipulation presented by the author of the *Gospel of Peter*. In fact, of the five-word form of the ruling used in the Akhmîm text, not even one of these words is found in the text of

---

conversation about Jesus's departure in Jerusalem, and a mention of Jesus's resurrection at the end. Again, however, there are of course differences, as Edo notes. Galbraith rightly notes, however, that it is common in early Christian accounts to find Jesus at the transfiguration standing on earth but with his head extending into heaven ("Whence the Giant Jesus," 483–86).

93. David W. Chapman, *Ancient Jewish and Christian Perceptions of Crucifixion* (Tübingen: Mohr Siebeck, 2008), 244–45.

Deuteronomy."[94] The closest parallels to the *Gospel of Peter*'s wording of the law are in Christian texts, Swete pointing out the similar wording in the *Apostolic Constitutions* and a report in Epiphanius's *Panarion*.[95] Foster concludes, probably correctly, that "this tradition drew upon Jewish reflections on Deut 21:23, but was developed in Christian circles into a form that best suited the apologetic agenda."[96] Indeed, it may be that the *Gospel of Peter* was the source of this formulation.[97] In any case, there is a certain distance from the language of the source in Deuteronomy, which is unusual given that this law in the *Gospel of Peter* is very important in the narrative.

The second point to note arises from the second reference to the law, where it is introduced by the curious citation formula "it was written for them" (γέγραπται αὐτοῖς). The translation is disputed. Foster has, for γέγραπται αὐτοῖς, "written *by* them," which is possible but not probable: it is grammatically unlikely,[98] and the context suggests that the anxiety among the Jews has arisen because of a command "for them" that they are obliged to obey. It is notable that, on either reading, the narrator puts some distance between himself and the law, rather as in the case of John's references to "your law" and "their law." However, while in the case of John these references are clearly to be understood alongside instances where scripture is clear testimony to Jesus and scriptural fulfillment is something unambiguously positive, it is difficult to find such counterbalancing examples in the *Gospel of Peter*.

Third, this close relation of the law to the Jewish people in the *Gospel of Peter*'s narrative, rather than being something the author himself appropriates, is confirmed shortly after this second reference. In *Gos. Pet.* 5.17, there is a specific reference to fulfillment that fits this application of scripture to the Jews, rather than providing evidence that scripture is shared between the author and the Jews in the narrative:

94. Foster, *Gospel of Peter*, 245. Strictly speaking, this is not quite true, as the word ἐπί appears in both, but in reference to the tree in Deuteronomy, and the corpse in the *Gospel of Peter*.

95. Swete, *Akhmîm Fragment*, 3, discussed in Foster, *Gospel of Peter*, 245.

96. Foster, *Gospel of Peter*, 245.

97. See, e.g., Marcus, "Gospel of Peter," on the possible influence of the *Gospel of Peter* on these later works.

98. E.g., Friedrich Blass, Albert Debrunner, and Robert Funk, *Greek Grammar of the New Testament and Other Early Christian Literature* (Chicago: University of Chicago Press, 1961), 102, consider that there is only one instance of the dative of agency in the New Testament.

And they brought everything to fulfillment (ἐπλήρωσαν πάντα) and heaped upon themselves the full measure of their sins (ἐτελείωσαν κατὰ τῆς κεφαλῆς αὐτῶν τὰ ἁμαρτήματα). (*Gos. Pet.* 5.17)

Here it is the people, the Jews, who fulfill "everything," presumably through the events just described immediately before *Gos. Pet.* 5.17: dividing his garments (4.12) and giving the gall and vinegar (5.16). The people's concern about the sunset law is an implicit admission that they have murdered Jesus (πεφονευμένῳ) and thereby broken the sixth commandment (οὐ φονεύσεις). The sun setting over Jesus then brings further infraction of the law (5.15). The events are thus fulfillments in the sense that the people's sinful actions contribute to the heaping up of their sins. Hence, like Matthew and Paul, the *Gospel of Peter* attests the biblical notion that God does not punish national sin immediately but delays until sin has reached its utmost limit.[99]

4.4 Interim Conclusion:
Scriptural Fulfillment in the Gospel of Peter and the Kerygma

The *Gospel of Peter* is a useful work to introduce into a comparative discussion of scriptural fulfillment because it, and the scholarship it has attracted, can help to draw attention to different kinds of fulfillment. In the *Gospel of Peter*, we have not so much a divine or christological fulfillment of scripture (e.g., in the cross and resurrection) but a fulfillment of a sum total of sins by the Jewish people, as we have seen especially in *Gos. Pet.* 5.17. There may be scriptural fulfillment, in that the "everything" (πάντα) that is fulfilled points back to sinful actions of the people, perhaps, as they act out typological or prophetic scenes of wickedness from scripture. There is no "positive" fulfillment of scripture, however, in the sense that scripture interprets what is being achieved in the death and resurrection of Jesus. The focus in the *Gospel of Peter's* crucifixion narrative is fulfillment by the people rather than by God.

CONCLUSION: THE GOSPEL OF PETER AND THE KERYGMA

As noted in the introduction to this chapter, the results of this survey—like the results of any study of the *Gospel of Peter's* theology—must be taken with a pinch of salt. The fact that we have only an excerpt of the work should be a

---

99. Matt 23:32, 34–36; 1 Thess 2:14–16. Cf. also Gen 15:16.

constant reminder that the interpreter can make only tentative observations. Declarations about the author such as "one thing is clear: he is a Docetist" have rightly been questioned.[100] On the other hand, just as positive generalizations are risky, negative comments about what the *Gospel of Peter* is not are also dangerous. What we might think the *Gospel of Peter* is avoiding or denying may have been implied or stated clearly in a part of the text that we do not have.

On Christology, whether the *Gospel of Peter* has a view of Jesus as a Jewish messiah is hard to discern. The Jews mock Jesus as a faux "king of Israel," which may imply ironically that he really is the king of Israel—or it may not. The author is consistent in the narrative in using the title "Lord" for Jesus, and so it is hard to discern what his christological outlook is and therefore whether he reflects the messianism of the kerygma.

Similarly, in terms of the death of Jesus, the crucifixion scene appears to be one of unalloyed gloom without any hint of soteriological value. Judgment predominates. On the other hand, there is salvation through Jesus's proclamation to the dead, an action to which the resurrection scene bears witness. In the 1920s, Harnack might have been thinking of the *Gospel of Peter* when he described the harrowing of hell in the second century as "almost the chief component of the redeemer's proclamation."[101] Certainly in our Akhmim fragment, the harrowing of hell is the main component of the *Gospel of Peter*'s soteriology, and to this extent, the *Gospel of Peter*'s theology is at some variance with the effective and vicarious death of the kerygma.

Again, there is some uncertainty and complexity in the *Gospel of Peter*'s attitude to scripture. But there is also an interesting contribution to the ways of interpreting the Old Testament in the second century. As our survey of this theme shows, the predominant sense of scriptural fulfillment in our Akhmim excerpt is—if the scriptural references are deliberate—that the Jews have fulfilled scriptural scenes about casting lots for the righteous one's clothes and giving gall and vinegar to him. The emphasis is on "the people" bringing their guilt to its full measure, such that the destruction of Jerusalem becomes inevitable. If there is a conscious allusion to Amos 8, and that is a big *if*, God may himself be directly fulfilling prophecy, though there is no reference to

100. J. Rendel Harris, *A Popular Account of the Newly Recovered Gospel of St Peter* (London: Hodder & Stoughton, 1893), 35, quoted in Paul Foster, "The Gospel of Peter," in *The Non-canonical Gospels*, ed. Paul Foster (London: Bloomsbury, 2008), 35.

101. Adolf von Harnack, *Marcion: Das Evangelium vom fremden Gott: Eine Monographie zur Geschichte der Grundlegung der katholischen Kirche*, 2nd ed. (Leipzig: Hinrichs, 1924), 169: "nahezu das Hauptstück der Verkündigung vom Erlöser."

fulfillment of scripture in the actual death and resurrection of Jesus. The fact that the law is written "for them" suggests that the author does not necessarily regard the Old Testament as Christian scripture.

Overall, conclusions about the extent to which the *Gospel of Peter* reflects the kerygma are necessarily provisional. In a sense, we are left with a series of question marks, partly because we have only an excerpt of the text, and partly because what does survive is often enigmatic. Jesus is not clearly designated as "Christ," but his messiahship might or might not be implied. As far as we can see, his death is not an "effective death" for the benefit of others in general, or a "vicarious death" (i.e., a *necessary* and *saving* death). The narration of Jesus's resurrection appearance points to salvation having taken place elsewhere. Scripture may be fulfilled in the *Gospel of Peter*'s passion narrative, but if so, it is by the sinful activities of Jesus's executioners rather than by God. But again, all of these points are true only as far as we can tell from our short fragment.

APPENDIX 1: JESUS'S BURIAL IN THE GOSPEL OF PETER

The first difference between the accounts of the burial of Jesus in the *Gospel of Peter* and the canonical Gospels is that Joseph of Arimathea requests Jesus's body before, not after, the crucifixion.[102] Joseph is introduced as "a friend of Pilate and of the Lord," and so Pilate in turn requests the body from Herod (*Gos. Pet.* 2.3–4). Herod remarks that if no one had requested the body, "we would have buried him, especially since the Sabbath is approaching" (2.5). After the crucifixion, the *Gospel of Peter* also adds the distinctive detail that those who take down Jesus's body "removed the nails from the hands of the Lord and placed him on the ground" (6.21). When the body is handed over to Joseph, the two essential elements follow: the burial proper and the sealing of the tomb. First, Joseph washes the body (a distinctive feature), wraps it in linen (as in the canonical Gospels), and places it in his tomb with the unparalleled name "Joseph's Garden" (6.24). Second, there is the extensive development of Matthew's guarding narrative. As in Matthew, Pilate grants permission for a guard, and so the tomb is sealed and the guard posted. In the *Gospel of Peter*, not only does Petronius guard the tomb with his men; they are accompanied by the elders and the scribes as well. Indeed, the Roman soldiers are guarding

---

102. In addition to the commentaries, see especially Henderson, *Gospel of Peter*, 123–53, on the burial.

"two by two on duty" (9.35).[103] Moreover, unlike in Matthew, where the guard is posted on the Saturday morning, in the *Gospel of Peter*, the guard is posted on the Friday afternoon, removing the possibility of a theft during the Friday night (8.30–9.34).[104] All who are there together roll the stone in front of the tomb. It is sealed with (reminiscent of the book of Revelation!) seven seals. The effect is that, by comparison with Matthew, there are an earlier posting of the guard (the chronological gap is closed), additional vigilance (with the additional watchers and specification of the guarding two by two), an emphasis on the size of the stone (rolled by everyone present), and sealing with seven-fold completeness. The *Gospel of Peter* therefore lays great stress on the action of the burial and the sealing, as a means of guaranteeing the veracity of the resurrection. It would therefore be an important part of the gospel message for the author of the *Gospel of Peter*. The attention drawn to the burial in the *Gospel of Peter* more than does justice to the reference to Jesus's burial in the early Christian kerygma.

Appendix 2: The Resurrection Appearances in the Gospel of Peter

The surprising feature of the resurrection narrative in the *Gospel of Peter* is that there are no appearances to male or female disciples. This is probably because the narrative breaks off where it does. The final line ("I, Simon Peter, and Andrew my brother took our nets and went off to the sea, and with us was Levi the son of Alphaeus whom the Lord. . . .") might well introduce an episode like John 21: "Afterward Jesus appeared again to his disciples, by the Sea of Galilee, in this way: Simon Peter, Thomas (also known as Didymus), Nathanael of Cana in Galilee, the sons of Zebedee, and two other disciples were together" (John 21:1–2). In any case, we cannot rule out the likelihood of Jesus appearing once or more to the disciples, given that we have no idea of how much more of the *Gospel of Peter* there was after our extant fragment.

We do, however, have a resurrection appearance; the surprising element is that the first witnesses to it are the soldiers and the elders, as well as, presumably, the scribes (*Gos. Pet.* 10.38; cf. 8.31). The appearance has already been described above. It is therefore the Roman guards and the Jewish authority

---

103. Henderson, *Gospel of Peter*, 141–42, notes that by comparison to Matthew, there are three additional references to guarding.

104. Henderson, *Gospel of Peter*, 131–32.

figures who see the gigantic Jesus and his angelic bearers: "When the soldiers saw this, they woke the centurion and the elders. (They were also on guard there.) As they were explaining what they had seen, they saw three men coming out from the tomb, two of them holding the other one aloft, and a cross following behind them" (10.38–39). Before the final scene at the lake, Mary and her friends are informed by an angelic figure that Jesus has risen, but the women are not themselves witnesses to the resurrection.

Chapter Nine

MARCION'S GOSPEL

Marcion's Gospel (ca. 150 CE) is unique among those discussed in this book, as it is the one work whose authorship is uncontroversial. Probably the most hotly debated aspect of the study of Marcion is the relation of his Gospel to canonical Luke, some arguing that Marcion is an abridgment of Luke, others that Luke is an expansion of Marcion, and still others that both are reworkings of a common source.[1] The discussion here will not get caught up in this question, as little in the present chapter depends on conclusions about source-critical matters.[2] The aim of this chapter is to examine Marcion's

---

1. E.g., respectively, in recent discussion, Michael Wolter, *The Gospel according to Luke*, 2 vols. (Waco, TX: Baylor University Press, 2016–2017); Markus Vinzent, *Marcion and the Dating of the Gospels* (Leuven: Peeters, 2014); Judith Lieu, *Marcion and the Making of a Heretic: God and Scripture in the Second Century* (Cambridge: Cambridge University Press, 2015). The description of Marcion as a mutilator of a preexisting Gospel of Luke first appears in Irenaeus, *Haer.* 1.27.2.

2. I take it that a text similar to our Luke was the source for Marcion. This is not the place for a full argument, but four points can suffice here. First, there is a prima facie plausibility that Marcion is an excerptor, given what we know of how he treated Paul's epistles. Second, on the theory of a source common to Luke and Marcion, or of Luke's dependence on Marcion, it would be peculiar that almost everything in Marcion is also in Luke. On the view of Marcionite priority, Luke's wholesale incorporation of Marcion's material would be odd (on certain versions of the theory) given the way he uses Mark (and perhaps Matthew), a source much more theologically congenial to him. On the theory of a common source, it is hard to see how different from Marcion's text that common source would have been, given the extensive verbatim agreement between Luke and Marcion. Third, there seem to be instances of specifically Lukan redaction or style in Marcion's Gospel. See Dieter Roth, *The Text of Marcion's Gospel* (Leiden: Brill, 2015), 437–38, and Wolter, *Gospel according to Luke*, 1:3. Such stylistic features can be recognized as Lukan from the evidence not just of the Gospel but also of Acts. Fourth, it appears that Marcion thought that the Gospel text that he had antecedently received had been corrupted. See Tertullian, *Marc.* 1.20.1, and Judith M.

theology—as it is reflected in his Gospel—of Jesus as the Christ, his death and resurrection, and whether these events are forecast in scripture.

The unique difficulty in this chapter is that no manuscript of Marcion's Gospel survives, and therefore the text can be reconstructed only from testimonia found in the accounts of Marcion's patristic opponents.[3] Our earliest source for the material reconstruction of the Gospel is Tertullian, whose *Against Marcion* dates in its final form to the early third century. After that, there is a gap until the anti-Marcionite portions of works by Ephrem and Epiphanius, along with the *Adamantius Dialogue*, all from the fourth century. Additionally, a later work of limited value is that of the Armenian author Eznik of Kolb (ca. 430–450), as well as the various other patristic authors who make more brief comments on Marcion. These works are also used in the reconstruction of Marcion's *Apostolos*, or Pauline corpus, and—to a more limited extent—of his *Antitheses*, a work that drew pointed contrasts between the Old Testament and Christ. Given the relative lateness of some of the patristic sources, it is often difficult to distinguish the views of Marcion himself from later Marcionite views.

On the positive side, however, we are particularly well served to study Marcion's Gospel at present because of the serendipitous arrival recently of both wide-ranging treatments of Marcion and focused studies of the text of Marcion's Gospel, which are part of a recent explosion of interest in him.[4] These have served to urge caution in how we might reconstruct Marcion's Gospel, but have also provided more clarity about his theology. Roth's text will be taken as a starting point for the investigation in this chapter. We also have the excellent text of Schmid for the *Apostolos*, and the knowledge that Marcion understood the Gospel and Paul in tandem.[5] In mitigation of the chronological difficulties of the sources, priority will be given to Tertullian, who is separated from Marcion by only two generations. Also employed will be a criterion of

---

Lieu, "Heresy and Scripture," in *Ein neues Geschlecht? Entwicklung des frühchristlichen Selbstbewusstseins*, ed. M. Lang (Göttingen: Vandenhoeck & Ruprecht, 2013), 94. Further see also *Marc.* 4.4.1; 4.4.4–5; 4.5.6. These passages are mentioned further in chapter 16.

3. The editions of the key texts used here are Ernest Evans, *Tertullian: Adversus Marcionem* (Oxford: Oxford University Press, 1972); Karl Holl and Jürgen Dummer, eds., *Epiphanius: Panarion haer. 34–64* (Berlin: de Gruyter, 1980), 107–86; G. W. Mitchell, ed. and trans., *S. Ephraim's Prose Refutations of Mani, Marcion and Bardaisan*, vol. 2 (London: Williams & Norgate, 1921); Kenji Tsutsui, *Die Auseinandersetzung mit den Markioniten im Adamantios-Dialog: Ein Kommentar zu den Büchern I–II* (Berlin: de Gruyter, 2004), 295–345.

4. Especially to be noted are Lieu, *Marcion*, and Roth, *Text*.

5. Ulrich Schmid, *Marcion und sein Apostolos: Rekonstruktion und historische Einordnung der marcionitischen Paulusbriefausgabe* (Berlin: de Gruyter, 1995), 313–44.

"multiple attestation" for Marcion's wording and views, especially attestation by Tertullian and Epiphanius, who both knew texts of Marcion.[6]

1. The Two Christs and Marcion's Gospel

Marcion is by no means hesitant about using the label "Christ," either in the Gospel or the *Apostolos*.[7] It is generally agreed by scholars that Marcion's Christology is distinctive because he in fact considers there to be two Christs, just as there are two gods.[8] These two gods are polar opposites: the Old Testament creator, the just god, is "a judge, wild and warlike," while the God and father of Jesus is called "the Stranger God" and is "mild and placid, only good and indeed supremely good."[9] The Christs of these two separate deities, or the "sons of the two gods," as Celsus calls them, reflect the character of their fathers.[10] As the title of one of Marcion's works, the *Antitheses*, suggests, it is necessary to reflect upon how Jesus and the creator's messiah are opposed in order to understand them. This section will therefore be structured in four parts, the first three of which focus on a key contrast between the two Christs, the fourth drawing attention to Marcion's reserve in attributing Jewish messianic epithets to Jesus.

1.1 David's Son and David's Antithesis

As noted in chapter 4 above, on Mark's Gospel, Davidic paternity is commonly assigned to figures titled "messiah" and features in the Dead Sea Scrolls

---

6. E.g., Lieu and Roth are in broad agreement, especially on the principle that an explicit statement about absence by Epiphanius, in conjunction with no reference in Tertullian, is a strong indication that a passage was not in Marcion's Gospel. See Judith M. Lieu, "Marcion and the Synoptic Problem," in *New Studies in the Synoptic Problem*, ed. P. Foster et al. (Leuven: Peeters, 2011), 734; Lieu, *Marcion*, 197. Lieu is probably slightly more optimistic than Roth overall, e.g., in the judgment that the healing of Jairus's daughter was absent from Marcion's Gospel, a point "predicated on the failure of any source to mention it" (Lieu, *Marcion*, 203 n. 51). Roth, on the other hand, classifies it as "unattested," i.e., deeming that there is absence of evidence rather than evidence of absence.

7. Contra Jason BeDuhn, *The First New Testament: Marcion's Scriptural Canon* (Salem, OR: Polebridge, 2013), 70, as his own text of, e.g., Gos. Marcion 24.26 shows.

8. Marcion's ditheism is reported already in Justin, *1 Apol.* 26.5; 58.1. See Gerhard May, "Marcion in Contemporary Views: Results and Open Questions," *SecCent* 6 (1987–1988): 138–39.

9. See Tertullian, *Marc.* 1.6.1, opposing the one, *iudicem ferum, bellipotentem*, with the other, *mitem, placidum et tantummodo bonum atque optimum*.

10. See Origen, *Cels.* 6.74.

(4Q252), Pss. Sol. 17–18, and 4 Ezra, as well as later in the Talmuds and targumim. This strand of messianic exegesis is prominent in Marcion's construction of the creator's Christ, whereas Jesus is kept strictly separate from such messianic tradition.

A Future Son of David

Ephrem gives evidence for the Marcionite view that the "messiah of the law" is "David's son" and "the exalted son of David."[11] Indeed, his surprise at discovering that Marcion(ites) believed this probably confirms its authenticity.[12] The messiah in the law, according to Ephrem's Marcion, is a "slayer" and "the shatterer of all."[13] The idea of the creator's messiah as a son of David may go back to Tertullian as well. There too the creator's Christ is a "warrior" (*Marc.* 3.13.1), as he also is in the *Adamantius Dialogue* (*Adam. dial.* 1.11). At the end of a lengthy discussion of Old Testament passages that Tertullian takes as proof of what Jesus as the son of David is bringing about, Tertullian concludes that Marcion is therefore not entitled to say that these things lie in the future (*Marc.* 3.20.10). The implication is that Marcion takes the son of David to be a figure still to come. This is confirmed elsewhere, when Tertullian states that, for Marcion, one Christ (i.e., Jesus) appeared under Tiberius, while the other is promised for the future (*Marc.* 1.15.6; also 3.23.1).[14]

Jesus as David's Antithesis

By contrast, Marcion's Jesus is not a figure who was predicted. For Marcion, Jesus suddenly descended to and appeared in Capernaum out of a clear blue sky.[15] Since Marcion's Jesus has no human parentage,[16] Marcion could not

11. Ephrem, *Prose Refutations*, xxxvii–xxxviii/82–83 (Mitchell, vol. 2).

12. Ephrem, *Prose Refutations*, xxxviii/82 (Mitchell, vol. 2): "But it is wonderful [i.e., extraordinary] to hear that John believes in David's son."

13. Ephrem, *Prose Refutations*, xlix–l/109 (Mitchell, vol. 2).

14. Tertullian, *Marc.* 5.8.4, also strongly implies the Davidic descent of the creator's messiah. See also Lieu, *Marcion*, 288, on Megethius taking Ps 2 this way.

15. On the suddenness, see the comments in Sebastian Moll, *The Arch-Heretic Marcion* (Tübingen: Mohr Siebeck, 2010), 64.

16. Tertullian seems to be countering Marcion, when he, Tertullian, responds that Paul's language of "likeness" should not be understood to refer to flesh that is not real (*Marc.* 5.14.1, on Rom 8:3; *Marc.* 5.20.3, on Phil 2:7). In terms of the Gospel, Marcion probably found support for his Christology in his version of Jesus's question: "Who is my mother and who is my brothers, if not (εἰ μή) those who hear my words and put them into practice?" (8.21): Roth's reconstruction of Marcion's formulation here is arguably more polemical than that of the

connect Jesus to the line of David, a point of concern for Tertullian.[17] By comparison with the thirteen verses mentioning David in Luke's Gospel, the first seven are absent from Marcion because he does not have 1:1–2:52 or 3:21–4:13.[18] Thereafter there are three passages with references to David.

It is unclear how Marcion might have understood Gos. Marcion/ Luke 6.3.[19] The same is true of Gos. Marcion 20.41–44.[20] Marcion does, however, seem to explain the two acclamations of Jesus as "Son of David" by the blind man begging outside Jericho as false (18.38–39): "Those at the front ordered him to be quiet" (18.39a)—and rightly so, Marcion thought.[21] Another interpretation of this incident may have been preserved in the *Antitheses*, with this passage pitted against 2 Sam 5.[22] In the latter, the Jebusites taunt David, stating that even their blind and lame citizens could see David off. David responds by conquering the town, and in the Greek text of 2 Sam 5:8, David exhorts his men: "everyone who strikes a Jebusite should attack with the dagger even the lame and the blind (τοὺς τυφλούς)." By contrast, Jesus cures the sight of the blind man. Hence an antithesis between David, the slayer of the blind, and Jesus, the healer of the blind.[23]

Overall, then, far from being great David's greater son, the Christ of the Stranger God is the antithesis of David. There is neither a genealogical nor a typological relationship between them.

---

other Gospels. Tertullian says, and Lieu agrees (*Marcion*, 223), that Marcion was able to take Jesus's question as a denial because his text starts the pericope at 8.20, without the reference to Jesus's biological mother and brothers in 8.19. In addition to the Pauline language of ὁμοίωμα, Marcion may also have used φάντασμα: it is not in itself a negative word, and the frequency of Tertullian's reference to it might suggest that the term goes back to Marcion himself.

17. Tertullian, *Marc.* 4.36.9–14.

18. Hence the references to David in Luke 1:27, 32, 69; 2:4, 11; 3:31 are not present according to Roth.

19. Verse numbers for Marcion's Gospel follow the Lukan versification, as is conventional.

20. On this passage, see Tertullian, *Marc.* 4.38.10. On the possibility that Marcion may have taken Jesus to be correcting the scribes' mistake in Gos. Marcion 20.41–44, see Dieter Roth, "Prophets, Priests, and Kings: Old Testament Figures in Marcion's Gospel and Luke," in *Connecting Gospels: Beyond the Canonical/Non-canonical Divide*, ed. Francis Watson and Sarah Parkhouse (Oxford: Oxford University Press, 2018), 51. BeDuhn, *First New Testament*, 76, is overconfident in assuming that Marcion takes David's actions and words as authoritative.

21. References in Tertullian, *Marc.* 4.36.9–10. While some take Jesus's forbearance (*sed patiens dominus*) as a possible explanation of Marcion's, I think this less likely.

22. Tertullian, *Marc.* 4.36.12–14, refers both to this passage and to Marcion falling into the antithetical ditch in his interpretation of the Gospel passage.

23. Lieu, *Marcion*, 281 n. 42, also notes Chrysostom's remark about Marcion's negative portrayal of David.

1.2 John's "Messiah in the Law" and the Stranger's Christ

Although scholars have sometimes speculated about rivalry between a community whose allegiance was to John the Baptist, on the one hand, and Jesus's disciples, on the other, the general picture in early Christian literature is that the two figures' interests were aligned and that John was "preparing the way" for Jesus. For Marcion, however, they are representatives of two different gods.

John the Baptist's "Messiah in the Law"

Marcion's Gospel does indeed speak of John the Baptist in the language of Isa 40 as a preparatory figure, quoting, "Behold I am sending my messenger ahead of you, who will prepare your way" (7.27).[24] In Marcion's view, Gos. Marcion 7.18–24 probably suggested that John is understood in the Gospel as the forerunner of the just god's messiah and a predecessor foretold in the scriptures of that creator god. Epiphanius's discussion attests something of this (*Pan.* 41.11.17, E9) and is confirmed by Tertullian, who focuses on Gos. Marcion 7.23: "Blessed is anyone who does not stumble on account of me." Marcion understood this as confirmation that John was disgruntled at Jesus and that the prophet therefore belonged to a different god.[25] Tertullian's exegesis of this same verse is directed against the idea that John was "hoping for, or thinking about a different Christ" (*Marc.* 4.18.5).[26] Similarly, Tertullian objects to Marcion's exegesis of 7.28 ("the least in the kingdom of God is greater than he") as meaning that John belongs to a different kingdom (*Marc.* 4.18.8).

Other sources confirm such an understanding of Gos. Marcion 7.18–35. Ephrem's *Prose Refutations* present Marcion's John as speaking of a "coming one," who is a figure other than Jesus.[27] In the *Adamantius Dialogue*, the

---

24. Apart from the initial οὗτος, Roth, *Text*, 416, prints the rest of the text of 7.27 in bold, i.e., assigning it the highest degree of certainty (ἐστι περὶ οὗ γέγραπται· ἰδοὺ ἀποστέλλω τὸν ἄγγελόν μου πρὸ προσώπου σου, ὃς κατασκευάσει τὴν ὁδόν σου).

25. Tertullian, *Marc.* 4.18.4; cf. Epiphanius, *Pan.* 44.11.17 E8. As Roth notes, there may have been a textual change in the Gospel text at 7.23 making this clear (*Text*, 416). Ephrem also has the application to John in *Prose Refutations*, xxxviii–xxxix/86 (Mitchell, vol. 2), and it is he who coins the expression "messiah in the law."

26. *Alium Christum sperans vel intellegens.* Similarly, Tertullian says in *Marc.* 4.18.8 that it would be ridiculous for a Christ who is not John's to bear witness to John in Jesus's quotation of Isa 40.

27. *Prose Refutations*, xxxvii–xxxviii/81–83 (Mitchell, vol. 2). The problem for Marcion, according to Ephrem, is therefore that Jesus seems to commend John, who is not "a reed

Marcionite Megethius took John's question, "Are you the one to come?" to mean that John did not recognize Jesus.[28] The sources are therefore in general agreement that, in contrast to Luke 7:18–35, for Marcion, John the Baptist was expecting and preparing the way for the creator's messiah, not Jesus.

The Stranger's Christ

For Marcion, then, John fails to recognize Jesus for who he is. John and Jesus are always distinguished and never in a sequential relationship for Marcion. There is nothing of the relation between John and Jesus in Luke's infancy narrative. The absence of the large block of material in Luke 3 means that Marcion has no account of Jesus's baptism.[29] Marcion seems to have understood the introduction to the Lord's Prayer (Gos. Marcion 11.1), which places John and Jesus in parallel, to mean that the disciples of Jesus and the disciples of John constituted separate groups who prayed to different gods.[30] Given what he does and does not include, then, it is understandable how Marcion may have regarded the material about John in his Gospel as antithetical rather than preparatory. The messiah anticipated by John is a quite separate figure from Jesus.

1.3 The Redeemer of Israel and the Savior of All

Tertullian attributes to Marcion the view that the two Christs are "a Jewish Christ destined by the creator for the regathering from exile of his people alone" and Jesus, "your Christ brought by the supremely good God for the liberation of the whole human race" (*Marc.* 3.21.1). The exclusive/inclusive

---

shaken by every wind." If Marcion takes John to have a faulty expectation about the "coming one," then John is indeed "shaken" contrary to what Jesus says; if John is not "shaken," i.e., is correct in his expectation, then Jesus is "the messiah of the law" and the son of David. Therefore, Marcion is in a cleft stick.

28. *Adam. dial.* 1.26.

29. The mistaken opinions about Jesus being John redivivus are included by Marcion (Gos. Marcion 9.7; 9.19) but stand in no tension with his wider tendency. The episode about John's authority and Jesus's authority (Gos. Marcion 20.1–8) could speculatively be seen as an ad hominem strategy.

30. Tertullian, *Marc.* 4.26.1: "one of his disciples approached him and said, 'Lord, teach us to pray, as John also taught his disciples,' because, as you will have it, he thought a different god must needs be prayed to in different terms." Roth presents the text of Gos. Marcion 11.1—κύριε, δίδαξον ἡμᾶς προσεύχεσθαι, καθὼς (καὶ) Ἰωάννης ἐδίδαξεν τοὺς μαθητὰς αὐτοῦ—as having the highest level of certainty.

or particular/universal contrast was probably principally derived by Marcion from Paul but seems also to be reflected in the text of his Gospel.[31]

Redeemer of Israel

We saw above that the messiah in the law, according to Ephrem's Marcion, is a "slayer" and "the shatterer of all."[32] Ephrem goes on to describe Marcion's understanding of this figure as "the just one,"[33] and (in worldly terms) "the greater of the [two] messiahs," "that subjugator of the nations," "the mighty one," and "the exalted one."[34] Presumably Marcion's view here is that this "exalted" messiah of the Jews is someone who will lead his people to victory in the earthly realm.[35] Marcion's view is also reflected in his imagined mockery of Tertullian's belief merely in the creator god who "promises the Jews their former estate, after the restitution of their country, and, when life has run its course, refreshment with those beneath the earth, in Abraham's bosom."[36] The image of Ephrem's "slayer" is reflected in Tertullian's view that Marcion took Old Testament prophecies of divine victory to refer to "a militant and armed warrior" (*Marc.* 4.20.4). On Marcion's Gospel text more specifically, Tertullian quite plausibly states that for Marcion "the one to redeem Israel" (24.21) was a designation of the creator's messiah.[37] Indeed, in Marcion's text, the rebuke

---

31. Lieu, *Marcion*, 286, cites it as possibly part of the *Antitheses*.

32. Ephrem, *Prose Refutations*, xlix–l/109 (Mitchell, vol. 2).

33. Though see the astute comments of Winrich Löhr, which may point to a more absolute moral opposition between the creator and the other God. This question need not detain us, though I think Löhr is correct. See his "Did Marcion Distinguish between a Just God and a Good God?," in *Marcion und seine kirchengeschichtliche Wirkung/Marcion and His Impact on Church History*, ed. Gerhard May and Katharina Greschat (Berlin: de Gruyter, 2002), 131–46.

34. Ephrem, *Prose Refutations*, l/110–11 (Mitchell, vol. 2).

35. Lieu, *Marcion*, 171: "Probably Marcion presented John as heralding a future coming of 'that Just One, and the greater of the (two) Messiahs,' by implication as the Saviour of the Jews." There is some suggestion of the creator rewarding the just in the underworld in Marcion's version of the parable of the rich man and Lazarus. See Löhr, "Did Marcion Distinguish between a Just God and a Good God?," 134: "the Marcionite Jesus is stressing the immense distance between his kingdom and the hell of the creator god. Indeed, it is Marcion who 'improves' upon Luke's text by replacing Abraham by Jesus and by explicitly telling us that even those that have pleased the creator have to enjoy their reward *apud inferos*."

36. Tertullian, *Marc.* 3.24.1.

37. Tertullian, *Marc.* 4.43.3, 5. For discussion, see Antonio Orbe, "Hacia la doctrina marcionítica de la redención," *Gregorianum* 74 (1993): 45–46.

"How foolish and slow-witted you are" may even have followed directly after the Emmaus road disciples' statement.[38]

The Savior of All

Again, Marcion would have derived his understanding of Jesus as a universal savior principally from Paul, but there is some evidence of this inclusivism being reflected in his Gospel text. Marcion's adaptation of Luke 13:38 (if that is what it is) is instructive. Luke has: "There will be weeping there, and gnashing of teeth, when you see Abraham, Isaac, and Jacob and all the prophets in the kingdom of God, but you yourselves thrown out." Marcion tellingly replaces "when you see *Abraham, Isaac, and Jacob and all the prophets* in the kingdom of God" with "when you see *all the righteous entering* the kingdom of God" (Gos. Marcion 13.28).[39] As we will see in the discussion of the resurrection below, there is also general agreement that Marcion's Gospel concluded with Jesus's command to the disciples to go and preach to all the nations. Luke's Gospel is known for its universalist tendency, and indeed this may have been what attracted Marcion to this Gospel in the first place, if indeed he had a choice.[40] Be that as it may, Moll accurately summarizes the situation: "Marcion thought of the Creator's Messiah, in accordance with the literal meaning of the Old Testament prophecy, as a great political and military leader, a warrior, destined by the Creator to re-establish the Jewish state. The Christ of the good God, however, has a completely different agenda."[41]

1.4 Jewish Messianic Epithets and Jesus the Christ

We have observed that Marcion does not avoid reference to Jesus as "Christ" in his Gospel. In Roth's minimalist text alone, there are perhaps six occurrences,

---

38. Roth states that 24.21a here is attested (*Text*, 435). The text between 24.21a and 24.25 is unattested, however, rather than definitely absent; hence such a sequence is only a possibility.

39. Roth, *Text*, 425.

40. On Marcion's possible choice, see further Ulrich Schmid, "Marcions Evangelium und die neutestamentlichen Evangelien: Rückfragen zur Geschichte und Kanonisierung der Evangelienüberlieferung," in May and Greschat, *Marcion und seine kirchengeschichtliche Wirkung*, 67–78, arguing that if Marcion had a choice, he may have selected Luke for its similar account of the eucharistic words to that of Paul.

41. Moll, *Arch-Heretic*, 63. See further *Adam. dial.* 2.4 on the universal/particular contrast.

and Schmid's text of Marcion's Paul has dozens of cases.[42] The title "Christ" in the Gospel is unproblematic for Marcion, then. On the other hand, there may be more of an unease with some of the explicitly Jewish dimensions of Jesus's messiahship:[43]

(1) As we have seen, the acclamation of Jesus as "son of David" appears to have been something that Marcion was concerned to justify or explain away.[44]

(2) We have also seen the way in which Jesus in Marcion's Gospel distances himself from the title "the coming one."[45]

(3) Of Luke's seven instances of ἐπιστάτης ("master," "chief," "governor"), one is not present, five are unattested, and one is printed with the lowest level of certainty by Roth, bracketed italics, that is: "where a source attests certain elements from verses, but where, despite some allusion to the reading, precise wording is not attested."[46]

(4) Absent from Marcion is the acclamation to Jesus on Palm Sunday: "Blessed is the king who comes in the name of the Lord!" (Luke 19:38).[47] We do not know why this material might be absent (nothing of Luke 19:29–46 is present). Irrespective of the reason(s), the effect is a reduction of reference to Jesus's kingship understood in scriptural terms, by comparison with other Gospels.

(5) Luke 23:2 has an accusation against Jesus: "We have found this man subverting our nation. He opposes payment of taxes to Caesar and claims to be messiah, a king." Epiphanius's text of Marcion does not have reference to "claims to be messiah, a king"; the sentence of the accusation reads there instead, "He *is destroying the Law and the Prophets*, opposing payment of taxes to Caesar and sending away wives and children."[48]

(6) In the next verse in Tertullian's text (Gos. Marcion 23.3), Pilate does not ask Jesus, "Are you *the king of the Jews?*" but rather, "Are you *the Christ?*"[49]

---

42. Gos. Marcion 9.20 (Peter's reply at Caesarea Philippi), 20.41 (in the *Davidssohnfrage*), 21.8 (many will come in my name claiming to be Χριστός), 22.67 (in the question at the trial), 23.2 (in Pilate's question), and in the statement on the Emmaus road about the necessity of the Christ's suffering (24.26).

43. Lieu, *Marcion*, 228: "his text may have avoided messianic epithets and appeals."

44. So also Lieu, *Marcion*, 228, for whom Marcion "interpreted Jesus' response to messianic acclamation as rejection or as temporary accommodation."

45. Marcion prefers ὁ ἐπερχόμενος: see sec. 2.3 below.

46. See Roth, *Text*.

47. Roth, *Text*, 430.

48. Lieu, *Marcion*, 217.

49. Tertullian, *Marc.* 4.42.1.

(7) Marcion's passion narrative may not have had the *titulus*. If that is the case, "Marcion may have felt uncomfortable with any suggestion that Jesus was crucified as 'King of the Jews' or as the Jewish Messiah."[50]

(8) According to Roth, Marcion's Gospel did not contain Jesus's promise to the thief: "Truly I tell you, today you will be with me in paradise" (Luke 23:43). I would imagine, then, that if 23:43 was absent, there is a good likelihood that the thief's request in 23:42 was also absent ("Jesus, remember me when you come into your kingdom"). This would remove another reference to Jesus's kingship.

While these points are not all clear indicators, and some features may not go back to Marcion himself, it is notable that none of Luke's three uses of the title ὁ βασιλεὺς τῶν Ἰουδαίων is attested, and the only reference to Jesus as a royal figure in Roth's text of Marcion's Gospel (see point 5 above, on 23.2, for which Roth gives the Lukan wording) is not attested in Epiphanius. As Lieu remarks on Tertullian's assessment: "Marcion found evidence in the Gospel that Jesus deliberately refused to identify himself with the Jews and their hopes."[51]

1.5 Interim Conclusion: Messiahship in Marcion's Gospel and the Kerygma

Marcion's conception of the two Christs is one of the most striking innovations in his theology. The son of the just god is still to come, but the son of the good God is of course Jesus who has come. Marcion's distinction between the two Christs has very little in common with possible pre-Christian Jewish notions of dual messiahship, in which the two messiahs work in tandem rather than in opposition.[52] In Marcion's Gospel, the "Christ" identified with Jesus is defined entirely in terms of his relation to the Stranger God rather than to anything in the human or creaturely sphere. He is not a Christ understood in scriptural terms, because that would be to understand him within the categories of the creator god. Rather, he is entirely new and unheralded. For Marcion, Jesus's

---

50. Lieu, *Marcion*, 217; Roth has the *titulus* as "unattested," though, rather than absent.

51. Lieu, *Marcion*, 228.

52. In the Rule of the Community, e.g., the messiahs of Aaron and Israel appear and act together (1QS IX, 11); cf. CD XII, 23; XIV, 19; XIX, 10–11. For discussion, see John J. Collins, *The Scepter and the Star: Messianism in the Light of the Dead Sea Scrolls*, 2nd ed. (Grand Rapids: Eerdmans, 2010), 79–83; by contrast, and for further treatment of these passages, see Martin Abegg, "The Messiah at Qumran: Are We Still Seeing Double?," *DSD* 2 (1995): 125–44. See also b. Sukkah 52a–b for the messiah ben Joseph and the messiah ben David.

messiahship does not tap into any scriptural discourse, except insofar as it stands in antithesis to that discourse and its messiah.

2. THE VICARIOUS DEATH OF JESUS IN MARCION'S GOSPEL

In contrast to Marcion's Christology or "messianology," his understanding of Jesus's death is more conventional. Lieu characterizes Marcion's Gospel, in terms that could be applied to many early Christian Gospels, as the "proclamation of a divine intervention narrated through the life, death and resurrection of one who alone could bring salvation."[53] Here, however, rather more than in the discussion of messiahship, we are hampered by conflicting reports among the fathers, perhaps as a result of their diverse interactions with Marcionites in different centuries and different places. Additionally, Tertullian becomes briefer in the latter sections of his treatment of the Gospel, making Marcion's passion narrative harder to reconstruct.[54] What the sources tend to agree upon is that in Marcion's theology, Jesus's death was (sec. 2.1) a real death and (sec. 2.2) an act of redemption, a purchase of another's property. Finally, we will consider (sec. 2.3) whether particular episodes in Marcion's Gospel narrative evoke, or would have been understood in terms of, his theology of redemption.

2.1 A Real Death

The first point to note is that Marcion does not appear to be nervous of speaking about a real death of Jesus. Certain passages in the *Apostolos* emphasize this, perhaps in particular 1 Cor 2:8 and Phil 2:8. On the former, Tertullian states: "the heretic argues that the princes of this world crucified the Lord, the Christ of his other (i.e., the higher) god" (*Marc.* 5.6.5). On the latter, Tertullian addresses Marcion and his minions by saying "that you yourselves have already stated your belief that a god has dwelt in human shape and in all the rest of what belongs to man's estate," and he takes as common ground between the two of them that God "did with such great humility so lay low the high estate of his majesty as to make it subject to death, even the death on a cross" (*Marc.* 2.27.2).

Tertullian therefore takes it as read that Marcion viewed the Stranger God as subjecting himself to death in Jesus, even if elsewhere Tertullian can ex-

---

53. Lieu, *Marcion*, 434.
54. Lieu, *Marcion*, 216.

press his bafflement that Marcion really accepted this understanding of Jesus's death.[55] How exactly Marcion conceived of Jesus's body is not easy to say, because it is a tangible but not a straightforwardly human body.[56] (We will return to this later in the discussion of the resurrection.) For now it is sufficient to note that references in Marcion's Gospel to crucifixion (24.7), suffering (24.26), death (9.22), and burial (23.50–53) need not be hastily explained away.

2.2 The Meaning of Jesus's Death in Marcion's Theology

To begin in the broadest terms, it is very likely that Marcion thought that the death of Jesus was an act of salvation.[57] According to Megethius in the *Adamantius Dialogue*, the good God had pity on human souls and came to rescue them, but the creator god plotted against him and decided to crucify Christ:

> MEGETHIUS: The demiurge, seeing the Good One dissolving his Law, plotted against him, *not realizing that the death of the Good One was the salvation of humanity* (μὴ εἰδὼς ὅτι ὁ θάνατος τοῦ ἀγαθοῦ σωτηρία ἀνθρώπων ἐγίνετο). (*Adam. dial.* 2.9)

Tertullian attributes similar language of Jesus's saving death to Marcion, noting that the good God "took the trouble himself to come down from the third heaven into these beggarly elements"; this is because the Stranger God had set his affection on "*man for whose sake he was even crucified in this prison house of the creator* (hominem . . . cuius causa in hac cellula creatoris etiam crucifixus est)."[58] Tertullian's Latin *cuius causa* echoes the New Testament terminology of Jesus's death ὑπέρ humanity.

This general kerygmatic language is made more precise by Marcion, who identified Jesus's death specifically as a purchase.[59] This can also be found in

---

55. Tertullian, *Marc.* 2.27.7: "I wonder if you do honestly believe that God was crucified."

56. Lieu, *Marcion*, 212, collects the evidence that Marcion's Jesus did have a body of some sort because he was touchable. See Tertullian, *Marc.* 4.9.5; 4.18.9; 4.20.13–14; *Pan.* 42.11.17 S10, S14; see also Moll, *Arch-Heretic*, 65.

57. Moll, *Arch-Heretic*, 67, 71; Lieu, *Marcion*, 262.

58. Tertullian, *Marc.* 1.14.2, referring here to the characteristically Marcionite third heaven and the crucifixion in the creator's prison house.

59. Conversely, most scholars have suggested that forgiveness and atoning sacrifice are less in evidence in Marcion's thought. See, e.g., Barbara Aland, "Sünde und Erlösung bei Marcion und die Konsequenz für die sogenannten beiden Götter Marcions," in *Was ist Gnosis? Studien zum frühen Christentum, zu Marcion und zur kaiserzeitlichen Philosophie*

all the major sources; here we will work backward from the latest to the earliest. There is a highly elaborate account of the process of redemption at the beginning of Eznik's account of Marcion.[60] Epiphanius attributes to Marcion an understanding of the crucifixion along these lines:

"Christ has redeemed (ἐξηγόρασεν) us from the curse of the law, by becoming a curse for us" [Gal 3:13]. Marcion says, "If we had been his, he would not have had to 'purchase' what was his own. Rather, 'purchasing' (ἀγοράσας), he went into an alien cosmos to redeem (ἐξαγοράσαι) us, because we were not his. For we were the creation of another, *and hence he purchased us, at the cost of his own life* (καὶ διὰ τοῦτο ἡμᾶς αὐτὸς ἠγόραζεν εἰς τὴν ἑαυτοῦ ζωήν). (*Pan.* 42.8.1–2)

As well as the Pauline term ἐξαγοράζω ("redeem"), then, Marcion appears to use the simpler everyday term ἀγοράζω ("buy"). The *Adamantius Dialogue* puts similar language into the mouth of the Marcionite Megethius, who comments on Gal 3:13 that "Paul says that Christ redeemed (ἐξηγόρασε) us—us *strangers*, clearly, then (δῆλον οὖν ὅτι ἀλλοτρίους). For no one ever buys (ἀγοράζει) what are their own!" (*Adam. dial.* 1.27). Ephrem has a very long and convoluted discussion, in which Marcionites allegedly keep changing their minds about whether Jesus snatched human souls from the creator or paid for them, equivocating between "violent robbery" and "purchase in humble fashion."[61]

This theology of liberation can be traced back to Tertullian's testimony. Tertullian's exegesis of Gal 5:1 in response to Marcion has perhaps been neglected as evidence for his understanding of the death of Jesus:[62] Tertullian takes "in [*or* by] this freedom, Christ set us free" (*qua libertate Christus nos manumisit*) as evidence that the manumitter can set only his own slaves free—obviously a dig at Marcion's idea that Christ had liberated the subjects of the creator god (*Marc.* 5.4.9). First Corinthians 6:20, in its variant reading, according to which we are bought at a *great* price, is also of interest to Marcion (*Marc.* 5.7.4). Furthermore, Tertullian disputes Marcion's interpretation of Gal 3:13, that, since the good God cannot have cursed Jesus, a different god hostile to him

---

(Tübingen: Mohr Siebeck, 2009), 341–54; Moll, *Arch-Heretic*, 70; Lieu, *Marcion*, 437. Epiphanius, *Pan.* 42.12.1 S16/24 may imply that Marcion deleted "for our sins" from 1 Cor 15:3.

60. Eznik, *De Deo* 358; cf. also 386, 398.

61. Ephrem, *Prose Refutations*, lx–lxi/132 (Mitchell, vol. 2).

62. In addition to passages discussed below, see also Tertullian, *Marc.* 1.17.1, with the verb *libero*.

must have done so.[63] Tertullian is clear elsewhere that, for Marcion, it is the creator god that subjected Christ to crucifixion.[64] Hence, a curse-bearing understanding of Jesus's death and a purchasing liberation go back to our earliest of the most substantial sources for Marcion's theology.[65] What Tertullian states or implies about Marcion's understanding of Gal 3:13 and 5:1 confirms that Marcion almost certainly held the view ascribed to him by Epiphanius and the *Adamantius Dialogue*.

Pauline statements of purchase such as Gal 3:13 and 1 Cor 6:20 and 7:23 were thus key for Marcion's understanding of redemption.[66] Not only that, they also confirmed his distinction between the two gods. The logic is that Christ could not have *bought* what was already his own, necessitating a purchase involving a buyer and a seller. The point of the "purchase" language for Marcion seems to suggest both the alien nature of the object of salvation and the cost at which the redemption came. The object of salvation is the human soul that, although the creator's, can be the recipient of divine mercy.[67]

2.3 Reflections in the Gospel

Is this understanding of redemption confined to the *Apostolos*, or is it also found in Marcion's Gospel and its interpretation? Perhaps one might assume not, given that some consider Luke to have no redemptive understanding of the death of Christ; Marcion's Gospel has only Lukan material and not even all of that. There are, however, five possible blocks of the material where Marcion's Gospel may have been understood as evincing a saving death.

---

63. Tertullian, *Marc.* 5.3.10: *Neque enim quia creator pronuntiavit, Maledictus omnis in ligno suspensus, ideo videbitur alterius dei esse Christus et idcirco a creatore iam tunc in lege maledictus.* "Because the Creator has given judgement, Cursed is everyone that hangeth on a tree, it will not follow from that that Christ belongs to another god and for that reason was already in the law made accursed by the Creator" (trans. Evans).

64. Tertullian, *Marc.* 3.23.5; 4.26.1; 5.6.7.

65. Enrico Norelli, "Note sulla soteriologia di Marcione," *Aug* 35 (1995): 283 n. 8, also notes Jerome's testimony.

66. See Orbe, "Hacia la doctrina marcionítica de la redención," 49–50, 57–59, as well as 62–63 on 1 Cor 6:20 and Gal 2:20; on Gal 3:13, see Moll, *Arch-Heretic*, 70 n. 126: "Although Schmid did not include this line in his reconstruction of Marcion's *Apostolos*, I believe it is very well attested in *Adam.* 1.27 and especially in Epiphanius, *Pan.* 42.8.1, which clearly states that Marcion used these words of the Apostle."

67. E.g., *Adam. dial.* 2.7.

The Parable of the Strong Man (Gos. Marcion 11.21–22)

Despite the contrasts that we have seen between gentle Jesus meek and mild, on the one hand, and the bloodthirsty messiah of the creator, on the other, there are hints that this is only part of the story. Lieu, for example, argues that the metaphor of conflict is central to Marcion's theology.[68] Marcion certainly seems to have understood the parable of the strong man (Gos. Marcion 11.21–22) as about the conflict between the creator (ὁ ἰσχυρός) and Jesus (ὁ ἰσχυρότερος). Tertullian writes as follows:

> Furthermore, if the parable of the "strong man armed," whom another "stronger" has overcome and whose property he has seized, is (thus Marcion) taken to be a parable about the creator, then it would be impossible for that creator to have still remained in ignorance of the God of glory while he was being overcome by him; nor could he have hanged on a cross that one against whom his strength was of no avail. (*Marc.* 5.6.7)

Marcion's interpretation of the parable in this way may explain why Tertullian names Marcion's Jesus ὁ ἐπερχόμενος ("the attacker"),[69] since in the parable this verb (ἐπέρχομαι) is used of the "stronger man" who comes upon the merely *strong* man and overpowers him.[70] The *Adamantius Dialogue* also has Jesus as "the stronger man" (ὁ ἰσχυρότερος).[71] The idea of two divine sons in conflict with one another, as already noted, is also attributed to Marcion by Celsus.[72]

There are three possible sections of the Gospel narrative that the parable of the strong man may be taken to interpret. First, the overpowering of the creator may take place in the course of Jesus's ministry, as he flouts the creator

68. Lieu, *Marcion*, 233: "The image of a conflict or of a battle is one of the principal metaphors of Marcion's soteriology."

69. This interpretation is confirmed in Tertullian, *Marc.* 4.26.12, according to which Marcion understood the parable to mean that "the creator was overcome by the God of another" (*creatorem ab alii deo subactum*).

70. *Pace* Evans, *Adversus Marcionem*, 385 n. 23, this verb would not have been (solely) derived from John the Baptist's question in Luke 7:19, where the epithet is merely ὁ ἐρχόμενος. See further Winrich Löhr, "Markion," *RAC* 24:160–61: "M. nannte ihn ὁ ἐπερχόμενος, vielleicht um die unerwartete, nicht vorhergekündete Art seines Erscheinens zu bezeichnen . . . oder in Aufnahme von Lc. 11, 22"; Lieu, *Marcion*, 233 n. 149.

71. *Adam. dial.* 1.4.

72. Origen, *Cels.* 6.74.

god's regulations: for Marcion, Jesus inter alia touches a leper in opposition to the creator's law (*Marc.* 4.9.3–5) and opposes his law of divorce, "teaching what is contrary to Moses and the creator" (*Marc.* 4.34.3).[73] The healing miracles can also be understood this way, as acts of kindness in antithesis to the acts of the creator (*Adam. dial.* 1.20).[74]

Two other possible scenes could come into play if Marcion was particularly interested in the stronger man seizing the strong man' property. Marcion could have taken the confiscation of the creator's booty to take place during the harrowing of hell, because the creator keeps those under his dominion in Hades after death.[75] Or Marcion might have understood the capture of the strong man's possessions to take place at the cross. Melito is ambiguous on which of these two ways he takes the parable; in any case, he understands humanity as the plunder (*Pasch.* lines 762–764). Unfortunately, we cannot be certain about how Marcion applied the parable, if indeed he did apply it to a particular event or narrative in the Gospel, but it is plausible to think that he understood the cross as the realization of this parable.

The Transfiguration (Gos. Marcion 9.28–36)

One of the most controversial pericopes in the interpretation of Marcion's Gospel—both in antiquity and in modern scholarship—is the transfiguration.[76] Drijvers, following leads in particular in Ephrem, identifies "Christ as warrior and merchant" in the transfiguration narrative.[77] On the warrior theme, first, Drijvers takes Ephrem's *Hymns against Heresies* to indicate that "Marcion apparently interpreted the Transfiguration as a defeat of the Creator, who is said to have been robbed"; his silence, in response the good God's injunction

---

73. See Winrich A. Löhr, "Die Auslegung des Gesetzes bei Markion, den Gnostikern und den Manichäern," in *Stimuli: Exegese und ihre Hermeneutik in Antike und Christentum; FS für Ernst Dassmann,* ed. Georg Schollgen and Clemens Scholten (Münster: Aschendorff, 1996), 77–95, for an overview of Marcion's understanding of the law (77–80) and for a list of infractions of the law in Jesus's ministry in Marcion's Gospel (79); on the latter, also Norelli, "Note sulla soteriologia di Marcione," 294.

74. On the healings, see further Ephrem, *Prose Refutations,* lviii/125–26 (Mitchell, vol. 2).

75. Tertullian, *Marc.* 5.6.7: *vasa eius occupavit.*

76. See especially Han J. W. Drijvers, "Christ as Warrior and Merchant: Aspects of Marcion's Christology," in *Papers Presented to the Tenth International Conference on Patristic Studies Held in Oxford 1987: Second Century,* ed. Elizabeth A. Livingstone, StPatr 21 (Leuven: Peeters, 1989), 73–85, and Norelli, "Note sulla soteriologia di Marcione," 281–305.

77. Drijvers, "Christ as Warrior and Merchant." Ephrem's *Prose Refutations* highlight both themes.

to listen to Jesus, is an admission of defeat.[78] At the same time, Marcion also pictured Jesus as intending to purchase souls, and this is the topic of conversation between Jesus and the two prophets.[79] For Drijvers, Moses and Elijah are threatened by force at the appearance of Jesus in his glory and are pressured into selling human souls to Jesus: "The price of that sale would be Jesus's blood, his death on the cross. That must have been Marcion's interpretation of the words in Luke 9,31: 'and they (Moses and Elijah) spoke of his decease which he should accomplish at Jerusalem.'"[80] Drijvers's reliance on the picture in Ephrem results from his view that Ephrem probably had direct acquaintance with the *Antitheses*.[81]

Attractive as this appears as a Marcionite exegesis of the transfiguration narrative, there are several problems with attributing such a view to Marcion. First, Norelli notes the absence of mercantile language from Tertullian's discussion of Gos. Marcion 9.28–36.[82] This is an important point, because Tertullian does engage with Marcion's view of the transfiguration at some length (running to over a thousand words of Latin). Second, Ephrem appears as much to be anticipating possible Marcionite views as refuting positions he knows to be those of Marcion; although he probably does attest the idea of a pact or deal, he is nevertheless a late source and so may be presenting the Marcionite views of his own day.[83] Third, although Epiphanius refers to a purchase, he does not

---

78. Drijvers, "Christ as Warrior and Merchant," 76–77.

79. See Lieu, *Marcion*, 169, 173, on Ephrem's reference to the view that on the mount of transfiguration, Jesus, Moses, and Elijah struck "a deal by which the Stranger purchased the souls of those to be saved from the Maker."

80. Drijvers, "Christ as Warrior and Merchant," 82–83.

81. Drijvers, "Christ as Warrior and Merchant," 81.

82. Norelli, "Note sulla soteriologia di Marcione," 294.

83. Ephrem's commentary on the *Diatessaron* does contain references to Jesus acting both by force and to a pact, but the former is part of a conditional clause, and the latter prefaced by an "or perhaps": see Carmel McCarthy, *Saint Ephrem's Commentary on Tatian's Diatessaron: An English Translation of Chester Beatty Syriac MS 709 with Introduction and Notes* (Oxford: Oxford University Press, 1993), 217–18 on Ephrem, *Comm. Diat.* 14.9. His hymns have a single, unexplained reference to "the robbed Just one" (*k'n' bzyz'*): see hymn 48.10, line 5 (Beck, 189 [Syriac], 168 [German]); now also Flavia Ruani, trans., *Éphrem de Nisibe: Hymnes contre les hérésies* (Paris: Les Belles Lettres, 2018), 282 and notes. Ephrem's *Prose Refutations* have lots of material, but it is far from clear. Much of the material that refers to both themes ("warrior" and "merchant") is framed as Ephrem's wondering about possible Marcionite responses and offering a rejoinder to those hypothetical responses. The length of the discourse about both themes does imply that these were real Marcionite views, but whether they can be traced back to the second century is another matter.

connect this with the transfiguration.[84] Finally, it may be that, as Norelli and Lieu suggest, Marcion emphasizes not the conversation Jesus had with Moses and Elijah but rather their distance (διαχωρίζεσθαι, in 9.33) and the heavenly voice's instruction to listen to Jesus alone (and therefore not to Moses and Elijah).[85] In sum, very little can be deduced from Marcion's understanding of the transfiguration for his conception of how the death of Jesus works.

I suggest that the reason for Ephrem's voluminous and tortuous discussion of "this pact agreed by Moses and the Stranger" (*hn' 'byd' dqsw dbyt mwš' 'm nwkry'*) lies in the tensions left in Marcion's soteriology.[86] He emphasized the purchase, but also the Stranger overcoming the creator. He retained the speech between Jesus and the prophets on the mount of transfiguration, but also stressed that the Stranger was unknown to the creator god. This leads to disagreement in the later sources: Ephrem thinks in terms of a pact, while Megethius argued that the creator "did not realize that the death of the Good One was the salvation of humanity." Ephrem may not be inventing when he talks of Marcionites in his day equivocating between martial and mercantile views of soteriology, but it is nevertheless very unclear whether Marcion himself thought in terms of a deal negotiated between the creator and the Stranger, or of the mount of transfiguration as the creator god's negotiating chamber.

The Eucharistic Words (Gos. Marcion 22.17–20)

The most promising evidence for a soteriological death in Luke's Gospel lies in the words of institution, and the same is probably true for Marcion's version. The precise detail of Marcion's eucharistic words is uncertain, but there is enough even in Roth's reconstruction for us to be fairly confident of something like the Lukan material:

22.17—[If the *Adamantius Dialogue* is attesting Marcion's Gospel, "cup" is attested]

22.18—Unattested

22.19—*taking the bread . . . he gave it (to them) . . . "This is my body (which is given for you)"*

22.20—"This is the cup, the . . . covenant in my blood."[87]

---

84. The *Adamantius Dialogue* does not touch upon the transfiguration.

85. Norelli, "Note sulla soteriologia di Marcione," 292–93.

86. Ephrem, *Prose Refutations*, xli/91 (Mitchell, vol. 2).

87. Roth, *Text*, 433.

Although fragmentary, this passage gives with tolerable clarity evidence for a soteriological understanding of Jesus's death, or at the very least the text is not merely consistent with but strongly suggestive of it.

To deal with the less secure case first, the statement in Gos. Marcion 22.19 that Jesus's body is "given for you," while uncertainly attested, is clearly consistent with the kerygmatic statements that we saw earlier: in the *Adamantius Dialogue*, the death of Jesus "was the salvation of humanity," and in Tertullian, it was "man for whose sake . . . he (Christ) was crucified." This idea seems to be picked up in Gos. Marcion 22.19: even if the "which is given for you" clause is weakly attested, there is a high probability that "taking the bread, he gave it . . . 'This is my body'" was present in Marcion's Gospel text.

Also probably present is the text's association of Jesus's blood with the covenant, which encourages a view of relationship with God created by Jesus's death, even if Marcion would not envisage an allusion to the covenant inauguration in Exodus. Other evidence suggests some importance in covenant language for Marcion. His *Apostolos* retains the "new covenant" language of 2 Cor 3:6, as well as the subsequent "not of the letter but of the spirit, for the letter kills but the spirit gives life." Tertullian states, apparently polemically, that "the new covenant/testament was to belong to none other than the one who promised it," that is, to the creator and not to the Stranger (*Marc.* 5.11.4), and his insistence that the old covenant prefigures the new may imply Marcion's acceptance of covenantal categories (*Marc.* 4.14.2). Marcion's text of Ephesians (or Laodiceans, as he has it) refers to the audience's pre-Christian state as "strangers to the covenants of the promise," which for Marcion probably is not a gloss on their separation from Israel but refers to their prior lack of acquaintance with the Stranger.[88] His text of Gal 4 may be instructive in that our earliest witness, Tertullian, gives a different reading for the text of the two women (Sarah and Hagar) who represent the two covenants (Gal 4:24): "for they are the two covenants (*testamenta*), or two 'demonstrations' (*ostensiones*), as we find he has translated it" (*Marc.* 5.4.8). While there is a risk in interpreting Marcion's textual modifications, it may be that he thought the Mosaic covenant not worthy of the name. There are in fact no attested references to the old covenant in the *Apostolos*, and indeed the reference in Gal 3:17 is removed.[89]

The "new" in Marcion's new covenant hints at what this covenant brings into being. The idea that Jesus introduces new legislation is multiply attested: in the *Adamantius Dialogue*, Megethius promises to prove "that the Demiurge

---

88. On the text, see Schmid, *Marcion und sein Apostolos*, 338.
89. Schmid, *Marcion und sein Apostolos*, 316.

instituted certain laws, and Christ others in opposition to him [i.e., to the Demiurge]"; when Adamantius asks him whether different and contradictory laws entail different gods, Megethius replies: "Why of course!"[90] Ephrem in the *Prose Refutations* also seems to be picking up the Marcionite view that Jesus abolished the old laws and put new ones in their place.[91] Tertullian refers to Marcion's theme of "new teachings" (*hae sunt novae doctrinae novi Christi* [*Marc.* 4.28.8]).

Finally, Kinzig has also argued that Marcion's works formed a trilogy, *Antitheses—Gospel—Apostolos*, which he called a "New Testament" (καινὴ διαθήκη).[92] Whatever the accuracy of this particular claim, Kinzig's observation about how Tertullian uses the term *testamentum* is noteworthy. Tertullian's fourth book in his *Against Marcion* begins as follows:

> Marcion imagined a certain "dowry," a work named, because it placed contrasts side by side, the *Antitheses*. It forced a separation of the law and the Gospel, a separation by which he distinguished between two gods opposed to one another, one of one document (*instrumentum*)—or, to use the more common term, "testament" (*testamentum*)—and one of the other. (*Marc.* 4.1.1)

Kinzig notes that one obvious way to read Tertullian's aside here is that he is offering *testamentum* as the more common word for what is meant by *instrumentum*.[93] Following a study of van der Geest, however, he makes two significant observations: (1) before writing against Marcion, Tertullian uses the word *testamentum* to mean "ordinance" or "regulation,"[94] but (2) when he comes to write *Against Marcion*, he uses *testamentum* also to refer to biblical books.[95]

---

90. *Adam. dial.* 1.9. In 1.10, Megethius implies that Jesus introduces new *dogmata*, and Eutropius characterizes Megethius's view as involving two *nomothesiai*.

91. Ephrem, *Prose Refutations*, lviii/127 (Mitchell, vol. 2).

92. Wolfram Kinzig, "Καινὴ διαθήκη: The Title of the New Testament in the Second and Third Centuries," *JTS* 45 (1994): 519–44. Against positioning the *Antitheses* first, see Winrich Löhr, "Problems of Profiling Marcion," in *Christian Teachers in Second Century Rome*, ed. Gregory H. Snyder (Leiden: Brill, 2020), 122.

93. Kinzig, "Καινὴ διαθήκη," 540.

94. Kinzig, "Καινὴ διαθήκη," 529.

95. Kinzig, "Καινὴ διαθήκη," 530 n. 51, ascribes the usage in Tertullian, *Marc.* 4.6.1 and 5.11.4 to Marcion; it is difficult to disentangle Marcion's and Tertullian's usage in these places, though in the latter case I think he is correct. His other reference, Tertullian, *Praescr.* 30.9 (see further Kinzig, "Καινὴ διαθήκη," 540), is also suggestive and may support his case on *Marc.* 4.6.1.

Kinzig takes this to reflect the influence of Marcion's own usage. He further argues that the reason for the glossing of *instrumentum* with *testamentum* (a gloss that Tertullian does not find necessary in his other usages of *instrumentum*) is that Tertullian is here adding Marcion's favored term. If van der Geest and Kinzig are correct about Tertullian's *Against Marcion* representing a watershed in his usage of *testamentum*, this is an excellent explanation of his gloss in *Marc.* 4.1.1. In that case, this gloss (*vel, quod magis usui est dicere, testamenti*) would therefore be more accurately (if rather clunkily) translated "or, to say what is more in *his* usage, 'testament.'"[96]

Overall, then, Marcion may well have attached significance to the covenant language in the words of institution, thereby assigning considerable importance to the death of Jesus.

The Crucifixion Narrative (Gos. Marcion 23)

It seems likely that the crucifixion narrative was relatively brief in Marcion's Gospel. After the statement of the crucifixion in Gos. Marcion 23.33, there is no text clearly attested until the darkness over the land in 23.44.[97] Indeed, Epiphanius's evidence suggests that Marcion's text jumped from 23.33–34 straight to 23.44 (skipping the mockery of Jesus and the mention of the two criminals).[98] Lieu's suggestion that Marcion viewed the darkness as indicative of the defeat of the creator's power is a plausible one; a related interpretation of the darkness and the tearing of the curtain is attested in Eznik of Kolb, who takes it as an act of mourning by the creator.[99] As seen in our discussion

---

96. Perhaps, though only perhaps, reflective of early Marcionite usage is the language in Eznik, *De Deo* 416: "They boast, 'From the pool we are covenanters from flesh-meat and from marriage.'" Cf. Eznik, *De Deo* 414, referring to the Marcionites' "covenant to virginity."

97. Roth, *Text*, 434. On 23.34a, it is worth noting that although in Roth's presentation of the text, he describes 23.34a as "attested by Ephrem and unattested by Tertullian and Epiphanius," this level of certainty about Ephrem was not anticipated in the commentary. Cf. Roth, *Text*, 408: "It is perhaps best simply to note the possibility that Ephrem attests v. 34a and that it is unattested by Tertullian and Epiphanius." The case of the division of the clothes in 23.34b is a more straightforward difference in the sources: "Attested as not present by Tertullian but present by Epiphanius" (Roth, *Text*, 434).

98. Lieu, *Marcion*, 217: There is a "possibility that Epiphanius' highly abbreviated summary of the crucifixion, division of garments, and darkening of the sun catalogues all that was included in his copy of Marcion's crucifixion narrative." Further, "thus Tertullian's and Epiphanius' silences may point to a truncated crucifixion account that would be congenial to Marcion's position" (Lieu, *Marcion*, 218).

99. Lieu, *Marcion*, 217–18; Eznik, *De Deo* 358.

of the *Gospel of Peter*, several works take the tearing of the veil as a kind of lamentation. In the end, however, we do not know how Marcion interpreted Gos. Marcion 23.44–45. What we can be more confident about, however, is that he understood the creator god as the agent behind the crucifixion and that Jesus bore a curse from that lesser deity; at the same time, however, he was purchasing human souls.

The Harrowing of Hell

Marcion's Gospel does not of course narrate the harrowing of hell, but if he believed in it, he would probably have placed the event after Jesus's death in Gos. Marcion 23.46. (It should be remembered that this time frame is not the only option.)[100] Löhr's systematic treatment of Marcion's theology summarizes this moment after the death of Jesus as follows: "After that he descended into the Underworld and so offered his salvation also to those who lived before his appearance on earth."[101] As discussed in connection with the *Gospel of Peter* above, at the time in which Marcion was active, this motif was becoming more and more standard among mid-second-century authors.[102] Indeed, Harnack comments that although for us the harrowing of hell is a relic of a bygone age, in Marcion's day it was almost the high point of Jesus's preaching.[103] Testimony to Marcion's belief in the harrowing of hell comes already in Irenaeus, who polemicizes against the idea that Jesus in Hades saved people like Cain and the Sodomites (*Haer.* 1.27.3). Although this rehabilitation of the old covenant sinners may be suspect—as also in the discussion of those behind the *Gospel of Judas* later (*Haer.* 1.31.1)—the basic theme of a descent to the underworld is a very uncontroversial one. In addition to Irenaeus's testimony, Ephrem and Epiphanius also attribute it to Marcion—although in Epiphanius's case, in terms that suggest dependence on Irenaeus.[104] Ephesians 4:8–10, where Jesus descends εἰς τὰ κατώτερα [μέρη] τῆς γῆς, may have encouraged Marcion in such a view: Schmid is confident that at least a fragment of this passage was

100. E.g., in *Questions of Bartholomew* 1, Jesus descends to hell when the sun is darkened during the crucifixion.

101. Löhr, "Markion," 24:161: "Daraufhin stieg er in die Unterwelt hinab . . . und bot so sein Heil auch jenen an, die vor seinem Erscheinen auf Erden lebten."

102. See discussion in chapter 8 above, on the *Gospel of Peter*.

103. Harnack, *Marcion*, 169.

104. Ephrem, *Prose Refutations*, xxxvii/81 (Mitchell, vol. 2); Epiphanius, *Pan.* 42.4.3–4. For other sources, see Lieu, *Marcion*, 45 n. 47.

in Marcion's *Apostolos*.[105] Strictly speaking, talk of the harrowing of hell is not an ascription of a soteriological nature to Jesus's death per se, but it does view Jesus's death as a necessary condition of that aspect of salvation.

2.4 Interim Conclusion: Jesus's Death in Marcion's Gospel and the Kerygma

In sum, the eucharistic words in Marcion's Gospel are suggestive of soteriological significance, in that they indicate a connection between the new covenant that Jesus instituted and his death. It is also fairly certain, since Marcion's Gospel from the beginning was embedded in a "canon" with the *Apostolos*, that the crucifixion narrative was originally understood in line with how Jesus's death is explained in Marcion's Pauline texts: that is, principally, that it is a redemption or purchase in which Jesus bears the curse pronounced in the creator god's law, thereby rescuing those who did not previously belong to him. Marcion's Gospel therefore clearly attests an effective and vicarious death like the kerygma.

3. THE RESURRECTION OF JESUS IN MARCION'S GOSPEL

After an account of the death of Jesus, the Gospel follows the conventional canonical narrative with an account of the burial (Gos. Marcion 23.50–53) and the women's visit to the tomb (24.1–3). The appearances of the angels to the women, the road to Emmaus episode, and the meeting with the Eleven are all attested,[106] and there is a good level of scholarly agreement that the Gospel ended with the sending of the disciples out into the world (i.e., at 24.47).[107] It is also reasonably clear that the resurrection is not a resurrection of human

---

105. Following Tertullian, *Marc.* 5.18.5, Schmid prints ἠχμαλώτευσεν αἰχμαλωσίαν, from Eph 4:8. Unfortunately, Tertullian is very brief on Marcion's text here.

106. Roth, *Text*, 435–36. Peter's visit to the tomb in 24.12 is less certain; Daniel A. Smith, "Marcion's Gospel and the Resurrected Jesus of Canonical Luke 24," *ZAC* 21 (2017): 49–50, is particularly skeptical.

107. Lieu, *Marcion*, 221: "It is likely that Marcion's 'Gospel' ended as does Tertullian's account, with Jesus 'sending the disciples to the nations of the world' . . . avoiding reference to his departure and to the disciples' return to Jerusalem." Similarly, Markus Vinzent, "Der Schluß des Lukasevangeliums bei Marcion," in May and Greschat, *Marcion und seine kirchengeschichtliche Wirkung*, 83–84, though he also sees 24.44–46 (except the Εἶπεν δὲ πρὸς αὐτούς at the beginning of 24.44) as "gestrichen."

flesh but is in some sense bodily: the tomb is empty (24.3), but Jesus's statement that a spirit does not have bones may imply the opposite of Luke 24:39, namely that he *is* a boneless spirit or phantasm (24.39).[108] There is no straightforward solution to this question.

More straightforwardly, Marcion follows the conventional chronology according to which the resurrection took place on the third day, as is seen both implicitly in the narrative and in explicit statements.[109] Given that the precise wording of the pericopes in the resurrection chapter eludes us,[110] we will be able to make only a few brief comments on the theological significance of the resurrection.

The *Apostolos* illuminates a great deal of how Marcion must have understood the resurrection. One could of course decant the resurrection theology of the *Apostolos* into chapter 24 of the Gospel holus-bolus, but that would probably not do justice to the way Marcion went about his exegesis. It is also possible that the resurrection of Jesus was understood in a distinctively Marcionite fashion as a climactic negation of the law of the creator god, who demanded death as the penalty for disobedience to his statutes; the necessity (δεῖ) of Jesus's death may have been to purchase souls, but the necessity of resurrection (δεῖ . . . ἐγερθῆναι [9.22]; δεῖ . . . ἀναστῆναι [24.7]) may have to do with Jesus not being bound finally by the terms of the creator's legislation. To these more speculative elements, we can briefly add two aspects of the significance of the resurrection that are probable and not just plausible.

3.1 The Resurrection as Vindication

A first point that may be theologically significant is that the resurrection vindicates Jesus's preresurrection teaching. First, the angel exhorts the women to remember what Jesus had taught in Galilee and how this teaching has now come to fulfillment (Gos. Marcion 24.6). They do indeed recall his words

108. Tertullian, *Marc.* 4.43.7, reports Marcion's view as follows. Luke's text reads "a spirit does not have flesh and bones as you see me having" (πνεῦμα σάρκα καὶ ὀστέα οὐκ ἔχει καθὼς ἐμὲ θεωρεῖτε ἔχοντα). Marcion does not delete any of the text, but reads it as "a spirit [*or* phantasm], in accordance with how you see I am, does not have flesh and bones." Smith acknowledges the difficulty of tracing this understanding back to Marcion; Lieu, *Marcion*, 220, also doubts Tertullian's report here.

109. On the former, after Jesus's death, the women keep the Sabbath (23.56) and then presumably visit early the next morning. Explicit statements are attested in 9.22 (μετὰ τρεῖς ἡμέρας ἐγερθῆναι) and 24.7 (καὶ τῇ τρίτῃ ἡμέρᾳ ἀναστῆναι).

110. A point highlighted in Lieu, *Marcion*, 218.

(24.8). Second, in contrast, there are the Emmaus road disciples who initially do not grasp the point. Marcion has different wording from Luke in Jesus's statement in 24.25: "You fools, slow to believe everything that I/he spoke to you."[111] The subsequent revelation of Jesus probably means that Cleopas and friend do understand him (24.31).

3.2 The Resurrection and the Commissioning of the Apostles

A second point worth noting is that the resurrection of Jesus is the occasion for the sending of the disciples out into the world. Hence the mission and expansion of Marcionism begin here. This positive valuation of the disciples by Jesus, in his entrusting them with evangelization, may serve to correct the negative picture of the disciples emphasized by some scholars.

3.3 Interim Conclusion: Jesus's Resurrection in Marcion's Gospel and the Kerygma

There is much that is controversial about the resurrection in Marcion—both in the primary sources and in the secondary literature. Questions about the kind of body Jesus possessed before and after the resurrection, however, need not detain us here. More to the point, we have two elements: vindication and mission. Marcion seems a good deal more interested in the death of Jesus, however, which is the revelation of a new kind of humility, than in his resurrection. They do not lend much support to the idea that the resurrection was a crucial element in Marcion's theology, so much so that he imparted that "resurrection mania" to great swathes of subsequent Christianity.[112] Vinzent's assessment of the significance of the resurrection to Marcion builds simply from the contents of Paul's letters, assuming that Marcion included particular sections and interpreted them in a particular way.[113] Since our discussion

---

111. Tertullian attests "he spoke" (*locutus est*), while Epiphanius (ἐλάλησα ὑμῖν) and the *Adamantius Dialogue* (ἐλαλήσα πρὸς ὑμᾶς) attest "I spoke." It is unclear why Roth prints the retroversion ἐλάληθη.

112. Marcion, he avers, "must have seen the gap between what he read in the Apostle, and what his contemporaries made out of his hero's core idea." See Markus Vinzent, *Christ's Resurrection in Early Christianity and the Making of the New Testament* (Farnham: Ashgate, 2011), 113. On the alleged "resurrection mania," see Vinzent, *Christ's Resurrection*, 111–25, more widely, and James Carleton Paget's review: "Marcion and the Resurrection: Some Thoughts on a Recent Book," *JSNT* 35 (2012), 74–102.

113. E.g., Vinzent, *Christ's Resurrection*, 115, according to which the resurrection is seem-

is focused specifically on the Gospel, we need to be content with what can be extracted from the reconstructed resurrection predictions and the fragmentary remains of Gos. Marcion 24. Despite the difficulty of the evidence, Marcion's understanding of the resurrection is quite in line with the kerygma as presented in chapter 2.

4. Christ and Scripture in Marcion's Gospel

There is a reasonably high level of agreement among scholars about Marcion's attitude to scripture. Although one still sometimes finds popular-level misunderstandings about Marcion simply excising Old Testament references, assessments such as this are comparatively rare.[114]

4.1 The Old Testament as Attestation of the Creator God

The first point to note, then, is that Marcion does not "abolish" the Old Testament *tout simple* or erase traces of it from his Gospel. The Old Testament is not irrelevant but is the essential dark background against which the light of Jesus is projected.[115] Crucial to Marcion's whole project is the identification of the antitheses, "which are designed to show the conflict and disagreement of the Gospel and the law," as Tertullian puts it (*Marc.* 1.19.4). This engagement with the Old Testament is continued by subsequent Marcionites, as is suggested by the *Adamantius Dialogue*.[116]

What the text of Marcion's Gospel has is a taste of the contrast between law and gospel that no doubt appeared in more extended fashion in the *Antitheses*. The particular instance where this probably becomes explicit in the Gospel text is where Jesus's healing of multiple lepers is compared to advantage with Elisha's healing of only one.[117] It seems likely that the statement about Elisha's

---

ingly fundamental to salvation because of passages such as Rom 6:1–7:6 in which new life is rooted in the resurrection of Jesus.

114. E.g., Walter C. Kaiser, *The Christian and the "Old" Testament* (Eugene, OR: Wipf & Stock, 1998), 270: "Marcion felt that all references to the Old Testament should be erased from the New Testament. Consequently, he took the 300 major direct quotes from the Old Testament and deleted them."

115. Moll, *Arch-Heretic*, is helpful in emphasizing the importance of the Old Testament in Marcion's thought. See also recently Roth, "Prophets, Priests, and Kings," 41–56.

116. Lieu, *Marcion*, 122.

117. Contra BeDuhn's interpretation (*First New Testament*, 76–77).

healing of one solitary Naaman (Luke 4:27) is inserted within the pericope of Jesus's healing of the ten lepers (between Gos. Marcion 17.12 and 17.14).[118] Other Gospel episodes are understood in opposition to Old Testament passages, and these may have been expounded as such in Marcion's *Antitheses*. (Hence the point about Jesus and David above.) In the main, however, as far as the "present" material is concerned, it is perhaps more that the same material is interpreted differently. The parable of the rich man and Lazarus, for example, identifies Hades as the place where the creator god rewards good and punishes evil, and the transfiguration emphasizes the separation of Jesus from Moses and Elijah.[119] There are numerous other references to scriptural figures where the meaning is less easily detectable (e.g., 6.3–4; 12.27; 11.47–48; 17.26, 28, 32).

4.2 Christ and Scriptural Fulfillment

Second, there is no pattern of scriptural promise that finds fulfillment in Jesus.[120] We have touched on this from a different angle in the discussion of the term "Christ" above and can now address it further via exploration of the Lukan passages deemed by Roth to be "not present" in Marcion. Here it is inevitable that some redaction-critical assessment of Marcion's "omissions" is necessary.[121]

There are twenty-two Lukan passages "not present" in Roth's reconstruction, albeit of very divergent lengths.[122] Although deducing rationales for the absences of certain pericopes from Marcion should be done with caution, in some cases it is feasible.[123] (Of course, this is on the assumption of Marcion's use of something like a Lukan base text.) Roughly half of the passages deemed

---

118. Adolf von Harnack, *Marcion: Das Evangelium vom fremden Gott; Eine Monographie zur Geschichte der Grundlegung der katholischen Kirche*, 2nd ed. (Leipzig, Hinrichs, 1924), 52; Lieu, *Marcion*, 210; Roth, *Text*, 427–28; contra BeDuhn, *First New Testament*, 77.

119. On these points, see Lieu, *Marcion*, 211, 230, and Roth, "Prophets, Priests, and Kings," 51–54.

120. This is a consistent feature of the heresiologists, appearing already in Justin, *1 Apol.* 58.1; *Dial.* 35.5.

121. As noted in n. 2 above, I take it that Marcion's Gospel is dependent upon Luke.

122. Roth (*Text*, 412–36) marks as "not present" Luke 1–2; 3:21–4:13; 8:19; 9:31b; 11:30–32; 11:49–51; 12:6; 13:1–9; 13:29–35; 15:11–32; 17:10b; 17:12b–13; 18:31–33; 19:29–46; 20:9–17; 20:37–38a; 21:18; 21:21–22; 22:16; 22:35–38; 22:50–51; and 23:43. I am therefore not including here instances of words and short phrases attested as "not present" in otherwise attested verses (see, e.g., Roth, *Text*, 415, on 6.36–37).

123. See, e.g., Lieu's remarks on speculative proposals for why Marcion may have omitted the parable of the lost son ("Marcion and the Synoptic Problem," 739).

absent by Roth might be suspected of associating Jesus too closely with scripture or scriptural fulfillment.

The birth narrative in Luke 1–2, for example, contains various examples of Jesus fulfilling scriptural promises (in the Magnificat, e.g., 1:55, and the Benedictus, e.g., 1:70, 72–73). The presentation of Jesus in the temple "according to the law of Moses" (Luke 2:22) might also come under similar suspicion. Next, Luke 3:21–4:13 contains the genealogy (which links Jesus to Adam, the patriarchs, David, et al.) and the temptation narrative in which Jesus cites scripture directly and approvingly. Marcion has a transfiguration narrative but, as we have already seen, probably without the statement that Moses and Elijah spoke of the exodus that Jesus was to fulfill (9.31), and perhaps emphasizing the separation of the prophets from Jesus (9.33).[124] Also absent are the positive comparisons between Jonah and Jesus, and between Solomon and Jesus (11.30–32).[125] Marcion eschews reference to everything written about the Son of Man being fulfilled (18.31–33), and the parable of the wicked tenants in which the son is preceded by other envoys in a sequence (20.9–17).[126] Moses attesting the general resurrection, and the characterization of "the God of Abraham, Isaac, and Jacob" as "the God of the living" are excluded (20.37–38). Among the eschatological woes, reference to fleeing to the mountains because the days of vengeance are written so as to be fulfilled (21.21–22) is excised. Luke 22:35–38's reference to Isa 53, which Jesus says must be fulfilled by him, also goes. If Marcion's Gospel is indeed an abridgment of Luke, this significant proportion of the "not present" material points to a tendency to remove references to Jesus's fulfillment of scripture.

One might add another case, not so much an absence of a textual block but a modification: Luke 24:25 has Jesus rebuking the disciples for not believing what *the prophets* have spoken; Marcion replaces the mention of prophets speaking with a reference to *Jesus himself* speaking.[127] "As a deliberate change it would both remove any reference to prophecy and would also reinforce Jesus's self-revelation by his word."[128] Although strictly speaking unattested, it is

---

124. Lieu, *Marcion*, 230.

125. Harnack, *Marcion*, 54. It may be that the references to judgment are an alternative (or additional) impulse for the deletion of this segment, however.

126. Both are "sicher gestrichen," according to Harnack, *Marcion*, 56.

127. Tertullian, *Marc.* 4.43.4, has *locutus est* (in reference to Jesus), while *Adam. dial.* 5.12 has ἐλάλησα (Jesus speaking). Epiphanius, *Pan.* 42.11.17, S77, also has the latter, referring to Marcion's replacement of the reference to the prophets. See Lieu, *Marcion*, 218–19: "it is highly likely that according to Marcion Jesus recalled Cleopas and his companion to his own earlier words rather than to those of the prophets (Luke 24:25)."

128. Lieu, *Marcion*, 219, who is not, however, convinced that it is a deliberate change.

highly likely therefore that Luke 24:27 ("And beginning with Moses and all the prophets, he explained to them what was said in all the scriptures concerning himself") was therefore absent.[129]

In sum, Lieu's suggestion that "his text may have avoided . . . appeals to prophetic fulfilment" seems to be more than warranted, indeed overly cautious.[130] Although Harnack may have exaggerated the extent of Marcion's "Streichungen und Correcturen," he seems still to be correct that the motivations for such omissions included inter alia the fact that "the OT cannot have prophesied anything which has been fulfilled in Christ."[131] Crucially for Marcion, Jesus was a *novum*: he arrives, like Athene from Zeus, fully grown from God and lands in an apocalyptically unexpected manner in Capernaum in the fifteenth year of Tiberius (Gos. Marcion 3.1; 4.31). There is a good deal of reference to scriptural material in his Gospel, but Marcion is careful neither to attribute to this material any role in testifying to the saving activity of Jesus nor to regard scripture as in any sense fulfilled by him.

4.3 Interim Conclusion: Christ and Scripture in Marcion's Gospel

To say that Christ is not the fulfillment of scripture is of course to express the point negatively. To put it positively, Marcion might have said that Christ was self-authenticating and self-interpreting. The negative point, however, is not only a negative one. The very identity of Jesus and the message of the Christian gospel cannot really be expressed solely in positive terms. Jesus is *defined* antithetically, just as to call the good God "the Stranger God" requires the other to which he is a stranger. "Marcion's presentation of Jesus as consistently challenging the Law" is not incidental;[132] that is who he is. The activity of the creator god forms the essential backdrop that is the foil for understanding Jesus.[133]

---

129. Lieu, *Marcion*, 218–19, though there is no reason why 24:26 should have been absent: ἔδει could be explained on other grounds.

130. Lieu, *Marcion*, 228. The claim in BeDuhn, *First New Testament*, 77, that "the 'missing' material relative to Luke does not confirm any concept contrary to Marcionism not found also in other passages retained in the Evangelion" is incorrect on this point, ignoring the well-known theme of scriptural fulfillment in Luke.

131. Harnack, *Marcion*, 64: "das AT kann nichts geweissagt haben, was sich in Christus erfüllt hat."

132. Lieu, *Marcion*, 227. I merely borrow Lieu's formulation here; no criticism is intended.

133. Similarly, Wolfgang A. Bienert, "Marcion und der Antijudaismus," in May and Greschat, *Marcion und seine kirchengeschichtliche Wirkung*, 201: "Sein [sc. Marcions] Christentum ist insofern—anders als im Barnabasbrief und bei Justin—nicht das 'wahre Israel' oder, wie im 'Kerygma Petrou,' ein neues, das 'dritte Geschlecht' aus Christen und Juden, sondern

CONCLUSION: MARCION'S GOSPEL AND THE KERYGMA

To conclude, we can briefly summarize the main points. The text of Marcion's Gospel is very like the Gospel of Luke in some respects, but it differs in important ways not only in content but also in how pericopes common to both might have been interpreted. Hence, on our first topic, a passage like Jesus's discussion of John the Baptist in Luke 7 in fact sets them in opposition to one another, John expecting a scriptural messiah and Jesus demonstrating himself to be a different kind of Christ. Similarly, he is David's antithesis rather than David's son. He is not "the one who was to redeem Israel" but a messiah sent from the heaven of the Stranger God. Marcion therefore bifurcates existing Christian tradition by distinguishing between the creator's scriptural messiah still to come and the messiah already sent by the supreme God in the person of Jesus. In taking this unprecedented step, Marcion is therefore a radical figure who departs significantly from the kerygma that is operating as the comparator in this study.

In his views of Jesus's death and resurrection, Marcion is in certain respects more conventional. They are both divine necessities (δεῖ), as they are in other Gospels. While he may shy away from cultic or sacrificial notions of atonement, Marcion taps into a well-established tradition of understanding Jesus's death as a redemptive purchase of humanity. The purchase motif was a central point for Marcion not only because it elucidated the function of Jesus's death but also because it comported well with his conception of two gods, the buyer and the vendor. The inauguration of a new covenant is, as in Luke, also an aspect of the death of Jesus and one that can be illuminated from hints of Marcion's view of covenant elsewhere.

Similarly, Jesus's resurrection was according to Marcion's Gospel "on the third day," as in the other narrative Gospels. Marcion's understanding of the nature of this resurrection is rather more difficult to fathom, because of the difficulties both in recovering his text and in interpreting his conception of Jesus's risen physiology—although in this latter case, at least, this is a common difficulty in understanding early Christian Gospels. In terms of its similarity to the early Christian kerygma, Marcion's understanding of Jesus's death and resurrection reflects that kerygma strongly.

Finally, Marcion is again clear in his position on the relation between Jesus's saving activity and scripture—which is to say that there is no relation. There is

---

eine neue Heilsgemeinde, die dennoch indirekt—als Antithese—dem Judentum verbunden bleibt." The formulation here seems to me to have it right.

fulfillment of scripture by the creator's messiah, who will come in the future to restore Israel's fortunes. Jesus, however, comes out of the blue and therefore demonstrates that the God he represents is a stranger to the material cosmos, its history, and its inhabitants. In this respect as well, Marcion differs starkly from some early Christian Gospels (such as Matthew or Luke, or the Egerton or Fayyum Gospels), although his position is not as original as his theory of dual messiahship. Marcion is close to other second-century views that pit Jesus against scripture, rather as we will see in the *Gospel of Thomas* or the *Gospel of the Egyptians*. Like these two other Gospels, Marcion's departs significantly from the "accordance with the scriptures" component of the kerygma.

APPENDIX 1: THE BURIAL OF JESUS IN MARCION'S GOSPEL

Irenaeus challenges Marcion with the question, "What body did those who buried him bury?"[134] The burial of Jesus is clearly attested in Marcion: there is strong evidence for him retaining both the burial narrative in the Gospel and Paul's reference to Jesus's burial (1 Cor 15:4) in the *Apostolos*.[135] In the Gospel in particular, there is attestation of almost every verse: the introduction of Joseph (Gos. Marcion 23.50), the reference to him not agreeing to the Sanhedrin's decision (23.51), the request for the body from Pilate (23.52), the wrapping and placing of the body in a rock-hewn tomb (23.53), and the women's visit (23.55).[136] Only 23.54 is not attested. This may be the result of the limitations of our sources; if it was absent, Marcion may have deliberately avoided a Jewish calendrical reference to Preparation Day and the Sabbath, but this is speculative. In any case, Marcion clearly adheres to the tradition of Jesus's burial as part of the *euangelion*.

APPENDIX 2: THE RESURRECTION APPEARANCES IN MARCION'S GOSPEL

As noted in section 4 above, the issue of the resurrection narrative is a complex one in Marcion. There is clear attestation of the appearance of Jesus to the two

---

134. Irenaeus, *Haer.* 4.33.2.

135. See the text in Roth, *Text*, 434, and Schmid, *Apostolos*, 326.

136. Lieu, *Marcion*, 218, notes the attestation of the burial, by both Tertullian and Epiphanius.

disciples on the Emmaus road (Gos. Marcion 24.13–32); it is interesting that 24.22–24 is unattested, meaning that the thought that Jesus might be the redeemer of Israel could be followed directly by the rebuke "O you, fools, slow in heart to believe." There are probably revelation and a recognition scene in 24.30–31, both of which are attested. As discussed previously, the references to Jesus's activity being presaged in scripture are the major casualties of Marcion's editorial activity (e.g., esp. 24.25); the narrative structure remains largely unchanged. However, since 24.32–36 is unattested, it is not clear whether the kerygma-like statement "the Lord has risen and has appeared to Peter" (Luke 24:34; cf. 1 Cor 15:4–5) was included in Marcion's Gospel. More certain is the fact that Marcion includes Jesus's appearance to the disciples en bloc in 24.36–47.

Chapter Ten

THE GOSPEL OF THOMAS

A s we will also see for the cases of the *Gospel of the Egyptians* and the *Gospel of Judas*, the major function of Jesus in the *Gospel of Thomas* is as a revealer. The major difference is that Jesus in the *Gospel of Thomas* is a speaker not of grand mythological schemes but of brief sentences and parables. Nor is there narration of the death and resurrection of Jesus such as we have seen in the Gospels treated so far. The opening of the Gospel introduces Jesus as the true "author" of the work:

> These are the secret sayings that the living Jesus spoke, and Didymus Judas Thomas wrote them down. And he said, "Whoever finds the interpretation of these sayings will not taste death." (prologue + *Gos. Thom.* 1)

The disciple Thomas, then, is less an author and more a scribe to the "living Jesus." The "sayings" are also thematized in the prologue, and the first saying proper emphasizes programmatically their soteriological import. Hence the gospel message of the *Gospel of Thomas* is not like the kerygma of, say, Mark. Nevertheless, there are allusions to some kerygmatic themes.

1. Jesus's Messiahship and the Gospel of Thomas

The *Gospel of Thomas* has a range of titles:

- "Lord": There is only one place where Jesus speaks clearly of being "lord"/"Lord," in the easy yoke saying in *Gos. Thom.* 90 where he talks of his mild "lordship" (ⲙⲛⲧϫⲟⲉⲓⲥ). There are two other uses of the title, in two adjacent sayings: in the former, Jesus commands the disciples to pray

363

to the Lord of the harvest (*Gos. Thom.* 73), and in the latter, Jesus—or just possibly another speaker—laments in an address to the Lord the paucity of true disciples (*Gos. Thom.* 74). In neither case is there a clear reference to Jesus, although that is a possibility.

- "Son of Man": The *Gospel of Thomas* contains a version of the saying in which the Son of Man/son of man has nowhere to lay his head, but the lack of context means that the referent is unclear (*Gos. Thom.* 86). Elsewhere the title is democratized to refer to true disciples (*Gos. Thom.* 106), and this is probably the sense in the earlier saying.[1]

More important are two titles of clear theological significance in the *Gospel of Thomas*:

- "Living one": In the prologue, Jesus is described as "the living Jesus," and he can also describe himself as "the living one" *tout simple*, in contrast to the dead prophets (*Gos. Thom.* 52). "Living" is an attribute that Jesus shares with the Father (*Gos. Thom.* 3, 37, 50) and that can also be extended to elect disciples (*Gos. Thom.* 11, 111; cf. 114).[2]
- "Son": Jesus's sonship is implied in a number of sayings where he talks of "the Father" or "my Father."[3] It is explicit in only a few. The "son of the Living One" in *Gos. Thom.* 37 is presumably Jesus, as is the son in *Gos. Thom.* 44. Whether Jesus is the son figure in the *Gospel of Thomas's* parable of the tenants (*Gos. Thom.* 65) is much debated; overall the identification is unlikely.[4]

Even if their christological significance is ambiguous, three of the "big four" titles of Jesus—Lord, Christ, Son of Man, Son (of God)—are included in the *Gospel of Thomas*. It is all the more striking, then, that "Christ" is absent. Nor are the distinctively Jewish messianic epithets "king of Israel" or "son of David" present. The use of the title "Son" in the *Gospel of Thomas* also does not give any hint of being used with any traditional messianic connotations. It appears only twice as a designation of Jesus. In the former case, the phrase

1. Simon Gathercole, *The Gospel of Thomas: Introduction and Commentary* (Leiden: Brill, 2014), 520, 583.

2. There are also cases where the reference is more ambiguous, e.g., *Gos. Thom.* 59 (probably Jesus, possibly the Father) and 111 (too close to call).

3. "The Father": *Gos. Thom.* 3, 27, 40, 44, 57, 69, 76, 79, 83, 96, 97, 98, 105, 113; "my Father": *Gos. Thom.* 62, 64, 99 bis.

4. See Gathercole, *Gospel of Thomas*, 460–61, for different views.

"the son of the Living One" is clearly stamped with the *Gospel of Thomas's* distinctive theology (*Gos. Thom.* 37). In the latter, its appearance within the Father-Son-Spirit triad bears the influence of the beginnings of early Christian Trinitarian thinking (*Gos. Thom.* 44). As noted above, "Son of Man" (*or* "son of man") appears but probably refers to human beings or disciples rather than specifically to Jesus.

As with some of the other works we are considering in this study, there is a negative attitude toward a Jewish worldview. The *Gospel of Thomas* criticizes the whole institution of circumcision (*Gos. Thom.* 53), not just of its misapplication to gentiles, for example. As we will explore shortly, the *Gospel of Thomas* gives a negative value to scripture per se (*Gos. Thom.* 52) and not just to its misinterpretation.[5] The whole period of Israel's history seems to have been a vacuum as far as true understanding is concerned, and the single reference to "the Jews" is unambiguously negative (*Gos. Thom.* 43).[6] The lack of interest in, or hostility to the idea of, Jesus as a Jewish messiah goes hand in hand with such views.

2. Jesus's Death in the Gospel of Thomas

On the *Gospel of Thomas's* lack of interest in Jewish messianism, there is no debate among scholars; a little more contested is how much reference there is to Jesus's death, and what the significance of the cross might be for the *Gospel of Thomas*. Patterson, in line with most scholars, assigns little importance to the death of Jesus in the *Gospel of Thomas*: "Thomas lacks a passion narrative and is almost completely devoid of interest in the death of Jesus."[7] By contrast, DeConick states: "The general opinion expressed by the majority of scholars, that *Thomas* is not interested in Jesus's death, is without merit."[8]

---

5. Cf. also *Gos. Thom.* 6, 14.

6. "They love the tree but hate its fruit, or love the fruit but hate the tree" (*Gos. Thom.* 43.3). Like the dog in the manger of the fable, the Pharisees and the Scribes not only reject the truth themselves but actively obstruct others as well (*Gos. Thom.* 39, 102). It may well be the case that adjacency to *Gos. Thom.* 39, on the one hand, and the context in Matthew's Gospel of the Matthean parallel, on the other, mean that the statement about the vine that will be uprooted (*Gos. Thom.* 40) is a statement specifically about Israel/Jews as well.

7. Stephen Patterson, "The View from across the Euphrates," *HTR* 104 (2011): 411.

8. April D. DeConick, *The Original Gospel of Thomas in Translation: With a Commentary and New English Translation of the Complete Gospel* (London: T&T Clark International, 2006), 189.

In the *Gospel of Thomas*'s saying about the succession from Jesus to James (*Gos. Thom.* 12), there is a fairly clear reference at least to Jesus's removal from the world, though without any significance attached to the death.[9] The *Gospel of Thomas* mentions the death of Jesus clearly (if implicitly) only once:[10]

> Jesus said, "Whoever does not hate his father and mother will not be able to be a disciple of mine. And whoever does not hate his brothers and sisters, and take his cross like me, will not be worthy of me." (*Gos. Thom.* 55)

Presumably the mention of Jesus's taking up his cross is a metaphor for his death, although it is possible it has some other meaning. Even though in context it is used in a metaphorical sense, the connection with "like me" suggests an allusion to Jesus's own crucifixion. Its significance here is that Jesus's rejection of the world's values (such as those expressed in the first half of the saying) and willingness to suffer as a result are to be a model for the attitudes of true disciples. For Patterson, this and this alone is the meaning of the death of Jesus in the *Gospel of Thomas*.[11]

For DeConick, by contrast, other sayings should be included as part of the picture: "Once the Gospel had incorporated the accretive sayings, L. 87 and 112, the crucifixion of Jesus and its imitation took on new meaning for the members of the later Thomasine community. . . . It was the ultimate model of the soul conquering the passions and the miserable state of embodiment. . . . Thus we find L. 56 immediately following."[12] We can consider, then, the relevance of *Gos. Thom.* 87 and 112 to the problem of Jesus's death:

> Jesus said, "Wretched is the body that depends on a body, and wretched is the soul that depends on these two." (*Gos. Thom.* 87)

---

9. The *Weggang* of Jesus is probably also implied in *Gos. Thom.* 38.2: "Days are coming when you will seek after me but will not find me." So also François Vouga, "Mort et résurrection de Jésus dans la Source des logia et dans l'Évangile de Thomas," in *Coptica—Gnostica—Manichaica: Mélanges offerts à Wolf-Peter Funk*, ed. Louis Painchaud and Paul-Hubert Poirier (Louvain: Peeters, 2006), 1015. I am less convinced of the motif's presence in *Gos. Thom.* 24 and 27, at least in any connection with Jesus's death, *pace* E. E. Popkes, "Die Umdeutung des Todes Jesu im koptischen Thomasevangelium," in *Deutungen des Todes Jesu im Neuen Testament*, ed. Jörg Frey and Jens Schröter, 2nd ed. (Tübingen: Mohr Siebeck, 2012), 531–32.

10. Or explicitly but indirectly, as Popkes puts it ("Umdeutung des Todes Jesu," 516).

11. Patterson, "View from across the Euphrates," 418–19.

12. DeConick, *Original Gospel of Thomas*, 189.

Jesus said, "Woe to the flesh that depends on the soul. Woe to the soul that depends on the flesh." (*Gos. Thom.* 112)

DeConick is correct that there is a reference here to "the miserable state of embodiment," but this stands almost in contradiction to her point about crucifixion. She notes that the verb translated "depends" above (ⲁϣⲉ/ⲟϣⲉ, from ⲉⲓϣⲉ) is the standard word used for crucifixion, but here this particular "hanging" or "crucifixion" is valued negatively. It is the subject of a woe, not something exhorted by Jesus. These sayings cannot have any relevance, then, for the interpretation of the crucifixion spoken of in Jesus's reference to carrying the cross in *Gos. Thom.* 55.

What of DeConick's highlighting of the juxtaposition of *Gos. Thom.* 55–56?

Jesus said, "Whoever does not hate his father and mother cannot be a disciple of mine. And whoever does not hate his brothers and sisters, and take his cross like me, will not be worthy of me." (*Gos. Thom.* 55)

Jesus said, "Whoever has come to know the world has found a corpse. And whoever has found the corpse is one of whom the world is not worthy." (*Gos. Thom.* 56)

Following Guillaumont, DeConick understands *Gos. Thom.* 56 to be about the mastery of the body, an idea similar to carrying one's cross. To get to this interpretation, however, she is required to make two changes to rectify two alleged mistranslations from a Semitic original.[13] The phrase translated above as "has found a corpse" is taken to mean "has mastered the body," on the grounds that the Syriac *mṣ'* can mean "to master," and Aramaic/Syriac *pgr* can mean a "body" in general and not just a dead one. It is a speculative theory indeed, however, to assume two hypothetical mistranslations in the now invisible process of transmission. There are in fact considerable difficulties not only with the supposition of an Aramaic/Syriac *Vorlage* but also with the two particular proposals mentioned here.[14]

---

13. DeConick, *Original Gospel of Thomas*, 192. Cf. also A. Guillaumont, "Les sémitismes dans l'Évangile selon Thomas: Essai de classement," in *Studies in Gnosticism and Hellenistic Religions Presented to Gilles Quispel on the Occasion of His 65th Birthday*, ed. R. van den Broek and M. J. Vermaseren (Leiden: Brill, 1981), 194; Guillaumont, "Sémitismes dans les logia de Jésus retrouvés à Nag-Hamâdi," *JA* 246 (1958): 117.

14. See Simon Gathercole, *The Composition of the Gospel of Thomas: Original Language and Sources* (Cambridge: Cambridge University Press, 2012), 19–125, on a Semitic original for the *Gospel of Thomas*, and 77–79, on these two specific points.

Passages where other scholars have detected references to Jesus's death include the parable of the tenants (*Gos. Thom.* 65), with or without the following saying about the rejected stone (*Gos. Thom.* 66),[15] as well as the saying about the destruction of the house (*Gos. Thom.* 71). Popkes, for example, in his study dedicated to the topic, sees the death of Jesus as at least reflected in these sayings. The parable of the tenants in its context in the *Gospel of Thomas*, however, probably does not have the same meaning as it does in the Synoptics. Standing as it does after two parables about the danger and fruitlessness of commerce, it is probably continuing along those lines rather than being concerned with salvation history.[16] Similarly, *Gos. Thom.* 71, "I will destroy this house, and no one will be able to build it," is probably a reference to the temple rather than the human body of Jesus.[17]

Unlike some of the Gospels considered in other chapters, there is a death here in the *Gospel of Thomas*. Jesus has a body derived from his human lineage.[18] Just as Jesus is indifferent to his biological family,[19] however, so also his death brings only his earthly, material existence to an end.[20] More fundamentally, Jesus is a "living one" who, like true disciples in the *Gospel of Thomas*,

---

15. DeConick, *Original Gospel of Thomas*, 214; similarly, Vouga, "Mort et résurrection," 1023 (and 1016–17), speaks of the necessary death of the Son of God, in relation to *Gos. Thom.* 65–66. Popkes is slightly less emphatic here, noting that with the combination of *Gos. Thom.* 65–66, "Beide Passagen scheinen somit ein Wissen um die Ablehnung bzw. den Tod zu dokumentieren" ("Umdeutung des Todes Jesu," 517). I could assent to this relatively soft conclusion but not to the way it is framed in Popkes's introduction, namely that this is a passage in which the death of Jesus is "thematisiert" ("Umdeutung des Todes Jesu," 514), which is much stronger than merely saying that it reflects knowledge of Jesus's death, or that it is "vorausgesetzt" ("Umdeutung des Todes Jesu," 542).

16. Gathercole, *Gospel of Thomas*, 457–63.

17. Gathercole, *Gospel of Thomas*, 477–80. Contra Popkes's tentative proposal ("Umdeutung des Todes Jesu," 520, 533), as DeConick notes, it is only when read through Johannine spectacles that one could arrive at a reference to Jesus's body here (*Original Gospel of Thomas*, 226).

18. Gregory J. Riley, *Resurrection Reconsidered: Thomas and John in Controversy* (Minneapolis: Fortress, 1995), 129.

19. See Risto Uro, "Asceticism and Anti-familial Language in the Gospel of Thomas," in *Constructing Early Christian Families: Family as Social Reality and Metaphor*, ed. H. Moxnes (London: Routledge, 1997), 217, who talks of a general "disregard of family ties" in the *Gospel of Thomas*; see further Gathercole, *Gospel of Thomas*, 160–61.

20. As Popkes rightly notes ("Umdeutung des Todes Jesu," 542): "In diesem neuen Gesamtkontext beendet der Tod Jesu nur dessen körperliche Existenz."

transcends physical death.[21] This is not because of a postmortem resurrection but rather because Jesus in his essence is immortally "living."[22]

The cross theme is of some importance in the *Gospel of Thomas*, but its significance lies only in the fact that a disciple of Jesus has to "take up his cross like me." In other words, it is the example of Jesus that is relevant. The death of Jesus is not in itself a saving event in the *Gospel of Thomas*.[23]

3. Jesus's Resurrection and the Gospel of Thomas

As we have seen, the *Gospel of Thomas* refers at the outset to Jesus as "the living Jesus" (*Gos. Thom.*, prologue). Elsewhere, this epithet alludes to resurrection: in Revelation Jesus is "the living one" (ὁ ζῶν), although he had been dead (Rev 1:18), and the same language is used in Luke's resurrection narrative when the angels ask the women why they are looking for "the living one" (τὸν ζῶντα) among the dead (Luke 24:5). In the context of the *Gospel of Thomas*, however, this designation is very unlikely to have the same sense.[24]

The *Gospel of Thomas* does not refer to any event that might suggest resurrection, and as we have noted, although there is a reference to the cross, the general thrust of the *Gospel of Thomas* points to Jesus transcending death. This transcendence means neither that there is no death nor that death is reversed but rather that Jesus and his followers are unaffected by a merely material death. This is reinforced by the negative attitude toward future resurrection:

21. On the disciples' transcendence of death, see Simon Gathercole, "'The Heavens and the Earth Will Be Rolled Up': The Eschatology of the Gospel of Thomas," in *Eschatologie—Eschatology: The Sixth Durham-Tübingen Research Symposium; Eschatology in Old Testament, Ancient Judaism and Early Christianity*, ed. H.-J. Eckstein, C. Landmesser, and H. Lichtenberger (Tübingen: Mohr Siebeck, 2011), 280–302.

22. Popkes, "Umdeutung des Todes Jesu," 533 ("Für das Thomasevangelium ist Jesus vielmehr *per se* der Lebendige"), and cf. also 542–43; Patterson, "View from across the Euphrates," 419: "In Thomas the 'living Jesus' is the *immortal* Jesus who brings to others the secret of immortality."

23. Rightly, Vouga, "Mort et resurrection," 1017.

24. Konrad Schwarz, "Der 'lebendige Jesus' im Thomasevangelium," in *Christ of the Sacred Stories*, ed. P. Dragutinović, T. Nicklas, and K. G. Rodenbiker (Tübingen: Mohr Siebeck, 2017), 234, rightly comments that the issue in the prologue is not the location of Jesus either preresurrection or postresurrection but the identification of him as "living" in the sense that he transcends death.

His disciples said to him, "When will the rest for the dead come, and when is the new world coming?"

He said to them, "That (rest) which you are seeking has come, but you do not know it." (*Gos. Thom.* 51)

The fact that Jesus's response, in keeping with his responses in the related controversies in *Gos. Thom.* 52–53, is negative suggests that there is no room in the *Gospel of Thomas's* theology for a future resurrection. This in turn makes a bodily resurrection of Jesus less likely.[25]

As indicated above, in the *Gospel of Thomas's* eschatology, the disciples relate to future eschatology as merely indifferent spectators:

Jesus said, "This heaven will pass away, as will the one above it. But the dead will not live, and the living will not die." (*Gos. Thom.* 11.1–2)

Jesus said, "The heavens and the earth will roll up in your presence; and he who lives from the Living One will not see death." (*Gos. Thom.* 111.1–2)

Here, the disciples are onlookers ("in your presence") at the dissolution of the cosmos, when "the heavens and the earth will roll up." This passive interpretation of "in your presence," where the elect are mere spectators, is required by the fact that however dramatic the events seem to be, they have no impact at all on what really counts: the dead stay dead, and the living are not threatened (11.2; 111.2).[26]

This transcendence of death for the true disciples is perhaps a useful paradigm for interpreting the impact of the crucifixion upon the prologue's "living Jesus" (Ἰησοῦς ὁ ζῶν, ⲓ̅ⲥ̅ ⲉⲧⲟⲛⲏ): compare the language used of the unaffected disciples who are "living ones" (ⲛⲉⲧⲟⲛⲏ) in *Gos. Thom.* 11 and in the singular "he who lives from the Living One" (ⲡⲉⲧⲟⲛⲏ ⲉⲃⲟⲗ ϩⲛ̅ ⲡⲉⲧⲟⲛⲏ) in *Gos. Thom.* 111. This analogy renders a resurrection as unnecessary for Jesus as it is for the true disciple, since the death of the physical element is apparently of no significance.

The basis for this is the eternity of the kingdom, which is almost coextensive with Jesus himself. Paradise is a sphere unaffected by the cycle of life and death (*Gos. Thom.* 19.3) and is a protological realm of light (*Gos. Thom.* 49–50) just as Jesus himself is the light (*Gos. Thom.* 77). The true disciple "stands in the beginning" and inhabits paradise and, for these reasons, "will not taste death" (*Gos. Thom.* 18–19). All the more will this be true, then, for Jesus.

---

25. I am not persuaded, however, that *Gos. Thom.* 71 is a denial of bodily resurrection, *pace* Riley, *Resurrection Reconsidered*, 154–56.

26. See Gathercole, "'Heavens and the Earth Will Be Rolled Up.'"

4. Jesus and Scripture in the Gospel of Thomas

The *Gospel of Thomas* has both a programmatic statement about alleged prior revelation and cases of Old Testament language being used. Before addressing these, however, the more positive statements about Jesus's own revelation and their implications will provide a useful contrast.

First, then, we have clear statements about Jesus's own revelation and its temporal boundedness:

> Jesus said, "I will give you what eye has not seen, what ear has not heard, what hand has not touched, and what has never occurred to the human mind." (*Gos. Thom.* 17)

> Jesus said, "Many times you have desired to hear these words that I speak to you, and you have no one else from whom to hear them. Days are coming when you will seek after me but will not find me." (*Gos. Thom.* 38)

> Jesus said, "Seek and you shall find. I now desire to tell you what I did not tell you before when you asked me. But now you do not seek it." (*Gos. Thom.* 92)

Jesus gives unprecedented revelation, then, in the course of his earthly ministry (*Gos. Thom.* 17; 38.1), even if his words are implied as living on into the present of the reader (prologue). There is also a tone of urgency about accepting this revelation in the present here (*Gos. Thom.* 38.2; 92.2).

Second, there is a negative counterpart to these sayings in Jesus's verdict upon scripture:

> His disciples said to him, "Twenty-four prophets spoke in Israel. And did all of them speak about you?"
> He said to them, "You have neglected the living one in front of you and spoken of the dead." (*Gos. Thom.* 52)

The disciples here ask a question about the relation between Jesus and scripture,[27] and their question in some ways reflects a position articulated in other Gospels. In Luke, for example, the risen Jesus explained to the disciples "in all the scriptures the things about him" (ἐν πάσαις ταῖς γραφαῖς τὰ περὶ ἑαυτοῦ

---

27. Help with both the form (a question) and meaning (Coptic ϩⲣⲁⲓ̈ ⲛ̄ϩⲏⲧⲕ̀ has the rough sense of "about you") of what the disciples say is at hand from a parallel in Augustine, *Leg.* 2.4.14. For the text and discussion, see Gathercole, *Gospel of Thomas*, 418.

[Luke 24:27]). Similarly, in John and the *Egerton Gospel*, Jesus says of Moses that he "wrote about me."[28] The position implied in the disciples' question is no artificial foil, then, but probably a view "out there" with which the *Gospel of Thomas* is intentionally engaging, though not necessarily in dialogue with another particular Gospel text.

In terms of the response to the disciples' question, some scholars have attempted to soften Jesus's answer. It has been taken variously as a criticism not of Israel's scripture per se but of *Heilsgeschichte*,[29] or as an antithetical hyperbole,[30] or as an exhortation to read scripture in the light of Jesus rather than vice versa.[31] Quispel even voices the impossible opinion "that the author of the *Gospel of Thomas* and the composers of its sources used the Old Testament and recognized it as Holy Scripture."[32] None of these positions is consistent with the wording of Jesus's response, however.[33] The use of "dead" as an epithet elsewhere in the *Gospel of Thomas* means that we have to view scripture neither in any positive light nor even amid the relativized *adiaphora*, but as pernicious.[34] As Watson has put it, Thomas "appears to sever the link with the scriptures, contrasting the living Jesus with the twenty-four dead prophets in Israel."[35]

The attitude expressed in *Gos. Thom.* 52 is consistent with the phenomena that we see in the actual allusions to scripture in the *Gospel of Thomas*. Logion 66 is one case in point:

Jesus said, "Show me the stone that the builders rejected—that is the cornerstone." (*Gos. Thom.* 66)

28. John 5:46: εἰ γὰρ ἐπιστεύετε Μωϋσεῖ, ἐπιστεύετε ἂν ἐμοί· περὶ γὰρ ἐμοῦ ἐκεῖνος ἔγραψεν. Although *P. Egerton* 2 frag. 1v lines 20–23 are very fragmentary, similar wording is likely.

29. Petr Pokorný, *A Commentary on the Gospel of Thomas: From Interpretations to the Interpreted* (London: T&T Clark, 2009), 97.

30. Reinhard Nordsieck, *Das Thomas-Evangelium: Einleitung—Zur Frage des historischen Jesus—Kommentierung aller 114 Logien* (Neukirchen-Vluyn: Neukirchener, 2004), 210.

31. DeConick, *Original Gospel of Thomas*, 184–85.

32. Gilles Quispel, "Das Thomasevangelium und das Alte Testament," in *Neotestamentica et Patristica: Eine Freundesgabe Herrn Prof. Dr. Oscar Cullmann zu seinem 60. Geburtstag überreicht* (Leiden: Brill, 1962), 243: "dass der Autor des Thomasevangeliums und die Verfasser seiner Quellen das Alte Testament benutzt und als Heilige Schrift anerkannt haben."

33. For elaborations of these views, and criticisms of them, see Gathercole, *Gospel of Thomas*, 414–16.

34. See Gathercole, *Gospel of Thomas*, 197, 149.

35. Francis Watson, *Gospel Writing: A Canonical Perspective* (Grand Rapids: Eerdmans, 2013), 608.

This saying directly follows the parable of the wicked tenants (*Gos. Thom.* 65) in the *Gospel of Thomas*, just as substantially the same saying follows the same parable in the Synoptic Gospels. The saying is of course a scriptural one, deriving ultimately from Ps 118:22 (117:22 LXX). This point is acknowledged by the Synoptic evangelists but not by the *Gospel of Thomas*, who simply introduces the stone saying in *Gos. Thom.* 66 with a fresh "Jesus said." Is this lack of acknowledgment because the *Gospel of Thomas* deliberately deletes the scriptural connection,[36] or does it simply reflect a distance from Old Testament scripture?[37] These two positions are very different: the former attributes a conscious redaction predicated upon direct and close acquaintance with the Old Testament, the latter a mere amnesia predicated upon the opposite, namely distance from it. The practice of Marcion raises the possibility that a conscious editorial deletion of some Old Testament material is at least conceivable.

Other examples to be brought into the discussion alongside *Gos. Thom.* 66 also come in parabolic material. The parable of the mustard seed (*Gos. Thom.* 20), for example, is more distant from its ultimate Old Testament source material than are the Synoptic versions.[38] Or again, in the case of the fragment of the parable of the seed growing secretly (*Gos. Thom.* 21.10), "the conclusion of the Markan parable alludes to Joel 4:13 LXX; the allusion is absent in Thomas."[39] Only the word for "sickle" (here ⲁⲥϩ; more commonly ⲟϩⲥ) survives from Joel through into the *Gospel of Thomas*.

As has commonly been noted, the Isaiah material in the parable of the wicked tenants features heavily in Matthew and Mark but is omitted by Luke, and (probably because the *Gospel of Thomas* is influenced by the Lukan formulation) not present in the *Gospel of Thomas*.[40] As has already been noted, *Gos. Thom.* 66, the saying about the rejected cornerstone, is formulated as a separate saying by the *Gospel of Thomas*, although still, as in the Synoptics, juxtaposed to the parable. In terms of the content of *Gos. Thom.* 66, in addition to Jesus

36. Robert M. Grant and David Noel Freedman, *The Secret Sayings of Jesus* (New York: Doubleday, 1960), 172.

37. Mark S. Goodacre, *Thomas and the Gospels* (Grand Rapids: Eerdmans, 2012), 189–90.

38. Cf. Mark 4:30–32 // Matt 13:31–32 // Luke 13:18–19 and *Gos. Thom.* 20 alongside Dan 4:12, 14, 20–21 and Ezek 17:23; 31:6. Mark takes over from the Old Testament the plural "branches" (cf. singular "branch" in *Gos. Thom.* 20.4) and the vocabulary and syntax of the birds under the shade of the tree (cf. "shelter for the birds of the air" in *Gos. Thom.* 20.4).

39. Watson, *Gospel Writing*, 281, further noting about the clause from Joel 4:13 that "in the Markan context the ὅτι-clause is redundant" (281 n. 184). See similarly Goodacre, *Thomas and the Gospels*, 189.

40. See Goodacre, *Thomas and the Gospels*, 190; Gathercole, *Composition of the Gospel of Thomas*, 188–94, and further my response to Kloppenborg in Gathercole, "Thomas Revisited: A Rejoinder to Denzey Lewis, Kloppenborg and Patterson," *JSNT* 36 (2014): 262–81.

being the speaker in the introduction, the main body of the saying is also more distant from the psalm by comparison with the near-verbatim use of the psalm by the Synoptic evangelists. Against Mark and Matthew but like Luke, the *Gospel of Thomas* includes only Ps 118:22 (the cornerstone saying) and omits Ps 118:23 ("the Lord has done this, and it is marvelous in our eyes").

Overall, three factors suggest that a distance of the *Gospel of Thomas* from scripture is more likely than deletion or suppression, however.

First, the relative brevity of some of the *Gospel of Thomas*'s sayings is not confined to any particular material. In the case of the parable of mustard seed (*Gos. Thom.* 20), for example, it is not just the Old Testament material that is compressed. In the statement preceding the scriptural language, the *Gospel of Thomas* is considerably shorter than, for example, Mark: "It is like a mustard seed, which [Mark + *when it is sown on the soil*] is the smallest of all seeds [Mark + *on the soil*]."[41] Again, in the parable of the tenants, there is abbreviation more widely, not just of the Isaiah material. The structure of the sequence is simplified into a tricolon: slave 1—slave 2—son (in contrast to the numerous slaves in Mark and Matthew, and the three slaves in Luke). Thereafter, the response of the tenants is shorter in the *Gospel of Thomas* than in the other three, and the reaction of the vineyard owner to the death of the son, for example, is absent. This explanation in terms of abbreviation of a general kind is quite consistent with the well-known reduction in length of Matthew's parable of the tares in the *Gospel of Thomas*.[42] In this parable (Matt 13:24–30 // *Gos. Thom.* 57), the central section of the parable (in Matthew, verses 26–28) is omitted, with the result that the parable no longer makes sense.[43]

Second, in the case of *Gos. Thom.* 17, we have a quasi-scriptural formula drifting into the mouth of Jesus, as in *Gos. Thom.* 66. This is a tendency that can be observed elsewhere without particular theological intention.[44]

---

41. Matthew is also long relative to the *Gospel of Thomas*; Luke is more comparable in length.

42. See, e.g., Goodacre, *Thomas and the Gospels*, 73–81; John P. Meier, "The Parable of the Wheat and the Weeds (Matthew 13:24–30): Is Thomas's Version (Logion 57) Independent?," *JBL* 131 (2012): 715–32.

43. The conclusion (Matt 13:30 // *Gos. Thom.* 57.4) is also much shorter in the *Gospel of Thomas*.

44. See Ramón Trevijano Etcheverría, "La valoración de los dichos no canónicos: El caso de 1 Cor 2.9 y Ev.Tom log. 17," in *Papers Presented at the Eleventh International Conference on Patristic Studies Held in Oxford 1991: Historica, Theologica et Philosophica, Gnostica*, ed. Elizabeth A. Livingstone, StPatr 24 (Leuven: Peeters, 1993), 410, on a possible tendency (citing Hebrews and Justin) of Old Testament language becoming attributed to Jesus.

Third, the enumeration of the "twenty-four prophets in Israel" in *Gos. Thom.* 52 probably reflects a distance from, rather than close acquaintance with, the Old Testament. This is because, as an enumeration of the *prophets*, it is a mistake; it is in fact a counting of the Old Testament *biblical books* also found in 4 Ezra, Victorinus of Pettau, and Numbers Rabbah.[45]

Finally, although there is occasional use of Old Testament language (e.g., "days are coming" in *Gos. Thom.* 38; cf., e.g., Mark 2:20), there is no detailed knowledge of biblical books apparent. There is some reference to Israel, the history of which is depicted as an unfortunate parenthesis of history: "Jesus said, 'From Adam to John the Baptist, there is no one among those born of women higher than John the Baptist'" (*Gos. Thom.* 46).[46] Indeed, Adam is the only named individual from the Old Testament (*Gos. Thom.* 46, 85). There is no evidence of direct engagement with the Old Testament here.

Overall, then, the disregard that the *Gospel of Thomas* shows toward the Old Testament is borne out in a lack of concern to preserve its language in this parabolic material, and indeed in a probable ignorance of what was scriptural, rather than in a deliberate concern to excise it. The attempt to excise not only marked quotations but Old Testament allusions as well from the Synoptic tradition would require vast learning.

Nor is there any preparatory or anticipatory myth that can be reconstructed for the *Gospel of Thomas*. It is possible that there is some kind of egressus-regressus scheme assumed in the statement of Jesus that "from me the all came forth, and the all reaches to me" (*Gos. Thom.* 77.1), but this is an isolated fragment, and also appears in the one saying in the *Gospel of Thomas* about which we are perhaps most uncertain about the original Greek form, because the rest of the saying (*Gos. Thom.* 77.2-3) appears in another place (*Gos. Thom.* 30) in the Oxford Oxyrhynchus fragment of this passage.[47] Again, *Gos. Thom.* 29.1 and 29.2, with their statements, "If the flesh has come into being because of the spirit" and "If the spirit came into being because of the body," have proven problematic because some scholars have taken both statements to be true, others have regarded them as alternatives, and others still see the *Gospel of Thomas* rejecting both (the last view, on balance, probably being correct).[48]

---

45. 4 Ezra 14.44-47; Victorinus, *Com. Apoc.* 4.5 (on Rev 5:8); Num. Rab. 28.21. See Gathercole, *Gospel of Thomas*, 416-17, for discussion and further rabbinic references.

46. The author's attitude to historical Israel is reflected in the verdicts on his Jewish contemporaries, as noted in sec. 1 above.

47. P. Oxy. I 1 recto lines 23-30.

48. See Gathercole, *Gospel of Thomas*, 335-36.

In the end, we cannot assume any particular mythological background for the *Gospel of Thomas* or indeed any myth at all.

All in all, the period before the advent of Christ's revelation is a vacuum as far as any revelation or preparation for revelation is concerned, with neither myth, nor legislation, nor prophecy anticipating what Jesus has revealed: the statement in *Gos. Thom.* 17 that what Jesus gives eye has not seen, nor ear heard, nor mind conceived, nor hand touched, assumes programmatic significance.

CONCLUSION: THE GOSPEL OF THOMAS AND THE KERYGMA

As is apparent from section 4 here, there is a strong degree of polemic against traditional Jewish and/or Christian theologoumena, such as resurrection, scripture, and circumcision (*Gos. Thom.* 51–53), as well as diet, prayer, and fasting (*Gos. Thom.* 6, 14). Consonant with that polemical thrust is the *Gospel of Thomas*'s divergence from a concern with the elements of the kerygma. We noted in the introduction above that there are allusions to some components of the kerygma. This is not so with Jesus's messiahship, however, since there is no reference to him as Christ, a title that—strikingly—does not appear. Nor is there any sense of Jesus being raised from the dead. There is a reference to the idea of prophetic witness to Christ (*Gos. Thom.* 52), but that idea is rejected. The theme of Jesus's death is taken up, but even then it is reconfigured and set in a new framework, with no hint of an effective or vicarious death.[49] In sum, then, the *Gospel of Thomas* diverges considerably from the kerygma on all four points.

---

49. Popkes, "Umdeutung des Todes Jesu," 539–40, talks about the absence of an Old Testament or Jewish understanding of death, with the *Gospel of Thomas* placing the theme in a new "Gesamtzusammenhang."

Chapter Eleven

THE GOSPEL OF TRUTH

One of the features that makes the *Gospel of Truth* such a fascinating work is its combination of the historical events of the gospel story with an elaborate cosmological myth that is the backdrop to those historical events. According to this protological myth, there is a spiritual universe, called "the All" (ⲡⲧⲏⲣϥ), which had originally existed within God, inside the Father. The All falls away from the divine somehow, leading to its ignorance of the Father. This ignorance in turn generates turmoil.[1] Next, the turmoil is pictured as condensing, solidifying into a blinding mist:

> Since the All sought after the one from whom it had come forth [i.e., the Father], and the All had been within the uncontainable and inconceivable one who surpasses all thought, ignorance of the Father brought about turmoil and fear. Now turmoil condensed like a mist, such that no one was able to see. For this reason, Error became powerful. (*Gos. Truth* 17.5–15)

The fall of the All leads to a twofold plight of ignorance and deficiency. The All therefore has both an ontological and an epistemological crisis: the All is deficient in its being and ignorant of true knowledge. The All, considered as a human plurality, is like empty jars (*Gos. Truth* 36.24) and ignorant of the Father (28.32–33).

If this is the twofold plight, the twofold solution is (1) revelation and (2) fullness, embodied in the savior Jesus, "being knowledge and perfection" (*Gos. Truth* 20.38–39). The Father reveals himself as and in the Son; this revelation is also expressed as the Word coming forth from the mind of the Father. The

---

1. *Gos. Truth* 17.9–11. Possible, though less probable, is the sense "she [i.e., ignorance] became (ⲁⲥⲣ̄) turmoil and fear."

restoration of the All consists of the Word/Son bringing revelation to supply knowledge to the ignorant All, and this is simultaneous with Jesus's filling up of the lack in the All's deficiency: "Since deficiency came about because the Father was not known, when the Father comes to be known, there will no longer be deficiency" (24.28–32). When the All is brought back to the Father, it receives its necessary replenishment, which the Father had retained in himself all along. This is the theological framework within which the identity and activity of Jesus are to be understood: as already noted, this myth is a kind of primeval theological backdrop to the historical events of Jesus's ministry and crucifixion.

As in previous chapters, the present discussion of the *Gospel of Truth* will analyze the reception of the themes of Jesus's messiahship, his death, the resurrection, and how these events relate to scripture.

1. Jesus as Christ in the Gospel of Truth

As we will see below in the discussion of the *Gospel of Philip*, Valentinian authors have an intensive interest in words and their explanations and etymologies. The *Gospel of Truth* begins with an explanation of the terms "gospel" and "savior" and goes on to elucidate the meanings of certain Christian terms and phrases: the "bosom of the Father" (John 1:18), for example, is the Holy Spirit (*Gos. Truth* 24.9–11), the "thought" and "grace" of the Father are one and the same (37.11–15), "Sabbath" is the perfect, heavenly day of salvation (32.23–30), and so on. Explanations are sometimes implied through a play on words, though these are hard to detect in the Coptic translation. (The Greek original does not survive.) It is often thought that lying behind the passage connecting anointing and mercy, which we shall look at shortly, are plays on the similarity of the Greek words for "oil" (ἔλαιον) and "mercy" (ἔλεος).[2] This serious-minded Valentinian linguistics is an important factor in the use of the Christ title in the *Gospel of Truth*.

The *Gospel of Truth* has two instances of the term "Christ." The first is fairly inconspicuous, appearing in conjunction with the name Jesus: "This gospel

---

2. Jacques E. Ménard, *L'Évangile de Vérité* (Leiden: Brill, 1972), 171, referring to Eric Segelberg, "Evangelium Veritatis: A Confirmation Homily and Its Relation to the Odes of Solomon," *Orientalia Suecana* 8 (1959): 13; see more recently, Matthew Novenson, *The Grammar of Messianism: An Ancient Jewish Political Idiom and Its Users* (Oxford: Oxford University Press, 2016), 237. The vowels (αι) and (ε) were probably pronounced identically.

of the one who was sought revealed his perfect ones by the Father's mercies, the hidden mystery, Jesus Christ" (*Gos. Truth* 18.11–16).[3] The passage goes on to elaborate Jesus's role as a revealer, but there is no particular sense that Jesus reveals qua Christ.

In the other place the title appears, however, it has more explicit significance. As Christ, the anointed one, Jesus in turn *anoints* with the pity of the Father and thereby makes perfect those who are troubled:

> The reason Christ was declared among them was so that those who were disturbed received a returning, and he might anoint them with the chrism. This chrism is the Father's mercy that he will bestow upon them. Those whom he has anointed are those who have become perfect. (*Gos. Truth* 36.13–20)

This passage takes as its point of departure the etymology of the Christ title, then, and its literal meaning of "anointed."[4] This motif and its various extensions are well established at the time the *Gospel of Truth* is written. References to God anointing Jesus are common, but this is not made explicit in the *Gospel of Truth*.[5] Also noticeable in early Christian literature is the transition from Jesus being anointed to his disciples sharing in that anointing. This appears as early as Paul: "Now it is God who makes both us and you stand firm in Christ (Χριστόν), having anointed (χρίσας) us" (2 Cor 1:21).[6] This is closer to what we find in the *Gospel of Truth*, the difference being that there Christ is actually the anointer: Jesus is the one to "anoint them with the chrism," but at the same time, "this chrism is the Father's mercy that he [Father or Son?] will bestow upon them." There is an anointing of disciples by Christ, but as is common in Coptic, the subjects of verbs in some sentences are unclear.

---

3. Since ⲓⲏⲥⲟⲩⲥ ⲡⲉⲭⲣⲓⲥⲧⲟⲥ is simply the regular formulation, the phrase should not necessarily be translated emphatically as "Jesus, the Christ."

4. See further Benoît Standaert, "L'Évangile de Vérité: critique et lecture," *NTS* 22 (1976): 256, and Novenson, *Grammar of Messianism*, 233. On anointing in the *Gospel of Truth*, see Einar Thomassen, *The Spiritual Seed: The "Church" of the Valentinians* (Leiden: Brill, 2006), 383–85.

5. E.g., Luke 4:18; Acts 10:38; Heb 1:8–9. See Novenson, *Grammar of Messianism*, 233–35 (noting also Acts 10:38).

6. First John also refers to Christians receiving the anointing (χρῖσμα) in 2:20 and 2:27, in close proximity to mentions of both the Christ and the antichrist (2:22). Later, not long after the *Gospel of Truth*, Theophilus, *Autol.* 1.12, makes the connection explicit: "We are called Christians (Χριστιανοί) because we are anointed (χριόμεθα)."

The reference to "anointing" and "perfection" gives shape to the illustration about the vessels that follows:

> Vessels that are full are "anointed" with a seal. But when the anointing of one is broken, the vessel becomes empty; and the cause of it becoming deficient is that its anointing has gone. For then a gust of wind can draw it off by the power of what is with it. But no seal is ever removed from the person who is without deficiency, nor is he ever emptied. (*Gos. Truth* 36.21–32)

This illustration is complex because the Coptic is difficult.[7] The most likely sense is a reference to a sealing of a full vessel.[8] The passage warns against breakage but ends with a note of assurance for those true disciples who can never be "deficient" or "emptied." In this passage in the *Gospel of Truth*, then, Jesus's identity as the Christ is a crucial element in the soteriological scheme, as Jesus's anointing of Christians almost certainly signifies the giving of the Spirit, a seal ensuring the security of the disciple's salvation.[9]

Although the Christ title is important in this passage in the *Gospel of Truth*, it is not among the most important christological titles in the Gospel, such as "Son" and "Logos."[10] The concordance is not an infallible guide, but by comparison with ten references to Jesus as "Son" and around eight titular instances

7. Wesley W. Isenberg, "The Gospel of Truth," in *Gnosticism: An Anthology*, ed. Robert M. Grant (London: Collins, 1961), 157, has a different interpretation again: "For the filled vessels are those which are customarily used for anointing. But when an anointing is finished, the vessel is usually empty, and the cause of its deficiency is the consumption of its ointment."

8. In addition to having the sense of anointing, Greek χρίω can mean "seal" both in the theological and quotidian domains. In the former case, the link is the Holy Spirit (Luke 4:18; Acts 10:38), who is both an anointing and a sealing (Eph 1:13–14). In the latter, the caulking of a ship is described as an anointing, in an analogy of Theophilus of Antioch (*Autol.* 1.12); similarly, Xenophon writes about doors made of palm wood but coated (κεχριμέναι) in asphalt (*Cyr.* 7.5.22).

9. See Kendrick Grobel, *The Gospel of Truth: A Valentinian Meditation on the Gospel* (New York: Abingdon, 1959), 169, and Einar Thomassen, "Baptism among the Valentinians," in *Ablution, Initiation, and Baptism: Late Antiquity, Early Judaism, and Early Christianity*, ed. David Hellholm et al. (Berlin: de Gruyter, 2011), 911, on the equivalence of the ointment and the Spirit.

10. On Christology in the *Gospel of Truth*, see, e.g., Sasagu Arai, *Die Christologie des Evangelium Veritatis: Eine religionsgeschichtliche Untersuchung* (Leiden: Brill, 1964); Andrew C. Robison, "The 'Evangelium Veritatis': Its Doctrine, Character, and Origin," *JR* 43 (1963): 234–43, esp. 236–37.

of "Logos" or "Word,"[11] the fact that there are only two mentions of the title "Christ" means that its relevance in the *Gospel of Truth* appears to be limited. The central soteriological themes of knowledge and filling can be elucidated without reference to the Christ title, although filling can be connected with it. Of the three levels of Valentinian discourse, the mythical, the historical, and the ritual, the last is not prominent in the *Gospel of Truth*.[12] Since the ritual dimension is the one most likely to elicit references to anointing, the obvious connections between the Christ title and the anointing of disciples have less importance in the *Gospel of Truth* than elsewhere. There is no explicit interest in the *Gospel of Truth* in the ritual practice of anointing or in an "apostolic succession" of anointing, both of which are more prominent in the *Gospel of Philip*, as we will see.

It is also noticeable, as we will see further in section 4, that there is no use of (Old Testament) scripture in connection with Jesus in the *Gospel of Truth*. As a result, while the Christ title has a certain degree of significance in the Gospel, it is not connected to the messianic exegetical tradition. That is, the *Gospel of Truth* does not activate the existing stock of prooftexts or themes in Jewish (and) Christian messianic discourse. The only exceptions are those themes that are part and parcel of early Christian literature, such as Jesus's identity as a savior figure.

2. Jesus's Vicarious Death in the Gospel of Truth

2.1 The Fact of Jesus's Death

The death of Jesus in the *Gospel of Truth* is a topic that has attracted considerable debate, principally over whether or to what degree it is physical and real.[13] Related to this question is the debate about whether the incarnation in the

---

11. These are hard to count, as it is not always clear when a reference to a "word" (ϣⲁϫⲉ) is christological and titular. Clear cases appear in *Gos. Truth* 16.34; 23.21; 23.33–34; 26.5; 35.30; 37.7–8; 37.11 (37.8 and 37.11 retain the Greek word ⲗⲟⲅⲟⲥ).

12. As Thomassen notes, the *Gospel of Truth* does not require the ritual dimension to make it comprehensible (*Spiritual Seed*, 165).

13. See, e.g., Arai, *Christologie des Evangelium Veritatis*, 93–96 ("Christus am Kreuz") and 100–105 ("Die Heilsbedeutung des Todes"); and see the discussion published following Barbara Aland, "Gnosis und Christentum," in *The School of Valentinus*, vol. 1 of *The Rediscovery of Gnosticism: Proceedings of the International Conference on Gnosticism at Yale, New Haven, Connecticut, March 28–31, 1978*, ed. Bentley Layton (Leiden: Brill, 1980), 330–50.

Gospel of Truth is real or merely apparent.[14] The passages referring to incarnation are tolerably clear in their talk of a real body of Jesus: especially telling
are the statements "his [sc. the Father's] love *made a body upon him*" (ⲁ ϭⲡ
ⲟⲩⲥⲱⲙⲁ ϩⲓⲱⲱϥ), and "when the Word, who is within those who speak it, came
into the middle region, it was not a mere voice *but made* [or, *became*] *a body*
(ⲁⲗⲗⲁ ⲁϥⲡ ⲟⲩⲥⲱⲙⲁ)."[15] Indeed, the contrast in the latter passage may even be
intended to *oppose* the idea of an incorporeal incarnation. On the other hand,
as will be discussed shortly, the reality of matter itself needs to be qualified.
The passages describing Jesus's death are similarly clear about the physicality
of Jesus, which is taken for granted in accounts of the crucifixion.

This section near the start of the Gospel is based on Rev 5 and probably
the Synoptic ransom saying. It begins with discussing the "children," who are
a symbol in some way for true disciples:

> In their hearts appeared the living book of the living, which is written in
> the thought and intellect of the Father and has from before the foundation
> of the All been in his impenetrable places. This book no one is able to take,
> since it is appointed that the one who does take it will be slaughtered. None
> of those who has believed for salvation was revealed until that book had
> come into their midst. The reason the merciful, faithful Jesus was patient,
> as he accepted his sufferings until he took up that book, was that he knew
> that his death meant life for the many.
>
> Just as when, before a will is opened, the estate of the householder who
> has died is secret, so it is in the case of the All that is hidden as long as the
> Father of the All is invisible (since he is unique of himself, the one from
> whom every place comes). For this reason, Jesus appeared and clothed
> himself with that book and was nailed to a tree. He published the decree of
> the Father on the cross.
>
> What magnificent teaching! He drags himself down to death, though
> clothed in eternal life! He stripped himself of his perishable rags and clothed
> himself with that imperishability that no one can take from him! He journeyed
> into the empty spaces of fear and passed through those who were stripped
> by oblivion, since he is knowledge and perfection. (*Gos. Truth* 19.34–20.39)

---

14. For some early debate, see Sasagu Arai, "Zur Lesung und Übersetzung des Evangelium Veritatis: Ein Beitrag zum Verständnis seiner Christologie," *NovT* 5 (1962): 216–18; see
Arai, *Christologie des Evangelium Veritatis*, 18, for a catalog of scholars on both docetic and
nondocetic sides at his time of writing.

15. *Gos. Truth* 23.30–31; 26.4–8. More ambiguous is *Gos. Truth* 31.4–6.

These assertions of Jesus wearing perishable rags, accepting his sufferings, being nailed to a tree, being slaughtered, and dragging himself down to death paint a picture of a real bodily figure.

The causes of Jesus's death can be described in different ways. At a theological level, the revelation that takes place in Jesus's death is obviously the Father's will. At the same time, it is the result of opposition to Jesus, and the *Gospel of Truth* sees both cosmic and human dimensions to this opposition. The crucifixion is the result both of Lady Error becoming enraged with Jesus and nailing him to a tree (*Gos. Truth* 18.21–24) and of "those wise in their own eyes" in the course of the incarnate ministry "hating" Jesus (19.18–26).

2.2 The Soteriological Significance of the Death as Revelation

As has already been noted, ignorance is one of the most basic ways in which the plight of the All and the individual person is described. It is the first consequence of the fall in the *Gospel of Truth*. Beyond what we saw earlier in the account of the fall, where ignorance generates "turmoil and fear" (*Gos. Truth* 17.10–11), that same ignorance means being in "great deficiency" (21.15–16) and induces a sleep-like state full of terrible nightmares (28.32–30.23). Hence the revelation of knowledge is an essential element of salvation.

This first passage employs the standard language for crucifixion, in the course of elucidating the revelatory significance of the cross:

> Therefore, Error grew furious at him and persecuted him,
>   but she was afflicted by him and brought to naught!
> He was nailed to a tree,
>   but became a fruit of the Father's knowledge!
> He did not wreak destruction in being eaten;
>   rather, he brought those who ate of him into being!
> They rejoiced in the discovery:
>   them he discovered in himself,
>   and him they discovered in themselves. (*Gos. Truth* 18.21–31)

Ironically, then, "grafting" Jesus onto a "tree" was good news, because in hanging on that tree, he became that tree's fruit. As the "fruit of the Father's knowledge" (i.e., fruit *that is* knowing the Father) Jesus reveals the truth. This is perhaps the main way in which the soteriology of the *Gospel of Truth* is expressed.

There is more play on words here, or development of the wood/tree language in a metaphorical direction. The Coptic term for "tree" here (ϣⲉ), like the Greek (ξύλον), is commonly used to mean "wood" or "tree," or "cross." Hence there is the potential for the cross to be a tree—which can bear fruit. As in John's Gospel, consuming the crucified Jesus is the way to salvation. In the *Gospel of Truth*, this eating is the acquisition of knowledge, both of Jesus and of oneself: "Them he discovered in himself, and him they discovered in themselves!"

Following immediately on from a passage about the hatred of Jesus by the "wise" is the description of his positive reception by the children (cf. Matt 11:25 // Luke 10:21). Here the focus of revelation is not on a fruit tree but on a book:

> After all of them [i.e., the "wise"], children came to him. To them belongs the knowledge of the Father. When they became strong, they learned the forms of the Father's face. They knew and were known. They received glory and gave glory. In their hearts appeared the living book of the living, which is written in the thought and intellect of the Father and has from before the foundation of the All been in his impenetrable places. This book no one is able to take, since it is appointed for the one who will take it and will be slaughtered. None of those who has believed for salvation was revealed until that book had come into their midst. The reason the merciful, faithful Jesus was patient, as he accepted his sufferings until he took up that book, was that he knew that his death meant life for the many. (*Gos. Truth* 19.27–20.14)

The possession by the "children" of the knowledge of the Father is therefore explicated in terms of the revelation they have received of "the living book of the living." In this book are written the hidden mysteries of the Father. As in Rev 5, Jesus is uniquely qualified to take up this scroll or book.[16] The death of Jesus is apparently either coterminous with, or inseparable from, his taking up the book of life. It is said here both that he "will take it and be slaughtered" and—apparently vice versa—that "he accepted his sufferings until he took up that book." The point is probably that the death of Jesus and the revelation of the book are one and the same event.

---

16. This book is identified with the scroll of Revelation in this passage. On the influence of Revelation, see Jacqueline A. Williams, *Biblical Interpretation in the Gnostic Gospel of Truth from Nag Hammadi* (Atlanta: Society of Biblical Literature, 1988), 37–44. There are echoes here both of Rev 5, where only Jesus is worthy to take the scroll (τὸ βιβλίον) and open it, and Rev 13:8 and 17:8 with the scroll or book (again, although usually rendered differently in English translations, βιβλίον) of life. Two of these three passages in Revelation also contain reference to Jesus as "slaughtered" (ἐσφάγης [5:9]; ἐσφαγμένου [13:8]), as does the *Gospel of Truth* here.

We saw in the discussion of *Gos. Truth* 18.21–31 that the knowledge that is gained in salvation is knowledge both of Jesus and of oneself. The arrival of the book here in *Gos. Truth* 19.27–20.14 is, even more richly, a revelation *in* Jesus's true disciples ("in their hearts appeared the living book of the living"), *among* them ("until that book had come into their midst"), and *of* them ("none . . . was revealed until that book had come into their midst").[17]

The passage continues with an illustration:

> Just as when before a will is opened the estate of the householder who has died is secret, so it is in the case of the All that is hidden as long as the Father of the All is invisible (since he is unique of himself, the one from whom every place comes). For this reason, Jesus appeared, clothed himself with that book, and was nailed to a tree. He published the testamentary disposition of the Father on the cross. (*Gos. Truth* 20.14–27)

The illustration of the will centers not so much on the death of the householder as on the will's hidden contents. Until a particular event takes place, the contents of the will and therefore the benefits accruing to the heirs will not be revealed. The householder in the illustration is not Jesus but the Father; the theme, however, suggests a revelatory death, and this is where the author immediately goes. Here Jesus actually *wears* the book in his death and thereby publishes the Father's "decree" (ⲆⲓⲀⲦⲀⲅⲘⲀ), or "testamentary disposition"; this Greek loanword refers to a royal decree in the four places in which it appears in the Bible, but in the papyri it can refer to an arrangement made in a will.[18] The publication of the Father's decree or testament and therefore of knowledge of him takes place on the cross, and so the thought in this passage is similar to what *Gos. Truth* 19–20 says about the book being revealed.

The passage goes on still further:

> What magnificent teaching! He drags himself down to death, though clothed in eternal life! He stripped himself of his perishable rags and clothed himself with that imperishability that no one can take from him! He journeyed into the empty spaces of fear and passed through those who were stripped by

---

17. On the different aspects of the book, see Thomassen, *Spiritual Seed*, 150–55.

18. For the former sense, see LXX Ezek 7:11; Esth 3:13; Wis 11:7; Heb 11:23. For the latter, see P. Oxy. X 1282 line 27; cf. P. Oxy. III 492 line 9 and III 493 line 6, where the verb διατάσσω is used in a testamentary setting. LSJ glosses the noun in this context as "testamentary disposition."

oblivion, since he is knowledge and perfection, proclaiming the things that are in the heart [. . .] the teaching for those who learn. Those who learn are those written in the book of the living. They learn their own selves as they receive from the Father a way back to him again. (*Gos. Truth* 20.27–21.8)

The poetic skill of the author here is more easily admired than understood. There is a clear reference to the crucifixion, understood as brought about by Jesus's own agency: this is no Johannine "lifting up"—in the *Gospel of Truth*, "he drags himself down." This death of Jesus is also a liberation from the corporeal flesh that he put on in the incarnation ("he stripped himself of his perishable rags"). Since matter is said in the *Gospel of Truth* to have been generated by "Error," such a view is hardly surprising. Jesus's death also involves or enables his entry into the realm of fear, a kind of hellish vacuum consisting of "empty spaces" and inhabited by "those who were stripped by oblivion." Given what we will see in section 2.4 below of the nature (for want of a better word) of the material world, this infernal vacuum is probably the material world: although the event is almost depicted as a kind of harrowing of hell, the reference is probably to Jesus's death on the cross as the salvation of the Father's children. Some uncertainty remains, and a lacuna in the text appears at a significant moment. Nevertheless, there is an important soteriological point that is clear. Jesus is a fitting savior in this author's theology, "since he is knowledge and perfection." As "knowledge," Jesus addresses the plight of ignorance, and as "perfection," he is the solution to the plight of deficiency. He provides salvation by "proclaiming the things that are in the heart [of the Father?]" in his death (*Gos. Truth* 20.39–21.1).

2.3 The Cross as Redemption

In addition to the revelatory dimension of Jesus's death, another passage probably echoes the ransom saying of Mark and Matthew:[19]

---

19. Mark 10:45; Matt 20:28. See Williams, *Biblical Interpretation*, 46–48. An alternative possibility is the eucharistic words of Jesus. This has been argued (specifically in connection with Matt 26:28) particularly by J. Christopher Edwards, *The Ransom Logion in Mark and Matthew: Its Reception and Its Significance for the Study of the Gospels* (Tübingen: Mohr Siebeck, 2012), 66–69. Edwards makes some good points, but his objections to an allusion to Mark 10:45 // Matt 20:28 are probably not persuasive (p. 68): (1) "there is no self-giving motif"—but Jesus accepts his sufferings knowing their saving results, and this is in connection with his mercy and faithfulness (rather than him simply being a victim); (2) while Edwards rightly notes that there is no explicit reference to redemption or ransom, a life-

The reason the merciful, faithful Jesus was patient, as he accepted his sufferings until he took up that book, was that he knew that his death meant life for the many. (*Gos. Truth* 20.10–14)

In the statement "his death meant life for the many" (ⲡⲓⲙⲟⲩ ⲛ̄ⲧⲟⲟⲧϥ̄ ⲟⲩⲱⲛϩ̄ ⲛ̄ϩⲁϩ ⲡⲉ), the cross is expounded more in redemptive terms. Although it is possible that life through the knowledge of revelation is still in view, perhaps a more obvious sense is of a life-for-life exchange. This language of redemption has been highlighted already in the prologue of the *Gospel of Truth*: "This Word is called 'savior,' the name of the work that he was to carry out for the redemption (ⲥⲱⲧⲉ) of those who did not know the Father" (16.37–17.1). In *Gos. Truth* 19.27–20.14, it is Jesus's death that secures or rescues the (presumably) otherwise forfeit lives of his disciples.

2.4 The Crucifixion as Cosmological Destruction

There is a further, more neglected dimension to the death of Jesus in the *Gospel of Truth*, namely, that in the crucifixion of Jesus, the material world is destroyed—with immediate revelatory and liberative consequences. This point needs to be argued in two parts, first clarifying the nature of matter and physicality in the *Gospel of Truth*, and second showing how this illuminates the meaning of the death of Jesus.

The Nature of Matter in the Gospel of Truth

We have so far accepted as highly probable that Jesus in the *Gospel of Truth* possesses a body of flesh. The passages touching upon Jesus's flesh and corporeality do, however, raise the question of what the nature of that flesh is.

As the introduction to this chapter has already briefly noted, the *Gospel of Truth* begins with a primeval myth of a "fall" as follows:

Since the All sought after the one from whom it had come forth, and the All had been within the uncontainable and inconceivable one who surpasses all thought, ignorance of the Father brought about turmoil and fear. Now

---

for-life exchange seems to be implied; (3) Edwards comments that "in Mark 10:45/Matthew 20:28 Jesus gives his life, but in GTr 20.13–14 Jesus' death is life." This is also true but hardly much of a contrast: in the Synoptic saying, Jesus giving his life means dying, and it is life for others, as the ransom language implies. Edwards is right, however, that an allusion (also?) to Matt 26:28 cannot be ruled out.

> turmoil condensed like a mist, such that no one was able to see. For this reason, Error (ⲡⲗⲁⲛⲏ) became powerful, and she worked upon her own matter (ϩⲩⲗⲏ) in vain. Not knowing the truth, she assumed a form (ⲡⲗⲁⲥⲙⲁ) that powerfully manufactured an attractive simulacrum of the truth.
>
> This, however, did nothing to diminish the uncontainable and inconceivable one, because turmoil and oblivion and the deceitful form (ⲡⲗⲁⲥⲙⲁ) were nothing, while the secure truth is unchangeable, imperturbable, and absolute beauty. Show nothing but contempt, then, for this Error! Hence, because she had no root, she was in a fog, ignorant of the Father, but still prepared there her works of oblivion and fear, so she could use them to entice those in the middle region and thereby imprison them. (*Gos. Truth* 17.4–36)

According to this protological myth, when the All falls out of the Father, it becomes ignorant of the Father. This ignorance in turn generates (or becomes) turmoil and fear. When the turmoil in turn condenses into a mist (*Gos. Truth* 17.11–14), that mist produces blindness. Through this blindness of the All, Lady Error grows powerful and works on her own matter (ϩⲩⲗⲏ); this matter seems to be the same as the condensed mist or fog. Therefore, she sets about sculpting herself to produce a material creation that is "a simulacrum of the truth" (ϫⲃ̄ⲃⲓⲱ ⲛ̄ϯⲧⲙⲛ̄ⲧⲙⲏⲉ [17.20–21]).[20] The author provides in the second paragraph cited above a kind of reassuring comment: to the enlightened, this is all insignificant.

As a result, in the protological backdrop to the historical activity of Jesus, physical "stuff" is the product of Error, indeed is Lady Error herself in material form: she came into being as a counterfeit image (ⲡⲗⲁⲥⲙⲁ). The metaphysical status of matter is therefore extremely precarious.

Elsewhere in the *Gospel of Truth*, this picture is reinforced. Error "is empty, since she has nothing in her" (*Gos. Truth* 26.26–27). Even though "she had no root" and "was in a fog, ignorant of the Father" (17.29–31), she still went about "preparing her works of oblivion and fear" (17.31–33). The world is a mere form: "When he [i.e., the Father] filled up the deficiency, he dissolved its form. Its form is the world that served it" (24.20–24).[21] The world is the "form" of deficiency and vanishes completely as soon as knowledge appears (24.28–32).

20. For Grobel, *Gospel of Truth*, 43, it is her own substance; cf. Bentley Layton, *The Gnostic Scriptures* (London: SCM, 1987), 253 n. 17c, where it belongs to her. Given that she undergoes some kind of transformation (ⲁⲥϣⲱⲡⲉ ϩⲛ ⲟⲩⲡⲗⲁⲥⲙⲁ), it is likely that she is working upon herself.

21. See also *Gos. Truth* 24.25–25.3; cf. 18.7–11.

The statement about the deficiency of matter (ⲡⲓⲱⲧⲱ ⲛ̄ϯⲉⲩⲗ︤ⲏ︥) probably means that matter simply *is* deficiency (35.9).

Given such theologoumena about the sensible world as mere deceptive image that is "nothing," a product of Lady Error who is mere vacuum with no root, it is tempting to draw the conclusion that the world of appearance and form is actually a privation of being, rather than having any ontological grip. Living in the cosmos according to the *Gospel of Truth* is like being in the Matrix.[22] A softer conclusion, which might also be consistent with the *Gospel of Truth*, is perhaps that matter has some kind of ontology but is fundamentally deceptive. Cut off from truth, it is a drifting mist that can only mislead.

Whichever way it is in the *Gospel of Truth*, however, all flesh and matter have a docetic character, either because it is unreal altogether or because it is bound to present itself falsely.

This helps to set up the question differently from the way the discussion of Jesus's incarnation and death in the *Gospel of Truth* is usually framed. Too often, the question seems to be whether the *Gospel of Truth* is orthodox or Gnostic: if it is orthodox, it cannot be docetic and so Jesus's body and death must have been real; if it is Gnostic, it must be docetic and so Jesus's body and death cannot have been real.[23] To pose the question this way is wrongheaded. The *Gospel of Truth* does not fit either of these approaches, because it is both docetic and nondocetic. (To put the point this way means of course that the term is not really appropriate to the Gospel.) The *Gospel of Truth* is not docetic, because Jesus took on a body, but in another sense, its theology is docetic, because matter is all illusory one way or another. Jesus's flesh is as real as flesh gets, but no flesh is (very) real, because the *Gospel of Truth* subscribes to a kind of pandocetism.[24] In this sense, Barbara Aland is right to emphasize that Jesus's body can only ever be "the false image of Error,"[25] but that does not mean it should be distinguished from any other human body.

Jesus's Death as the Destruction of Error's Creation

In addition to the revelatory and redemptive aspects of salvation provided by the cross, the conclusions just noted about the *Gospel of Truth*'s metaphysics mean that there may also be a cosmological component to the death of Jesus.

22. A reference to the film *The Matrix*, in which the characters inhabit a computer-generated reality.

23. See, e.g., the discussion after Aland's paper "Gnosis und Christentum."

24. I owe the term "pandocetism" to discussion of the *Gospel of Truth* with Dr. Mark Bonnington in the Durham New Testament Seminar.

25. Aland, "Gnosis und Christentum," 327: "das lügenhafte Gebilde der πλανή."

The first relevant passage is from the series of couplets already cited above, and the first couplet in particular:

> Error grew furious at him and persecuted him,
> but she was afflicted by him and brought to naught!
>
> (*Gos. Truth* 18.22–24)

As in the sentences that follow immediately after this one, there is a parallelism here between the first two clauses and the latter two. Given the cosmology of the *Gospel of Truth*, it is an attractive prospect to see here a direct connection between Error's persecution of Jesus and her own destruction. Since matter belongs to Lady Error herself, the connection between the cross and the destruction of Error appears to be:

(1) Error attacks Jesus, but her only access is to attacking his physical body,
(2) ergo in attacking Jesus's fleshly body, she is destroying matter that is actually her own self.

This move is made by Barbara Aland and perhaps also Einar Thomassen in their explanations of the "Christus victor" motif and the conquest of Error in the *Gospel of Truth*. Aland comments that Lady Error's crucifixion of Jesus is in fact a suicidal move: "Inasmuch as she does it, she is only persecuting and killing her own work, the deceitful image of the body, and thereby destroys herself. Thus God triumphs over the Nothing on the cross."[26] Thomassen says something similar in slightly different terms, assigning more agency to Jesus than to Error: "the Saviour must himself adopt the condition of empirical existence. This means he has to die; but in dying he also annuls the form of existence that is the cause of death."[27] Jesus's clothing of himself in flesh, then, is not merely for the purpose of revelation but also so that by the destruction of that flesh the nothingness that constitutes that flesh would be destroyed.

This connection is not made explicit in *Gos. Truth* 18.22–24 quoted above, and so this particular cosmological understanding of salvation in the *Gospel*

---

26. Aland, "Gnosis und Christentum," 327: "Aber indem sie das tut, verfolgt und tötet sie nur ihr eigenes Werk, das lügenhafte Gebilde des Körpers, und richtet sich damit selbst zugrunde. Am Kreuz triumphiert Gott also über das Nichtige." Cf. also similar formulations at 329. The point is disputed by H. Koester in the discussion appended to the essay (344–45).

27. Thomassen, *Spiritual Seed*, 154.

of Truth has not gained a lot of currency. There is a related, neglected passage, however, that may be able to bolster this theory:

> When the Word, who is within those who speak him, came into the middle region, he was not a mere voice but took a body. A great disturbance occurred among the vessels, with some being emptied and others being half filled, some being replenished and others being poured out, some remaining sealed, others getting broken. All the spaces were moved and disturbed because they did not have fixture and stability.
>
> Error grew anxious, not knowing what to do; she grieved and mourned, slashing herself (ⲉⲥⲱⲥϩ̄ ⲙ̄ⲙⲁⲥ) because she had no understanding. Since knowledge, which brings destruction to her and all her emanations, approached her, Error proved empty because she has nothing in her. (*Gos. Truth* 26.4–27)

The neglect of this passage in connection with *Gos. Truth* 18.22–24 and the cosmological consequences of Jesus's coming is probably a result of the difficulty of translating it. The key reference to Error "slashing herself" (ⲉⲥⲱⲥϩ̄ ⲙ̄ⲙⲁⲥ) has been variously rendered instead as "she was beside herself" (Isenberg),[28] or as "(she) cried out" (Layton);[29] closer are the renderings of "afflicting itself" (Attridge and MacRae) or "attacking herself" (Meyer).[30] Certainly the Coptic is unusual, as the root verb (ⲱϩⲥ)[31] usually means "to harvest."[32] However, it has a wider semantic field than English "harvest," as in the examples supplied by Crum of a garment being "cut" or "slashed" into pieces, as well as the metaphorical usage of persecutors being "mown down" in judgment;[33] it is cognate

---

28. Isenberg, "Gospel of Truth," 152, has the phrase "beside itself," without the personification.

29. Layton, *Gnostic Scriptures*, 258, perhaps reading the verb ⲱϣ?

30. Harold W. Attridge and George W. MacRae, "The Gospel of Truth," in *Nag Hammadi Codex I (The Jung Codex)*, ed. Harold W. Attridge (Leiden: Brill, 1985), 1:95; Marvin W. Meyer, ed., *The Nag Hammadi Scriptures* (New York: HarperOne, 2007), 41.

31. The transposition of ⲱϩⲥ as ⲱⲥϩ is very common. See W. E. Crum, *A Coptic Dictionary* (Oxford: Clarendon, 1939), 538b, and for post-Crum examples, Gos. Phil. 52.30, 31 (ⲱⲥϩ) and the noun in *Gos. Thom.* 21.10: "he came quickly with his sickle (ⲁⲥϩ) in hand." N. B. the scribal correction ⲧⲁⲱ⟦ϩ⟧ⲥϩ in *Gos. Thom.* 63.2, where the scribe deletes the former ϩ.

32. See Crum, *Coptic Dictionary*, 538b–539a, and the examples in the footnotes above.

33. Hans J. Polotsky, *Manichäische Homilien*, vol. 1 of *Manichäische Handschriften der Sammlung A. Chester Beatty* (Berlin: Kohlhammer, 1934), 15 (cited by Crum).

with the noun for sickle (variously, ⲟⲣⲥ, ⲁⲥⲣ, ⲁⲣⲥ).[34] Nor is there an obvious alternative Coptic root that could be seen here.

The reference, then, seems to be to self-destructive activity on the part of Lady Error. In this passage, the Word appeared and caused such distressing bewilderment to her that she slashes herself.

There is a certain comparable pattern in the two statements:

Gos. Truth 18.22–24	Gos. Truth 26.19–22
"Error grew furious at him	"Error grew anxious,
and persecuted him,	not knowing what to do;
but she was afflicted by him and brought	she grieved and mourned,
to naught!"	slashing herself."

While one cannot be certain, and *Gos. Truth* 26.4–27 is not explicitly connected specifically with Jesus's death, there is a strong probability that the combined force of the metaphorical language in the larger passages taken together indicates a destruction of Error through Jesus's physical death. This destruction comes not only through the divine plan of revelation but is also by her own hand. In her persecution of Jesus, she ends up slashing herself (26.4–27) and thereby is afflicted and destroyed (18.21–31). Her persecution of Jesus consists of putting to death the only dimension of Jesus to which she has access, namely his physical body that is actually composed of *her* own substance. Hence her attack on Jesus's body is in fact an attack on herself.

In sum, although this aspect of Jesus's death as cosmic destruction is not as prominent as the revelatory, there is a strong probability of its presence in the *Gospel of Truth*.

2.5 Interim Conclusion: Jesus's Death in the Gospel of Truth and the Kerygma

We can summarize in three points.

First, although we saw that Jesus appears in the *Gospel of Truth* to be in possession of real flesh, any talk of a real incarnation or a real death must be tempered by the observation that for the *Gospel of Truth* matter is not real. Hence everything material is in a sense to be understood docetically. On the other hand, nor can one say that Jesus does not take on a body of flesh.

---

34. Perhaps an English analogy is the verb "harrow," whose primary context is agricultural but which can also mean "to tear, lacerate, wound." See *OED*, s.v. "harrow," v. 1, §3a.

Second, in terms of the significance of Jesus's death, we have seen, from the echo of the ransom saying (Mark 10:45) in the words "his death meant life for the many," that the *Gospel of Truth*'s author is well aware of, and sympathetic to, a traditional understanding of Jesus's death as effective and vicarious. It goes well beyond this, however, and the saving effect is described through closely overlapping motifs. The death of Jesus is perhaps above all an event of revelation, in which knowledge of the Father is made known. This is expressed through the metaphors of the revelatory fruit hanging on a tree, a fruit that is Jesus himself, and of the book that is the exclusive property of Jesus and that is revelatory *in, among,* and even *of* the true disciples. It is published on the cross, and in his death on the cross, Jesus proclaims the knowledge of the Father. It could even be said that Jesus's death in the *Gospel of Truth* deals with sin. Forgiveness seems to be equivalent to the filling of the deficiency: in Jesus, fullness comes to the sinner, in order to bring salvation: "The reason that incorruptibility breathed forth and went after the one who had sinned was so he would come to rest. For forgiveness is what is left for the light in the deficiency, the word of the fullness" (*Gos. Truth* 35.24–29). Because the *Gospel of Truth* appears to have a tightly integrated theological system, the death of Jesus is related to almost every facet of the work.

Third, there is the probable cosmological effect of Jesus's death in Lady Error's suicidal attack on Jesus's material form. This theme is not as clear as the revelation of knowledge when Jesus hangs on the tree and takes up the book. The two key passages that describe the response of Error to Jesus (*Gos. Truth* 18.22–24; 26.19–22) taken together appear to indicate this additional dimension to the cross in the *Gospel of Truth*. In sum, the *Gospel of Truth* has all the ingredients of vicarious death in which the death of Jesus is necessary for salvation and is interpreted as the deliberate action of Jesus.

3. JESUS'S RESURRECTION AND THE GOSPEL OF TRUTH

Not many scholars talk nowadays of resurrection in the *Gospel of Truth*. Most standard expositions of the book make no mention of it at all. However, one does find occasional references to it in the scholarly literature. McGuire comments as if uncontroversially:

> Through his suffering and death on the cross, Christ became a "fruit of the knowledge of the Father" and published the decree (*diatagma*) of the Father.

Through his resurrection, he passed from perishability to imperishability, and called the "living ones written in the Book of the Living."[35]

There are three passages that have been proposed as potential references to the resurrection of Jesus, which we can examine in turn.

3.1 Potential Resurrection Passages in the Gospel of Truth

Gospel of Truth 20.27–39

The first of the three passages is alluded to in McGuire's comment quoted above and comes in a poetic discussion of the work of Jesus:

> What magnificent teaching! He drags himself down to death, though clothed in eternal life! He stripped himself of his perishable rags and clothed himself with that imperishability that no one can take from him! He journeyed into the empty spaces of fear and passed through those who were stripped by oblivion, since he is knowledge and perfection, proclaiming the things that are in the heart. (*Gos. Truth* 20.27–39)

Grobel saw in the statement of "that imperishability that no one can take from him" a reference to the risen Christ.[36] This is probably the most likely possibility for a reference to resurrection in the Gospel: Jesus clothing himself with imperishability comes after the reference to death, and there is a clear allusion to 1 Cor 15:53–54.[37] On the latter point, however, an allusion to 1 Cor 15 is not in itself a strong indicator, as the *Gospel of Truth*'s treatment of New Testament material often consists of "transposition" and "transformation."[38]

On the other hand, the "clothing with imperishability" in the *Gospel of Truth* might suggest resurrection because after death what is acquired is a body

---

35. Anne McGuire, "Conversion and Gnosis in the 'Gospel of Truth,'" *NovT* 28 (1986): 348; cf. also p. 353: "Through his teaching, death, and resurrection, he reveals the inconceivable God to be Father and enables those who are His to turn from ignorance to gnosis, anxiety and rootlessness to repose." Or again, on p. 347: "This knowledge is revealed not only through the teaching of Jesus Christ, but also through his death on the cross and his resurrection."

36. Grobel, *Gospel of Truth*, 69.

37. See Williams, *Biblical Interpretation*, 55–58.

38. See, e.g., Williams, *Biblical Interpretation*, 7, describing the *Gospel of Truth*'s use of Rev 5 as "transposing certain conceptions therein with the result that the eschatological context of the passage in Rev has been transformed," and further pp. 190–99.

of a different species (perishable vs. imperishable) but the same genus (clothing, i.e., a body). The difficulty here is that amid the metaphorical "clothes himself with that imperishability," there is no clear reference to a body: it is not clear that clothing in both cases is bodily. Furthermore, in the *Gospel of Truth* overall, imperishability and the material are opposites, as we saw earlier in the discussion of the death of Jesus. On the metaphysical assumptions of the *Gospel of Truth*, according to which the material has no real existence except of a negative kind, stripping off the perishable rags of Lady Error and being clothed with imperishability are probably the same thing. Therefore, the death and resurrection of Jesus are probably one and the same event.

Gospel of Truth 30.12–31

The following passage is seen by Wilson and Ménard as alluding to the resurrection of Jesus:[39]

> And it is good for the one who turns himself back and wakes up, and blessed is he who has opened the eyes of the blind.
>
> And the Spirit, rushing from waking him up, ran after him and gave his hand to the one who was lying flat on the ground, and stood him up on his feet as he had not yet risen up. He enabled them to understand the knowledge of the Father and the revelation of the Son. For when they saw him and heard him, he granted them the taste and the smell and the grasp of the beloved Son. (*Gos. Truth* 30.12–31)

There is a prima facie attractiveness to seeing resurrection here on the basis of (1) the Spirit raising "him" up (cf. Rom 1:4; 8:11), (2) the standard resurrection language (ⲧⲱⲟⲩⲛ in 30.23), and (3) the mention of "grasping" the Son (cf. Matt 28:9 and John 20:17?).

On the other hand, the major difficulty with taking this as a reference to Jesus in the *Gospel of Truth* is the immediate context. The author has just been writing of those who do not know the Father, and of how their lives are like a nightmarish unreality consisting of violent and irrational dreams (*Gos. Truth* 28.32–29.32). When one abandons ignorance, however, one wakes up or rises up. On waking, it becomes clear that the dream had no reality. This

---

39. So Robin McL. Wilson, *The Gnostic Problem: A Study of the Relations between Hellenistic Judaism and the Gnostic Heresy* (London: Mowbray, 1958), 160: "it evidently refers to the resurrection of Jesus"; and Ménard, *Évangile de Vérité*, 139, perhaps less confidently.

is the immediate prelude to the account of the Spirit waking the prone figure and setting him upright; hence it is obvious that this is not a reference to the resurrection of Jesus. Additionally, although depending on how one divides the units of the text, it is probable that the one who is raised up is enabled by the Spirit "to understand the knowledge of the Father and the revelation of the Son." It would be odd to say that in his own resurrection, Jesus came to understand the revelation of the Son.

The background to this passage is more likely to be second-century understandings of the creation of Adam. Hence, for example, Irenaeus's report of creation according to Saturninus/Saturnilus is described in very similar terms:

> When he [i.e., man] had been made, and what was formed could not stand erect because of the angels' weakness but wriggled like a worm, the Power above took pity on him because he was made in its likeness, and it sent a spark of life which raised the man and made him upright and made him live. (Irenaeus, *Haer.* 1.24.1)[40]

The thought of an initially inert or not yet upright human, who is only later enlivened, appears in numerous other places.[41] The parallel in Irenaeus, along with the incongruity about understanding the revelation of the Son noted above, makes it apparent that a resurrection of Christ is not in view here.[42] As Attridge and MacRae comment, what this is really about is the "new creation of the human being who receives the revelatory Gnosis."[43]

Gospel of Truth 30.32–31.13

Finally, another passage alludes to John's resurrection narrative:

> When he appeared, he gave them understanding of the inconceivable Father. He breathed into them what is in Thought, doing his will. And re-

---

40. Trans. Robert M. Grant, *Gnosticism: An Anthology* (London: Collins, 1961), 31.

41. E.g., Irenaeus, *Haer.* 1.30.6; *Ap. John* (NHC II) 19.10–15; *Nat. Rulers* 87.33–88.10; Hippolytus, *Haer.* 5.7.6.

42. Nor, however, is Jesus clearly the one effecting the resurrection, *pace* Arai, *Christologie*, 79.

43. Attridge and MacRae, "Gospel of Truth," 86; similarly McGuire, "Conversion and Gnosis," 353 n. 44: "GTr 30.6–26 may be read as a reinterpretation of Gnostic readings of the Genesis account of the creation of Adam. Especially suggestive is the image of the one who could not rise without Gnosis."

ceiving the light, many were turned to him. The material ones, however, were strangers and did not see his likeness and did not know him. For he came by means of the form of flesh, yet nothing blocked his path because his indestructibility meant that he could not be grasped. Furthermore, he spoke what was new because he spoke what was in the heart of the Father, and brought forth the word that had no deficiency. (*Gos. Truth* 30.32–31.13)

This passage has been credited with a reference to resurrection on two counts. First, there is the reference to Jesus breathing into the disciples, an event clearly evocative of John 20:22.[44] Williams submits this as only a possibility, however, and in view of the *Gospel of Truth*'s frequent transposition of New Testament material, there is little to commend the idea that a reference to John's Gospel on its own would carry its context with it into the *Gospel of Truth*. Second, it has been suggested that coming in the form of flesh, with nothing blocking the way (cf. John 20:19, 26?), evokes a postresurrection context.[45] Again, however, this cannot be assumed, for the same reason: the Johannine setting should not be presumed to be carried over into the *Gospel of Truth*. Judging by the context, the incarnation seems more likely to be in view.

Conclusion

There is thus no compelling evidence for anything more than resurrection *imagery*. Allusions may be made to 1 Cor 15 or John 20, but it is entirely in keeping with the *Gospel of Truth*'s approach to the New Testament that such language is transposed into another context.

3.2 Interim Conclusion: Jesus's Resurrection in the Gospel of Truth and the Kerygma

It has been averred by some that there is no need for resurrection in the *Gospel of Truth* because of the accomplishment of the death of Jesus. As Barbara Aland has commented, "The cross documents the self-ruination of the Nothing. It is the triumph of God over the Nothing. There is no talk of a resurrection.

---

44. Williams, *Biblical Interpretation*, 113.

45. So Robert M. Grant, *Gnosticism and Early Christianity* (New York: Columbia University Press, 1966), 131: "after his resurrection he 'came in flesh of similitude' (p. 31.4); 'nothing could obstruct his course' (p. 31.5; see also John 20.19, 26)."

The cross correlates with the meaning of the resurrection."[46] This may have rather too much of an a priori feel: as we have seen, scholars have made similar assertions about the Gospel of John despite the fact that there are two chapters of resurrection appearances on top of other allusions to the resurrection in Jesus's teaching there. On the other hand, in the case of the *Gospel of Truth*, it appears to be accurate.

In sum, it is hard to see how the *Gospel of Truth* could entertain the idea of Jesus taking on any sort of material form again, given the work's metaphysical and cosmological presuppositions about matter being a product of Error. Despite the Valentinian interest in resurrection in other literature, such as the obvious example of the *Treatise on the Resurrection*, the *Gospel of Truth* is not fired by such interest. The *Gospel of Truth* therefore does not reflect the kerygma on this point in the way that its interest in the death of Jesus does.

4. Scripture and the Gospel of Truth

As we saw in the introduction, the myth in the *Gospel of Truth* is in some sense a past reality that maps on to the historical events of Jesus's saving activity. If this is the case, might there be an element of scriptural fulfillment in the *Gospel of Truth*? Unfortunately, there does not seem to be any antecedent textual revelation.[47] This is not to say that the *Gospel of Truth* rejects other texts; it contains dozens of allusions to the New Testament.[48] As far as the Old Testament is concerned, there is just one potential allusion of an implicit nature.[49] Layton takes the passage in which Jesus "was nailed to a tree and became the fruit of the knowledge of the Father" as part of a contrast in the context between

46. Aland, "Gnosis und Christentum," 329: "Das Kreuz dokumentiert die Zugrunde-richtung des Nichtigen durch sich selbst. Es ist Triumph Gottes über das Nichtige. Von Auferweckung ist nicht die Rede. Das Kreuz entspricht dem Sinngehalt der Auferweckung."

47. There are other "texts" mentioned in the *Gospel of Truth*: the "living book of the living" is an important concern, and one analogy used to describe it is a human last will and testament (19.34–21.25). Cf. also the "living book" in *Gos. Truth* 22.37–23.18.

48. See the marginalia in Layton, *Gnostic Scriptures*, 253–64.

49. Layton, *Gnostic Scriptures*, 259, 261, suggests some other possible scriptural allusions: Gen 3:5, as a possible source for the macarism "blessed is the one who has opened the eyes of the blind!" (*Gos. Truth* 30.14–16), and Gen 2:7, as perhaps lying behind the phrase ογπλαсμα ἤγγχικοn, possible but more tenuous. The use of Gen 2:7 is almost certainly indirect, via John 20:22. For discussion, see Williams, *Biblical Interpretation*, 109–13: she labels direct use from Genesis as "possible" but the influence of John as "probable."

the tree of the cross and the tree of the knowledge of good and evil.[50] This is probable, because of the reference to Jesus as the fruit of the knowledge of the Father on the tree, the fruit that "does *not* bring ruin," in contrast presumably to the tree of knowledge in Genesis that did (*Gos. Truth* 18.11–33).[51] This may be the tip of an exegetical iceberg, but it is unclear what the particular iceberg might be. There may be presupposed here a wider discourse about the fall, expressible in terms other than those found expounded in the *Gospel of Truth*. Or alternatively, there may be a kind of law/gospel contrast. The contrast might even be with an account of the fall that it rejects altogether, as "not *X* but *Y*" obviously does not presuppose that the author views the source of *X* as authoritative. It is hard to assess one solitary case.

Rather than there being any appeal to external prophecy due for fulfillment, in the *Gospel of Truth* the backstory to the activity of the incarnate Jesus in history is written into the text itself, in the mythological backdrop. This protological myth is not "promise" or precursory testimony in some other way but rather is part of the Gospel itself.[52] A partial analogy in this respect is John, where the Gospel's prologue functions as a kind of backdrop to the action of the Gospel, although John also makes extensive use of Israel's scripture as well.[53]

CONCLUSION: THE GOSPEL OF TRUTH AND THE KERYGMA

We can sum up the individual contributions of these four sections. First, there seems to be agreement among commentators on the *Gospel of Truth* that any significance of the Christ title is to be sought within the work itself, in relation to wider usage in Valentinian literature, and in the context of broader early Christian usage. There is overlap between the New Testament and the *Gospel of Truth* in their application of anointing imagery from the Christ title and further to Christians. On the other hand, the *Gospel of Truth* has no interest in the messiah as connected to Israel and its biblical and postbiblical tradition,

---

50. Layton, *Gnostic Scriptures*, 254, noting Gen 2:17 and 3:7.

51. There is some debate over the translation of the passage, on whether the fruit does not destroy or is not destroyed. Scholars tend to assume the former. See Grobel, *Gospel of Truth*, 53; Ménard, *Évangile de Vérité*, 89; and Attridge and MacRae, "Gospel of Truth," 51.

52. See further Simon Gathercole, "*Praeparatio Evangelica* in Early Christian Gospels," in *Connecting Gospels: Beyond the Canonical/Non-canonical Divide*, ed. Francis Watson and Sarah Parkhouse (Oxford: Oxford University Press, 2018), 17–20.

53. I am grateful to Francis Watson, in the response to the conference version of the article noted above, for this observation.

and strikes out in a new direction in seeing Jesus qua Christ primarily as the agent of spiritual anointing. There is no sense that the *Gospel of Truth* retains an interest in scriptural discourse, in "the grammar of messianism."[54] This is borne out further in the final section, the discussion of the Old Testament in the *Gospel of Truth*, where there is apparently little relation between the two. Nor is there much indication of any interest in resurrection; indeed, a return on Jesus's part to an embodiment in Lady Error's fabricated matter would be quite out of place in the *Gospel of Truth*.

More positively, however, the *Gospel of Truth* does have a strong interest in the saving death of Jesus. In that respect, it corresponds to the kerygma. That death is the death of a embodied figure, the incarnate Word who "was not a mere voice but took a body" (*Gos. Truth* 26.4–8) and who subsequently was crucified and died (19.34–20.39). This death consists of revelation (sec. 2.2), redemption (sec. 2.3), and—through the suicidal attack of Lady Error on her own material—cosmological destruction (sec. 2.4). This last element is not quite as clear as the others, but if it is there, it represents the *Gospel of Truth*'s most original contribution to the presentation of Jesus's death in early Christian Gospels.

54. Referring here to the title of Novenson's book.

Chapter Twelve

THE GOSPEL OF PHILIP

Although there are only a few sayings of Jesus in the *Gospel of Philip*, Christ and his saving activity are still the focus of the work. The Gospel is not narrative in form, but it does presuppose a narrative outline of Jesus's earthly career, albeit from some perspectives an unconventional one. Jesus is straightforwardly the seed of Joseph (Gos. Phil. 73.8–19),[1] and there is a denial of the virgin birth, or at least of the conception by the Holy Spirit (55.23–36): the Father is said to have united with the virgin, but she is "the virgin who came down."[2] Jesus was baptized, with one of the references to the event expressing Jesus's need to fulfill all righteousness.[3] There are allusions to various canonical Gospel passages, such as the parable of the good Samaritan (78.7–9) or the Johannine Jesus's statement about eating and drinking his flesh and blood (57.3–5). The name "Jesus" is commonly used, along with "Lord," "Son of Man," and "Son"; furthermore, "(the) man" is perhaps employed in some kind of titular or ideal sense.[4] The figure of Jesus, his career, and saving activity, then, are instantly recognizable and connect the subject matter of the *Gospel of Philip* with that of other early Christian Gospels. This chapter is also placed deliberately next to the treatment of the *Gospel of Truth* in the previous chapter, as the *Gospel of Truth* and the *Gospel of Philip* both seem likely to be

---

1. This point is made without qualification, and a theological point is deduced from the fact.

2. Gos. Phil. 71.4–5. Shortly afterward, there is mention that "Christ was born of a virgin," but in the logion as a whole, this is contrasted with Adam's birth from two virgins, "the Spirit and the virgin earth": hence the term "virgin" appears to be one of the many words in the *Gospel of Philip* that needs to be decoded. See further section 4 of this chapter, on scripture in the *Gospel of Philip*, for further discussion of the Gospel's cryptography.

3. Gos. Phil. 70.34–71.3; 72.29–73.1.

4. For Jesus (perhaps) as "the man," see Gos. Phil. 54.31–55.5; 62.35–63.4.

products of the Valentinian movement. As in previous chapters, the focus in this discussion of the *Gospel of Philip* will be on the reception of the four familiar themes of Jesus as Christ, his saving death and resurrection, and their fulfillment of scripture.

1. THE CHRIST TITLE IN THE GOSPEL OF PHILIP

In contrast to only two instances in the *Gospel of Truth*, the title "Christ" appears twenty-two times in the surviving text of the *Gospel of Philip*, and "messiah" (ʍⲉⲥⲥⲓⲁⲥ) on a further three occasions.[5] Two of the Christ references are designations not of Jesus per se but of disciples.[6] The *Gospel of Philip*, as we shall see, is also unusual (though not unique) among the Nag Hammadi Codices, in using the term "Christian" (7×). Some of the statements in the *Gospel of Philip* are more immediately explicable as purposeful uses of the Christ title than others.[7]

1.1 The Mission of Christ

The coming of a Christ figure is a common collocation in both the New Testament and in prior Jewish literature.[8] One substantial set of uses of the Christ title in the *Gospel of Philip*, accounting for eight of the twenty instances referring to Jesus (rather than Christians), is in reference to his coming:[9]

Ever since Christ came, the world has been created, cities have been adorned, and the dead have been carried off. (Gos. Phil. 52.9–11)

Before Christ came, there was no bread in the world, just as Paradise where Adam lived had many trees to feed the wild animals but had no wheat to feed man. Man fed like the wild animals. But when Christ, the perfect man,

---

5. Christ: Gos. Phil. 52.19, 35; 55.6, 11; 56.4, 7, 9, 13; 61.30, 31; 62.9, 10, 12, 15; 67.27; 68.17, 20; 69.7; 70.13; 71.19; 74.16; 80.1. Messiah: Gos. Phil. 56.8; 62.8, 11.

6. Gos. Phil. 61.31; 67.27.

7. One instance, not discussed below, is in a simple reference to "Jesus Christ" (Gos. Phil. 80.1).

8. John 4:25; 7:27, 31, 41–42; 1 Tim 1:15; 1 John 4:2; 5:6; 2 John 7; cf. *mšyḥ* and *bwʾ* in CD-B XIX, 10–11; 1QS IX, 11; 4Q252 V, 3.

9. Including references (not discussed at length in this chapter) to "before Christ (came)" (Gos. Phil. 68.17–22) and to the purpose of his birth (71.18–21).

came, he brought bread from heaven so that man could be fed with human food. (Gos. Phil. 55.6–14)

The relationship between Christ's coming and "the world has been created, cities have been adorned, and the dead have been carried off" is not immediately obvious.[10] The former passage (52.9–11) does makes sense in the *Gospel of Philip*, however, when taken together with the discussion of sacrifice in the latter (55.6–14). Probably both excerpts are discussing a new, humanly civilized creation, which fits in the *Gospel of Philip* when one observes there that before Christ, human beings ate like animals, worshiped animals, and even *were* animals in human form.[11] When "Christ, the perfect man, came," he (metaphorically) established a properly functioning humanity, with decorated cities rather than wilderness where wild animals live, and with the dead being taken away rather than left unburied.[12]

Three more passages thematize the coming of Christ as a savior:

Christ came to ransom some, to rescue others, and to redeem still others. He ransomed strangers and made them his own. (Gos. Phil. 52.35–53.3)

Before Christ, some came forth from where they could no longer go in, and others went into a place from which they could no longer come out. But Christ came, and those who had gone in he brought out, and those who had gone out he brought in. (Gos. Phil. 68.17–22)

Had the female not separated from the male, she would not have died with the male. His separation marked the beginning of death. Therefore, Christ came to put right the separation that had existed from the beginning, to reunite the two and to give life and union to those who had died in the separation. (Gos. Phil. 70.9–17)

In the *Gospel of Philip*, then, the coming of Christ is an epoch-defining moment; the same event is expressed elsewhere in connection with Christ's birth

10. Hence Schenke attaches "since Christ came" to what precedes, but this seems syntactically less likely, even if "he is alive since Christ came" is theologically more apropos. See Hans-Martin Schenke, ed. and trans., *Das Philippus-Evangelium (Nag-Hammadi-Codex II, 3)* (Berlin: Akademie, 1997), 14–15.

11. Eating like animals: Gos. Phil. 55.6–14; worshiping animals: 54.36–55.4 (cf. 62.35–63.4); being animals: 81.7–8.

12. Cf. also Gos. Phil. 60.15–34.

(Gos. Phil. 71.18–21). Before Christ came, there was inescapable dislocation ("some came forth from where they could no longer go in, and others went into a place from which they could no longer come out"), death and disunity (Adam's and Eve's "separation became the beginning of death"). After Christ came, and not only post hoc but also propter hoc, these plights were addressed. Beyond the fact that the *Gospel of Philip* is tapping into a conventional collocation of "Christ" and "coming," sometimes with a soteriological explanation (e.g., 1 Tim 1:15), it is not clear that there is much particularly connected with the Christ title here, since elsewhere it is "Jesus" who is said to have come to bring salvation.[13]

1.2 Etymological Interpretations of "Messiah" and "Christ"

Besides reference to Christ's coming, the other main locus of the *Gospel of Philip*'s reference to Jesus as "Christ" is in the work's thematization of the term's meaning (accounting for nine or ten of the twenty references).[14] The *Gospel of Philip*, like other Valentinian literature, has an intense interest in the potential theological significance of names and titles.

Some of the explanations can still be enigmatic, however, as here:

"Jesus" is a hidden name, "Christ" is a manifest name. Therefore, Jesus is not a word in any language, but Jesus is his name, by which he is called. His name "Christ," however, is in Aramaic *Messias* but in Greek *Christos*.[15] Perhaps everyone else has a word for it in their own language. "Nazarene" is a manifestation of what is hidden. Christ has everything in him, whether man or angel or mystery or Father. (Gos. Phil. 56.3–15)

The main point made here is that Christ is a kind of relative title, particular to Greek because it is a translation of a Semitic-language original, and which

---

13. Gos. Phil. 63.24; 73.23–27; cf. "Son of Man" in Mark 10:45; Matt 20:28; Luke 19:10.

14. It is unclear whether Gos. Phil. 56.3–13 and 56.13–15 are really connected, and whether the reference to "Christ" in Gos. Phil. 56.13–15 has particular significance, or could not merely be substituted for "Jesus" or "the Lord." Hence nine or ten.

15. For the translation "Aramaic" here, it should be remembered that the distinction between Aramaic and Syriac is in any case an early-modern rather than an ancient one. I am grateful to Dr. Peter Williams for pointing out to me that the distinction goes back only to Tremellius in the sixteenth century. See also Bas van Os, "Was the Gospel of Philip Written in Syria?," *Apocrypha* 17 (2006): 87–93, esp. 91–93, concluding that the reference is to "Aramaic as the language of the apostles" (93).

could potentially be a different word in each language. The *Gospel of Philip* deduces this from the fact that "'Jesus' is a hidden name, 'Christ' is a manifest name." Presumably, then, *Christos* is a title that is "manifest" as a word publicly available already in the Greek language.[16] A possible explanation of "Jesus" being a hidden name is that—in contrast to being a part of a language's quotidian lexicon, like *Christos*—it is something that was revealed specially by God, which would make sense if the author knew of the angelic announcement in Matt 1:20–21 and/or Luke 1:30–31. This is not particularly far-fetched, given the *Gospel of Philip*'s knowledge of the Gospels more broadly. On this scenario, "hidden" means not permanently secret but something like a biblical "mystery" (μυστήριον), which was hidden but has now been revealed.

We do not yet have an interpretation of the title "Christ," but this comes in another, similar passage:

> The apostles who came before us called him "Jesus, Nazoraean, messiah," which means "Jesus, Nazoraean, Christ." The last name is "Christ," the first is "Jesus," and the one in the middle is "Nazarene." "Messiah" has two meanings, both "Christ" and "measured." "Jesus" in Hebrew means "redemption." "Nazara" means "truth," and so "Nazarene" means "truth." The Christ is the one who is "measured," and so "Nazarene" and "Jesus" are measured. (Gos. Phil. 62.6–18)

Here the interpretation is not of the Greek word *Christos* but of the Semitic *Messias*. It is not clear what the significance of Christ being the *last* name is: perhaps the order is alphabetical (ι, υ, χ). The interpretation of the Semitic *Messias* as "measured" does not come out of thin air: just as there is an Aramaic verb *mšḥ* meaning "anoint," there is also a different verb, spelled identically, that means "to measure."[17] Van Unnik provides a possible explanation of the

---

16. Tertullian offers this as a possibility that an opponent might entertain in *Marc.* 3.15: "If in your opinion the name of Christ is a common noun, just as the name of god is, with the result that it is permissible for the sons of each of two gods to be called Christ, as also for each <of those gods> to be called father <and> lord, assuredly reason will controvert this proposition. . . . The name of Christ, which comes not from nature but from revelation, becomes the peculiar property of him by whom it is known to have been fore-ordained." See Ernest Evans, *Tertullian: Adversus Marcionem* (Oxford: Clarendon, 1972), 214 (text) and 215 (for the translation cited here).

17. According to the CAL database, http://cal.huc.edu/, it is a widely attested verb across a number of different Aramaic dialects (e.g., Qumran, Targumic, Samaritan, Syriac, and Christian Palestinian Aramaic).

connection between Jesus and "measuring," alluding to Irenaeus's quotation of a predecessor: "And the person spoke well when he said, 'The immeasurable Father is himself measured in the Son, for the Son is the measure of the Father, since he also comprehends him.'"[18] If this sense is carried by the reference to Messiah meaning "measured," it could be an allusion to the incarnation.

There is also the etymological connection of Christ and the anointing of disciples:

> By the Holy Spirit we are born again, and equally we are born through Christ—it is by both. We are anointed by the Spirit. When we are born, we are united. No one can see himself either in the water or in a mirror without light. Nor, conversely, can you see yourself in the light without water or mirror. Hence baptism must be in both, in light and water—the light is the chrism. (Gos. Phil. 69.4–14)

The use of the term "Christ" here does not appear to be accidental, because of the connection with anointing. The statement "we are anointed by the Spirit" seems to be an explanation of the dual agency of rebirth, through the Spirit and Christ in unison ("it is by both"). Here we have the first hint of the etymologizing of the Greek term Christ, which is developed in the final passage:

> The chrism is superior to baptism. For from the chrism we are called "Christians" (not because of the baptism), and Christ was named after the chrism. For the Father anointed the Son, the Son anointed the apostles, and the apostles anointed us. Whoever is anointed has everything—the resurrection, the light, the cross, and the Holy Spirit. The Father has given him this from the bridal chamber, and the person received it. The Father was in the Son, and the Son was in the Father. This is the kingdom of heaven. (Gos. Phil. 74.12–24)

Here we have an interpretation of the Christ title widespread in other early Christian literature, as we saw above in the discussion of the *Gospel of Truth* where

---

18. Irenaeus, *Haer.* 4.4.2: *Et bene qui dixit ipsum immensum Patrem in Filio mensuratum: mensura enim Patris Filius, quoniam et capit eum* (Rousseau and Doutreleau, 4/2, 420–21). See further Willem C. van Unnik, "Three Notes on the Gospel of Philip," in *Patristica, Gnostica, Liturgica*, part 3 of *Sparsa Collecta* (Leiden: Brill, 1983), 239. To van Unnik's example, we can add a fragment of Theodotus, which compares earthly bodies with heavenly realities, and states that the latter are bodiless by comparison. By the same token, however, those heavenly forms are "measured and perceptible" by comparison with the Son, as the Son is by comparison with the Father (Clement of Alexandria, *Exc.* 11).

Jesus qua Christ anoints his disciples. The *Gospel of Philip* takes this further: Jesus is anointed by the Father, and he anoints others.[19] There is an apostolic succession of Father, Son, apostles, and "us" Valentinians, and all three cognate terms appear here: Christ (ⲭⲣⲓⲥⲧⲟⲥ), Christian (ⲭⲣⲓⲥⲧⲓⲁⲛⲟⲥ), and chrism (ⲭⲣⲓⲥⲙⲁ). "Chrism" is seen as the root term from which the other two derive, because, although the anointing relationship is asymmetrical, both Christ and the Christian are recipients of anointing. This commonality between Christ and the Christian is developed in two other passages, which are perhaps more surprising.

1.3 The Democratization of the Christ Title

There are several points at which the *Gospel of Philip* indicates that Jesus represents humanity as a whole. In one logion, for example, a clearly christological reference appears in connection with Christ's death and the preceding sacrificial cult: "God is a man-eater. Therefore, the man is sacrificed to him. Before the man was sacrificed, wild beasts were sacrificed because the recipients of the sacrifices were not gods" (Gos. Phil. 62.35–63.4). Perhaps more surprising is the way in which the true disciple can also be a Christ. There are two passages that, in different ways, develop this theme.

In this first passage, the particular visionary soteriology of the *Gospel of Philip* comes to expression:

> It is impossible for anyone to see anything in reality unless that person becomes like the object. It is not like this for the man in the world. He sees the sun without becoming a sun, and he sees the sky and the earth and everything else without becoming those things.
>
> But this is how it is in the truth: in fact, you saw something of the beyond, and you became like those there; you saw the Spirit, and you became Spirit; you saw Christ, and you became a Christ; you saw the Father, and you will become Father. Therefore, [in this realm] you see everything but you do not see yourself, but there you see yourself. For what you see is what you become. (Gos. Phil. 61.20–35)

Here, just as Jesus came and appeared in such a way that he could be seen (Gos. Phil. 57.28–32), the converse of this is that the human visionary assumes the nature of the object of vision in order to be able to see it. The passage begins

19. Cf. Heb 1:8–9; Luke 4:18; Acts 4:26–27. See Matthew V. Novenson, *The Grammar of Messianism* (Oxford: Oxford University Press, 2017), 233–35.

by contrasting the normal state of affairs in this world with what happens "in reality." Activity in the latter sphere is encapsulated in the concluding aphorism: "For what you see is what you become." On seeing Christ, the disciple becomes a Christ.

A second passage offers a different reason for the disciple having the right to the title:

> Truth has not come into the world naked but has come in types and images. The world cannot receive it any other way. There is rebirth along with an image of rebirth; truly one must be reborn by the image. What is it? The resurrection. The image must rise by the image, the bridal chamber, and its image must come, by the image, into the truth that is the restoration.
>
> This is necessary not only for those who have gained the name of the Father and the Son and the Holy Spirit but also for those who have gained them for you. If one does not gain them for himself, the name will also be taken from him. A person receives them in the chrism of the [. . .] of the cross's power. This power the apostles called "the right" and "the left." For the person is no longer a Christian but is a Christ. (Gos. Phil. 67.9–27)

The explanation of the Christian becoming a "Christ" that lies closest to hand is that the person "receives them [i.e., Father, Son, and Holy Spirit] in the chrism." The chrism is almost certainly not purely metaphorical but evokes the Valentinian ritual context. Despite a lacuna, it seems clear enough that "the cross's power" is somehow involved in the saving event, as, earlier on in the section cited, are rebirth and resurrection. Whether there is a specific logical relation between "the right and the left" and labeling the disciple as a "Christ" is not certain. It would seem in keeping with the hermeneutic of the *Gospel of Philip* to see the cross, by virtue of its shape (whether T or †), as uniting "right and left": one of Jesus's missions, according to a passage shortly after this one, is to resolve such dualities.[20] (Differences between such opposites as "right and left" are not real or ultimate because the elements in the pairings are compresent, according to Gos. Phil. 53.14–20.) In this sense, the Christ title may mark the perfect disciple as embodying union and oneness—in this passage, the union of image with image, which takes place in the restoration in the bridal chamber.

Overall, then, the application of the Christ title to Christians means, to make an obvious point, that it is no longer the unique preserve of a single

20. Gos. Phil. 67.30–35: the passage is, however, very lacunose.

person. This is because of the resolution of dichotomies. In the first passage, it is the resolution of the dichotomy of seer and seen, of the visionary and that divine realm that is the object of vision. In the second passage, there is the resolution of the image above and the image below in the bridal chamber and of the right and the left in (probably) the cross. Christ, as a son, not a creature, has the ability to generate. Hence Christ, the perfect man, generates others to be like him, and so they are entitled to the label.

1.4 Interim Conclusion: The Gospel of Philip's Christ and the Kerygma

The Christ title is therefore of major significance in the *Gospel of Philip*, in contrast to its relatively minor place in the theologically similar *Gospel of Truth*. Three principal contexts of the title together account for all but one of the uses of the Greco-Coptic "Christ," and two of the three references to the term *Messias*:[21] (1) the mission of Jesus, in which Jesus's earthly activity is summarized; (2) the philological investigation, so beloved of the Valentinians, of the meaning of the Christ title, and its origins in the Semitic term "messiah"; and (3) the distinctive application of the title to Jesus's disciples as well. The importance of the Christ title is reflected not only in the three references to the Semitic *Messias* but also in ten references to "chrism" (ⲭⲣⲓⲥⲙⲁ), twelve uses of the verb "anoint" (ⲧⲱϩⲥ̄), and three instances of "ointment" (ⲥⲟϭⲛ̄). There are also seven references to "Christian," and as far as I am aware, the *Gospel of Philip* accounts for all but one of the mentions of the term "Christian" in the Nag Hammadi Codices and is the only Nag Hammadi work to make positive use of the title.[22] These statistics are striking in a work only about two-thirds of the length of the Gospel of Mark. The degree of intentional deployment of the title is also noticeable, given the clustering of the usage in the three contexts noted.

The usage of "Christ" in the *Gospel of Philip* is in part conventionally Christian: the first set of references, alluding to Christ's mission, draws on familiar language especially in John's Gospel and the New Testament epistles.[23] The etymologizing is partly found already in earlier Christian literature, as noted, but

---

21. As noted, there is a bare reference to "Jesus Christ" in Gos. Phil. 80.1, and one of the instances of *Messias* simply says it is equivalent to "Christ."

22. The term also appears in *Testim. Truth* 31.22–32.3: "Foolish people think in their hearts that if they make the confession, 'We are Christians,' in word but not in power, giving themselves over to ignorance and to a human death (ignorant of where they are going and of who Christ is), they will live!"

23. As already noted, in John 4:25; 7:27, 31, 41–42; 1 Tim 1:15; 1 John 4:2; 5:6; 2 John 7.

the democratization of the title to include disciples is original. There are also familiar Christian collocations, such as references to Christ coming and being a savior.[24] This language, while also very common, is found in Judaism, but the *Gospel of Philip* does not display any interest in a scripturally rooted grammar of messianism. It is notable that, as in the *Gospel of Truth*, the *Gospel of Philip* does not employ the Old Testament in its portrayal of Christ. Since the *Gospel of Philip* does not activate the discourse of Jewish messianic exegesis, therefore, it marks a departure in this respect from the early Jewish-Christian kerygma.

2. THE VICARIOUS DEATH OF JESUS IN THE GOSPEL OF PHILIP

The *Gospel of Philip* demonstrates knowledge of the circumstances of Jesus's death, though in view of the author's obvious knowledge of the written Gospels, he knows more than he tells. What can be seen from the *Gospel of Philip* is that Jesus presumably instituted the Eucharist at his last supper. He is then crucified, and on the cross, he utters the cry of dereliction.[25] His crucifixion was accompanied by the tearing, from top to bottom, of the curtain of the Jerusalem temple.[26] This curtain is understood, more explicitly than in other Gospels, as the curtain in front of the holy of holies.[27]

There are certain difficulties in addressing the question of how the *Gospel of Philip* interprets the death of Jesus, mainly because of the *Gospel of Philip*'s elliptical style and disconnected structure. Some references to Jesus's death are brief and fragmentary, as we have seen, but nevertheless constitute prima facie evidence for a soteriological understanding of the crucifixion. One passage, for example, contains a list of saving blessings: "Whoever is anointed has everything—the resurrection, the light, the cross, and the Holy Spirit" (Gos. Phil. 74.18–21); another passage has a reference to "the power of the cross" (67.24); in two others, Jesus's death is described as a sacrifice, probably in a positive sense at least in one case.[28] There are more substantial passages that may be able to fill out this picture.

24. For Christ's coming, see, e.g., John 4:25; 1 Tim 1:15; 1 John 4:2.

25. Eucharist: Gos. Phil. 58.10–11; 63.21–24; 67.27–30; 75.14–26. Crucifixion: Gos. Phil. 67.24; 68.28; 73.12, 15; 74.20; 84.33. Cry of dereliction: Gos. Phil. 68.26–29.

26. Gos. Phil. 70.1–4; 85.5–10.

27. Gos. Phil. 85.1–5: the identity of the *katapetasma* as the inner curtain is clear from the exclusive nature of access behind it.

28. Gos. Phil. 54.34–55.5 might be negative; on the other hand, the rationale in Gos. Phil. 62.35–63.4 is a characteristic of God, albeit the curious one that he is a "man-eater."

2.1 The Cry of Dereliction and the Reordering of Resurrection and Death

The *Gospel of Philip* includes a version of the cry of dereliction, slightly modified and with a pesher appended to it:

"My God, my God, why O Lord have you forsaken me?" He said this on the cross, because he had left that place. (Gos. Phil. 68.26–29)

This is notable because there appear to be at least two characters involved. First, the "Lord" who forsakes the figure to which he had previously been connected is presumably the same as the one who "left that place," that is, departed from the cross. Second, there is the "he" left behind who utters the cry and then (presumably) dies.

The most satisfactory explanation of this duality is that of Painchaud, who understands the cry of dereliction in the light of other Valentinian accounts in which the spiritual savior departs from the fleshly body.[29] In the interpretation of Ptolemy's followers as preserved in Irenaeus, for example, the cry of dereliction signifies that the lower Sophia is abandoned by the light.[30] Although the *Gospel of Philip* does not allude here to a mythological dimension, the reference to the departed "Lord" indicates that the savior has forsaken the material body.[31] Nor is this exclusively Valentinian: in the Gnostic Justin's *Book of Baruch*, for example, Jesus left his soul and material body on the cross, while his spirit ascended to the Father.[32] As we saw earlier, there is probably a similar scenario in the *Gospel of Peter*.

Such an interpretation of the crucifixion facilitates understanding of one of the most mysterious statements in the *Gospel of Philip*:

29. Louis Painchaud, "Le Christ vainqueur de la mort dans l'Évangile selon Philippe: Une exégèse valentinienne de Matt. 27:46," *NovT* 38 (1996): 382–92.

30. Painchaud, "Le Christ vainqueur," 389–90, citing especially Irenaeus, *Haer.* 1.8.2. Similarly, Einar Thomassen, "How Valentinian Is the Gospel of Philip?," in *The Nag Hammadi Library after Fifty Years*, ed. John D. Turner and Anne McGuire (Leiden: Brill, 1997), 269. Painchaud also makes the intriguing suggestion that the defeat of death at the cross is already suggested in the preceding statement about Adam and Eve in Gos. Phil. 68.22–26 ("Le Christ vainqueur," 384–86).

31. Painchaud, "Le Christ vainqueur," 390.

32. Hippolytus, *Haer.* 5.26.29–31. See further discussion of the phenomenon in Matti Myllykoski, "Die Kraft des Herrn: Erwägungen zur Christologie des Petrusevangeliums," in *Das Evangelium nach Petrus: Texte, Kontexte, Intertexte*, ed. Thomas Kraus and Tobias Nicklas (Berlin: de Gruyter, 2007), 301–26.

Those who say that the Lord first died and then rose are wrong. For he first rose and then died. Unless someone first obtains resurrection, he cannot die. As surely as God lives, he would [. . .]. (Gos. Phil. 56.15–20)

While there are some aspects of the death of Jesus in the *Gospel of Philip* that overlap with more traditional interpretations, this passage has a more subversive flavor. It appears not to be simply a playful statement. It is introduced as a correction of a serious error (ϲⲉⲣ̄ⲡⲗⲁⲛⲁ), in a formula that appears several times in the *Gospel of Philip* in correction of the views of other mistaken groups,[33] including in a correction of the view of general death and resurrection in that order.[34] The subsequent oath formula, "As surely as God lives," reinforces the grave tone of the statement, even if we cannot see exactly what the oath is. The point is clearly to say that there is something profoundly wrong with the kerygmatic account of Good Friday and Easter Sunday.

This is a surprising development. Discussion of the meaning of resurrection will be deferred to the appropriate point later, because it appears to be resurrection that is more fundamentally recast. We can simply anticipate in brief that later discussion by noting that it is not merely by virtue of his divine parentage in eternity that Jesus "rises" before his death. Almost certainly there is a specific event alluded to here, possibly his redemption at his baptism,[35] but more probably the spiritual ascension of the Lord from the cross—a better candidate for a "rising" again to where he was before.[36] There is a similar insistence in the *Excerpts from Theodotus* that life must rise up and depart before Jesus's bodily death can take place:[37]

He died at the departure of the Spirit that had descended upon him at the Jordan. Not that it became separate; rather it was withdrawn in order that death might also operate on him, since how could the body have died when life was present in him? For in that case, death would have prevailed over the savior himself, which is absurd! (*Exc.* 61.6)[38]

33. The verb ⲣ̄-ⲡⲗⲁⲛⲁ appears in correction of the views that "Mary conceived by the Holy Spirit" (Gos. Phil. 55.24) and that "there is a man above and one above him" (67.37–38).

34. Gos. Phil. 73.1–5: "Those who say that they first die and then rise are deceived. If they do not first receive resurrection while they are alive, they die and do not receive anything." Cf. Gos. Phil. 52.15–18: "A gentile does not die, for he has never lived such that he could die. The one who has believed in the truth has received life and is at risk of dying because he is alive."

35. In Gos. Phil. 73.5–8, which is tied closely to 73.1–5 cited above, baptism brings new life.

36. Painchaud, "Le Christ vainqueur," 391.

37. Painchaud, "Le Christ vainqueur," 390.

38. Trans. Casey, modified; see R. P. Casey, *The Excerpta ex Theodoto of Clement of*

This resurrection of life to where it was before thus helps us understand how death can come afterward. The cry of dereliction testifies to the fact that the Spirit or life (Theodotus), or the light (followers of Ptolemy), or "my Power" (the *Gospel of Peter*), or the Lord (the *Gospel of Philip*) has departed, and this departure precedes death and makes death possible. The savior relinquishes his material body and ascends, leaving the body behind to perish.

2.2 The Regathering of the Psychic Substance

What then is the purpose of Jesus's coming and death? The first passage to touch upon the theme is as important as it is difficult:

> Christ came to ransom some, to rescue others, and to redeem still others. He ransomed strangers and made them his own. He set apart those who were his own, those whom he had laid down as deposits by his own will. It was not only when he appeared that he laid down his soul (ⲯⲩⲭⲏ) as he willed to do, but ever since the world began he has laid down his soul when he wills. Then he came early to take it up since it had been laid down as deposits. It fell among thieves, and they took it captive. He rescued it, however, and redeemed both those who are good in this world and those who are evil. (Gos. Phil. 52.35–53.14)

In addition to the vagueness of the opening statement (where it is hard to tell whether it is specifically Jesus's death that is accomplishing the ransom, rescue, and redemption), the difficulty is that the language appears on the surface to refer to the idea of the preexistent Jesus dying in some sense: "ever since the world began he has laid down his soul when he wills." The language evokes the Johannine language of "laying down the soul/life."[39]

It is probable, however, that this repeated action of laying down the soul "when he wills" is not a reference to a death but rather is a transposition of the Johannine language to refer to the depositing of Christ's psychic material in human beings. Wilson is probably correct to observe that "if Christ be considered pre-existent, and ψυχή in John be taken in the sense of 'soul,' not of 'life,' we have only to interpret τίθημι as meaning the depositing of souls in

---

Alexandria: Edited with Translation, Introduction and Notes (London: Christophers, 1934), 80 (text), 81 (translation).

39. τίθημι τὴν ψυχήν: cf. in both the *Gospel of Philip* and Coptic John ⲕⲱ ⲛ̄ⲧⲯⲩⲭⲏ. John 10:11, 15, 17; 13:37–38 and 1 John 3:16 all have the idiom ⲕⲱ ⲛ̄ⲧⲯⲩⲭⲏ in the Sahidic translation. On ⲕⲱ as a translation equivalent for τίθημι, see further W. E. Crum, *A Coptic Dictionary* (Oxford: Clarendon, 1939), 94b, 96a–b, 97b–98b.

bodies to reach something like the present passage."[40] There is overlap, then, with this analogy:

> No one hides an important and precious object in something important, but many times one casts countless thousands into something worth an assarion. So it is with the soul. It is a precious thing but has come to be in a despicable body. (Gos. Phil. 56.20–26)

The "many times" in which the valuable element has been cast into its worthless casing may therefore correspond to the many occasions "ever since the world began . . . when he wills" when souls have entered bodies, deposited there by the savior.

Both the fact that the singular soul that Jesus lays down is called "deposits" *plural* (ⲛ̄ⲧⲁⲩⲕⲁⲁⲥ ⲛ̄ⲛⲉⲟⲩⲱ), and that therefore the laying down of deposits and the laying down of his soul are the same event, strongly suggest that "those who were his own" and "his soul" are one and the same:

(1) those who were his own, those whom he had laid down as deposits;

(2) It was not only when he appeared that <u>he laid down his soul . . .</u>;

(3) but ever since the world began <u>he has laid down his soul . . .</u>;

(4) he came early to take it up since <u>it had been laid down as deposits</u>.

(Gos. Phil. 53.5–11)

In other words, Jesus has been depositing soul-stuff, or psychic material, throughout history (3), and his incarnation, "when he appeared," is at one level another instance of that (2). Thereafter, he took all the psychic stuff up again (4). This makes good sense in light of what we saw in the cry of dereliction earlier. There Jesus rises up before the death takes place, and there is talk of the Lord ascending. It is probably then that Jesus gathers up the psychic substance: "he came early/first/beforehand (ⲛ̄ϣⲟⲣⲡ) to take it up since it had been laid down as deposits" (Gos. Phil. 53.10–11). This is what he "rescued" from the thieves who had got hold of it. His death then makes sense as the completion of this rescue, as he separates the gathered psychic substance from his physical matter on the cross, by departing from the body.[41]

40. Robin McL. Wilson, *The Gospel of Philip: Translated from the Coptic Text, with an Introduction and Commentary* (London: Mowbray, 1962), 72.

41. Cf. Clement of Alexandria, *Exc.* 61–62, 64.

2.3 Revelation and Ascension in the Tearing of the Curtain

The tearing of the curtain contains clear soteriological symbolism, and there appear to be three main points in this regard: (1) the opening of the curtain is revelatory, (2) the rending marks a departure of divinity from the temple, leading to its destruction, and (3) the completeness of the tear illustrates the universal scope of salvation. The main passage comes near the end of the Gospel:

> The bedchamber is hidden: it is "the holy of the holy." The curtain at first concealed how God managed creation. If the curtain tears, however, those within are revealed. Then this house will be left desolate, and indeed will be destroyed. All divinity will flee from these places, but not into the holy of holies. For it will not mix with the unalloyed light and the unfading fullness. Instead it will be under the wings of the cross and under its arms. This ark will bring salvation when the cataclysm of the flood overwhelms them.
>
> Those who belong to the priestly tribe will be able to enter within the curtain with the high priest. This is why the curtain was not torn at the top alone: otherwise it would be open only to those of the upper realm. Nor was it only the bottom that was torn—then it would be revealed only to those in the lower realm. No, it split from top to bottom, and opened up for us below, so we could enter the hidden truth.
>
> This is what is truly "mighty and glorious," though we have access to it by means of weak and contemptible types. They are contemptible by comparison with the perfect glory. There is glory that surpasses glory, and power that surpasses power. For this reason, the perfections and the secrets of the truth have opened up to us. The "holy of holies" has been uncovered, and the bedchamber has invited us within. (Gos. Phil. 84.21–85.22)

The first paragraph above refers to the peculiar content of what is concealed but now revealed: "The curtain at first concealed how God managed creation. If the curtain tears, however, those within are revealed." Notably, although material creation is not the work of the supreme deity (Gos. Phil. 75.2–6), he does—by the agency of the Holy Spirit—nevertheless administer it: "The archons thought that it was by their own power and will that they did what they did, but the Holy Spirit was secretly working everything out through them as he willed!"[42] The divine management of creation was concealed but has now been illuminated. The spiritual puppeteer hidden behind the curtain

42. Gos. Phil. 55.14–19; cf. 59.18–23; 60.28–34.

is now unveiled, or rather, since it is "those within" who are revealed, the idea is probably that the archons are seen for what they really are—mere inferior puppets. Although the archons had distorted the true workings of the world and its language, now God's activity can be decoded by the Valentinian savant. Furthermore, according to the third paragraph cited above, with the rending of the veil, "the perfections and the secrets of the truth have opened up to us" (Gos. Phil. 85.18–19). Hence there is unambiguous revelatory symbolism in the rending of the veil.

Second, still in the first paragraph cited above, judgment accompanies revelation: "If the curtain tears, however, those within are revealed. Then this house will be left desolate, and indeed will be destroyed." The departure of divinity (however understood)[43] from the temple removes that institution's raison d'être, and so its days are numbered. Here the *Gospel of Philip* taps into the familiar motif of the flight of a god before his or her temple is destroyed.[44]

Third and finally, the completeness of the tear from top to bottom (Gos. Phil. 70.1–4; 85.5–10) indicates the scope of salvation. The rending of the top means that "those of the upper realm" are redeemed, and similarly the bottom means that "those of the lower realm"—among whom the author includes himself—are saved. The movement of the tear along the y-axis enables the ascent of those below,[45] and this vertical ascent (now possible because of the tearing) is presumably the same as the entry into the bridal chamber, the motif that frames (at the beginning and end of the passage cited above) this discussion of the temple curtain.

The close connection of the death of Jesus with the tearing of the veil probably indicates that the crucifixion is related to these three motifs. In sum, then,

43. Matthew Twigg, "Esoteric Discourse and the Jerusalem Temple in the Gospel of Philip," *Aries* 15 (2015): 68, probably correctly takes this to refer to an inferior god, who prior to the revelation of Jesus was taken to be the one true God. So also in Isenberg's translation, "(inferior) godhead": Wesley W. Isenberg, "The Gospel of Philip," in *Nag Hammadi Codex II,2–7, together with XIII,2*, Brit. Lib. Or.4926(1), and P. Oxy. 1, 654, 655*, ed. Bentley Layton (Leiden: Brill, 1989), 1:211.

44. On this motif, see the discussions of the tearing of the veil in chapters 4–6 on the Synoptic Gospels above, and bibliography in John S. Kloppenborg, "*Evocatio Deorum* and the Date of Mark," *JBL* 124 (2005): 419–50.

45. Gos. Phil. 69.25–70.4: "Baptism contains both resurrection and redemption. Redemption is in the bridal chamber, and the bridal chamber is in what is higher than [. . .] You will not find its [. . .] those who pray are [. . .] Jerusalem [. . .] Jerusalem, they [. . .] Jerusalem, awaiting [. . .]. These are called 'the holy of holies' [. . .] curtain was torn [. . .] the bridal chamber, unless the image [. . .] above. For the reason its curtain tore from top to bottom is that it was necessary for some from below to go upward."

the death of Jesus has the soteriological effects of revelation (as in the *Gospel of Truth*) and elevation. If this veil symbolism is to be harmonized with the cry of dereliction discussed earlier, the point may be that the elevation of "those below" is *symbolized* by the tearing of the veil, and *effected* on the cross where Jesus redeems the psychic realm.

2.4 The Eucharist and Participation

For the *Gospel of Philip*, as for Luke and Paul, the Eucharist was inaugurated in an event during Jesus's ministry: "He said on that day in the Eucharist. . . ."[46] There are two passages in particular that connect the Eucharist and the saving significance of Jesus's death:

> The "Eucharist" is Jesus. For in Aramaic it is called *pharisatha*, which means "spread out," for Jesus came to crucify the world. (Gos. Phil. 63.21–24)

> The cup of prayer has wine and has water. It is laid down as a type of the blood for which the Eucharist is celebrated. It is filled by the Holy Spirit, and is a possession of the completely perfect man. Whenever we drink it, we receive the perfect man to ourselves. (Gos. Phil. 75.14–26)

Here we encounter statements in the *Gospel of Philip* about aspects of salvation that, at least by implication (in the reference to crucifixion), are effects of Jesus's death. The reference to the Eucharist also strongly suggests that the crucifixion is something in which disciples participate.

What of this claim in the first statement that Jesus crucified the world? The impulse for the language is clearly Gal 6:14, where the cross is the means by which the world is crucified for Paul.[47] Thomassen is probably right to say that the crucifixion in Gos. Phil. 63.21–24 is the crucifixion of matter.[48] The world as a physical entity was a mistaken creation at the outset, and true disciples are born and nourished from outside, transcend it, and are destined to escape it.[49] One might draw a parallel between the action of Jesus here in the *Gospel*

---

46. Gos. Phil. 58.10–11; cf. also 67.27–30.

47. Cf. also 1 Jeu 1: "The living Jesus said to his apostles, 'Blessed is he who has crucified the world and has not let the world crucify him.'" For text, see Carl Schmidt and Violet MacDermot, *The Books of Jeu and the Untitled Text in the Bruce Codex* (Leiden: Brill, 1978), 1.15–2.2.

48. Thomassen, "How Valentinian Is the Gospel of Philip?," 274–75.

49. Transcendence: Gos. Phil. 53.21–23. Escape: 65.27–32; 66.16–20; 86.6–7, 11–13.

of Philip and a passage in the Valentinian *Treatise on the Resurrection*, where "the savior swallowed up death . . . for he set aside the perishable world" (*Treat. Res.* 45.14–17). We have also seen the cosmological effect of Jesus's death in the *Gospel of Truth.* Hence it appears that the death of Jesus's material body in the *Gospel of Philip* marks the neutralizing of the material cosmos for Christians, and it is in that sense that "Jesus came to crucify the world."

The "Eucharist" (ⲉⲩⲭⲁⲣⲓⲥⲧⲓⲁ), which for Valentinians, too, meant bread and wine, is a means of participation in that action of Jesus.[50] First, there is a theological wordplay connecting the eucharistic bread and the death of Jesus: Eucharist = Jesus = *pharisatha.*[51] In this example of Valentinian philology, the point is that *pharisatha* has a double meaning. It can refer to eucharistic bread: in the Syriac Peshitta translation of Acts 2:46 and elsewhere, the disciples daily broke *pryst'* in their houses.[52] The term can also mean "stretching out," however, as is indicated by the Aramaic *prs'yt,* which can refer to a stretching out of the body.[53]

Second, in addition to this theological wordplay, there is "type" language involved. (The theology of types and images in the *Gospel of Philip* will be explored more in section 4.) In the second excerpt above, the cup "is laid down as a type of the blood for which the Eucharist is celebrated" (Gos. Phil. 75.14–17)—that is, the wine is a symbol of the blood of Jesus. The "perfect man" that

---

50. For the bread and wine, see Gos. Phil. 74.36–75.2; 77.2–7. Gos. Phil. 75.14–26 strongly implies that it involved diluted wine (as was normal for wine drunk in antiquity). In Gos. Phil. 67.27–30, the Eucharist follows baptism and chrism and is therefore clearly a part of the ritual life of the author and his audience.

51. For the equation of Jesus and the Eucharist, cf. Ign. *Smyrn.* 7.1: "The Eucharist is the flesh of our savior Jesus Christ" (τὴν εὐχαριστίαν σάρκα εἶναι τοῦ σωτῆρος ἡμῶν Ἰησοῦ Χριστοῦ).

52. Van Unnik, "Three Notes on the Gospel of Philip," 241, also citing additional later sources with this sense. See further Robert Payne Smith, *Thesaurus Syriacus* (Oxford: Clarendon, 1879), 3278, s.v. *"prys'," "pryst'."*

53. For this sense of *pharisatha,* see *prs'yt* in CAL (http://cal.huc.edu/). CAL alludes to lexica citing the *Acta Martyrum,* for which see Emil Rödiger, *Chrestomathia Syriaca,* 3rd ed. (Halle: Orphanotropheum, 1892), 81 line 15. Carl Brockelmann, *Lexicon Syriacum,* 2nd ed. (Halle: Max Niemeyer, 1928), 600, has the gloss *"expanso corpore,"* and Payne Smith, *Thesaurus Syriacus,* 3280, has a gloss *"cum membris extensis,"* which would fit the context of the *Gospel of Philip* well. It is less likely that there is an allusion to emanation here, *pace* Thomassen, "How Valentinian Is the Gospel of Philip?," 275. In connection with Jesus, similar language is used, e.g., in the *Epistle of Barnabas* in reference to the crucifixion: when Moses stretched out (ἐξέτεινεν) his hands, he was making a sign of the cross and pointing forward to Christ (*Barn.* 12.1–2), as does God when through the prophet he says that he has stretched out (διεπέτασα) his hands to Israel (12.4).

is received by drinking the cup (in the second paragraph cited above) might be equated with the human over whom the cosmos holds no sway.

In sum, participation in the Eucharist—in the "flesh" and "blood" of Jesus, which are in reality the Word and the Holy Spirit (Gos. Phil. 52.6–7)—is a participation in the separation of the material from the psychic or spiritual that Jesus effected for himself on the cross.[54] The neutralizing of the cosmos that Jesus accomplished on the cross takes place in—or is recapitulated in— the Christian's partaking of the cup of Jesus's blood. This drinking is also the means by which the "perfect man" is received.

2.5 Interim Conclusion:
Jesus's Death in the Gospel of Philip and the Kerygma

As noted at the beginning, there are some difficulties in understanding the *Gospel of Philip*'s view of the death of Jesus. There is no extended discussion, and it is difficult to disentangle the cross from other events: Thomassen, for example, emphasizes how the *Gospel of Philip* appears to see different actions of Jesus as duplicating the effects of other episodes, such that the incarnation, baptism and death can be seen as one single undifferentiated "Christ event."[55] This will be discussed further shortly in connection with the resurrection.

For now, some of the strands about the death of Jesus in the *Gospel of Philip* can be drawn together, although the difficulties mean that conclusions will require a liberal sprinkling of uses of "perhaps" and "possibly." The cry of dereliction attests to an ascension of the Lord who thereby leaves the material Jesus behind to die. This is probably not an action solely of significance to Jesus himself but is the means of ascension of the psychic substance that Jesus has been laying down since the beginning and has now gathered up. Jesus is said to have rescued this psychic substance that had fallen among thieves; this rescue is presumably the same as the separation of soul from bodily matter on the cross. Perhaps in Jesus, the psychic substance, that is, the souls of the elect, is united with Spirit, since "the soul's partner is the Spirit" (Gos. Phil. 70.23–24) and Jesus's blood is Spirit (57.6–7).[56] One possible qualification here is that it

54. Thomassen, "How Valentinian Is the Gospel of Philip?," 275, commenting that those who participate in the Eucharist share in this redemptive separation.

55. Einar Thomassen, *The Spiritual Seed: The "Church" of the Valentinians* (Leiden: Brill, 2006), 94–95.

56. Hugo Lundhaug, *Images of Rebirth: Cognitive Poetics and Transformational Soteriology in the Gospel of Philip and the Exegesis on the Soul* (Leiden: Brill, 2010), 240, comes to a very similar conclusion in his discussion of the resurrection in the *Gospel of Philip*, where

is not the death per se that effects this rescue but Jesus's premortem ascension from the cross. The tearing of the curtain, in addition to signifying a revelatory dimension of Jesus's crucifixion, also by its vertical direction indicates that those below can ascend. This may, again, also take place during the process of the crucifixion rather than by the death proper. The Eucharist is significant as the means of participation, from the earthly standpoint, in the events of the crucifixion: through it—as well as through baptism and the chrism—come the effects of the death, including the destruction of the material realm and the reception of the Spirit because the eucharistic cup "is filled by the Holy Spirit" (Gos. Phil. 75.18). As does the *Gospel of Truth*, then, the *Gospel of Philip* presents the crucifixion as an important event of saving significance, of an effective and vicarious nature.

3. The Resurrection of Jesus in the Gospel of Philip

The resurrection of Jesus in the *Gospel of Philip* is complex, just as is his death. We need to ask both whether there is any sort of resurrection and, if so, what kind of resurrection it is. Some scholars are happy to speak of Jesus's rising again in the *Gospel of Philip*, and the language of resurrection is frequent there, but the question is whether the category dies the death of a thousand qualifications.[57]

3.1 The Death/Resurrection Reversal

The only passage in which the personal resurrection of Jesus is explicitly addressed is one touched upon already in the discussion of the cross in the *Gospel of Philip*:

> Those who say that the Lord first died and then rose are wrong. For he first rose and then died. Unless someone first obtains resurrection (ⲭⲡⲉ ⲧⲁⲛⲁⲥⲧⲁⲥⲓⲥ), he cannot die. As surely as God lives, he would [. . .]! (Gos. Phil. 56.15–20)

Wilson's explanation of the priority of resurrection is a sensible one, noting that the sequence "arise" then "die" can be explained because the verb "arise"

---

at the resurrection, or—as I put it here—at the ascension with Jesus, "it is the transformed soul that rises together with the Holy Spirit."

57. Thomassen, *Spiritual Seed*, 97–98, talks of Jesus's resurrection.

can have the sense of "appear on the scene."[58] While sensible, however, such a view does not do justice to the language that the *Gospel of Philip* uses: in an early Christian context, it is a stretch to take the noun (ἀνάστασις) in such a way. The *Gospel of Philip*'s language of "obtaining resurrection," quoted above, suggests something quite different from "coming on the scene."

A second possibility is that the "risen life" that must precede "death" is a regeneration that occurs at Jesus's baptism:

> Jesus appeared [. . .] the Jordan, the fullness of the kingdom of heaven. He who [was born] before the All was born again, he who was anointed in the beginning was anointed again, he who was redeemed in turn redeemed. (Gos. Phil. 70.34–71.3)

To all appearances, then, the baptism of Jesus is a regeneration.[59] The "new life" from the baptism is, therefore, different from biological, earthly life,[60] but it is also distinct in some respect from his eternal begetting ("before the All") by the Father.[61] It is therefore a viable candidate for the occasion of Jesus "rising" or "obtaining resurrection" in Gos. Phil. 56.15–20, quoted above.

---

58. Wilson, *Gospel of Philip*, 85–86. See, e.g., ἀνίστημι employed of Judas the Galilean "arising" (Acts 5:37; cf. 7:18; Heb 7:11, 15).

59. Thomassen, *Spiritual Seed*, 100: "the Saviour was both reborn, re-anointed and re-redeemed in the Jordan."

60. Life and death in the *Gospel of Philip* are not biological categories: to understand them this way is to fall under the spell of the distorted words in this world. "Life and death" are a pairing that is not ultimately real, a duality that will ultimately be resolved into its origin (Gos. Phil. 53.14–23).

61. This understanding of Jesus's resurrection as regeneration finds support in the *Gospel of Philip*'s statements about Christians' resurrections. (1) The Gospel uses resurrection more generally to talk about new life found in the present age: a Christian who "has believed in the truth has received life and is at risk of dying because he is alive," in contrast to a "gentile" who cannot die because he has never lived (Gos. Phil. 52.15–19): this is clearly the new spiritual life of the believer. (2) The same language used of Jesus is also used of Christians: as Christ "obtains resurrection" (ϫⲡⲉ ⲧⲁⲛⲁⲥⲧⲁⲥⲓⲥ), so "while we are in this world, we must obtain resurrection (ϫⲡⲟ ⲛ̄ⲧⲁⲛⲁⲥⲧⲁⲥⲓⲥ)" (Gos. Phil. 66.16–21). This latter passage is clearly referring to a spiritual event that occurs in the present realm. (3) Jesus's resurrection and the resurrections of believers are the subjects of the same polemic; the *Gospel of Philip* also criticizes those who get the deaths and resurrections of believers confused: "Those who say that they first die and then rise are deceived. If they do not first receive resurrection (ϫⲓ . . . ⲛ̄ⲧⲁⲛⲁⲥⲧⲁⲥⲓⲥ) while they are alive, they die and do not receive anything" (Gos. Phil. 73.1–5). What happens at Jesus's baptism is therefore similar to what happens to Christians, in that it is the reception of a new kind of life additional to biological life, and, crucially, it *precedes* death.

A third possibility—discussed already in section 2.1 above—is that the "resurrection" is the ascension of the Lord mentioned in the gloss on the cry of dereliction: "'My God, my God, why O Lord have you forsaken me?' He said this
on the cross, because he had left that place [. . .]." (Gos. Phil. 68.26–29). This
also constitutes a new ascended life, elevated above material existence.[62]

It is difficult to decide between these latter two possibilities, and indeed
if Thomassen's approach is correct, it may be a mistake to try to distinguish
between baptism and this redemption from the cross.[63] One hint that might
favor a reference to the crucifixion is that the *Gospel of Philip's* insistence that
the "Lord" rose first matches the point that, according to the cry of dereliction,
it was the "Lord" who forsook the material Jesus on the cross.

Is there, then, space still for a postmortem resurrection as well? As noted in
section 2, the statement of reordered death and resurrection is indeed a solemn
one, framed as a correction of a serious error by deviants (сєрⲡⲗⲁⲛⲁ) and accompanied by the oath "As surely as God lives. . . ." There are, however, other
passages that could be interpreted as referring to a resurrection of Jesus.

3.2 Resurrection Imagery

There are three other places that are potentially relevant to the resurrection
of Jesus.

The first continues the discussion of Jesus laying down his soul, with treatment of his taking it up again:

> He [i.e., Christ] set apart those who were his own, those whom he had laid
> down as deposits by his own will. It was not only when he appeared that
> he laid down his soul as he willed to do, but ever since the world began he
> has laid down his soul when he wills. Then he came early/first/beforehand
> (ⲛ̄ϣⲟⲣⲡ) to take it up since it had been laid down as deposits. It fell among
> thieves, and they took it captive, but he rescued it and redeemed those who
> are good in this world and those who are evil. (Gos. Phil. 53.4–14)

---

62. Elliot R. Wolfson, "Becoming Invisible: Rending the Veil and the Hermeneutic of
Secrecy in the Gospel of Philip," in *Practicing Gnosis: Ritual, Magic, Theurgy and Liturgy
in Nag Hammadi, Manichaean and Other Ancient Literature; Essays in Honor of Birger A.
Pearson*, ed. April D. DeConick, Gregory Shaw, and John D. Turner (Leiden: Brill, 2013),
126, appears to take a view similar to this.

63. Similarly, Lundhaug, *Images of Rebirth*, 230–31, takes the premortem resurrection
to be "chrismation by means of the crucifixion" as well as Jesus's baptism, which is also
associated with chrismation.

The language of Jesus taking up his soul, as already noted, is an echo of John 10:17: "The reason my Father loves me is that *I lay down my life/soul and then take it up again.*"[64] This Johannine language is embedded in a narrative in the *Gospel of Philip* with three elements: (1) Jesus on a number of occasions disperses his psychic substance in the world—"not only when he appeared . . . but ever since the world began"; (2) this is then taken captive ("it fell among thieves"), and so (3) Jesus comes to recover it. There is no particular sense of resurrection here, and indeed the recovery, as argued earlier in the discussion of the crucifixion in the *Gospel of Philip*, appears to take place on the cross.

A second passage does relate Christ to the resurrection:

Some are afraid of being raised naked. That is why they want to be raised in the flesh. They do not know that those who bear flesh are the naked ones! Those who [. . .] naked [. . .] are not naked. "Flesh and blood cannot inherit the kingdom of God." What is that flesh that does not inherit? That which clothes us. What, though, is the flesh that does inherit? That of Jesus and his blood. That is why he said, "The one who does not eat my flesh and drink my blood has no life in him." What is this flesh? His flesh is the Word—and his blood is the Holy Spirit. Whoever receives these has food and drink and clothing. (Gos. Phil. 56.26–57.8)

The discussion here is not about Christ's resurrection, however, but about the mode of postmortem existence that believers will assume: when they "rise," they will be constituted as Word and Holy Spirit.

Third, there is the comparison between the bestial sacrifices offered "BC" and the sacrifice of Christ:

There are powers existing that give [. . .] man, not wanting him to be saved, so they become a [. . .]. For if man is saved, sacrifices [. . .] and they offered up wild beasts to the powers. For those to whom they offered up sacrifices were beasts. The animals were offered up alive, but when they had been offered they were dead. Man they offered up to God dead, but he lived. (Gos. Phil. 54.31–55.5)

This final statement is suggestive and seems to have a christological reference, but of course it gives no content to the sense in which the man "lived."

---

64. ἐγὼ τίθημι τὴν ψυχήν μου, ἵνα πάλιν λάβω αὐτήν.

3.3 Interim Conclusion:
Jesus's Resurrection in the Gospel of Philip and the Kerygma

In view of the strong language about resurrection preceding death, and the separation of the spirit or soul from the body at the cry of dereliction, it seems probable that for the *Gospel of Philip*, there is no sense that Jesus's body rises.[65] Wolfson is on the mark in speaking of "the resurrection which occurs at the crucifixion with the separation [sc. from the body] of the Logos and the Holy Spirit."[66] Perhaps if (per Gos. Phil. 56.34–57.7) disciples are to be constituted as Word and Holy Spirit when they are raised, the same applies to Jesus as well.[67]

One further qualification may be in order. As Thomassen recognizes, it is extremely difficult to pry apart the different moments in Jesus's earthly career in the *Gospel of Philip*. If Thomassen's "layered" interpretation of the *Gospel of Philip* is right, then "putting all the pieces together, one is therefore led to the conclusion that Gos. Phil. collapses the incarnation, baptism and crucifixion of Jesus into one single act."[68] Resurrection in the *Gospel of Philip* is not part of any conventional sequence; rather, incarnation and birth, baptism, anointing, crucifixion, resurrection, and unification are more like "a single, indissoluble event."[69]

In sum, for the *Gospel of Philip*, there is an ascension already at the cross. Since "the Lord" left the cross before the death of the material speaker of the cry of dereliction, it is hard to find space for a resurrection after death. It is difficult to imagine the *Gospel of Philip* wanting a physical ("hylic" or "choic") frame to be raised, since matter for the *Gospel of Philip* is intrinsically perish-

---

65. So, e.g., Lundhaug, *Images of Rebirth*, 241, on the fact that the material body does not rise.

66. Wolfson, "Becoming Invisible," 115.

67. On the resurrection of disciples, see the helpful remarks in Lundhaug, *Images of Rebirth*, 238, where he notes that it is necessary for us to have Jesus's flesh and blood in Eucharist because by his flesh and blood (Word and Spirit), we rise, or again (Lundhaug, *Images of Rebirth*, 239): "Gos. Phil.'s solution to the problem of the resurrection of the flesh thus seems to be based on its identification of the flesh of Christ with the Logos."

68. Thomassen, *Spiritual Seed*, 94–95. Thomassen goes on to extend this to resurrection as well (p. 98), though the Coptic passage upon which this is apparently based does not point in this direction. Thomassen (p. 96) takes the ⲁϥϭⲱⲧⲉ in 70.34–71.3 in the sense of "was redeemed," but this misses the fact that the pattern hitherto in this logion, "was born, was born again, was anointed, was anointed again," is precisely broken in the last part: ⲡⲉⲛⲧⲁⲩ...ϥ, ⲡⲁⲗⲓⲛ ⲁⲩ...ϥ then ⲡⲉⲛⲧⲁⲩ...ϥ, ⲡⲁⲗⲓⲛ ⲁⲩ...ϥ, but then ⲡ[ⲉⲛ]ⲧⲁⲩⲥⲟⲧϥ ⲡⲁⲗⲓⲛ ⲁϥϭⲱⲧⲉ. Perhaps significantly, resurrection is not mentioned alongside the incarnation and crucifixion in Thomassen's conclusion on the *Gospel of Philip* (p. 102). It remains possible, however, that the rebirth and reanointing in *Gos. Phil.* 70.34–71.3 have some kind of resurrection in mind.

69. Thomassen, *Spiritual Seed*, 98.

able (Gos. Phil. 75.2–10). Resurrection for Valentinian Christians does come in the flesh—the *Gospel of Philip* even asserts that "resurrection in *this* flesh is *necessary*" (57.18)—but that flesh is composed of Word and Spirit.[70] In consequence, it is tempting to conclude that the *Gospel of Philip* is being at best playful and at worst rather disingenuous here. As Lundhaug comments: "One indeed gets the impression that Gos. Phil. is here in a sense sailing under false flag, giving the impression of affirming the doctrine of the resurrection of the flesh, and thus conforming to accepted dogma, while arguing what in reality amounts to the opposite."[71] In sum, then, the *Gospel of Philip* departs from the model of the kerygma employed in this study, in that it does not distinguish between resurrection and the cross but rather deliberately polemicizes against the kerygmatic order of the death of Jesus followed by his resurrection.

4. THE GOSPEL OF PHILIP AND SCRIPTURE

As this chapter has remarked upon several times, the *Gospel of Philip* has much in common theologically with the *Gospel of Truth*. There are hints of a myth in the *Gospel of Philip*, although the myths of the two works are difficult to compare because protology plays a far more minor role in the *Gospel of Philip*.[72] There is therefore not much of a sense of what we saw in the *Gospel of Truth*: a backdrop, functioning as a kind of "Old Testament," embedded within the work as a primeval myth that is then acted out in the historical realm in Jesus's ministry. The *Gospel of Philip* is also quite different from the *Gospel of Truth* in its use, across the whole work, of scriptural language and imagery.

4.1 The Dispersion of Truth in the World

As a backdrop to the discussion of scripture in the *Gospel of Philip*, it will be useful first to consider the primeval dispersion of truth into the world, a motif mentioned numerous times in the *Gospel of Philip*. As we will see, the *Gospel of*

---

70. The emphasis on Christ's flesh as true flesh by comparison with ours in A. (Ton) H. C. van Eijk, "The Gospel of Philip and Clement of Alexandria: Gnostic and Ecclesiastical Theology on the Resurrection and the Eucharist," *VC* 25 (1971): 94–120, is perhaps based on an overoptimistic reading of the very lacunose *Gos. Phil.* 68.31–37.

71. Lundhaug, *Images of Rebirth*, 384. It might be more accurate, given the strong language in the text itself, to say that the *Gospel of Philip* provides insiders with a way of affirming the doctrine while meaning something else; an outsider reading the work would be much more doubtful.

72. For myth in the *Gospel of Philip*, see Gos. Phil. 61.1–3; 81.14–31; cf. also 63.5–11.

Philip attempts to construct a kind of plausibility structure for its soteriology through the exploration of analogous phenomena in the world external to the text. There are some programmatic statements to this effect:

> The truth, however, has given birth to names in this world for our sake. We cannot learn about the truth without names. The truth is singular and is multiple, and it teaches this singular thing in multiple ways, out of kindness to us. (Gos. Phil. 54.13–18)

> The truth is sown everywhere and has existed from the beginning. There are many who see it being sown but few who see it harvested. (Gos. Phil. 55.19–22)

> For now we have what are revealed of creation. We say, "They are mighty and glorious, but contemptible weak things are obscure." But this is how it is with what are revealed of the truth: they may be "contemptible and weak," but it is "the mighty and glorious" who are obscure. The mysteries of truth are manifest as types and images. (Gos. Phil. 84.14–21; cf. 67.9–12; 85.10–15)

In this sense, then, there has been a vast quantity of prior disclosure, in "types and images," of the truth. On the other hand, there is a tension here in that the names that things currently possess are treacherous:

> The names that are given to things of this world are very deceptive. For they turn the mind from what is genuine to what is not. (Gos. Phil. 53.23–27)

> The archons wanted to deceive man, since they saw that he possessed kinship with what are truly good. Therefore, they took the names of good things and attached them to what are not good, so that by the names they could deceive him and bind people to what are not good. (Gos. Phil. 54.18–25)

The labels that are attached to phenomena in this world, then, are highly misleading, because these labels have been swapped around by hostile forces.

Alongside these programmatic statements, there are particular examples that the *Gospel of Philip* sees as illuminating. Fatherhood, human marriage, and sex are frequently mentioned. Money being kept in a cheap purse is illustrative of the relation of body to soul (Gos. Phil. 56.20–26). Kissing, and the conception and birth to which it leads, is emblematic of the "holy kiss" that leads to grace being "conceived" in the group (59.3–6). Other parabolic motifs are introduced without specific explication.[73] Exploration of metaphors and analogies is the basis for the procedure of much of the *Gospel of Philip*.

There is specific semitechnical vocabulary used to identify the relationship between the phenomena and the realities to which they point, as has been hinted above. The "cup of prayer," which contains wine and water, is a "type" (ⲦⲨⲠⲞⲤ) of the blood (Gos. Phil. 75.14–25); image language (ⲉⲓⲔⲰⲚ) is used to describe the physical, earthly person in contrast to the heavenly angelic counterpart (65.1–26), and the *Gospel of Philip* also implies that sex is an "image," as is human accomplishment in general (72.4–17). As in the passage cited above (84.14–21), these earthly instances of "images" and "types" are in some sense representations of "the mysteries of truth" (Ⲙ̄ⲘⲨⲤⲦⲎⲣⲒⲞⲚ Ⲛ̄ⲦⲀⲖⲎⲐⲈⲒⲀ) in the supramundane realm.

4.2 Scriptural Images and Types

Some of these images and types are scriptural.[74] One of the most elaborated images is the temple, and its layout comes to the fore initially. The *Gospel of Philip* has three buildings for sacrifice, each a "house" (Ⲏⲉⲓ): the "holy," the "holy of holy," and the "holy of holies" (Gos. Phil. 69.14–22). As we saw in the discussion of the crucifixion of Jesus, the curtain appears in two passages that echo the New Testament tradition of the tearing.[75] The latter pericope also mentions the ark, suggesting a connection and perhaps a typological relation between the wings (of the cherubim) over the ark and the "wings of the cross" (84.33).[76] In two passages, animal sacrifice is mentioned, as characteristic of the time before the revelation of Christ; the sacrificial system is cast in negative terms as involving offerings to animal deities and those who are not gods.[77] In this respect, the temple with its "places of sacrifice" (69.14–15) might be a good example of a fragment of truth sown in the world but distorted: it has elements that point to the ultimate reality of salvation, but it also functioned as a center for idolatrous worship. There is antecedent revelation in the dispersion of truth

73. E.g., Gos. Phil. 58.14–17.

74. One could add here traditional biblical turns of phrase, such as "As surely as God lives" (Gos. Phil. 56.19–20), which appears numerous times (with "Lord" instead of "God") in the Old Testament but not in the New Testament.

75. Gos. Phil. 69.35–70.4; 84.23–29.

76. The sequence of thought is a little unclear, but after the wings in Gos. Phil. 84.33, the ark is then mentioned in 84.34. The passage goes on to talk about the ark, but the ark of the covenant is fused with Noah's ark (each is a κιβωτός in the Septuagint and the NT, and the Greek word comes into the Coptic of the *Gospel of Philip* here).

77. Gos. Phil. 55.1–2; 63.1–4.

in the world, but the light of that revelation has been mischievously refracted by the influence of the archons.

Finally, there is a good deal of material in the *Gospel of Philip* about Adam and Eve in paradise from the early chapters of Genesis.[78] Paradise has two significant trees, one bearing foul fruit and the other bearing fair—"one bears animals and the other bears humans" (Gos. Phil. 71.22–29). The negatively valued tree is the tree of knowledge, which brought death for Adam, and the saving tree is the tree of life in the middle of the garden: this is an olive tree whence comes the oil of chrism used in the Valentinian rite (73.15–19).

There are three distinct moments of the beginning of Genesis reflected in the *Gospel of Philip*. Loosely along the lines of Gen 1–2, Adam's creation came about from two virgins, "the Spirit and the virgin earth" (Gos. Phil. 71.16–18). The reference to the Spirit is reflected in Adam's soul coming from breath and his elevation through being given spirit (70.22–26). Echoing Gen 3, the fall is pictured in two distinct ways, both resulting in death. In more traditional terms, death came with the words "eat this and do not eat that" (Gos. Phil. 74.11), because Adam ate from the wrong tree, the tree of knowledge, which killed him;[79] this "tree of knowledge" is identified also as the law, which provides knowledge but cannot save (74.5–12). Or again, the fall is understood as a result of the separation of Adam from Eve, who was formerly within Adam; when they separated, death appeared.[80] Recalling elements of Gen 4, Eve gives birth, though Cain, at least, is the product of Eve's adultery with the serpent; this parentage is reflected in his murder of Abel (Gos. Phil. 60.34–61.12). Further on in the primeval history, the *Gospel of Philip* also refers (directly or indirectly) to Gen 17: Abraham's circumcision "teaches us" (ⲉϥⲧⲁ[ⲙⲟ] ⲙ̄ⲙⲟⲛ) about the destruction of the flesh (Gos. Phil. 82.26–29).

4.3 Discontinuities between Scripture and the Gospel of Philip

Although elements of scripture, such as Abraham's circumcision, can be instructive as images or "types," the sense in which scripture functions as testimony to reality is subject to three quite serious qualifications.

---

78. Other possible Old Testament allusions include, in Meyer's version, Sophia called a "pillar of salt," echoing Lot's wife, but this translation is based on a restoration (Gos. Phil. 59.33–34). See Marvin Meyer, ed., *The Nag Hammadi Scriptures* (New York: HarperOne, 2007), 167. There is also a fleeting reference to the Sabbath but again in a lacunose passage (52.34).

79. Gos. Phil. 74.3–12; cf. 71.24–26.

80. Gos. Phil. 68.22–24; 70.9–12, 20–22.

First, in places, the *Gospel of Philip*'s creation narrative appears to be correcting the traditional account. The creation of the world came about as a mistake, through an inferior deity (Gos. Phil. 75.2–6). Similarly, as noted, Eve's extraction from Adam is regarded by the *Gospel of Philip* as an unfortunate fall rather than as part of the divine purpose.[81]

Second, and relatedly, the institutions of Israel's history that in scripture are identified as divinely ordained are not necessarily taken as such in the *Gospel of Philip*. This is most clearly evident in the portrayal of the cult, where sacrifices are not offered to God. Instead, as already noted, the *Gospel of Philip* refers to human beings (without distinction) as offering animal sacrifices to bestial archontic powers.[82] Although the passage has lacunae, the main point is fairly clear:

> There are powers existing that give [. . .] man, not wanting him to be saved, so they become a [. . .]. For if man is saved, sacrifices [. . .] and they offered up wild beasts to the powers. For those to whom they offered up sacrifices were beasts. The animals were offered up alive, but when they had been offered they were dead. Man they offered up to God dead, but he lived. (Gos. Phil. 54.31–55.5)

Similarly, what is *probably* a reference to the death of Jesus marks the end of a period that was *certainly* characterized by a sacrificial system that was not directed toward the true deity:

> God is a man-eater. Therefore, the man is sacrificed to him. Before the man was sacrificed, wild beasts were sacrificed because the recipients of the sacrifices were not gods. (Gos. Phil. 62.35–63.4)

In this example, then, the cult and temple are not veiled anticipations but— again—seriously distorted types. God's status is not so degraded that he eats animals. In fact, he is at the very top of the food chain and so can be pleased only with a human sacrifice—and not just any human but probably the perfect human, "*the* man" Jesus. Israel's worship is directed to demonic archons not just when the nation strays and worships Molech but precisely in the temple

---

81. In Gen 2:22, God takes the woman out of man. Again, the birth of Cain is the result of Adam knowing Eve (Gen 4:1), a point that may be "corrected" by the *Gospel of Philip*. Cf., e.g., *Ap. John* (NHC II) 13.19–20: "Do not suppose it is as Moses said. . . ."

82. See the preliminary discussion of this theme in sections 1.1 and 3.2 above.

worship prescribed in scripture. This is what for the *Gospel of Philip* characterizes the era before Christ, "when we were Hebrews" (Gos. Phil. 52.21–22).

Third, there is little sense of Genesis being referred to *as* scripture. It is hard
to say that the Genesis narrative has any privileged status over and above other
images and types mentioned in the *Gospel of Philip*. In this respect, the *Gospel
of Philip* differs markedly from the attitude in the canonical Gospels and (as
far as one can tell) the *Egerton Gospel*, for example. In the *Gospel of Philip*,
the images drawn from Genesis are also subject to the distorting influence
of "worldly names." There is certainly no clear sense in the *Gospel of Philip*
of testimony to salvation through Jesus in this scriptural material. There may
perhaps be a contrast between law and gospel of some sort implied in the two
trees: the tree of the knowledge of good and evil, which is identified with the
law, brings death, while the olive tree (the tree of life?) from which the chrism
comes brings resurrection (Gos. Phil. 73.15–19).[83] Confusingly, however, the
tree of knowledge can also be spoken of positively (74.1–5). In any case, however distorted and bewildering these earthly symbols might be, they can be
understood to point to truth. Now that the curtain separating the holy of holies
has been torn apart, the mysteries of divine operation are revealed.[84] Virtuoso
Valentinian interpreters, who "have come to know what is correct" (53.34–35),
are capable of undeception.

Conclusion: The Gospel of Philip and the Kerygma

In terms of the reception of the themes of Jesus's messiahship, his death and
resurrection, and the "according to the scriptures" motif, the *Gospel of Philip*
is one of the hardest Gospels to evaluate. Some of the themes are marked by a
degree of ambiguity, although others can be understood adequately.

First, the *Gospel of Philip* is enthusiastic in its use of "Christ" language
in connection with Jesus. This usage is not eccentric but appears in familiar
collocations: in the pairing of "Jesus Christ," for example, and particularly
in connection with his coming. Like John's Gospel, the *Gospel of Philip* also
includes the Greek transliteration of the Semitic form (*Messias*). On the other
hand, there are no particular scriptural prooftexts involved in the construction

---

83. The Coptic of Gos. Phil. 73.15–19 can certainly be read as identifying the tree of life
with the olive tree, though this is not certain. Nevertheless, the fact that the olive chrism
brings *resurrection* strongly suggests this identification.

84. Gos. Phil. 84.23–29; 85.10–13.

of this messianic identity. The scriptural discourse that is prominent in the canonical Gospels is not employed. Novenson summarizes the picture elsewhere with reference to "the participation by ancient Jews and Christians in a common scriptural discourse in texts about their respective messiahs," but the *Gospel of Philip* does not activate this common scriptural discourse.[85]

Second, there is some ambiguity about the death of Jesus, although some points are clear. There is certainly a crucifixion, because the cross is mentioned several times. What appears to happen on the cross is a separation of, on the one hand, the perishable material body of Jesus that dies and, on the other hand, the pneumatic and/or psychic nature of Jesus that departs from the cross. In this departure or ascension, it appears that Jesus redeems psychic substance, that is, redeems the souls of the elect. The vertical rending of the temple curtain symbolizes the vertical ascent of true disciples with Jesus in this crucifixion. They are thereby separated from the world in a manner similar to Jesus's separation from the world on the cross. There is therefore considerable emphasis in the *Gospel of Philip* on the way in which Jesus's death effects redemption, a redemption in which the Valentinian disciple participates through the Eucharist. This redemption consists of the fact that Jesus has crucified the world in the course of his experience on the cross. Because it attests an effective and vicarious understanding of Jesus's death, therefore, the *Gospel of Philip* does reflect the kerygma on this point.

Third, the theme of resurrection does seem to be reshaped in accord with the polemical statement against those who believe that Jesus died before he rose. As Elaine Pagels is doubtless correct to note, the understanding of resurrection *ritual* has impacted the understanding of Christ's death and life.[86] There is use of what has previously been resurrection language, such as the Johannine phrase "taking up the soul again" (John 10:17), but—as we saw in the case of the *Gospel of Truth*—the resurrection language is transposed to another theological context. There is also difficulty in disentangling the distinct events of Jesus's ministry, as they are frequently rolled up together. It does not seem possible to identify a distinct resurrection of Jesus that takes place after his death. Rather, the "rising" of Jesus in the *Gospel of Philip* seems most appropriately to label the ascension of the Lord from the cross prior to the death of the material Jesus.

---

85. Novenson, *Grammar of Messianism*, 1.

86. Elaine Pagels, "Ritual in the Gospel of Philip," in *The Nag Hammadi Library after Fifty Years: Proceedings of the 1995 Society of Biblical Literature Commemoration*, ed. John D. Turner and Anne McGuire (Leiden: Brill, 1997), 286–87.

Fourth and finally, there is ambivalence toward the idea of scriptural testimony. On the one hand, scripture contains "types" and "images": as we saw, Abraham's circumcision was a type of image of the destruction of the flesh, and the temple and its veil are in some sense images of the truth. However, this is subject to three serious qualifications. For a start, scripture needs to be corrected; if taken at face value, it is and always has been false. Additionally, Israel's worship in the Old Testament is actually directed toward bestial archons. Finally, there is no sense that scripture is a kind of privileged type, qualitatively different from all the other distorted images in the world. To use the traditional terminology, if it does reveal once it has been decoded, it is a part of *general* revelation rather than *special* revelation. Nor are the death and resurrection fulfillments of a prophetic scripture.

Chapter Thirteen

THE GOSPEL OF JUDAS

The *Gospel of Judas* focuses on Jesus's revelation, setting this in the last days of Jesus before the Passover. The work begins with a relatively traditional-sounding introduction that recounts Jesus's miraculous activity, his calling of the disciples, and his eschatological teaching. However, the *Gospel of Judas* is also subversive in a number of ways and not only in its identification of Judas as the special recipient of Jesus's revelation. Jesus's disciples are derided by Jesus for celebrating the Eucharist and are condemned as murderous and sexually deviant priests. In the revelation itself, the world is not created by the highest deity. The supreme, transcendent being, "the Great Invisible Spirit," spawns or emanates further spiritual beings in the upper echelons of the heavenly hierarchy. A corrupt heavenly "cosmos" comes into existence somehow, and demonic forces create a reflection of this in the cosmos below, and along with it generate Adam and Eve. Like the *Gospel of the Egyptians* and the *Apocryphon of John*, which are theologically similar to it, the *Gospel of Judas* opposes the canonical pictures both of creation and the activity of Jesus, as we shall see. The focus of this chapter, however, will as usual be on the extent to which this Gospel reflects the model and its four components of messiahship, vicarious death, resurrection, and scriptural fulfillment.

1. THE CHRIST TITLE IN THE GOSPEL OF JUDAS

The use of "Christ" language in the *Gospel of Judas* is, as far as I am aware, un-paralleled. The title appears only once, and that is in a list of demonic rulers:[1]

---

1. See Lance Jenott, *The Gospel of Judas: Coptic Text, Translation, and Historical Interpretation of "the Betrayer's Gospel"* (Tübingen: Mohr Siebeck, 2011), 212–14, on this line. See also

> The first is [. . .]th who is called "Christ."
> The [second] is Harmathōth, who [. . .].
> The third is Galila.
> The fourth is Ïōbēl.
> The fifth is Adōnaios.
> These are the five who ruled over the underworld, and were pre-
> eminent over chaos. (*Gos. Jud.* 52.4–14)

The first difficulty comes in the text, in the first name of the first ruler. In the Coptic text, we can read "The first" (пϣορπ), and one needs then to supply пє (cf. "is"), which almost certainly appears in a lacuna. Thereafter, scholars have read either "[S]ēth" or "[Ya]ōth" or "[Ath]ōth."[2] As to what the vowel is, I am not confident that it is legible. The main sources for reconstructing the name are therefore parallel lists in other related texts, of which there are a large number: the four manuscripts of the *Apocryphon of John* (each containing more than one list), a Gnostic gem, two manuscripts of the *Gospel of the Egyptians*, and two versions of the Ophite diagram recorded in Origen's *Contra Celsum*. It is hard to come up with a positive answer to the question, however, because of variations in both the order and content of the lists, lacunae in some of the relevant places, and even variation across different manuscripts of the same work.

What emerges from table 1 below is that "Seth" is a very unlikely suggestion, although it seems to be based, for some editors, on traces of ink that suggested an "e" before "th."[3] This is not clear, however.

What is clear is that the reading "Seth" (сне) is unlikely because it does not appear in other lists. The table shows that the closest affinities to the list of rulers in the *Gospel of Judas* are found in the *Gospel of the Egyptians* and in the first list in the *Apocryphon of John*. The most likely conjecture for the *Gospel of Judas*, therefore, is either "Athōth" or "Iaōth." "Haōth" in the Codex III text of the *Apocryphon of John* is something of an outlier.

Jenott, *Gospel of Judas*, 96, 213, for a synopsis, and the helpful synopses in John D. Turner, "The Sethian Myth in the Gospel of Judas," in *The Codex Judas Papers*, ed. A. D. DeConick (Leiden: Brill, 2009), 95–133, esp. 113, 116.

2. Rodolphe Kasser, Marvin Meyer, and Gregor Wurst, eds., *The Gospel of Judas* (Washington, DC: National Geographic, 2006), 38, and Marvin Meyer, "The Gospel of Judas," in *The Nag Hammadi Scriptures*, ed. Marvin Meyer (New York: HarperCollins, 2007), 767; also Johanna Brankaer and Hans-Gebhard Bethge, eds., *Codex Tchacos: Texte und Analysen* (Berlin: de Gruyter, 2012), 278 (Seth); April D. DeConick, *The Thirteenth Apostle: What the Gospel of Judas Really Says*, rev. ed. (London: Continuum, 2009), 118 (Athōth); Jenott, *Gospel of Judas*, 174–75 (Yaōth). Turner, "Sethian Myth in the Gospel of Judas," 116, reads "[Ath]ēth." See further the apparatus criticus in Jenott, *Gospel of Judas*, 174.

3. E.g., Bethge and Brankaer, *Codex Tchacos*, 278.

In the end, however, it does not greatly matter, because the *Gospel of Judas* does not identify any particular characteristics of the first archon, even though other texts do.[4] There may be connotations associated with the different readings: Iaōth evokes the Hebrew divine name, whereas Athōth may evoke the Egyptian god Thoth, especially given the second name in the *Gospel of Judas*'s list "Harmathōth," that is, Hermes-Thoth: some Greeks identified their Hermes with Egyptian Thoth.[5]

Others have questioned the reading "Christ," which appears as usual as the *nomen sacrum* x̄c̄. Jenott, for example, proposes a corruption from the Greek word for "ram" (κριός), although his hypothesis is rather overelaborate.[6] More plausibly, Turner suggests that the *nomen sacrum* x̄c̄ is a contraction not of *Christos* ("Christ") but of *chrēstos* ("good"); hence Athōth/Iaōth would then be "the good one." The *nomen sacrum* contraction x̄c̄ is more naturally read as *Christos*, however: whatever we might imagine the original text to have been, the current text would have been read as a reference to "Christ," and we probably have to be content with that.

In sum, however, there is not a great deal to be discovered from the identification of "Christ" with Athōth/Iaōth. A possible explanation for the identification may lie in the fact that in one text of the *Apocryphon of John*, Yaldabaoth unites the seven *powers* in his thought with the seven *authorities* accompanying him: united with the first authority in the list, Athōth, then is the first power, "goodness" or possibly "Christness" (ⲧⲙⲛⲧⲭⲣ̄ⲥ̄).[7] Another possible explanation is that in the Berlin text of the *Apocryphon of John*, Yaldabaoth-Saklas becomes "Christ" over the other powers. Other manuscripts have "Lord," however, and so the Berlin text looks like a simple transcriptional error.[8]

---

4. In the different texts of the *Apocryphon of John*, e.g.: in NHC II 11.26–27, Athōth has a sheep's face, in BG 41.18 Ïaōth has a lion's face (as does Aōth in NHC III 17.22), while in NHC II 10.29–30, Athōth is referred to possibly as the "reaper" (although the reading is not certain).

5. E.g., the cult center of Thoth was known by the Greek name Hermopolis, and Thoth like Hermes was sometimes called three times great. See, e.g., George Hart, ed., *The Routledge Dictionary of Egyptian Gods and Goddesses*, 2nd ed. (London: Routledge, 2005), 158.

6. It requires two corruptions in sequence: κριός → κύριος → κ̄c̄→ x̄c̄. See Jenott, *Gospel of Judas*, 214.

7. *Ap. John* II 12.15–16: ⲙⲛⲧⲭⲣ̄ⲥ̄ is usually taken as a contraction of ⲙⲛⲧⲭⲣⲏⲥⲧⲟⲥ, "goodness," but could also be taken as a contraction of ⲙⲛⲧⲭⲣⲓⲥⲧⲟⲥ. The fact that the Coptic word is an abstract noun (ⲙⲛⲧ-), however, makes a christological sense in the *Apocryphon of John* less likely. Cf. also the ambiguity in *Ap. John* (NHC II) 6.23, 25, 26 (and parallels) and BG 49.13 and parallels.

8. *Ap. John* BG 42.19, misreading κ̄c̄ for x̄c̄. The two are easily confused. See, e.g., the different manuscript readings of 1 Cor 10:9.

	1	2	3
Gos. Jud. 52.4–11	[. . .]ⲉ = ⲭ(ⲣⲓⲥⲧⲟ)ⲥ [. . .]th = "Christ"	ⲅ̄ⲁⲣⲙⲁⲑⲱⲑ Harmathōth	ⲅⲁⲗⲓⲗⲁ Galila
Gos. Eg. NHC III 58.7–22*	Ath[ōth]	Harmas	[. . .]
Ap. John: list 1† NHC II 10.29–34 BG 40.5–11 NHC III 16.20–25	 Athōth Iaōth Haōth	 Harmas Hermas Harmas	 Kalila-Oumbri Galila Galila
Ap. John: list 2‡ NHC II 11.18–33 BG 41.18–42.6 NHC III 17.20–18.6	 Athōth Ïaōth Aōth	 Elōaiou Elōaios Elōaios	 Astaphaios Astaphaios Astophaios
Ap. John: list 3§ NHC II 12.16–25 BG 43.13–44.4 NHC IV 19.17–26	 Athōth Ïaōth A[th]ō[th]	 Elōaiō Elōaios Elōaios	 Astraphaiō Astaphaios Astraphaios
P. Berlin 20915¶	[Ialda]baōth	Sabaōth	Adōnaios
Jasper Gem**	Ia	Iaō	Sabaōth
Ophite diagram†† Irenaeus version Origen version Celsus version	 Ialdabaoth Hōraios Michaēl	 Iao Ailōaios Souriēl	 Sabaoth Astaphaios Raphaēl

Table 1: Archon Names in Gnostic Lists

Notes: Restorations are not marked, except in the first column. Only the first seven in each list are included.

*Alexander Böhlig and Frederik Wisse, eds., *Nag Hammadi Codices III, 2 and IV, 2: The Gospel of the Egyptians (the Holy Book of the Great Invisible Spirit* (Leiden: Brill, 1975), 122–25. The *Gospel of the Egyptians* has a list of twelve. The text of the list in NHC IV 69–70 is largely lacunose: only the ninth and a fragment of the tenth names survive.

† Frederik Wisse and Michael Waldstein, eds., *The Apocryphon of John: Synopsis of Nag Hammadi Codices II,1; III,1 and IV,1 with BG 8502,2* (Leiden: Brill, 1995), 64–67. Only the eighth name survives in the fragments of NHC IV.

‡ Wisse and Waldstein, *Apocryphon of John*, 70–73. No names in NHC IV survive.

§ Wisse and Waldstein, *Apocryphon of John*, 74–75. No names survive in NHC III. Those in NHC IV in this list are heavily restored and so conjectural.

4	5	6	7
ïⲱⲃⲏⲗ Ïōbēl	ⲁⲁⲱⲛⲁⲓⲟⲥ Adōnaios		
Ïōbēl	Adōnaios = Sabaōth	[. . .]	[. . .]
Ïabēl Ïōbēl Ïōbēl	Adōnaiou = Sabaōth Adōnaios Adōnaios	Kaïn Sabaōth Sabaōth	Abel Kaïnan Kaïnan-Kasin
Ïaō Ïaō Ïazō	Sabaōth Adōnaios Adōnaios	Adōnin Adōni Adōnin	Sabbede Sabbataios Sabbadaios
Iaō Ïaō Ïaō [. . .] Adōnai	Sanbaōth Sabaōth Sabaōth Elōaios Elōai	Adōnein Adoni Adōnein Ōraios Ōreos	Sabbateōn Sabbataios [. . .] [. . .] Astapheos
Adoneus Gabriēl	Eloeus Sabaōth Thauthabaōth	Horeus Iaō Erathaōth	Astaphaeus Ialdabaōth Onoēl Thartharaōth/Thaphabaōth

¶ Gesine Schenke Robinson, Hans-Martin Schenke, and Uwe-Karsten Plisch, eds., *Das Berliner "Koptische Buch" (P 20915): Eine wiederhergestellte frühchristlich-theologische Abhandlung* (Leuven: Peeters, 2004), 1:257.

** Campbell Bonner, "An Amulet of the Ophite Gnostics," in *Commemorative Studies in Honor of Theodore Leslie Shear*, Hesperia Supplements 8 (Princeton: American School of Classical Studies at Athens, 1949), 43–46, 444.

†† Irenaeus, *Haer.* 1.30.5; Celsus: in *Cels.* 6.30; Origen: *Cels.* 6.31.

More significance can be gleaned from the context. The statement that these five "ruled . . . preeminent over chaos" (if that is the right translation) probably alludes to the initial state of the world,[9] "formless and void" in Genesis, and to *Chaos* as the ultimate source of the world in certain strands of Greek cosmogony.[10] The "underworld" that these angels also govern is probably the material world of everyday existence. Nevertheless, they are relatively inferior in the cosmic "lower-archy." The supreme demons Saklas and Nimrod-Yaldabaoth generate twelve angels, then these angels consort with twelve rulers, and together these twenty-four beings generate these five angels. It appears that Saklas and the five angels are the creators of the material Adam and Eve (*Gos. Jud.* 52.14–21).

In sum, this is obviously an extreme case of how the Christ title is used, not only disconnected from the figure of Jesus but assigned a different role altogether, and a negative one at that. It is hard to know the motivation for this usage. Possibly this Christ figure, as first in the list, is seen as a leading agent of Saklas and/or Nimrod-Yaldabaoth, rather like the Christ of the creator in Marcion's system. Possibly the title is seen as too much associated with Judaism to be redeemable and so could for that reason take on a negative association.

2. The Death of Jesus and the Gospel of Judas

The death of Jesus in the *Gospel of Judas* is an event of little significance; indeed, one can only speak of a death of Jesus from a certain point of view, as we will see. The crucifixion is not narrated. Some light is shed on what happens in the final two episodes. Taking the second and concluding passage first, we can note that the text ends with Judas's "betrayal" of Jesus:

> Just then there was a disturbance among the Jews [. . .]. Their chief priests were angry that Jesus had gone to his lodging place to pray. Some of the scribes were there looking to arrest him at prayer, for they feared the people, because the people all held him as a prophet. They approached Judas.

9. In agreement with the translation offered here, Jenott, *Gospel of Judas*, 175, has "chiefs over chaos." Cf. Bethge and Brankaer, *Codex Tchacos*, 279, who take the phrase not as "preeminent (ⲛϭⲟⲣⲡ) over chaos" but as "formerly over chaos" ("zuvor über das Chaos"); also Kasser, Meyer, and Wurst, *Gospel of Judas*, 39: "first of all over chaos."

10. E.g., Hesiod, *Theog.* 116–138, where Chaos is the first "thing" to come into existence (ἤτοι μὲν πρώτιστα Χάος γένετ᾿·); then Erebos and Night come from Chaos (ἐκ Χάεος δ᾿ Ἔρεβός τε μέλαινά τε Νὺξ ἐγένοντο·), and Aether and Day from Night, and so on.

"Why are you here?" they asked him. "You are Jesus's disciple."

He answered them according to their wish. Judas received money and handed [him] over to them. (*Gos. Jud.* 58.6–26)

The picture here is fairly conventional, with allusions to the Synoptic Gospels (and especially Matthew) in the reference to the attempt to arrest Jesus, and its delay because of Jesus's popularity.[11]

More illuminating is the preceding passage, where Jesus forecasts what will happen:

[Jesus speaking:] "Tomorrow, the one who bears me will be tormented. Truly I say to you [pl.], no human mortal hand will sin against me. Truly, [I] say to you [sg.], Judas, [those who] offer up sacrifice to Saklas [. . .] all, since [. . .] everything that is evil. But you will be greater than them all.[12] For you will sacrifice the man who carries me around. Already your horn has become exalted, your anger has burned, your star has passed overhead, and your mind has [. . .].

. . .

"Behold, everything has been told to you. Lift up your eyes and behold the cloud and the light that is in it, and the stars that surround it. The star that is the leader—that is your star."

Judas lifted up his eyes and saw the cloud of light. Then he [i.e., Jesus] leapt into it. Those who stood underneath heard a voice coming from the cloud, which said: ". . . great generation [. . .]." [. . .] and [. . .]. And Judas stopped looking at Jesus. (*Gos. Jud.* 56.6–58.6)

Three points are notable here.

First, there is the repeated, threefold stress on how the crucifixion will have no effect upon Jesus. (1) It is the *one who bears* Jesus (ⲡⲉⲧⲣ̄ϥⲟⲣⲉⲓ ⲙ̄ⲙⲟⲓ̈ [56.6–7]) who will be tormented, hence Jesus distances himself from the agony of crucifixion. (2) In contrast, no sin will be committed against the "real" Jesus per se in the betrayal and crucifixion: "no human mortal hand will sin[?] against me" (*Gos. Jud.* 56.9–10).[13] (3) In terms similar to the first reassurance about the

---

11. See Simon Gathercole, "Matthean or Lukan Priority? The Use of the NT Gospels in the Gospel of Judas," in *Judasevangelium und Codex Tchacos*, ed. E. E. Popkes and G. Wurst (Tübingen: Mohr Siebeck, 2012), 291–302.

12. Or, "You will do more," i.e., Judas will be *worse*.

13. The text is very corrupt here, however, so certainty about the text is impossible.

torment, Jesus reaffirms the fact that it is Jesus's "carrier" who will be crucified: "For you will sacrifice the man who carries me around" (*Gos. Jud.* 56.20–22). Clearly there is a distinction between Jesus's speaking "I" and the physical body that will endure the crucifixion.

Second, the passage offers a potential explanation for this. On the initial discovery of the text, it looked as though it might be Judas who jumps into the cloud, whereas there is now general agreement that it is Jesus. This event is a kind of transfiguration, in which Jesus enters the cloud and then speaks from within it. But it probably also alludes to the account of the ascension in Acts: "After he said this, he was taken up before their very eyes, and a cloud hid him from their sight" (Acts 1:9). After Jesus enters the cloud, he speaks from there but does not say or do anything else on the ground. There is a strong possibility, then, that the carried Jesus, his immaterial or spiritual being, has been removed at this point from the earthly sphere. If this is right, and we cannot be sure because of the fragmentary nature of the text, the disconnection between Jesus's true nature and the crucified carrier is complete. At the very least, though, the *Gospel of Judas* stops short theologically of saying that Jesus is threatened by a death, just as it also stops short narratively of describing the crucifixion. Clearly there is no thought here of an effective death.

Finally, we can return to the scene at the beginning of the Gospel, in which Jesus encounters his disciples assembled. It is notable that when Jesus sees the disciples "giving thanks" (ⲣ̄-ⲉⲩⲭⲁⲣⲓⲥⲧⲓ) over the bread, he laughs and explains his laughter on the grounds that the disciples are worshiping another god (*Gos. Jud.* 33.26–34.18).[14] The disciples then ask why he is laughing at their "thanksgiving," or "Eucharist" (ⲉⲩⲭⲁⲣⲓⲥⲧⲓⲁ). The point is therefore probably a polemic against the "Eucharist," which by the time of the composition of the *Gospel of Judas* is already for some (e.g., Ignatius and Justin) a conventional term referring to the commemoration of Jesus's saving death.[15]

---

14. Similarly, the disciples have a vision of priests wallowing in slaughter as they call upon Jesus's name (*Gos. Jud.* 38.1–39.25), and Jesus interprets this vision as a vision of the disciples themselves, although the slaughter in this case is not Jesus's death but the figurative "sacrifice" of their congregations whom the disciples lead astray (39.25–40.7).

15. So also Jenott, *Gospel of Judas*, 191. For the use of εὐχαριστ- language in a technical sense, see, e.g., *Did.* 9–10; Ign. *Phld.* 4.1; Ign. *Smyrn.* 6.2; Justin, 1 *Apol.* 66.1; 67.5; *Dial.* 41.1, 3; 117.1; *Acts John* 110.

3. Jesus's Resurrection and the Gospel of Judas

There is even less to say about the resurrection of Jesus in the *Gospel of Judas*, presumably because there is no such event. Since the final event recorded before the *subscriptio* is "Judas received money and handed [him] over to them," we have even less reference to resurrection than to death—none at all, in fact. If the suggestion above about Jesus's removal to the cloud is accepted, this would mean that the physical body crucified no longer had any relationship to Jesus at all, and so would hardly be a candidate for resurrection. Indeed, on any view of the *Gospel of Judas*, it is hard to imagine the viability of a resurrection for the bodily Jesus. That body is merely a participant in the earthly version of the "corruption" (ⲫⲑⲟⲣⲁ) pictured in the heavenly realms (*Gos. Jud.* 50.13–14). The grand finale of the Gospel narrative is not resurrection but Judas selling Jesus for thirty pieces of silver, or here just "some money."

4. Fulfillment of Scripture and the Gospel of Judas

The *Gospel of Judas* is replete with scriptural characters and locations. The text begins with the action defined chronologically in relation to the Passover festival (33.5–6). Biblical categories of "righteousness" and "transgression" are introduced in the prologue (33.10–13). Parts of the theogony and cosmogony are introduced with the formula, "Let there be" (ⲙⲁⲣⲉϥϣⲱⲡⲉ or ⲙⲁⲣⲟⲩϣⲱⲡⲉ), on one occasion answered by "and it was so" (ⲁⲩⲱ ⲁⲥϣⲱⲡⲉ).[16] The creations include light, two luminaries, heavens, firmaments, and a cosmos. These heavenly aeons are populated by Adamas, Seth and his generation, Nimrod, "Christ," Yobel (Hebrew for "Jubilee"), Adonaios (cf. Hebrew *'dny*), Michael, and Gabriel.[17] Adam and Eve are created with the words, "Let us make man according to the likeness and according to the image," and earth is populated by "the twelve tribes of Israel," and in general by "Adam with his generation."[18]

---

16. *Gos. Jud.* 47.16–17; 48.1–2; 48.10 (sg. ⲙⲁⲣⲉϥϣⲱⲡⲉ); 48.6; 51.5 (pl. ⲙⲁⲣⲟⲩϣⲱⲡⲉ). For ⲁⲩⲱ ⲁⲥϣⲱⲡⲉ, see 48.2–3; cf. also 48.10 (ⲁⲩⲱ ⲁϥϣⲱⲡⲉ).

17. Adamas, Seth, and his generation: *Gos. Jud.* 48.21–49.6; "Christ," "Yobel," and "Adonaios": 52.6–11; Michael and Gabriel: 53.20, 23. Nimrod appears in *Gos. Jud.* 51.12–13, 17 as one of Saklas's demonic associates: the spelling "Nebro" in the *Gospel of Judas* reflects the Greek spelling Νεβρωδ in the Septuagint of Gen 10:8–9; 1 Chr 1:10; Mic 5:6.

18. The creation of Adam and Eve: *Gos. Jud.* 52.14–21; "the twelve tribes of Israel": *Gos. Jud.* 55.8–9. For Adam and his generation, see *Gos. Jud.* 53.11–12, and cf. 56.5–6: "the whole generation of the earthly Adam."

There is even a notion of fulfillment:

> Jesus said, "Truly I say to you, when the stars over them have all completed their courses, and when Saklas has completed the times that have been appointed for him, their leading star will come with the generations, and what has been spoken of will be fulfilled.
>
> "Then they will commit sexual immorality in my name, and will kill their children and [. . .] evil and [. . .] the aeons that bring their generations, presenting them to Saklas. After that, [. . .]rael will come bringing the twelve tribes of Israel from [. . .] and all the generations that sinned in my name will serve Saklas. And {and} your star will ru[le] over the thirteenth aeon." After this, Jesus laughed.
>
> "Master, wh[y are you laughing?]" asked Judas.
>
> [Jesus] replied [and said], "I am not laughing [at yo]u [pl.] but at the error of the stars, because these six stars were deceived with these five warriors, and all these will perish with their creations." (*Gos. Jud.* 54.15–55.22)

In this passage, there is a sense, perhaps surprisingly given the picture of the cosmos elsewhere in the book, of the stars following an orderly pattern. Parallel to this, Saklas has a limited time of activity, after which his power will presumably be annulled. After the stars and Saklas have run their courses, "what has been spoken of will be fulfilled" (54.23–24). This may be a reference to the speech of the generations that have just been mentioned, hence the translation of Kasser, Meyer, and Wurst: "they will finish what they said they would do."[19] Perhaps more likely is a reference to the fulfillment of some of Jesus's own speech. He has previously spoken of events that would fit into this context, such as the disciples' own sin (38.12–40.26), which matches closely what immediately follows the reference to fulfillment: "Then they will commit adultery in my name, and they will kill their children and . . . evil" (54.24–55.1). Or again, other possibilities include Jesus's teaching about the stars and the kingdom, or about Judas's destiny.[20]

There is no indication, however, of any positive reference to the fulfillment of Israel's scripture, and it would be very surprising if there were, given the picture of the creator god Saklas and his minions.

19. Kasser, Meyer, and Wurst, *Gospel of Judas*, 42.
20. *Gos. Jud.* 45.12–46.2 and 46.18–47.1, respectively.

CONCLUSION: THE GOSPEL OF JUDAS AND THE KERYGMA

Overall, some of what emerges from the *Gospel of Judas* is not unexpected, given its wider theological profile. It shares with other Gnostic works a rejection of the idea that Jesus might die and rise again, as well as having a distaste for the Old Testament. Some of these themes we will encounter in the *Gospel of the Egyptians*. On the other hand, the reference to "Christ" as the byname of a demon is genuinely unexpected, although there are some parallels with Marcion's concept of the creator god's warlike Christ figure.

There is thus almost no interest in the kerygma as it is represented in the earlier Christian sources we examined in chapters 2 and 3. Indeed, to the extent that there is interest in the model, it is of a negative kind, in the radical treatment of the Christ title and the polemical attitude to Jesus's death represented in its treatment of the Eucharist.

Chapter Fourteen

THE COPTIC GOSPEL OF THE EGYPTIANS

The Nag Hammadi *Gospel of the Egyptians*, or perhaps more properly the *Egyptian Gospel*, is also known as the Holy Book of the Great Invisible Spirit.[1] It can be divided into four parts and a conclusion.[2] First, it begins with the enumeration of a bewildering array of deities who come into being as part of the heavenly bureaucracy. The prime being is the Great Invisible Spirit, who emanates a trinity of Father, Mother, and Son, each of whom in turn becomes differentiated into eight elements, and so on (*Gos. Eg.* III 40.12–56.22). The second section, which begins after an interval of five thousand years, describes the emergence of the demonic realm (56.22–59.1). The demonic beings who arrive on the scene include figures such as Saklas ("Fool") and Nebrouel ("Nimrod-God"). In the wake of the activity of these demons, third (59.1–64.9), the divine Seth undertakes to rescue his seed, who are the heavenly spirits or identities of his elect disciples on earth. Eventually Seth comes himself to earth, fused with the person of Jesus. The last section of the work (64.9–68.1) is concerned with the ritual activities of the group, which involve baptism and a series of "renunciations." A conclusion (68.1–69.5) describes how Seth himself wrote

---

1. *Gos. Eg.* III 69.6, ⲡⲉⲩⲁⲅⲅⲉⲗⲓⲟⲛ ⲛ̄ⲣⲙ̄ⲛ̄ⲕⲏⲙⲉ, suggests the sense "Egyptian Gospel." The title "the Holy Book of the Great Invisible Spirit" appears in *Gos. Eg.* III 69.18–20.

2. The work survives in two manuscripts from the Nag Hammadi hoard, and both probably date to the fourth or fifth century. The textual base for the analysis here is primarily Codex III, though Codex IV is used especially for the corresponding portion of Codex III where there is a large lacuna (pp. 45–48), and occasionally in other places where the readings seem preferable; in addition, each of the two texts is continually needed to supply gaps in the other. Unless otherwise specified, references are to Codex III. I have used the Coptic text printed in Alexander Böhlig and Frederik Wisse, eds., *Nag Hammadi Codices III,2 and IV,2: The Gospel of the Egyptians (the Holy Book of the Great Invisible Spirit)* (Leiden: Brill, 1975), while also consulting the facsimile edition in a few difficult places.

the Gospel, and a colophon contains the book's various titles and a scribal note (69.6–20).[3]

The specific religious outlook of the *Egyptian Gospel* corresponds to what we know of the Gnostics. This is evident partly from what is said of the nature of the creator god and his creation. The two "generating spirits of earth" (*Gos. Eg.* III 57.17–19) are both evil figures, with Nebrouel explicitly called a demon.[4] The other, Saklas, declares, "I, I am God, and apart from me there is no other!" (58.24–26), making it clear that the infernal realm that he inhabits is utterly separated from the higher plane of the Great Invisible Spirit and his emanations. An evil creator, rather than one who is good, or simply ignorant, is a hallmark of Gnostic sects. The cast of characters also resembles those in other Gnostic works: the Great Invisible Spirit and Barbelo, on the one hand, and Saklas, Nimrod, and the list of the sentinels of hell, on the other (58.7–22), correspond closely to the dramatis personae of, for example, the *Gospel of Judas*. As in other Gnostic texts, then, the goal of salvation in the *Gospel of the Egyptians* is not the redemption of the world but total liberation from the material realm, which—like its creators—is evil. The salvation of the individual involves both knowledge and the ritual practices that are delineated at the end of the Gospel.

As in the case of the *Gospel of Judas*, we will not see a great deal of connection with the elements of the kerygma, although the greater complexity of the *Gospel of the Egyptians* demands a treatment slightly longer than that of the previous chapter.

1. "CHRIST" IN THE GOSPEL OF THE EGYPTIANS

The problem in the *Egyptian Gospel* lies not in identifying a Christ figure but in the plurality of children, Sons, and Christs. We will focus here on the beings labeled Jesus or as "Christ" or a similar title, going sequentially through the unfolding of the pantheon in the *Gospel of the Egyptians*.[5]

---

3. For another account of the structure, see the summary statement in John D. Turner, "The Holy Book of the Great Invisible Spirit," in *The Nag Hammadi Scriptures*, ed. Marvin Meyer (New York: HarperOne, 2007), 247–51.

4. Cf. *Gos. Eg.* IV 69.3–4 where some of the text is better preserved and may suggest the sense that Saklas and Nebrouel together constitute a single begetting spirit.

5. I am leaving aside here the Christology of the colophon, which is clearly appended by the scribe (NHC III 69.8–20): "Grace, understanding, perception and wisdom be with him who wrote: beloved Eugnostus in the Spirit—in the flesh my name is Concessus—and my

1.1 The Initial Sequence of Emanations

As noted in the introduction, the Great Invisible Spirit generates the first triad:[6]

Great Invisible Spirit
↓
Father   Mother   Son

If the additional phrase in Codex IV's account of this process is to be accepted, then this is not so much an emergence of separate beings but an emanation of the Spirit's own being: Father, Mother, and Son are said to have "come forth from themselves" (*Gos. Eg.* IV 50.26–27).

From the same place of this first triad's origin comes a power called Domedon Doxomedon, who produces what seems to be a mirror image of this first triad, a mirror image in that it consists of the same dramatis personae but in reverse order:[7]

Great Invisible Spirit → Domedon Doxomedon
↓   ↓
Father   Mother   Son   Son   Mother   Father

A third process is the emanation of three Ogdoads or Eights:[8]

Great Invisible Spirit
↓
Father Ogdoad   Mother Ogdoad   Son Ogdoad

These may not be different from the first triad; rather this process may be filling out, or introducing differentiation into, the component figures of the first triad:

---

fellow luminaries in incorruptibility. Jesus Christ, the Son of God and savior. ICHTHUS. The divinely written and holy book of the Great Invisible Spirit. Amen. *The Holy Book of the Great Invisible Spirit. Amen.*"

6. *Gos. Eg.* III 41.7–12 // IV 50.23–51.2.

7. *Gos. Eg.* III 41.13–23 // IV 51.2–15.

8. *Gos. Eg.* III 41.23–43.8 // IV 51.15–53.3.

Great Invisible Spirit

↓

Father Ogdoad:	Mother Ogdoad:	Son Ogdoad:
Thought	Mother[9]	The seven
Reason[10]	Virginal Barbelo	powers
Incorruptibility	[?]Epititiōch[. . .]kaba[11]	of the
Eternal Life	Adonai	great light
Will	Memeneaimen	of the
Intellect	[?]Karb[. . .]akrōbōriarōr[12]	seven voices
Foreknowledge	uninterpretable power	
androgynous Father	ineffable Mother	The word/Word

Next, a child comes onto the scene and is located within the Domedon Doxomedon aeon:[13]

This mysterious "Triple Male Child" has in fact already been mentioned in passing as having come for the sake of the first Ogdoad (*Gos. Eg.* III 42.5–7).

Thus far, then, we have (1) a "Son" (ϣΗΡЄ) figure from the first emanated triad, (2) a mirrored "Son" projected from the Domedon Doxomedon aeon, and an eightfold distinction introduced (perhaps) into the first Son, the completion of which is (1*) the Word (ΠϢΑΧЄ). Finally, there is also (3) the "(Triple) Male Child."

9. The identity of the Mother as the first element is clearer in the copy in Codex IV.

10. This could also be a reference to another (!) Word.

11. It appears that in Codex III, the name of the third element begins "Epititiōch[. . .]," and in Codex IV the name ends "[. . .]kaba."

12. It appears that in Codex III, the name of the third element begins "Karb[. . .]," and in Codex IV, the name ends "[. . .]akroboriaor."

13. *Gos. Eg.* III 43.8–17 // IV 53.3–15.

1.2 The Presentations of Praise

After roughly one-sixth of the total surviving text, which has consisted of the first sequence of emanations, a new set of divine beings comes into existence. This second set comes into being because, in each case, one of the already existing divinities gives praise to the rest of the pantheon and requests a new divinity for itself.

The first request to the Great Invisible Spirit, from the three Ogdoads, results in the emanation of "silent silence," as well as a host of other beings, including the offspring of the male generation (*Gos. Eg.* III 44.14–19).

The second request is from the "Triple Male Child," and intriguingly this child is said to be the offspring "of the Great Christ." This is not a terribly helpful piece of information at this point, because this Great Christ has not yet been mentioned. We are told, however, that this Great Christ has been anointed by the Great Invisible Spirit:

> Then the Triple Male Child of the Great Christ, whom the [Great] Invisible Spirit—whose power was given the name Ainōn—had anointed, gave praise to the Great Invisible Spirit and his male virgin Yōēl. (*Gos. Eg.* III 44.22–27)

Hence the *Gospel of the Egyptians* is clearly tapping into the etymology of "Christ" as do some New Testament epistles and the Valentinian Gospels already discussed. There may even be some kind of connection between anointing and baptism here, since at this point, the Great Invisible Spirit (or his power) is suddenly given the title "Ainōn." This is sometimes interpreted as meaning "praising" (from Greek αἰνέω), but Ainōn ("Springs") is also the name of a place where John the Baptist baptized (John 3:23).[14]

A later passage elaborates upon the description of the Great Christ, identifying him as "the undefiled child Telmaēl Telmachaēl Ēli Ēli Machar Sēth, the living power" (*Gos. Eg.* IV 59.18–21). I take it that the second part of this name is a corruption of the cry of dereliction, "Eli Seth lama sabachthani"; if so, this might hint at some kind of connection of the figure with Jesus.

Another statement about the son of the Great Christ (presumably still "the Triple Male Child") appears shortly afterward: "'[. . .]aia[. . .]thaōthōsth[. . .],' who is the son of the Great Christ, who in turn is the son of the Ineffable

---

14. Cf. John's spelling Αἰνών and Aramaic *'ynwn*: for this consonantal spelling, see Jastrow, 1072a.

Silence" (*Gos. Eg.* IV 60.6–9). More accessible names for the Great Christ's son are, later, "'Autogenes' [i.e., 'Self-Generated'], who is also the 'Word.'"[15]

The result of this second request is unclear because of gaps in the manuscripts, but it may well be the appearance of "the child Ēsēphēch," later identified as "the keeper of the glory" and "the child of the child."[16] This designation "the child of the child" adds weight to the probability that Ēsēphēch appears as an emanation (at the gift of the Great Invisible Spirit in *Gos. Eg.* IV 56.8–11) of the Triple Male Child.

Hence this possible genealogy:

the Ineffable Silence
↓
the Great Christ
(Telmaēl Telmachaēl Ēli Ēli Machar Sēth)
↓
the Triple Male Child
(= Autogenes = the Word)
↓
the child Ēsēphēch
(Child of the Child)

Autogenes here, who is the principal character who is labeled "god" (ⲚⲞⲨⲦⲈ), also has a male partner who is a "man," namely Adamas. (He is still a supramundane being, however.) The name is clearly an allusion to the biblical Adam, but its ending makes his name mean "indomitable" or "unconquerable" (Greek ἀδάμας). Autogenes and Adamas mingle, and as a result, a "Word of Man" or "human word" came to be (*Gos. Eg.* III 49.16–22).

Adamas also, independently of Autogenes, generates a son from himself—as the gift of all the powers, to whom Adamas made his request. This son is, per the biblical narrative, called Seth (cf. Gen 4:25). Perhaps as a result of a descent of the Great Christ (*Gos. Eg.* III 54.18–55.1), the spiritual church comes into being (55.1–11). (The descent is not a descent to planet earth but to another supramundane plane lower than the Great Christ's natural habitat.) This church consists of the spiritual selves of the elect and so can also be called the seed of the Father (54.6–11). Seth presents praise and requests this seed for

15. *Gos. Eg.* III 49.16–18 // IV 61.18–19.
16. Respectively, *Gos. Eg.* IV 56.20–22 ("the child Ēsēphēch"); IV 59.24–25 ("the keeper of the glory"); III 50.3 // IV 62.2–3 ("the child of the child").

himself (55.16–56.3). At this request, Plēsithea appears (56.4–13). The Greek components of her name appropriately suggest both abundance (πλησ-) and divinity (-θεα), because she is "the glorious mother, the four-breasted virgin," so she is at the same time both a pure virgin and ultrafertile. She granted Seth his seed. This marks the culmination of the series of perfect emanations, before things turn bad.

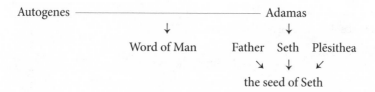

As an interim report, we can first recall the various Christlike emanations we noted in the first series in section 1.1: (1) a "Son" (ϣⲏⲣⲉ) figure from the first emanated triad, who is probably filled out as an Ogdoad, the completing element of which is (1*) the Word; (2) a mirrored "Son" from Domedon Doxomedon; and (3) the "Triple Male Child," now identified as the Word and Autogenes. To this we can now add from section 1.2 (leaving aside the host of anonymous triple male offspring): (4) "the Great Christ," who properly belongs in sequence before the Triple Male Child who is his son; (5) "the child Ēsēphēch," who is "child of the child"; (6) the "Word of Man" or "human word"; and (7) Seth, whose connection with Jesus becomes apparent later.

1.3 The Three Parousias

Suddenly in the narrative, although reportedly "after five thousand years," evil comes on to the scene.[17] For some reason, rulers over Chaos and hell are needed, and first a cloud, identified as material Sophia, appears, and somehow by her will demonic creators come forth:[18]

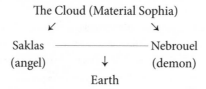

---

17. *Gos. Eg.* III 56.22–23 // IV 68.5.
18. *Gos. Eg.* III 56.26–57.19 // IV 68.9–69.4.

The principal demon, "Saklas the great angel," enclosed in his own realm and believing that he was the ultimate reality, claimed that he is the only god (*Gos. Eg.* III 58.23–59.1). He was duly informed from above, however, "There are the Man and the Son of Man" (59.1–4). It is plausible to assume that Adamas is "the Man" (as he has already been labeled), and Seth the Son of Man.

After this dark side of the heavenly realms is apparent, the process of salvation begins and is accomplished by the three comings of Seth. We will return to this in more detail when we come to consider the reception of Jesus's death in the *Gospel of the Egyptians*. For now, we can note that one climactic moment is the coming of Seth "through a body generated by the Word that the Great Seth mysteriously prepared for himself through the virgin" (*Gos. Eg.* III 63.10–13). A similar combination comes in the description of baptism, which is instituted in part by "the incorruptible one generated by the Word, (and) the living Jesus, and the Great Seth who clothed himself with him" (63.25–64.3).[19]

The "(and)" in parenthesis here is because the account of the incarnation is garbled in at least one of the Coptic texts:

NHC III 63.9–13
and by baptism, through
(1) a body generated by the Word that
(2) the Great Seth mysteriously prepared for himself through the virgin.

NHC IV 74.24–29
and by baptism of the body through
(1) the one generated by the Word, he whom
(2) the Great Seth mysteriously prepared for himself through the virgin.

NHC III 63.22–64.3
Through her, he decreed the holy baptism that surpasses heaven by
(1) the incorruptible one generated by the Word (and)
(2) the living Jesus and
(3) the Great Seth who clothed himself with him.

NHC IV 75.11–17
Through her, he established the holy one and the baptism that surpasses heaven by
(1) the holy one and
(2) the incorruptible one
(3) and the living, Word-generated Jesus, the one with whom the Great Seth clothed himself.

The most elegant solution to this puzzle is that there are simply two elements in the incarnation, namely the heavenly Seth and the bodily Jesus. This is

19. Here I am going against the translation in the critical edition, which identifies the body and Jesus and Seth: "the incorruptible, Logos-begotten one, even Jesus the living one, even he whom the Great Seth has put on" (Codex III: Böhlig and Wisse, *Nag Hammadi Codices*, 146), or "the holy one and the incorruptible one, even Jesus who has been begotten by a living word" (Codex IV: Böhlig and Wisse, *Nag Hammadi Codices*, 147).

apparent in both texts of the former passage cited above, although there are variations in the two accounts. In the latter passage, the difficulty is that we are presented with a list of items separated by "and" (ⲙⲛ̄), which would suggest distinct beings—three in Codex III and four in Codex IV. It is quite possible here, however, that in Codex III, (1) the incorruptible one generated by the Word, and (2) the living Jesus, are one and the same. Support for this might arise from the presence of Codex IV's third item in the list, "the living, Word-generated Jesus" in a single phrase. Hence, the Greek might well originally have referred to only two beings, (1) the incorruptible, living Jesus generated by the Word, and (2) Seth. The difficulties here are twofold. In the first place, this is what neither of the Coptic texts reads. Second, while this may be the most elegant way for the reader—armed with Occam's razor—to cut through the difficulties, the *Gospel of the Egyptians* has such a multiplicity of beings elsewhere that Occam's razor may not be the best tool for analyzing the work.

In either case, it may well not be accurate to say here that "Jesus is the embodiment of Seth on earth," or that the relation between Seth and Jesus is equated with that between the soul and the body.[20] The difficulty with the former is that what appears to be envisaged is more a union of Seth and Jesus than Jesus representing Seth; the problem with the latter is that the *Egyptian Gospel* pictures the Jesus figure as a distinct being in some sense ("the living Jesus"), rather than merely a physical shell.[21]

1.4 The Baptismal Discourse

This leads us into the final section (*Gos. Eg.* III 64.9–68.1), which a number of scholars consider the real focus of the book. After the account of the establishment of baptism, there is a large list of appearances, presumably of those who appeared at that prototypical baptism of the incarnate Seth-Jesus.

The first figure to appear is the great attendant "Yesseus Mazareus Yessedekeus" (ⲓⲉⲥⲥⲉⲟⲥ ⲙⲁⲍⲁⲣⲉⲟⲥ ⲓⲉⲥⲥⲉⲇⲉⲕⲉⲟⲥ). The first two names are clearly a

---

20. So, respectively, Böhlig and Wisse, *Nag Hammadi Codices*, 21, and Bentley Layton, *The Gnostic Scriptures: A New Translation with Annotations and Introductions* (New York: Doubleday, 1987), 116 n. 75c.

21. Although in *Gos. Eg.* III 63.10–11 we have the "Word-begotten body," in *Gos. Eg.* III 63.25–64.3 the figure whom Seth puts on is the "incorruptible Word-begotten one, Jesus the living one." To call Jesus "the living one" suggests rather more than a mere physical body assumed by Seth. In Codex IV, the point is even clearer, since we do not have the phrase "Word-begotten body" in the first place: the reference is rather, as already noted above, to "the baptism of the body through the one generated by the Word" (*Gos. Eg.* IV 74.24–26).

bastardization of "Jesus of Nazareth."[22] He is called "the living water."[23] He appears again in the hymn at the end of this final section of the work (*Gos. Eg.* III 66.8–68.1),[24] again called "living water."[25] In this hymn, he emerges not just as one among many objects of vision, as in the earlier passage, but rather as an extremely exalted figure, "child of the child" (66.11), perfect and self-begotten (66.23–24). There may be an identification, via this title "child of the child," with Esephech noted earlier.

In the second section of this hymn,[26] Jesus, "God of silence," the "Son," is addressed.[27] This raises the (unanswerable) question of whether there is some kind of identity or relationship between Jesus and Yesseus Mazareus Yessedekeus: both are addressed in similar terms, with sequences of vowels, the frequently occurring phrase "truly truly," and as "existing forever."[28]

1.5 Interim Conclusion: The Egyptian Gospel's "Christ" and the Kerygma

Congratulations if you are still with me. In sum, we have the following figures who reflect elements associated with Jesus Christ:

1. the "Son" in the first triad—
   filled out as an Ogdoad, the final component of which is (1*) the Word
2. a mirrored "Son" from Domedon Doxomedon,
3. the "Triple Male Child," that is, Word, or Autogenes,
4. "the Great Christ," father of (3) the Triple Male Child,

---

22. The last is less well understood. Meyer, *Nag Hammadi Scriptures*, 265 n. 71, proposes a corruption of Ἰησοῦς + ὁ δίκαιος. Another possibility, in view of the baptismal context, is ἐν σοὶ εὐδόκησα. Or perhaps a corrupted phrase about Jesus's connection with Jesse is a possibility: e.g., Ἰεσσαὶ δὲ ἐγέννησεν (Matt 1:6). One can only speculate here.

23. *Gos. Eg.* III 64.11–12 // IV 75.26–27.

24. In *Gos. Eg.* III 66.10, the name appears in full, in vocative form; in *Gos. Eg.* IV 78.10, the name appears first just as ιεϲϲεοϲ, with the full three-part name appearing in 78.12–13, in nominative form.

25. *Gos. Eg.* III 66.11 // IV 78.13.

26. It is possible that this section is spoken antiphonally: thus Meyer's translation of ϩⲛ ⲕⲉⲥⲙⲏ in *Gos. Eg.* III 66.27 as "in another voice." See Meyer, *Nag Hammadi Scriptures*, 268. If this is the case, however, the version in Codex IV would have misunderstood the reference.

27. *Gos. Eg.* III 67.15–17 // IV 80.1–4. The passage in *Gos. Eg.* III 65.10–18 about "the Great Seth," "Jesus the author of life," and "the one who came forth and crucified the contents of the law" will be dealt with in the discussion of the death of Jesus below.

28. *Gos. Eg.* III 66.19 (ⲡⲉⲧϣⲟⲟⲡ ϣⲁ ⲁⲛⲏϩⲉ ⲉⲛⲉϩ) // 67.26 (ⲡⲉⲧϣⲟⲟⲡ ϣⲁ ⲉⲛⲉϩ).

5. "the child Ēsēphēch," "Child of the Child," that is, of (3) the Triple Male Child,

6. the "Word of Man," or "human word,"

7. Seth,

8. the "body generated by the Word," through which Seth comes,

9. the living Jesus,

10. Yesseus Mazareus Yessedekeus.

This is admittedly a maximal list, and some identifications may be possible, such as between the two "Words" (1*) and (3). Furthermore (8) and (9) may perhaps be identified. It is also highly schematic, and so some figures might be, if not identified, at least blurry in their distinction: hence it looks very much as though the Great Christ is identified as Telmaēl Telmachaēl Ēli Ēli Machar Sēth (*Gos. Eg.* IV 59.16–21), whereas elsewhere the Triple Male Child, who is child of the Great Christ, is called by the same set of *nomina barbara*.[29]

Contrary to the *Gospel of Judas*, the Christ figure in the *Egyptian Gospel* is positive, and the connection with anointing is retained: as we have seen, he is "the Great Christ, whom the Great Invisible Spirit had anointed." On the other hand, there is nothing to suggest that Jesus here is to be identified with the "Great Christ" figure or any of the other sons featured in the theogonic material earlier in the book. This is similar to the disconnect in the *Gospel of Judas*. The same phenomenon is seen in other Gnostic works, such as the Three Forms of First Thought (or Trimorphic Protennoia) where the "Christ" is mentioned several times, and Jesus only once at the end in a fashion unrelated to the references to Christ, or again in the *Apocryphon of John* where there are frequent references to the Christ, but Jesus is not named at all in the short recension except in a postscript, "Jesus Christ Amen."[30] It seems highly probable that in the *Gospel of the Egyptians*, the Great Christ is split from the figure of Jesus. Jesus is rather lower than the Great Christ in the chain of being, separate from the Great Christ by several stages of begetting.[31] Nor is there any sense of messianic biblical exegesis used in connection either with Jesus or with the Christ figure. The scriptural discourse that constitutes messiah-talk in the kerygma is left behind for reasons that will be seen further in the final section of this chapter.

---

29. *Gos. Eg.* III 62.2–4 // IV 73.12–14.

30. The phrase appears at the end of the text in NHC II and IV, but not in the texts in NHC III and the Berlin Gnostic Codex.

31. He is associated less with Christ than with Seth, and—as we will see in section 3 of this chapter—is "the one whom the Great Seth put on" (*Gos. Eg.* III 64.2–3).

2. A Death of Jesus in the Gospel of the Egyptians?

As noted in the discussion of the Christ title in the *Egyptian Gospel*, there is a three-part *Heilsgeschichte* in the work. Seth is sent off and goes through a series of parousias,[32] first a cataclysm, or flood, and second a conflagration: the former seems to be patterned on the biblical flood of Gen 7, a specific reference for the second is less clear.[33] The third of the three parousias is "the judgment of the archons and powers and authorities" and is given more extensive description,[34] as it is a climactic redemptive act "to save what had gone astray" (*Gos. Eg.* III 63.8–9). As noted in the discussion of "Christ," there is some kind of incarnation here: one text at least refers to "a body generated by the Word that the Great Seth mysteriously prepared for himself through the virgin."[35] This two-natures incarnation later appears to be recast as tripartite: baptism is instituted "(1) by the incorruptible one generated by the Word and (2) the living Jesus and (3) the Great Seth who clothed himself with him."[36] The question, discussed earlier, of whether this tripartition is actually only a two-natures incarnation is hard to resolve.

The role of this variegated incarnate unity is a crucifixion, but an active crucifying rather than a passive death:

> Through him [i.e., the living Jesus], he [i.e., Seth] nailed the powers of the thirteen aeons and confirmed those who bring forth and those who take away, equipping them with the armory of knowledge of the truth in unconquerable, incorruptible power.[37]

Later a clearly related statement appears, in a list of who dwells in the four luminaries. The second is Oroïaēl:

> The second light Oroïaēl, the place of the Great Seth, and of Jesus to whom life belongs, the one who came and crucified what was in (Cod. III)/under (Cod. IV) the law.[38]

---

32. *Gos. Eg.* III 62.24–25 // IV 74.9–10.

33. In the first, the Greek loanword κατακλυσμός, also used of the flood in Gen 7, is employed. Cf. the flood, fire, and punishment in *Apoc. Adam* 69.2–77.18.

34. *Gos. Eg.* III 63.7–64.9 // IV 74.21–75.24.

35. *Gos. Eg.* III 63.9–13; cf. IV 74.24–29.

36. *Gos. Eg.* III 63.25–64.3; cf. IV 75.14–17.

37. *Gos. Eg.* III 64.3–9; cf. IV 75.18–24.

38. *Gos. Eg.* III 65.16–18 // IV 77.12–15.

The activity of this incarnate Seth has consequences both at the supramundane level (in the first passage) and in the earthly realm (in the second). The nailing of the powers of the thirteen aeons in the former (*Gos. Eg.* III 64.3–9), probably identical with "the judgment of the archons and powers and authorities" mentioned earlier (63.7–8), is a liberation of the seed of Seth from the threat of danger. In contrast, the second passage speaks of the crucifixion of what is oppressed on the earthly plane, by the law, or perhaps—per Codex III—the crucifixion of its contents.

It is notable in all this, however, that there is no suggestion of a death of a redeemer figure. The "nailing" and "crucifying" is all done *by*, not *to*, the incarnate Seth. Here the *Gospel of the Egyptians* draws exclusively upon traditional formulations of how, through Jesus, forces opposing God and human beings are crucified (e.g., Gal 6:14; Col 2:14). There is a reticence here not shown by, for example, the *Gospel of Truth* or the canonical Gospels, a desire to distance the divine Seth—as well as the living Jesus—from death. We might expect to find that the *Egyptian Gospel* was closer to other "classic Gnostic" texts. And that is indeed what we do find: just as the *Gospel of Judas* stops short theologically of saying that Jesus is threatened by death and stops short narratively of describing the crucifixion, so the *Gospel of the Egyptians* confines itself to talking of Jesus's/Seth's crucifying in the active rather than passive voice. Hence the *Egyptian Gospel* is clearly cognizant of ideas about Jesus's death but chooses to configure Jesus as the crucifier rather than the crucified.

3. RESURRECTION AND THE GOSPEL OF THE EGYPTIANS

As is the case in the *Gospel of Judas*, which neither refers in advance to a resurrection, nor announces, nor narrates any appearances, in the same way there is no place in the *Gospel of the Egyptians* for a resurrection of Jesus. The designation "the living Jesus" does not relate to resurrection but is suggestive of Jesus as eternally living and as a source of life.[39] There has been no sign of a death, and so a resurrection could not be expected.[40]

---

39. Cf. *Gos. Thom.* prologue.

40. One enigmatic passage toward the end of the *Gospel of the Egyptians* contains the invocation: "You, O Son, are my place of rest ĒS ĒS O E, formless one who exists among the formless beings, existing, raising up the man in whom you will purify me for your life, in accordance with your name that never fails" (*Gos. Eg.* III 67.16–22). The identity of the raised man here is unclear, however. It is unlikely to be that of the "Son" who is addressed here.

4. Scripture and the Gospel of the Egyptians

4.1 Salvation History in the Gospel of the Egyptians

As is discussed in the treatment of the crucifixion in the *Gospel of the Egyptians*, there is a narrative of salvation, even of a sort of *Heilsgeschichte*, in the work.[41] The section of the myth before the fall already has some potential soteriological relevance in that immediately prior to the account of Chaos and Hades, there has been a sense of an interim conclusion at the arrival of Seth's seed, which later becomes a key agent, as well as object, of salvation.

Furthermore, the Great Seth accomplishes salvation not by a purely vertical intersection into the fallen realm but by passing through the series of three advents (ⲛ̄ⲡⲁⲣⲟⲩⲥⲓⲁ) mentioned earlier.[42] While these are difficult to conceptualize, Seth's first advent is through a "flood," and this flood is a typological precursor (ⲧⲩⲡⲟⲥ) of the end of the world (*Gos. Eg.* III 61.1–3). His second coming, as it were, is through a fiery conflagration. The third and final advent, which consists of the Great Seth's union with Jesus, and his baptism and nailing, is certainly a climactic event of decisive relevance for the institution of the saving baptism. By incorporating the incarnation into this threefold advent scheme (cf. the Three Forms of First Thought), then, the activity of Jesus is set in a soteriological sequence.

4.2 The Colophon

At the end of the book, we have a colophon by the author:

> This is the book that the Great Seth wrote and that he deposited in lofty mountains on which the sun has not risen, nor can it. Since the days of the prophets and the apostles and the preachers (ⲝⲓⲛ ⲛⲉϩⲟⲟⲩ ⲛ̄ⲛⲉⲡⲣⲟⲫⲏⲧⲏⲥ ⲙⲛ̄ ⲛⲁⲡⲟⲥⲧⲟⲗⲟⲥ ⲙⲛ̄ ⲛ̄ⲕⲏⲣⲩⲝ), the name has in no way entered human thought, nor could it, nor have human ears heard it.
>
> The Great Seth composed this book letter by letter over one hundred and thirty years and deposited it in the mountain called "Charaxio," so that, at

---

41. For additional discussion of the Gospel of Egyptians and scripture, see Simon Gathercole, "*Praeparatio Evangelica* in Early Christian Gospels," in *Connecting Gospels: Beyond the Canonical/Non-canonical Divide*, ed. Francis Watson and Sarah Parkhouse (Oxford: Oxford University Press, 2018), 24–27.

42. *Gos. Eg.* III 63.4–9; cf. 61.1–15.

> the end of the times and the seasons—by the will of the divine Autogenes and the whole Pleroma, through the gift of the untraceable, unthinkable love of the Father—he [*or possibly* "it"][43] may come forth (ϥ<ε>ⲡⲣⲟⲉⲗⲟⲉ ⲉⲃⲟⲗ) and appear to this incorruptible, holy race. (*Gos. Eg.* III 68.1–21)

The author of this Gospel is Seth, then, who labored over its composition for 130 years. Three possible implications can be drawn from the concealment of the truth in Mount Charaxio. First, this concealment has ensured that the truth has been preserved: the text is perhaps stored inside the mountain so that it would escape damage from the flood and the conflagration.[44] Second, the hiddenness means that there is a polemic here against the notion that there may have been other true testimony to Jesus either antecedently (in its reference to the "prophets"), or after him (in its statement about the "apostles and preachers"). Third, if the *Egyptian Gospel* itself functions as any sort of *praeparatio evangelica*, it is only in an entirely retrospective manner, because of its prior hiddenness.

In addition to this, there are three further implications of this colophon, arising from the fact of Seth's authorship.

First, by identifying its date of composition in some kind of mysterious primordial past, the *Gospel of the Egyptians* gives itself an antiquity *as* Gospel. The message of these Gnostics is that their Gospel possesses its authority as an ancient discourse: it is not a jumped-up newcomer, nor is it coordinated with *another* authoritative work testifying in advance to its message. This Gospel text alone is where the truth lies. From this point of view, appeal to scripture ("prophets") as advance testimony to the Gospel would be superfluous.

Second, because the *Egyptian Gospel's* author is Seth, a further implication may be that the text has greater antiquity than the Old Testament: after all, Seth (like the Seth of Genesis) must predate by some considerable time Moses, the

---

43. "The book" (ⲧⲃⲓⲃⲗⲟⲥ in Codex III) is feminine and so it is clear that from the point of view of the Coptic text, the masculine subject of the "coming forth" is *not* "the book." (Codex IV uses the masculine ϫⲱⲱⲙⲉ.) In the Greek original, however, "the book" may have been the subject. It is possible, and in some ways would make sense, to imagine that it is the book that is hidden but then comes forth at the end. As the text stands, however, the author Seth is to come forth at the end of ages, and probably he makes more sense as the subject of the revealing of the incorruptible holy race. This finds no exact parallel with the earlier material in the *Gospel of the Egyptians* but would comport with it.

44. Cf. Josephus, *Ant.* 1.70–71, which refers to the inscription of Adam's and Seth's secrets on stone and brick to preserve them from both flood and fire. Cf. further early Christian references in Meyer, *Nag Hammadi Scriptures*, 526.

author of the oldest portion of scripture. The "prophets" here stand for the Old Testament, which is not old at all: it is a Johnny-come-lately by comparison with this *Gospel of the Egyptians*. The title's reference to Egypt may also aim to accentuate the antiquity of the work, not just because Egypt is an ancient civilization but in particular because of the celebrated fact of Egypt preserving such ancient texts: as Barclay has commented, "the extreme antiquity of Egyptian records had been a trope since Herodotus."[45]

Finally, a quirk of this authorship by Seth is that the Gospel, despite having been written (presumably) long years ago, narrates from the point of view of the reader's present what *has* taken place. The reader observes that the coming of Seth-Jesus and his, or their, saving activity have already come to pass, and baptism has already been instituted. In the middle of the baptismal liturgy, if that is what it is, there is a future-tense statement relating more directly to "those worthy of the invocation and words of renunciation of the five seals in the baptism of running water" in the reader's present.[46] The result of this is something of a muddle: the work becomes a preemptive or proleptic description of what Seth will have accomplished and that "the prophets and the apostles and the preachers" have not grasped—even though it is hard to argue that these three groups had arrived before the dramatic date of composition. It is tempting to think that the more coherent account in the *Revelation of Adam* has been somewhat mangled in the *Gospel of the Egyptians*, which has put the account of salvation in the past tense, and inserted into this coda a polemic against other early (Jewish and?) Christian groups.

Conclusion: The Gospel of the Egyptians and the Kerygma

In conclusion, we can summarize. First, the question of the Christ figure in the *Egyptian Gospel* is one of rather overwhelming complexity, given the extreme plurality of sons, children, and Words, alongside the Great Christ, the living Jesus, and Yesseus. There is still a connection in the author's mind between the Christ and anointing, although the scriptural discourse within which messiah categories have historically been formulated is not present. In terms of the death and resurrection, there is no clear indication of either, although the

---

45. John Barclay, "The Politics of Contempt: Judaeans and Egyptians in Josephus's *Against Apion*," in *Negotiating Diaspora: Jewish Strategies in the Roman Empire*, ed. John Barclay (London: Bloomsbury, 2004), 111 n. 6.

46. *Gos. Eg.* III 65.26–66.8.

language of crucifixion is employed; it is used, however, in a context where the living Jesus is Seth's agent in nailing "the powers of the thirteen aeons," with no hint of an effective death of Jesus or of a Christ figure.[47] Seeing an Old Testament scripture that is prophetic of the Christ event is impossible both because of the lack of scriptural imagery in the messiah discussion and because in the days of the prophets no one knew the truth. There is none of the explicit contradiction of scripture that we see in, for example, the *Apocryphon of John's* refrain that Moses got things wrong.[48] The claim, however, is that this *Gospel of the Egyptians*, by comparison with the Old Testament, has chronological precedence, was written by a superior—indeed heavenly—author, and is the repository of truthful content that has been providentially preserved.

47. *Gos. Eg.* III 64.3–9; cf. IV 75.18–24.
48. See *Ap. John* II 13.18–23; 22.22–25; 29.6–10.

Part Three

COMPARISON AND CONCLUSION

—

Chapter Fifteen

A COMPARISON OF
EARLY CHRISTIAN GOSPELS (THESIS 1)

A s a reminder of part I, its initial chapter established the set of comparanda that constitute, for the purposes of the present book, the class of early Christian Gospels to be compared: Mark, Matthew, Luke, John, the *Gospel of Peter*, Marcion's Gospel, the *Gospel of Thomas*, the *Gospel of Truth*, the Coptic *Gospel of Philip*, the *Gospel of Judas*, and the Coptic *Gospel of the Egyptians*. As discussed especially in chapter 2, no scholar can compare whole entities, and so the aim of the exercise here is to compare the various early Christian Gospels *with respect to* a particular criterion or comparator. The comparator in this case takes the form of a composite model, with "model" defined as *a simplified description of a process or system*, along the lines of Jonathan Z. Smith's usage. The model employed as comparator is the early Christian kerygma, as preserved in 1 Cor 15, the components of which are (1) the identity of Jesus as the Christ, (2) the vicarious death and (3) resurrection of Jesus, and (4) the fulfillment of scripture in these two events. As argued in chapter 3 in connection with the "salience" of the comparator, these components and the model they comprise are important elements in other early Christian works (e.g., Hebrews, 1 Peter, and Revelation), not just in Paul. Now that the descriptive task has also been undertaken (in part II), we can engage in the comparison proper.

This chapter will therefore proceed through the individual components of the model, drawing out material from the preceding descriptive chapters, in order to identify where the various Gospels are similar to and different from each other with respect to these elements of the comparator. Some scholars prize similarities over differences, and vice versa, but both are essential parts of any comparison.[1] As Segal has stated, "Differences begin only where sim-

---

1. Cf. the oft-cited but rather prejudicial remark that similarities are what make comparisons possible but differences are what make them interesting. See, e.g., Fitz J. P. Poole,

ilarities end and can therefore be found only by pressing similarities as far as they will go."[2] He elsewhere remarks, conversely, "To compare phenomena is necessarily to find differences as well as similarities. Even if one were seeking only similarities, one would know that one had found them all only at the point at which no further differences could be converted into similarities."[3]

A third product of comparison to be explored in addition to similarity and difference is *absence*, that is, where a feature present in one comparandum is not found in another. The importance of such absences is noted by Indologist Wendy Doniger:

> We cannot, to borrow the Zen koan, hear the sound of one hand clapping; we cannot hear sameness. But through the comparative method we can see the blinkers that each culture constructs for its retelling of myths. Comparison makes it possible for us literally to cross-examine cultures, by using a myth from one culture to reveal to us what is not in a telling from another culture, to find out the things not "dreamt of in your philosophy."[4]

Doniger describes such an absence here, following Sherlock Holmes's *The Adventure of Silver Blaze*, as "the dog that didn't bark," a trope also employed by Jonathan Z. Smith:

> In religious disclosure, the unexpected is not only the surprising occurrence (a burning bush), it may as well be *the lack of occurrence of an expected el-*

"Metaphors and Maps: Towards Comparison in the Anthropology of Religion," *JAAR* 54 (1968): 417; William E. Paden, "Elements of a New Comparativism," *MTSR* 8 (1996): 9. Interestingly, Paden dropped this statement from his later revision of this essay in Kimberley C. Patton and Benjamin C. Ray, eds., *A Magic Still Dwells: Comparative Religion in the Postmodern Age* (Berkeley: University of California Press, 2000), 182–92.

2. Robert A. Segal, "Classification and Comparison in the Study of Religion: The Work of Jonathan Z. Smith," *JAAR* 73 (2005): 1184.

3. Robert A. Segal, "In Defense of the Comparative Method," *Numen* 48 (2001): 349–50; cf. also Segal's statement on p. 358: "While the comparative method can be used to find differences as well as similarities, the method itself seeks similarities and finds differences only when the similarities cease."

4. Wendy Doniger, *The Implied Spider: Politics and Theology in Myth* (New York: Columbia University Press, 2011), 36. Cf. Doniger, *Other Peoples' Myths: The Cave of Echoes* (New York: Macmillan, 1988), 136: "It is easier to understand the role of an animal in one culture if we can see where it does not appear in another, and we can notice the lacuna left by an animal in one culture if we see where it does appear in another." She continues here with the Zen koan analogy.

ement which, as in the case of Sherlock Holmes, provides a "clue" to which one's thought and attention may be directed.[5]

The present chapter, then, will seek to classify the different Gospels under examination *with respect to* how they are similar to or different from, or indeed have no reference to, the four components of the comparator. This will aim to demonstrate thesis 1 mentioned in the introduction: *The four New Testament Gospels share key elements of theological content that mark them out from most of the noncanonical Gospels.*

1. Jesus's Messiahship

As discussed in chapter 2, the term "messiah" is not a fixed, technical term but an idiom that could be used to refer to a figure belonging to a particular field of discourse. Jewish authors could employ the term in a manner that presumed that the "messiah" was a recognizable category, even if the word did not refer to a figure with certain essential characteristics and a set job description. To recap the point made in chapter 2, "Jewish messianism was not so much a tradition of ideas as a tradition of exegesis."[6] Messiah discourse consisted not of a "concept" but of "a body of tradition which could be used to articulate it,"[7] or "a common set of scriptural source texts."[8] As Novenson remarks, "all ancient messiah texts, Jewish or Christian, are the product of the reinterpretation of scriptural oracles in the light of the experience of their respective authors."[9] In addition to the exegesis of specific, individual passages, there are optional *themes* in Jewish messianic discourse (often derived from a combination of different scriptural passages), such as the question of the messiah's paternity, his kingship, or the like.

---

5. Jonathan Z. Smith, *Map Is Not Territory: Studies in the History of Religions* (Leiden: Brill, 1978), 301. Emphasis mine.

6. Richard J. Bauckham, *The Testimony of the Beloved Disciple* (Grand Rapids: Baker, 2007), 234.

7. John J. Collins, *The Scepter and the Star: Messianism in Light of the Dead Sea Scrolls*, 2nd ed. (Grand Rapids: Eerdmans, 2010), 77.

8. Matthew V. Novenson, *The Grammar of Messianism: An Ancient Jewish Political Idiom and Its Users* (Oxford: Oxford University Press, 2017), 14.

9. Novenson, *Grammar of Messianism*, 184; cf. *Grammar of Messianism*, 1, which talks of "participation by ancient Jews and Christians in a common scriptural discourse in texts about their respective messiahs."

In light of this basic, minimal description, we can proceed to classify how different early Christian Gospels reflect this approach and thereby evaluate the extent to which different Gospel texts in similar or different ways do or do not activate this "tradition of exegesis" (Bauckham), "body of tradition" (Collins), or "reinterpretation of scriptural oracles" (Novenson) and reflect messianic exegesis.

The classification here will be threefold, noting (1.1) Gospels incorporating messianic exegesis and themes, (1.2) Gospels with other positive applications of "Christ" to Jesus, and (1.3) Gospels not connecting Jesus and "Christ."

1.1 Gospels Incorporating Messianic Exegesis and Themes

First, we can consider those Gospels that not only use the term "messiah" but also activate messianic discourse. We have seen that this is the case in Mark, which uses Dan 7 (cf. 1 Enoch and 4 Ezra), Zech 13 (cf. CD-B), and Ps 2 (cf., e.g., Psalms of Solomon), as well as giving a specifically messianic interpretation to passages already understood in a more general eschatological sense. Matthew shares with Mark the use of Dan 7 and Zech 13 and supplements this with messianic interpretation of Isa 42 and 53 (cf. 1 Enoch; Targum), Mic 5 (cf., e.g., Targum), and Zech 9 (cf. Psalms of Solomon; *Testaments of the Twelve Patriarchs*?). Luke does the same, echoing his predecessors' uses of Ps 2, Isa 53, and Dan 7, while also employing Isa 61 (cf. Dead Sea Scrolls) and Ps 89 (cf. Dead Sea Scrolls; Mishnah; Targum). John's usage echoes the Synoptics' use of Dan 7, while also branching out to Ezek 34–37 and perhaps Zech 3, along with a different kind of usage of Isa 52:13–53:12. In terms of themes, the canonical Gospels employ the terminology of Son of God, Son of Man, and (in the case of the Synoptics) Son of David. Further idioms echo Jewish messianic discourse, such as Matthew's use of the "throne of glory" in connection with Jesus (cf. 1 Enoch) or Luke's collocations of "Christ" with "Lord" and "king." John's extensive interest in the "signs" of the messiah is rather more well attested in wider Jewish messianism than is often recognized.

The other Gospel that particularly employs a degree of messianic discourse is Marcion's Gospel. The important difference here is that this exegetical tradition is applied not to the Stranger God's Christ (i.e., Jesus) but to the creator god's messiah. John the Baptist, who for Marcion is a representative of the creator god, was to "prepare the way" for that demiurge's messiah (Gos. Marcion 7.27 ← Exod 23:20//Mal 3:1). The son-of-David question (Gos. Marcion 22.41–44), with its exegesis of Ps 110, may have been taken as a correction of the view that Jesus was a descendant of David, while confirming that Davidic descent was to be a characteristic of the creator's messiah.[10] The supposition in the Gospel that Jesus was "the one destined to redeem Israel" (Gos. Marcion 24.21) was likewise probably thought to be a description of the creator's messiah.[11] This demiurge's messiah is, according to Tertullian and Ephrem, a figure destined to come in the future, who will be a descendant of David and a warrior-king who will regather Israelites from the diaspora.[12]

The hard case in this discussion is the *Gospel of Peter*. It might seem overgenerous to regard the *Gospel of Peter* as a marginal case, because Christ language does not appear in the Gospel. On the other hand, it might seem overly harsh, because of the *Gospel of Peter*'s fragmentary nature and its use of phrases such as "Son of God" and "king of Israel" in connection with Jesus. As we have seen, however, the *Gospel of Peter* may have a negative attitude to scriptural categories and institutions: the law was "written *for them*" (*Gos. Pet.* 5.15), that is, for the Jewish people; the Passover is "*their* festival" (2.5); perhaps reflecting a certain authorial distance, the temple has to be specified by the narrator as the "the temple in Jerusalem" (5.20). While the *Gospel of Peter* appears to endorse the application of the "Son of God" title to Jesus, the phrase "king of Israel" is used only mockingly by the people (3.6–4.12). We must, with our present knowledge of the state of the *Gospel of Peter*'s text, be cautious about attributing to the author the conviction that Jesus is the Jewish messiah, although this remains a possibility. Even then, there is little evidence of traditional messianic exegesis in the text we have.

1.2 Other Positive Application of the Term "Christ" to Jesus

Other Gospels share the positive usage of the word "messiah" as a designation of Jesus, while not tapping into traditional messianic discourse. This is especially true of the *Gospel of Truth* and the *Gospel of Philip*. Both Gospels put its etymology to work to explain their theologies of anointing. In the *Gospel of Truth*, the emphasis is on how Jesus, as Christ, anoints disciples with the Father's mercy. The *Gospel of Philip* has an apostolic succession of anointing flowing from Father, to Son, to the disciples, to "us." The anointing language is

---

10. Dieter Roth, "Prophets, Priests, and Kings: Old Testament Figures in Marcion's Gospel and Luke," in *Connecting Gospels: Beyond the Canonical/Non-canonical Divide*, ed. Francis Watson and Sarah Parkhouse (Oxford: Oxford University Press, 2018), 51.

11. Tertullian, *Marc.* 4.43.3.

12. A future figure: Tertullian, *Marc.* 1.15.6; descent from David: *Marc.* 5.8.4; Ephrem, *Prose Refutations*, xxxvii–xxxviii/82–83 (Mitchell, vol. 2); warrior: *Marc.* 3.13.1; 4.20.4; *Adam. dial.* 1.11; regathering: *Marc.* 3.21.1.

extensive, including the Greek words for "Christian" and "chrism" (ⲭⲣⲓⲥⲧⲓⲁⲛⲟⲥ, ⲭⲣⲓⲥⲙⲁ), as well as Coptic anointing language (ⲧⲱϩⲥ̄, ⲥⲟϭⲛ̄). Additionally, the *Gospel of Philip* extends its "Christ" language to disciples, as well as understanding the messiah title as derived not only from the verb for "anoint" but also from the homonymous Aramaic verb *mšḥ*, meaning "measure." In neither of these two Gospels is Jesus's identity as the Christ explained by reference to traditionally messianic passages of scripture or by distinctively messianic themes elaborated from scriptural sources, but nevertheless "Christ" language is very much given a constructive theological role.

As noted already in section 1.1, the usage of messiah language in Marcion's Gospel is more complex because Marcion's theology incorporates both a "good" Christ, identified with Jesus, as well as another "just" or even evil messiah who is Jesus's antithesis. Although Marcion seems nervous about applying to Jesus such designations as "king of the Jews" (Luke 23:33) and "the one destined to redeem Israel" (Luke 24:21), the Gospel and the *Apostolos* display no such reserve about the title "Christ," which is used freely. This positive use of Christ language for Jesus, however, is not accompanied by traditional messianic discourse to explicate his identity and role.

1.3 Gospels Not Connecting Jesus and "Christ"

Several Gospels do not connect Jesus with the term "messiah," although there are various different kinds of disconnection. In the case of the *Gospel of Thomas*, the term "Christ" does not appear either in the Greek fragments or the Coptic text. Given the anti-Jewish tenor of the work and its disparagement of scripture (*Gos. Thom.* 52), this is not necessarily surprising and indeed appears to be deliberate.

More surprising is the absence of the title from the *Gospel of Peter*, although, as has often been said already, this may not be significant given the fragmentary nature of the text. (The same is also true, incidentally, of the *Gospel of Mary*, and a similar caveat again applies.) On the one hand, this absence is unremarkable given that the *Gospel of Peter* consists only of passion and resurrection narratives, where one might not expect to find much usage of messiah language.[13] On the other hand, however, the *Gospel of Peter* shows a marked preference for the title "Lord" (13×).

Most remarkable of all is the *Gospel of Judas's* usage of the term "Christ" to designate a demon, one of "the five who ruled over the underworld, and were

---

13. As noted in chapter 8, in the canonical parallels that overlap with what survives of the *Gospel of Peter*, there is not a great deal of reference to the Christ title either.

preeminent over chaos" (*Gos. Jud.* 52.4–14). As in Marcion's theology, which has a warlike messiah of the creator god, there is a radical dissociation of Jesus from the Christ figure in the *Gospel of Judas.*

In contrast, the theologically similar *Gospel of the Egyptians* decouples Jesus from "Christ" language in a different manner. Amid its vast array of deities, "the Great Christ" appears early on in the account of the theogony. We may deduce two characteristics of this figure, although because of the uncertainty of some of the Coptic relative clauses, it is impossible to be sure. First, this figure seems to be anointed by the Great Invisible Spirit (*Gos. Eg.* III 44.22–27), and there is thus a nod to the literal meaning of "Christ." Second, this Christ figure could be the one designated as "the son of the Ineffable Silence" (IV 60.6–9). The Jesus figure, by contrast, occupies a rather later position in the sequence of emanations, in a phase separated from the arrival of the Great Christ by an interval of "five thousand years" (III 56.22–23) and the outbreak of evil (III 56.22–59.9); thereafter, Seth goes through a series of three advents, in (probably) the last of which he is united with Jesus (III 63.23–64.3).

1.4 Jesus's Messiahship: Conclusion

The different treatments of messiah/Christ language in these Gospels result in the classification of Matthew, Mark, Luke, and John as resembling the model (as well as each other) most closely, in their absorption not only of messiah language but also of Jewish messianic discourse with its particular scriptural passages and broader messianic themes. It is in these works where the similarity is strongest. The *Gospel of Peter* fragment does not contain messiah language, but this may be coincidental. Marcion's Gospel also makes use of messianic themes but in connection with its other messiah figure, not with Jesus.

The *Gospel of Truth* and the *Gospel of Philip* are different from these works that make use of messianic exegesis but are similar to each other in their treatments of the "Christ" language, exploiting not the term's scriptural associations but its linguistic connotations. The *Gospel of the Egyptians* also takes a similar philological approach in its reference to the Great Christ who, like Marcion's redeemer of Israel, is not identified with Jesus; the Great Christ is anointed by the supreme deity, the Great Invisible Spirit. The *Gospel of Judas* also decouples Jesus from the Christ title, identifying the "Christ" figure as a demon. With the exception of the *Gospel of Thomas* and the *Gospel of Peter*, all these noncanonical Gospels make use of Christ language, but some necessitate a slight correction to the *Lex Novenson* that early Christian messiah discourse is part of the great project of scriptural interpretation. In the cases of these noncanonical Gospels, the Christ language is part of other discourses, with the *Gospel of Peter* constituting a tantalizingly ambiguous borderline case.

2. Jesus's Vicarious Death

To recall Versnel's definition of "vicarious" in reference to death, such a death is "any deliberately sought or accepted death that is—or is *a posteriori* interpreted as—both unconditionally required and explicitly intended to guarantee the salvation of another or others from present or impending doom or death."[14] As we also noted, a further aspect of the kerygma's understanding of Jesus's death is that this salvation occurs at least to a degree through dealing with sins, whether that is understood as the *removal of*, or *making amends for*, or *forgiveness of* sin(s), or *bearing the (theological) consequence of* the sins of others or some other *protection from the future consequences of* sins.

2.1 Gospels with a Vicarious Understanding of Jesus's Death

As we have seen, Mark and Matthew have a clearly vicarious interpretation of the death of Jesus, as is apparent from the ransom saying (Mark 10:45; Matt 20:28). The two very similar versions of this saying in Matthew and Mark are not statements of Jesus's general activity as a redeemer. In accord with the formulaic syntax and vocabulary of ransom discourse, Mark and Matthew are making specific reference to the way in which Jesus's life is a necessary payment for the lives of "the many"; Mark 8:35–38 and Matt 16:25–27 illuminate further the eschatological background to the ransom language, as argued in chapters 4–5. Matthew explicitly specifies in the eucharistic words that Jesus's death effects the forgiveness of sins: the sins of God's people were flagged up at the beginning of the Gospel as a plight that Jesus came to address (Matt 1:21). Mark very probably assumes the same idea implicitly:[15] his reference to the "blood of the covenant" probably implies purification or forgiveness (as assumed not just by Matthew but also by Hebrews and the targumim), and his allusion to Isa 53:12 (Jesus's blood is "poured out" for "many") probably

---

14. Henk S. Versnel, "Making Sense of Jesus' Death: The Pagan Contribution," in *Deutungen des Todes Jesu im Neuen Testament*, ed. Jörg Frey and Jens Schröter, 2nd ed. (Tübingen: Mohr Siebeck, 2012), 226–27. For Versnel, "vicarious" is apparently interchangeable with "soteriological."

15. E.g., Catherine Sider Hamilton, *The Death of Jesus in Matthew: Innocent Blood and the End of Exile* (Cambridge: Cambridge University Press, 2017), 222 n. 97.

amplifies that idea. Similarly, as argued in chapter 4, it is probably human sin that endangers the lives of the many and therefore provides the explanation for why the ransom is necessary, though this point is not made explicit. The earthquake that rouses the dead during the crucifixion in Matt 27 additionally indicates that for Matthew the cross is life-giving.

The Gospel of Luke and Marcion's Gospel do not contain the ransom saying but do nevertheless still see the covenant as inaugurated by Jesus's blood; this should not be underestimated since for both evangelists "covenant," importantly, embraces the whole sphere of divine-human relations. For both Luke and Marcion (as well as for Matthew and Mark), then, the eucharistic words identify the death of Jesus as the means by which God's relationship to human beings is restored (or in Marcion's case, initiated). This takes place against the backdrop of Luke's and even Marcion's warnings about future doom (e.g., 12:8–10). For Marcion, there was apparently an emphasis, especially brought out in his explanation of Gal 3:13, that the death of Jesus was a purchase of those belonging to another (i.e., the creator); although this theme is not clearly reflected in the Gospel, his passion narrative was probably meant to be understood in light of it. In any case, if Jesus's death is necessary for the (re)establishment of the covenant in Luke and Marcion, the cross is clearly vicarious.

Just as Mark and Matthew mention "the blood of the covenant," Luke refers similarly to "the new covenant in my blood" and thereby may imply purification. Indeed, Luke's distinctive reference to the advent of the "*new* covenant," which in Jer 31:31–34 entails forgiveness of sins, may further point to an interest in forgiveness. In Luke, moreover, the covenant is an overarching framework within which the forgiveness of sins occurs (Luke 1:68–79). The idea is certainly not emphasized, however. An allusion to Isa 53:12c ("he poured out his life unto death") is not as likely in Luke's eucharistic words as in the other Synoptics, but he does instead have an explicit, heavily marked quotation of Isa 53:12d ("and he was numbered with the transgressors") in the same scene.

In Marcion, the "new covenant" motif is probably less evocative of the scriptural background, and his Gospel also lacks the further illumination of the covenant motif from the infancy narrative and Acts. As a result, Marcion does not connect the motifs of covenant and the forgiveness of sins. Indeed, most scholars have suggested on other grounds that forgiveness and atoning sacrifice are less in evidence in Marcion's thought.[16] It may be no accident that

---

16. See, e.g., Barbara Aland, "Sünde und Erlösung bei Marcion und die Konsequenz für die sogenannten beiden Götter Marcions," in *Was ist Gnosis? Studien zum frühen Christentum, zu Marcion und zur kaiserzeitlichen Philosophie* (Tübingen: Mohr Siebeck, 2009),

none of the passages in Paul that connect Jesus's death with sins is attested in Marcion's *Apostolos*.[17] This must not be overemphasized, however, since lack of attestation is not evidence of absence and may be the result of our patchy information. In any case, Marcion's emphasis in his "new covenant" language in his Gospel is more on the discontinuity of the new dispensation.

A vicarious understanding of Jesus's death is also obvious in John's Gospel, with its great variety of statements in which the death of Jesus obtains or secures the lives of those whom the Father has entrusted to the Son. The necessity of Jesus's death is repeatedly stated or implied (e.g., John 3:14–15; 12:23–24). As Moody Smith notes of Jesus in John, "he is greeted as the lamb of God who takes away the sin of the world (1:29; cf. verse 34); out of his love God *gave* him (3:16; cf. Romans 5:8); Jesus gives his flesh for the life of the world (6:51); Jesus is said to die for the people (*hyper tou laou*), that the nation (*ethnos*) not perish (11:51)."[18] To these can be added the way in which Jesus "draw[s] all people" to himself in his death (12:30–34) and lays down his life for his friends (15:13). This salvation is not merely the preservation of life but the provision of "life—and that in abundance" (10:10).

Moreover, there is also very probably an understanding of the removal of sin in Jesus's death, when one connects John the Baptist's characterization of Jesus as "the Lamb of God who takes away the sin of the world" (John 1:29) together with the symbolic footwashing (13:1–10) and Jesus's sanctification of his disciples through his self-consecration (17:19); this aspect of Jesus's death is especially clear when one reads the Gospel alongside 1 John.[19]

The *Gospel of Truth* is also emphatically clear on the saving effect of Jesus's death. This is most obvious in Jesus's role as revealer, a role that comes to the fore in his crucifixion (e.g., *Gos. Truth* 20.14–27): Jesus's revelation of knowledge addresses one of the two key components of the human plight, namely ignorance.[20] There are also additional hints, such as the ransom-like language of the Gospel's statement that Jesus's death meant life for many (20.10–14). Most distinctively, the *Gospel of Truth* appears to regard Jesus's death as the

---

341–52; Sebastian Moll, *The Arch-Heretic Marcion* (Tübingen: Mohr Siebeck, 2010), 70; Judith M. Lieu, *Marcion and the Making of a Heretic: God and Scripture in the Second Century* (Cambridge: Cambridge University Press, 2015), 437.

17. Gal 1:4; 1 Cor 15:3b has "Christ died," perhaps without "for our sins"; Rom 3:25–26; 4:25; Eph (Marcion: Laodiceans) 1:7; Col 2:14.

18. D. Moody Smith, *The Theology of the Gospel of John* (Cambridge: Cambridge University Press, 2010), 115, 116.

19. It is clearer still if one sees John 1:29 drawing on a particular text form of Isa 53.

20. The other is deficiency.

obliteration of the illusory material world, insofar as Error's assault upon Jesus in the crucifixion is a suicidal move in which she attacks matter that is in fact her own substance (26.4–27). As noted, the *Gospel of Truth* also speaks of forgiveness, and this may be a consequence of Jesus's death (35.24–29).

Despite the *Gospel of Philip*'s pointed aversion to the conventional construal of Jesus's death and resurrection, the *Gospel of Philip* does appear to assign a particular soteriological function to Jesus's death. This is hard to define but appears to involve the rescue of psychic, or "soul," material and the raising of this soul-stuff to a supernal realm.

2.2 Gospels with Other Understandings of Jesus's Death

To begin with the *Gospel of Peter*, this Gospel fragment does not reveal any saving effects of the crucifixion. Jesus's death prefaces salvation, however, in the sense that after Jesus dies, he descends to the underworld to preach the good news to the dead. This is the soteriological focus of the *Gospel of Peter*, as far as we can tell.

The *Gospel of Thomas* does refer to the departure of Jesus (*Gos. Thom.* 12) but does not display much interest in his death. The emphasis is on "the living Jesus" (prologue; cf. 52, 59). The most that can be said is that the obligation upon the disciple to "take up his cross like me," the one clear reference in the *Gospel of Thomas* to Jesus's death, implies an exemplary understanding of it (55). This does not amount to a vicarious understanding, however.[21] Nor does the *Gospel of Thomas* show anything more than a passing interest in sin or sins (14, 104). The whole construction of the *Gospel of Thomas* demonstrates that it is not the events of Jesus's death and resurrection (which are not narrated) that bring salvation. Instead, as the opening of the Gospel makes clear, understanding Jesus's words is the means by which the true disciple transcends death (prologue + 1).

2.3 Gospels without Jesus's Death

Like the *Gospel of Thomas*, neither the *Gospel of the Egyptians* nor the *Gospel of Judas* narrates Jesus's death. In fact, the *Gospel of the Egyptians* has no reference to it at all and makes Jesus the crucifier instead of the crucified (*Gos. Eg.*

---

21. See Versnel's criticism ("Making Sense of Jesus' Death," 230 n. 64) of an argument that "the philosophical death is vicarious in the sense that it works as an example to be imitated or emulated" as "a peculiar and actually inaccurate application of that term."

III 64.3–9). Although the *Gospel of Judas* does not describe Jesus's death, we will return in the next chapter to look at two ways in which it is discussed.

2.4 Jesus's Vicarious Death: Conclusion

In summary, those Gospels that can be classified together as holding to a vicarious understanding of Jesus's death are the Gospels of Mark, Matthew, Luke, John, and Marcion, as well as the *Gospel of Truth* and the *Gospel of Philip*. The *Gospel of Thomas* and the *Gospel of Peter* do refer to Jesus's death but do not specify any saving significance in it: these, along with the *Gospel of Judas* and the *Egyptian Gospel*, fall into the category of dogs that did not bark.

3. JESUS'S RESURRECTION

We can recall the kerygma's assumptions about the resurrection of Jesus set out in chapter 2.

First, the resurrection is an event distinct from Jesus's death, as is clear from the "third day" interval: the resurrection is not a translation of Jesus's soul or spirit at his death. Second, the risen Jesus appears to a series of witnesses. Third, the resurrection is a "gospel" event and therefore has a purpose in the divine plan of salvation.

3.1 Bodily Resurrection on the Third Day

The narrative Gospels treated here (Matthew, Mark, Luke, John, the *Gospel of Peter*, and Marcion's Gospel) all recount a sequence of Jesus dying on a Friday and rising again on Sunday, that is, on the third day according to an inclusive reckoning. They therefore maintain a distinction between the death and the resurrection. Even Mark's truncated account has the declarations "he has been raised" and "he is not here." Additionally, all the narrative Gospels to some degree seem to affirm a bodily rising, with the possible exception of Marcion's Gospel: there is some ambiguity in Gos. Marcion 24, where the evidence about Jesus's bones is difficult to assess, although Jesus does also eat. We have also seen in the appendices to the respective chapters that the risen Jesus makes appearances. Even Mark's Gospel *refers* to an appearance in Mark 16:7 ("you will see him"), although the appearance is not narrated. Despite the peculiarity of Jesus's risen appearance in the

Gospel of Peter, the resurrection there is still bodily (as the tomb is empty). Finally, all attribute theological significance to the resurrection, with the implications variously being the fulfillment of Jesus's promises (all six narrative Gospels); the vindication of Jesus (e.g., Mark, John, Marcion) and his messianic appointment (esp. Matthew); the transformation of the disciples (e.g., Luke and John); a reconstitution of the disciples for mission (e.g., the canonical Gospels and Marcion); revelation of Jesus's identity (e.g., Luke and John); the triumph over death (e.g., Matthew); the announcement of triumph by the harrowing of hell (*Gospel of Peter*); or the dawning of a new era (e.g., Matthew and Mark).

3.2 Absence of Reference to Resurrection

Given that they abstain from saying that Jesus really died, it is unsurprising that the *Gospel of Judas* and the *Gospel of the Egyptians* have no interest in talking about any resurrection of Jesus.

The *Gospel of Truth* gives the impression that Jesus's death is at the same time a kind of "resurrection" and that as Jesus dies he clothes himself in imperishability when his material body is destroyed (*Gos. Truth* 20.27–39). Certainly, the author would not countenance any resumption of a material body, which would according to the *Gospel of Truth*'s theology be illusory and constituted by error and deficiency. Similarly, the *Gospel of Philip* does not allow for a resurrection as taking place *after* death; rather, Jesus rises from the cross, as (probably) his spirit departs for the upper realms and leaves his physical body behind to perish.

Finally, the *Gospel of Thomas* displays no interest or belief in Jesus's resurrection. Jesus's title "the living one" or "the living Jesus" refers to Jesus's transcendence of physical death, rather than his passage through death and out the other side.

3.3 Jesus's Resurrection: Conclusion

In sum, the Gospels that take the resurrection as a distinctive event with soteriological significance are those that have a Gospel *narrative*: Matthew, Mark, Luke, John, the *Gospel of Peter*, and Marcion's Gospel. The *Gospel of Philip* diverges in significant ways from this sense of the resurrection, while the others—the *Gospel of Thomas*, the *Gospel of Judas*, the *Egyptian Gospel*, and probably the *Gospel of Truth*—apparently pay no attention to it.

4. A Gospel Message "according to the Scriptures"

Each of the descriptive chapters above has also provided an assessment of how the early Christian Gospels understand the good news—and the death and resurrection of Jesus in particular—as prefigured in scripture, such that the gospel events constitute the fulfillment of that scripture. There are certain Gospels that insist on such an idea, while others display different attitudes to scripture.

4.1 Positive Interest in Scriptural Fulfillment

The first group of Gospels comprises those that, as we have seen, are strongly invested in the idea that the death and resurrection of Jesus are the fulfillment of God's purposes communicated in scripture. Matthew and John press very strongly the point that certain events in their respective Gospels take place, by divine intent, to fulfill scripture. Mark does this to a lesser degree and often invokes scripture in more subtle and allusive ways, although Matthew and Mark both employ the "strike the shepherd" oracle to point explicitly to God's fulfillment of scripture in Jesus's death. Luke is commonly described as having a theology of "proof from prophecy" or "proclamation from prophecy": the events are "in accord with what is ordained" (Luke 22:22).[22] The canonical Gospels especially make use of the Psalms to illuminate the suffering and circumstances of the crucifixion. The Synoptics employ Ps 118 and Dan 7 as prophetic specifically of Jesus's death and vindication, as well as using—in varying degrees—Isa 53 to explain the cross and Ps 110 to interpret the resurrection. All four highlight the death and resurrection of Jesus as God's fulfillments of scripture.[23]

Again, the incompleteness of the extant *Gospel of Peter* is frustrating in its ambiguity. On the one hand, it declares a certain ambivalence to scripture in its description of the law and the festivals as decidedly the property of the Jewish people rather than of Jesus. On the other, it is possible that the *Gospel of Peter* alludes suggestively to scriptural fulfillment. Such fulfillment

---

22. For an early instance of the now common former phrase, see Paul Schubert, "The Structure and Significance of Luke 24," in *Neutestamentliche Studien für Rudolf Bultmann*, ed. Walther Eltester (Berlin: Alfred Töpelmann, 1954), 165–86; for its adaptation into the latter, see Darrell L. Bock, *Proclamation from Prophecy and Pattern: Lucan Old Testament Christology* (Sheffield: Sheffield Academic, 1997).

23. See further the excursus on Acts for evidence for divine fulfillment in Luke's thought (e.g., Acts 3:18).

may merely be the people's accumulation of their full quantity of sin (e.g., in the maltreatments of Isa 50), while it is also a possible though not necessary conclusion from the evidence that the darkening of the sun may be a divine activity. Even then we do not have the death and resurrection of Jesus per se identified as scriptural fulfillments; indeed, if God brings about the darkness over the land, this event thereby ensures that Jesus's death takes place *contrary* to the law as the *Gospel of Peter* understands it. As with the other themes, however, we are hampered by the fragmentary nature of what the Akhmim excerpt can tell us.

4.2 Absence of Scriptural Fulfillment

By contrast, the *Gospel of Truth* displays a noticeable lack of interest in scripture. Its own protological discourse functions as a kind of "Old Testament," and the gospel events of Jesus's death, revelation of the truth, and swallowing up of deficiency take place in accordance with the myth of the Father's thought extending to the All and reabsorbing the All back into himself. The other work fitting most closely in this category is the *Gospel of Judas*, where there is also no positive reference to Jewish scripture. The *Gospel of Peter* may also belong in this grouping, as noted above.

The contrast with the works noted in section 4.1 above is clearer in those Gospels that do display an interest in scripture, but an interest of a negative kind. Most clear on this point are the *Gospel of Thomas* and the *Gospel of the Egyptians*. For the former, Israel's scripture belongs to the realm of the dead (*Gos. Thom.* 52), and nothing can be allowed to eclipse the uniqueness and sufficiency of Jesus's own revelation (e.g., *Gos. Thom.* 17, 38). For the *Egyptian Gospel*, scripture, like Christian apostles, does not contain "the name": the revelation contained within the Gospel itself is an "Old*er*" Testament, having been penned by Seth (*Gos. Eg.* III 68.1–21). Marcion and his Gospel unquestionably do not see Jesus's activity as prophesied in, or a fulfillment of, scripture. For Marcion, as for the *Gospel of Thomas*, the exclusive emphasis is on Jesus's own self-authenticating revelation.

Like Marcion's Gospel, the *Gospel of Philip* does not hold to a notion of scriptural fulfillment, but nor is it uninterested in scripture. For the *Gospel of Philip*, scripture does not have any privileged status but rather is part of the general dispersion of truth in the world that is misleading because demonic forces have distorted reality through the confusion of language. Once the initiated cryptographer gets to work, however, the truth can be decoded from the false messages that the world (including scripture) broadcasts.

4.3 Scriptural Fulfillment: Conclusion

Overall, then, both the death and resurrection of Jesus are understood as fulfillments in the canonical Gospels. This theme constitutes a significant example of the distinctiveness of Mark, Matthew, Luke, and John vis-à-vis the others discussed here. The *Gospel of Peter* is only a possible, partial exception, as far as we can tell: it is possible that some of the events accompanying the death of Jesus are fulfillments of scripture, but the death per se and the resurrection are not clearly marked as prophetic fulfillments in the text that has come down to us.

CONCLUSION: COMPARING EARLY CHRISTIAN GOSPELS (THESIS 1)

The aim of the comparison here has been to classify different early Christian Gospels rather than to make evaluative criticisms of the kind made by F. F. Bruce and Robert M. Grant (as noted in the introduction). The latter sorts of evaluations compare the canonical Gospels with the "speculative" apocryphal Gospels that are characterized by "perversion" and "distortion."[24]

The aim of this chapter has rather been to show that the four canonical Gospels are the only works treated here that clearly contain all four elements of the model. Part of the comparison has drawn attention not only to places where certain Gospels resemble elements of the model but also to places where there is a lack of resemblance and where particular components may be called absent.

The argument has of course not been that the canonical Gospels are the only works to include *any* of the four principal elements of the kerygma. It is not that Matthew, Mark, Luke, and John are the only works that refer to Jesus as Christ or that describe Jesus's death as a vicarious act of salvation, and so on. As noted throughout the descriptions of chapters 8–14, various noncanonical Gospels describe Jesus's death as a saving event (e.g., the *Gospel of Truth* or the *Gospel of Philip*). Similarly, some ascribe soteriological significance to Jesus's resurrection (e.g., Marcion's Gospel and the *Gospel of Peter*).

However—and here we reach an important conclusion—the noncanonical Gospels are all "dogs that didn't bark" at certain key points. With respect to

---

24. "Speculative": F. F. Bruce, "The Gospels and Some Recent Discoveries," *Faith & Thought* 92 (1962): 154; and Robert M. Grant, "Two Gnostic Gospels," *JBL* 79 (1960): 6. "Perversion": Robert M. Grant and David Noel Freedman, *The Secret Sayings of Jesus* (New York: Doubleday, 1960), 20. "Distortion": Grant, "Two Gnostic Gospels," 3.

the elements of the comparator, we encounter in the noncanonical Gospels what Smith labeled "*the lack of occurrence of an expected element* which, as in the case of Sherlock Holmes, provides a 'clue' to which one's thought and attention may be directed."[25] Most clearly, none of them signals the death and resurrection of Jesus as prophetic fulfillments (sec. 4). Relatedly, none of them employs traditional messianic exegesis and themes, except Marcion—and then only in connection with the creator's messiah, not as applied to Jesus (sec. 1). While there is more of a focus in some extracanonical Gospels on (sec. 2) the vicarious death of Jesus, the *Gospel of Judas* and the *Gospel of the Egyptians*, as well as the *Gospel of Thomas* and (as far as we can see) the *Gospel of Peter*, do not have it. Similarly, while there is (sec. 3) interest in the resurrection and its significance in the narrative Gospels studied here, the soteriological importance of the resurrection as a distinct event is absent from the others (*Thomas, Truth, Philip, Egyptians,* and *Judas*). The *Gospel of Peter* is very interesting as a borderline case that comes closest to containing some of the kerygmatic elements: it may imply an interest in Jewish messianism, and while not attesting a saving death of Jesus, it may have understood some of the circumstances around Jesus's death as foretold in scripture.

Hence, the first goal of the book has been reached, that of arguing for thesis 1 mentioned in the introduction:

The four New Testament Gospels share key elements of theological content that mark them out from most of the noncanonical Gospels.

The comparison here has of course been limited to the works that were selected in chapter 1 as the class of early Christian Gospels, but of these only Mark, Matthew, Luke, and John reflect the full kerygma outlined in chapter 2.[26] It was also shown in chapter 3 that the elements of the kerygma were historically important theologoumena. In other words, the comparator is a salient one. Having dealt with the first thesis in this present chapter, the argument will next conclude with a historical proposal that seeks to provide some explanations for the results.

---

25. As cited in the introduction to this chapter, Smith, *Map Is Not Territory*, 301. Emphasis mine.

26. Therefore, the composite *Diatessaron* also reflects the kerygma fully just as the collected fourfold Gospel does.

Chapter Sixteen

THE RECEPTION OF THE KERYGMA IN EARLY CHRISTIAN GOSPELS (THESIS 2)

The previous chapter concluded that there are important elements of the theological content of the New Testament Gospels that unite them and that mark them out from most of the noncanonical Gospels. Thus far, then, the argument has merely been a *relative* case—in Smith's terms, a comparison that has taken place in the scholar's mind. The aim up to this point has been to *classify* the various Gospels with respect to the comparator and to *identify resemblances* rather than drawing any historical conclusions. Hence the claim in thesis 1: *The four New Testament Gospels share key elements of theological content that mark them out from most of the noncanonical Gospels.*

The present chapter aims to go beyond this and to enter the historical sphere. Recognizing the distinction between resemblance (covered in the previous chapter) and relation, this chapter aims to venture a thesis about the latter.[1] Hence the second thesis noted in the introduction: *The reason why the four New Testament Gospels are theologically similar to one another is that they—unlike most others—follow a preexisting apostolic "creed" or preached gospel.* In this chapter, then, we are dealing with influence ("genealogical" comparison) rather than merely engaging in "analogical" comparison as in chapter 15.[2] In short, it deals with the historical reception of the kerygma in the early Christian Gospels that we have been examining.

---

1. On the distinction, see Simon Gathercole, "Resemblance and Relation: Comparing the Gospels of Mark, John and Thomas," in *The New Testament in Comparison: Validity, Method, and Purpose in Comparing Traditions*, ed. John Barclay and Benjamin White (London: Bloomsbury, 2020), 173–92.

2. On the terms "genealogical" and "analogical," see Jonathan Z. Smith, *Drudgery Divine: On the Comparison of Early Christianities and the Religions of Late Antiquity* (Chicago: University of Chicago Press, 1990), 47–51; Troels Engberg-Pederson, "The Past Is a Foreign

The case for this second thesis will be made in seven steps across various short sections:

1. The first section will make a case that the kerygma outlined in chapter 2 had a kind of normative status for a number of early Christians.
2. The second section will trace the influence of that kerygma upon Mark.
3. The third section examines the influence of the kerygma upon Matthew and Luke via Mark and by other means.
4. The fourth section applies a similar method to the different case of John.
5. The fifth section treats the reception of the kerygma in *Peter*, Marcion, and *Thomas*.
6. The sixth section examines how the Valentinian Gospels (the *Gospel of Truth* and the *Gospel of Philip*) absorb aspects of existing Gospels and respond to elements of the kerygma.
7. The final section traces the reception of the components of the kerygma in the Gnostic Gospels (the *Gospel of Judas* and the *Gospel of the Egyptians*) along similar lines.

Obviously, each of the early Christian Gospels here has a complex history of origin. A fuller account of the emergence of the Valentinian Gospels, for example, would involve tracing the development of and influences upon the Valentinian movement in general. This chapter will be limited in focusing on the various Gospels' knowledge and receptions of the kerygma.

1. A "Canonical" Kerygma prior to the Gospels

The first section, then, seeks to make the case that, for a number of early Christians, the kerygma outlined in chapter 2 had a kind of normative status and was strongly influential. The argument here for this influence, as in chapters 2–3, is not a claim about the Pauline formulation per se but about the kerygma to which Paul is merely one witness.

At the outset, we can recall the argument, in chapter 3 (sec. 1), for the *antiquity* of the kerygma. Paul attaches to his summary of the gospel in 1 Cor 15 a statement that he himself "received" it, just as he says in Gal 1 that he began after his conversion to preach the same gospel that he had sought to obliter-

---

Country: On the Shape and Purposes of Comparison in New Testament Scholarship," in Barclay and White, *New Testament in Comparison*, 41–61.

ate. On almost any dating of the Gospels, the kerygma therefore antedates the composition of all the written early Christian Gospels that are extant.

Similarly, as also shown in chapter 3 (sec. 2), the kerygma was *widespread*. Paul reports that the other apostles proclaimed it: after listing the various other witnesses to Jesus's resurrection, he notes "whether, then, it is I or they, this is what we preach, and this is what you believed" (1 Cor 15:11). Additionally, the components of the kerygma are all attested as important themes not only in Paul but also in Hebrews, 1 Peter, and the book of Revelation. The antiquity of the kerygma and its wide dispersion are of course related.

Furthermore, many early Christian authors display a concern for the preservation of this kerygma and for repelling what were deemed to be false claims about it or dangerous inferences from it. The examples below are provided as illustrations of debate *around* the elements of the kerygma and as instances of what were deemed to be true and false implications of it. The point is not that these authors are defending the precise details of the kerygma per se.

First, defense against divergent views of the identity of Jesus is a focus of concern. Paul writes in general terms in 2 Corinthians about those who preach "another Jesus" (ἄλλον Ἰησοῦν) and "a different gospel" (εὐαγγέλιον ἕτερον) as false apostles and servants of Satan (2 Cor 11:4, 13–15). More specifically, the Synoptic Jesus issues warnings in the Gospels about false messianic claimants (e.g., Mark 13:5–6, 21–23; and parr.). First John emphasizes as a criterion of the true gospel that "every spirit that confesses that Jesus Christ has come in the flesh is from God," with the alternative coming from the antichrist (1 John 4:2–3). Similarly, 2 John 7 bemoans the "many deceivers, who do not acknowledge Jesus Christ as coming in the flesh." Additionally, Jude identifies opponents who are perverting (μετατίθημι) the grace of God and—whether directly or by implication—denying the Lord (Jude 4).

Second, on the death of Jesus, Paul is apparently concerned in 1 Cor 1–2 about dilution of the saving power of the cross: the message of Christ's death cannot be contaminated with "wisdom"—"lest the cross of Christ be rendered ineffective" (1 Cor 1:17).[3] Similarly, in Paul's eyes, a concession to works of the law as a means of righteousness is tantamount to denying the purpose of Christ's death (Gal 2:21). In Hebrews, the idea that apostates could come back to repentance is impossible, because it would mean "crucifying the Son of God for themselves all over again" (Heb 6:6). Second Peter 2 polemicizes against

---

3. Cf. Paul's positive statement in the following verse, that the cross is the power of God for those who are being saved (1 Cor 1:18).

false teachers who introduce destructive *haireseis* and "deny the sovereign Lord who bought them" (2 Pet 2:1).

Similarly, on the resurrection, in 1 Cor 15 Paul is deeply concerned that "some of you say that there is no resurrection of the dead," which for Paul would imply that "Christ has not been raised either" (1 Cor 15:12–13). He therefore instructs the Corinthians: "come rightly back to your senses, and stop sinning!" (1 Cor 15:34). Conversely, the opponents in 2 Timothy believe in *too much* resurrection as already having happened (2 Tim 2:17–18).

In more general terms, Galatians is an obvious case in which Paul disparages a third party (the "troublers") who have introduced "a different gospel" and so overturn (μεταστρέφω) the gospel of Christ and are accursed as a result (Gal 1:6–9). The effect of the Galatians believing this other gospel is, or would be, their fall from grace (5:4). Paul establishes the *kanōn* "neither circumcision nor uncircumcision amounts to anything—only new creation does" as a means of guarding the gospel (6:15–16). Or again, against an extreme Paulinist view, Jas 2 asks "what is the use" of such a view (Jas 2:14–16) and pronounces "faith alone" as dead, useless, and the same as what demons have (2:18–26). The book of Revelation attacks the Balaamites and Nicolaitans in Pergamum (Rev 2:14–16) and the Jezebelites in Thyatira (2:20–25). The Pastoral Epistles constantly warn about false teaching and contain instructions to guard the gospel. Other places are concerned not with clear and present dangers but with future threats, as in Paul's speech to the elders in Miletus (Acts 20:29–30). Other passages deal more with hypothetical, potential false teaching (Col 2:8–23; cf. Eph 4:14).

Such counterattacks, polemics, and warnings differ starkly from the ways in which Paul discusses *adiaphora* such as celebrations of special days or eating certain food (Rom 14–15) or whether to marry (1 Cor 7). Jude distinguishes between those destined for destruction and those who waver and should be treated mercifully (Jude 22). On matters *adiaphora*, believers are not to judge one another (Matt 7:1–3; Rom 14:10; Jas 4:12). The distortion or dilution of points touching upon the kerygma, however, is a different matter from such lower-level issues. The phrase "touching upon" is deliberate here: again, the point is not that the bare elements of the kerygma per se are being disputed. Rather, authors such as Paul see certain claims as *tantamount to* undermining such central tenets as the death of Christ (1 Cor 1:17; Gal 2:20) or his resurrection (1 Cor 15:12–13).

What this means is that none of the written Gospels emerged in a theological vacuum at the beginning, only subsequently in the late second or third or fourth centuries to enter a world of theological prejudice in which Christians developed criteria of orthodoxy. There were theological criteria in operation, in and around the preached apostolic gospel, *even before the compositions of any written Gospels.* These theological criteria were, inter alia, embedded in the kerygma and its component elements. All the Gospels—"canonical" and "apocryphal" alike—emerged from a situation in which there were already established, though also developing,[4] norms of what constituted authentic apostolic proclamation. Though it may sound odd to put it this way, in an important sense, a "canon"—that is, a standard of teaching—*preceded* the composition of the Gospels, and the authors of Gospels, deliberately or unconsciously, reflected this preached gospel, or (whether deliberately or unconsciously) they did not.

2. The Kerygma and Mark's Gospel

Beginning with Mark's Gospel, the point here is that the resemblance of Mark's theology to that of the kerygma is substantial enough that the similarity cannot be a coincidence. Indeed, as noted in chapter 4, some scholars have remarked on the similarity. For Moody Smith, Mark encapsulates the "primitive Christian idea that the kerygma as presently announced fulfils the past prophetic scriptures (e.g., in I Cor. 15:3ff)," and for Joel Marcus, Mark "reflects the primitive Christian conviction that Christ died and was raised on the third day in accordance with the scriptures (see 1 Cor 15:3–4)."[5] Similarly, Best summarizes Mark's teaching about the necessity of Jesus's death as judgment, and about forgiveness and new community through the cross and resurrection, concluding, "what Mark thereby preaches is not the kerugma of Phil ii.5–11; it lies nearer that of I Cor xv.3,4."[6]

Naturally, Mark is not just restating the kerygma in the bald form in which Paul does in 1 Cor 15; Mark's Gospel is an extended narrative. Even if Mark is doing more than reannouncing the kerygma, however, he is not doing less.

---

4. By using the word "developing," I am alluding here to the manner in which the controversies reflected in, e.g., Galatians and 1 John lead to further clarifications of how the good news is to be understood.

5. D. Moody Smith, "The Use of the Old Testament in the New," in *The Use of the Old Testament in the New and Other Essays: Studies in Honor of William Franklin Stinespring,* ed. J. M. Efird (Durham, NC: Duke University Press, 1972), 42; Joel Marcus, *The Way of the Lord: Christological Exegesis of the Old Testament in the Gospel of Mark* (Louisville: Westminster John Knox, 2003), 153.

6. Ernest Best, *The Temptation and the Passion: The Markan Soteriology* (Cambridge: Cambridge University Press, 1965), 191.

As Eugene Boring notes after a reference to 1 Cor 15:3-5, Mark is "extending the term 'gospel' to embrace not only the church's kerygma about Jesus but to include Jesus's own words and deeds."[7] This extension of the narrative is itself connected to the kerygma, however. It is not just anyone who happened to give his life as a ransom for many: it is the Jesus who is identified as the scriptural Jewish messiah not only in the passion narrative but through the course of the whole body of Mark's Gospel.

The point here is not that Mark is reflecting the influence specifically of the Pauline phrasing of the kerygma. As noted in chapter 4, Mark neither has an explicit statement of Jesus's death for sins nor uses the particular Pauline phrase "on the third day" (τῇ ἡμέρᾳ τῇ τρίτῃ): he speaks instead of the resurrection "after three days" (μετὰ τρεῖς ἡμέρας) and about the resurrection of the temple "within three days" (διὰ τριῶν ἡμερῶν) or "in three days" (ἐν τρισὶν ἡμέραις). In fact, we do not (or at least, I do not) really know the extent of specifically Pauline influence, and for the purposes of the present study, a conclusion is of no particular relevance.[8] The main point is that, whether under the influence of Paul or independently or both, Mark's Gospel (like Paul) bears the imprint of a kerygma that predates the composition of that Gospel.

3. The Kerygma and the Gospels of Matthew and Luke

In the cases of Matthew and Luke, we can speak more confidently of literary influence. Matthew and Luke take over the kerygmatic theology of Mark, but they also appear to display independent influence of the kerygma. As Mark did before them, Matthew and Luke construct narratives that not only report the events of the kerygma but also identify who the Christ is.

Matthew's treatment of the death of Jesus illustrates his dependence but not his total dependence upon Mark. Matthew takes over Mark's "ransom" saying and his words at the Last Supper but also makes explicit the point that Christ died *"for sins"* in his statement that Christ's blood, the blood of the covenant, "is poured out for many *for the forgiveness of sins*" (Matt 26:28). This is not the formulation in 1 Corinthians, but it may reflect kerygmatic language that also finds its way into Col 1:14 ("redemption, the forgiveness of

---

7. M. Eugene Boring, *Mark: A Commentary* (Louisville: Westminster John Knox, 2006), 31.

8. See the recent debate in, e.g., Joel Marcus, "Mark—Interpreter of Paul," *NTS* 46 (2000): 473-87, and Michael Kok, "Does Mark Narrate the Pauline Kerygma of 'Christ Crucified'? Challenging an Emerging Consensus on Mark as a Pauline Gospel," *JSNT* 37 (2014): 139-60.

sins") and Eph 1:7 ("redemption through his blood, the forgiveness of sins"). Matthew might, alternatively, be reflecting Old Testament and early Jewish ideas of atonement (e.g., in Jer 31) or may be picking up the Markan language about John the Baptist's promise of forgiveness for sins (Mark 1:4) and taking it as fulfilled in Jesus's death. Be all that as it may, Matthew in any case clearly emerges in a context in which the kerygma is present, most clearly following the kerygma as it is embedded in Mark's Gospel but in other ways as well.

The same can be said of Luke. Luke also emerges from a context in which the kerygma has been incorporated into Mark's Gospel, and bears the influence of the kerygma indirectly via Mark. Additionally, as in the case of Matthew, there is some indication of other source material independent of Mark. As noted in the discussion of the resurrection and the appearances in Luke's Gospel, a number of scholars note the striking similarity between Paul's formulation and how Luke describes Jesus's appearance to Peter:

1 Cor 15:4–5	Luke 24:34
ὅτι ἐγήγερται	ὅτι ὄντως ἠγέρθη ὁ κύριος
τῇ ἡμέρᾳ τῇ τρίτῃ κατὰ τὰς γραφὰς	καὶ ὤφθη Σίμωνι
καὶ ὅτι ὤφθη Κηφᾷ	
that he has been raised	that the Lord really was raised
on the third day according to the scriptures	and he appeared to Simon.
and that he appeared to Cephas.	

Both the report-like form (hence the introduction with ὅτι in each case) and the content are similar. Obviously, the sequence of resurrection followed by appearance is the same. Paul and Luke also employ the same verbs, in the latter case (ὤφθη) in exactly the same form, followed by Cephas/Simon in the dative. Eckstein notes that Luke reflects the kerygma that assigns a primacy to Peter.[9] Alkier comments, on Luke 24:34: "That the resurrected Crucified One was seen by Simon Peter is formulated in the exact same way as Paul hands it down in 1 Cor 15."[10] A direct influence is possible but by no means

---

9. Hans-Joachim Eckstein, "Die Wirklichkeit der Auferstehung Jesu," in *Die Wirklichkeit der Auferstehung*, ed. Hans-Joachim Eckstein and Michael Welker (Neukirchen-Vluyn: Neukirchener, 2002), 3–4; cf. Christopher Bryan, *The Resurrection of the Messiah* (Oxford: Oxford University Press, 2011), 114. Similarly, James M. Robinson, "Jesus from Easter to Valentinus (or to the Apostles Creed)," *JBL* 101 (1982): 8.

10. Stefan Alkier, *The Reality of the Resurrection: The New Testament Witness* (Waco, TX: Baylor University Press, 2013), 132. Cf. also François Bovon, *Luke* (Minneapolis: Fortress, 2002–2012), 3:376; Eckstein, "Die Wirklichkeit der Auferstehung Jesu," 12.

certain. Becker, for example, concludes that Luke formulates this statement in the language of the kerygma, although not from 1 Cor 15 directly but from tradition common to both.[11]

In sum, Luke, like Matthew, has access to the kerygma directly from Mark but also from other now unknown sources, oral or written. In both Matthew's and Luke's cases, they have a very positive reception of all the components of the kerygma.

4. THE KERYGMA AND JOHN'S GOSPEL

There is now a considerable level of scholarly agreement that John's Gospel is influenced by the Synoptics.[12] Arguments for the influence of (especially) Mark upon John have been made on a number of fronts, ranging from the details of verbatim agreement,[13] to treatments of individual themes,[14] to more general considerations of size and shape.[15] Scholars have, for example, recently employed the language of John's *relecture* of Mark.[16] At the very least, John is acquainted with Mark. Further, Goodacre makes a strong case for John knowing all the Synoptics.[17]

---

11. Jürgen Becker, *Die Auferstehung Jesu Christi nach dem Neuen Testament: Ostererfahrung und Osterverständnis im Urchristentum* (Tübingen: Mohr Siebeck, 2007), 50.

12. See especially Eve-Marie Becker, Helen Bond, and Catrin Williams, eds., *John's Transformation of Mark* (London: Bloomsbury, 2021).

13. Mark Goodacre, "Parallel Traditions or Parallel Gospels? John's Gospel as a Reimagining of Mark," in Becker, Bond, and Williams, *John's Transformation of Mark*, 77–89.

14. E.g., the messianic secret, on which see Troels Engberg-Pedersen, *John and Philosophy: A New Reading of the Fourth Gospel* (Oxford: Oxford University Press, 2017), 312–20, and Goodacre, "Parallel Traditions or Parallel Gospels," 86–88.

15. On size, Robert Morgenthaler, *Statistik des neutestamentlichen Wortschatzes* (Zurich: Gotthelf-Verlag, 1958), 164, gives the word counts as 11,242 (Mark) and 16,150 (John); cf. Matthew's 18,305 and Luke's 19,428 words. On structure, see Harold W. Attridge, "John and Mark in the History of Research," in Becker, Bond, and Williams, *John's Transformation of Mark*, 16, and Goodacre, "Parallel Traditions or Parallel Gospels," 84–85.

16. Jean Zumstein, "The Johannine 'Relecture' of Mark," in Becker, Bond, and Williams, *John's Transformation of Mark*, 23–29. Similarly, Andreas Dettwiler, "Le phénomène de la relecture dans la tradition johannique: Une proposition de typologie," in *Intertextualités: La Bible en échos*, ed. D. Marguerat and A. Curtis (Genève: Labor et Fides, 2000), 185–200. See discussion in Jörg Frey, *Die Herrlichkeit des Gekreuzigten* (Tübingen: Mohr Siebeck, 2013), 499–500.

17. Goodacre, "Parallel Traditions or Parallel Gospels," 80–81, 83–84, drawing in part on Streeter. See also Goodacre's forthcoming book on John's indebtedness to the Synoptics, previewed in the 2016–2017 Speaker's Lectures in Biblical Studies at the University of Oxford.

John therefore knows the kerygma through Mark and probably also through Matthew and Luke. Like these others, however, he displays a knowledge of the kerygma in the most distinctive features of his Gospel as well. The Synoptics are hardly John's only sources, and therefore the author of the Fourth Gospel would have been acquainted with the kerygma from other sources as well. To take the death of Jesus as an example, we have seen how the vicarious function of Jesus's death is explicated through John the Baptist's cry of "the lamb of God who takes away the sin of the world" (John 1:29), the bread of life and good shepherd discourses in John 6 and 10, Caiaphas's prophecy (11:49–52), the seed that dies (12:23–24), the death of Jesus as "attraction" (12:30–34), the footwashing (13:3–15), "laying down life for one's friends" (15:13), Jesus's consecration for and of the disciples (17:19), narrative substitutions in John 18, and perhaps Passover imagery (John 19; cf. 1:29). Few of these are paralleled in the Synoptics: Matthew employs the Davidic shepherd motif, and some of the Synoptics with varying degrees of emphasis probably employ Barabbas as a narrative substitution. Most of the Johannine material about the cross, however, is distinctive to John while also emphasizing strongly the existing theme of a vicarious death including the removal of sin. The same is true of the resurrection narratives, which reinforce the tradition of Jesus's bodily resurrection on the third day and his appearance to witnesses, but with little narrative overlap with the Synoptics. John's *relecture* of the kerygma has very similar theological content but is expressed in a quite different manner.

The Fourth Gospel therefore clearly emerges from a context in which the kerygma and its components are well known. John is an instance of a Gospel that *retells*—in both senses—the story of the kerygma. It retells the kerygma in the sense of repeating the same story of Jesus as the messiah who dies a vicarious death and rises again according to scripture. It also retells that kerygma in a manner that, however indebted the Gospel is to the Synoptics, is quite different from them.[18]

---

18. See the helpfully balanced comments in D. Moody Smith, *The Theology of the Gospel of John* (Cambridge: Cambridge University Press, 2010), 115, 116. N. B. also Michel Gourgues, "'Mort pour nos péchés selon les Écritures': Que reste-t-il chez Jean du Credo des origines? Jn 1,29, chaînon unique de continuité," in *The Death of Jesus in the Fourth Gospel*, ed. Gilbert Van Belle (Leuven: Leuven University Press, 2007), 181–98, which reflects on how John uses the same words as the kerygma to describe a different reality and vice versa, while also using the same words to describe the same reality.

5. THE KERYGMA AND THE GOSPELS OF PETER, MARCION, AND THOMAS

5.1 The Gospel of Peter

As has frequently been observed in the course of this book, the *Gospel of Peter* constitutes something of an enigma. We can note initially that there is general scholarly agreement that it probably knows all four canonical Gospels, including elements of Matthean and Lukan redaction alongside distinctively Johannine motifs such as the reference to *crurifragium*.[19] The Gospel also exhibits considerable interest in the death and resurrection of Jesus, regardless of whether the author recognized them as part of a kerygma. Whether because he is following closely the narrative chronology of a prior Gospel, or because he has in mind Jesus rising on the "third day" (or both), the author sticks closely to the kerygmatic presentation of the resurrection. Further, he clearly seeks to bolster early Christian claims about the resurrection for his own apologetic purposes.[20]

On the other areas, however, our conclusions are more negative, or at least need to hedged about with uses of the subjunctive and "perhaps." There is no clear acceptance or rejection of the Christ title. The *Gospel of Peter* similarly does not refer to a vicarious death in our fragment, but our evidence is limited here. Again, the Gospel perhaps has independent knowledge of scripture, but there is a shift away from a divine fulfillment of scripture and toward the people's fulfillment of the maximal limit of their sins: the law belongs to the people but not to the author. There is also no hint in our excerpt of the resurrection being a fulfillment of scripture, although we do not have the whole resurrection narrative. Just as we noted in chapter 1 that the *Gospel of Peter* is on the border of being sufficiently long to be included in this book, so its content makes it a marginal case in what we can say about its stance toward the elements of the kerygma. Perhaps it is no accident that the *Gospel of Peter* is the one Gospel for which we have evidence of its early, if short-lived, use alongside canonical Gospels.[21]

---

19. Paul Foster, *The Gospel of Peter: Introduction, Critical Edition and Commentary* (Leiden: Brill, 2010), 115–47.

20. See especially Timothy P. Henderson, *The Gospel of Peter and Early Christian Apologetics: Rewriting the Story of Jesus' Death, Burial, and Resurrection* (Tübingen: Mohr Siebeck, 2011).

21. See Serapion's testimonium in Eusebius, *Hist. eccl.* 6.12.2–6.

5.2 Marcion's Gospel

We have more definite knowledge of Marcion. Irrespective of whatever oral proclamation was current in his day, Marcion had access to the kerygma in the Pauline letters known to him and very probably in his Lukan *Vorlage* as well.[22] (He may have known other Gospels as well: indeed, as a rich and well-travelled elite, he could have had easy access to various Christian texts.) The evidence indicates that Marcion regarded both his Pauline and Gospel texts as corrupted and in need of editorial restoration, however. On the former point, Tertullian reports, "I declare that Marcion's [Gospel] is adulterated, Marcion that mine is."[23] On the latter point, Tertullian writes, "In the end, he emended what he regarded as corrupt."[24] As far as the message and theology of Marcion are concerned, his followers allegedly claimed that "he did not so much make up a new rule by his separation of the law and the gospel, as restore an adulterated rule back again."[25] Hence Marcion first encountered a Gospel, a *regula*, and a cluster of Pauline epistles all informed by the kerygma, but eventually he came to regard them all as corrupted and in need of restoration to their former untainted glory.

Marcion's interpretation of the elements of the kerygma as they came down to him involved the following: (1) His bifurcation of messiahship meant that Jesus remained Christ but a Christ detached from Jewish messianic discourse. Marcion must have been conscious that his own reading of both the Gospel and the Pauline epistles as referring to two messiahs was not an idea present in these sources as they had come down to him but was something that required "restoration." (2) The death and (3) the resurrection of Christ continued to have significance for him, although he may have had a complex understanding of Christ's risen body that is not now known to us.[26] Finally, (4) Marcion's kerygma, or *regula*, could not be "according to the scriptures," because for

---

22. See chapter 9, n. 2 above, for a summary of reasons for Marcion having something like our canonical Luke before him.

23. *Marc.* 4.4.1: *Ego Marcionis affirmo adulteratum, Marcion meum.*

24. *Marc.* 4.5.6: *Denique emendavit quod corruptum existimavit.* Cf. *Marc.* 4.4.4–5, according to which Marcion accuses the Gospel (of Luke) in wider use of being "interpolated by the protectors of Judaism" (*interpolatum a protectoribus Iudaismi*); hence Tertullian refers to Marcion as *emendator . . . evangelii* and (as in *Marc.* 4.5.6) his activity as *emendatio.*

25. *Marc.* 1.20.1: *Aiunt enim Marcionem non tam innovasse regulam separatione legis et evangelii quam retro adulteratam recurasse.*

26. Additionally, he may have had a reduced emphasis on the forgiveness of sins especially in his edition of the epistles of Paul.

him the law and the gospel were antithetical rather than correlative. While not explicit as far as we can tell from his Gospel itself, Marcion unquestionably does not see Jesus's activity as presaged in scripture. Marcion almost certainly removed the notion of Christ's fulfillment of scripture from his Gospel *Vorlage*, as is clear he did with the Pauline epistles: when one observes which Lukan passages are absent from or modified in Marcion's Gospel, it is tolerably clear that some of his editing of both Gospel and *Apostolos* was guided by a similar method. On the issue of the fulfillment of scripture, then, Marcion was in sharp disagreement with the kerygma under discussion here.

5.3 The Gospel of Thomas

This approach to scripture is similar in the *Gospel of Thomas*, at least in its theology if not in its editorial method (about which we know very little). The editor or author of the *Gospel of Thomas* is aware of (at least) Matthew and Luke in some form, as well as of some of Paul's letters.[27] Hence the author knows the narrative of Christ's death and resurrection according to the scriptures. The *Gospel of Thomas*'s acquaintance with more "orthodox" forms of Christian religiosity is further evident from his engagement in debate on topics such as prayer, fasting, almsgiving, and food (*Gos. Thom.* 6, 14), as well as resurrection, the relation of Jesus to scripture, and circumcision (*Gos. Thom.* 51–53).

Against this background, what is most clear in relation to the kerygma is that the *Gospel of Thomas* takes a position—seemingly in deliberate opposition to a view held by others—that scripture belongs to the realm of the dead (*Gos. Thom.* 52). For the *Gospel of Thomas*, as for Marcion, nothing can be allowed to eclipse the uniqueness and self-interpreting sufficiency of Jesus's own revelation (e.g., *Gos. Thom.* 17, 38). In this respect, the author opposes the kerygma. Additionally, it is unlikely to be coincidental that in the entire Gospel, there is no mention of the Christ title: while it remains possible that the absence of "Christ" from the *Gospel of Peter* is mere happenstance, this is less likely in the *Gospel of Thomas*, which is both complete and over three times longer than what has survived of the *Gospel of Peter*. (There is also a possible sideswipe at Jesus's resurrection in *Gos. Thom.* 51, although the polemic here is directed at "rest for the dead" rather than against the resurrection of Jesus

27. Mark S. Goodacre, *Thomas and the Gospels* (Grand Rapids: Eerdmans, 2012); Simon Gathercole, *The Composition of the Gospel of Thomas: Original Language and Influences* (Cambridge: Cambridge University Press, 2012).

per se.) Similarly, that there is only passing, implicit reference to Jesus's death and no reference at all to the resurrection appears to be deliberate.

In sum, regardless of whether the author or editor was conscious of taking a stance on the kerygma *as such*, the *Gospel of Thomas*'s attitude to the elements of that kerygma is a mixture of omission (of "Christ" and of his resurrection), indifference (to Jesus's death), and opposition (to scriptural fulfillment).

6. The Kerygma and the Gospel of Truth and the Gospel of Philip

There is a broad scholarly majority in favor of the view that the Valentinians produced both the *Gospel of Truth* and the *Gospel of Philip*.[28] We can identify the *Gospel of Truth* and the *Gospel of Philip* as Valentinian because there is a preexisting school or church from which they emerged and that is characterized by a distinctive style and theology.

6.1 The Gospel of Truth

In the case of the *Gospel of Truth*, we have a testimonium to a Gospel of Truth by Irenaeus, who describes the work as emanating from the school of Valentinus. As discussed in chapter 1, the manuscripts of the *Gospel of Truth* from Nag Hammadi do not have *subscriptiones* with a title, but the opening words of the work are "The gospel of truth," and opening words can function as titles. Furthermore, the Nag Hammadi text, which in one of the manuscripts is well preserved, shares various characteristic and even distinctive Valentinian motifs. In terms of literary style, it employs etymology and wordplay. Prominent, too, are theological themes such as the plight of ignorance and deficiency, the solutions to which are the anointing of disciples and the disciple's unification with the "name"—the name itself being a key theme for Valentinian Christology and theology proper.[29] Overall the soteriology is like that of the *Excerpts*

---

28. See especially Einar Thomassen, *The Spiritual Seed: The "Church" of the Valentinians* (Leiden: Brill, 2006). For earlier discussion, see Einar Thomassen, "How Valentinian Is the Gospel of Philip?," in *The Nag Hammadi Library after Fifty Years: Proceedings of the 1995 Society of Biblical Literature Commemoration*, ed. John D. Turner and Anne McGuire (Leiden: Brill, 1997), 251–79, and, most recently, Geoffrey Smith, trans., *Valentinian Christianity: Texts and Translations* (Oakland: University of California Press, 2020), which includes both the *Gospel of Truth* and the *Gospel of Philip*.

29. On these, see Thomassen, *Spiritual Seed*, 383–85.

from Theodotus.[30] Matter comes about as a result of ignorance, rather than from a perfect, good God or from an evil demiurge such as that of the Gnostic system (on which more below). There are passages that make good sense against the background of a tripartition of the material, psychic, and spiritual. The whole scheme is based on the triunity of protological myth, salvation in history, and ritual, although the *Gospel of Truth* is muted (but not silent) on the last of these. In these respects, while it has its own particularities, the *Gospel of Truth* has a level of agreement with known Valentinian literature that is unlikely to be coincidental.

The *Gospel of Truth* is a curiously freestanding text. It cites no other literature and does not have any polemic. It does clearly know the canonical Gospels, however, as well as some of Paul's epistles and the book of Revelation. The author is therefore obviously aware of the main themes of the kerygma, although he may not have recognized them as constituting what some Christians regarded as a kerygma. The use of the Christ title and its application to Jesus clearly emerge from common Christian usage, but there is no exploitation of Jewish messianic discourse. Whether this is a deliberate choice is hard to say, but it is notable that despite the great quantity of New Testament allusions in the *Gospel of Truth*, there are barely any from the Old Testament.

The *Gospel of Truth*'s presentation of the vicarious death of Jesus, while also developing in a distinctive direction, relies heavily on traditional language: first, the statement that "he knew that his death means life for the many" (*Gos. Truth* 20.13–14) is redolent of the ransom saying in particular; second, language in the same discourse about a scroll that no one can take except the one who was slaughtered is a clear reference to Rev 5. In contrast to the situation with the "Christ" language, therefore, the author seems happily to absorb the soteriological dimensions of Jesus's death from the writings that he already knows, while also developing the vicarious death motif with a distinctively Valentinian style (e.g., through play on the word "tree") and theological approach (e.g., in the cross as revelation of knowledge).

The author also knows the resurrection discourse of 1 Cor 15: the statement that Jesus "clothed himself with that imperishability that no one can take from him" is a clear allusion to 1 Corinthians: "For the perishable must clothe itself with the imperishable, and the mortal with immortality. When the perishable has been clothed with the imperishable, and the mortal with immortality . . ." (1 Cor 15:53–54). Here, however, it is less certain what the *Gospel of Truth* is doing with the resurrection language.

30. Thomassen, *Spiritual Seed*, 154–55, 163–65.

Overall, then, we know a good deal about the *Gospel of Truth*'s sources and therefore about the author's knowledge of the elements of the kerygma. Regardless of whether he recognized these themes as belonging to a kerygma as such, the author transposes the Christ language from messianic discourse into the Valentinian framework and constructs a mythological backdrop for Jesus's historical activity in place of a scriptural setting. On the nature of Jesus's messiahship, therefore, and on his death and resurrection as fulfillments of scripture, the *Gospel of Truth* is (consciously or unconsciously) inattentive to the kerygma.

6.2 The Gospel of Philip

The *Gospel of Philip* does not have the advantage of a patristic testimonium, but there are still strong reasons for assigning it to the Valentinians.[31] We have the characteristic etymological interest. The demiurge is merely incompetent, rather than either perfect or evil. The supreme God did not create the cosmos, as in Gen 1; nor was it made by a demon (see the Gnostic view in sec. 7 below). Rather, "The world came into being by a mistake. For the one who made it wanted to make it imperishable and immortal. He failed and did not succeed in what he had hoped" (Gos. Phil. 75.2–6). We see evidence again of a soteriology expressed as protological myth, salvation in history, and ritual; just as the *Gospel of Truth* gave less attention to ritual, the *Gospel of Philip* gives less attention to the myth, but all three are present.[32] The human plight consists of being the offspring only of the female, and not of the male, and thus being in a deficient state (52.21–24).[33] Salvation consists in, among other things, the unification of the empirical self with the "image" above (58.10–14), and the union in the bridal chamber.[34] Jesus himself is in need of redemption, which takes place at his baptism (70.34–71.3),[35] and this supplies the pattern for the redemption of the elect. Like the *Gospel of Truth*, then, the *Gospel of Philip* can be identified as Valentinian through the presence of various salient and distinctive themes.

---

31. Or rather we do have a reference and a quotation in Epiphanius (*Pan.* 36.13.2), but apparently to a different *Gospel of Philip*.

32. Cf. Thomassen, "How Valentinian Is the Gospel of Philip?," 254: "*Gos. Phil.* does not deal with protology." If "deal with" means "discuss at length," then, true, but it is mentioned. The primeval sowing of truth (Gos. Phil. 55.19–22) and the distortion of it by the archons (54.18–25) could be noted, for example.

33. Cf. Clement of Alexandria, *Exc.* 68.

34. Cf. Clement of Alexandria, *Exc.* 68, 79. See Thomassen, "How Valentinian Is the Gospel of Philip?," 254–55.

35. Cf. Clement of Alexandria, *Exc.* 22.6–7; *Tri. Trac.* 124.32–125.11.

6. The Kerygma and the Gospel of Truth and the Gospel of Philip

The *Gospel of Philip* is much less coy than the *Gospel of Truth* about its attitude to existing Christian tradition. There is clear opposition to various opinions with which the author disagrees. The author might be described as adopting a stance of "critical inheritance" toward the canonical Gospels:[36] it can both quote the Gospel of Matthew positively, for example, and on another occasion criticize the notion of a virgin birth.[37]

In terms of the kerygma, there is further critical polemic in the Gospel's treatment of the death-resurrection sequence. As discussed in chapter 12, the *Gospel of Philip* has a surprising twist on the standard sequence of Easter events: "Those who say that the Lord first died and then rose are wrong (ⲥⲉⲣ̄ⲡⲗⲁⲛⲁ). For he first rose and then died. Unless someone first obtains resurrection, he cannot die. As surely as God lives, he would [. . .]!" (Gos. Phil. 56.15–20). In this respect, the *Gospel of Philip* is notable not just for going its own way but for deliberately polemicizing *against* a more conventional sequence. The *Gospel of Philip*'s position seems to be that the resurrection takes place immediately before Jesus's death, in the sense that Jesus's spirit rises to the supernal realm from the body, which he leaves upon the cross to perish as a result.[38] We noted in chapter 12 above the close parallel that Louis Painchaud drew between the *Gospel of Philip* and Theodotus: "[the Spirit] was withdrawn in order that death might also operate on him, since how could the body have died when life was present in him? For in that case, death would have prevailed

---

36. On the concept of critical inheritance, see Chris Keith, "'If John Knew Mark': Critical Inheritance and Johannine Disagreements with Mark," in Becker, Bond, and Williams, *John's Transformation of Mark*, 31–49, esp. 37–40.

37. Quotations: e.g., Gos. Phil. 68.8–13; 83.12–13; on the virgin birth: 55.23–27.

38. How much the *Gospel of Philip*'s view here reflects a broader Valentinian perspective is unclear, but there is an emphasis on spiritual language in talk of the resurrection in other texts. For example, the likes of Lazarus and the widow of Nain's son whom Jesus raised were only images of "the spiritual/pneumatic resurrection" (Clement of Alexandria, *Exc.* 7). In the context of the resurrection "on the third day," Heracleon interprets the phrase "in three days" in John 2:19 as meaning that the third is "the spiritual day" (Heracleon, frag. 15). Rheginus is informed by his teacher that the "spiritual resurrection" is "that which swallows up the psychic/animate and the sarkic alike" (*Treat. Res.* 45.39–46.2). For a Valentinian, after all, a spiritual resurrection would inevitably be *more* real than a material one. Similarly, later in the *Excerpts from Theodotus*, the result of Jesus's resurrection (ἀναστὰς ὁ κύριος) is that he proclaims the good news to the righteous "in rest," apparently a heavenly locale (Clement of Alexandria, *Exc.* 18). The promise "I will go ahead of you into Galilee" is also understood allegorically: "He goes ahead of all things and hints that he will raise up the soul that is invisibly saved and will restore it to where he is now going ahead" (Clement of Alexandria, *Exc.* 61).

over the savior himself, which is absurd!" (*Exc.* 61.6).[39] Just as the *Excerpts from Theodotus* insist on the withdrawal of the Spirit before Jesus's death as an important doctrinal point (to avoid absurdity), so the *Gospel of Philip* insists that the sequence of death *then* resurrection is a serious theological error. The author of the *Gospel of Philip* thereby has a sharply disapproving reception of the structure of the kerygma.

7. The Kerygma and the Gospel of Judas and the Gospel of the Egyptians

Like the Valentinian works just discussed, the *Gospel of Judas* and the *Egyptian Gospel* also belong to an identifiable school, that of the Sethian or "classic" Gnostics.[40] I am taking "Gnostic" here in the specific sense that it has both in the neo-Platonist circle of Plotinus and in the earliest of the fathers (Irenaeus, Hippolytus, et al.), where Gnostics are distinguished from Valentinians and others.[41]

7.1 The Gospel of Judas

In the case of the Gnostic affiliation of the *Gospel of Judas*, we have a testimonium in which Irenaeus assigns the work to a Gnostic group (*Haer.* 1.31.1). The supreme being in the Gospel, as in a number of Gnostic works, is the "Great Invisible Spirit" (cf., e.g., the *Apocryphon of John*). Alongside this Spirit, there is Barbelo, from whose aeon Jesus originates. Barbelo is also a distinctively Gnostic figure, present in (again) the *Apocryphon of John*, as well as in *Zostrianus* and *Allogenes*, which are identified by Porphyry as Gnostic works.[42] The demiurge in the *Gospel of Judas*, in contrast to that of the Valentinian literature

---

39. Trans. Casey, modified; see R. P. Casey, *The Excerpta ex Theodoto of Clement of Alexandria: Edited with Translation, Introduction and Notes* (London: Christophers, 1934), 80 (text), 81 (translation).

40. The term "school," however, may imply too singular an entity: Edwards talks in terms of "a congeries of obscure and related sects": Mark J. Edwards, "Gnostics and Valentinians in the Church Fathers," *JTS* 40 (1989): 34.

41. On the whole issue of the distinction, see Edwards, "Gnostics and Valentinians in the Church Fathers," and Edwards, "Neglected Texts in the Study of Gnosticism," *JTS* 41 (1990): 26–50, as well as David Brakke, *The Gnostics: Myth, Ritual, and Diversity in Early Christianity* (Cambridge: Harvard University Press, 2010).

42. Porphyry, *Vit. Plot.* 16.

above, appears very much to be evil. Nimrod, or Yaldabaoth, is introduced as follows: "And behold, an [angel] appeared out of the cloud with his face pouring forth fire. His appearance was polluted with blood, and his name was 'Nimrod,' which interpreted means 'apostate'" (*Gos. Jud.* 51.12–14). The other demiurgic figure, Saklas, is similarly negative.[43] In this respect, they are like the Gnostic creator described as evil (κακός) in Plotinus's school.[44] The list of demonic rulers created by Nimrod-Yaldabaoth and Saklas conforms in general, if not in exact detail, to other comparable lists in the *Apocryphon of John*, as well as in Sethian and Ophite lists: as in most such lists, Adonai(os), that is, the Jewish God, is one of these evil archons.[45] The true seed, that is, the elect Gnostics, are the generation of Seth, whereas the world is defined as "corruption" (*Gos. Jud.* 50.13–14) with no prospect of redemption; indeed, the text suggests nothing but the destruction of the world (55.21–22). This is in keeping with Porphyry's statement that, for the Gnostics, the world reflects the character of its creator and is therefore also evil.

This helps to make sense of why the *Gospel of Judas* describes the last days of Jesus as it does. We have noted that one of the five archons over the underworld is Adonaios, just as another is "[. . .]th who is called 'Christ.'" It may well be that the Christ title's association with the Jewish God is a reason for the author to consign messiahship to an evil domain.

The death of Jesus is also a theme with which the *Gospel of Judas* critically engages, in a manner probably informed by the Gnostic author's views of creation and materiality. Since the *Gospel of Judas* ends with the betrayal, the crucifixion is not narrated, but it is discussed. Notably, some of Jesus's last words make it clear that the executioners do not land any blows upon him. Negatively, Jesus states, "no mortal hand will sin against me" in the crucifixion (*Gos. Jud.* 56.8–11). More positively, after Judas's action, Jesus says to him, "the one who carries me about will be tormented" (56.6–8), and states that Judas's betrayal effectively means that "you will sacrifice the man who carries me around" (56.18–22). Since Jesus belongs to another realm ("the aeon of Bar-

---

43. He creates those who rule over the underworld (ⲁⲙⲛⲧ[ⲉ] in *Gos. Jud.* 55.13). Cf. *Gos. Jud.* 55.10–11, "and all the generations that sinned in my name will serve Saklas," and *Gos. Jud.* 56.12–18, "Judas, [those who] offer up sacrifice to Saklas . . . all, since [almost three lines missing] everything that is evil."

44. Plotinus, *Enn.* 2.9: this division is titled by Porphyry both Πρὸς τοὺς Γνωστικούς (*Vit. Plot.* 16) and Πρὸς τοὺς κακὸν τὸν δημιουργὸν τοῦ κόσμου καὶ τὸν κόσμον κακὸν εἶναι λέγοντας (*Vit. Plot.* 24).

45. *Gos. Jud.* 52.4–11. For further information on these lists, and a synopsis, see chapter 13, sec. 1 (table 1) above.

belo"), his real essence will not be affected by the trivialities of what happens in the material domain.

Furthermore, these statements about the insignificance of the crucifixion for Jesus are not merely clarificatory but appear to be polemical. A combative tone is especially evident in the early part of the Gospel, which shows reaction against other contemporaneous communities. On the first narrated day, "When Jesus [met] them [i.e., the disciples] sitting together and giving thanks (ϥ-ⲉⲩⲭⲁⲣⲓⲥⲧⲓ) over the bread, he laughed," and the disciples then ask why he is laughing at their "thanksgiving," or "Eucharist" (ⲉⲩⲭⲁⲣⲓⲥⲧⲓⲁ). Jesus explains that the disciples are worshiping another god (*Gos. Jud.* 33.26–34.18). The point is therefore probably a polemic against the Eucharist. As noted in chapter 13, by the time of the composition of the *Gospel of Judas*, "Eucharist" is in some circles a conventional term referring to the commemoration of Jesus's death: it is already used in a technical sense in the *Didache*, Ignatius, and Justin.

In sum, then, in addition to presenting a radically different assessment of what is going on at the crucifixion, the *Gospel of Judas* also mocks those Christians who engage in ritual commemoration of Jesus's death. Regardless of whether the Gnostic author is familiar with the message of the kerygma as such, he shows a sharply polemical aversion to Jesus's identity as the Christ and to the idea of the cross as theologically significant, and is also entirely indifferent to (and almost certainly dismissive of) any notion of Jesus's resurrection.

7.2 The Gospel of the Egyptians

The *Egyptian Gospel* contains many similar marks of belonging to a Gnostic group. As in the *Gospel of Judas* and elsewhere, the supreme being is the Great Invisible Spirit; one of the titles this work gives itself is "The Holy Book of the Great Invisible Spirit." Alongside this Spirit, again, is Barbelo, together with a succession of spirits, including Seth and his indestructible seed, who are the elect generation. Again, there is a list of demonic figures that conforms loosely to the lists noted above, in the *Apocryphon of John*, the Ophite diagrams, and the Sethian list in the Berlin Codex. Others in the dramatis personae of the *Gospel of the Egyptians* are Ephesech/Esephech, Domedon/Doxomedon, and the Triple Male Child, who also appear in, for example, *Zostrianus* (as noted above, one of the revelations mentioned by Porphyry as Gnostic). These features are unknown in Valentinian literature, while the *Gospel of the Egyptians* and a cluster of other Gnostic texts have frequent reference to them. As in the *Gospel of Judas*, the creator is evil and indeed is probably identified with "the devil" (*Gos. Eg.* III 61.17). While they have their own particular interests, the *Egyptian Gospel* and the *Gospel of Judas* share Gnostic features that are both salient and distinctive.

The negativity of the Christ title in the *Gospel of Judas*, however, is not reflected in the *Egyptian Gospel*. As we have seen, the *Gospel of the Egyptians* does have a constructive reception of the title in its characterization of one of the supreme heavenly emanations, "the Great Christ." This figure is not identified with Jesus, however, and the term is not set within any Jewish messianic discourse. The positive use of the title together with an insouciant lack of application of it to Jesus implies a certain absence of concern (either positive or negative) with the kerygma.

There is perhaps a clearer concern implied in the account of the crucifixion in the Gospel. There are of course two different ways in which crucifixion can be employed in early Christian literature—literal and metaphorical. Jesus is literally crucified. Metaphorically, Christians in general are crucified in their former selves (Rom 6:6; Gal 5:24), Paul is crucified to the world and vice versa (Gal 6:14), and God nails to the cross "the written record, with its decrees, that was against us" (Col 2:14). The *Egyptian Gospel* employs two metaphorical references, stating that through Jesus, Seth "nailed the powers of the thirteen aeons," and that Jesus "came and crucified that which was in [*or* under] the law."[46] Both of these references may pick up Col 2.[47] It is possible that this particular use of crucifixion language is a careful selection of the metaphorical over the literal, especially where the agency in the crucifying is attributed in both places to Jesus/Seth. The *Gospel of the Egyptians* thus focuses exclusively on an active nailing of hostile powers to the cross, to the exclusion of the literal crucifixion of Jesus. This is after all what one might expect from a Gospel reflecting a classic Gnostic outlook, as we saw in the case of the *Gospel of Judas*.

More pointed still is the statement toward the end of the *Egyptian Gospel*:

This is the book that the Great Seth wrote and that he deposited in lofty mountains upon which the sun has not risen, nor can it. Since the days of the prophets and the apostles and the preachers, the name has in no way entered their minds, nor could it have, and their ears did not hear it. (*Gos. Eg.* III 68.1–9)

---

46. "In the law" (*Gos. Eg.* III 64.3–4; 65.17–18); "under the law" (*Gos. Eg.* IV 75.18–19; 77.13–15).

47. In the former case, the nailing (cf. Col 2:14) of the aeons leads to triumph over them (cf. 2:15). In the latter, the connection between "the law" and "the written record with its decrees" is obvious.

This passage is notable in characterizing both (presumably Israelite) prophets and Christian apostles and teachers as ignorant of the "name."[48] The *Egyptian Gospel's* statement is noteworthy for our purposes for two reasons. First, it dismisses prophetic scripture as containing nothing of the truth. Second, it makes the same claim about the Christian "apostles and the preachers" (ⲛⲁⲡⲟⲥⲧⲟⲗⲟⲥ ⲙⲛ̄ ⲛ̄ⲕⲏⲣⲩⲝ) and therefore implicitly interacts with a kerygma. While we cannot leap from the Greco-Coptic word ⲕⲏⲣⲩⲝ to the kerygma under discussion in the present book, the *Egyptian Gospel* clearly sets itself against what it regards as the apostolic message and its omission of the name. At the same time, the *Gospel of the Egyptians* denies what is crucial to the kerygma, namely the identification of Jesus as the Christ and the death and resurrection of Jesus as fulfillments of scripture.

Conclusion

As noted, then, the previous chapter concluded with the first thesis of this book, namely that *the four New Testament Gospels share key elements of theological content that mark them out from most of the noncanonical Gospels*. This chapter has been concerned with thesis 2: *The reason why the four New Testament Gospels are theologically similar to one another is that they—unlike most others—follow a preexisting apostolic "creed" or preached gospel.*

The elements of this second thesis, which have been synthesized in this final chapter, are threefold.

First, we have seen that for a number of early Christians, there was a very old kerygmatic "creed"—easily old enough to predate the composition of all written Christian Gospels (canonical or noncanonical). We saw this creed attested in Paul's first letter to the Corinthians. Chapter 2 also showed that this kerygma was not merely a Pauline message but one that was shared among his fellow apostles, and one whose themes were all taken as important not just in Paul but also in Hebrews, 1 Peter, and Revelation. We saw earlier in the present chapter (sec. 1) that the themes touching upon this kerygma were subjects that early Christian writers were concerned to defend against what were perceived to be threatening variants. In other words, the first and early second

---

48. Possible referents for the name are that of Domedon Doxomedon, which at the beginning of the Gospel is described as the "unrevealable name" (*Gos. Eg.* III 43.8–20), or Yesseus Mazareus Yessedekeus—the "glorious name" (66.8–12, with 66.22–25?), or the Son's name "ES ES O E," which appears shortly before the declaration cited above (67.16–17).

centuries were not a theologically innocent melting pot of Gospels that only later were subject to prejudicial evaluation. Criteria of true and false teaching were already embedded in the kerygma and developing in the writings of the New Testament.

Second, the canonical Gospels emerge from a context in which this kerygma circulated, and they follow that kerygma. In Mark's case, for example, the similarity is too striking to be coincidental. Mark probably followed an oral form of early Christian preaching and whatever written sources available to him that may also have been influenced by the kerygma. Matthew and Luke accessed the kerygma partly from Mark and partly from other sources. The same is true of John. In the introduction, I noted Ehrman's contention that "the history of the engagement"—the battle over what constituted the shape of early Christianity—had to be "rewritten" to justify the idea that Matthew, Mark, Luke, and John reflected "the views of the apostolic Churches."[49] It is of course true, from a fourth-century perspective, that "Matthew, Mark, Luke and John all tell the story as the proto-orthodox had grown accustomed to hearing it."[50] The point of the present book is also to argue that Matthew, Mark, Luke, and John all tell the story—the story of the kerygma—as many had grown accustomed to hearing it *already when these Gospels were first composed*.

Third, the other Gospels discussed here, either consciously or unconsciously, do not follow the kerygma all the way. It is difficult to *show* unconscious omissions or divergences; it is much easier to show those cases where it is clearly deliberate. Such cases are found, for example, in Marcion's bifurcation of messiahship and opposition to the idea of Jesus's fulfillment of scripture, the *Gospel of Judas*'s polemic against Jesus's dying and the Eucharist, the *Gospel of Philip*'s polemical alteration of the kerygmatic sequence, or the charges against scripture in the *Gospel of Thomas* and the *Egyptian Gospel*. On the other hand, the *Gospel of Truth* contains little if anything in the way of polemic, although it has no scriptural framework in its depictions of Jesus's messiahship and the saving death of Jesus. Similarly, the *Gospel of Peter* does not obviously reflect inner-Christian debate, although, again, there is a notable absence of reference in our surviving text to Jesus's vicarious death and resurrection as fulfillments of scripture.

Finally, some of these noncanonical Gospels were assessed as belonging to particular, identifiable movements in early Christianity. The *Gospel of Thomas*

---

49. This language comes from Bart D. Ehrman, "Christianity Turned on Its Head: The Alternative Vision of the Gospel of Judas," in *The Gospel of Judas*, ed. Rodolphe Kasser, Marvin Meyer, and Gregor Wurst (Washington DC: National Geographic, 2006), 118.

50. Again, Ehrman, "Christianity Turned on Its Head," 118.

and the *Gospel of Peter*, according to our current knowledge, cannot be assigned to particular groups. Marcion's Gospel, however, clearly belongs, with his *Apostolos* and *Antitheses*, to a defined movement. Similarly, chapters 11 and 12, along with section 6 above, pointed out some important similarities between the *Gospel of Truth* and the *Gospel of Philip*, resemblances that constitute part of the evidence for seeing them as products of the Valentinians. Similarly, chapters 13 and 14, with section 7 above, highlighted some of the points that the *Gospel of Judas* and the *Gospel of the Egyptians* hold in common, points that are a consequence in part of their shared (Sethian or classic) Gnostic origin.[51]

These classifications of Valentinian and Gnostic Gospels provide an analogy to a key aim of this book, which has been to identify a distinctive theological profile in the four canonical Gospels. This is not because they are the products of a single cohesive community but because they emerge from a movement characterized by certain key theological tenets, including those of the apostolic kerygma under discussion here. If Paul is correct in 1 Cor 15:11, and we have seen in chapter 3 evidence that he is, then this kerygma is that of all the apostles.[52] The Four Gospels, whatever else they may be seeking to do, also happen to follow the theological position of that apostolic kerygma—that Jesus is the messiah who, in fulfillment of Israel's scripture, died a vicarious death and rose again on the third day.

---

51. See further Gathercole, "Resemblance and Relation," 173–92. On the Valentinians and Gnostics respectively, see especially Thomassen, *Spiritual Seed*, and Brakke, *Gnostics*.

52. See the related argument of Louis Ayres, "Continuity and Change in Second-Century Christianity: A Narrative against the Trend," in *Christianity in the Second Century: Themes and Developments*, ed. J. Carleton Paget and J. M. Lieu (Cambridge: Cambridge University Press, 2017), 106–21.

BIBLIOGRAPHY

Abegg, Martin. "The Messiah at Qumran: Are We Still Seeing Double?" *DSD* 2 (1995): 125–44.

Achtemeier, Paul J. "The Christology of 1 Peter: Some Reflections." Pages 140–54 in *Who Do You Say That I Am? Essays on Christology in Honor of Jack Dean Kingsbury*. Edited by Mark Allan Powell and David R. Bauer. Louisville: Westminster John Knox, 1999.

———. *1 Peter: A Commentary on First Peter*. Minneapolis: Fortress, 1996.

Adams, Edward. *Parallel Lives of Jesus: Four Gospels—One Story*. London: SPCK, 2010.

Adams, Sean A., and Seth M. Ehorn, eds. *Composite Citations in Antiquity*. London: Bloomsbury, 2018.

Ådna, Jostein. "The Servant of Isaiah 53 as Triumphant and Interceding Messiah." Pages 189–224 in *The Suffering Servant: Isaiah 53 in Jewish and Christian Sources*. Edited by Bernd Janowski and Peter Stuhlmacher. Translated and supplemented by Daniel P. Bailey. Grand Rapids: Eerdmans, 2004.

Ahearne-Kroll, Stephen P. *The Psalms of Lament in Mark's Passion: Jesus' Davidic Suffering*. Cambridge: Cambridge University Press, 2007.

Ahn, Sanghee M. *The Christological Witness Function of the Old Testament Characters in the Gospel of John*. Milton Keynes: Paternoster, 2014.

Aland, Barbara. "Gnosis und Christentum." Pages 330–50 in *The School of Valentinus*. Vol. 1 of *The Rediscovery of Gnosticism: Proceedings of the International Conference on Gnosticism at Yale, New Haven, Connecticut, March 28–31, 1978*. Edited by Bentley Layton. Leiden: Brill, 1980.

———. "Sünde und Erlösung bei Marcion und die Konsequenz für die sogenannten beiden Götter Marcions." Pages 341–52 in *Was ist Gnosis? Studien zum frühen Christentum, zu Marcion und zur kaiserzeitlichen Philosophie*. Tübingen: Mohr Siebeck, 2009.

Aland, Kurt. *Synopsis Quattuor Evangeliorum*. 5th ed. Stuttgart: Deutsche Bibelgesellschaft, 2005.

Alexander, Philip S. "The King Messiah in Rabbinic Judaism." Pages 456–73 in *King and Messiah in Israel and the Ancient Near East*. Edited by J. Day. Sheffield: Sheffield Academic, 1998.

Alkier, Stefan. *The Reality of the Resurrection: The New Testament Witness*. Waco, TX: Baylor University Press, 2013.

Allison, Dale C. "Darkness at Noon." Pages 79–105 in *Studies in Matthew: Interpretation Past and Present*. Grand Rapids: Baker, 2005.

———. *The New Moses: A Matthean Typology*. Edinburgh: T&T Clark, 1993.

———. "The Scriptural Background of a Matthean Legend: Ezekiel 37, Zechariah 14, and Matthew 27." Pages 162–73 in *Life beyond Death in Matthew's Gospel: Religious Metaphor or Bodily Reality?* Edited by Wim Weren, Huub van de Sandt, and Joseph Verheyden. Leuven: Peeters, 2011.

Anderson, Charles A. "'Time, Time, Time. See What's Become of It': Factors on the Temporal Relation of Aorist Participles and Verbs in the New Testament." Paper presented at the Annual Meeting of the Society of Biblical Literature. Washington DC, 19 November 2006.

Anderson, Hugh. "The Old Testament in Mark's Gospel." Pages 280–306 in *The Use of the Old Testament in the New and Other Essays: Studies in Honor of William Franklin Stinespring*. Edited by J. M. Efird. Durham, NC: Duke University Press, 1972.

Arai, Sasagu. *Die Christologie des Evangelium Veritatis: Eine religionsgeschichtliche Untersuchung*. Leiden: Brill, 1964.

———. "Zur Lesung und Übersetzung des Evangelium Veritatis: Ein Beitrag zum Verständnis seiner Christologie." *NovT* 5 (1962): 214–18.

Ashton, John. *Understanding the Fourth Gospel*. Oxford: Oxford University Press, 2007.

Askeland, Christian. "A Coptic Papyrus without John 21?" Pages 93–108 in *The New Testament in Antiquity and Byzantium: Traditional and Digital Approaches to Its Texts and Editing; A Festschrift for Klaus Wachtel*. Edited by H. A. G. Houghton, David C. Parker, and Holger Strutwolf. Berlin: de Gruyter, 2020.

Attridge, Harold W. "From Discord Rises Meaning." Pages 1–19 in *The Resurrection of Jesus in the Gospel of John*. Edited by Craig R. Koester and Reimund Bieringer. Tübingen: Mohr Siebeck, 2008.

———. "John and Mark in the History of Research." Pages 9–22 in *John's Transformation of Mark*. Edited by Eve-Marie Becker, Helen Bond, and Catrin Williams. London: Bloomsbury, 2021.

Attridge, Harold W., and George W. MacRae. "The Gospel of Truth." Pages 55–117 in *Nag Hammadi Codex I (The Jung Codex)*. Vol. 1. Edited by Harold W. Attridge. Leiden: Brill, 1985.

Aubert, Bernard. *The Shepherd-Flock Motif in the Miletus Discourse (Acts 20:17–38) against Its Historical Background*. New York: Lang, 2009.

Augenstein, Jörg. "'Euer Gesetz'—Ein Pronomen und die johanneische Haltung zum Gesetz." *ZNW* 88 (1997): 311–13.

Augustin, Philipp. *Die Juden im Petrusevangelium: Narratologische Analyse und theologiegeschichtliche Kontextualisierung*. Berlin: de Gruyter, 2015.

Aune, David E. *Revelation 17–22*. Grand Rapids: Zondervan, 1998.

Ayres, Louis. "Continuity and Change in Second-Century Christianity: A Narrative against the Trend." Pages 106–21 in *Christianity in the Second Century: Themes and Developments*. Edited by J. Carleton Paget and J. M. Lieu. Cambridge: Cambridge University Press, 2017.

Barclay, John. "The Politics of Contempt: Judaeans and Egyptians in Josephus's *Against Apion*." Pages 109–27 in *Negotiating Diaspora: Jewish Strategies in the Roman Empire*. Edited by John Barclay. London: Bloomsbury, 2004.

Barclay, John, and Benjamin White, eds. *The New Testament in Comparison: Validity, Method, and Purpose in Comparing Traditions*. London: Bloomsbury, 2020.

Barrett, C. K. *Acts 1–14*. ICC. Edinburgh: T&T Clark, 2004.

———. "Cephas and Corinth." Pages 28–39 in *Essays on Paul*. Philadelphia: Westminster, 1982.

———. "Christianity at Corinth." *BJRL* (1964): 269–97.

———. *The Gospel according to St. John*. 2nd ed. London: SPCK, 1978.

———. "Luke/Acts." Pages 231–44 in *It Is Written: Scripture Citing Scripture; Essays in Honour of Barnabas Lindars, SSF*. Edited by D. A. Carson and H. G. M. Williamson. Cambridge: Cambridge University Press, 1988.

———. "The Old Testament in the Fourth Gospel." *JTS* 48 (1947): 155–69.

Bauckham, Richard J. *The Climax of Prophecy: Studies on the Book of Revelation*. Edinburgh: T&T Clark, 1993.

———. *Gospel of Glory: Major Themes in Johannine Theology*. Grand Rapids: Baker, 2015.

———. "James, 1 and 2 Peter, Jude." Pages 303–17 in *It Is Written: Scripture Citing Scripture; Essays in Honour of Barnabas Lindars, SSF*. Edited by D. A. Carson and H. G. M. Williamson. Cambridge: Cambridge University Press, 1988.

———. *Jesus and the God of Israel: God Crucified and Other Studies on the New Testament's Christology of Divine Identity*. Carlisle: Paternoster, 2008.

———. *The Testimony of the Beloved Disciple*. Grand Rapids: Baker, 2007.

———. *The Theology of the Book of Revelation*. Cambridge: Cambridge University Press, 1993.

Baxter, Wayne. "Healing and the 'Son of David': Matthew's Warrant." *NovT* 48 (2006): 36–50.

———. *Israel's Only Shepherd: Matthew's Shepherd Motif and His Social Setting*. London: Bloomsbury, 2012.

Beale, Gregory K. *The Book of Revelation: A Commentary on the Greek Text*. Grand Rapids: Eerdmans, 1998.

———. "Revelation." Pages 318–36 in *It Is Written: Scripture Citing Scripture; Essays in Honour of Barnabas Lindars, SSF*. Edited by D. A. Carson and H. G. M. Williamson. Cambridge: Cambridge University Press, 1988.

Beck, Edmund, ed. *Des heiligen Ephraem des Syrers Hymnen contra Haereses*. Leuven: Peeters, 1957.

Becker, Eve-Marie, Helen Bond, and Catrin Williams, eds. *John's Transformation of Mark*. London: Bloomsbury, 2021.

Becker, Jürgen. *Die Auferstehung Jesu Christi nach dem Neuen Testament: Ostererfahrung und Osterverständnis im Urchristentum*. Tübingen: Mohr Siebeck, 2007.

BeDuhn, Jason. *The First New Testament: Marcion's Scriptural Canon*. Salem, OR: Polebridge, 2013.

Bell, H. Idris, and T. C. Skeat. *Fragments of an Unknown Gospel and Other Early Christian Papyri*. London: The British Museum, 1935.

Bennett, W. J. "The Son of Man Must . . ." *NovT* 17 (1975): 113–29.

Berman, Samuel A. *Midrash Tanhuma-Yelammedenu: An English Translation of Genesis and Exodus from the Printed Version of Tanhuma-Yelammedenu with an Introduction, Notes, and Indexes*. Hoboken: Ktav, 1996.

Best, Ernest. *The Temptation and the Passion: The Markan Soteriology*. Cambridge: Cambridge University Press, 1965.

Beutler, Johannes. *A Commentary on the Gospel of John*. Grand Rapids: Eerdmans, 2017.

———. "Resurrection and the Remission of Sins: John 20:23 against Its Traditional Background." Pages 237–51 in *The Resurrection of Jesus in the Gospel of John*. Edited by Craig R. Koester and Reimund Bieringer. Tübingen: Mohr Siebeck, 2008.

Bienert, Wolfgang A. "Marcion und der Antijudaismus." Pages 191–205 in *Marcion und seine kirchengeschichtliche Wirkung/Marcion and His Impact on Church History*. Edited by Gerhard May and Katharina Greschat. Berlin: de Gruyter, 2002.

Bieringer, Reimund. "Das Lamm Gottes, das die Sünde der Welt hinwegnimmt (Joh 1,29): Eine kontextorientierte und redaktionsgeschichtliche Untersuchung auf dem Hintergrund der Passatradition als Deutung des Todes Jesu im Johannesevangelium." Pages 199–232 in *The Death of Jesus in the Fourth Gospel*. Edited by Gilbert Van Belle. Leuven: Leuven University Press, 2007.

Billings, Bradley S. *Do This in Remembrance of Me: The Disputed Words in the Lukan Institution Narrative (Luke 22.19b–20); An Historico-Exegetical, Theological and Sociological Analysis*. London: Bloomsbury, 2006.

Bitel, A. P. "Quis ille Asinus aureus? The Metamorphoses of Apuleius' Title." *Ancient Narrative* 1 (2000–2001): 208–44.

Black, Mark. "The Messianic Use of Zechariah 9–14 in Matthew, Mark, and Pre-Markan Tradition." Pages 97–114 in *Scripture and Traditions: Essays on Early Judaism and Christianity in Honor of Carl Holladay*. Edited by Patrick Gray and Gail R. O'Day. Leiden: Brill, 2008.

Blanton, Thomas R., IV. "Saved by Obedience: Matthew 1:21 in Light of Jesus' Teaching on the Torah." *JBL* 132 (2013): 393–413.

Blass, Friedrich, Albert Debrunner, and Robert Funk. *Greek Grammar of the New Testament and Other Early Christian Literature*. Chicago: University of Chicago Press, 1961.

Bock, Darrell L. "The Function of Scripture in Mark 15.1–39." Pages 8–17 in *The Gospel of Mark*. Vol. 1 of *Biblical Interpretation in Early Christian Gospels*. Edited by Thomas R. Hatina. London: T&T Clark, 2006.

———. *Luke*. Leicester: Inter-Varsity, 1994.

———. *Proclamation from Prophecy and Pattern: Lucan Old Testament Christology*. Sheffield: Sheffield Academic, 1997.

Bockmuehl, Markus. *Ancient Apocryphal Gospels*. Louisville: Westminster John Knox, 2017.

Bockmuehl, Markus, and James Carleton Paget, eds. *Redemption and Resistance: The Messianic Hopes of Jews and Christians in Antiquity*. Cambridge: Cambridge University Press, 2009.

Boer, Martinus C. de. *Johannine Perspectives on the Death of Jesus*. Kampen: Kok Pharos, 1996.

Böhlig, Alexander, and Frederik Wisse. "Introduction." Page 208 in *The Nag Hammadi Library in English*. Edited by J. M. Robinson. Leiden: Brill, 1977.

———, eds. *Nag Hammadi Codices III, 2 and IV, 2: The Gospel of the Egyptians (the Holy Book of the Great Invisible Spirit)*. Leiden: Brill, 1975.

Bond, Helen. "A Fitting End? Self-Denial and a Slave's Death in Mark's Life of Jesus." *NTS* 65 (2019): 425–42.

Bonner, Campbell. "An Amulet of the Ophite Gnostics." Pages 43–46 and 444 in *Commemorative Studies in Honor of Theodore Leslie Shear*. Hesperia Supplements 8. Princeton: American School of Classical Studies at Athens, 1949.

Boor, C. de. *Neue Fragmente des Papias, Hegesippus und Pierius in bisher unbekannten Excerpten aus der Kirchegeschichte des Philippus Sidetes*. Leipzig: Hinrichs, 1888.

Boring, M. Eugene. *Mark: A Commentary*. Louisville: Westminster John Knox, 2006.

Botner, Max. *Jesus Christ as the Son of David in the Gospel of Mark*. Cambridge: Cambridge University Press, 2019.

Bovon, François. *Luke*. 3 vols. Minneapolis: Fortress, 2002–2012.

Boyarin, Daniel. "'After the Sabbath' (Matt. 28:1)—Once More into the Crux." *JTS* 52 (2001): 678–88.

Brakke, David. *The Gnostics: Myth, Ritual, and Diversity in Early Christianity*. Cambridge: Harvard University Press, 2010.

Brankaer, Johanna, and Hans-Gebhard Bethge, eds. *Codex Tchacos: Texte und Analysen*. Berlin: de Gruyter, 2012.

Braude, William G., trans. *The Midrash on Psalms*. New Haven: Yale University Press, 1959.

——, trans. *Pesikta Rabbati: Discourses for Feasts, Fasts, and Special Sabbaths*. New Haven: Yale University Press, 1968.

Braude, William G. (Gershon Zev), and Israel J. Kapstein, trans. *Pesikta de-Rab Kahana: R. Kahana's Compilation of Discourses for Sabbaths and Festal Days*. 2nd ed. Philadelphia: Jewish Publication Society, 2002.

Breytenbach, Cilliers. "Das Markusevangelium, Psalm 110,1 und 118,22f.: Folgetext und Prätext." Pages 197–222 in *The Scriptures in the Gospels*. Edited by Christopher M. Tuckett. Leuven: Leuven University Press, 1997.

——. "Narrating the Death of Jesus in Mark." *ZNW* 105 (2014): 153–68.

Brockelmann, Carl. *Lexicon Syriacum*. 2nd ed. Halle: Max Niemeyer, 1928.

Brooke, George J. "The Amos-Numbers Midrash (CD 7.13b–8.1a) and Messianic Expectation." *ZAW* 92 (1980): 397–404.

——. "The Messiah of Aaron in the Damascus Document." *RevQ* 15 (1991): 215–30.

Brown, Raymond E. *The Death of the Messiah: From Gethsemane to the Grave*. London: Geoffrey Chapman, 1994.

——. *The Gospel according to John*. 2 vols. New York: Doubleday, 1966–1970.

——. *The Gospel and Epistles of John: A Concise Commentary*. Collegeville, MN: Liturgical, 1988.

Bruce, F. F. "The Gospel of Thomas." *Faith and Thought* 92 (1961): 3–23.

——. "The Gospel of Thomas." Pages 110–56 in *Jesus and Christian Origins outside the New Testament*. London: Hodder & Stoughton, 1974.

——. "The Gospels and Some Recent Discoveries." *Faith and Thought* 92 (1962): 149–67.

——. "The Kerygma of Hebrews." *Int* 23 (1969): 3–19.

——. "Paul and Jerusalem." *TynBul* 19 (1968): 3–25.

Brunson, Andrew. *Psalm 118 in the Gospel of John: An Intertextual Study on the New Exodus Pattern in the Theology of John*. Tübingen: Mohr Siebeck, 2003.

Bryan, Christopher. *The Resurrection of the Messiah*. Oxford: Oxford University Press, 2011.

Bryan, Steven M. "Consumed by Zeal: John's Use of Psalm 69:9 and the Action in the Temple." *BBR* 21 (2011): 459–74.

Bultmann, Rudolf. "Bekenntnis- and Liedfragmente im ersten Petrusbrief." Pages 1–14 in *Coniectanea Neotestamentica XI: In honorem A. Fridrichsen*. Lund: Gleerup, 1947.

——. *Das Evangelium des Johannes*. Göttingen: Vandenhoeck & Ruprecht, 1986.

——. *Theology of the New Testament*. 2 vols. London: SCM, 1952–1955.

Burchard, Christoph. "Markus 15,34." *ZNW* 74 (1983): 1–11.

Burke, Tony. *Secret Scriptures Revealed: A New Introduction to the Christian Apocrypha*. London: SPCK, 2013.

Burridge, Richard. *What Are the Gospels? A Comparison with Graeco-Roman Biography*. 2nd ed. Grand Rapids: Eerdmans, 2004.

Bynum, William R. *The Fourth Gospel and the Scriptures: Illuminating the Form and Meaning of Scriptural Citation in John 19:37*. Leiden: Brill, 2012.

Byrne, Brendan. "Jesus as Messiah in the Gospel of Luke: Discerning a Pattern of Correction." *CBQ* 65 (2003): 80–95.

Campbell, Douglas. "The Story of Jesus in Romans and Galatians." Pages 97–124 in *Narrative Dynamics in Paul: A Critical Assessment*. Edited by Bruce W. Longenecker. Louisville: Westminster John Knox, 2002.

Carey, Holly J. *Jesus' Cry from the Cross: Towards a First-Century Understanding of the Intertextual Relationship between Psalm 22 and the Narrative of Mark's Gospel*. London: Bloomsbury, 2009.

Carleton Paget, James. "The Definition of the Term 'Jewish Christian'/ 'Jewish Christianity.'" Pages 289–324 in *Jews, Christians and Jewish Christians in Antiquity*. Tübingen: Mohr Siebeck, 2010.

———. "Marcion and the Resurrection: Some Thoughts on a Recent Book." *JSNT* 35 (2012): 74–102.

Carpinelli, Francis G. "'Do This as *My* Memorial' (Luke 22:19): Lucan Soteriology of Atonement." *CBQ* 61 (1999): 74–91.

Carroll, John T. *Luke: A Commentary*. Louisville: Westminster John Knox, 2012.

———. "Luke's Crucifixion Scene." Pages 108–24 and 194–203 in *Reimaging the Death of the Lukan Jesus*. Edited by Dennis D. Sylva. Frankfurt am Main: Hain, 1990.

Carson, D. A. *The Gospel according to John*. Grand Rapids: Eerdmans, 1991.

———. "John and the Johannine Epistles." Pages 245–64 in *It Is Written: Scripture Citing Scripture; Essays in Honour of Barnabas Lindars, SSF*. Edited by D. A. Carson and H. G. M. Williamson. Cambridge: Cambridge University Press, 1988.

———. *Matthew*. Grand Rapids: Zondervan, 1995.

Carson, D. A., and H. G. M. Williamson, eds. *It Is Written: Scripture Citing Scripture; Essays in Honour of Barnabas Lindars, SSF*. Cambridge: Cambridge University Press, 1988.

Casey, P. Maurice. *From Jewish Prophet to Gentile God*. Cambridge: James Clarke, 1991.

Casey, R. P. *The Excerpta ex Theodoto of Clement of Alexandria: Edited with Translation, Introduction and Notes*. London: Christophers, 1934.

Catchpole, David R. *Resurrection People: Studies in the Resurrection Narratives of the Gospels*. London: Darton, Longman & Todd, 2000.

Cathcart, Kevin, and Robert P. Gordon. *The Targum of the Minor Prophets*. Edinburgh: T&T Clark, 1990.

Chapman, David W. *Ancient Jewish and Christian Perceptions of Crucifixion*. Tübingen: Mohr Siebeck, 2008.

Charles, R. H. *A Critical History of the Doctrine of a Future Life in Israel, in Judaism, and in Christianity*. London: A. & C. Black, 1899.

Charlesworth, James H., ed. *Damascus Document II*. Vol. 3 of *The Dead Sea Scrolls: Hebrew, Aramaic, and Greek Texts with English Translations*. Tübingen: Mohr Siebeck, 2006.

Charlesworth, Scott. *Early Christian Gospels: Their Production and Transmission*. Florence: Edizioni Gonnelli, 2016.

———. "The Gospel Manuscript Tradition." Pages 28–61 in *The Content and Setting of the Gospel Tradition*. Edited by Mark Harding and Alanna Nobbs. Grand Rapids: Eerdmans, 2010.

———. "Indicators of 'Catholicity' in Early Gospel Manuscripts." Pages 37–48 in *The Early Text of the New Testament*. Edited by C. E. Hill and M. J. Kruger. Oxford: Oxford University Press, 2012.

Charlier, J.-F. "L'exégèse johannique d'un précepte légal: Jean VIII 17." *RB* 67 (1960): 503–15.

Chester, Andrew. *Messiah and Exaltation: Jewish Messianic and Visionary Traditions and New Testament Christology.* Tübingen: Mohr Siebeck, 2007.

———. "The Sibyl and the Temple." Pages 37–69 in *Templum Amicitiae: Essays on the Second Temple Presented to Ernst Bammel.* Edited by William Horbury. Sheffield: Sheffield Academic, 1991.

Chilton, Bruce. *The Isaiah Targum.* Edinburgh: T&T Clark, 1987.

Coggins, Richard J., and Michael A. Knibb. *The First and Second Books of Esdras.* Cambridge: Cambridge University Press, 1979.

Cohen, A., trans. *Ecclesiastes.* Vol. 8 of *Midrash Rabbah.* London: Soncino, 1939.

Collins, John J. *The Scepter and the Star: Messianism in the Light of the Dead Sea Scrolls.* 2nd ed. Grand Rapids: Eerdmans, 2010.

———. "The Works of the Messiah." *DSD* 1 (1994): 98–112.

Combs, J. R. "A Walking, Talking Cross: The Polymorphic Christology of the Gospel of Peter." *EC* 5 (2014): 198–219.

Cotter, Wendy. "Greco-Roman Apotheosis Traditions and the Resurrection Appearances in Matthew." Pages 127–53 in *The Gospel of Matthew in Current Study.* Edited by David E. Aune. Grand Rapids: Eerdmans, 2001.

Cover, Michael. *Lifting the Veil: 2 Corinthians 3:7–18 in Light of Jewish Homiletic and Commentary Traditions.* Berlin: de Gruyter, 2015.

Cranfield, Charles E. B. *The Gospel according to St Mark.* Cambridge: Cambridge University Press, 1959.

———. "St Mark 16.1–8 (Parts I and II)." *SJT* 5 (1952): 282–98, 398–414.

Crawford, Matthew. "Diatessaron, a Misnomer? The Evidence from Ephrem's Commentary." *EC* 4 (2013): 362–85.

Creed, J. M. "The Conclusion of the Gospel according to Saint Mark." *JTS* 31 (1930): 175–80.

Crossan, John Dominic. *The Birth of Christianity.* Edinburgh: T&T Clark, 1998.

Croy, N. Clayton. *The Mutilation of Mark's Gospel.* Nashville: Abingdon, 2003.

Crum, W. E. *A Coptic Dictionary.* Oxford: Clarendon, 1939.

Cuany, Monique. "Jesus, Barabbas and the People: The Climax of Luke's Trial Narrative and Lukan Christology (Luke 23.13–25)." *JSNT* 39 (2017): 441–58.

Daise, Michael A. "Quotations with 'Remembrance' Formulae in the Fourth Gospel." Pages 75–93 in *Abiding Words: The Use of Scripture in the Gospel of John.* Edited by Alicia D. Myers and Bruce G. Schuchard. Atlanta: SBL Press, 2015.

Daly-Denton, Margaret. *David in the Fourth Gospel: The Johannine Reception of the Psalms.* Leiden: Brill, 2000.

———. "The Psalms in John's Gospel." Pages 119–37 in *The Psalms in the New Testament.* Edited by Steve Moyise and Maarten J. J. Menken. London: T&T Clark, 2004.

Danby, Herbert. *The Mishnah: Translated from the Hebrew with Introduction and Brief Explanatory Notes.* Oxford: Oxford University Press, 1933.

Daniélou, Jean. *The Theology of Jewish Christianity: A History of Early Christian Doctrine before the Council of Nicaea.* London: Darton, Longman & Todd, 1964.

Davies, W. D., and D. C. Allison. *The Gospel according to Saint Matthew.* 3 vols. Edinburgh: T&T Clark, 1988–1997.

Decock, Paul B. "The Breaking of Bread in Luke 24." *Neot* 36 (2002): 39–56.

DeConick, April D. *The Original Gospel of Thomas in Translation: With a Commentary and New English Translation of the Complete Gospel.* London: T&T Clark, 2006.

———. *The Thirteenth Apostle: What the Gospel of Judas Really Says*. Rev ed. London: Continuum, 2009.

Denaux, A. *Studies in the Gospel of Luke: Structure, Language and Theology*. Münster: LIT Verlag, 2010.

Denker, Jürgen. *Die theologiegeschichtliche Stellung des Petrusevangeliums: Ein Beitrag zur Frühgeschichte des Doketismus*. Frankfurt am Main: Herbert Lang, 1975.

Denyer, Nicholas. "Mark 16:8 and Plato, Protagoras 328d." *TynBul* 57 (2006): 149–50.

Dettwiler, Andreas. "Le phénomène de la relecture dans la tradition johannique: Une proposition de typologie." Pages 185–200 in *Intertextualités: La Bible en échos*. Edited by D. Marguerat and A. Curtis. Geneva: Labor et Fides, 2000.

Dibelius, Martin. "Die alttestamentlichen Motive in der Leidensgeschichte des Petrus- und des Johannes-Evangeliums." Pages 125–50 in *Abhandlungen zur semitischen Religionskunde und Sprachwissenschaft: FS Wolf Wilhelm Grafen von Baudissin*. Edited by W. Frankenberg and F. Küchler. Giessen: Töpelmann, 1918.

———. *Studies in the Acts of the Apostles*. London: SCM, 1956.

Dietzfelbinger, Christian. *Das Evangelium nach Johannes*. Zurich: TVZ, 2001.

Diggle, James, et al., eds. *The Cambridge Greek Lexicon*. Cambridge: Cambridge University Press, 2021.

Dillon, Richard J. *From Eye-Witnesses to Ministers of the Word: Tradition and Composition in Luke 24*. Rome: Pontificio Istituto Biblico, 1978.

Dodd, C. H. *The Apostolic Preaching and Its Developments*. London: Hodder, 1936.

———. "ΙΛΑΣΚΕΣΘΑΙ, Its Cognates, Derivatives and Synonyms in the Septuagint." *JTS* 32 (1931): 352–60.

———. *The Interpretation of the Fourth Gospel*. Cambridge: Cambridge University Press, 1968.

Dodds, E. R. *Pagan and Christian in an Age of Anxiety: Some Aspects of Religious Experience from Marcus Aurelius to Constantine*. Cambridge: Cambridge University Press, 1965.

Doniger, Wendy. *The Implied Spider: Politics and Theology in Myth*. New York: Columbia University Press, 2011.

———. *Other Peoples' Myths: The Cave of Echoes*. New York: Macmillan, 1988.

———. "Post-modern and -colonial -structural Comparisons." Pages 63–74 in *A Magic Still Dwells: Comparative Religion in the Postmodern Age*. Edited by Kimberley C. Patton and Benjamin C. Ray. Berkeley: University of California Press, 2000.

Dowd, Sharyn, and Elizabeth Struthers Malbon. "The Significance of Jesus' Death in Mark." *JBL* 125 (2006): 271–97.

Dozemann, Thomas B. *Exodus*. Grand Rapids: Eerdmans, 2009.

Drijvers, Han J. W. "Christ as Warrior and Merchant: Aspects of Marcion's Christology." Pages 73–85 in *Papers Presented to the Tenth International Conference on Patristic Studies Held in Oxford 1987: Second Century*. Edited by Elizabeth A. Livingstone. StPatr 21. Leuven: Peeters, 1989.

Du Plessis, Isak J. "The Saving Significance of Jesus and His Death on the Cross in Luke's Gospel—Focussing on Luke 22:19b–20." *Neot* 28 (1994): 523–40.

Dunderberg, Ismo. *The Beloved Disciple in Conflict? Revisiting the Gospels of John and Thomas*. Oxford: Oxford University Press, 2006.

Dupont, J. "ΑΝΕΛΗΜΦΘΗ (Act. 1.2)." *NTS* 8 (1962): 154–57.

Eckstein, Hans-Joachim. "Die Wirklichkeit der Auferstehung Jesu." Pages 1–30 in *Die*

Wirklichkeit der Auferstehung. Edited by Hans-Joachim Eckstein and Michael Welker. Neukirchen-Vluyn: Neukirchener, 2002.

Edersheim, Alfred. *The Life and Times of Jesus the Messiah*. 8th ed. 2 vols. London: Longmans, 1907.

Edo, Pablo M. "A Revision of the Origin and Role of the Supporting Angels in the Gospel of Peter (10:39b)." *VC* 68 (2014): 206–25.

Edwards, J. Christopher. *The Ransom Logion in Mark and Matthew: Its Reception and Its Significance for the Study of the Gospels*. Tübingen: Mohr Siebeck, 2012.

Edwards, Mark J. "Gnostics and Valentinians in the Church Fathers." *JTS* 40 (1989): 26–47.

———. "Neglected Texts in the Study of Gnosticism." *JTS* 41 (1990): 26–50.

Edwards, Robert G. T. "The Theological Gospel of Peter?" *NTS* 65 (2019): 496–510.

Efird, J. M., ed. *The Use of the Old Testament in the New and Other Essays: Studies in Honor of William Franklin Stinespring*. Durham, NC: Duke University Press, 1972.

Ehrman, Bart D. "Christianity Turned on Its Head: The Alternative Vision of the Gospel of Judas." Pages 77–120 in *The Gospel of Judas*. Edited by Rodolphe Kasser, Marvin Meyer, and Gregor Wurst. Washington, DC: National Geographic, 2006.

———. *Lost Christianities: The Battles for Scripture and the Faiths We Never Knew*. Oxford: Oxford University Press, 2003.

Eijk, A. (Ton) H. C. van. "The Gospel of Philip and Clement of Alexandria: Gnostic and Ecclesiastical Theology on the Resurrection and the Eucharist." *VC* 25 (1971): 94–120.

Elliott, J. Keith. "The Last Twelve Verses of Mark: Original or Not?" Pages 80–102 in *Perspectives on the Ending of Mark: 4 Views*. Edited by David A. Black. Nashville: Broadman & Holman, 2008.

Elliott, John H. *1 Peter*. New York: Doubleday, 2000.

Engberg-Pedersen, Troels. *John and Philosophy: A New Reading of the Fourth Gospel*. Oxford: Oxford University Press, 2017.

———. "The Past Is a Foreign Country: On the Shape and Purposes of Comparison in New Testament Scholarship." Pages 41–61 in *The New Testament in Comparison: Validity, Method, and Purpose in Comparing Traditions*. Edited by John Barclay and Benjamin White. London: Bloomsbury, 2020.

Eubank, Nathan. "A Disconcerting Prayer: On the Originality of Luke 23:34a." *JBL* 129 (2010): 521–36.

———. *Wages of Cross-Bearing and Debt of Sin: The Economy of Heaven in Matthew's Gospel*. Berlin: de Gruyter, 2013.

Evans, C. F. "I Will Go before You into Galilee." *JTS* 5 (1954): 3–18.

———. *Resurrection and the New Testament*. London: SCM, 1970.

Evans, Craig A. "Messiahs." Pages 537–42 in vol. 1 of *Encyclopedia of the Dead Sea Scrolls*. Edited by Lawrence H. Schiffman and James C. VanderKam. Oxford: Oxford University Press, 2000.

———. "A Note on the 'First-Born Son' of 4Q369." *DSD* 2 (1995): 185–201.

———. "Zechariah in the Markan Passion Narrative." Pages 64–80 in *The Gospel of Mark*. Vol. 1 of *Biblical Interpretation in Early Christian Gospels*. Edited by Thomas R. Hatina. London: T&T Clark, 2006.

Evans, Ernest, ed. and trans. *Tertullian: Adversus Marcionem*. Oxford: Clarendon, 1972.

Farrer, Austin. *The Revelation of St. John the Divine*. Oxford: Clarendon, 1964.

Ferguson, Anthony. "The Elijah Forerunner Concept as an Authentic Jewish Expectation." *JBL* 13 (2018): 127–45.

Fiedler, Peter. *Das Matthäusevangelium*. Stuttgart: Kohlhammer, 2006.

Field, Frederick. *Notes on Select Passages of the Greek Testament: Chiefly with Reference to Recent English Versions*. Oxford: E. Pickard Hall & J. H. Stacy, 1881.

———. *Origen: Hexapla*. Oxford: Clarendon, 1875.

Fitzmyer, Joseph A. *Luke the Theologian: Aspects of His Teaching*. New York: Paulist, 1989.

Forestell, J. Terence. *The Word of the Cross: Salvation as Revelation in the Fourth Gospel*. Rome: Biblical Institute Press, 1974.

Foster, Paul. "The Gospel of Peter." Pages 30–42 in *The Non-canonical Gospels*. Edited by Paul Foster. London: Bloomsbury, 2008.

———. *The Gospel of Peter: Introduction, Critical Edition and Commentary*. Leiden: Brill, 2010.

———. "Passion Traditions in the Gospel of Peter." Pages 47–68 in *Gelitten—Gestorben—Auferstanden*. Edited by T. Nicklas, A. Merkt, and J. Verheyden. Tübingen: Mohr Siebeck, 2010.

———. "Paul and Matthew: Two Strands of the Early Jesus Movement." Pages 86–114 in *Paul and the Gospels: Christologies, Conflicts and Convergences*. Edited by Michael Bird and Joel Willitts. London: Bloomsbury, 2011.

France, R. T. *The Gospel of Mark*. Grand Rapids: Eerdmans, 2002.

———. *The Gospel of Matthew*. Grand Rapids: Eerdmans, 2007.

———. *Jesus and the Old Testament*. London: Tyndale, 1971.

Fredriksen, Paula. *Paul, the Pagans' Apostle*. New Haven: Yale University Press, 2017.

Freedman, Harry, trans. *Genesis*. Vols. 1–2 of *Midrash Rabbah*. London: Soncino, 1939.

Frey, Jörg. *Die Herrlichkeit des Gekreuzigten*. Tübingen: Mohr Siebeck, 2013.

———. "Edler Tod—wirksamer Tod—stellvertretender Tod—heilschaffender Tod: Zur narrativen und theologischen Deutung des Todes Jesu im Johannesevangelium." Pages 65–94 in *The Death of Jesus in the Fourth Gospel*. Edited by Gilbert Van Belle. Leuven: Leuven University Press, 2007.

———. *The Glory of the Crucified One: Christology and Theology in the Gospel of John*. Waco, TX: Baylor University Press, 2018.

Frey, Jörg, and Jens Schröter, eds. *Deutungen des Todes Jesu im Neuen Testament*. 2nd ed. Tübingen: Mohr Siebeck, 2012.

Frey, Jörg, Jens Schröter, and E. E. Popkes, eds. *Das Thomasevangelium: Entstehung—Rezeption—Theologie*. Berlin: de Gruyter, 2008.

Friedlander, Gerald. *Pirkê de Rabbi Eliezer (The Chapters of Rabbi Eliezer the Great)*. London: Kegan Paul, 1916.

Gäbel, Georg. *Die Kulttheologie des Hebräerbriefes: Eine exegetisch-religionsgeschichtliche Studie*. Tübingen: Mohr Siebeck, 2006.

Galbraith, Deane. "Whence the Giant Jesus and His Talking Cross? The Resurrection in Gospel of Peter 10.39–42 as Prophetic Fulfilment of LXX Psalm 18." *NTS* 63 (2017): 473–91.

Gamel, Brian K. "Salvation in a Sentence: Mark 15:39 as Markan Soteriology." *JTI* 6 (2012): 65–78.

Garland, David. *A Theology of Mark's Gospel: Good News about Jesus the Messiah, the Son of God*. Grand Rapids: Zondervan, 2015.

Gathercole, Simon. "The Alleged Anonymity of the Canonical Gospels." *JTS* 69 (2018): 447–76.

———. *The Composition of the Gospel of Thomas: Original Language and Sources*. Cambridge: Cambridge University Press, 2012.

———. *Defending Substitution: An Essay on Atonement in Paul*. Grand Rapids: Baker, 2015.

———. *The Gospel of Judas*. Oxford: Oxford University Press, 2007.

———. *The Gospel of Thomas: Introduction and Commentary*. Leiden: Brill, 2014.

———. "'The Heavens and the Earth Will Be Rolled Up': The Eschatology of the Gospel of Thomas." Pages 280–302 in *Eschatologie—Eschatology: The Sixth Durham-Tübingen Research Symposium; Eschatology in Old Testament, Ancient Judaism and Early Christianity*. Edited by H.-J. Eckstein, C. Landmesser, and H. Lichtenberger. Tübingen: Mohr Siebeck, 2011.

———. "Matthean or Lukan Priority? The Use of the NT Gospels in the Gospel of Judas." Pages 291–302 in *Judasevangelium und Codex Tchacos*. Edited by E. E. Popkes and G. Wurst. Tübingen: Mohr Siebeck, 2012.

———. "The Nag Hammadi Gospels." Pages 199–218 in *Die Nag-Hammadi Schriften in der Literatur und Theologiegeschichte des frühen Christentums*. Edited by J. Schröter and K. Schwarz. Tübingen: Mohr Siebeck, 2017.

———. "Named Testimonia to the Gospel of Thomas: An Expanded Inventory and Analysis." *HTR* 105 (2012): 53–89.

———. "Other Apocryphal Gospels and the Historical Jesus." Pages 250–68 in *The Oxford Handbook of Early Christian Apocrypha*. Edited by Andrew Gregory and Christopher M. Tuckett. Oxford: Oxford University Press, 2015.

———. "*Praeparatio Evangelica* in Early Christian Gospels." Pages 15–40 in *Connecting Gospels: Beyond the Canonical/Non-canonical Divide*. Edited by Francis Watson and Sarah Parkhouse. Oxford: Oxford University Press, 2018.

———. *The Preexistent Son: Recovering the Christologies of Matthew, Mark, and Luke*. Grand Rapids: Eerdmans, 2006.

———. "Resemblance and Relation: Comparing the Gospels of Mark, John and Thomas." Pages 173–92 in *The New Testament in Comparison: Validity, Method, and Purpose in Comparing Traditions*. Edited by John Barclay and Benjamin White. London: Bloomsbury, 2020.

———. "Son of Man in Mark's Gospel." *ExpTim* 115 (2004): 366–72.

———. "Thomas Revisited: A Rejoinder to Denzey Lewis, Kloppenborg and Patterson." *JSNT* 36 (2014): 262–81.

———. "The Titles of the Gospels in the Earliest New Testament Manuscripts." *ZNW* 104 (2013): 33–76.

Giambrone, Anthony. "'Why Do the Scribes Say' (Mark 9:11): Scribal Expectations of an Eschatological High Priest and the Implications of Jesus' Transfiguration." *RB* 128 (2021): 201–35.

Giblin, Charles H. "Structural and Thematic Correlations in the Matthean Burial-Resurrection Narrative (Matt. XXVII.57–XXVIII.20)." *NTS* 21 (1974–1975): 406–20.

Gillingham, Susan. *A Journey of Two Psalms: The Reception of Psalms 1 and 2 in Jewish and Christian Tradition*. Oxford: Oxford University Press, 2013.

Gnilka, Joachim. *Das Evangelium nach Markus*. 2nd ed. Neukirchen: Neukirchener Verlag, 2015.

———. *Das Matthäusevangelium*. 2 vols. Freiburg: Herder, 1986–1988.

Goodacre, Mark. "Parallel Traditions or Parallel Gospels? John's Gospel as a Re-imagining of Mark." Pages 77–89 in *John's Transformation of Mark*. Edited by Eve-Marie Becker, Helen Bond, and Catrin Williams. London: Bloomsbury, 2021.

———. "Prophecy Historicized or Tradition Scripturalized? Reflections on the Origin of the Passion Narratives." Pages 37–51 in *The New Testament and the Church: Essays in Honour of John Muddiman*. Edited by John Barton and Peter Groves. London: Bloomsbury, 2015.

———. *Thomas and the Gospels*. Grand Rapids: Eerdmans, 2012.

Goodenough, Erwin R. *Symbolism in the Dura Synagogue II*. Vol. 10 of *Jewish Symbols in the Greco-Roman Period*. New York: Pantheon, 1964.

Gordon, Robert P. "Targumists as Eschatologists." Pages 113–30 in *Congress Volume: Göttingen 1977*. Edited by John Emerton. Leiden: Brill, 1978.

Gourgues, Michel. "'Mort pour nos péchés selon les Écritures': Que reste-t-il chez Jean du Credo des origines? Jn 1,29, chaînon unique de continuité." Pages 181–98 in *The Death of Jesus in the Fourth Gospel*. Edited by Gilbert Van Belle. Leuven: Leuven University Press, 2007.

Grant, Robert M., ed. *Gnosticism: An Anthology*. London: Collins, 1961.

———. *Gnosticism and Early Christianity*. New York: Columbia University Press, 1966.

———. "Two Gnostic Gospels." *JBL* 79 (1960): 1–11.

Grant, Robert M., and David Noel Freedman. *The Secret Sayings of Jesus*. New York: Doubleday, 1960.

Green, Joel B. "The Death of Jesus, God's Servant." Pages 1–28 and 170–73 in *Reimaging the Death of the Lukan Jesus*. Edited by Dennis D. Sylva. Frankfurt am Main: Hain, 1990.

———. "'Salvation to the End of the Earth' (Acts 13:47): God as Saviour in the Acts of the Apostles." Pages 83–106 in *Witness to the Gospel: The Theology of Acts*. Edited by I. H. Marshall and D. Peterson. Grand Rapids: Eerdmans, 1998.

Gregory, Andrew F. *The Gospel according to the Hebrews and the Gospel of the Ebionites*. Oxford: Oxford University Press, 2017.

Gregory, Andrew F., and C. Kavin Rowe, eds. *Rethinking the Unity and Reception of Luke and Acts*. Columbia: University of South Carolina Press, 2010.

Grimm, Werner. *Weil ich dich liebe: Die Verkündigung Jesu und Deuterojesaja*. Frankfurt am Main: Lang, 1976.

Grobel, Kendrick. *The Gospel of Truth: A Valentinian Meditation on the Gospel*. New York: Abingdon, 1959.

Guillaumont, A. "Les sémitismes dans l'Évangile selon Thomas: Essai de classement." Pages 190–204 in *Studies in Gnosticism and Hellenistic Religions Presented to Gilles Quispel on the Occasion of His 65th Birthday*. Edited by R. van den Broek and M. J. Vermaseren. Leiden: Brill, 1981.

———. "Sémitismes dans les logia de Jésus retrouvés à Nag-Hamâdi." *JA* 246 (1958): 113–23.

Gurtner, Daniel M. "The 'House of the Veil' in Sirach 50." *JSP* 14 (2005): 187–200.

———. "The Rending of the Veil and Markan Christology: 'Unveiling' the ‛ΥΙΟΣ ΘΕΟΥ (Mark 15:38–39)." *BibInt* 15 (2007): 292–306.

———. *The Torn Veil: Matthew's Exposition of the Death of Jesus*. Cambridge: Cambridge University Press, 2007.

Hagner, Donald A. *Matthew*. 2 vols. Waco, TX: Word, 1993–1995.

Hamilton, Catherine Sider. *The Death of Jesus in Matthew: Innocent Blood and the End of Exile*. Cambridge: Cambridge University Press, 2017.

Hamilton, Neill Q. "Resurrection Tradition and the Composition of Mark." *JBL* 84 (1965): 415–21.

Hann, Robert R. "Christos Kyrios in PsSol 17.32: 'The Lord's Anointed' Reconsidered." *NTS* 31 (1985): 620–27.

Harnack, Adolf von. *Marcion: Das Evangelium vom fremden Gott; Eine Monographie zur Geschichte der Grundlegung der katholischen Kirche.* 2nd ed. Leipzig: Hinrichs, 1924.

Harris, J. Rendel. *A Popular Account of the Newly Recovered Gospel of St Peter.* London: Hodder & Stoughton, 1893.

Hart, George, ed. *The Routledge Dictionary of Egyptian Gods and Goddesses.* 2nd ed. London: Routledge, 2005.

Hasitschka, Martin. "The Significance of the Resurrection Appearance in John 21." Pages 311–28 in *The Resurrection of Jesus in the Gospel of John.* Edited by Craig R. Koester and Reimund Bieringer. Tübingen: Mohr Siebeck, 2008.

Hatina, Thomas R., ed. *The Gospel of Mark.* Vol. 1 of *Biblical Interpretation in Early Christian Gospels.* London: T&T Clark, 2006.

Hay, David. *Glory at the Right Hand: Psalm 110 in Early Christianity.* Atlanta: Society of Biblical Literature, 1973.

Hays, Richard B. *Echoes of Scripture in the Gospels.* Waco, TX: Baylor University Press, 2016.

———. *Reading Backwards: Figural Christology and the Fourfold Gospel Witness.* Waco, TX: Baylor University Press, 2014.

Head, Peter M. *How the New Testament Came Together.* Cambridge: Grove Books, 2009.

———. "On the Christology of the Gospel of Peter." *VC* 46 (1992): 209–24.

Hebert, G. "The Resurrection-Narrative in St. Mark's Gospel." *SJT* 15 (1962): 66–73.

Hedrick, C. H. "Christian Motifs in the 'Gospel of the Egyptians': Method and Motive." *NovT* 23 (1981): 242–60.

Henderson, Timothy P. *The Gospel of Peter and Early Christian Apologetics: Rewriting the Story of Jesus' Death, Burial, and Resurrection.* Tübingen: Mohr Siebeck, 2011.

Hengel, Martin. "The Old Testament in the Fourth Gospel." Pages 380–95 in *The Gospels and the Scriptures of Israel.* Edited by Craig A. Evans and W. R. Stegner. Sheffield: Sheffield Academic, 1994.

———. *Studies in Early Christology.* Edinburgh: T&T Clark, 1995.

Hengel, Martin, and Anna Maria Schwemer. *Jesus und das Judentum.* Tübingen: Mohr Siebeck, 2007.

———. *Paul between Damascus and Antioch: The Unknown Years.* London: SCM, 1997.

Hengel, Martin, with D. P. Bailey. "The Effective History of Isaiah 53 in the Pre-Christian Period." Pages 75–146 in *The Suffering Servant: Isaiah 53 in Jewish and Christian Sources.* Edited by Bernd Janowski and Peter Stuhlmacher. Translated and supplemented by Daniel P. Bailey. Grand Rapids: Eerdmans, 2004.

Herzer, Jens. "The Riddle of the Holy Ones in Matthew 27:51b–53: A New Proposal for a Crux Interpretum." Pages 142–57 in *The Synoptic Gospels.* Vol. 1 of *"What Does the Scripture Say?" Studies in the Function of Scripture in Early Judaism and Christianity.* Edited by Craig A. Evans and H. Daniel Zacharias. London: Bloomsbury, 2012.

Hieke, Thomas. "Das Petrusevangelium vom Alten Testament her gelesen: Gewinnbringende Lektüre eines nicht-kanonischen Textes vom christlichen Kanon her." Pages 91–115 in *Das Evangelium nach Petrus: Texte, Kontexte, Intertexte.* Edited by Thomas Kraus and Tobias Nicklas. Berlin: de Gruyter, 2007.

Himmelfarb, Martha. *Jewish Messiahs in a Christian Empire: A History of the Book of Zerub-babel*. Cambridge: Harvard University Press, 2017.

Hofius, Otfried. "The Fourth Servant Song in the New Testament Letters." Pages 163–88 in *The Suffering Servant: Isaiah 53 in Jewish and Christian Sources*. Edited by Bernd Janowski and Peter Stuhlmacher. Translated and supplemented by Daniel P. Bailey. Grand Rapids: Eerdmans, 2004.

Holl, Karl, and Jürgen Dummer, eds. *Epiphanius: Panarion haer. 34–64*. Berlin: de Gruyter, 1980.

Holladay, Carl R. "Acts as Kerygma: λαλεῖν τὸν λόγον." *NTS* 63 (2017): 153–82.

Hooker, Morna D. *Endings: Invitations to Discipleship*. London: SCM, 2003.

———. *The Gospel according to St. Mark*. London: A. & C. Black, 2001.

———. "Mark." Pages 220–30 in *It Is Written: Scripture Citing Scripture; Essays in Honour of Barnabas Lindars, SSF*. Edited by D. A. Carson and H. G. M. Williamson. Cambridge: Cambridge University Press, 1988.

———. *Not Ashamed of the Gospel: New Testament Interpretations of the Death of Christ*. Carlisle: Paternoster, 1994.

———. *The Son of Man in Mark*. London: SPCK, 2007.

Horbury, William. "Herod's Temple and 'Herod's Days,'" in idem, ed. *Templum Amicitiae*, 103–49.

———. *Jewish Messianism and the Cult of Christ*. London: SCM, 1998.

———. "The Messianic Associations of the 'Son of Man.'" *JTS* 36 (1985): 34–55.

———. *Messianism among Jews and Christians: Biblical and Historical Studies*. London: Bloomsbury, 2003.

———, ed. *Templum Amicitiae: Essays on the Second Temple Presented to Ernst Bammel*. Sheffield: Sheffield Academic, 1991.

Horrell, David G. "The Catholic Epistles and Hebrews." Pages 122–35 in *Redemption and Resistance: The Messianic Hopes of Jews and Christians in Antiquity*. Edited by Markus Bockmuehl and James Carleton Paget. Cambridge: Cambridge University Press, 2009.

———. "Jesus Remembered in 1 Peter? Early Jesus Traditions, Isaiah 53, and 1 Peter 2.21–25." Pages 123–50 in *James, 1 & 2 Peter, and Early Jesus Traditions*. Edited by Alicia J. Batten and John S. Kloppenborg. London: Bloomsbury, 2014.

———. "The Product of a Petrine Circle? A Reassessment of the Origin and Character of 1 Peter." *JSNT* 86 (2002): 29–60.

———. "Who Are 'the Dead' and When Was the Gospel Preached to Them? The Interpretation of 1 Pet 4.6." *NTS* 48 (2003): 70–89.

Horst, Pieter W. van der. "Can a Book End with γάρ? A Note on Mark xvi.8." *JTS* 23 (1972): 121–24.

———. "Once More: The Translation of οἱ δέ in Matthew 28.17." *JSNT* 27 (1986): 27–30.

Hurtado, Larry W. *The Earliest Christian Artifacts: Manuscripts and Christian Origins*. Grand Rapids: Eerdmans, 2007.

———. "The Greek Fragments of the Gospel of Thomas as Artefacts: Papyrological Observations on Papyrus Oxyrhynchus 1, Papyrus Oxyrhynchus 654 and Papyrus Oxyrhynchus 655." Pages 19–32 in *Das Thomasevangelium: Entstehung—Rezeption—Theologie*. Edited by Jörg Frey, Jens Schröter, and E. E. Popkes. Berlin: de Gruyter, 2008.

———. *Lord Jesus Christ: Devotion to Jesus in Earliest Christianity*. Grand Rapids: Eerdmans, 2003.

Isenberg, Wesley W. "The Gospel of Philip." Pages 142–215 in *Nag Hammadi Codex II,2–7, together with XIII,2*, Brit. Lib. Or.4926(1), and P. Oxy. 1, 654, 655.* Vol. 1. Edited by Bentley Layton. Leiden: Brill, 1989.

———. "The Gospel of Truth." Pages 146–61 in *Gnosticism: An Anthology.* Edited by Robert M. Grant. London: Collins, 1961.

Iverson, Kelly. "A Further Word on Final γάρ." *CBQ* 68 (2006): 79–94.

Jamieson, Robert B. *Jesus' Death and Heavenly Offering in Hebrews.* Cambridge: Cambridge University Press, 2019.

Janowski, Bernd. "He Bore Our Sins: Isaiah 53 and the Drama of Taking Another's Place." Pages 48–74 in *The Suffering Servant: Isaiah 53 in Jewish and Christian Sources.* Edited by Bernd Janowski and Peter Stuhlmacher. Translated and supplemented by Daniel P. Bailey. Grand Rapids: Eerdmans, 2004.

Janowski, Bernd, and Peter Stuhlmacher, eds. *The Suffering Servant: Isaiah 53 in Jewish and Christian Sources.* Translated and supplemented by Daniel P. Bailey. Grand Rapids: Eerdmans, 2004.

Janse, Sam. *"You Are My Son": The Reception History of Psalm 2 in Early Judaism and the Early Church.* Leuven: Peeters, 2009.

Jantsch, Torsten. *Jesus, der Retter: Die Soteriologie des lukanischen Doppelwerks.* Tübingen: Mohr Siebeck, 2017.

Jenott, Lance. *The Gospel of Judas: Coptic Text, Translation, and Historical Interpretation of "the Betrayer's Gospel."* Tübingen: Mohr Siebeck, 2011.

Jeremias, Joachim. *The Eucharistic Words of Jesus.* Oxford: Basil Blackwell, 1955.

Jipp, Joshua W. "Luke's Scriptural Suffering Messiah: A Search for Precedent, a Search for Identity." *CBQ* 73 (2010): 255–74.

Johnson, Luke Timothy. "The Christology of Luke-Acts." Pages 145–61 in *Contested Issues in Christian Origins and the New Testament.* Leiden: Brill, 2013.

———. "Luke 24:1–11: The Not-So-Empty Tomb." *Int* 46 (1992): 57–61.

Johnston, Jeremiah J. *The Resurrection of Jesus in the Gospel of Peter: A Tradition-Historical Study of the Akhmîm Gospel Fragment.* London: Bloomsbury, 2015.

Jonge, Marinus de. "Jewish Expectations about the 'Messiah' according to the Fourth Gospel." *NTS* 19 (1973): 246–70.

Juel, Donald H. *Messiah and Temple: The Trial of Jesus in the Gospel of Mark.* Atlanta: Society of Biblical Literature, 1977.

———. *Messianic Exegesis: Christological Interpretation of the Old Testament in Early Christianity.* Minneapolis: Fortress, 1988.

Kaiser, Walter C. *The Christian and the "Old" Testament.* Eugene, OR: Wipf & Stock, 1998.

Karrer, Martin. *Der Gesalbte: Die Grundlagen des Christustitels.* Göttingen: Vandenhoeck & Ruprecht, 1990.

Karris, Robert J. *Luke, Artist and Theologian: Luke's Passion Account as Literature.* New York: Paulist, 1985.

Kasser, Rodolphe, Marvin Meyer, and Gregor Wurst, eds. *The Gospel of Judas.* Washington, DC: National Geographic, 2006.

Kaufman, Ryan. "Does 𝔓66 Suggest a Vorlage Lacking John 21?" Academia. https://independent.academia.edu/RyanKaufman1.

Keith, Chris. "'If John Knew Mark': Critical Inheritance and Johannine Disagreements with Mark." Pages 31–49 in *John's Transformation of Mark.* Edited by Eve-Marie Becker, Helen Bond, and Catrin Williams. London: Bloomsbury, 2021.

Kelhoffer, James A. *Miracle and Mission: The Authentication of Missionaries and Their Message in the Longer Ending of Mark*. Tübingen: Mohr Siebeck, 2000.

Kimbell, John. *The Atonement in Lukan Theology*. Newcastle: Cambridge Scholars, 2014.

Kinzig, Wolfram. "Καινὴ διαθήκη: The Title of the New Testament in the Second and Third Centuries." *JTS* 45 (1994): 519–44.

Kirk, G. S., J. E. Raven, and M. Schofield. *The Presocratic Philosophers*. 2nd ed. Cambridge: Cambridge University Press, 1983.

Kloppenborg, John S. "*Evocatio Deorum* and the Date of Mark." *JBL* 124 (2005): 419–50.

Klumbies, Paul-Gerhardt. "Himmelfahrt und Apotheose Jesu in Lk 24,50–53." *Klio* 89 (2007): 147–60.

Knibb, Michael A. *Essays on the Book of Enoch and Other Early Jewish Texts and Traditions*. Leiden: Brill, 2008.

———. "Interpreter of the Law." Pages 383–84 in vol. 1 of *Encyclopedia of the Dead Sea Scrolls*. Edited by Lawrence H. Schiffman and James C. VanderKam. Oxford: Oxford University Press, 2000.

———. "Martyrdom and Ascension of Isaiah." Pages 143–76 in vol. 2 of *The Old Testament Pseudepigrapha*. Edited by J. H. Charlesworth. Garden City, NY: Doubleday, 1985.

Knowles, Michael P. *Jeremiah in Matthew's Gospel: The Rejected Prophet Motif in Matthean Redaction*. Sheffield: JSOT Press, 1993.

Knox, W. L. "The Ending of St. Mark's Gospel." *HTR* 35 (1942): 13–23.

Koester, Craig R. "The Death of Jesus and the Human Condition: Exploring the Theology of John's Gospel." Pages 141–57 in *Life in Abundance: Studies of John's Gospel in Tribute to Raymond E. Brown*. Edited by John Donahue. Collegeville, MN: Liturgical, 2005.

———. "Jesus' Resurrection, the Signs, and the Dynamics of Faith in the Gospel of John." Pages 47–74 in *The Resurrection of Jesus in the Gospel of John*. Edited by Craig R. Koester and Reimund Bieringer. Tübingen: Mohr Siebeck, 2008.

———. "Messianic Exegesis and the Call of Nathanael (John 1:45–51)." *JSNT* 39 (1990): 23–34.

———. *Symbolism in the Fourth Gospel: Meaning, Mystery, Community*. Minneapolis: Fortress, 2003.

———. *The Word of Life: A Theology of John's Gospel*. Grand Rapids: Eerdmans, 2008.

Koester, Craig R., and Reimund Bieringer, eds. *The Resurrection of Jesus in the Gospel of John*. Tübingen: Mohr Siebeck, 2008.

Koester, Helmut. "Apocryphal and Canonical Gospels." *HTR* 73 (1980): 105–30.

Kok, Michael. "Does Mark Narrate the Pauline Kerygma of 'Christ Crucified'? Challenging an Emerging Consensus on Mark as a Pauline Gospel." *JSNT* 37 (2014): 139–60.

Konradt, Matthias. *Das Evangelium nach Matthäus*. Göttingen: Vandenhoeck & Ruprecht, 2015.

———. *Israel, Church, and the Gentiles in the Gospel of Matthew*. Waco, TX: Baylor University Press, 2014.

Kraus, Thomas, and Tobias Nicklas, eds. *Das Evangelium nach Petrus: Texte, Kontexte, Intertexte*. Berlin: de Gruyter, 2007.

Kraus, Wolfgang. "Zur Aufnahme und Funktion von Gen 14,18–20 und Ps 109 LXX im Hebräerbrief." Pages 459–74 in *Text—Textgeschichte—Textwirkung: Festschrift zum 65. Geburtstag von Siegfried Kreuzer*. Edited by Thomas Wagner, Jonathan Miles Robker, and Frank Ueberschaer. Münster: Ugarit-Verlag 2014.

Krosney, Herb. *The Lost Gospel: The Quest for the Gospel of Judas Iscariot*. Washington, DC: National Geographic, 2006.

Krosney, Herb, Marvin Meyer, and Gregor Wurst. "Preliminary Report on New Fragments of Codex Tchacos." *EC* 2 (2010): 282–94.

Kruse, Colin. *The Gospel according to John: An Introduction and Commentary*. Grand Rapids: Eerdmans, 2004.

Lampe, G. W. H. *A Patristic Greek Lexicon*. Oxford: Clarendon, 1961.

Lane, Eugene N. *The Monuments and Inscriptions*. Vol. 1 of *Corpus Monumentorum Religionis Dei Menis*. Leiden: Brill, 1971.

Lanier, Gregory. *Old Testament Conceptual Metaphors and the Christology of Luke's Gospel*. London: Bloomsbury, 2018.

Lappenga, Benjamin. "Whose Zeal Is It Anyway? The Citation of Psalm 69:9 in John 2:17 as a Double Entendre." Pages 141–60 in *Abiding Words: The Use of Scripture in the Gospel of John*. Edited by Alicia D. Myers and Bruce G. Schuchard. Atlanta: SBL Press, 2015.

Larsen, Matthew D. C. *Gospels before the Book*. Oxford: Oxford University Press, 2018.

Layton, Bentley. *The Gnostic Scriptures: A New Translation with Annotations and Introductions*. New York: Doubleday, 1987.

Le Donne, Anthony. "Greater Than Solomon: Orality, Mnemonics and Scriptural Narrativization in Luke." Pages 96–113 in *The Gospel of Luke*. Vol. 3 of *Biblical Interpretation in Early Christian Gospels*. Edited by Thomas Hatina. London: Bloomsbury, 2010.

Lehrman, S. M., trans. *Exodus*. Vol. 3 of *Midrash Rabbah*. London: Soncino, 1939.

Levey, Samson H. *The Messiah: An Aramaic Interpretation; The Messianic Exegesis of the Targum*. New York: Ktav, 1974.

———. "The Targum to Ezekiel." *HUCA* 46 (1975): 139–58.

Liebengood, Kelly D. *The Eschatology of 1 Peter: Considering the Influence of Zechariah 9–14*. Cambridge: Cambridge University Press, 2014.

Lieu, Judith M. "Heresy and Scripture." Pages 81–100 in *Ein neues Geschlecht? Entwicklung des frühchristlichen Selbstbewusstseins*. Edited by M. Lang. Göttingen: Vandenhoeck & Ruprecht, 2013.

———. *Marcion and the Making of a Heretic: God and Scripture in the Second Century*. Cambridge: Cambridge University Press, 2015.

———. "Marcion and the Synoptic Problem." Pages 731–51 in *New Studies in the Synoptic Problem*. Edited by P. Foster, A. Gregory, J. S. Kloppenborg, and J. Verheyden. Leuven: Peeters, 2011.

———. "Messiah and Resistance in the Gospel and Epistles of John." Pages 97–107 in *Redemption and Resistance: The Messianic Hopes of Jews and Christians in Antiquity*. Edited by Markus Bockmuehl and James Carleton Paget. Cambridge: Cambridge University Press, 2009.

———. "Narrative Analysis and Scripture in John." Pages 144–63 in *The Old Testament in the New Testament: Essays in Honour of J. L. North*. Edited by Steven Moyise. Sheffield: Sheffield Academic, 2000.

———. Review of *The Grammar of Messianism: An Ancient Jewish Political Idiom and Its Users*, by Matthew V. Novenson. *Theology* 121 (2018): 294–95.

Lightfoot, J. B. *St. Ignatius, St. Polycarp*. Part 2 of vol. 2 of *The Apostolic Fathers*. London: Macmillan, 1889.

Lincoln, Andrew T. *The Gospel according to St John*. London: Continuum, 2005.

———. "'I Am the Resurrection and the Life': The Resurrection Message of the Fourth Gospel." Pages 122–44 in *Life in the Face of Death: The Resurrection Message of the New Testament*. Edited by Richard N. Longenecker. Grand Rapids: Eerdmans, 1998.

————. "The Promise and the Failure: Mark 16:7, 8." *JBL* 108 (1989): 283–300.

Lindemann, Andreas. "Die Osterbotschaft des Markus: Zur theologischen Interpretation von Mk 16.1–8." *NTS* 26 (1979–1980): 298–317.

Loader, William. *Jesus in John's Gospel: Structure and Issues in Johannine Christology.* Grand Rapids: Eerdmans, 2017.

Löhr, Hermut. "Jesus and the Ten Words." Pages 3135–54 in *Handbook to the Study of the Historical Jesus.* Edited by Tom Holmén and Stanley Porter. Leiden: Brill, 2010.

Löhr, Winrich A. "Did Marcion Distinguish between a Just God and a Good God?" Pages 131–46 in *Marcion und seine kirchengeschichtliche Wirkung/Marcion and His Impact on Church History.* Edited by Gerhard May and Katharina Greschat. Berlin: de Gruyter, 2002.

————. "Die Auslegung des Gesetzes bei Markion, den Gnostikern und den Manichäern." Pages 77–95 in *Stimuli: Exegese und ihre Hermeneutik in Antike und Christentum; FS für Ernst Dassmann.* Edited by G. Schollgen and C. Scholten. Münster: Aschendorff, 1996.

————. "Markion." *RAC* 24:147–73.

————. "Problems of Profiling Marcion." Pages 109–33 in *Christian Teachers in Second Century Rome.* Edited by Gregory H. Snyder. Leiden: Brill, 2020.

Lührmann, Dieter. *Das Markusevangelium.* Tübingen: Mohr Siebeck, 1987.

Luijendijk, AnneMarie. "Reading the *Gospel of Thomas* in the Third Century: Three Oxyrhynchus Papyri and Origen's *Homilies.*" Pages 241–67 in *Reading New Testament Papyri in Context.* Edited by C. Clivaz and J. Zumstein. Leuven: Peeters, 2011.

Lundhaug, Hugo. *Images of Rebirth: Cognitive Poetics and Transformational Soteriology in the Gospel of Philip and the Exegesis on the Soul.* Leiden: Brill, 2010.

Lunn, Nicholas P. *The Original Ending of Mark: A New Case for the Authenticity of Mark 16:9–20.* Cambridge: James Clarke, 2014.

Luz, Ulrich. *Matthew: A Commentary.* 3 vols. Minneapolis: Fortress, 2001–2007.

————. *Studies in Matthew.* Grand Rapids: Eerdmans, 2005.

Magness, J. Lee. *Sense and Absence: Structure and Suspension in the Ending of Mark's Gospel.* Atlanta: Scholars Press, 1986.

Mainville, Odette. "De Jésus à l'Église: Étude rédactionelle de Luc 24." *NTS* (2005): 192–211.

Mansfeld, Jaap. *Prolegomena: Questions to Be Settled before the Study of an Author or a Text.* Leiden: Brill, 1994.

Manson, T. W. *Studies in the Gospels and Epistles.* Manchester: Manchester University Press, 1962.

Mara, Maria Grazia. *Évangile de Pierre: Introduction, texte critique, traduction, commentaire et index.* Paris: Cerf, 2006.

Marcus, Joel. "The Gospel of Peter as a Jewish Christian Document." *NTS* 64 (2018): 473–94.

————. *Mark 8–16.* New Haven: Yale University Press, 2009.

————. "Mark—Interpreter of Paul." *NTS* 46 (2000): 473–87.

————. *The Way of the Lord: Christological Exegesis of the Old Testament in the Gospel of Mark.* Louisville: Westminster John Knox, 2003.

Marguerat, Daniel. *The First Christian Historian: Writing the "Acts of the Apostles."* Cambridge: Cambridge University Press, 2004.

Markschies, Christoph, and Jens Schröter, eds. *Evangelien und Verwandtes.* Vol. 1 of *Antike christliche Apokryphen in deutscher Übersetzung.* Tübingen: Mohr Siebeck, 2012.

Marsh, John. *Saint John*. London: Penguin, 1968.

Martin, Dale B. "The Possibility of Comparison, the Necessity of Anachronism and the Dangers of Purity." Pages 63–77 in *The New Testament in Comparison: Validity, Method, and Purpose in Comparing Traditions*. Edited by John Barclay and Benjamin White. London: Bloomsbury, 2020.

Martyn, J. Louis. *History and Theology in the Fourth Gospel*. Louisville: Westminster John Knox, 2003.

Matera, Frank J. "The Death of Jesus according to Luke: A Question of Sources." *CBQ* 47 (1985): 469–85.

May, Gerhard. "Marcion in Contemporary Views: Results and Open Questions." *SecCent* 6 (1987–1988): 129–51.

May, Gerhard, and Katharina Greschat, eds. *Marcion und seine kirchengeschichtliche Wirkung/Marcion and His Impact on Church History*. Berlin: de Gruyter, 2002.

McArthur, Harvey K. "'On the Third Day.'" *NTS* 18 (1971): 81–86.

McCant, Jerry. "The Gospel of Peter: Docetism Reconsidered." *NTS* 30 (1984): 258–73.

McCarthy, Carmel. *Saint Ephrem's Commentary on Tatian's Diatessaron: An English Translation of Chester Beatty Syriac MS 709 with Introduction and Notes*. Oxford: Oxford University Press, 1993.

McGuire, Anne. "Conversion and Gnosis in the 'Gospel of Truth.'" *NovT* 28 (1986): 338–55.

McHugh, John F. *John 1–4: A Critical and Exegetical Commentary*. London: Bloomsbury, 2009.

McNally, Robert E., ed. *Scriptores Hiberniae Minores*. Part 1. Turnhout: Brepols, 1973.

McWhirter, Jocelyn. "Messianic Exegesis in the Fourth Gospel." Pages 124–48 in *Reading the Gospel of John's Christology as Jewish Messianism*. Edited by Benjamin Reynolds and Gabriele Boccaccini. Leiden: Brill, 2018.

Meier, John P. "The Parable of the Wheat and the Weeds (Matthew 13:24–30): Is Thomas's Version (Logion 57) Independent?" *JBL* 131 (2012): 715–32.

Ménard, Jacques E. *L'Évangile de Vérité*. Leiden: Brill, 1972.

Menken, Maarten J. J. "The Minor Prophets in John." Pages 79–96 in *The Minor Prophets in the New Testament*. Edited by Maarten J. J. Menken and Steve Moyise. London: Bloomsbury, 2009.

———. *Old Testament Quotations in the Fourth Gospel: Studies in Textual Form*. Leuven: Peeters, 1996.

———. "The Quotation from Isa 40,3 in John 1,23." *Bib* 66 (1985): 190–205.

Meshorer, Ya'akov. *A Treasury of Jewish Coins: From the Persian Period to Bar Kochba*. Jerusalem: Yad Ben-Zvi, 2001.

Metzger, Bruce M. *A Textual Commentary on the Greek New Testament*. 2nd ed. Stuttgart: Deutsche Bibelgesellschaft, 1994.

Meyer, Marvin. "The Gospel of Judas." Pages 755–69 in *The Nag Hammadi Scriptures*. Edited by Marvin Meyer. New York: HarperCollins, 2007.

———, ed. *The Nag Hammadi Scriptures*. New York: HarperCollins, 2007.

Miller, Merrill P. "The Function of Isa 61:1–2 in 11Q Melchizedek." *JBL* 88 (1969): 467–69.

Miller, R. C. "Mark's Empty Tomb and Other Translation Fables in Classical Antiquity." *JBL* 129 (2010): 759–76.

Minnen, Peter van. "The Akhmim Gospel of Peter." Pages 53–60 in *Das Evangelium nach*

Petrus: Texte, Kontexte, Intertexte. Edited by Thomas Kraus and Tobias Nicklas. Berlin: de Gruyter, 2007.

Mitchell, G. W., ed. and trans. *S. Ephraim's Prose Refutations of Mani, Marcion and Bardaisan.* Vol. 2. London: Williams & Norgate, 1921.

Mitchell, Margaret M. "On Comparing, and Calling the Question." Pages 95–124 in *The New Testament in Comparison: Validity, Method, and Purpose in Comparing Traditions.* Edited by John Barclay and Benjamin White. London: Bloomsbury, 2020.

Mittmann-Richert, U. *Der Sühnetod des Gottesknechts: Jesaja 53 im Lukasevangelium.* Tübingen: Mohr Siebeck, 2008.

Moessner, David P. "Suffering, Intercession and Eschatological Atonement: An Uncommon View in the Testament of Moses and in Luke-Acts." Pages 202–27 in *The Pseudepigrapha and Early Biblical Interpretation.* Edited by James H. Charlesworth and Craig A. Evans. Sheffield: Sheffield Academic, 1993.

Moffitt, David. *Atonement and the Logic of Resurrection in the Epistle to the Hebrews.* Leiden: Brill, 2011.

Moll, Sebastian. *The Arch-Heretic Marcion.* Tübingen: Mohr Siebeck, 2010.

Moloney, Francis J. *The Gospel of John.* Collegeville, MN: Liturgical, 1998.

Montanari, Franco, ed. *The Brill Dictionary of Ancient Greek.* Leiden: Brill, 2015.

Moo, Douglas J. *The Old Testament in the Gospel Passion Narratives.* Sheffield: Almond, 1983.

Morgan, Robert. Review of *Die Deutung des Todes Jesu im Markusevangelium,* by A. Weihs. *JTS* (2008): 273–74.

Morgenthaler, Robert. *Statistik des neutestamentlichen Wortschatzes.* Zurich: Gotthelf-Verlag, 1958.

Morris, Leon. *The Book of Revelation: An Introduction and Commentary.* Grand Rapids: Eerdmans, 1987.

———. *Gospel according to John.* Grand Rapids: Eerdmans, 1971.

Motyer, Stephen. "The Rending of the Veil: A Markan Pentecost?" *NTS* 33 (1987): 155–57.

Mounce, Robert H. *The Book of Revelation.* Rev. ed. Grand Rapids: Eerdmans, 1998.

Moyise, Stephen. *The Old Testament in the Book of Revelation.* London: Bloomsbury, 1995.

Mutschler, Bernhard. *Irenäus als johanneischer Theologe: Studien zur Schriftauslegung bei Irenäus von Lyon.* Tübingen: Mohr Siebeck, 2004.

Myers, Alicia D., and Bruce G. Schuchard, eds. *Abiding Words: The Use of Scripture in the Gospel of John.* Atlanta: SBL Press, 2015.

Myllykoski, Matti. "Die Kraft des Herrn: Erwägungen zur Christologie des Petrusevangeliums." Pages 301–26 in *Das Evangelium nach Petrus: Texte, Kontexte, Intertexte.* Edited by Thomas Kraus and Tobias Nicklas. Berlin: de Gruyter, 2007.

Nachmanson, E. *Der griechische Buchtitel: Einige Beobachtungen.* Darmstadt: Wissenschaftliche Buchgesellschaft, 1969.

Nagel, Peter. "'Das (Buch) nach Philippus': Zur Titelnachschrift Nag Hammadi Codex II,3: p. 86,18–19." *ZNW* 99 (2008): 99–111.

———. *Evangelien und Apostelgeschichten aus den Schriften von Nag Hammadi und verwandtes Kodizes: Koptisch und Deutsch.* Vol. 1 of *Codex apocryphus gnosticus Novi Testamenti.* Tübingen: Mohr Siebeck, 2014.

Needham, Rodney. "Polythetic Classification: Convergence and Consequences." *Man* 10 (1975): 349–69.

Neusner, Jacob. "Comparing Judaisms." *HR* 18 (1978): 177–91.

Neyrey, Jerome. *The Passion according to Luke: A Redaction Study of Luke's Soteriology*. New York: Paulist, 1985.

Nickelsburg, George W. E. *1 Enoch 1: A Commentary on the Book of 1 Enoch, Chapters 1–36; 81–108*. Minneapolis: Fortress, 2001.

———. *Resurrection, Immortality, and Eternal Life in Intertestamental Judaism and Early Christianity*. Exp. ed. Cambridge: Harvard University Press, 2006.

Nickelsburg, George W. E., and James VanderKam. *1 Enoch: The Hermeneia Translation*. Minneapolis: Fortress, 2012.

———. *1 Enoch 2: A Commentary on the Book of 1 Enoch, Chapters 37–82*. Minneapolis: Fortress, 2011.

Nicklas, Tobias. "Angels in Early Christian Narratives on the Resurrection of Jesus: Canonical and Apocryphal Texts." Pages 293–311 in *Angels: The Concept of Celestial Beings—Origins, Development and Reception*. Edited by F. V. Reiterer, T. Nicklas, and K. Schöpflin. Berlin: de Gruyter, 2007.

———. "Die 'Juden' im Petrusevangelium (PCair 10759): Ein Testfall." *NTS* 47 (2001): 206–21.

———. "Die Leiblichkeit der Gepeinigten: Das Petrusevangelium und frühchristliche Märtyrerakten." Pages 195–220 in *Martyrdom and Persecution in Late Ancient Christianity*. Edited by J. Leemans. Leuven: Peeters, 2011.

———. "Die Prophetie des Kajaphas: Im Netz johanneischer Ironie." *NTS* 46 (2000): 589–94.

———. "Resurrection in the Gospels of Matthew and Peter: Some Developments." Pages 26–41 in *Life beyond Death in Matthew's Gospel: Religious Metaphor or Bodily Reality?* Edited by Wim Weren, Huub van de Sandt, and Joseph Verheyden. Leuven: Peeters, 2011.

Niese, Benedikt, ed. *Flavii Iosephi Opera*. Vol. 6. Berlin: Weidmann, 1894.

Nolland, John. *Luke*. 3 vols. Waco, TX: Word, 1989–1993.

Nongbri, Brent. "P. Bodmer 2 as Possible Evidence for the Circulation of the Gospel according to John without Chapter 21." *EC* 9 (2018): 345–60.

Nordsieck, Reinhard. *Das Thomas-Evangelium: Einleitung—Zur Frage des historischen Jesus—Kommentierung aller 114 Logien*. Neukirchen-Vluyn: Neukirchener, 2004.

Norelli, Enrico. "Note sulla soteriologia di Marcione." *Aug* 35 (1995): 281–305.

Novakovic, Lidija. *Raised from the Dead according to Scripture: The Role of the Old Testament in the Early Christian Interpretations of Jesus' Resurrection*. London: Bloomsbury, 2012.

Novenson, Matthew V. *Christ among the Messiahs: Christ Language in Paul and Messiah Language in Ancient Judaism*. Oxford: Oxford University Press, 2012.

———. *The Grammar of Messianism: An Ancient Jewish Political Idiom and Its Users*. Oxford: Oxford University Press, 2017.

———. "Jesus the Messiah: Conservatism and Radicalism in Johannine Christology." Pages 109–24 in *Portraits of Jesus in John*. Edited by Craig R. Koester. London: Bloomsbury, 2018.

———. "Whose Son Is the Messiah?" Pages 72–84 in *Son of God: Divine Sonship in Jewish and Christian Antiquity*. Edited by Garrick Allen, Kai Akagi, Paul Sloan, and Madhavi Nevader. Winona Lake, IN: Eisenbrauns, 2019.

———. "Why Does R. Akiba Acclaim Bar Kokhba as Messiah?" *JSJ* 40 (2009): 551–72.

O'Brien, Kelli S. *The Use of Scripture in the Markan Passion Narrative*. London: Bloomsbury, 2010.

Odeberg, Hugo. *The Fourth Gospel: Interpreted in Its Relation to Contemporaneous Religious Currents in Palestine and the Hellenistic-Oriental World.* Uppsala: Almqvist & Wiksell, 1929.

Oegema, Gerbern S. *The Anointed and His People: Messianic Expectations from the Maccabees to Bar Kochba.* Sheffield: Sheffield Academic, 1994.

Omerzu, Heike. "'My Power, Power, You Have Left Me': Christology in the Gospel of Peter." Pages 163–88 in *Connecting Gospels: Beyond the Canonical/Non-canonical Divide.* Edited by Francis Watson and Sarah Parkhouse. Oxford: Oxford University Press, 2018.

Orbe, Antonio. "Hacia la doctrina marcionítica de la redención." *Gregorianum* 74 (1993): 45–74.

Os, Bas van. "Was the Gospel of Philip Written in Syria?" *Apocrypha* 17 (2006): 87–93.

Paden, William E. "Elements of a New Comparativism." *MTSR* 8 (1996): 5–14.

———. "Elements of a New Comparativism" (revised version). Pages 182–92 in *A Magic Still Dwells: Comparative Religion in the Postmodern Age.* Edited by Kimberley C. Patton and Benjamin C. Ray. Berkeley: University of California Press, 2000.

Pagels, Elaine. *The Gnostic Gospels.* New York: Vintage Books, 1979.

———. "Ritual in the Gospel of Philip." Pages 280–92 in *The Nag Hammadi Library after Fifty Years.* Edited by John D. Turner and Anne McGuire. Leiden: Brill, 1997.

Painchaud, Louis. "Le Christ vainqueur de la mort dans l'Évangile selon Philippe: Une exégèse valentinienne de Matt. 27:46." *NovT* 38 (1996): 382–92.

Painchaud, Louis, and Paul-Hubert Poirier, eds. *Coptica—Gnostica—Manichaica: Mélanges offerts à Wolf-Peter Funk.* Leuven: Peeters, 2006.

Painter, John. "The Light Shines in the Darkness." Pages 21–46 in *The Resurrection of Jesus in the Gospel of John.* Edited by Craig R. Koester and Reimund Bieringer. Tübingen: Mohr Siebeck, 2008.

———. *The Quest for the Messiah: The History, Literature and Theology of the Johannine Community.* 2nd ed. Edinburgh: T&T Clark, 1993.

Parker, David C. *The Living Text of the Gospels.* Cambridge: Cambridge University Press, 1997.

Parsons, Kathryn Pyne. "Three Concepts of Clusters." *Philosophy and Phenomenological Research* 33 (1973): 514–23.

Parsons, Peter J. *City of the Sharp-Nosed Fish: Greek Lives in Roman Egypt.* London: Weidenfeld & Nicholson, 2007.

Patterson, Stephen J. "The Gospel of Thomas and Historical Jesus Research." Pages 663–84 in *Coptica—Gnostica—Manichaica: Mélanges offerts à Wolf-Peter Funk.* Edited by Louis Painchaud and Paul-Hubert Poirier. Leuven: Peeters, 2006.

———. "The View from across the Euphrates." *HTR* 104 (2011): 411–31.

Patton, Kimberley C., and Benjamin C. Ray, eds. *A Magic Still Dwells: Comparative Religion in the Postmodern Age.* Berkeley: University of California Press, 2000.

Payne Smith, Robert. *Thesaurus Syriacus.* Oxford: Clarendon, 1879.

Pearson, Birger A. *Gnosticism and Christianity in Roman and Coptic Egypt.* London: T&T Clark International, 2004.

Pesch, Rudolf. *Das Markusevangelium.* 3rd ed. Freiburg: Herder, 1984.

Peterson, Jeff. "The Extent of Christian Theological Diversity: Pauline Evidence." *ResQ* 47 (2005): 1–12.

Pitre, Brant. *Jesus and the Last Supper*. Grand Rapids: Eerdmans, 2015.

Plevnik, Joseph. "The Eyewitnesses of the Risen Jesus in Luke 24." *CBQ* 49 (1986): 90–103.

Pokorný, Petr. *A Commentary on the Gospel of Thomas: From Interpretations to the Interpreted*. London: Continuum, 2009.

Polotsky, Hans J. *Manichäische Homilien*. Vol. 1 of *Manichäische Handschriften der Sammlung A. Chester Beatty*. Berlin: Kohlhammer, 1934.

Poole, Fitz J. P. "Metaphor and Maps: Towards Comparison in the Anthropology of Religion." *JAAR* 54 (1986): 411–57.

Popkes, E. E. "Die Umdeutung des Todes Jesu im koptischen Thomasevangelium." Pages 513–43 in *Deutungen des Todes Jesu im Neuen Testament*. Edited by Jörg Frey and Jens Schröter. 2nd ed. Tübingen: Mohr Siebeck, 2012.

Proctor, Mark. "'After Three Days He Will Rise': The (Dis)Appropriation of Hosea 6.2 in the Markan Passion Predictions." Pages 131–50 in *The Gospel of Mark*. Vol. 1 of *Biblical Interpretation in Early Christian Gospels*. Edited by Thomas R. Hatina. London: T&T Clark, 2006.

Quarles, Charles L. *Matthew*. Nashville: Broadman & Holman, 2017.

Quispel, Gilles. "Das Thomasevangelium und das Alte Testament." Pages 243–48 in *Neotestamentica et Patristica: Eine Freundesgabe Herrn Prof. Dr. Oscar Cullmann zu seinem 60. Geburtstag überreicht*. Leiden: Brill, 1962.

Reeves, Keith H. *The Resurrection Narrative in Matthew: A Literary-Critical Examination*. Lewiston, NY: Mellen, 1993.

Reinhartz, Adele. "'And the Word Was God': John's Christology and Jesus's Discourse in Jewish Context." Pages 69–91 in *Reading the Gospel of John's Christology as Jewish Messianism*. Edited by Benjamin Reynolds and Gabriele Boccaccini. Leiden: Brill, 2018.

Reynolds, Benjamin. *The Apocalyptic Son of Man in the Gospel of John*. Tübingen: Mohr Siebeck, 2008.

Reynolds, Benjamin, and Gabriele Boccaccini, eds. *Reading the Gospel of John's Christology as Jewish Messianism*. Leiden: Brill, 2018.

Richard, Earl. "Jesus' Passion and Death in Acts." Pages 125–52 and 204–10 in *Reimaging the Death of the Lukan Jesus*. Edited by Dennis D. Sylva. Frankfurt am Main: Hain, 1990.

Riley, Gregory J. *Resurrection Reconsidered: Thomas and John in Controversy*. Minneapolis: Fortress, 1995.

Ringgren, Helmer. "Luke's Use of the Old Testament." *HTR* 79 (1986): 227–35.

Robertson, A. T. *A Grammar of the Greek New Testament in the Light of Historical Research*. London: Hodder & Stoughton, 1919.

Robinson, J. A. "Lecture on the Gospel according to Peter." Pages 11–36 in *The Gospel according to Peter, and the Revelation of Peter: Two Lectures on the Newly Discovered Fragments Together with the Greek Texts*, by J. A. Robinson and M. R. James. London: Clay, 1892.

Robinson, J. A., and M. R. James. *The Gospel according to Peter, and the Revelation of Peter: Two Lectures on the Newly Discovered Fragments Together with the Greek Texts*. London: Clay, 1892.

Robinson, James M. "Jesus from Easter to Valentinus (or to the Apostles Creed)." *JBL* 101 (1982): 5–37.

———, ed. *The Facsimile Edition of the Nag Hammadi Codices: Codex I*. Leiden: Brill, 1977.

Robison, Andrew C. "The 'Evangelium Veritatis': Its Doctrine, Character, and Origin." *JR* 43 (1963): 234–43.

Rödiger, Emil. *Chrestomathia Syriaca*. 3rd ed. Halle: Orphanotropheum, 1892.

Rooke, Deborah W. "Jesus as Royal Priest: Reflections on the Interpretation of the Melchizedek Tradition in Heb 7." *Bib* 81 (2000): 81–94.

Roth, Dieter. "Prophets, Priests, and Kings: Old Testament Figures in Marcion's Gospel and Luke." Pages 41–56 in *Connecting Gospels: Beyond the Canonical/Non-canonical Divide*. Edited by Francis Watson and Sarah Parkhouse. Oxford: Oxford University Press, 2018.

———. *The Text of Marcion's Gospel*. Leiden: Brill, 2015.

Roukema, Riemer. *Jesus, Gnosis and Dogma*. London: Bloomsbury, 2010.

Rousseau, Adelin, and Louis Doutreleau, eds. *Irenée de Lyon: Contre les hérésies*. 5 vols. Paris: Cerf, 1969–1982.

Rowe, C. Kavin. *Early Narrative Christology: The Lord in the Gospel of Luke*. Berlin: de Gruyter, 2006.

Ruani, Flavia, ed. and trans. *Éphrem de Nisibe: Hymnes contre les hérésies*. Paris: Les Belles Lettres, 2018.

Rusam, Dietrich. *Das Alte Testament bei Lukas*. Berlin: de Gruyter, 2003.

Schenke, Hans-Martin, ed. and trans. *Das Philippus-Evangelium (Nag-Hammadi-Codex II, 3)*. Berlin: Akademie, 1997.

Schenke Robinson, Gesine, Hans-Martin Schenke, and Uwe-Karsten Plisch, eds. *Das Berliner "Koptische Buch" (P 20915): Eine wiederhergestellte frühchristlich-theologische Abhandlung*. Vol. 1. Leuven: Peeters, 2004.

Schiffman, Lawrence H., and James C. VanderKam, eds. *Encyclopedia of the Dead Sea Scrolls*. 2 vols. Oxford: Oxford University Press, 2000.

Schmalzriedt, Egidius. *Peri Physeos: Zur Frühgeschichte der Buchtitel*. Munich: Wilhelm Fink, 1970.

Schmid, Ulrich. *Marcion und sein Apostolos: Rekonstruktion und historische Einordnung der marcionitischen Paulusbriefausgabe*. Berlin: de Gruyter, 1995.

———. "Marcions Evangelium und die neutestamentlichen Evangelien: Rückfragen zur Geschichte und Kanonisierung der Evangelienüberlieferung." Pages 67–78 in *Marcion und seine kirchengeschichtliche Wirkung/Marcion and His Impact on Church History*. Edited by Gerhard May and Katharina Greschat. Berlin: de Gruyter, 2002.

Schmidt, Carl, and Violet MacDermot. *The Books of Jeu and the Untitled Text in the Bruce Codex*. Leiden: Brill, 1978.

Schneiders, Sandra M. "Touching the Risen Jesus." Pages 153–76 in *The Resurrection of Jesus in the Gospel of John*. Edited by Craig R. Koester and Reimund Bieringer. Tübingen: Mohr Siebeck, 2008.

Schröter, Jens. "Die Funktion der Herrenmahlsüberlieferungen im 1. Korintherbrief: Zugleich ein Beitrag zur Rolle der 'Einsetzungsworte' in frühchristlichen Mahltexten." *ZNW* 100 (2009): 78–100.

———. *From Jesus to the New Testament: Early Christian Theology and the Origin of the New Testament Canon*. Waco, TX: Baylor University Press, 2013.

———. "Sterben für die Freunde: Überlegungen zur Deutung des Todes Jesu im Johannesevangelium." Pages 263–87 in *Religionsgeschichte des Neuen Testaments: Festschrift für Klaus Berger zum 60. Geburtstag*. Edited by Axel von Dobbeler, Kurt Erlemann, and Roman Heiligenthal. Tübingen: Francke, 2000.

———. "Sühne, Opfer, Stellvertretung: Zur Verwendung der analytischer Kategorien zur Deutung des Todes Jesu." Pages 51–71 in *Deutungen des Todes Jesu im Neuen Testament*. Edited by Jörg Frey and Jens Schröter. 2nd ed. Tübingen: Mohr Siebeck, 2012.

Schubert, Paul. "The Structure and Significance of Luke 24." Pages 165–86 in *Neutestamentliche Studien für Rudolf Bultmann*. Edited by Walther Eltester. Berlin: Alfred Töpelmann, 1954.

Schuchard, Bruce. "Form versus Function: Citation Technique and Authorial Intention in the Gospel of John." Pages 23–46 in *Abiding Words: The Use of Scripture in the Gospel of John*. Edited by Alicia D. Myers and Bruce G. Schuchard. Atlanta: SBL Press, 2015.

Schwarz, Konrad. "Der 'lebendige Jesus' im Thomasevangelium." Pages 223–46 in *Christ of the Sacred Stories*. Edited by P. Dragutinović, T. Nicklas, and K. G. Rodenbiker. Tübingen: Mohr Siebeck, 2017.

Schweizer, Eduard. "Concerning the Speeches in Acts." Pages 208–16 in *Studies in Luke-Acts*. Edited by Leander Keck and J. Louis Martyn. Nashville: Abingdon, 1966.

Segal, Robert A. "Classification and Comparison in the Study of Religion: The Work of Jonathan Z. Smith." *JAAR* 73 (2005): 1175–88.

———. "In Defense of the Comparative Method." *Numen* 48 (2001): 339–73.

Segelberg, Eric. "Evangelium Veritatis: A Confirmation Homily and Its Relation to the Odes of Solomon." *Orientalia Suecana* 8 (1959): 3–42.

Senior, Donald P. "The Lure of the Formula Quotations: Re-assessing Matthew's Use of the Old Testament with the Passion Narrative as a Test Case." Pages 89–115 in *The Scriptures in the Gospels*. Edited by Christopher M. Tuckett. Leuven: Leuven University Press, 1997.

———. *The Passion of Jesus in the Gospel of Matthew*. Collegeville, MN: Liturgical, 1990.

Setzer, Claudia. "Resurrection in the Gospel of Matthew: Reality and Symbol." Pages 43–56 in *Life beyond Death in Matthew's Gospel: Religious Metaphor or Bodily Reality?* Edited by Wim Weren, Huub van de Sandt, and Joseph Verheyden. Leuven: Peeters, 2011.

Sheridan, Ruth. "The Testimony of Two Witnesses: John 8:17." Pages 161–85 in *Abiding Words: The Use of Scripture in the Gospel of John*. Edited by Alicia D. Myers and Bruce G. Schuchard. Atlanta: SBL Press, 2015.

———. "They Shall Look upon the One They Have Pierced: Intertextuality, Intra-textuality and Anti-Judaism in John 19:37." Pages 191–210 in *Searching the Scriptures: Studies in Context and Intertextuality*. Edited by Craig A. Evans and Jeremiah J. Johnston. London: Bloomsbury, 2015.

Siliezar, Carlos. *Creation Imagery in the Gospel of John*. London: Bloomsbury, 2015.

Simon, Maurice, trans. *Esther and Song of Songs*. Vol. 9 of *Midrash Rabbah*. London: Soncino, 1939.

Slotki, Judah J., trans. *Numbers*. Vols. 5–6 of *Midrash Rabbah*. London: Soncino, 1939.

Smith, D. Moody. *The Theology of the Gospel of John*. Cambridge: Cambridge University Press, 2010.

———. "The Use of the Old Testament in the New." Pages 3–65 in *The Use of the Old Testament in the New and Other Essays: Studies in Honor of William Franklin Stinespring*. Edited by J. M. Efird. Durham, NC: Duke University Press, 1972.

Smith, Daniel A. "Marcion's Gospel and the Resurrected Jesus of Canonical Luke 24." *ZAC* 21 (2017): 41–62.

———. *Revisiting the Empty Tomb: The Early History of Easter*. Minneapolis: Fortress, 2010.

———. "Revisiting the Empty Tomb: The Post-mortem Vindication of Jesus in Mark and Q." *NovT* 45 (2003): 123–37.

Smith, Geoffrey, trans. *Valentinian Christianity: Texts and Translations*. Oakland: University of California Press, 2020.

Smith, Jonathan Z. *Drudgery Divine: On the Comparison of Early Christianities and the Religions of Late Antiquity*. Chicago: University of Chicago Press, 1990.

———. *Imagining Religion: From Babylon to Jonestown*. Chicago: University of Chicago Press, 1982.

———. "In Comparison a Magic Dwells." Pages 23–44 in *A Magic Still Dwells: Comparative Religion in the Postmodern Age*. Edited by Kimberley C. Patton and Benjamin C. Ray. Berkeley: University of California Press, 2000.

———. *Map Is Not Territory: Studies in the History of Religions*. Leiden: Brill, 1978.

Snodgrass, Klyne R. "Streams of Tradition Emerging from Isaiah 40:1–5 and Their Adaptation in the New Testament." *JSNT* 8 (1980): 24–45.

Soards, Marion L. *The Speeches in Acts: Their Content, Context, and Concerns*. Louisville: Westminster John Knox, 1994.

Söding, Thomas. "Der Gehorsam des Gottessohnes: Zur Christologie der matthäischen Versuchungserzählung (4,1–11)." Pages 711–49 in *Jesus Christus als die Mitte der Schrift: Studien zur Hermeneutik des Evangeliums*. Edited by Christof Landmesser, Hans-Joachim Eckstein, and Hermann Lichtenberger. Berlin: de Gruyter, 1997.

Spilsbury, Paul. "The Apocalypse." Pages 136–46 in *Redemption and Resistance: The Messianic Hopes of Jews and Christians in Antiquity*. Edited by Markus Bockmuehl and James Carleton Paget. Cambridge: Cambridge University Press, 2009.

Standaert, Benoît. "'Evangelium Veritatis' et 'Veritatis Evangelium': La question du titre et les témoins patristiques." *VC* 30 (1976): 138–50.

———. "L'Évangile de Vérité: critique et lecture." *NTS* 22 (1976): 243–76.

Stanton, Graham. *The Gospels and Jesus*. 2nd ed. Oxford: Oxford University Press, 2002.

Stempvoort, P. A. van. "The Interpretation of the Ascension in Luke and Acts." *NTS* 5 (1958–1959): 30–42.

Stone, Michael E. *Fourth Ezra*. Minneapolis: Fortress, 1990.

Strauss, Mark L. *The Davidic Messiah in Luke-Acts: The Promise and Its Fulfillment in Lukan Christology*. Sheffield: Sheffield Academic, 1995.

Stuckenbruck, Loren T. *1 Enoch 91–108*. Berlin: de Gruyter, 2007.

Sweet, John. *Revelation*. London: SCM, 1990.

Swete, H. B. *The Akhmîm Fragment of the Apocryphal Gospel of St. Peter*. London: Macmillan, 1893.

Swetnam, James. "No Sign of Jonah." *Bib* 66 (1985): 126–30.

Sylva, Dennis D. "Death and Life at the Center of the World." Pages 153–69 and 211–17 in *Reimaging the Death of the Lukan Jesus*. Edited by Dennis D. Sylva. Frankfurt am Main: Hain, 1990.

———, ed. *Reimaging the Death of the Lukan Jesus*. Frankfurt am Main: Hain, 1990.

Syreeni, Kari. "Resurrection or Assumption? Matthew's View of the Post-mortem Vindication of Jesus." Pages 56–78 in *Life beyond Death in Matthew's Gospel: Religious Metaphor or Bodily Reality?* Edited by Wim Weren, Huub van de Sandt, and Joseph Verheyden. Leuven: Peeters, 2011.

Tannehill, Robert C. "The Functions of Peter's Mission Speeches in the Narrative of Acts." *NTS* 37 (1991): 400–414.

Telford, William R. *The Theology of the Gospel of Mark*. Cambridge: Cambridge University Press, 1999.

Theobald, Michael. "Der johanneische Osterglaube und die Grenzen seiner narrativen Vermittlung (Joh 20)." Pages 93–123 in *Von Jesus zum Christus: FS P. Hoffmann*. Edited by R. Hoppe and U. Busse. Berlin: de Gruyter, 1998.

Thiessen, Matthew. "The Many for One or One for the Many? Reading Mark 10:45 in the Roman Empire." *HTR* 109 (2016): 447–66.

Thiselton, Anthony C. *The First Epistle to the Corinthians*. Grand Rapids: Eerdmans, 2000.

Thomassen, Einar. "Baptism among the Valentinians." Pages 895–915 in *Ablution, Initiation, and Baptism: Late Antiquity, Early Judaism, and Early Christianity*. Edited by David Hellholm, Tor Vegge, Øyvind Norderval, and Christer Hellholm. Berlin: de Gruyter, 2011.

———. "How Valentinian Is the Gospel of Philip?" Pages 251–79 in *The Nag Hammadi Library after Fifty Years*. Edited by John D. Turner and Anne McGuire. Leiden: Brill, 1997.

———. *The Spiritual Seed: The "Church" of the Valentinians*. Leiden: Brill, 2006.

Thompson, Marianne Meye. *John: A Commentary*. Louisville: Westminster John Knox, 2015.

Thyen, Hartwig. *Das Johannesevangelium*. 2nd ed. Tübingen: Mohr Siebeck, 2015.

Tischendorf, C., ed. *Apocalypses Apocryphae: Moses, Esdrae, Pauli, Iohannis item Mariae Dormitio*. Leipzig: H. Mendelssohn, 1851.

Toit, David S. du. "Heil und Unheil: Die Soteriologie des Markusevangeliums." Pages 186–208 in *Sōtēria: Salvation in Early Christianity and Antiquity; Festschrift in Honour of Cilliers Breytenbach*. Edited by David S. du Toit, Christine Gerber, and Christiane Zimmermann. Leiden: Brill, 2019.

Tregelles, S. P. *Account of the Printed Text of the Greek New Testament*. London: Samuel Bagster, 1854.

Trevijano Etcheverría, R. "La valoración de los dichos no canónicos: El caso de 1 Cor 2.9 y Ev.Tom log. 17." Pages 406–14 in *Papers Presented at the Eleventh International Conference on Patristic Studies Held in Oxford 1991: Historica, Theologica et Philosophica, Gnostica*. StPatr 24. Edited by Elizabeth A. Livingstone. Leuven: Peeters, 1993.

Tsutsui, Kenji. *Die Auseinandersetzung mit den Markioniten im Adamantios-Dialog: Ein Kommentar zu den Büchern I–II*. Berlin: de Gruyter, 2004.

Tuckett, Christopher M. "The Christology of Luke-Acts." Pages 133–64 in *The Unity of Luke-Acts*. Edited by Joseph Verheyden. Leuven: Leuven University Press, 1999.

———. "Forty Other Gospels." Pages 238–53 in *The Written Gospel*. Edited by Markus Bockmuehl and Donald A. Hagner. Cambridge: Cambridge University Press, 2005.

———. *The Gospel of Mary*. Oxford: Oxford University Press, 2007.

———, ed. *The Scriptures in the Gospels*. Leuven: Leuven University Press, 1997.

Turner, John D. "The Holy Book of the Great Invisible Spirit." Pages 247–51 in *The Nag Hammadi Scriptures*. Edited by Marvin Meyer. New York: HarperOne, 2007.

———. "The Sethian Myth in the Gospel of Judas." Pages 95–133 in *The Codex Judas Papers*. Edited by A. D. DeConick. Leiden: Brill, 2009.

Turner, John D., and Anne McGuire, eds. *The Nag Hammadi Library after Fifty Years*. Leiden: Brill, 1997.

Twigg, Matthew. "Esoteric Discourse and the Jerusalem Temple in the Gospel of Philip." *Aries* 15 (2015): 47–80.

Tzoref, Shani. "The Use of Scripture in the Community Rule." Pages 203–34 in *A Companion to Biblical Interpretation in Early Judaism*. Edited by Matthias Henze. Grand Rapids: Eerdmans, 2012.

Ulrich, Eugene, ed. *Isaiah–Twelve Minor Prophets*. Vol. 2 of *The Qumran Biblical Scrolls: Transcriptions and Textual Variations*. Leiden: Brill, 2013.

Unnik, Willem C. van. "Three Notes on the Gospel of Philip." Pages 238–43 in *Patristica, Gnostica, Liturgica*. Part 3 of *Sparsa Collecta*. Leiden: Brill, 1983.

Uro, Risto. "Asceticism and Anti-familial Language in the Gospel of Thomas." Pages 216–34 in *Constructing Early Christian Families: Family as Social Reality and Metaphor*. Edited by H. Moxnes. London: Routledge, 1997.

Vaganay, L. *L'Évangile de Pierre*. Paris: Gabalda, 1930.

Van Belle, Gilbert, ed. *The Death of Jesus in the Fourth Gospel*. Leuven: Leuven University Press, 2007.

———. "The Signs of the Messiah in the Fourth Gospel: The Problem of a 'Wonder-Working Messiah.'" Pages 159–78 in *The Scriptures of Israel in Jewish and Christian Tradition: Essays in Honour of Maarten J. J. Menken*. Edited by Bart J. Koet, Steve Moyise, and Joseph Verheyden. Leiden: Brill, 2013.

Vermes, Geza. *The Complete Dead Sea Scrolls in English*. Rev. ed. London: Penguin, 2004.

Versnel, Henk S. "Making Sense of Jesus' Death: The Pagan Contribution." Pages 213–94 in *Deutungen des Todes Jesu im Neuen Testament*. Edited by Jörg Frey and Jens Schröter. 2nd ed. Tübingen: Mohr Siebeck, 2012.

———. "Quid Athenis et Hierosolymis? Bemerkungen über die Herkunft von Aspekten des 'Effective Death.'" Pages 162–96 in *Die Entstehung der jüdischen Martyrologie*. Edited by Jan Willem van Henten, B. A. G. M. Dehandschutter, and H. J. W. van der Klaauw. Leiden: Brill 1989.

Vielhauer, Philipp. "On the Paulinism of Acts." Pages 33–50 in *Studies in Luke-Acts: Essays Presented in Honor of Paul Schubert*. Edited by Leander E. Keck and J. Louis Martyn. Nashville: Abingdon, 1966.

Vinzent, Markus. *Christ's Resurrection in Early Christianity and the Making of the New Testament*. Farnham: Ashgate, 2011.

———. "Der Schluß des Lukasevangeliums bei Marcion." Pages 79–94 in *Marcion und seine kirchengeschichtliche Wirkung/Marcion and His Impact on Church History*. Edited by Gerhard May and Katharina Greschat. Berlin: de Gruyter, 2002.

———. *Marcion and the Dating of the Gospels*. Leuven: Peeters, 2014.

Vorholt, Robert. *Das Osterevangelium: Erinnerung und Erzählung*. Freiburg: Herder, 2013.

Vouga, François. "Mort et résurrection de Jésus dans la source des logia et dans l'Évangile de Thomas." Pages 1009–24 in *Coptica—Gnostica—Manichaica: Mélanges offerts à Wolf-Peter Funk*. Edited by Louis Painchaud and Paul-Hubert Poirier. Leuven: Peeters, 2006.

Vygotsky, Lev. *Thought and Language*. Rev. and exp. ed. Cambridge: MIT Press, 2012.

Wahlde, Urban C. von. "The Interpretation of the Death of Jesus in John against the Background of First-Century Jewish Eschatological Expectations." Pages 555–65 in *The Death of Jesus in the Fourth Gospel*. Edited by Gilbert Van Belle. Leuven: Leuven University Press, 2007.

Walker, Norman. "After Three Days." *NovT* 4 (1960): 261–62.

Wallace, Daniel B. *Greek Grammar beyond the Basics: An Exegetical Syntax of the New Testament*. Grand Rapids: Zondervan, 1997.

Walton, Steve. *Leadership and Lifestyle: The Portrait of Paul in the Miletus Speech and 1 Thessalonians*. Cambridge: Cambridge University Press, 2000.

Wasserman, Tommy. "The 'Son of God' Was in the Beginning (Mark 1:1)." *JTS* 62 (2011): 20–50.

Watson, Francis. *Gospel Writing: A Canonical Perspective*. Grand Rapids: Eerdmans, 2013.

Watson, Francis, and Sarah Parkhouse, eds. *Connecting Gospels: Beyond the Canonical/ Non-canonical Divide*. Oxford: Oxford University Press, 2018.

Watts, Rikki E. *Isaiah's New Exodus and Mark*. Tübingen: Mohr Siebeck, 1997.

Wayment, Thomas A. "A Reexamination of the Text of P.Oxy. 2949." *JBL* 128 (2009): 375–82.

Weidemann, Hans-Ulrich. "Eschatology as Liturgy: Jesus' Resurrection and Johannine Eschatology." Pages 277–310 in *The Resurrection of Jesus in the Gospel of John*. Edited by Craig R. Koester and Reimund Bieringer. Tübingen: Mohr Siebeck, 2008.

Weiss, Haim. "A Double Edged Sword—The Power of Bar-Kosibah: From Rabbinic Literature to Popular Culture." Pages 341–56 in *The Reception of Ancient Virtues and Vices in Modern Popular Culture: Beauty, Bravery, Blood and Glory*. Edited by Eran Almagor and Lisa Maurice. Leiden: Brill, 2017.

Wengst, Klaus. *Das Johannesevangelium: Neuausgabe in einem Band*. Stuttgart: Kohlhammer, 2019.

Wenham, John W. "When Were the Saints Raised? A Note on the Punctuation of Matthew xxvii.51–3." *JTS* 32 (1981): 150–52.

Weren, Wim. "Matthew's Stories about Jesus' Burial and Resurrection (27:55–28:20) as the Climax of His Gospel." Pages 189–200 in *Life beyond Death in Matthew's Gospel: Religious Metaphor or Bodily Reality?* Edited by Wim Weren, Huub van de Sandt, and Joseph Verheyden. Leuven: Peeters, 2011.

Weren, Wim, Huub van de Sandt, and Joseph Verheyden, eds. *Life beyond Death in Matthew's Gospel: Religious Metaphor or Bodily Reality?* Leuven: Peeters, 2011.

White (Crawford), Sidnie. "A Comparison of the A and B Manuscripts of the Damascus Document." *RevQ* 12 (1987): 537–53.

Wilckens, Ulrich. "Kerygma und Evangelium bei Lukas (Beobachtungen zu Acta 10.34–43)." *ZNW* 49 (1958): 223–37.

———. "The Tradition-History of the Resurrection of Jesus." Pages 51–76 in *The Significance of the Message of the Resurrection for Faith in Jesus Christ*. Edited by C. F. D. Moule. London: SCM, 1968.

Williams, Catrin H. "'He Saw His Glory and Spoke about Him': The Testimony of Isaiah." Pages 53–80 in *Honouring the Past and Shaping the Future: Religious and Biblical Studies in Wales; Essays in Honour of Gareth Lloyd Jones*. Edited by Robert Pope. Leominster: Gracewing, 2003.

———. "Johannine Christology and Prophetic Traditions: The Case of Isaiah." Pages 92–123 in *Reading the Gospel of John's Christology as Jewish Messianism*. Edited by Benjamin Reynolds and Gabriele Boccaccini. Leiden: Brill, 2018.

———. "Patriarchs and Prophets Remembered: Framing Israel's Past in the Gospel of John." Pages 187–212 in *Abiding Words: The Use of Scripture in the Gospel of John*. Edited by Alicia D. Myers and Bruce G. Schuchard. Atlanta: SBL Press, 2015.

Williams, Jacqueline A. *Biblical Interpretation in the Gnostic Gospel of Truth from Nag Hammadi*. Atlanta: Society of Biblical Literature, 1988.

Williams, Martin. *The Doctrine of Salvation in the First Letter of Peter*. Cambridge: Cambridge University Press, 2011.

Willitts, Joel. "David's Sublation of Moses: A Davidic Explanation for the Mosaic Christology of the Fourth Gospel." Pages 203–25 in *Reading the Gospel of John's Christology as Jewish Messianism*. Edited by Benjamin Reynolds and Gabriele Boccaccini. Leiden: Brill, 2018.

———. *Matthew's Messianic Shepherd-King: In Search of 'The Lost Sheep of the House of Israel.'* Berlin: de Gruyter, 2007.

———. "Paul and Matthew: A Descriptive Approach from a Post–New Perspective Interpretative Framework." Pages 62–85 in *Paul and the Gospels: Christologies, Conflicts and Convergences*. Edited by Michael Bird and Joel Willitts. London: Bloomsbury, 2011.

Wilson, Benjamin. *The Saving Cross of the Suffering Christ: The Death of Jesus in Lukan Soteriology*. Berlin: de Gruyter, 2016.

Wilson, Robin McL. *The Gnostic Problem: A Study of the Relations between Hellenistic Judaism and the Gnostic Heresy*. London: Mowbray, 1958.

———. *The Gospel of Philip: Translated from the Coptic Text, with an Introduction and Commentary*. London: Mowbray, 1962.

Winger, J. Michael. "When Did the Women Visit the Tomb: Sources for Some Temporal Clauses in the Synoptic Gospels." *NTS* 40 (1994): 284–88.

Wischmeyer, Oda. *Liebe als Agape: Das frühchristliche Konzept und der moderne Diskurs*. Tübingen: Mohr Siebeck, 2015.

Wisse, Frederik, and Michael Waldstein, eds. *The Apocryphon of John: Synopsis of Nag Hammadi Codices II,1; III,1 and IV,1 with BG 8502,2*. Leiden: Brill, 1995.

Witetschek, Stephan. "Peter in Corinth? A Review of the Evidence from 1 Corinthians." *JTS* 69 (2018): 66–82.

Wolfson, Elliot R. "Becoming Invisible: Rending the Veil and the Hermeneutic of Secrecy in the Gospel of Philip." Pages 113–35 in *Practicing Gnosis: Ritual, Magic, Theurgy and Liturgy in Nag Hammadi, Manichaean and Other Ancient Literature; Essays in Honor of Birger A. Pearson*. Edited by April D. DeConick, Gregory Shaw, and John D. Turner. Leiden: Brill, 2013.

Wolter, Michael. *Das Lukasevangelium*. Tübingen: Mohr Siebeck, 2008.

———. "Der Heilstod Jesu als theologisches Argument." Pages 297–313 in *Deutungen des Todes Jesu im Neuen Testament*. Edited by Jörg Frey and Jens Schröter. 2nd ed. Tübingen: Mohr Siebeck, 2012.

———. *The Gospel according to Luke*. 2 vols. Waco, TX: Baylor University Press, 2016–2017.

———. "Jesu Tod und Sündenvergebung bei Lukas und Paulus." Pages 15–35 in *The Reception of Paulinism in Acts*. Edited by D. Marguerat. Leuven: Peeters, 2009.

Wrede, W. "The Task and Methods of New Testament Theology." Pages 68–116 in *The Nature of New Testament Theology*. Edited and translated by Robert Morgan. London: SCM, 1973.

Wright, David F. "Apocryphal Gospels: The 'Unknown Gospel' (Pap. Egerton 2) and the Gospel of Peter." Pages 207–32 in *The Jesus Tradition outside the Gospels*. Vol. 5 of *Gospel Perspectives*. Edited by David Wenham. Sheffield: JSOT Press, 1985.

———. "Apologetic and Apocalyptic: The Miraculous in the Gospel of Peter." Pages 401–18 in *Miracles of Jesus*. Vol. 6 of *Gospel Perspectives*. Edited by David F. Wright and Craig L. Blomberg. Sheffield: JSOT Press, 1986.

Wright, N. T. "Early Traditions and the Origin of Christianity." *STRev* 41 (1998): 125–40.

———. *Judas and the Gospel of Jesus: Have We Missed the Truth about Christianity?* Grand Rapids: Baker, 2006.

———. *The Resurrection of the Son of God.* London: SPCK, 2003.

Yarbro Collins, Adela. "The Appropriation of the Psalms of Individual Lament by Mark." Pages 223–41 in *The Scriptures in the Gospels.* Edited by Christopher M. Tuckett. Leuven: Leuven University Press, 1997.

———. *Mark: A Commentary.* Minneapolis: Fortress, 2007.

———. "Mark's Interpretation of the Death of Jesus." *JBL* 128 (2009): 545–54.

———. "The Signification of Mark 10:45 among Gentile Christians." *HTR* 90 (1997): 371–82.

Zangenberg, Jürgen. "'Bodily Resurrection' of Jesus in Matthew?" Pages 217–31 in *Life beyond Death in Matthew's Gospel: Religious Metaphor or Bodily Reality?* Edited by Wim Weren, Huub van de Sandt, and Joseph Verheyden. Leuven: Peeters, 2011.

Zehnle, Richard. "The Salvific Character of Jesus' Death in Lucan Soteriology." *TS* 30 (1969): 420–44.

Zelyck, Lorne. *The Egerton Gospel (Egerton Papyrus 2 + Papyrus Köln VI 255): Introduction, Critical Edition, and Commentary.* Leiden: Brill, 2019.

Zimmermann, Johannes. *Messianische Texte aus Qumran: Königliche, priesterliche und prophetische Messiasvorstellungen in den Schriften von Qumran.* Tübingen: Mohr Siebeck, 1998.

Zimmermann, Ruben. "Jesus—the Divine Bridegroom? John 2–4 and Its Christological Implications." Pages 358–86 in *Reading the Gospel of John's Christology as Jewish Messianism.* Edited by Benjamin Reynolds and Gabriele Boccaccini. Leiden: Brill, 2018.

Zuber, Beat. *Jalkut Schimoni zu Josua.* Berlin: de Gruyter, 2017.

Zumstein, Jean. "Jesus' Resurrection in the Farewell Discourses." Pages 103–26 in *The Resurrection of Jesus in the Gospel of John.* Edited by Craig R. Koester and Reimund Bieringer. Tübingen: Mohr Siebeck, 2008.

———. "The Johannine 'Relecture' of Mark." Pages 23–29 in *John's Transformation of Mark.* Edited by Eve-Marie Becker, Helen Bond, and Catrin Williams. London: Bloomsbury, 2021.

———. "L'interprétation de la mort de Jésus dans les discours d'adieu." Pages 95–119 in *The Death of Jesus in the Fourth Gospel.* Edited by Gilbert Van Belle. Leuven: Leuven University Press, 2007.

———. "L'interprétation johannique de la mort du Christ." Pages 2119–38 in *The Four Gospels: Festschrift for Frans Neirynck.* Edited by F. Van Segbroeck, C. M. Tuckett, G. Van Belle, and J. Verheyden. Leuven: Leuven University Press, 1992.

———. "The Purpose of the Ministry and Death of Jesus in the Gospel of John." Pages 331–46 in *The Oxford Handbook of Johannine Studies.* Edited by Judith Lieu and Martinus C. de Boer. Oxford: Oxford University Press, 2018.

Zyl, Hermie C. van. "The Soteriological Meaning of Jesus' Death in Luke-Acts: A Survey of Possibilities." *Verbum et Ecclesia* 23 (2002): 533–57.

Index of Authors

Index of Subjects

Index of Scripture and Other Ancient Sources

Hellenistic Jewish Authors

Philo

Flavius Josephus

Rabbinic and Later Jewish Literature